Fish Flies

Volume II

Terry Hellekson

Illustrated by Wanda Prunty
Fly Plates Photographed by Jim Schollmeyer

A major work dealing with the ultimate level of the angler's art—fly tying.
The techniques, tools, materials, and proven patterns for hundreds of flies

Share the experience—it's catching.

Published in 1995 by Frank Amato Publications, Inc.
P. O. Box 82112, Portland, Oregon 97282
(503) 653-8108

ISBN: 1-57188-024-0

Fly plate photographs taken by Jim Schollmeyer

Book Design : Terry Hellekson

Printed in HONG KONG

1 3 5 7 9 10 8 6 4 2

Contents

Foreword

When I first became involved in fly tying in the mid 1960s, my mind was a sponge for any and all tying information, whether it were techniques, materials or patterns. As a result of a long association with Theodore Gordon Flyfishers in New York I had the good fortune to have excellent teachers: Ken Bay, Ed Koch, Larry Solomon, Eric Leiser, Ted Niemeyer, Poul Jorgensen, Charlie DeFeo and others less well known but many equally as skilled as those mentioned. I bought all the instructional books I could find and read and reread them incessantly. I passed quickly through the stages of "creating" my own patterns to recreating the standard patterns to experimentation with imitation. I adopted, rejected and readopted theory after theory, from exact imitation to impressionism to use of fluorescence and a host of others.

About a half dozen years after I started tying I fancied myself something of an authority and began teaching others to tie. A year or so thereafter I realized several things: 1. while I could tie a decent fly, I was far from an authority on any aspect of tying; 2. there was little truly "new" in fly tying, yet there was much to learn; 3. most of what was heralded as a "revolutionary, new development" was, in fact, something old revisited with a different material.

About this same time I was working as editor for the *Field & Stream* Book Club, and in that capacity I reviewed a new book called *Popular Fly Patterns* by a new writer named Terry Hellekson. I was impressed with the work and chose his book as a major selection of the book club. Terry went on to continue making fly tying and fly tying materials his lifework. I went on to become involved in computer based education. We both remained passionate about fly fishing and fly tying.

I had thought little about the book or Terry since that time until recently when the "information superhighway" reconnected us through our common interest in fly fishing and fly tying. It was only because we recognized through our e-mail communications a common thinking with respect to fly tying and its history that we became reacquainted.

I had been frustrated for years by the periodic "discoveries" in the world of fly tying; frustrated to the point that I began questioning and almost immediately rejecting anything with the words "new fly tying development" or "new material." Through pragmatics, I had reduced the number of pattern designs I carried to a double handful, varying sizes and colors to achieve what I needed in the way of imitation. I'd chalked up my attitudes to experience (read "advancing age") and a tendency toward curmudgeon-hood.

By and large, I had kept my beliefs and attitudes about tying to myself and concentrated more on honing my tying skills rather than chasing after each "new" material or design that came down the road. For example, to this day you will not find in my fly boxes a beadhead, a flashback, a cul de canard or a Waterwisp™. With a few notable exceptions, my flies are tied with fur and feathers. The maddening (or, perhaps, intriguing) thing about all of this is that I am still catching as many fish as I've caught, and, at the risk of being immodest, when I am with others, not too many people catch more than I.

Terry, on the other hand, had never given up his relentless and energetic research into tying and its origins or his acquisition of in-depth knowledge on and experimentation with most new developments in tying and materials. I was delighted to find he would confirm many of the conclusions I'd reached over the years, as well as bring clarification to a few other vagaries by which I'd long been bothered. When Terry asked me to write a few introductory words to this volume I was both happy and flattered.

As each of us, you and I, become more involved in the art of fly tying and the sport of fly fishing, we tend to become to one degree or another researchers and scholars of the origins, artifacts, literature or sciences associated with these activities. The ability of our art and our sport to generate first interest, then enjoyment, then curiosity (my wife would add "obsession") is I think one of the reasons we love fly tying and fly fishing. There is also a risk in all of this: the quest for knowledge can overwhelm and numb the passion that brought us there in the first place. In other words, we risk becoming so introspective and analytical about the way we tie or how and where we fish, that we forget that fun was the reason we started tying or fishing.

Another tendency that occurs early in the evolution of the fly fisher is to speculate that it would be truly wonderful to be able to make a living doing the things we enjoy the most, which, of course, would be something allied with fly fishing. The speculation, unfortunately, doesn't hold up well when it comes in contact with reality, because the facts are: 1. fly fishing is, for most of us, an escape from the rigors of our jobs; and 2. once most people begin performing an activity for the purpose of earning a living, it generally ceases to be truly enjoyable for them.

Terry is an exception to both these situations. He has made fly tying and fly fishing his career; yet he doesn't for a minute let us forget tying and fishing are fun. Furthermore, he helps us remember a great deal of our fun can be derived from and enhanced by increasing our knowledge of tying and fishing. Although Terry and I have never fished together, I can tell from his correspondence that each day of fishing for him, as it is for me, is a day of discovery and learning.

Because he grew up in a fly tying environment, Terry's two-volume set, *Fish Flies*, is the product of a virtual lifetime of research and experience. The books, taken together, make order of the informational chaos that fly tying has, for many of us, threatened to become. Terry is not one to mince words on subjects he knows thoroughly, nor does he accept that which has been previously written as fact. The reader seeking to find confirmation of long held opinions on patterns, materials and people associated with fly tying will not find it in these pages. With respect to most problems and situations involving fly tying, Terry has, in the popular vernacular "Been there. Done that. And has the T-shirt to prove it." Where he hasn't been and done to his own demanding standards, he's sought out experts as consultants or as alter egos to verify and codify his thinking. In summary, much of what *Fish Flies* has to say is truly "new."

Through our correspondence, I've learned from Terry that a great deal of what he has written is information which was not only new to him, but which in several instances was shockingly new. In other words, he uncovered information as a result of his research which he either did not expect to find or which soundly refuted long held beliefs. His writing says,

"Here are the facts as I have found them. They may be different than what you've been told. Nonetheless, these *are* the facts. Form your own conclusions or accept mine."

On the one hand, Terry holds up a few of the popular new theories and materials for scrutiny they cannot long endure, but he is also fair in giving endorsement to other new developments which his experience has shown will benefit fly tyers and fishermen. Similarly, he is not shy in pointing to a bit of tarnish on the haloes of some of those to whom fly tying/fishing sainthood has been granted over the years, while simultaneously singling out other less well-known names for the recognition they have truly earned. In each case, his basis for evaluation is either that which is verifiable fact or has stood the test of time as a worthwhile contribution to the arts of fly tying and fly fishing.

The *Volume I* chapters on materials, dyeing and hooks alone are worth the reading. Couple these with the chapters on fish food forms and their imitations, then add *Volume II* on patterns and you have in two books a virtual encyclopedia of the fly tyer's art. While the set will take its place as a reference work, the books' chapters also read well in large topical bites, providing comprehensive information on the subjects each addresses. Because he has traveled and fished all over the world, Terry's work carries little of the regional bias from which so many preceding works have suffered. The pattern lists, for example, while specifically applicable in the U.S. carry an international flavor reflective of Terry's experience and contacts.

A word of caution to the reader: any work as intentionally exhaustive as **Fish Flies** will be scrutinized for omissions, and because of this scrutiny apparent omissions may be found. A bit of thought will reveal, however, that while a locally or fleetingly popular pattern may have been omitted from the listings, little of substance associated with the origins or techniques of fly tying has been omitted from the text. In addition, Terry tacitly asks his readers to accept his experience as their guide to the art of tying. To this extent, he also asks us to grant him the privilege of holding informed opinion. In any endeavor so highly individualistic as fly tying, personal preference as to tools, techniques and materials is certain to evolve. The reader is invited to question and to disagree with the suggestions and instruction implicit in the text. Before disregarding any suggestion, however, he or she should also consider the depth of experience on which Terry's advice is based and perhaps reconsider, as Terry has, the wisdom and correctness of that which previously has been a standard.

What Terry has accomplished for me with **Fish Flies** is to highlight the importance of at least considering and evaluating each purportedly "new" development in tying rather than disregarding it without examination as I had previously done. I really don't expect to find much that is truly new, but I now know I can anticipate finding things that are at least worthwhile. He has also reaffirmed that the key to understanding and evaluating all that will appear in fly fishing and fly tying in the future is to know and understand all that has been a part of fly fishing and fly tying in the past.

Eric W. Peper
Atlanta, Georgia

Introduction

This volume is a continuation of the most complete reference work yet to be compiled on the subject of fish flies, hence the title. It lists fly patterns that cannot all be found in any other available reference material. While it reintroduces many of the older proven patterns, it also brings to light many new and relatively unknown ones.

As a young man my thoughts and opinions about fly fishing in general were often rejected. I cannot count the number of times I was told that I was too young and lacked the experience to offer such tokens of wisdom. One day I awakened to find that all of a sudden I was being told I was old fashioned and I was not in tune with how things are being done these days. Not that I allowed this to cause any loss of sleep, but there were periods while I was behind my fly tying vise where I gave some serious thought to all of this. Incidentally, I have always found some particle of salvation while emptily gazing at the jaws of my vise.

This is when I came to realize that there was much wisdom in the saying, "The more things change the more they actually stay the same." Not that there is a point where one reaches a knowing level where everything there is to know about fly fishing is achieved—that will never come to pass. It would probably require us to develop the ability to have dialogue with the game fish that we prey upon and I feel confident that man will regress back into the Stone Age before that ever happens.

We have to realize that fly fishing is not unlike a long partially-traveled road of enlightenment. It holds for us any number of detours and side roads. One has to conclude that perhaps the earth was purposely made round so we don't see too far down this road of discovery at any one time.

Many of us have elected to take a side road marked "fly tying" and have discovered that it is not a real side road at all. We have learned that it is an artery paralleling that of the first road and sharing almost the same level of importance and has its own partially disclosed wonderments. Both of these roads offer us moments where we are disconnected and far away from everyday practical matters. We find that we are better able to focus on more important things that happen to be connected with fishing and fish flies, such as dressing or casting a fly.

When viewed by others, these are often things of minor importance, yet others will appear to have been fitted with magnified rose-colored glasses and will view things quite differently. I have been on these roads for many years and have ventured up more than my share of side roads. Somewhere along the journey I lost my rose-colored glasses and have had to start trying to view things in a more arranged manner.

In Volume One a sketch is presented of where this road possibly started; it discusses some perceptions of color and reveals dye formulas for the adventurous fly tier; it expresses opinions on fly tying tools and deals with many of our fly tying hooks as they are used today. Then it goes into some of the basic techniques of fly tying, giving specific patterns for dry flies, wet flies and nymphs; following up with a comprehensive selection of patterns for mayflies, stoneflies and caddisflies and depicting them in their respective cycles of life.

After reviewing the contents of Volume Two you will discover that I have taken you on additional roads. You might even come to realize the similarity of many roads—finding out how many are joined by semantics and practice. I have continued my practice of not specifying fly patterns which have no suitable substitutes for their materials. I have refrained from specifying materials which are here today and gone tomorrow, i.e., some of the magic dubbings that are often just shimmering optimism. These flash-in-the-pan materials have been left to the discretion of the individual tier—allowing substitutions as whims dictate.

A good example of the "here today, gone tomorrow" syndrome is Miclon. This is a material that I was assured would always be available. Later I learned, after this book was written, that it was an imported product and the company had gone out of business. The good news is that after visiting a number of craft shops I finally came to realize what the material really was. Simple macramé cord when unraveled matched it perfectly. The white appears white until the fibers are freed and then in natural sunlight you realize that they are really translucent. A few pennies will get you a lifetime supply of this stuff—I use it extensively. Try it and I am sure you will discover many new uses.

I am a strong believer in experimenting with most of these newer materials, however, I try and keep it all in focus, realizing they may be gone tomorrow. I know that progress can only be brought about with our experiments—that's part of the unending fun of it all. It is really too bad that more of our truly talented imagineers are never discovered or recognized when they are discovered.

I have tried very hard to give credit as appropriate, however, I cannot discount the possibility of a few references being incorrect. I have expended equal effort to giving the fly patterns as correctly as possible. Some patterns and their origins have been lost in the haze of antiquity and we will never know all with certainty.

Chapter 13

Terrestrials

Summer brings with it a population of warm-weather-loving insects that we call terrestrials. They breed and hatch on dry land as opposed to most of our aquatic insects who favor water. In those areas where they are prevalent, fly fishermen await the annual hopper season. These big mouthfuls can rival most any of the other hatches which might be coming off the water at the time. For many that were exposed to "fishing pox" in their youth, then scrummed by the imperiling fever, hoppers from the fields provided temporary relief.

I have often seen lackadaisical anglers waiting for the sun to hit the fields in the morning so they can catch their daily supply of grasshoppers. Hoppers just don't want to move until the warmth of the sun has dried the dewdrops from their wings. One of the many advantages a fly fisherman has over the bait guys is that their bait is already in their fly boxes. We are often further outfitted with not only our hopper patterns, but with proper ants, tiny beetles and inchworm patterns made up in their likeness. Ever try putting one of these naturals on a bait hook?

Anglers have a tendency to get entrenched in their habits. They recognize one particular insect and associate it with only one stream or lake. As an example, I have had friends tell me how good ant or beetle patterns work on a particular stream here in

California, yet they never consider their use when they venture to central Oregon or other destinations. They become obsessed with using only the local patterns. This is without question a good practice, however, we should regard the terrestrials as "universal gold" and fish them wherever we might be. Without any hesitation, I know that either an ant or beetle pattern will work for me whether I'm fishing Yellow Creek here in California or the Letort in Pennsylvania. Remember, terrestrial means earthly or worldly.

Ants

Ants are no doubt the most successful of all the social insects and are believed to have evolved from wasps. They are colony makers and have inhabited the warmer environments of the earth for at least 100 million years. These insects have some 5,000, or perhaps as many as 10,000, species. They are very adaptive and are found everywhere. I have come to believe, maybe I'm wrong, that what fly fishermen deal with is primarily the subfamily *Myrmicinae*, or more commonly known in my area as timber ants. It would be purposeless for us as anglers to try and extend the montage of Latin names and other classifications further. We know that those found on the kitchen counter are just uninvited guests and are not what we are interested in.

White ants are another form of insect that play a significant role in the diet of fish in some areas. These are actually termites, belonging to the order Isoptera, and are not ants at all. This is a misnomer based on superficial similarities in their appearance. At maturity they leave their nest in swarms, this is when they become probable fish food. It is common for the angler-entomologist to confuse these with ants due to the darker coloring of the reproducing adults. I personally don't find it essential to start splitting frog hairs over such technicalities. I am sure the fish don't.

Plate 1   ## Autumn Ant
Hooks: AC80000BR, TMC100 or DAI1180, sizes 12-16.
Thread: Black.
Tail: Black hackle barbs.
Body: Dubbed with #1 black Bunny-Blend. Body should be tied in two distinctive lumps to simulate the shape of an ant's body.
Wings: Furnace hen hackle tips tied delta wing style.
Hackle: Black tied on as a collar.

This is a good dressing for almost any area. It is my favorite ant pattern for fast water conditions. I sometimes substitute dark moose or porcupine bristles for the tailing material. It was originated by Lloyd Byerly of Salem, Oregon.

Flying Black Ant

Hooks: AC80000BR, TMC100 or DAI1180, sizes 10-16.
Thread: Black.
Tail: Black hackle barbs.
Butt: Black ostrich.
Body: Black floss.
Wings: Grizzly hackle tips tied delta wing style.
Hackle: Dyed black tied on as a collar.

Fur Ant, Black

Hooks: AC80000BR, TMC100 or DAI1180, sizes 12-18.
Thread: Black.
Body: Dubbed with #1 black Bunny-Blend. Body should be tied in two distinctive lumps to simulate the shape of an ant's body.
Hackle: Sparse black tied in at the center joint.

Fur Ant, Cinnamon

Hooks: AC80000BR, TMC100 or DAI1180, sizes 12-18.
Thread: Brown.
Body: Dubbed with #24 brown Bunny-Blend. Body should be tied in two distinctive lumps to simulate the shape of an ant's body.
Hackle: Sparse brown tied in at the center joint.

Hardshell Black Ant

Hooks: You can use any number of hook models for this pattern. Depending on the model, I tie these in sizes 8-16.
Thread: Black.
Body: Build an underbody with heavy thread. Most any thread is usable. I usually try and clear out some of those odds and ends as color at this point is of no concern. Wrap your thread in two distinctive segments in the shape of an ant's body. You only need to build up the intended finished shape about half way. Tie off and give a coat of deep penetrating head cement.

After a few minutes drying time, apply a coat of fast drying black gloss enamel.

Remove any excess from the center joint. Allow to dry and continue to build additional ant bodies. I usually build a season's supply at one time and allow the lot to dry overnight.

On day two I go through and apply additional enamel, generally concentrating on the top side and not getting in too much of a rush. By applying this filling (shaping) application in the morning they have adequate time to dry well enough to be handled by afternoon.

Now you are ready for the finishing coat. You will possibly note that you have accumulated a lot of irregular shapes. So, this time apply your enamel, filling the voids, much like sculpting a clay figure. Allow these to dry overnight.

Day three finds me inspecting my finished bodies and doing whatever touch up necessary.
Legs/Hackle: Natural black hen hackle tied on at the front as a collar and tied back.

Variations of this include tying-in your hackle at the center joint in which case you need to compensate for this by providing slightly more space when constructing the body. I suggest using a slightly longer-shanked hook. Another variation has red enamel applied to the front joint of the body. Still other variations include hackle tip wings tied flat over the body; legs made from rubber hackle, deer hair used for legs and tied-in at either the center joint or in front, and just about any other type of minor configuration of leg materials the tier desires.

I have to strongly recommend only tying a simple collar of hackle at the front of the fly. I believe that the body silhouette is the most important feature of this fly. The action of the softer hen hackle may have a role in all of this. It is just icing on the cake and cannot hurt. I have experimented with other colors, such as brown, but none have been found to be as effective as basic black.

Last season while fishing the upper Yuba River I was overrun by a group of yuppies and their ingenuous young guide. After politely telling them to walk around me and distance themselves from the water I was fishing, I noticed that one of the young ladies really had not understood the meaning of "get." She positioned herself about fifty feet below me and was attempting to fish some worthless water. Her setup, as assembled by their high priced guide, consisted of a strike indicator as big as the largest of horse apples and a large bright green Woolly Worm. This was a great rig for August, with low, gin clear water and heavily pounded wary fish.

As I watched out of the corner of my eye I got to thinking, "Gosh, this could be any one of my daughters being treated so callously." It was apparent that their mediocre guide had other priorities. I worked myself down to where she was standing, all the time praying that she would not hit herself in the head and do harm with the strike indicator. I helped her remove her lethal weapon and tied on a Hardshell Black Ant. Then I proceeded to coach her upstream to the water that I was about to fish. Instructions were given as to where a fish might be awaiting her offering and on about her third cast she was hooked up with a nice rainbow.

After allowing her to play the fish for several minutes, I assisted by netting the fish. Then she was disheartened to see me release the fish for another day. She complained, "How am I going to get my friends to believe I caught it?" She

went on, "I've never caught a fish before, that was my first one." I sympathized with her and gave her a couple more ants and moved on up stream.

That evening when I went out to eat I ran into the group again. The woman was thrilled to see me. I was her confirming witness to catching the only fish in the group that day. Of course I did not try and correct her when she again related the story of the twenty-four inch rainbow, even though it had grown six or seven inches. Who could dampen the excitement of a freshly born, freshly christened fly fisher.

Encounters such as this add to my enjoyment of fly fishing. I just thank the stars that someone was around when I was young and inexperienced and gave me some ants.

Plate 1 **Lively's Black Ant**
Hooks: AC80000BR, TMC100 or DAI1180, sizes 12-16.
Thread: Black.
Body: Dyed black deer tied in two distinctive humps.
Legs: Deer hair pulled out from rear hump and projecting from center of body.

If you were one of the regular readers of *Pennsylvania Angler* a couple of decades ago you came to know Chauncy Lively. His wealth of tying information educated fly fishermen with unique patterns that have since proven to be productive across the country.

Beetles

Although I have not had a lot of experience with fishing beetle imitations, I have to stop and think when I read of them. Why have I given them so little attention? There are more than 250,000 known species, that figure represents more than one-quarter of all known animal species.

The most prominent characteristic of the beetle is their hardened, sheath-like front wings, which in most beetles cover their entire abdomen when they are not in flight. The patterns given here have been proven producers in most parts of the country. With a little investigation and experimentation you can develop any number of patterns for your own area.

Plate 1   Black Beetle

Hooks: TMC921 or DAI1310, sizes 14-18.
Thread: Black.
Body: Dubbed with #1 black Bunny-Blend.
Legs: Dyed black saddle hackle. Select hackle which has fine-textured barbs and a fine stem. Wrap about 4 or 5 turns over the body and tie off at head.
Shellback: Dyed black turkey quill section tied in at rear. Pull hackle barbs down to the sides and pull quill section forward and tie off at the head. Quill section should be tied in so that shiny side is up when fly is completed. While pulling hackle barbs downward, clip off even with the hook point.

Black Foam Beetle

Hooks: AC80000BR, TMC100 or DAI1180, sizes 8-16.
Thread: Black.
Body: Dubbed with #1 black Bunny-Blend.
Legs: Natural black hen hackle tied on as a collar and clipped off on top.
Shellback: Black closed cell foam.
Head: Butt end of shellback.

There is no end to what one can do with closed cell foam. I tie all of my bugs with white foam and then decorate them with waterproof marking pens.

Ants are also very good candidates for this type of fly. Play around with some.

Crowe Beetle

Hooks: AC80000BR, TMC100 or DAI1180, sizes 12-18.
Thread: Black.
Body: Dubbed with #1 black Bunny-Blend.
Shellback: Black deer hair tied in at the rear and pulled forward after body is completed.
Legs: Deer hair form the shellback pulled out on each side.
Head: Butts from shellback.

This is a variation of the Deer Hair Beetle that many favor.

Plate 1   Crown Beetle

Hooks: AC80000BR, TMC100 or DAI1180, sizes 10-14.
Thread: Brown.
Body: Dubbed with #9 orange Bunny-Blend.
Legs: Brown hackle wrapped through thorax and clipped off on top.
Shellback: Natural brown bucktail tied in at the rear and pulled over the body after it has been completed.
Head: Butts from shellback.

Originated by Lester McGiven of Salt Lake City, Utah, in 1989.

Crystal Beetle

Hooks: AC80000BR, TMC100 or DAI1180, sizes 12-16.
Thread: Black.
Body: Peacock herl.
Legs: Crystal Hair pulled out from shellback.
Shellback: CH16 dark olive Crystal Hair tied in at the rear and pulled over the body after it is completed.

Crystal Beetles have been, in general, used for more than a decade now. They are tied in many colors by just changing colors of the Crystal Hair being used.

Deer Hair Beetle

Hooks: AC80000BR, TMC100 or DAI1180, sizes 10-16.
Thread: Brown.
Body: Dubbed with #31 tan Bunny-Blend.
Legs: Deer hair pulled out from shellback.
Shellback: Natural deer hair tied in at the rear and pulled over the back after body is completed.
Head: Butts from deer hair.

This is probably our oldest method of constructing beetle imitations. The deer hair and body colors can be changed to match whatever strikes your fancy.

Plate 1   Japanese Beetle

Hooks: AC80000BR, TMC100 or DAI1180, sizes 10-16.
Thread: Brown.
Body: Dubbed with #24 brown poly.
Legs: Brown hackle wrapped through thorax and clipped off on top.
Shellback: Brown raffia. Raffia should be tied in at the rear of the thorax area and folded back so it reaches the end of the hook. It is then lacquered.

I was given this pattern by Doug Ralston of Farmington, New Mexico. He developed it while he was living in New York and found it to also be productive after relocating out here in the west in 1970.

Plate 1   Ladybird

Hooks: TMC921 or DAI1640, size 14.
Thread: Black.
Body: Dubbed with #1 black Bunny-Blend.
Shellback: Natural deer hair pulled over the body. Apply orange enamel and allow to dry, then apply tiny black spots.
Head: Black ostrich herl.

Ladybird is the common name given to the ladybug by entomologists. Were you to observe one of these on display in a fly fishing shop you would probably regard it as something gimmicky. That might well be the case in some areas.

While fishing a favored stream along the Pacific Crest Trail not too many years ago I noticed a large bush overhanging the stream was literally covered with thousands of bugs. After a closer examination I realized what I was witnessing was a major hatch of these little critters and as they hatched a good percentage was falling to the water and floating away in the tumbling current. There was little I could do about it as I had nothing that even came close to simulating them.

That winter while browsing through one of my gardening magazines I saw an advertisement for ladybugs. Sounded silly at the time, but I guess they eat the aphids and some other garden pests. What struck me was the fact that these bugs were being sold by the thousands from a small Sierra foothill town in the general area of where I had fished that past summer.

That was enough to inspire me to get behind the vise and make an attempt to duplicate them. My past observations told me that I did not need anything that floated very well so I proceeded in tying them as you see here. A little investigation told me that I could probably use four spots on their backs if I wanted to get close to duplicating them. The bug books told me seven but two on each side just works out fine.

Since that time I have been armed to the teeth with these easy-to-tie beetles. I fish them as a drowned insect at a dead drift and the fish eat them up. I have only had the opportunity of fishing them in northern California and southern Oregon but they are on my list to carry everywhere.

Mann's Black Beetle

Hooks: AC80000BR, TMC100 or DAI1180, sizes 12-18.
Thread: Black.
Body: Black ostrich herl.
Legs: Black deer hair tied in at the front with three pieces extending out each side.

Shellback: Black raffia tied in at the rear and pulled over the body after it is completed.

Originated by Leonard Mann of Denver, Colorado.

Plate 1   Peacock Beetle

Hooks: AC80000BR, TMC100 or DAI1180, sizes 12-18.
Thread: Black.
Body: Peacock herl.
Legs: Brown hackle wrapped through thorax and clipped off on top.
Shellback: Brown raffia.
Head: Raffia folded back and tied off at the rear.

This pattern has been around for as long as I have. It is one that my father always had with him and fished in the surface film on those hot summer afternoons when all else was at a stand still.

Crickets

After what Walt Disney did for Jiminy Cricket's career I hope you do not get too emotional when I say, "I hate these damn bugs." They are a fly tier's nightmare, they love to eat most any furs or feathers they can get into. Don't let that cute little hopping and jumping around, and chirping fool you as I was fooled for so many years. What I had been blaming moths for turned out to be crickets.

Most crickets have a single annual generation. Eggs are laid in the autumn, then hatch out as tiny nymphs that look like miniature adults. The nymphs usually just eat leaves and roots and go through a series of molts until they reach the adult stage. The best known type are the dark, cylindrical field crickets, imitations of these are just as rewarding to the fly fisherman as hoppers.

Plate 1 ## Brown Field Cricket

Hooks: TMC5212 or DAI1280, sizes 10-16.
Thread: Dark brown.
Ribbing: Black saddle clipped to shape.
Body: Brown poly yarn.
Wings: Mottled dark brown turkey tail sections tied over the body.
Legs: Knotted dark pheasant tail barbs.
Head and Collar: Dyed dark brown deer hair spun on and clipped, leaving a small Muddler-style head and a collar. Collar should be sparse and only extend over the top and sides.

Originated by Nicholas Erickson of Buena Park, California, in 1980.

Letort Cricket

Hooks: TMC5212 or DAI1280, sizes 10-16.
Thread: Black.
Body: Black poly yarn.
Wings: Dyed black turkey quill sections tied over the body.
Head and Collar: Dyed black deer hair spun on and clipped, leaving a small Muddler-style head and a collar. Collar should be sparse and only extend over the top and sides.

Originated around 1960 by Ed Shenk.

Hoppers

As I have already mentioned at the beginning of this chapter, hoppers are very important to fly fishermen. Along with grasshoppers we also have their close cousins which gives us a real complex bag of bugs. This includes the locust (cicada) and katydid, plus the already mentioned crickets. In all honesty I believe the fly fisherman is wise to only concentrate his efforts on hopper-like patterns and not go off the deep end worrying about some of the cousins. I find it amusing when I see cicada patterns offered commercially. As if fly fishermen weren't challenged enough, there are those who want to suggest we make it even harder. Cicadas, order Homoptera, have the longest life cycle of any insect known. One species only hatches out into an adult every thirteen years and another every seventeen years. Speaking of taking long shots, this really amplifies the word "optimism." Highly suppositional offerings such as this only confuses the casual or novice angler. Hopper and cricket patterns will adequately fill your needs should a cicada pattern ever be dictated.

I have cast an imitation hoppers on the water in the middle of the day, when no other form of life was stirring, and had some very explosive reactions from lurking fish. From out of nowhere, with no display of politeness whatsoever, fish will attack a hopper as if it were their last meal. You will seldom experience a gentle slurping take. When you do, it is usually just a dink which is not worth worrying about anyway. Carry hopper patterns in the summer and use them when all others are napping.

Plate 1 ### Dave's Hopper
Hooks: TMC5212 or DAI1280, sizes 8-14.
Thread: Brown.
Tail: Dyed red deer hair.
Body: Yellow yarn with a small loop extending out over the tail.
Ribbing: Brown saddle hackle clipped to shape.
Wings: Yellow deer hair tied over the body with overwings of mottled brown turkey quill sections.
Legs: Knotted pheasant tail barbs.
Head and Collar: Natural deer hair spun on and clipped, leaving a half collar over the top and sides and a head shaped more in the likeness of a hopper than a Muddler.

Originated by Dave Whitlock.

Plate 1 ### Flutter Winged Hopper, Red
Hooks: TMC5262 or DAI1720, sizes 10-14.
Thread: Brown.
Body: Dark elk or deer hair secured parallel to the hook with figure eight wrappings of thread. Body should extend past bend of hook.
Wings: Dyed red bucktail with overwings of natural brown bucktail. Wing is tied divided in a semi-spent V.
Hackle: Brown tied on as a collar and trimmed off on bottom.

Plate 1 ### Flutter Winged Hopper, Yellow
Hooks: TMC5262 or DAI1720, sizes 10-14.
Thread: Tan.
Body: Light elk or deer hair secured parallel to the hook with figure eight wrappings of thread. Body should extend past bend of hook.
Wings: Dyed yellow bucktail with overwings of natural brown bucktail. Wing is tied divided in a semi-spent V.
Hackle: Ginger or ginger variant tied on as a collar and trimmed off on the bottom.

Tying what you see on the water is what the Flutter Winged Hoppers are about. When a hopper misjudges its landing site and ends up water-bound it is not long before it realizes its predicament. In this stressful atmosphere

the wings part for additional buoyancy and natural stability on the water.

Prove it to yourself and do as I did. Catch a live hopper and cast it upon the water. At first it will use its long and powerful hind legs to try and swim, then you will see the wings part as it tires. At a very young age I came to realize this and I also started questioning how might the fish observe such an intruder from their vantage point.

After observing these guys on land it was easy to determine that I was basically dealing with two different colors, red and yellow. I tie these generally in size 12 and go up to a size 10 on the larger, faster-moving rivers. Size 14s are correct for spring creeks and where a more delicate presentation is more in tune with the conditions.

Jacklin's Hopper
Hooks: TMC5262 or DAI1720, sizes 6-14.
Thread: Yellow.
Tail: Dyed red deer hair.
Ribbing: Brown saddle clipped to shape.
Body: Fluorescent green yarn.
Wings: Natural gray goose quill sections tied over the body.
Head and Collar: Light elk hair tied forward and then pulled back to form a bullet head and collar.

Originated by Bob Jacklin of West Yellowstone, Montana.

Plate 1 ### Joe's Hopper
Hooks: TMC5262 or DAI1720, sizes 6-14.
Thread: Brown.
Tail: Red hackle barbs.
Ribbing: Brown saddle hackle clipped to shape.
Body: Yellow poly yarn.
Wings: Mottled brown turkey quill sections tied over the body.
Hackle: Brown and grizzly tied on as a collar mixed.

Also known as the Michigan Hopper. Joe Brooks popularized this pattern, hence the name change. This is probably the oldest known hopper pattern.

Lawson's Hopper

Hooks: TMC5212 or DAI1280, sizes 8-14.
Thread: Yellow.
Body: Light elk or deer hair secured parallel to the hook with figure eight wrappings of thread. Body should extend past bend of hook.
Wing: Dyed yellow elk hair tied over the body with an overwing of a pair of lacquered mottled brown hen saddle feathers.
Head and Collar: Natural brown elk hair tied forward and then pulled back to form a bullet head and collar.

Originated by Mike Lawson. Also known as the Henry's Fork Hopper. Variations of this pattern also include legs of knotted rubber hackle or pheasant tail feather barbs.

Plate 1   Letort Hopper

Hooks: TMC5212 or DAI1280, sizes 10-16.
Thread: Yellow.
Body: Yellow poly yarn.
Wings: Mottled brown turkey quill sections tied over the body.
Head and Collar: Natural deer hair spun on and clipped, leaving a small Muddler-style head and a collar. Collar should be sparse and only extend over the top and sides.

Originated about 1960 by Ed Shenk.

Plate 1   MacHopper

Hooks: TMC5212 or DAI1280, sizes 8-10.
Thread: Yellow.
Body: Extend yellow braided macramé cord.
Wings: Strands of CH04 yellow Crystal Hair tied over the body with an overwing of mottled fly film tied flat.
Legs: Knotted yellow rubber hackle or pheasant tail feather barbs tied in at each side.

Head and Collar: Natural deer hair that has been overdyed yellow. Hair is tied forward and then pulled back to form a bullet head and collar.

Originated by Al Troth of Dillon, Montana.

Plate 1   Parahopper

Hooks: TMC5212 or DAI1280, sizes 8-14.
Thread: Brown.
Hackle Post: Single upright wing of white calf tail tied short.
Body: Dubbed with raccoon fur.
Wings: Mottled brown turkey quill sections tied over the body.
Hackle: Grizzly tied parachute style.

Originated by Buz Buszek of Visalia, California. This is actually a spin-off of the King's River Caddis that Buz developed. He recommended it in the smaller sizes for such places as Hot Creek. Today this pattern also has legs included on many variations. Buz also had his Buz Hopper which never gained much popularity.

Plate 1   Pheasant Hopper

Hooks: TMC5212 or DAI1280, sizes 8-14.
Thread: Yellow.
Tail: Dark moose hair.
Ribbing: Furnace saddle hackle trimmed to shape.
Body: Yellow poly yarn.
Wings: Golden pheasant tail feather sections tied over the body.
Head and Collar: Natural deer hair spun on and clipped, leaving a half collar over the top and sides and a head shaped more in the likeness of a hopper than a Muddler.

Inchworms

Not much has been put down on paper about the inchworm, or measuring-worm if you like, as a practical bug for the fly fisherman to imitate. *Terrestrial Fishing*, 1990, by Ed Koch addresses them, however, and I have also seen mail-order catalogs through the years give some wondrous hype regarding these worms.

The inchworm belongs to the family Gemetridae and is the larvae of some 1,300 species of geometrid moths that are found in North America. The adults seldom if ever serve any significant role in the diet of our game fish, however, the worms or caterpillars are readily consumed when opportunities arise. The northeastern states have populations of these species which are bright green in color. The color may very well add to their attractiveness to both fish and angler alike inasmuch as this is where our attentions have been directed to date.

While the inchworm enjoys its off and on again popularity with eastern fly fishermen, the West Coast harbors a similar morsel. The larvae of the oak moth can be found at lower elevations. Although they have been eradicated for the most part in populated areas, they can certainly be found in the wild. To come upon a mature oak tree positioned beside a stream in the spring can be rewarding. Rewarding if there happens to be a population of worms. This does not occur as often as we would like—even when planned. Not that there is a shortage of these little worms, they just don't purposely select trees bordering our favored streams as we would like. Now I don't go out of my way seeking out these creatures, it is an affair that occurs through happenstance.

Here in northern California the Feather and North Fork of the Feather Rivers, and the North Fork of the Yuba and Trinity Rivers have been my best finds. I understand that the upper Sacramento River has its share also. I am sure that through collective effort other areas could be identified.

The first couple of times I came across these little tannish worms as they were clinging precariously to the leaves and branches of oak trees I was unprepared. It was either the second or third time out that I began to realize they were, for a brief period, an important fish food. As they tumble from their sacrificial perches in the oaks, landing in the water, they float rather well as they attempt to wiggle to a place of safety. This has a tendency to drive fish crazy and they selectively feed on them for an indefinite time.

Green Inch Worm

Hooks: TMC5212 or DAI1280, sizes 10-12.
Thread: Cream or pale yellow.
Body: Dyed insect green deer hair secured parallel to the hook with figure eight wrappings of thread. Body should extend past bend of hook.

 Tan Inch Worm

Hooks: TMC5212 or DAI1280, sizes 10-12.
Thread: Tan.
Body: Light elk or deer hair secured parallel to the hook with figure eight wrappings of thread. Body should extend past bend of hook.

Chapter 14

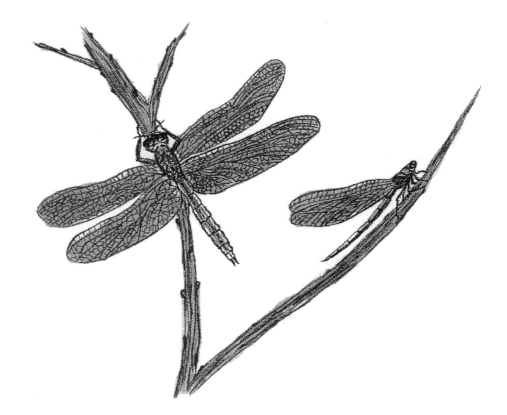

Damselflies and Dragonflies: Order Odonata

Some refer to these creatures as "flying egg beaters." Others use such names as "devil's darning needle" or "mini choppers." The later making reference to a small helicopter of course. Many of us as kids were plagued with old wives tales about the certainty of them sewing up our lips should we get out of line.

The Odonata is a well recognized member of the planet and is found from the Arctic region to the Tropics which is cause for a large variation in life cycles. There are more than 400 species to be found here in North America. They favor slow moving backwaters and eddies of streams and the shorelines of lakes, sloughs and ponds. Kick up a weed bed along a shoreline of any one of these and you are bound to stir up some life. It has been my experience that mosquitoes inhabit the same waters and because of their earlier emergence, a signal is sent up. It is time to examine the water more closely for nymph populations; they feed rather heavily on both the larvae and adult stages of the mosquito and are occasionally used for abatement purposes.

Like with caddisflies, breeding normally takes place over land. You may see the male and female flying joined together. The male may accompany the female, grasping her behind the head, to the water when she deposits her eggs in weed beds or other debris. I have witnessed large fish erupt from nowhere along the shoreline trying to seize them at this time. Their lunge can be so strong and out of control that they temporarily beach themselves in the shallower portions of a shoreline.

After a week of frustration up north on Oregon's Crane Prairie Reservoir, a surly old friend of mine came to me seeking the answer to these hovering little guys. Much has been debated over the years among fishermen concerning how imitations could best be made. This is a cyclic reaction many anglers anguish over each season. We can send men to the moon, engineer graphite fly rods out of dirt, yet we cannot properly suspend a dragonfly or damselfly imitation in a hovering position over the water.

Any fly fisherman who has spent the summer on the banks of our streams, lakes and ponds can relate to this. It is not uncommon to see a fish come completely out of the water in pursuit of one of these large morsels. They continue to display their presence all summer long. Every year I observe a new color, one that I did not know existed previously, then I never see the color repeated. Just last summer I saw one which looked as if it had just left the paint shop, it was a beautiful metallic fluorescent red. It landed on the tip of my rod while I was changing flies and I became so preoccupied with it that I almost forgot I was fishing.

In this chapter I will not be able to give you my secret for a hovering damselfly or dragonfly, however, we are going to get into some nymph and adult patterns which I know you will be able to put to good use. The damsels and dragons represent two suborders, Anisoptera (dragonflies) and Zygoptera (damselflies). For simplicity's sake we will approach them in that fashion.

Dragonflies: Suborder Anisoptera

Nymphs

Assam Dragon

This pattern is located in Chapter 9 for a purpose. It probably represents a small mouse or lemming more than a dragonfly nymph. Charles Brooks, the originator, always found that it was more effective when fished in fast water where the fish had little or no opportunity for examination. My experiences also tell me it is more effective where dragonflies are not commonly found.

Plate 2 ## Beaverpelt
Hooks: AC80050BR, TMC200R or DAI1270, sizes 4-8.
Thread: Black.
Body: Dubbed with beaver fur with guard hairs left in.
Legs: Pheasant rump hackle tied on as a collar and tied back.

Originated by Don E. Earnest, retired fisheries biologist with Washington State Department of Game, to suggest large dragonfly nymphs. This is the original dressing and there are several variations. See Chapter 9.

Burke's Dragon
Hooks: TMC5263 or DAI1720, sizes 6-10.
Thread: Olive.
Tail: Dyed olive elk hair tied short with olive marabou tied on top. Tail should be tied long Woolly Bugger style.
Body: Dubbed with a 50/50 blend of #19 olive and #20 dark olive Bunny-Blend.
Wingcase: Ringneck pheasant tail feather barbs.
Legs: Dyed olive barred teal barbs tied in at each side.
Eyes: Black mono.
Head: Dubbed through the eyes with body blend.

Originated by Andy Burke of Redding, California. This pattern is also referred to as the Dragon Bugger due to the longer tail.

Floating Dragon
Hooks: TMC5263 or DAI1720, sizes 6-8.
Thread: Brown.
Tail: Tuft of dyed brown grizzly marabou.
Body: Dyed brown deer hair spun on and clipped to shape with emphasis on a flat top and bottom.
Legs: Dyed brown grizzly marabou tied in at each side.
Wingcase: Mottled dark brown turkey tail feather section tied over the thorax. Trim a V on the end and lacquer.
Eyes: Black mono.
Head: Dubbed with brown rabbit.

Originated by Randall Kaufmann of Portland, Oregon. This fly can also be tied on other colors, i.e., olive or black to meet your local conditions.

Gierach Dragon
Hooks: AC80050BR, TMC200R or DAI1270, sizes 6-8.
Thread: Black.
Ribbing: Flat gold tinsel.
Body: Dubbed with hare's mask fur.
Wingcase: Dyed dark brown deer hair tied upside-down with mottled dark brown turkey tail feather section tied short.
Legs: Ringneck pheasant flank barbs tied in at each side.
Eyes: Black mono.
Head: Dubbed with hare's mask fur.

Originated by John Gierach.

Plate 2 ## Great Green Dragon
Hooks: TMC5263 or DAI1720, sizes 8-10.
Thread: Black.
Body: Dark olive chenille.
Legs: Natural black hen hackle wrapped through thorax. Trim off on top before mounting wingcase.
Wingcase: Natural gray duck shoulder feather tied over the thorax. Feather should have tip cut out, leaving a V, and then lacquered.
Eyes: Black mono.

Howell's Dragon
Hooks: TMC300, DAI2340 or DAI2370, sizes 6-10.
Thread: Brown.
Tail: Grizzly marabou tied short.
Body: Brown chenille with tan chenille woven up the belly.
Legs: Two turns of furnace hen hackle tied on as a collar and clipped off on top and bottom.
Wingcase: Two mottled dark brown turkey tail feather sections tied over the thorax. Trim a V on the end and lacquer.
Eyes: Black mono.
Head: Brown fur dubbed through eyes.

Originated by Joe Howell of Idleyld Park, Oregon.

Plate 2   Lake Dragon

Hooks: TMC5263 or DAI1720, sizes 6-8.
Thread: Olive.
Tail: Tuft of dyed olive grizzly marabou.
Ribbing: Copper wire.
Body: Dubbed with a blend of 50% olive rabbit fur and the remainder a mixture of one part each green, purple, rust, brown, blue, olive and amber goat.
Legs: Brown pheasant rump barbs tied in at each side.
Wingcase: Mottled dark brown turkey tail feather section tied over the thorax. Trim a V on the end and lacquer.
Eyes: Black mono.
Head: Dubbed with same mixture used for body.

Originated by Randall Kaufmann of Portland, Oregon. Don't get too emotional should you not be able to come up with all of the colors for the dubbing mixture. The design is excellent and you should attempt to meet your own local demands.

This is one of those designs that you can tie in varying shades. To tie from a dark olive to a very pale olive would not be eccentric by any means. I have seen such variations all within the same lake—naturally, this is caused by differing chemical compositions.

Plate 2   Peacock Dragon

Hooks: TMC5263 or DAI1720, sizes 6-10.
Thread: Black.
Tail: Ringneck pheasant rump barbs tied short.
Ribbing: Reverse wrap with fine gold wire.
Abdomen: Peacock herl over an underbody of either dark olive floss or yarn.
Thorax: Dubbed with muskrat fur with guard hairs left in.
Legs: Pick out guard hairs from thorax.
Eyes: Black mono.
Head: Peacock herl wrapped through eyes.

Whit's Dragon Nymph

Hooks: TMC5263 or DAI1720, sizes 6-10.
Thread: Olive.
Ribbing: Fine gold wire.
Shellback: Olive Swiss straw or raffia.
Body: Dubbed with a blend of #20 dark olive Bunny-Blend and clear Antron.
Legs: Dyed olive grizzly hen hackle barbs tied in at each side.
Eyes: Black mono.
Head and Wingcase: The Swiss straw or raffia is folded back through the eyes and tied off behind the eyes.

Originated by Dave Whitlock. This pattern is often tied on a salmon fly hook. Naturally, this pattern can be tied in other appropriate colors.

Adults

Plate 2   Deer Hair Dragon

Hooks: AC80000BR, TMC100 or DAI1180, sizes 4-10.
Thread: Black.
Wings: Two pair of grizzly hackle tips tied spent.
Extended Body: Natural brown bucktail secured parallel to the hook with figure eight wrappings of thread. Body should extend well past bend of hook.

Hackle: Grizzly wrapped through the base of the wings.
Wingcase: Thin tan closed cell foam tied in behind the wings and pulled over the thorax and tied off at the head.
Head: Butt end of foam protruding over eye of hook.

This style of adult dragonfly has been with us for many years. The use of foam is an added feature. Previously the wingcase was deer hair tied in the same fashion. Many fly tiers are using pearl Crystal Hair for wings which may or may not be an improvement. Obviously you can change the deer hair colors to meet your local conditions.

As a trout pattern I have rarely seen or had word of any anglers having very much success with this pattern. If tied elegantly and with great care it is certain to embellish your fly box.

Damselflies: Suborder Zygoptera

Nymphs

It has been my experience that the damselfly nymphs reign supreme even when other hatches are taking place. As the waters warm in the spring and early summer their activity becomes very rewarding to those anglers who are tuned in and filled with anticipation.

Last season while fishing a small lake in mid April I observed what appeared to be an iridescent blue carpet shimmering some yards from me. It was a nature photographer's dream shot—my camera had been left behind. Upon making a closer confirming examination it was clear that thousands of adult damsels were emerging in this selected area and were using a large weed bed to rest upon while they dried themselves. By mid morning the air was filled with *Callibaetis* in extraordinary numbers coupled with darting damsels. The fish were not giving any indication of etiquette or selectivity as they gorged themselves on something. For a period I was dumbfounded, thinking, "What are these fish going for—the sky?" It was not a prolonged mystery however. Between the five of us, those using damsel nymphs were taking more than their share of fish—even with a *Callibaetis* spinner fall of textbook version underway.

Using a floating line and slowly swimming our nymphs a few inches below the surface made five fly fishermen jubilant enough to want to try it another day.

Aspen Damsel, Dark
Hooks: TMC300, DAI2340 or DAI2370, sizes 10-12.
Thread: Olive.
Tail: Two olive ostrich herl tips tied short.
Ribbing: Heavy olive thread.
Abdomen: Dubbed thin with #18 light olive Bunny-Blend.
Thorax: Light olive saddle hackle wrapped through the thorax and clipped short.

Plate 2   Aspen Damsel, Light
Hooks: TMC300, DAI2340 or DAI2370, sizes 10-12.
Thread: Tan.
Tail: Tan ostrich herl tips tied short.
Ribbing: Heavy tan thread.
Abdomen: Dubbed thin with #3 cream Bunny-Blend.
Thorax: Cream saddle hackle wrapped through the thorax and clipped short.

Originated by Billie Dawson of Golden, Colorado, in 1980.

Giant Damsel

Hooks: TMC9395 or DAI2220, sizes 6-10.
Thread: Olive.
Tail: Dyed olive grizzly hen hackle barbs.
Body: Black and olive variegated wool yarn.
Hackle: Dyed olive grizzly hen tied on as a collar and tied back.
Head: Olive chenille.

Originated by Jim Cope of Bend, Oregon. I have found that I can duplicate the yarn body with a 50/50 blend of olive and black lambs wool or goat. Well, it is close.

Green Damsel, Brooks

Hooks: TMC5263 or DAI1720, sizes 8-10.
Thread: Olive.
Tail: Three peacock sword feather barbs.
Ribbing: Oval gold tinsel.
Body: Dubbed with #19 olive Bunny-Blend.
Hackle: Dyed olive hen hackle tied on as a collar.

Originated by Charlie Brooks. Like Polly, Charlie also varied the shades of olive used when tying this pattern. This could involve a green, olive green to a bright yellowish-green olive.

Green Damsel, Polly's

Hooks: TMC5263 or DAI1720, sizes 8-10.
Thread: Olive
Tail: Light golden olive marabou tied short.
Ribbing: Heavy olive thread.
Body: Dubbed with #21 golden olive Bunny-Blend.
Legs: Dyed olive barred teal barbs tied beard style.
Wingcase: Golden olive marabou tied in at the head and extending over the thorax.

This pattern was originated by E.H. "Polly" Rosborough. This is one of the patterns that Polly enjoyed playing around with. You can either brighten the body color with yellow or darken it with gold colored fur.

June Damsel

Plate 2

Hooks: TMC300, DAI2340 or DAI2370, sizes 10-12.
Thread: Olive.
Tail: Dyed olive grizzly marabou tied short.
Ribbing: Heavy yellow thread.
Body: Olive floss well tapered.
Legs: Dyed olive speckled guinea fowl barbs tied beard style.
Wingcase: Tuft of dyed olive grizzly marabou tied over the thorax.

Originated by Donald "Les" Malcolm of Oroville, California.

Marabou Damsel, Borger

Hooks: AC80000BR, TMC100 or DAI1180, sizes 10-12.
Thread: Olive.
Tail: Light olive marabou with brown marabou tied on top.
Abdomen: Dubbed with olive and brown marabou mixed.
Wingcase: Peacock herl.
Thorax: Dubbed with olive and brown marabou mixed.

Originated by Gary Borger.

Marabou Damsel, Kaufmann

Plate 2

Hooks: AC80050BR, TMC200R or DAI1270, sizes 8-12.
Thread: Olive.
Tail: Olive marabou tied short.
Ribbing: Copper wire.
Body: Dubbed with olive marabou.
Wingcase: Olive marabou tied over the thorax.

Mountain Damsel

Hooks: TMC300, DAI2340 or DAI2370, sizes 10-12.
Thread: Olive.
Tail: Dyed olive goose biots tied short.
Ribbing: Fine gold wire.
Shellback: Olive marabou.
Body: Thinly dubbed with #20 dark olive African Angora goat.
Wingcase: Olive marabou tied over the thorax and extending one-third.

The two preceding patterns were originated by Randall Kaufmann.

Ostrich Damsel

Hooks: TMC300, DAI2340 or DAI2370, sizes 10-12.
Thread: Tan.
Tail: Three tan ostrich herl strands. These are secured at the end much like the Zygo Damsel.
Ribbing: Oval gold tinsel.
Abdomen: Dubbed with #31 tan Bunny-Blend.
Thorax: Tan ostrich herl.
Legs: Brown Hungarian partridge tied beard style.

 ## Zygo Damsel Nymph, Dark

Hook: TMC921, DAI1640, DAI1310 or DAI1330, sizes 12-14.
Thread: Olive.
Extended Body/Tail: Olive marabou.
Wingcase: Olive raffia.
Thorax: Dubbed with #19 olive Bunny-Blend.
Legs: Olive hen hackle barbs tied beard style.
Eyes: Black mono.

Zygo Damsel Nymph, Light

Hook: TMC921, DAI1640, DAI1310 or DAI1330, sizes 12-14.
Thread: Tan.
Extended Body/Tail: Tan marabou.
Wingcase: Natural raffia.
Thorax: Dubbed with #31 tan Bunny-Blend.
Legs: Ginger hen hackle barbs tied beard style.
Eyes: Black mono.

The Zygo Damsel Nymphs were originated by Walter Voeller of Sacramento, California. Walter is one of those free spirits who winters here in California and summers in Montana. He is one of the most contemptible cusses that I know—just wants to fish.

I like his nymphs though. I have never fished with any other damsels that have a more natural "damsel action" in the water than these. They are remarkable. Most other imitations with extended bodies are stiff and have literally no action in the water. These come alive.

The tail is formed by tying thread in a small knot around the marabou and a fine spot of Krazy Glue to secure the thread.

Adults

Blue Damsel

Hooks: AC80000BR, TMC100 or DAI1180, sizes 10-12.
Thread: Black.
Wings: White bucktail tied spent.

Extended Body: Dyed blue deer hair secured parallel to the hook with figure eight wrappings of thread. Body should extend well past bend of hook.
Hackle: Light cast grizzly tied on as a collar and trimmed off on bottom.

Braided Butt Blue Damsel

Hooks: AC80000BR, TMC100 or DAI1180, sizes 10-12.
Thread: Black.
Wings: Narrow white hackle tips tied spent.
Extended Body: Braided butt material. Color with waterproof marker. Body should extend well past bend of hook.
Wingcase/Thorax: Dubbed with #35 blue poly.
Wingcase/Hackle Post: Blue elk hair.
Hackle: Blue dun tied parachute style around base of wingcase.

Plate 2   Crystal Damsel, Blue

Hooks: AC80000BR, TMC100 or DAI1180, sizes 10-12.
Thread: Black.
Wings: CH01 pearl Crystal Hair tied spent.
Extended Body: CH13 blue Crystal Hair secured parallel to the hook with figure eight wrappings of thread. Body should extend well past bend of hook.
Hackle: Blue dun wrapped through base of wings.

Crystal Damsel, Green

Hooks: AC80000BR, TMC100 or DAI1180, sizes 10-12.
Thread: Olive.
Wings: CH01 pearl Crystal Hair tied spent.
Extended Body: CH10 light green Crystal Hair secured parallel to the hook with figure eight wrappings of thread. Body should extend well past bend of hook.
Hackle: Olive wrapped through base of wings.

Plate 2   Parachute Blue Damsel

Hooks: AC80050BR, TMC200R or DAI1270, sizes 12-14.
Thread: White.
Extended Body: Braided butt material. Color with waterproof marker. Body should extend well past bend of hook.
Wingcase/Thorax: Blue deer hair.
Hackle: Grizzly tied parachute style around base of wingcase.
Head: Butts of wingcase.

Chapter 15

Leeches and Worms:
Order Annelida

This order includes earthworms, freshwater worms, leeches, and marine worms. It would take years of research to attempt to cover these creatures. The *Polychaeta* alone are known for sixty-four families with about sixteen hundred genera and more than ten thousand species. Whether you are a fresh or saltwater fly fisherman, these creatures are important fish food.

Anglers for centuries have depended on the plain old garden variety earthworm *(Lumbricidae)* as fish bait. More recently fly fishermen have been made aware of the freshwater worm *(aeolosoma)* which the fish have better access to than does the bait fisherman. The color of these worms can vary from translucent to high opalescent or to very dark.

The *Hirudinea* group comprises about two hundred and ninety species of leeches. In size these leeches vary from microscopic to two feet or more. Aquatic leeches swim with undulating movements. It is not uncommon for a leech to be mistaken for a crane fly larvae or other aquatic insect form. I believe that none of our fish take the time to dissect any of these underwater creatures, they strike instinctively based on size, silhouette, color and movement alone thus leaving us with a considerable number of options.

It has been my experience that most dedicated fly fishermen who use leech patterns to any extent only fish them religiously in the morning before the sun reaches the water, on cloudy overcast days, in the evening after the sun has left the water or at night.

Garden Hackle.

Although the number of patterns I offer here may appear to be few, you should consider a full range of sizes and colors when tying any leech design. I suggest that you also think of the eels and small water snakes when creating any of these critters. Also see Duck Lake Woolly Worm, Chapter 8 and Ultimate, Ghost, Egg Sucking, Bunny and Lead Eye Leeches in Chapter 20. Although I have included these in other chapters, many have applications for other game fish as well.

Plate 2 Articulated Leech

Hooks: TMC800B or DAI2451, sizes 1/0-8. Two hooks are used for this pattern.
Thread: Black.
Body: Black yarn.
Hackle: Black marabou and CH02 black Crystal Hair.

Following are step-by-step instructions for tying the Articulated Leech:

Step 1. Black Dacron or monofilament loop is tied onto first hook. Second hook is strung through the loop and tied snug with thread with the bend and point of the hook up.

Step 2. Remove first hook from vise and secure trailer hook in vise. Wrap body to the center of the hook shank with black yarn and tie off. Tie in black marabou and wrap one full turn and tie off.

Step 3. Finish completing the body with black yarn and tie in a collar of black marabou at the front. Spin on sparse collar of CH02 black Crystal Hair in front of the marabou.

Step 4. Remove the hook from the vise and repeat the same on the front hook. When the fly is completed clip off the bend on the first hook.

This leech pattern is a producer. It was first tied by Mike Montaigna of Olema, California. Since it was first introduced in 1985 it has become an immediate success wherever used. It has accounted for record catches not only on the West Coast, but has also come away with very high marks in the Great Lakes area. Although this pattern has been stereotyped as a steelhead and salmon pattern here in the West, it is effective for most any game fish. Big, black and ugly does it every time, however, other colors are encouraged.

Now I want to give you some further "articulated thoughts" that I know many of you will put to good use. First study the simple designs of the Articulated Leech and the Marabou Leech. Now go to Chapter 23 and look at a Waddington shank. If this does not excite a fellow leecher nothing will.

Bunny Leech, Black

Hooks: TMC9395, DAI2220 or DAI1750, sizes 2-10.
Thread: Black.
Tail: Strip of dyed black rabbit. Over this is tied six strands of CH02 black Crystal Hair.
Body: Strip of dyed black rabbit wrapped forward.
Topping: Six strands of CH02 black Crystal Hair.
Head: Black.

Bunny Leech, Brown

Hooks: TMC9395, DAI2220 or DAI1750, sizes 2-10.
Thread: Brown.
Tail: Strip of dyed reddish-brown rabbit. Over this is tied six strands of CH25 copper brown Crystal Hair.
Body: Strip of dyed reddish-brown rabbit wrapped forward.
Topping: Six strands of CH25 copper brown Crystal Hair.
Head: Brown.

Bunny Leech, Gray

Hooks: TMC9395, DAI2220 or DAI1750, sizes 2-10.
Thread: Gray.

Tail: Strip of natural gray rabbit. Over this is tied six strands of CH01 pearl Crystal Hair.
Body: Strip of natural gray rabbit wrapped forward.
Topping: Six strands of CH01 pearl Crystal Hair.
Head: Gray.

The natural gray rabbit referred to in this pattern is also called "chinchilla." It is a natural gray with the guard hairs having dark tips. There is also a natural brown or fawn color with dark tips which ties up into a very fine leech pattern.

Plate 2   Bunny Leech, Olive

Hooks: TMC9395, DAI2220 or DAI1750, sizes 2-10.
Thread: Olive.
Tail: Strip of dyed olive rabbit. Over this is tied six strands of CH15 olive Crystal Hair.
Body: Strip of dyed olive rabbit wrapped forward.
Topping: Six strands of CH15 olive Crystal Hair.
Head: Olive.

If at all possible try and obtain rabbit for this pattern which has been overdyed olive either on a light cast natural brown or gray. It is the overall elusion portrayed in the finished fly that makes this type of pattern more effective.

The fur strips used for the body of these patterns should be cut across the skin rather than down. This allows the hair to lay back naturally when properly wrapped.

Ever since Zonkers became popular in Colorado an interest has been taken by fly tiers in finding other applications for rabbit fur strips. Larry Walker of Golden, Colorado, got me thinking along this line, in fact he sent me a device for cutting the rabbit strips from full hides. As you can see, some of us don't mess around and take all of this rather seriously.

He mentioned that they were trying different approaches for leech patterns and made some suggestions. This got me inspired and I also started experimenting. My son Stan and I embarked on this in 1980 and these are the patterns we have finally settled on after more than a decade of trial and error. Also see Chapter 20 for some of the other Bunny Leech patterns we are real happy with. There have been a number of leech patterns developed across the country using rabbit fur strips. Many of these patterns are very similar and yet others have a little bit of different flavor.

I give most of the credit for Bunny Leech patterns to Larry Walker who planted some very productive seeds in the minds of many. Larry himself is no slouch when it comes to fly tying and creativity. Many take his ideas and end up calling them their own. As a fly tying artist I would rate Larry in the top 2% in the entire Rocky Mountain Region.

His humbleness often makes it hard to extract some of his broad knowledge, however, he is always willing to share once the ice is broken.

Canadian Blood Leech

I am not certain that I want to get into this pattern or not, but interest shown dictates someone needs to. No matter how I represent it someone is going to be upset. During the past thirty years there have been stories of this mysterious special Canadian mohair yarn which would make most any fly fisherman set up and pay attention. One author stated:

"The original Canadian brown mohair yarn has become something of a legend in the Northwest and the tiers who possess skeins treat them with as much respect as a collector of fine art would a Picasso."

This is strictly merchandising tactics which emerged from the Boise, Idaho, area in the late 1970s. I agree that some of these yarns might well be collector items—they are one-of-a-kind, and seldom, if ever, will be duplicated again. These yarns are somewhat like fashion apparel and the ladies do buy them just for that reason. They are referred to as novelty yarns within that particular trade. Certainly there is a difficulty in locating this material in some of the fantasized colors that fly tiers want. Gullibility, blind naive trust, I cannot find the words that best suits this situation. See Quebec Mohair Yarn, Chapter 5.

Another endlessly repeated story is, *"This pattern was developed in the Kamloops region of British Columbia for the remote interior lakes. It has become a popular fly in the U.S. as well."* This is a bit of imagination coming from someone who apparently never fished this region. The reader eats up the mystique of "British Columbia" and "remote lakes" like a bee going after honey.

I can tell you from my own personal knowledge that it certainly does not take something very special to catch fish in this particular area. In Akehurst Lake for example, a large body of water, the resort owner pays the kids a dollar for every five gallon bucket of fish they bring to him. He says the kids do very well with just a piece of white string tied on a hook. The area suffers an overpopulation and not enough fishing pressure rather than the lack of some specialty pattern.

I am certain I have not settled this issue, just added fuel to the fire. So here we have two stories floating around. One story gives credence to a Canadian mohair yarn and the other to an area in Canada. Neither makes any sense and just confuses the issue—as they may well be intended to do. See Mohair Leech that follow in this chapter.

Chamois Leech, Black

Hooks: TMC5263 or DAI1720, sizes 4-12.
Thread: Black.
Tail/Back: Strip of black chamois.
Body: Dubbed with #1 black Bunnytron.

Chamois Leech, Brown

Hooks: TMC5263 or DAI1720, sizes 4-12.
Thread: Brown.
Tail/Back: Strip of natural chamois.
Body: Dubbed with #25 reddish-brown Bunnytron.

Chamois Leech, Dark Brown

Hooks: TMC5263 or DAI1720, sizes 4-12.
Thread: Black.
Tail/Back: Strip of dark brown chamois.
Body: Dubbed with #26 dark brown Bunnytron.

The Chamois Leeches are very easy to tie and should be taken seriously by any fly fisherman who fishes lakes. Fish will eat these best on overcast days. They were developed by Arnold Bostos of Mankato, Minnesota.

To obtain the colors for the chamois strips, use waterproof markers. Note how the strip is first tied in at the rear, pulled forward over the body and tied down, leaving a portion protruding over the head. This gives the imitation a more natural movement in the water when retrieved.

Plate 2 — Davis Leech, Black

Hooks: TMC5263 or DAI1720, sizes 6-10.
Thread: Black.
Tail: Grizzly marabou tip.
Body: Dubbed with #1 black Bunnytron.
Wing: CH02 black Crystal Hair tied over the body and extending to the end of the tail with an overwing of grizzly marabou. Marabou should only extend to the end of the body.

Davis Leech, Brown

Hooks: TMC5263 or DAI1720, sizes 6-10.
Thread: Black.
Tail: Dyed brown grizzly marabou tip.
Body: Dubbed with #24 brown Bunnytron.
Wing: CH25 copper brown Crystal Hair tied over the body and extending to the end of the tail with an overwing of dyed brown grizzly marabou. Marabou should only extend to the end of the body.

Davis Leech, Olive

Hooks: TMC5263 or DAI1720, sizes 6-10.
Thread: Black.
Tail: Dyed olive grizzly marabou tip.
Body: Dubbed with #21 golden olive Bunnytron.
Wing: CH16 dark olive Crystal Hair tied over the body and extending to the end of the tail with an overwing of dyed olive grizzly marabou. Marabou should only extend to the end of the body.

Howard Ross of Portola, California, gave me some of these in 1969 to try in Davis Lake. Davis Lake is situated just 8 miles north of Portola and is noted for some rather large fish mostly being taken on a variety of Woolly Worms or Woolly Buggers. Since that time I have used these flies with very good success and I can see now why the locals have kept these leech patterns to themselves.

Filoplume Leech

Hooks: TMC5263 or DAI1720, sizes 6-10.
Thread: Black.
Tail: Dyed black filoplume with a few strands of CH02 black Crystal Hair.
Body: Dyed black filoplumes wrapped individually over the body. Be careful—

stems are frail and will break with too much pressure.

This is basically a Troth Leech without a haircut. Al Troth tied this pattern in the early 1970s, but he trimmed the top and bottom flat leaving only the sides. This pattern is also tied in a natural gray and a natural gray overdyed brown or dark brown.

Plate 2 — Henry's Lake Leech

Hooks: TMC9395, DAI2220 or DAI1750, sizes 6-12.
Thread: Brown.
Tail: Reddish-brown marabou.
Ribbing: Brown saddle hackle clipped to pencil shape.
Body: Reddish-brown chenille.

This is the original Henry's Lake Leech, however, there is a multitude of variations using this same design. When I am visiting Idaho this is the one that I feel most confident with.

Plate 2 — Howells' Leech

Hooks: TMC9395, DAI2220 or DAI1750, sizes 6-12.
Thread: Black.
Ribbing: Copper wire.
Body: Dubbed with #1 black African Angora goat.
Wing: One dyed black marabou plume mounted flat over the body and tied down with ribbing.

Gary Howells of Richmond, California, originated this pattern for Henry's Lake and now it has gained favor wherever used. This pattern is also tied in a reddish-brown. Gary Howells is the maker of some of the finest bamboo fly rods ever made. That is an all-encompassing statement, but true—just ask someone who has the privilege of owning one.

Lectric Leech

Hooks: TMC5263 or DAI1720, sizes 4-10.
Thread: Black.
Tail: Dyed black marabou.
Shellback: Peacock herl.
Sides: Pearl Flashabou.
Body Hackle: Black tied palmer style over the body.
Body: Dubbed with #1 black Bunnytron.

This is a design created by Dave Whitlock and can be tied in several colors. First tie in the tail; tie in the hackle; tie in the peacock so the tips extend to the end of the tail, and then tie in the Flashabou at each side with it also trailing back to the end of the tail. Dub the body, then pull the peacock over the back and the Flashabou up each side and tie off at the front. Finally, wrap the hackle and finish off the head.

Marabou Leech

Hooks: TMC9395, DAI2220 or DAI1750, sizes 2-10.
Thread: Brown.
Tail: Reddish-brown marabou.
Body: Reddish-brown chenille.
Center Wing: Reddish-brown marabou.
Wing: Reddish-brown marabou.

Of all the many leech patterns this one has been the most productive. I generally fish this in black and on overcast days. The last time I used this on California's Milton Reservoir the fish treated it unlike any conventional text book logic, they ate my fly on the top just as it hit before it could sink. Needless to say, in the excitement I lost one hell of a lot of flies that afternoon and stopped when my last leech was gone.

Matuka Leech, Marabou

Hooks: TMC9395, DAI2220 or DAI1750, sizes 4-10.

Thread: Black.
Ribbing: Copper wire.
Body: Dubbed with FB47 olive/black Fly Brite.
Wing: Dyed black marabou. Select a matching pair of marabou plumes and strip off the barbs on one side and tie on edge over the body using the copper wire ribbing.

Matuka Leech, Rabbit

Hooks: 79580, TMC9395, DAI2220 or DAI1750, sizes 4-10.
Ribbing: Copper wire.
Body: Black mohair yarn.
Wing: Dyed black rabbit fur strip tied over the back using the copper wire ribbing.

Plate 2   Mini Leech

Hooks: TMC5263 or DAI1720, sizes 10-14.
Thread: Tan.
Tail: Tan marabou.
Body: Tan ostrich herl.

The Mini Leech is most often tied in natural gray and lighter colors, even white, and proves itself best on a very slow retrieve.

From the three leech patterns I have just listed you can tie colors and sizes of your own choice. I sincerely believe that good basic colors and sizes joined with someone doing his or her thing on the other end can be one of our more effective forms of fly fishing.

Plate 2   Mohair Leech

Hooks: TMC9395, DAI2220 or DAI1750, sizes 2-10.
Body: Leech yarn or mohair yarn.

This style of fly basically consists of a body which has been picked out and made shaggy. You have the option of wrapping your yarn as fat as you want, maintaining a leech profile of course, and then picking it out. When you tie in your yarn leave the tag end stringing out the back like a tail, then during the picking out process this should be frayed (picked) out.

For those of you who want mixed or variegated colors first twist the two colors together before wrapping. Because of the composition of these yarns they will blend easily when picked out. One would swear that the fly was either tied with a mixed blend of dubbing or a variegated novelty yarn.

This is probably the most rational approach to the mysterious Canadian Blood Leech or Canadian Brown Leech for a variegated design. The basic colors tiers seek range from a reddish-brown, crimson red, to a purple. Many will interpret shades of either violet or maroon in between the crimson red and the purple. Usually two strands of these basic colors are used along with one strand of black. Now the secret is out, maybe.

Bart Bancroft is the only one I know of who has mohair yarn specifically for fly tying. He says that he tried to supply some of the earlier requests for variegated colors but the requirements became so moronic and unreasonable that he totally stays away from it now. The fourteen colors that he currently offers probably exceeds what we need.

Mohair / Marabou Leech

Tied same as the Mohair Leech except has a marabou tail of the same color as the body.

My Leech

Hooks: TMC9395, DAI2220 or DAI1750, sizes 6-10.
Thread: Black.
Ribbing: Copper wire.

Body: Black chenille.
Hackle: Dark brown tied on as a collar and tied back and down.
Tail and Shellback: Dark brown marabou tied in at the rear (forming the tail) and pulled over the back. All is secured with ribbing.

Originated in 1967 by Jim Dexter of LaPine, Oregon.

Ozark Leech, Black
Hook: TMC9395, DAI2220 or DAI1750, sizes 6-10.
Thread: Black.
Tail: Black marabou tied long.
Ribbing: Flat gold tinsel.
Body: Black chenille.

Plate 2 ### Ozark Leech, Brown
Hook: TMC9395, DAI2220 or DAI1750, sizes 6-10.
Thread: Brown.
Tail: Brown marabou tied long.
Ribbing: Flat gold tinsel.
Body: Brown chenille.

Ozark Leech, Gray
Hook: TMC9395, DAI2220 or DAI1750, sizes 6-10.
Thread: Black.
Tail: Gray marabou tied long.
Ribbing: Flat silver tinsel.
Body: Gray chenille.

Ozark Leech, Olive
Hook: TMC9395, DAI2220 or DAI1750, sizes 6-10.
Thread: Olive.
Tail: Golden olive marabou tied long.
Ribbing: Flat gold tinsel.
Body: Olive chenille.

Originated by Eric Bibbs of Tulsa, Oklahoma. I never realized that the heartland of American had such excellent fishing until I visited Tulsa in 1980. Heading east out of Tulsa there is water and more water. After crossing the entire state it is a refreshing sight. With this water comes excellent fishing. They have trout all right, but I had my most excitement with the striped bass and Ozark Leeches.

Pheasant Leech

Hooks: TMC9395, DAI2220 or DAI1750, sizes 6-10.
Thread: Brown.
Tail: Dyed brown pheasant rump barbs tied long.
Ribbing: Reverse wrapped with fine gold wire.
Body: Brown horse hair wrapped over an underbody of brown floss.
Hackle: Dyed brown pheasant rump barbs tied in at each side and extending just past the end of the hook.

Originated by Art Benning of Grand Junction, Colorado.

San Juan Worm

Hooks: DAI1130 or DAI1150, sizes 10-16.
Thread: To match body color.
Body: Section of chenille to simulate shape of the natural. This particular chenille is a flock product and known under such names as Plush Chenille, Ultra Chenille, etc. Best colors are: scarlet red, crimson red, reddish-brown, brown, dark brown, tan and black.

San Juan Worm, Looped

Tied same as above, but the body material is looped up and is only attached to the hook at the front and back as per illustration.

Uinta Leech, Black

Hooks: TMC9395, DAI2220 or DAI1750, sizes 2-10.
Thread: Red.
Tail: Dyed black long fine bucktail mixed with FB02 black Fly Brite.
Body: MHY02 black mohair yarn.
Wing: Sparse black marabou tied over the body and extending the length of the body.
Topping: Very sparse FB02 black Fly Brite.
Head: Red.

Uinta Leech, Brown

Hooks: TMC9395, DAI2220 or DAI1750, sizes 2-10.
Thread: Orange.
Tail: Natural brown long fine bucktail mixed with FB53 brown/orange blended Fly Brite.
Body: MHY05 dark brown and MHY11 orange stone mohair yarn mixed.
Wing: Sparse dark brown marabou tied over the body and extending the length of the body.
Topping: Very sparse FB53 brown/orange Fly Brite.
Head: Orange.

Uinta Leech, Gray

Hooks: TMC9395, DAI2220 or DAI1750, sizes 2-10.
Thread: Black.
Tail: Dyed black long fine bucktail mixed with FB26 gray Fly Brite.
Body: MHY02 black and MHY07 gray mohair yarn mixed.
Wing: Sparse dark gray marabou tied over the body and extending the length of the body.
Topping: Very sparse FB26 gray Fly Brite.
Head: Black.

The body of the two previous patterns are constructed by first twisting the two colors together before wrapping. After the body is wrapped it is picked out same as the Mohair Leech.

Uinta Leech, Olive

Hooks: TMC9395, DAI2220 or DAI1750, sizes 2-10.
Thread: Yellow.
Tail: Dyed olive long fine bucktail mixed with FB25 brown Fly Brite.
Body: MHY10 golden olive mohair yarn.
Wing: Sparse dark olive marabou tied over the body and extending the length of the body.
Topping: Very sparse FB25 brown Fly Brite.
Head: Yellow.

The Uinta Leeches were created by Kevin Adler of Provo, Utah. He first used them in Utah's Strawberry Reservoir in 1979 and they have since been used in literally dozens of lakes throughout the country.

Kevin states he ties these leeches in a host of colors but finds he fishes these four patterns more regularly and with the most conviction. He tries to use contrasting colored heads as he feels the fish zero in on his fly best when given this as a target.

Variegated Leech, Dark

Hooks: TMC300 or DAI2220, sizes 4-8.
Thread: Dark brown.
Tail: Brown marabou topped with dark brown marabou.
Body: Brown chenille.
Center Wing: Brown marabou topped with dark brown marabou.
Wing: Brown marabou topped with dark brown bucktail.

Variegated Leech, Light

Hooks: TMC300 or DAI2220, sizes 4-10.
Thread: Brown.
Tail: Tan marabou topped with reddish-brown marabou.
Body: Tan chenille.
Center Wing: Tan marabou topped with reddish-brown marabou.
Wing: Tan marabou topped with natural brown bucktail.

Ron Bennington's idea of mixing up the colors a bit does in fact give these patterns the illusion of more than simple movement as these flies are worked through the water.

Plate 2 Woolly Bugger, Black

Hooks: TMC5263 or DAI1720, sizes 4-12.
Thread: Black.
Tail: Black marabou tied equal to one and one half the length of the body. Strands of CH02 black Crystal Hair is tied in on top of the marabou.
Body: Black chenille.
Hackle: Black tied palmer style over the body.

The Woolly Bugger has been like a person without a country, left wandering around for years. In this case, without a name—but a good one was finally found and stuck. As you can see, the Woolly Bugger is simply a variation of the Woolly Worm and with its longer tail has stepped up in status, from that of a common wet fly to a leech (close to it anyway). You might even say it is a Henry's Lake Leech without a clipped body.

Countless tiers have been playing with variations for many generations and no one or one hundred fly tiers can begin to take credit here. Some of the more popular color combinations are listed below, however, if you feel something will work better for you, go for it. Also see Woolly Worms, Chapter 8, for other color ideas.

Woolly Bugger, Brown

Hooks: TMC5263 or DAI1720, sizes 4-12.
Thread: Brown.
Tail: Brown marabou tied equal to one and one half the length of the body. Strands of CH25 copper brown Crystal Hair is tied in on top of the marabou.
Body: Brown chenille.
Hackle: Brown tied palmer style over the body.

Woolly Bugger, Golden Olive

Hooks: TMC5263 or DAI1720, sizes 4-12.
Thread: Tan.
Tail: Golden olive marabou tied equal to one and one half the length of the body. Strands of CH18 golden olive Crystal Hair is tied in on top of the marabou.
Body: Yellow chenille.
Hackle: Ginger tied palmer style over the body.

This could very well be the Henry's Lake secret. It has the color.

Woolly Bugger, Olive

Hooks: TMC5263 or DAI1720, sizes 4-12.
Thread: Olive.
Tail: Olive marabou tied equal to one and one half the length of the body. Strands of CH15 olive Crystal Hair is tied in on top of the marabou.
Body: Olive chenille.
Hackle: Dyed olive grizzly tied palmer style over the body.

Woolly Bugger, Purple

Hooks: TMC5263 or DAI1720, sizes 4-12.
Thread: Black.
Tail: Purple marabou tied equal to one and one half the length of the body. Strands of CH19 purple Crystal Hair are tied in on top of the marabou.
Body: Purple chenille.
Hackle: Black tied palmer style over the body.

The five preceding patterns have proven to be the most successful. There are a considerable number of localized favorites.

Woolly Bugger, Crystal

Tied the same as the Woolly Bugger except Crystal Chenille is used for the body.

Woolly Bugger, Stan's

Tied same as the Woolly Bugger except has shellback of CH01 pearl Crystal Hair which also extends over the length of the tail.

Wiggler, Light

Hook: DAI1330, sizes 12-22.
Thread: Tan.
Body: Strip of natural chamois.
Legs: Sparse ginger hen hackle tied on as a collar and tied back.

Originated by Charlie Brooks. Charlie developed this design, and I emphasize "design" not pattern, to try and interest fish during those periods of, literally, no activity.

Using a waterproof marking pen, he would color the chamois from black to light gray and all shades in between. Naturally, the hackle colors would be changed accordingly. This fly would probably be better named the Brooks Wiggler. Taking advantage of size and color variations with most designs will often make the day.

Chapter 16

Midges: Order Diptera

The term midge is interpreted differently by a great many people. To some it takes on the meaning of something very tiny or small. Others try to associate it with the insect order Diptera. Experienced fly tiers find themselves confronted with not only the Diptera, but a triad or more of other like imitations. It is very possible that one could tie a Diptera imitation and find that it simulates a micro caddis, a Trico or other tiny mayfly. Frustrating as hell isn't it? Press on, it will all work itself out.

This chapter is fundamentally dedicated to the Diptera, however, there are patterns which may or may not properly fit into this category. They are included on basis of their smaller size, coupled with what their intended use has been perceived to be in the past.

As a young man, with good eyes and endless energy, tying commercially I thoroughly enjoyed doing the midges. At that time fly fishermen on the West Coast showed very little interest in the real small flies. It was always an uphill battle for me to keep a supply of hackle in sizes 12 and 14, as that was the fly sizes most demanded.

There I was with all of this hackle, either too large or too small, and praying for something to use it on. Quite by accident I met some people from the Denver area up at Rough and Ready one Saturday afternoon. We struck up a conversation and before I knew it I had talked myself into more than three months work tying midges for their shop. I believe they may have thought they were taking advantage of the situation. Little did they know that I already had the materials readily available. You see, small hackle has always been in rather short supply.

After I got into it I soon realized that by-darn I was making good money. At least better than the average commercial tier could expect in those days. How great it was. Tying these little 18, 20 and 22s, requiring very little material whatsoever, and producing more flies in a 4 hour work day than I ever did in 8 or 10 hours with other flies. This led to my tying for other shops in the Rocky Mountain area and, you guessed it, total burn out after a couple of years.

We in the fly fishing fraternity have often elected to focus our attention on only a portion of the Diptera order of flies and have unconsciously broken the others out into separate categories of their own. We use the common name "midge" most often when dealing with this order. Commercially we further confuse this by referring to any fly tied on a size 16 or smaller hook as a midge. In the scientific world the common name most frequently used is "true flies." This order is all-encompassing and includes thousands of species.

Besides the midges, this order also includes mosquitoes, craneflies, gnats, the common housefly, horseflies, deerflies, etc. All of these flies have a complete metamorphosis. Their young are called larvae, not nymphs. These flies have two sets of wings, one set developed and the other undeveloped and carried on the thorax. This chapter primarily deals with the midges (Chironomidae), mosquitoes (Culicidae) and the crane flies (Tipulidae). I have also included some general purpose patterns which have proven productive.

Midges: Family Chironomidae

Some say that there are over a thousand species of these tiny insects alone. I do not feel the angler has to be too concerned about this large number. Here again, size, color and shape is where your emphasis should be placed. It has been my experience that I really do not have to give a hoot about a particular species or subspecies. There are those who spend a lifetime studying this one family alone, but I feel it is of no significant benefit to the angler.

I am sure all of you have seen these little guys buzzing over the water, often in big swarms, and felt helpless due to their tiny size. The thought has to cross any thinking person's mind, "do fish really bother with something so small?" I believe it would be safe to say that fish do not expend much energy pursuing the adults, but the juveniles are another story. Because of their abundance fish do feed on them regularly. God only knows what a fish is thinking when it does take your tiny dry off the surface. There are a number of other small insects that fish may selectively seek out. If it is dry fly action you are after, one can tie a range of colors in sizes 16-24 and cover literally thousands of different species of insects. Just keep it simple with a tail, body and hackle, tying various subtle colors. Let's face it, the fish have little opportunity to examine a tiny dry, where their cousins under the surface can be more closely scrutinized.

I have fished stillwaters in most parts of the west and have developed personal techniques that may interest you. I cannot recall ever comparing what I do, or do differently from others, but I have had some reasonable success.

I am very partial to a light, sensitive rod, 3 to 5 weight, and a floating line. I have never found a sink tip line to be of any advantage for this particular style of fishing. Using a twelve foot conventional tapered leader finds me building on to it with additional tippet material. Depending on the clarity and depth of the water, my finished leader will range from fourteen to twenty feet or more.

From the limited research I have done, it would indicate that a great many of the species we think we are simulating hatch from the mud and other sediment on the lake bottom. The larvae does not seek out the weed beds until they reach the pupae stage just before hatching. Hence, my opting for the longer leaders.

Unlike the more active species, i.e., damsels and mosquitoes, these flies should be retrieved very slowly. I mean an inch at a time. Try to fix in your mind just what your fly might be doing with every minute twitch of the rod tip or faint stripping of the line. When you think you are going slow enough, slow it down even more. Try not to go to sleep and be ready for even the slightest nudge. This form of fishing takes considerable steadfastness and the ability to focus on what you are doing, much like a stalking animal, which in fact you are. Be deliberate and untiring.

Because of the complexities of these tiny insects we as fly fishermen have really not progressed in our development of a great variety of patterns. In areas where they have a strong following you will find anglers using midge patterns not only in lakes but in streams also. Personally, I have not had extensive experience with them, or to the level many of my friends have. You may see much more creativity in some areas with patterns used. I have been to places where one would get the impression there was a pattern of the week society cranking out variations. I believe that most of the great successes with this type of fly has more to do with presentation rather than the pattern being used—be it stream or stillwater.

As simple and fruitful as most of these designs are, I can strongly recommend that you attempt to develop some patterns of your own. The material requirements are minimal and the rewards can be fantastic. You might well be amazed at what a bit of fur and fluff can do when bound to a tiny hook. Midges are more than worth our attention as they are available to the fish as larvae, pupae and adults throughout the year.

For what it is worth, some species can fly more than 50 miles per hour.

Al's Rat

Hooks: TMC500U or DAI1140, sizes 18-22.
Thread: Brown.
Abdomen: Brown thread.
Thorax: Dubbed with sparse muskrat fur.

Originated by Al Miller of Allentown, Pennsylvania. On first seeing this pattern most are sure to say, "is that all?" Well if you fish Pennsylvania's Little Lehigh this may fill your needs. Ed Vatza, one of Al's friends, sent me this pattern after I got wind of it. They have been fishing it religiously for a number of years. They will tell you that size 20 is probably best and it can be tied in most any color just as long as it is brown. They admit to violating the "any color as long as it is brown edict" and have strayed off and tied other variations. These include the Lab Rat (white), Army Rat (olive), Commie Rat (red), and the Pinko Commie Rat (pink). Hey, they work.

Plate 3 Bent Emerger, Gray
Hooks: AC80200BR, TMC2457 or DAI1150, sizes 16-18.
Thread: Black.
Ribbing: Black thread.
Abdomen: Gray floss.
Budding Wing: Clear (white) Miclon.
Wingcase: Natural gray duck quill section tied over the thorax.
Thorax: Dubbed with muskrat fur.

Bent Emerger, Olive
Hooks: AC80200BR, TMC2457 or DAI1150, sizes 16-18.
Thread: Olive.
Ribbing: Yellow thread.
Abdomen: Olive floss.
Budding Wing: Clear (white) Miclon.
Wingcase: Dyed olive duck quill section tied over the thorax.
Thorax: Dubbed with #19 olive Bunny-Blend.

Plate 3 Bent Emerger, Red
Hooks: AC80200BR, TMC2457 or DAI1150, sizes 16-18.
Thread: Red.
Ribbing: Gray thread.
Abdomen: Red floss.
Budding Wing: Clear (white) Miclon.
Wingcase: Dyed red duck quill section tied over the thorax.
Thorax: Dubbed with #4 red Bunny-Blend.

The Bent Emergers were originated by Leroy Bentley of Colorado Springs, Colorado.

Plate 3 Black Midge Pupa
Hook: AC80000BR, TMC100 or DAI1180, sizes 16-20.
Thread: Black.
Tail: Black hackle barbs.
Abdomen: Black floss.
Thorax: Dubbed with #1 black Bunny-Blend.
Antennae: Black hackle barbs.

You will find that this pattern is easy to tie and can be real effective in the early morning or evening hours.

Black Midge Pupa
Hooks: TMC5212 or DAI1710, sizes 12-14.
Thread: Gray.
Head: Black ostrich herl tied in at the rear of the body.
Legs: Light cast grizzly tied on as a collar and tied back. This is mounted at the rear of the body.
Body: Dubbed with muskrat fur. Body should be well tapered with the thicker portion at the rear.

E. H. "Polly" Rosborough brought us this pattern. This fly is tied reversed on the hook.

Blood Worm
Hook: DAI1273, sizes 16-22.
Thread: Brown.
Abdomen: Red larva lace.
Thorax: Dubbed with #25 reddish brown lambs wool.

Effective or productive are both understatements about how well this pattern yields action. I have hooked into some sizable steelhead on the Yuba River with this fly and have yet to beach one. Others have told me they have had good success, however, they are not sure if it is being taken as tiny fragmentary bits of egg mass or a midge. I guess there are no absolutes in fly fishing.

Cain's Fur Midge

Hooks: AC80200BR, TMC2457 or DAI1510, sizes 14-20.
Thread: Black.
Ribbing: Closely wrapped with fine silver wire
Abdomen: Dubbed with beaver fur.
Thorax: Dubbed with #1 black lambs wool.

Chung's RS-2

See Chapter 9.

Griffith's Gnat

Hooks: AC80000BR, TMC100 or DAI1180, sizes 14-24.
Thread: Black.
Body: Peacock herl.
Hackle: Grizzly tied palmer style over the body.

Originated by George Griffith. This little fly has had such an outstanding success that it has become popular internationally. It is known in Europe as the Grey Palmer.

 Griffith's Gnat, Sparkle

Tied same as the preceding except it has a wing of clear (white) Miclon tied over the body. Many prefer this dressing due to its increased visibility.

 Hare Quill Midge

Hooks: AC80050BR, TMC200R or DAI1270, sizes 16-22.
Thread: Black.
Abdomen: Stripped peacock quill.
Thorax: Dubbed with hare's mask fur.

When I tie this little guy it is one of the few times I do not reverse wrap a quill type body with fine wire. They are so simple to tie and I want as little weight on this one as possible. I don't even apply cement. Fish in the surface film in the shadows during the day and expect the unexpected.

Invincible

Hooks: TMC921 or DAI1310, sizes 16-22.
Thread: Black.
Body: Dubbed with #1 black lambs wool.
Wing: Small bunch of imitation barred lemon woodduck barbs tied over the body.

Another of the Charlie Brooks patterns that he fished generally as an emerger. He dressed the wing with the smallest amount of paste type floatant.

Metallic Midge, Dark Olive

Hooks: TMC921 or DAI1510, sizes 16-20.
Thread: Black.
Body: CH16 dark olive Crystal Hair wrapped over a tapered underbody of white floss.
Head: Peacock herl.

Metallic Midge, Golden Olive

Hooks: TMC921 or DAI1510, sizes 16-20.
Thread: Black.
Body: CH18 golden olive Crystal Hair wrapped over a tapered underbody of white floss.
Head: Peacock herl.

Metallic Midge, Olive

Hooks: TMC921 or DAI1510, sizes 16-20.
Thread: Black.
Body: CH15 olive Crystal Hair wrapped over a tapered underbody of white floss.
Head: Peacock herl.

The Metallic Midges were developed in central Oregon. They are regarded as just the ticket for some of the deeper lakes with chironomid.

Miracle Nymph

Hooks: TMC921 or DAI1510, sizes 16-18.
Thread: Black.
Ribbing: Copper wire.
Body: White floss over an underbody of fully tapered black floss.

The so-called "miracle" of this fly is that the body changes to a dull gray color when wet. This fly was originated for the South Platte River in Colorado.

Plate 3 Palomino Midge, Dark Pupa

Hooks: TMC921 or DAI1310, sizes 16-22.
Thread: Black.
Abdomen: Fine black Ultra or Plush Chenille.
Wingcase: White (clear) Miclon or Z-Lon tied over the thorax.
Thorax: Dubbed with dyed black muskrat fur.
Head: Butts of wingcase extending over hook eye.

Plate 3 Palomino Midge, Dark Adult

Hooks: TMC921 or DAI1310, sizes 16-22.
Thread: Black.
Abdomen: Fine black Ultra or Plush Chenille
Thorax: Peacock herl.
Hackle: Black wrapped through the thorax.

Palomino Midge, Light Pupa

Hooks: TMC921 or DAI1310, sizes 16-22.
Thread: Gray.
Abdomen: Fine gray Ultra or Plush Chenille.
Wingcase: White (clear) Miclon or Z-Lon tied over the thorax.
Thorax: Dubbed with muskrat fur.
Head: Butts of wingcase extending over hook eye.

Palomino Midge, Light Adult

Hooks: TMC921 or DAI1310, sizes 16-22.
Thread: Gray.
Abdomen: Fine gray Ultra or Plush Chenille.
Thorax: Peacock herl.
Hackle: Grizzly wrapped through the thorax.

The Palomino series of midges can be tied in a variety of successful colors. Those I have given have proved to be the most successful for me and others. I first learned of these flies while fishing the Miracle Mile section of the North Platte River in Wyoming. Note how the abdomen of these patterns is tied extended body style.

Red Midge Pupa

Hooks: TMC5212 or DAI1710, sizes 12-14.
Thread: Red.
Head: Natural dark gray ostrich tied in at the rear of the body.
Legs: Light cast grizzly tied on as a collar and tied back.
Ribbing: Heavy red thread.
Body: Dubbed with #4 red Bunny-Blend. Body should be well tapered with thicker portion at the rear.

Tan Midge Pupa

Hooks: TMC5212 or DAI1710, sizes 12-14.
Thread: Tan.
Legs: Light cast grizzly tied on as a collar and tied back.
Ribbing: Heavy tan thread.
Body: Dubbed with #31 tan Bunny-Blend.

The two preceding patterns were originated by E. H. "Polly" Rosborough. They are tied reversed on the hook.

Serendipity

Hooks: AC80250BR, TMC2487 or DAI1510, sizes 16-22.
Thread: Gray.
Body: Red polypropylene yarn. Twist tightly before and while wrapping to give good segmented effect.
Head: Clipped deer hair.

Were you to display this pattern in Europe you would here it referred to as a Buoyant Buzzer rather than a Serendipity. The Europeans tie this pattern in a number of different body colors to represent a number of species of emerging pupae. The buoyancy of the hair allows the fly to rest in the water with just its nose sticking up. The deer hair can be clipped off in differing amounts to obtain different floating qualities. This pattern was developed as a stillwater pattern and when used in that fashion it can be really effective. There are literally dozens of Buoyant Buzzer-type patterns available in Europe.

In this country you will see this pattern also tied in different colors, however, wire of different colors may also be seen used by some tiers. Naturally this destroys the floating qualities of this creation—but if it works?

TDC

Hooks: TMC3761 or DAI1560, sizes 12-16.
Thread: Black.
Ribbing: Wrapped closely with fine flat silver tinsel.
Body: Dubbed with #1 black lambs wool. Body should be tied well down on the bend of the hook and tapered towards the head.

Thorax: Black ostrich, six turns.
Collar: White ostrich, two turns.

This pattern was developed by Dick Thompson of Seattle, Washington, for fishing the low land lakes of western Washington and Oregon. Dick is a fishery research biologist and developed this pattern to imitate the chironomid pupae which emerge from the bottom of the lakes in the west. It is suggested that this pattern be dressed in two versions—one with a rather fat taper and the other with a slender taper. This difference can decide your success from one area to another. So, as you can see, it amounts to more than just fishing with a TDC.

Some amateur fly tiers tie this pattern with a black chenille body. This only further reduces its effectiveness inasmuch as it is not possible to get a proper taper (silhouette) with chenille. Maybe this is one of those patterns that should not be fiddled with and left in its present form. Dick has already done the qualified research on this one for us.

Mosquito: Family Culicidae

I believe that, more than any other member of this order of insects, the mosquito is the most prevalent of them all. They are found from Alaska to Greenland, and in tropical regions of Africa and South America, and all points in between. These intolerable little pests are virtually everywhere, ranging from seashore to altitudes of at least 13,000 feet. Within North America there are 30 known species alone. Are they an important fish food? You bet. That is why I have been so encouraged to spend considerable time examining these darn worrisome pests.

Up until the early 1960s I didn't really think of a mosquito as anything other than a single species. A mosquito was a mosquito. One summer while fishing the Larmie River in northern Colorado I kept seeing these large creamy-colored, mosquito-like insects flying around in a lethargic manner. They were not aggressive in any sense of the word, you could brush them off and they appeared to be too dumb to return. I had come to the conclusion that they might not be mosquitoes at all.

That night in camp after I had gotten all snuggled down in my sleeping bag I began to itch and itch and itch. At first I thought I might have gotten into a patch of poison ivy. I concluded that those imperceptible little creatures had bitten me several hundred times that day. Needless to say, I had a crummy night.

Some time later I was in Wyoming on another fishing expedition, we had heard of a small lake on BLM land that had monstrous rainbows in it. We drove for what seemed to be hours and finally found a body of water nestled in some sage brush flats with nothing else in sight. Sure enough, we found public access and a gravel parking lot with a boat launching site. I hurriedly set up and started out around the perimeter of the little lake, kicking through the tall grass and started to work out some line. Suddenly I realized that I was being bit by mosquitoes, then more mosquitoes. Hell, I was being attacked like you see killer bees attacking on the movie screen.

I could not get back to the car fast enough. I got in, closed the door, then I realized that they really meant business—they had followed me into the car. We began killing what was on us and around us in the car. I got the brunt of the bites, I had charged into the grass first while my partner, Jerry, was still getting his act together. We lingered there for about ten minutes before the coast looked clear enough to get out to the gravel parking lot. No problem there, I guess mosquitoes don't like hot gravel parking lots.

Our only alternative was to avoid the grass and wade into the lake using the boat launching site. But first I had to make a few casts. Now some fish start smelling in this little story. On about my third or forth cast I hooked into and beached a thirteen and a half pound rainbow. It was so chrome bright that one would subconsciously look for sea lice. Taken on a size 14 Hornberg before it even had a chance to sink. That turned out to be one hell of a lake, a bit far to drive, but worth it. Incidentally, that water had the biggest population of mosquito larvae I had ever seen—and they were big. Using a size 12 with a 3X long shank hook would have been called for, so my tiny Hornberg wasn't out of place—just at the right place at the right time.

These two experiences got me to thinking and doing some intense reading. With more than 350 species in the world, they are certainly something the fly fisherman should give attention to. There is more to a mosquito than just his bite. The typical life cycle of a mosquito is much like that of other aquatic insects. The eggs are deposited at night in shallow water, usually fresh water but a few species use brackish or saltwater. After one or a few days they hatch into legless, aquatic larvae, and are commonly known as "wigglers." During this period they feed on plant life and other micro insects. By their active wiggling the larvae come frequently to the surface and breathe, and then sink lazily to the bottom. After one or more weeks the larvae molt finally and turn into pupae.

Like the larvae the pupae are active wigglers, but, unlike them, are buoyant and float naturally just at the surface. After a few days they hatch from the surface and spend an average of ten days as adults. As you can see many generations can be produced during a favorable season.

Mosquitoes are very well known by science and literally thousands of pages have been written about them. I find it odd that this area has been so neglected by the fly fishing community. The work has been done for us, yet we have chosen to almost ignore it. The few patterns we do have only simulate a couple of species and more-or-less lean towards a stereotype. Someone years ago convinced us that a coloring of black and white was the common makeup of the mosquito. As I looked at this closer I found that was only partially true. In fact, if found in the majority of our often frequented fly fishing areas they would be considered rare.

The closest thing I had to simulating the larvae in the Wyoming lake was a Light Cahill nymph that I had with me just by chance. After I lost it, some hackle quickly got clipped off our dry flies of similar color. It all worked out and new approaches to the mosquito patterns were developed and have been in use for more than twenty years now. First I am going to list the patterns which I have developed, then give you the patterns which others have found productive.

Light Mosquito Larva
Hooks: AC80050BR, TMC200R or DAI1270, sizes 14-16.
Thread: Tan.
Tail: Dyed imitation barred lemon woodduck barbs.
Body: Dubbed with #3 cream Bunny-Blend and made slightly fuller in the thorax area.
Head: Tan.

Light Mosquito Pupa
Hook: TMC5212 or DAI1280, sizes 14-16.
Thread: Tan.
Tail: Tan marabou tied short and sparse.
Ribbing: Heavy tan thread over the abdomen.
Abdomen: Dubbed with #31 tan Bunny-Blend.
Thorax: Dubbed with #27 ginger Bunny-Blend.
Legs: Dyed imitation barred lemon woodduck barbs tied beard style.

Light Adult Mosquito
Hooks: AC80000BR, TMC100 or DAI1180, sizes 12-18.
Thread: Tan.
Tail: Light ginger hackle barbs.
Ribbing: Tan thread.

Body: Dubbed with #3 cream poly.
Wing: Barred mallard tip tied flat over the body.
Hackle: Light ginger tied on as a collar.

Medium Mosquito Larva
Hooks: AC80050BR, TMC200R or DAI1270, sizes 14-16.
Thread: Gray.
Tail: Dyed gray barred mallard barbs.
Body: Dubbed with #12 light gray Bunny-Blend and made slightly fuller in the thorax area.
Head: Gray.

Medium Mosquito Pupa
Hook: TMC5212 or DAI1280, sizes 14-16.
Thread: Gray.
Tail: Light gray marabou tied short and sparse.
Ribbing: Heavy gray thread over the abdomen.
Abdomen: Dubbed with #12 light gray Bunny-Blend.
Thorax: Dubbed with #13 gray Bunny-Blend.
Legs: Dyed blue dun barred mallard barbs tied beard style.

Medium Adult Mosquito

Hooks: AC80000BR, TMC100 or DAI1180, sizes 12-18
Thread: Gray.
Tail: Dyed blue dun grizzly hackle barbs.
Ribbing: Gray thread.
Body: Dubbed with #12 light gray poly.
Wing: Barred mallard tip tied flat over the body.
Hackle: Dyed blue dun tied on as a collar.

Plate 3   Dark Mosquito Larva

Hooks: AC80050BR, TMC200R or DAI1270, sizes 14-16.
Thread: Black.
Tail: Grizzly hen hackle barbs.
Body: Dubbed with #13 gray Bunny-Blend and made slightly fuller in the thorax area.
Head: Black.

Plate 3   Dark Mosquito Pupa

Hook: TMC5212 or DAI1280, sizes 14-16.
Thread: Black.
Tail: Grizzly marabou tied short and sparse.
Ribbing: Heavy black thread over the abdomen.
Abdomen: Dubbed with #13 gray Bunnytron.
Thorax: Dubbed with #14 dark gray Bunnytron.
Legs: Grizzly hen hackle barbs tied beard style.

Plate 3   Dark Adult Mosquito

Hooks: AC80000BR, TMC100 or DAI1180, sizes 12-18.
Thread: Black.
Tail: Dyed dark blue dun grizzly hackle barbs.
Ribbing: Heavy light gray thread.
Body: Dubbed with #13 gray poly.
Wing: Barred mallard tip tied flat over the body.
Hackle: Grizzly tied on as a collar.

Other Mosquito Patterns

California Mosquito
(Wet Fly Design)
Hooks: TMC3769 or DAI1550, sizes 10-16.
Thread: Black.
Tail: Scarlet red hackle barbs.
Ribbing: Black floss.
Body: White floss.
Wings: Two grizzly hen hackle tips tied on edge in a V over the body.
Hackle: Grizzly hen hackle tied on as a collar and tied back.

Please note that the wings are mounted behind the hackle collar. I never thought much of this mosquito variation until I learned of its success when hen hackle was used.

Mosquito
(Wet Fly Design)
Hooks: TMC3769 or DAI1550, sizes 10-16.
Thread: Black.
Tail: Grizzly hackle barbs.
Body: Light and dark moose mane.
Hackle: Grizzly tied on as collar and tied back and down.
Wings: Grizzly hackle tips tied on edge over the body.

Both of the preceding patterns are also tied as dry flies. I have a preference for them as wets over the dries. They have always served my fishing needs better when fished in the surface film.

Plate 3   Mosquito Larva

Hooks: TMC5262 or DAI1720, sizes 14-16.
Thread: Gray.
Tail: Speckled guinea fowl barbs.
Ribbing: Gray thread.

Body: Medium gray yarn.
Legs: Speckled guinea fowl barbs tied in at the throat and kept short.
Head: Gray.
Eyes: Tiny black dots.

This is probably the last fly pattern that Polly Rosborough designed. It was inspired by the backwaters of his favored river, the Williamson.

Plate 3   Mosquito Larva
Hooks: TMC3761 or DAI1560, sizes 14-18.
Thread: Black.
Tail: Grizzly hackle barbs.
Abdomen: Stripped peacock quill.
Thorax: Peacock herl.
Head: Black.

Plate 3   Mosquito Larva
Hooks: TMC3761 or DAI1560, sizes 14-16.
Thread: Black.
Tail: Grizzly hackle barbs.
Antennae: Grizzly hackle barbs.
Abdomen: Stripped grizzly hackle stem.
Thorax: Grizzly saddle hackle wound over the thorax and clipped to shape.

Head: Black.
Plate 3   Mosquito Larva
Hooks: AC80050BR, TMC200R or DAI1270, sizes 14-20.
Thread: Black.
Tail: Grizzly hen hackle barbs tied short.
Body: Peacock quill wrapped over a tapered underbody of dubbed muskrat fur.
Antennae: Grizzly hen hackle barbs tied short.

Mosquito Pupa
Hooks: AC80050BR, TMC200R or DAI1270, sizes 14-20.
Thread: Olive.
Tail: Tuft of grizzly marabou tied short.
Ribbing: Copper wire.
Abdomen: Peacock quill.
Thorax: Peacock herl.
Budding Wings: Grizzly hen hackle tips tied on edge over the body and extending half way.

The two preceding patterns were originated by Randall Kaufmann.

Crane Flies: Family Tipulidae

These flies have the general appearance of a large mosquito. As Abe Snake would describe them, "They are Texas mosquitoes—the biggest you have ever seen." These are the largest members of the Diptera order. The bodies of the varied species range from a quarter to one inch long. Contrary to popular belief, most crane fly species do not live in streams or lakes. They are found around damp mossy areas, rotting wood, and generally moist ground. In early summer I can walk out onto my well mulched lawn and they fly up clumsily by the hundreds.

There are a few species that use water as a breeding ground, these species have similar traits to other Diptera in this regard. Although considered few in number in most areas, we in the western part of the country should give them our attention.

No one in fly fishing has yet to come up with a reasonably good imitation of the adult crane fly. I mean one that can be fished with and give you the opportunity to use it for a second fish. What I have seen is some very realistic attempts that would make one fearsome of handling them while trying to attach them to your leader. My personal attempts have all resulted in a disaster of sorts—they're just too damn fragile. If an adult pattern is found to be necessary, and I seriously doubt it ever would, I recommend trying one of the larger Spider or Variant patterns to fill this void.

The larvae is a different story. Get out and collect samples in your area before wasting a minute behind the vise. You will find that the larvae range in color from cream to dark olive and all shades in-between. These are the guys you really want to tie.

Adult Crane Fly

Hooks: AC80000BR, TMC100 or DAI1180, size 10.
Thread: Brown.
Tail/Body Extension: Brown polypropylene yarn. Burn end to keep from fraying out.
Legs: Six brown pheasant tail feather barbs. Knot these in two places.
Body: Dubbed with #24 brown poly.
Hackle: Undersized ginger tied on as a collar.
Wings: Pair of light blue dun hackle tips tied flat over the body. These may also be tied spent or semi-spent.

This represents my best attempt at the adult. I hate the legs—they foul my tippets if I am not careful.

Crane Fly Larva

Hooks: TMC300 or DAI2340, sizes 4-12.
Thread: Gray.
Tail: Small tuft of light gray marabou.
Ribbing: Heavy gray thread.
Abdomen: Dubbed with a 50/50 blend of #3 cream and #12 light gray African Angora goat.
Thorax: Dubbed with #13 gray African Angora goat.

This is a pattern I carry with me for many of my local waters. If I were on my way to the Gunnison River in southern Colorado you can bet they would have a dark olive abdomen and black thorax.

Other Midge Patterns

Horse Hair Midges

One of the nicer materials to tie with is horse hair. I had an occasion where I found myself in need of some midge patterns, I really didn't know where I was going and started experimenting with a good number of materials. I came across a stash of horse hair that I had left over from some woven body flies I had been working on months before. My goal was to create something tiny yet with a segmentation in the body. The horse hair did the trick and also gave me bugs that provided a deceptive illusion that I was sure would trick some fish.

I have found that on waters like Idaho's Silver Creek conventional dry flies and nymphs often have little appeal to some of the local trout. Through extensive trial and error I found that midges fished in the surface film did the trick when the general activity on the water would tell most of us something different. Fish would be rolling and appear to be sipping something off the top. Even with the tiniest of dries and 6X or 7X tippets, which extended my leaders to sixteen feet, I was unsuccessful. This is the point where my friends come in and tell me that my bright fly line might be spooking the fish.

To make a long story short, I found that by fishing my HH Midges in sizes 16 or 18, all at once I was in command of the situation. Using 4X and 5X tippets on nine to twelve foot leaders is acceptable. And that misconception about line color is just a bunch of wind. I still contend that line and leader shadow is the culprit and this can be largely overcome by proper presentation. See Chapter 2.

I fish these general purpose patterns on waters all over the west. When I can walk away from an afternoon on the fly fishing only section of the South Platte River in Colorado saying, "what a great day this has been," I know something is working in my favor.

Black HH Midge

Hooks: AC80200BR, TMC2457 or DAI1150, sizes 16-18.
Thread: Black.
Tag: Black floss.
Body: Black horse hair wrapped well down into the bend of the hook.
Legs: Black hen hackle barbs tied beard style.
Wingcase: Black ostrich herl

Brown HH Midge

Hooks: AC80200BR, TMC2457 or DAI1150, sizes 16-18.
Thread: Brown.
Tag: Brown floss.
Body: Brown horse hair wrapped well down into the bend of the hook.
Legs: Brown hen hackle barbs tied beard style.
Wingcase: Brown ostrich herl.

Cream HH Midge

Hooks: AC80200BR, TMC2457 or DAI1150, sizes 16-18.
Thread: Pale yellow.
Tag: Pale yellow floss.
Body: Cream horse hair wrapped well down into the bend of the hook.
Legs: Cream hen hackle barbs tied beard style.
Wingcase: Yellow ostrich herl.

Golden HH Midge

Hooks: AC80200BR, TMC2457 or DAI1150, sizes 16-18.
Thread: Orange.
Tag: Yellow floss.
Body: Golden brown horse hair wrapped well down into the bend of the hook.
Legs: Brown hen hackle barbs tied beard style.
Wingcase: Tan ostrich herl.

Gray HH Midge

Hooks: AC80200BR, TMC2457 or DAI1150, sizes 16-18.
Thread: Gray.
Tag: Gray floss.
Body: Gray horse hair wrapped well down into the bend of the hook.
Legs: Blue dun hen hackle barbs tied beard style.
Wingcase: Natural gray ostrich herl.

Olive HH Midge

Hooks: AC80200BR, TMC2457 or DAI1150, sizes 16-18.
Thread: Olive.
Tag: Olive floss.
Body: Olive horse hair wrapped well down into the bend of the hook.
Legs: Olive hen hackle barbs tied beard style.
Wingcase: Peacock herl.

Wrap an underbody on these patterns with the same floss as used for the tag.

Spider Dry Flies

Spider dry flies are tied to represent tiny hovering insects of all types. Their popularity has been hampered only by the availability of proper hackle so one can tie them correctly. Hackle is best tied as sparse as possible so it needs to be of the best, stiffest quality. Spider hackle is tied two times larger (longer) than normal. In other words, size 10 hackle is used for a size 14 hook. Tail length is proportioned accordingly.

Adams Spider

Hooks: TMC921 or DAI1310, sizes 14-18.
Thread: Black.
Tail: Brown and grizzly hackle barbs mixed and tied long.
Body: Dubbed with muskrat fur.
Hackle: Oversized brown and grizzly tied in as a collar mixed.

Badger Spider

Hooks: TMC921 or DAI1310, sizes 14-18.
Thread: Black.
Tail: Badger hackle barbs tied long.
Body: Black saddle hackle stem.
Hackle: Oversized badger tied on as a collar.

Black Spider

Hooks: TMC921 or DAI1310, sizes 14-18.
Thread: Black.
Tail: Black hackle barbs tied long.
Body: Black saddle hackle stem.
Hackle: Oversized black tied on as a collar.

Blue Dun Spider

Hooks: TMC921 or DAI1310, sizes 14-18.
Thread: Gray.
Tail: Blue dun hackle barbs tied long.
Body: Dubbed with muskrat fur.
Hackle: Oversized blue dun tied on as a collar.

Brown Spider

Hooks: TMC921 or DAI1310, sizes 14-18.
Thread: Brown.
Tail: Brown hackle barbs tied long.
Body: Brown saddle hackle stem.
Hackle: Oversized brown tied on as a collar.

Elk Hair Spider

Hooks: TMC921 or DAI1310, sizes 14-18.
Thread: Tan.
Tail: Light elk hair.
Hackle/Body: Light elk hair.

This unusually constructed pattern can be very effective if put together properly. The use of a hair evener is almost unavoidable to insure the tips of all the hair used are perfectly even—at least close anyway.

The tail should be tied in at the center of the hook shank. The hackle consists of two small bunches of hair. First spin on a bunch with the butts to the rear of the hook and then a second bunch with the butts towards the front. The second bunch should be packed closely against the first bunch. Finished hackle should have hair tied in at favorable opposing directions which allows each bunch of hair to support the other.

Furnace Spider

Hooks: TMC921 or DAI1310, sizes 14-18.
Thread: Black.
Tail: Furnace hackle barbs tied long.
Body: Dubbed with #1 black poly.
Hackle: Oversized furnace tied on as a collar.

Ginger Spider

Hooks: TMC921 or DAI1310, sizes 14-18.
Thread: Tan.
Tail: Ginger hackle barbs tied long.
Body: Dubbed with #27 ginger poly.
Hackle: Oversized ginger tied on as a collar.

Grizzly Spider

Hooks: TMC921 or DAI1310, sizes 14-18.
Thread: Black.
Tail: Grizzly hackle barbs tied long.
Body: Grizzly saddle hackle stem.
Hackle: Oversized grizzly tied on as a collar.

Skater Spider

This is a fly design rather than a fly pattern. Edward Hewitt, one of the more inventive fly fishermen of times past, created this type of fly around 1935. Skater Spiders are tied on regular dry fly hooks in sizes 14 and smaller. They have no body or tail and have oversized hackles wrapped over the shank of the hook. Hackle should be long, about the size of a silver dollar, after it has been wrapped. Hewitt's first Skaters were tied with large stiff spade hackles. Today we often have the option of using large saddle hackles which do the job equally well. They can be tied in any color or combination of colors you fancy. They should be dressed heavy with several turns of hackle and using several feathers when necessary.

With a long rod that will handle a light line and tippet and a breeze to assist you, these flies can be skated across the surface of the water with ease. Hewitt called this form of fly fishing "butterfly fishing." Some say he believed that larger trout would mistake the skated spider for a butterfly.

Troth Hair Spider

Hooks: AC80000BR, TMC100 or DAI1180, sizes 12-14.
Thread: Yellow.
Tail: Deer hair tied rather heavy.
Body: Yellow thread.
Hackle: Deer hair spun as a collar.

Originated by Al Troth of Dillon, Montana. The deer hair hackle on this pattern is tied in with the butts toward the rear of the hook. It is then pushed up in front and tied in place while forming the head. This style of tying the spider with deer hair affords the tier the opportunity to change colors of thread and hair to simulate a variety of hatches.

Variant Dry Flies

Once you have tied a Spider the tying of a Variant is a piece of cake. Personally, I would fish a Variant pattern over a Spider. As you can see they have the same basic characteristics as the Spiders with one exception—they have wings. I know there are those who will argue that wings really do not make a difference. The fish view our flies from the bottom and not the top as we do. I agree wholeheartedly with that assessment, however, I feel that I am smarter than a fish and if I can see them, that is all that counts. I am fishing with the fly, not the fish. In all seriousness though, I have concluded that just possibly, from a distant angle, a fish may have some sight advantage. It makes me feel better to know that I have covered all of the bases.

The wings on Variants are kept short—they are not oversized like the hackles and tails. The hooks I recommend have a shorter shank than normal, so keep your wings about the same length as the hook shank and your flies will be well proportioned.

Badger Variant

Hooks: TMC921 or DAI1310, sizes 14-16.
Thread: Black.
Wings: Natural gray duck quill sections tied upright and divided.
Tail: Badger hackle barbs tied long.
Ribbing: Gray thread.
Body: Black floss.
Hackle: Oversized badger tied on as a collar.

Black Variant

Hooks: TMC921 or DAI1310, sizes 14-16.
Thread: Black.
Wings: White duck quill sections tied upright and divided.
Tail: Black hackle barbs tied long.
Body: Black floss.
Hackle: Oversized black tied on as a collar.

Blue Variant

Hooks: TMC921 or DAI1310, sizes 14-16.
Thread: Gray.
Wings: Natural light gray duck quill sections tied upright and divided.

Tail: Dyed light blue grizzly hackle barbs tied long.
Body: Dark peacock quill.
Hackle: Oversized dyed light blue grizzly tied on as a collar.

Brown Variant

Hooks: TMC921 or DAI1310, sizes 14-16.
Thread: Brown.
Wings: Furnace hackle tips tied upright and divided.
Tail: Brown hackle barbs tied long.
Ribbing: Orange thread.
Body: Tan floss.
Hackle: Oversized brown tied on as a collar.

Cream Variant

Hooks: TMC921 or DAI1310, sizes 14-16.
Thread: White.
Wings: Barred mallard barbs tied upright and divided.
Tail: Cream hackle barbs tied long.
Ribbing: Pale yellow thread.
Body: White floss.
Hackle: Oversized cream tied on as a collar.

Donnelly's Dark Variant

Hooks: TMC921 or DAI1310, sizes 14-16.
Thread: Black.
Wings: Furnace hackle tips tied upright and divided.
Tail: Brown hackle barbs tied long.
Body: Dubbed with muskrat fur.
Hackle: Oversized brown and grizzly tied on as a collar mixed.

Donnelly's Light Variant

Hooks: TMC921 or DAI1310, sizes 14-16.
Thread: White.
Wings: Badger hackle tips tied upright and divided.
Tail: Light ginger hackle barbs tied long.
Body: Dubbed with #3 cream poly.
Hackle: Oversized light ginger tied on as a collar.

The two preceding patterns were originated by Roy Donnelly.

Dun Variant

Hooks: TMC921 or DAI1310, sizes 14-16.
Thread: Gray.
Wings: Natural gray duck quill sections tied upright and divided.
Tail: Blue dun hackle barbs tied long.
Body: Dubbed with muskrat fur.

Hackle: Oversized blue dun tied on as a collar.

Furnace Variant

Hooks: TMC921 or DAI1310, sizes 14-16.
Thread: Black.
Wings: Natural dark gray duck quill sections tied upright and divided.
Tail: Brown hackle barbs tied long.
Body: Dubbed hare's mask fur.
Hackle: Oversized furnace tied on as a collar.

Ginger Variant

Hooks: TMC921 or DAI1310, sizes 14-16.
Thread: Tan.
Wings: Dyed imitation barred lemon woodduck barbs tied upright and divided.
Tail: Ginger hackle barbs tied long.
Body: Dubbed with #3 cream poly.
Hackle: Oversized ginger tied on as a collar.

Hair Wing Variant

See H&L Variant, Chapter 7.

Multi-Color Variant

Hooks: TMC921 or DAI1310, sizes 14-16.
Thread: Black.
Wings: Natural gray duck quill sections tied upright and divided.
Tail: Cree hackle barbs tied long.
Ribbing: Black thread.
Body: Light orange floss.
Hackle: Oversized cree tied on as a collar.

Red Variant

Hooks: TMC921 or DAI1310, sizes 14-16.
Thread: Black.
Wings: Dyed imitation barred lemon woodduck barbs tied upright and divided.
Tail: Furnace hackle barbs tied long.
Body: Dark peacock quill.
Hackle: Oversized furnace tied on as a collar.

The hackle and tail material on the original dressing for the Red Variant called for the color "coch-y-bondhu." This is essentially a furnace with black tips on the barbs, try finding some in suitable quality and size. Furnace is bad enough.

Tails on Spiders and Variants obviously play a significant role. I must refer you back to Chapter 7 and again remind you of the "float line" on a conventional dry fly. This partially applies when dealing with this style of fly also. The only significant difference is oversized hackle and tail. These features consequently elevate the hook above the familiar float line as previously discussed.

You are certainly going to find yourself in need of proper tail material compatible with these designs. Most likely hackle barbs of suitable length and stiffness are going to be in short supply. I have tried most hairs and find them too stiff, they invariably want to penetrate the surface and drown your fly. The paint brush bristles I spoke of elsewhere are also ideal for this type of tail.

Chapter 17

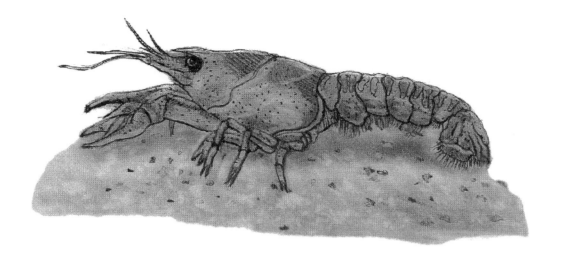

Crustaceans

Crustacean is the common name for aquatic arthropod animals with jaws and two pairs of antennae that constitute the class *Crustacea.* They are among the most successful animals and are found in both freshwater and saltwater—they have survived millenniums. Crustaceans have an external skeleton and a body made up of segments. Although most crustaceans are small, they have a wide range of body forms and habits and consist of about 26,000 species. I won't even attempt to get into this horrendous entanglement.

I find myself carrying a wide number of patterns that fall within the category of crustaceans. These mainly consist of very small shrimp and scud patterns. The larger patterns, i.e., crayfish, do not normally find a place in my fly boxes unless I know that I will be visiting waters where they are present. They take up too much room that could be devoted to other hopeful morsels.

One point that I do feel has to be made about crustacean patterns is that we often ignore them. We become so preoccupied with aquatic insect imitations we have a tendency to forget that other life forms might exist, life forms that the fish may well be more prone to eating that day than what we might be offering in the way of a bug. I know that I am guilty of this and when I have confronted other anglers I find that we share that commonality.

When crustaceans are available, fisheries management personnel are quick to tell you of the tremendous growth rates that fish can achieve when they are in such an environment. My own unscientific observations confirm this when I see trout that more closely resemble the shape of a football than they do a fish.

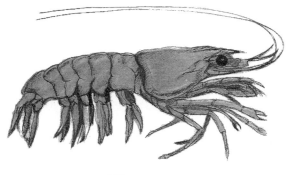

Shrimp

For years shrimp have been threaded on the hooks of bait fishermen. Various sand shrimp (Crangon), grass shrimp (Palaemonetes), and ghost shrimp (Callianassa), as well as edible shrimp (Penaeus) are used. The colors of shrimp vary greatly so you cannot depend on it as a means of identification. Shrimp belong to the order Decapoda which means ten footed. Shrimp are structurally similar to lobsters and crayfish, but they lack enlarged pincers and are flattened in width rather than height.

They have eight pair of appendages on their thorax; three pair at the front called maxillipeds which are mouthparts used for feeding, then five pair at the rear that are called pereipods and used for walking. The abdomen has another five pair of swimming legs, called pleopods, and a fan-like tail.

We have fly tiers here on the West Coast that really get into designing and tying various forms of shrimp. It is amazing to realize just how some of these tiers can devise methods for using any number of different sorts of materials. These masters of tolerance for tedium create specimens that deserve a place in a showcase rather than in the water.

Shrimp range in size from one half inch up to eight inches. The imitations I offer here seldom, if ever, exceed two or three inches. All of these patterns have been proven effective for trout, salmon and steelhead. There are other patterns in Chapter 20, i.e., the Polar Shrimps which are shrimp in name only and simulate egg masses far better. Chapter 22 has over one hundred Spey fly patterns that are also shrimp-like in their design.

Plate 3 **Barbied Shrimp**
Hook: AC80500BL or AC80501BL, sizes 2-8.
Thread: Black.
Antennae: Dyed black squirrel tail tied split.
Ribbing: Oval gold tinsel.
Body: Rear half, orange chenille and front half, red chenille.

Rear Body Hackle: Dyed black pheasant rump tied palmer style over the rear half of the body.
Front Body Hackle: Black hackle tied palmer style over the front half of the body.
Wings: Dyed black squirrel tail tied over the body.
Head: Black and tied large.
Eyes: Red dots.

Originated by Frederic Nicholas Kozy for the Russian River. This is a winter pattern that Fred thinks highly of. He uses it in the lower part of the river and the bay. He says *"It's just the thing for those mixed up fish who haven't decided where they are going."* Fred's "barbecued shrimp" has taken many kings over thirty pounds while they are still in their decision making process.

Bighorn Shrimp

Hooks: TMC3769 or DAI1550, sizes 8-16.
Thread: Tan.
Tail: Light ginger hackle barbs.
Shellback: Clear plastic strip.
Ribbing: Copper wire.
Body: Dubbed with a 50/50 blend #31 tan and #9 orange Bunnytron. Pick out belly for legs.

Bodega Shrimp, Black

Hooks: AC80500BL or AC80501BL, sizes 1-4.
Thread: Black.
Tip: Oval silver tinsel.
Ribbing: Oval silver tinsel.
Body: Dubbed with #1 black lambs wool.
Body Hackle: Black tied palmer style over the body.
Hackle: Black tied on as a collar and tied back and slightly parted at the top.
Wing: Sparse black bucktail tied over the body and tied down at back with ribbing.
Topping: Small bunch of CH02 black Crystal Hair. Tied down with wing.
Head: Black.

Plate 3 Bodega Shrimp, Brown

Hooks: AC80500BL or AC80501BL, sizes 1-4.
Thread: Brown.
Tip: Oval gold tinsel.
Ribbing: Oval gold tinsel.
Body: Dubbed with #25 reddish brown lambs wool.
Body Hackle: Brown tied palmer style over the body.
Hackle: Brown tied on as a collar and tied back and parted slightly at the top.
Wing: Natural brown bucktail tied over the body and tied down at back with ribbing.
Topping: Small bunch of CH32 copper Crystal Hair. Tied down with wing.
Head: Brown.

Bodega Shrimp, Chartreuse

Hooks: AC80500BL or AC80501BL, sizes 1-4.
Thread: Fluorescent green.
Tip: Oval gold tinsel.
Ribbing: Oval gold tinsel.
Body: Dubbed with #57 fluorescent chartreuse lambs wool.
Body Hackle: Fluorescent chartreuse tied palmer style over the body.
Hackle: Fluorescent chartreuse tied on as a collar and tied back and slightly parted at the top.
Wing: Chartreuse bucktail tied over the body and tied down at back with ribbing.
Topping: Small bunch of CH11 green Crystal Hair. Tied down with wing.
Head: Fluorescent green.

Bodega Shrimp, Olive

Hooks: AC80500BL or AC80501BL, sizes 1-4.
Thread: Olive.
Tip: Oval gold tinsel.
Ribbing: Oval gold tinsel.
Body: Dubbed with #21 golden olive lambs wool.
Body Hackle: Golden olive tied palmer style over the body.
Hackle: Dark ginger tied on as a collar and tied back and slightly parted at the top.
Wing: Dyed olive natural brown bucktail tied over the body and tied down at back with ribbing.
Topping: Small bunch of CH16 dark olive Crystal Hair. Tied down with wing.
Head: Olive.

Bodega Shrimp, Orange
Hooks: AC80500BL or AC80501BL, sizes 1-4.
Thread: Fluorescent orange.
Tip: Oval gold tinsel.
Ribbing: Oval gold tinsel.
Body: Dubbed with #10 orange stone lambs wool.
Body Hackle: Dark ginger tied palmer style over the body.
Hackle: Dark ginger tied on as a collar and tied back and parted slightly at the top.
Wing: Dyed orange natural brown bucktail tied over the body and tied down at back with ribbing.
Topping: Small bunch of CH25 copper brown Crystal Hair. Tied down with wing.
Head: Fluorescent orange.

Bodega Shrimp, Pink
Hooks: AC80500BL or AC80501BL, sizes 1-4.
Thread: Fluorescent pink.
Tip: Oval silver tinsel.
Ribbing: Oval silver tinsel.
Body: Dubbed with #54 fluorescent hot pink lambs wool.
Body Hackle: White tied palmer style over the body.
Hackle: Pink tied on as a collar and tied back and parted slightly at the top.
Wing: Pink bucktail tied over the body and tied down at back with ribbing.
Topping: Small bunch of CH03 red Crystal Hair. Tied down with wing.
Head: Fluorescent pink.

This series was developed by Thomas Bret of Occidental, California.

Brown Legged Shrimp
Hooks: AC80500BL, AC80501BL, TMC7999 or DAI2441, sizes 2-6.
Thread: Gray.
Body: Oval silver tinsel.
Body Hackle: Brown tied palmer style over the body.
Shellback: Dyed gray bucktail. The natural tips of the bucktail should extend from the rear of the fly and be equal to the length of the body.
Head: Gray.

Eyes: Tiny red dots.

This is another of the shrimp patterns generated from the basic design of the Horner Shrimp.

Plate 3 Crystal Shrimp, Black
Hook: DAI2151 or DAI2161, sizes 1-10.
Thread: Black.
Antennae: Dyed black monofilament.
Eyes: Silver bead chain.
Body: Extra large CC02 black Crystal Chenille.
Ribbing: Dyed black monofilament.
Tail and Shellback: Dyed black raffia.
Head: Black.

Crystal Shrimp, Brown
Hook: DAI2151 or DAI2161, sizes 1-10.
Thread: Brown.
Antennae: Dyed brown monofilament.
Eyes: Brass bead chain.
Body: Extra large CC25 copper brown Crystal Chenille.
Ribbing: Dyed brown monofilament.
Tail and Shellback: Dyed brown raffia.
Head: Brown.

Crystal Shrimp, Olive
Hook: DAI2151 or DAI2161, sizes 1-10.
Thread: Olive.
Antennae: Dyed brown monofilament.
Eyes: Brass bead chain.
Body: Extra large CC20 olive Crystal Chenille.
Ribbing: Dyed brown monofilament.
Tail and Shellback: Dyed olive raffia.
Head: Olive.

Crystal Shrimp, Orange
Hook: DAI2151 or DAI2161, sizes 1-10.
Thread: Orange.
Antennae: Dyed brown monofilament.
Eyes: Brass bead chain.
Body: Extra large CC05 orange Crystal Chenille.
Ribbing: Dyed brown monofilament.
Tail and Shellback: Dyed orange raffia.
Head: Orange.

Crystal Shrimp, Pink

Hook: DAI2151 or DAI2161, sizes 1-10.
Thread: Fluorescent pink.
Antennae: Dyed red monofilament.
Eyes: Silver bead chain.
Body: Extra large CC08 pink Crystal Chenille.
Ribbing: Dyed red monofilament.
Tail and Shellback: Dyed pink raffia.
Head: Fluorescent pink.

Crystal Shrimp, Red

Hook: DAI2151 or DAI2161, sizes 1-10.
Thread: Red.
Antennae: Dyed red monofilament.
Eyes: Silver bead chain.
Body: Extra large CC03 red Crystal Chenille.
Ribbing: Dyed red monofilament.
Tail and Shellback: Dyed red raffia.
Head: Red.

When I designed these shrimp patterns I selected raffia for the shellbacks because of the duller color of this material when it is dyed. The contrast between the body and the shellback is perfect, as it gives these little creatures more of a natural appearance in the water. Inasmuch as I find them most effective when fished at a dead drift in slower moving water I know the fish are having a closer look at them before the take. Now you are getting close to knowing one of my secret flies.

Estuary Shrimp, Black

Hooks: AC80500BL, AC80501BL, TMC7999 or DAI2441, sizes 2/0-8.
Thread: Fluorescent fire orange.
Tail: Black calf tail and CH02 black Crystal Hair mixed.
Ribbing: Pearl tinsel or clear flat monofilament.
Body: Dubbed with #1 black Bunnytron.
Hackle: Black tied on as a collar and tied back and down.

Wing: Small bunch of CH02 black Crystal Hair mixed with black calf tail tied over the body.
Topping: Small bunch of fluorescent fire orange calf tail tied short.
Head: Fluorescent fire orange.

Estuary Shrimp, Green

Hooks: AC80500BL, AC80501BL, TMC7999 or DAI2441, sizes 2/0-8.
Thread: Fluorescent green.
Tail: Fluorescent chartreuse calf tail and CH23 chartreuse Crystal Hair mixed.
Ribbing: Pearl tinsel or clear flat monofilament.
Body: Dubbed with #57 fluorescent chartreuse Bunnytron.
Hackle: Fluorescent chartreuse tied on as a collar and tied back and down.
Wing: Fluorescent chartreuse calf tail mixed with CH23 chartreuse Crystal Hair tied over the body.
Topping: Small bunch of white calf tail tied short.
Head: Fluorescent green.

Estuary Shrimp, Orange

Hooks: AC80500BL, AC80501BL, TMC7999 or DAI2441, sizes 2/0-8.
Thread: Fluorescent orange.
Tail: Orange calf tail and CH05 orange Crystal Hair mixed.
Ribbing: Pearl tinsel or clear flat monofilament.
Body: Dubbed with #9 orange Bunnytron.
Hackle: Orange tied on as a collar and tied back and down.
Wing: Orange calf tail mixed with CH06 orange Crystal Hair and tied over the body.
Topping: Small bunch of white calf tail tied short.
Head: Fluorescent orange.

Estuary Shrimp, Pink

Hooks: AC80500BL, AC80501BL, TMC7999 or DAI2441, sizes 2/0-8.
Thread: Fluorescent pink.
Tail: Pink calf tail and CH08 pink Crystal Hair mixed.
Ribbing: Pearl tinsel or clear flat monofilament.
Body: Dubbed with #28 pink Bunnytron.

Hackle: Pink tied on as a collar and tied back and down.
Wing: Pink calf tail mixed with CH08 pink Crystal Hair and tied over the body.
Topping: Small bunch of white calf tail tied short.
Head: Fluorescent pink.

Estuary Shrimp, Tan

Hooks: AC80500BL, AC80501BL, TMC7999 or DAI2441, sizes 4-8.
Thread: White.
Tail: Fox squirrel tail and CH25 copper brown Crystal Hair mixed.
Body: Flat gold tinsel.
Hackle: Natural gray pheasant rump tied on as a collar and tied back and down.
Wing: Fox squirrel tail mixed with CH25 copper brown Crystal Hair and tied over the body.
Topping: Greenish-gray pheasant rump barbs.
Head: White.

These are the shrimp patterns of Les Johnson of Seattle, Washington. Some minor evolutionary changes have taken place since these patterns were first tied which has only made his basic principles even more fruitful. These patterns may also have the wing tied down at the rear forming a shellback. When tied in a range of sizes these flies will work under just about any conditions, from saltwater to freshwater conditions in the Rockies and beyond. Most will have trouble obtaining ribbing materials for these patterns, so just undo pearl braided Mylar piping and use the strands.

Horner's Silver Shrimp

Hooks: AC80500BL, AC80501BL, TMC7999 or DAI2441, sizes 2/0-8.
Thread: Black.
Tail: Dyed gray bucktail.
Body: Oval silver tinsel wrapped over a well tapered white floss underbody.
Body Hackle: Grizzly saddle hackle tied palmer style over the body.
Shellback: Dyed gray bucktail.

Head: Black tied extra large.
Eyes: White with black centers.

This pattern was created in 1938 by Jack Horner of San Francisco, California. Jack also tied a similar pattern, the Saltwater Shrimp, which had no grizzly hackle (legs) and used barred teal for the tail and shellback. The Orange Legged Shrimp is a variation of this pattern. The grizzly hackle is substituted with fluorescent orange hackle. Also see Horner's Deer Hair, Chapter 7.

Horny Shrimp

Hooks: DAI2151 or DAI2161, sizes 1-6.
Thread: Fluorescent fire orange.
Tail: Salmon marabou mixed with CH03 red Crystal Hair.
Eyes: Black monofilament.
Body: Fluorescent pink chenille.
Body Hackle: Orange tied palmer style over the body.
Wing: Red marabou mixed with CH03 red Crystal Hair tied over the body.
Head: Fluorescent fire orange.
Note: Use Kozy Kote to finish the head and extend your application of cement back over a portion of the wing.

This is a good fly to use in estuaries holding fish prior to their journey upstream. It is my understanding that this pattern is a creation of Joe Butorac.

Kispiox Shrimp

Hooks: AC80500BL, AC80501BL, TMC7999 or DAI2441, sizes 2/0-4.
Thread: Fluorescent fire orange.
Ribbing: Copper wire.
Shellback: CH07 fire orange Crystal Hair with clear plastic over the top. Leave butt ends of Crystal Hair extending out over the eye of the hook for feelers.
Body: Dubbed with #52 Bunnytron.
Body Hackle: Orange saddle hackle tied palmer style over the body. Do not strip off the butt marabou (fluff) and tie in by the butt with concave side towards the rear.
Eyes: Brass bead chain.

This is an extremely good pattern originated by Mike Craig. This pattern benefits from an underbody of lead wire, however, this must be adjusted to suit your water conditions.

Plate 3 Lively Shrimp, Gray
Hooks: DAI2151 or DAI2161, sizes 1-8.
Thread: Black.
Ribbing: Monofilament.
Tail: Grizzly marabou with CH14 dark blue Crystal Hair tied on top.
Shellback: Gray bucktail.
Body: Dubbed with #13 gray Bunnytron.
Body Hackle: Grizzly tied palmer over the body.
Feelers: Black hackle stems.
Eyes: Black mono.

Lively Shrimp, Olive
Hooks: DAI2151 or DAI2161, size 1-8.
Thread: Olive.
Ribbing: Monofilament.
Tail: Golden olive marabou with CH15 olive Crystal Hair tied on top.
Shellback: Olive bucktail.
Body: Dubbed with #19 olive Bunnytron.
Body Hackle: Golden olive tied palmer style over the body.
Feelers: Golden olive hackle stems.
Eyes: Black mono.

Lively Shrimp, Orange
Hooks: DAI2151 or DAI2161, sizes 1-8.
Thread: Orange.
Ribbing: Monofilament.
Tail: Orange marabou with CH06 orange Crystal Hair tied on top.
Shellback: Natural brown bucktail.
Body: Dubbed with #52 fluorescent orange Bunnytron.
Hackle: Dyed orange grizzly tied palmer style over the body.
Feelers: Dyed orange grizzly hackle stems.
Eyes: Black mono.

Lively Shrimp, Pink
Hooks: DAI2151 or DAI2161, sizes 1-8.
Thread: Fluorescent pink.
Ribbing: Monofilament.
Tail: Fluorescent hot pink marabou with CH04 red Crystal Hair tied on top.
Shellback: Fluorescent hot pink bucktail.
Body: Dubbed with #54 fluorescent hot pink Bunnytron.
Body Hackle: Fluorescent hot pink tied palmer style over the body.
Feelers: Fluorescent hot pink hackle stems.
Eyes: Black mono.
Note: The shellbacks on these shrimp patterns should be given a coat of clear Kozy Koat after the fly is completed. The feelers are made from the same feathers as used for the hackle. When the barbs are stripped off it leaves a segmented effect on the remaining stem.

The Lively Shrimp patterns were developed by Kenneth Lively of Menlo Park, California. At one time Ken tied these in over a dozen colors but has narrowed it down to those listed above as the best suited for steelhead and salmon. Ken is an engineer for General Electric and his vocation causes him to travel constantly from Anchorage to Los Angeles. He has always carried with him a rather complete leather case of fly tying gear. In 1964, after reading an article in a magazine he has made a science out of shrimp patterns.

Nyerges Shrimp
Hooks: TMC9395 or DAI2220, size 10.
Thread: Dark olive.
Tail: Brown hackle barbs.
Body: Dark olive chenille.
Legs: Brown hackle tied over the body then clipped to zero on top and sides.

Originated by Gil Nyerges of Clinton, Washington, for use in eastern Washington lakes. Also known as the Nyerges Nymph.

Pink Shrimp
Hooks: AC80500BL, AC80501BL, TMC7999 or DAI2441, sizes 4-6.
Thread: White.
Tail: Pair of fluorescent hot pink hackle tips tied together on edge.
Shellback: Fluorescent hot pink bucktail.
Ribbing: Oval silver tinsel.

Body: Dubbed with #28 pink lambs wool.
Body Hackle: Fluorescent hot pink tied palmer style over the body.
Head: White.
Eyes: Tiny red dots.
Note: Body color variations include #4 red lambs wool or silver diamond braid.

This pattern first appeared on northern California's Russian River about 1960. Since that time it has been popular on all major waters which become discolored during the winter-runs.

Reiff's Shrimp

Hooks: DAI2151 or DAI2161, sizes 1-6.
Thread: Red.
Body: Dubbed with #10 orange stone African Angora goat. Body should be picked out after the fly is finished for a "shaggy" effect.
Shellback/Tail: Red bucktail. This is tied-in at the head and wrapped aft and then back to the head forming five figure eights.
Hackle: Long scarlet red hackle barbs tied in at the throat and extending to the point of the hook.
Eyes: Insect mounting pins.

Created by Dan Reiff of Bellevue, Washington. Dan's creative idea of using these pins for eyes is a new one on me. His eyes are intended to be black, if the pin heads you find are other than that, use a waterproof marker to get the color. Mono eyes work as well on this pattern.

Plate 3 Salmon River Spring Wiggler

Hooks: AC80500BL, AC80501BL, TMC7999 or DAI2441, sizes 4-8.
Thread: Orange.
Body: CC06 orange Crystal Chenille tied fat.
Shellback/Tail: Dyed orange fox squirrel tail. This hair is tied in at the head and again at the rear of the body allowing the natural tips to extend out for the tail.
Head: Orange.

This shrimp-like pattern is popular in the Great Lakes area. See Spring's Wiggler patterns in Chapter 20.

Plate 3 Taintor Shrimp

Hooks: TMC3769 or DAI1550, sizes 8-14.
Thread: Black.
Tail: Ringneck pheasant tail feather barbs.
Shellback: Natural gray goose quill section.
Legs: Grizzly saddle hackle tied palmer style over the body. After the fly is completed trim to a taper running from the bend of the hook towards the eye of the hook.
Body: Dubbed with #57 fluorescent chartreuse lambs wool.

We all have moments in our lives that others pass off very casually, yet we remember vividly. One afternoon a dapper little gray haired man pranced into the shop in Ogden, Utah, wearing a very loud plaid sports jacket and catching the attention of everyone. None of us were expecting anyone to come through the front door and introduce themself as Bob Taintor. Hell, he had been dead for years. When I related this to Bob he just grinned. He went on to tell of the cold winters he had been spending in St. Paul, Minnesota, for the past twenty years and thanked us for tying and carrying his shrimp pattern. To me this was like turning back the pages of history at least thirty or more years. I felt extremely pleased with myself when I learned that I had been tying his shrimp pattern exactly as he had intended. You see, the body color was well ahead of its time and to suggest this pattern for trout was folly.

Troth Shrimp

Hooks: TMC3769 or DAI1550, sizes 10-16.
Thread: Olive.
Tail: Cream hackle barbs.
Shellback: Clear plastic strip.
Ribbing: Clear monofilament.
Body: Dubbed with #19 olive Bunnytron.

Originated by Al Troth of Dillon, Montana.

Trueblood's Otter Shrimp

Hooks: TMC3769 or DAI1550, sizes 6-14.
Thread: Tan.
Body: Dubbed with pale otter belly fur mixed with a little natural cream-white seal fur.

This is the original dressing for this pattern. It was originated in 1950 by Ted Trueblood of Nampa, Idaho. It is also known as the Otter Nymph. Ted also tied this fly using belly fur from a fox squirrel, pine squirrel and yes, even a common house cat. Today it is tied with brown Hungarian partridge tail and legs tied beard style. Is it still Ted's Otter Shrimp?

Plate 3   Werner Shrimp

Hooks: TMC5262 or DAI1280, sizes 8-14.
Thread: Brown.
Shellback/Tail: Well marked, fine textured blacktail deer hair.
Body: Dubbed with #19 olive African Angora goat.
Legs: Brown saddle hackle tied palmer style over the body and pulled down. Strip the barbs from one side and keep sparse.

Originated by Mary Stewart and popularized by Werner Schmid, both of Vancouver, British Columbia. There are some key factors that go into the make-up of this pattern that have been long forgotten. The hook should be at least 1X or 2X long. The deer hair should be of very fine texture. Coarse hair increases the buoyancy of the fly. The legs (hackle) should be sparse and enhanced by stripping the barbs off one side of the hackle stem before it is wrapped. Barbs should be kept long.

As you can see, this is not just another tied down caddis pattern posing as a shrimp as some have made it out to be.

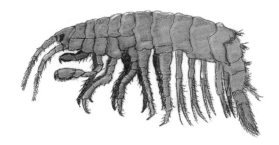

Mussel Shrimp (Scuds)

Scud, from the word scudding, is the common name used by some for these freshwater shrimp-like creatures because of their swift swimming, darting habits. In the world of science they are more commonly known as mussel shrimp (Ostracoda).

There are more than 50 species of freshwater scuds in North America. They are tiny with the largest reaching one inch long but most only a quarter inch. They are shrimp-like in appearance, hence the erroneous name of freshwater shrimp. A novice fly fisherman will normally associate the word "shrimp" with either saltwater or something found in the frozen food section of his local super market. When you mention "scud" you are most likely to get a grimacing glance as if you had said "mud." Dealing with the unknown will often create the impression of something slime-like and undesirable.

Their bodies are smooth and segmented. Their colors vary from pale creamish to pale gray to light olive. Scuds are most common among aquatic vegetation, they are good swimmers and will rapidly depart when disturbed by a wading angler. When they dart away their bodies are straight. I tie my scud patterns on both straight and curved shank hooks. With the straight shank hooks I find that a trout is more prone to chase after and strike at these little imitations when they are being stripped (in a swimming position).

Those patterns tied on curved hooks more closely represent the dead fetal position. I normally only resort to these when I detect them in any significant numbers. In lakes and ponds it is rather frivolous to even consider their use. Remember, gravity sucks and they sink into the bottom and become obscure to any passing fish. In streams the current will often carry them along and here is where you can be rewarded by fishing your imitation at a dead drift.

There is probably very little that you can do to be innovative with respect to scud pattern designs. You can pick up most any book with scud patterns in it and you will generally see a pattern with hackle barbs for the tail; dubbed bodies of all colors and types of dubbing material; clear monofilament for ribbing; clear plastic strip for shellback, and more hackle barbs for the unnecessary antennae. Then if they are over an inch long, you've got a shrimp and not a scud. Naturally you are going to see all sorts of regional names attached to the same thing. It is amazing what some can do with the four letter word scud. So, as you can see, you need to really examine the scuds in your area for color and size and then take it from there.

Cream Scud

Hooks: AC80000BR, TMC5210 or DAI1170, sizes 10-18.
Thread: Cream.
Ribbing: Clear monofilament.
Body: Dubbed with #3 cream African Angora goat. Pick out belly for legs.
Shellback: Natural raffia.

Gray Scud

Hooks: AC80000BR, TMC5210 or DAI1170, sizes 10-18.
Thread: Cream.
Ribbing: Clear monofilament.
Body: Dubbed with #12 light gray African Angora goat. Pick out belly for legs.
Shellback: Light gray raffia.

Olive Scud

Hooks: AC80000BR, TMC5210 or DAI1170, sizes 10-18.
Thread: Cream.
Ribbing: Clear monofilament.
Body: Dubbed with #18 light olive African Angora goat. Pick out belly for legs.
Shellback: Light olive raffia.

Ostrich Scud

Hooks: AC80050BR, TMC200R or DAI1270, sizes 12-18.
Thread: Gray.
Ribbing: Clear monofilament.
Shellback: Clear plastic strip.
Body: Natural gray ostrich herl.

Originated by Fred Arbona and can be tied in as many colors as you can find shades of ostrich.

Super Scud

Hooks: TMC5263 or DAI1720, sizes 4-10.
Thread: Olive.
Ribbing: Fine gold wire.
Shellback: Barred lemon woodduck barbs mixed with CH15 olive Crystal Hair.
Body: Dubbed with a 50/50 blend of #21 golden olive Bunnytron and #9 orange African Angora goat.

Originated by John Shewey of Bend, Oregon.

Plate 3 — Terry's Scud

Hooks: AC80000BR, TMC5210 or DAI1170, sizes 10-18.
Thread: Cream.
Ribbing: Clear monofilament.
Body: A blend of 1 part each of the following colors of African Angora goat: #2 white, #6 yellow, #18 light olive. Pick out belly for legs.
Shellback: Light elk hair mixed with CH01 pearl Crystal Hair.

I came up with this pattern to eliminate some of the guess work often encountered when fishing larger lakes with known scud populations. Large impoundments often have more than one species and different chemical compositions within the same body of water. This will naturally vary the specific colors of the scud population from one area to another. I always start out with this pattern and then change only when I single out a specific color. Rarely a change takes place.

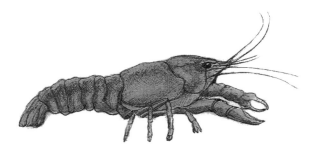

Crayfish

Crayfish belong to the order Decapoda and in the northern hemisphere we only have the family Astaeidae. I have been fascinated by crayfish ever since I saw my first one as a small boy while summering on the Truckee River, in northern California. Some have referred to them as a "poor man's" lobster. I have memories of boiling them up on the river bank and spending the day eating them like popcorn. Crayfish are also regionally known as crawfish, crab, or grass crab. In Florida and the Caribbean the spiny lobster is known as crayfish which further adds to the confusion.

Crayfish favor temperate climates and are an important food source for trout and bass in many parts of North America. There are numerous species. I have found them in swift streams, sluggish rivers, and in lakes and ponds. Their colors range from cream to black. The color I see predominantly in northern California is bright reddish orange. In such places as the Gunnison River in Colorado they are very dark, almost black.

Most crayfish have a short life span. As a rule males die at the end of the second summer and females at the beginning of their third summer. Most fishermen are seldom aware of the crayfish's presence. They are light-sensitive and therefore most active at night. Should you kick over a rock that is being used as cover, they will scurry away backwards and seek cover elsewhere under another rock or rubble.

A crayfish grows by periodically discarding their hard-shell and forming a new one. This molting may occur eight times or more during the first year of life. For a brief period after the hard shell has been discarded, the new shell is very soft and pliable. Their color is usually very pale, cream, light tan to light gray. As their new shell hardens, they become darker in color. Before this is when game fish find them the most delectable. It has been my experience that fish are more readily aware of this cycle than we might give them credit for. A small light-colored imitation which simulates this more palatable state has always been more productive for me rather than when the crayfish's color has darkened.

Plate 3

Baby Crawfish

Hooks: TMC5262 or DAI1280, sizes 8-12.
Thread: Tan.
Body: Dubbed with #3 cream Bunnytron.
Pincers: Light ginger hen hackle trimmed to shape.
Eyes: Black mono.
Antennae: Brown hackle stems.
Legs: Light ginger hackle (lacquered).
Shellback/Tail: Light elk hair.

Of all the crayfish patterns available, and there are many, this is the one I go for first.

Clouser's Crayfish

Hooks: TMC5263 or DAI1720, sizes 4-12.
Thread: Gray.
Antenna (tied as tail): Ringneck pheasant tail feather barbs.
Pincers: Brown hen hackle barbs tied in under the shellback.
Body: Dubbed with #3 cream lambs wool.
Legs: Light ginger hackle.
Shellback/Tail: Mottled brown turkey quill section.

Originated by Bob Clouser.

Crawdaddy

Hooks: TMC5263 or DAI1720, sizes 4-8.
Thread: Black.
Body: Dubbed with #12 light gray lambs wool.
Legs: Grizzly hackle wrapped through the thorax.
Eyes: Black mono.
Pincers/Shellback: Gray squirrel tail.
Tail: Grizzly marabou tied short.

Developed by Charles Overstreet of Reno, Nevada.

Plate 3

Jim's Crayfish

Hooks: TMC9395 or DAI2220, sizes 6-8.
Thread: Brown.
Body: Dubbed with #31 tan lambs wool.
Ribbing: Copper wire.
Pincers/Shellback: Dyed orange fox squirrel tail.
Legs: Brown hackle wrapped through thorax.

Tail: Two brown hen hackle tips tied flat.

Originated by Jim Victorine of Loomis, California.

Mystic Crayfish

Hooks: TMC5263 or DAI1720, sizes 4-6.
Thread: Black.
Ribbing: Copper wire.
Body: Dubbed with #24 brown African Angora goat.
Pincers: Dark brown hen hackle trimmed to shape.
Eyes: Black mono.
Legs: Brown hackle.
Shellback/Tail: Dark brown raffia.

Originated by Rich Bergan of San Carlos, California.

Plate 3

Skip's Dad

Hooks: TMC5262 or DAI1280, sizes 6-12.
Thread: Tan.
Ribbing: Fine copper wire.
Body: Dubbed with #31 tan Bunnytron.
Pincers: Ringneck tail feather barbs.
Eyes: Lead.
Legs: Light ginger hackle.
Tail: Butt ends of tail feather barbs trimmed to shape.

Originated by Skip Morris of Portland, Oregon. Most of you will like this one—it's so easy.

Plate 3

Whitlock's Crayfish

Hooks: TMC300 or DAI2220, sizes 2-8.
Thread: Orange.
Eyes: Black mono.
Antennae: Two dark moose hairs.
Pincers: Dyed orange mottled hen body feathers.
Body: Dubbed with #10 orange lambs wool.
Legs: Dyed orange grizzly hackle.
Shellback/Tail: Orange raffia or Swiss Straw.
Note: Black detailed markings are made with waterproof marker.

Originated by Dave Whitlock of Cotter, Arkansas.

Chapter 18

Streamers

As a rule, streamers or bucktails are designed to simulate various kinds of minnows or baitfish. The exception would be those dressed as attractor type patterns. Possibly the most sought after staple in the diet of any game fish is another fish. Credit for this style of fly cannot be given to any specific person. Minnow imitations were being used in Britain in the early 1800s with no recognition given as it was not recognized as a form of fly fishing. Early settlers brought the knowledge with them to this country and primitive bucktails are known to have been tied for smallmouth bass as early as the 1870s. They were being offered commercially in the early 1890s. Mr. William Scripture of Rome, New York, was experimenting and tying streamers just after 1900.

Around 1902 fly tier Herbert L. Welch in Maine is credited with some of our first streamer patterns. His investigative undertakings were perceptive for the time. He possibly fashioned some of the first long shank hooks more befitting the design of this type of fly.

Here again another gifted woman pops up in fly tying history. Carrie Gertude Stevens, also from Maine, should share the limelight with Welch. Stevens was one of the more prolific fly tiers of her time. Many of her designs live on today as a tribute to her talents, patterns such as her Gray Ghost have become famous the world over.

Some have objected to calling a streamer a fly. Their interpretation is a streamer is a "streamer" and not a fly at all. Following this line of reasoning would make those who make these creations "streamer tiers" and not fly tiers. Hence, those using them would be streamer fishermen and not fly fishermen. This is just more of the Victorian era way of thinking that contributes to the problem with communications amongst ourselves. It has to be worrisome to the new fly fisherman. Don't we owe them more regarding the future of the sport than this type of antiquated approach?

It was only during the 1960s when stillwater fly fishing came into vogue in Britain that a streamer fly was even accepted into their arsenal of flies, and then only for stillwater. Even today, were you to suggest using one in England on one of their streams you would be frowned upon. They still insist on maintaining the old chalkstream snobbery. In their way of looking at this, it is not fly fishing. Looking north to Scotland you will find that they are much like we are in their thinking, however, very little interest has been developed.

Some of the more colorful patterns originated in the New England states. Much of this has to do with a carry-over of thinking by the immigrants from Europe. Many of these patterns carry with them a taste of Victorian era Atlantic salmon flies yet they are unique in their own right. You will find a mixed bag of both the old and the new in this chapter.

When you get down to splitting hairs, the word "streamer" originally applied to feather winged patterns. The use of hair or bucktail for the wings is a variation which took place on a broader scale in the 1930s. To this day there are those who will not agree with our calling a bucktail streamer a streamer. This is more misplaced snobbery, however, this time it is coming from this side of the Atlantic. By not understanding what a true streamer design consists of, some novice anglers have made misclassifications. To some, the Woolly Bugger represents their interpretation of a streamer. The long tail on this type of fly is just that, an extended tail on a wet fly. To be even more correct, they are probably more akin to leech patterns. See Chapter 15.

There are others who attempt to extend this classification to Mylar-like body creations which have minnow patterns painted on them much like bass plugs. These creations are not flies at all and for that reason have been omitted, they belong to another category of lures along with their cousins, the Flatfish, spinners, spoons, etc. The key ingredient that constitutes a streamer is the wing or wings. The wings streaming over the body of the fly gives it the name, "streamer." This includes feathers, hair or even fur strips as found on Zonker-like patterns. We have evolved beyond a single line of thinking, leaving only a very small minority in our dust.

With the passage of time more and more fly fishermen are beginning to realize the importance of streamers. Often novice fly fishermen don't take the time to develop the skills needed to be successful with this fly design. I find that I have to change my entire way of thinking when I have a streamer on the other end of my line. I have to keep telling myself, "It's a minnow—not a bug." If you work a little harder and manipulate your fly properly, not allowing the fish a close examination, success will be yours.

Many fly fishermen specialize in the use of streamer flies and consider them to be the total answer to seducing larger fish. Apparently the larger fish I seek out are for the most part nocturnal in their feeding habits. I have always done better after the sun leaves the water in the evening, before it hits the water in the early morning and with the aid of a full moon. I have also had rewards with streamers in the fall when large trout are feeding heavily on baitfish just before winter sets in. For those fly fishermen who can think of more than just trout, these flies are very productive on bass and other game fish.

As some say, "Big flies, big fish."

Streamer Fly Parts

1. Tail
2. Wings
3. Body
4. Ribbing
5. Hackle
6. Cheeks
7. Tip
8. Tag
9. Shoulder
10. Butt

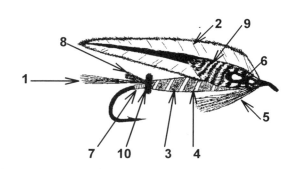

Streamer Fly Proportions

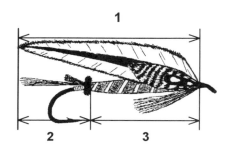

1. Wings. Equal to length of body and tail.
2. Tail. Equal to half the body length, plus or minus.
3. Body. Equal to hook shank less head.

Because of the varied hook shank lengths that streamers can be tied on you must realize that there are no proportion standards for streamers. I have provided this as guidance only.

Most fly tiers will find the following patterns beneficial. Many of our salmon and steelhead patterns were derived from some of the classics, you will find that some have been with us for almost a century. Care has been taken to give dressings for these patterns as close to the original as possible. Many streamer patterns are steeped in American fly fishing days of old. So much of what we do in fly tying today bore its roots in this collective gathering of fly artists. I sincerely wish that I was more knowledgeable and better qualified so I could better give this group the respect they deserve.

Many of the patterns in this chapter can also be tied in tandem style. I discuss the merits of tandem style flies in Chapter 23. Whether you are fishing a lake, a pond in Maine or an estuary on the Pacific Coast, the design application is much the same.

AA Special

Plate 4

Hooks: TMC9395 or DAI2220, sizes 2-8.
Thread: Orange.
Tail: Black hackle barbs.
Body: Copper diamond braid.
Throat: Yellow calf tail tied in and extending to the point of the hook.
Wing: Orange bucktail tied over the body with overwings of natural brown bucktail and dyed dark brown bucktail.
Head: Orange.

Originated by Albert Alexander of Paradise, California, for the browns in Lake Oroville.

Alaska Mary Ann

Hooks: TMC5263 or DAI1720, sizes 4-8.
Thread: Black.
Tail: Red hackle barbs.
Ribbing: Flat silver tinsel.
Body: White floss well tapered.
Wing: White bucktail tied over the body and extending to the end of the tail.
Cheeks: J.C. or substitute.
Head: Black.

Originated in 1922 by Frank Dufresne. See Chapter 20 for steelhead variation.

Alexandra

Plate 4

Hooks: TMC5263 or DAI1720, sizes 2-6.
Thread: Black.
Tail: Red goose quill section.
Ribbing: Oval silver tinsel.
Body: Embossed silver tinsel.
Hackle: Black tied on as a collar and tied back and down.
Wing: Bunch of peacock herl strands tied over the body and extending slightly past the tail.
Head: Black.

Originated by Frier Gulline of Montreal, Canada in 1929. This is

thought to have been a variation on an English wet fly pattern.

Allie's Favorite

Hooks: TMC5263 or DAI1720, sizes 4-6.
Thread: Black.
Tip: Flat silver tinsel.
Ribbing: Flat silver tinsel.
Body: Red floss wrapped thin.
Throat: Small sparse bunch of black hackle barbs with a small bunch of orange hackle barbs tied over and follow by a bunch of white bucktail extending the length of the hook.
Wing: Bunch of peacock herl strands tied over the body with an overwing of two orange saddle hackles with black saddle hackles tied in at each side.
Cheeks: J.C. or substitute.
Head: Black with red band at base of wing.

Originated by Carrie G. Stevens. She named this pattern after Allie W. French of Willimantic, Connecticut.

American Beauty

Hooks: TMC9395 or DAI2220, sizes 2-10.
Thread: Black.
Body: Flat silver tinsel.
Wings: White bucktail tied over the body with overwings of two red saddle hackles with a light blue saddle tied in at each side.
Cheeks: J.C. or substitute.
Head: Black.

Andy's Smelt

Hooks: TMC9395 or DAI2220, sizes 6-12.
Thread: Black.
Tail: Red duck quill section.
Body: Flat silver tinsel.
Wing: White calf tail tied over the body with an overwing of a single dyed blue barred mallard flank feather tied flat.
Head: Black.

Plate 4 ## Anson Special

Hooks: TMC5262 or DAI1280, sizes 4-8.
Thread: Black.
Tip: Flat silver tinsel.
Tail: Red hackle barbs tied sparse and short.
Ribbing: Flat silver tinsel.
Body: Peacock herl.
Hackle: Red tied on as a sparse collar and tied back and down. Barbs should be rather long.
Wing: White bucktail tied over the body and extended slightly past tail.
Shoulders: Barred teal tied in at each side of the wing and extending one-third the wing length.
Cheeks: J.C. or substitute.
Head: Black.

Originated by Anson Bell.

Ashdown Green

Hooks: TMC5263 or DAI1720, sizes 4-6.
Thread: Black.
Tail: Red section of goose quill.
Ribbing: Oval gold tinsel.
Body: Dubbed with #32 claret lambs wool.
Hackle: Claret tied on as a collar and tied back and down.
Wings: White goose quill sections tied over the body and extending just past the tail.
Head: Black.

Originated by Ashdown H. Green, this British Columbia pattern is recorded being used as early as 1889 on the Cowichan River. It is now tied with white bucktail for the wing and there are many variations.

Aunt Ider

Hooks: TMC5263 or DAI1720, sizes 2-6.
Thread: Black.
Ribbing: Oval silver tinsel.
Body: Flat silver tinsel.
Throat: White bucktail with strand of peacock herl tied over and extending the length of the wing.
Wings: Small bunch of yellow bucktail tied over the body with an overwing of four grizzly saddle hackles.
Shoulders: Silver pheasant tied in at each side and extending one-third the wing length.
Cheeks: J.C. or substitute.
Head: Black.

Originated by Frank Congdon of Middletown, Connecticut.

Plate 5 ## Baby Smelt

Hooks: TMC5263 or DAI1720, sizes 4-10.
Thread: White.
Body: Flat silver tinsel.
Wing: Fluorescent pink bucktail tied over the body with barred teal tied in on each side.
Head: White.

Originated by Bob Bouchea.

Ballou Special

Hooks: TMC5263 or DAI1720, sizes 2-8.
Thread: Black.
Tail: Golden pheasant crest curved downward.
Body: Flat silver tinsel.
Wing: Small bunch of red bucktail tied over the body and extending just past the tail with an overwing of two white marabou feathers tied flat.
Topping: Dozen strands of peacock herl.
Cheeks: J.C. or substitute.
Head: Black.

Originated in 1921 by A. W. Ballou of Litchfield, Maine. He is given credit for originating the first marabou streamers.

Barnes Special

Hooks: TMC9395 or DAI2220, sizes 2-8.
Thread: Red.
Ribbing: Oval silver tinsel.
Body: Flat silver tinsel.

Wings: Small bunch of red bucktail tied over the body with overwings of small bunch of white bucktail and two yellow saddle hackles with grizzly saddles tied in at their sides.
Hackle: Long white tied on as a collar and tied back.
Head: Red.

Originated by C. Lowell Barnes of Sebago Lake, Maine. This is a variation of the Hurricane. Optional jungle cock eyes or hackle tips were at one time used for tail.

Bartlett's Special

Hooks: TMC5263 or DAI1720, sizes 2-6.
Thread: Black.
Tail: Golden pheasant crest tied short and curved up.
Ribbing: Flat silver tinsel.
Body: Black floss with a thin taper.
Throat: Yellow hackle barbs.
Wings: Four white saddle hackles tied over the body.
Topping: Golden pheasant crest with a very narrow section (3 barbs) of dark blue turkey quill.
Head: Black.

Originated by Arthur Bartlett of Presque Isle, Maine. This is basically a variation of the Black Ghost.

Barton Special

Hooks: TMC5262 or DAI1280, sizes 4-8.
Thread: White.
Tail: Red duck quill section.
Body: Flat silver tinsel.
Throat: Red hackle barbs.
Wings: Yellow calf tail tied over the body with a barred mallard flank feather tied in at each side.
Shoulders: Dyed red barred mallard breast feather tied in at each side.
Head: Painted silver.
Eyes: Yellow with red centers.

Battenkill Shiner

Hooks: TMC300, DAI2340 or DAI2370, sizes 6-8.
Thread: Black.
Tip: Red floss.

Tail: Gray hackle barbs.
Ribbing: Flat silver tinsel.
Body: White floss well tapered.
Throat: Small bunch of gray hackle barbs.
Wings: Two blue saddle hackles tied over the body with badger saddles tied in at each side.
Cheeks: J.C. or substitute.
Head: Black.

Originated by Lew Oatman of Shushan, New York, to simulate the shiners in the Battenkill River in Vermont.

 Bauman

Hooks: TMC300, DAI2340 or DAI2370, sizes 4-8.
Thread: Black.
Tail: Section of black and white barred lemon woodduck.
Ribbing: Flat gold tinsel.
Body: Orange floss well tapered.
Throat: Red hackle barbs.
Wing: White bucktail tied over the body with an overwing of yellow bucktail.
Topping: Peacock sword feather barbs tied one half the length of the wing.
Cheeks: J.C. or substitute.
Head: Black.

Originated by Arthur Bartlett of Presque Isle, Maine, and named after Art Bauman.

Bear, Black

Hooks: TMC5263 or DAI1720, sizes 4-10.
Thread: Black.
Tail: Gray squirrel tail tied half the length of the body.
Body Hackle: Black tied palmer style over the body.
Body: Black chenille.
Wing: Gray squirrel tail tied over the body.
Head: Black.

Bear, Brown

Hooks: TMC5263 or DAI1720, sizes 4-10.
Thread: Brown.
Tail: Fox squirrel tail tied half the length of the body.
Body Hackle: Brown tied palmer style over the body.
Body: Brown chenille.
Wing: Fox squirrel tail tied over the body.
Head: Brown.

I first came across the Bear patterns in Wyoming. They have a reputation for taking their share of larger fish.

Belknap

Hooks: TMC5263 or DAI1720, size 8.
Thread: Yellow.
Tail: Crimson red hackle barbs.
Body: Flat gold tinsel over a tapered underbody of yellow floss.
Wing: White calf tail tied over the body.
Topping: Two narrow sections of barred mallard flank.
Cheeks: J.C. or substitute.
Head: Yellow.

Originated by Ray Salminen of West Acton, Massachusetts.

Bell Special

Hooks: TMC5263 or DAI1720, sizes 4-8.
Thread: Black.
Body: Flat silver tinsel.
Throat: Three red hackle tips.
Wing: Dozen strands of white ostrich herl tied over the body with an overwing of six strands of brown ostrich herl.
Topping: Strands of peacock herl.
Head: Black.

Originated by Anson Bell of Pittsburg, New Hampshire.

Binn's Streamer

Hooks: TMC5263 or DAI1720, sizes 6-8.
Thread: Black.
Tail: White bucktail with a small bunch of red bucktail tied on top.
Ribbing: Oval silver tinsel.
Body: Dubbed with #6 yellow lambs wool.
Hackle: Red and white tied on as a collar and tied back and down.

Wing: White bucktail tied over the body with an overwing of yellow bucktail.
Shoulders: Guinea fowl feathers tied in at each side.
Head: Black.

Originated in 1937 by Frier Gulline as a wet fly. By 1940 it was converted to a streamer.

Black Angus

Hooks: TMC300, DAI2340 or DAI2370, sizes 2-6.
Thread: Black.
Tail: Four black neck hackles tied on edge and curved out.
Body Hackle: Black marabou tied palmer style over the body.
Body: Black floss.
Collar and Head: Dyed black deer hair spun on and clipped to shape.

Originated by Eric Leiser.

Black Beauty

Hooks: TMC300, DAI2340 or DAI2370, sizes 2-10.
Thread: Black.
Tail: Red hackle barbs.
Ribbing: Flat gold tinsel.
Body: Dark green floss tied thinly tapered.
Throat: Red hackle barbs.
Wings: Four black saddle hackles tied over the body.
Cheeks: J.C. or substitute.
Head: Black.

Black and White

Hook: DAI2220, sizes 6-10.
Thread: Black.
Tail: Crimson red hackle barbs tied sparse.
Body: Flat silver tinsel.
Throat: Pink bucktail mixed with crimson red hackle barbs and extending just past the hook. Hackle barbs should be half the length of the bucktail.
Wings: Four white saddle hackles tied over the body with a black saddle tied in at each side. The barbs on the lower portion of the black saddle are stripped off. When wing is properly positioned you have a black upper half and a white lower half showing from the outside.

Shoulders: Dyed black duck body feather tied in at each side and extending one-third the wing length.
Cheeks: J.C. or substitute.
Head: Black.

Originated by Austin Hogan of Fultonville, New York. This is a stunning fly when it is completed.

Blackbird

Hooks: TMC5263 or DAI1720, sizes 4-10.
Thread: Black.
Tail: Black hackle barbs tied long.
Ribbing: Oval gold tinsel.
Body: Dubbed with #1 black lambs wool.
Throat: Black hackle barbs tied long.
Wing: Dyed black squirrel tied over the body and extending to the end of tail.
Cheeks: J.C. or substitute. Well marked grizzly hackle tips will also dignify this pattern.
Head: Black.

Originated by William Reynolds of Sturbridge, Massachusetts. There are several variations of this pattern known under different names.

Plate 4   Black Ghost

Hooks: TMC300, DAI2340 or DAI2370, sizes 2-10.
Thread: Black.
Tail: Yellow hackle barbs tied one-third the length of the body.
Ribbing: Flat silver tinsel.
Body: Black floss.
Hackle: Yellow hackle barbs tied in at the throat.
Wings: Four white saddle hackles tied over the body.
Cheeks: J.C. or substitute.
Head: Black.

This pattern was originated in 1927 by Herbert L. Walsh of Mooselookmeguntic, Maine. This is one of the classics.

Plate 4   Black Nose Dace

Hooks: AC80050BR, TMC200R or DAI1720, sizes 4-10.
Thread: Black.
Tag: Red yarn.
Ribbing: Oval silver tinsel.
Body: Flat silver tinsel.
Wing: White bucktail tied over the body with an overwing of black bucktail, then natural brown bucktail is tied on top. The black bucktail should only be three quarters the length of the other portions.
Head: Black.

Originated by Art Flick of Westkill, New York.

Blonde Bucktails

The Blonde Bucktails were popularized by Joe Brooks. Some he had a hand in originating and some he did not. It is difficult to know where to draw the line. They were first known to us as "Argentine Blondes" due to a magazine article he had written introducing the flies. The large color recount of his trip to Argentina displayed large trout that would make any fisherman begrudgingly envious. Later Harry Darbee gave us successful accounts of how many of these patterns worked wonders on Canada's Margaree for Atlantic salmon. Here on the West Coast many Pacific salmon and steelhead fly fishermen discovered their value as well. Need I mention the numbers of stripers and largemouth bass they have accounted for also. Forget the stigma of these being only saltwater flies and look to their other uses.

Blonde, Argentine
Hooks: TMC811S or DAI2546, sizes 4/0-1/0.
Thread: White.
Tail: White bucktail.
Body: Flat silver tinsel.
Wing: Light blue bucktail.
Head: Blue.

Blonde, Black
Hooks: TMC811S or DAI2546, sizes 4/0-1/0.
Thread: Black.
Tail: Black bucktail.
Body: Flat silver tinsel.
Wing: Black bucktail.
Head: Black.

Blonde, Blue
Hooks: TMC811S or DAI2546, sizes 4/0-1/0.
Thread: White.
Tail: Blue bucktail.
Body: Flat silver tinsel.
Wing: Blue bucktail.
Head: Blue.

Blonde, Brunette
Hooks: TMC811S or DAI2546, sizes 4/0-1/0.
Thread: Yellow.
Tail: Natural brown bucktail.
Body: Flat gold tinsel.
Wing: Natural brown bucktail.
Head: Yellow.

Blonde, Honey
Hooks: TMC811S or DAI2546, sizes 4/0-1/0.
Thread: Yellow.
Tail: Yellow bucktail.
Body: Flat gold tinsel.
Wing: Yellow bucktail.
Head: Yellow.

Blonde, Irish
Hooks: TMC811S or DAI2546, sizes 4/0-1/0.
Thread: White.
Tail: Light green bucktail.
Body: Flat silver tinsel.
Wing: Dark green bucktail.
Head: Green.

Blonde, Katydid
Hooks: TMC811S or DAI2546, sizes 4/0-1/0.
Thread: White.
Tail: White bucktail.
Body: Flat silver tinsel.
Wing: Green bucktail.
Head: Green.

Blonde, Mickey Finn
Hooks: TMC811S or DAI2546, sizes 4/0-1/0.
Thread: Yellow.
Tail: Yellow bucktail.
Body: Flat silver tinsel.
Wing: Red bucktail with an overwing of yellow bucktail.
Head: Yellow.

Blonde, Pink
Hooks: TMC811S or DAI2546, sizes 4/0-1/0.
Thread: White.
Tail: Pink bucktail.
Body: Flat gold tinsel.
Wing: Pink bucktail.
Head: White.

Blonde, Platinum
Hooks: TMC811S or DAI2546, sizes 4/0-1/0.
Thread: White.
Tail: White bucktail.
Body: Flat silver tinsel.
Wing: White bucktail.
Head: White.

Blonde, Strawberry
Hooks: TMC811S or DAI2546, sizes 4/0-1/0.
Thread: White.
Tail: Red bucktail.
Body: Flat silver tinsel.
Wing: Orange bucktail.
Head: Red.

Blue Devil
Hooks: TMC5263 or DAI1720, sizes 6-8.
Thread: Black.
Tip: Flat silver tinsel.
Ribbing: Flat silver tinsel.
Body: Black floss thinly tapered.

Throat: Orange hackle barbs with white bucktail tied over and extending to the bend of the hook.
Wings: Strands of peacock herl tied over the body with an overwing of two orange saddles with dark blue saddles tied in at each side.
Shoulders: Brownish-gray Hungarian partridge tied in at each side.
Cheeks: J.C. or substitute.
Head: Black with a red band at the base of the wing.

Originated in 1923 by Carrie G. Stevens.

Blue Marabou

Hooks: TMC300, DAI2340 or DAI2370, sizes 2-8.
Thread: Black.
Tail: Fire orange hackle barbs tied short.
Ribbing: Flat gold tinsel.
Body: Gray floss.
Throat: Small bunch of green bucktail extending to end of hook.
Wings: White bucktail tied over the body and extending to the end of the tail with an overwing of two light blue marabou feathers.
Shoulders: Badger saddle hackles tied in at each side and extending almost to end of wings.
Cheeks: J.C. or substitute.
Head: Black.

Originated by Paul Kukonen of Worcester, Massachusetts.

Blue Smelt

Hooks: TMC300, DAI2340 or DAI2370, sizes 2-8.
Thread: Black.
Body: Flat silver tinsel.
Wing: White bucktail tied over the body with an overwing of blue bucktail.
Topping: Strands of peacock herl.
Cheeks: J.C. or substitute.
Head: Black.

Blue Smolt

Hooks: TMC300, DAI2340 or DAI2370, sizes 2-10.
Thread: Black.
Body: Silver Mylar piping slipped over the body and tied in at the rear with red thread.
Tail: Ends from body frayed out.
Wing: White bucktail tied over the body with overwings of blue bucktail and barred mallard flank feather tied flat.
Hackle: Red calf tail tied in at the throat.
Head: Black.

Bolshevik

Hooks: TMC5263 or DAI1720, sizes 6-8.
Thread: Black.
Tail: Golden yellow hackle tip.
Body: Flat silver tinsel.
Throat: Natural brown bucktail extending to end of hook.
Wings: Red saddle hackles tied over the body with a furnace saddle tied in at each side.
Cheeks: J.C. or substitute.
Head: Black.

Originated in 1925 by Fred Flower of Oquossoc, Maine.

Brown Bucktail

Hooks: TMC5263 or DAI1720, sizes 4-14.
Thread: Black.
Ribbing: Oval silver tinsel.
Body: Flat silver tinsel.
Hackle: Crimson red hackle barbs tied in at the throat.
Wing: Natural brown bucktail.
Head: Black.

Brown Falcon

Hooks: TMC5263 or DAI1720, sizes 6-8.
Thread: Black.
Tip: Oval silver tinsel.
Butt: Red floss.
Body: Embossed silver tinsel with red floss wrapped at the front and rear. In other words, a tinsel body with equal portions of floss wrapped at each end.
Wing: White bucktail tied over the body with an overwing of yellow bucktail. White and yellow portions should be equal. Tie brown saddle hackles at each side that extend almost to the end of the wing.

Cheeks: J.C. or substitute.
Head: Black.

Brown Ghost

Hooks: TMC5263 or DAI1720, sizes 4-8.
Thread: Black.
Tip: Flat silver tinsel.
Ribbing: Flat silver tinsel.
Body: Dark brown floss.
Throat: Golden pheasant crest feather extending half the body length and curved up with white bucktail tied over and extending just past the hook with strands of peacock herl tied in last.
Wings: Golden pheasant crest tied slightly longer than hook and curved up with two brown saddle hackles tied in at each side.
Shoulders: Dyed brown barred teal feather tied in at each side.
Cheeks: J.C. or substitute.
Head: Black.

This variation of the Gray Ghost was originated by Gardner Percy of Portland, Maine.

Branchu

Hooks: TMC300, DAI2340 or DAI2370, sizes 2-10.
Thread: Red.
Tail: Golden pheasant crest.
Body: Dubbed with #9 orange African Angora goat. Pick out and make shaggy.
Wing: Barred lemon woodduck flank feather tied flat over the body.
Cheeks: J.C. or substitute.
Hackle: Cree hen hackle tied on as a collar and tied back.
Head: Red.

Plate 5 ## Bucktail Silver

Hooks: TMC300, DAI2340 or DAI2370, sizes 4-6.
Thread: Black.
Body: Embossed silver tinsel.
Throat: Red Amherst crest tied with curve up.
Wings: White bucktail tied over the body with a badger neck hackle tied in at each side.
Cheeks: J.C. or substitute.
Head: Black.

Originated in 1933 by Ray Bergman of Nyack, New York.

Bullhead

Hooks: AC80500BL or AC80501BL, sizes 2/0-6.
Thread: Black.
Tail: White bucktail.
Body: Dubbed with #3 cream African Angora goat.
Gills: Dubbed with #4 red Bunny-Blend.
Wing: Black ostrich herl.
Collar and Head: Natural deer body hair.
Note: Wing should extend to the end of tail and tied down at the rear of the body. The top of the head is colored black using a waterproof marking pen.

This pattern was originated by Al Troth of Dillon, Montana. More than twenty years of success with this pattern has made me a believer. I now add a small bunch of CH02 black Crystal Hair over the ostrich.

Bumblepuppy No. 1

Hooks: TMC5263 or DAI1720, sizes 4-6.
Thread: Red.
Lower Tip: Flat silver tinsel.
Upper Tip: Red floss.
Tail: Red goose quill section.
Butt: Red chenille.
Ribbing: Flat silver tinsel.
Body: White chenille.
Hackle: Badger tied on as a collar and tied back and down.
Wings: White bucktail tied over the body with an overwing of white goose quill sections.
Shoulders: Barred teal feathers tied in at each side.
Cheeks: J.C. or substitute tied parallel to body.
Head: Red.

My source for this pattern was *Streamer Fly Tying and Fishing* by Joseph D. Bates, Jr. I have made some minor adjustments in the pattern as he relates it so if one wanted to tie it today there would be no limiting factors to overcome.

Here are some of the comments Bates makes concerning this creation:

"This historic fly, originally tied both as a bucktail and as a streamer, evidently is the first of all modern patterns of this type. Originated by the famous Theodore Gordon, creator of the popular Quill Gordon and father of the American dry fly, the Bumblepuppy actually is not one fly but rather several related patterns developed by Mr. Gordon over many years prior to his death in 1915."

Bates lost all credibility with that mouthful. See Chapter 1. Bate's book was written in 1950 and others have picked up on this, unchallenged, and taken it upon themselves to allow their imaginations to expand even further.

Further on, Bates' comments that the flies were originally tied on wet fly hooks because long hooks were not available during Gordon's lifetime.

Herbert L. Welch was tying on long shanked hooks during this time frame and Bates confirms this in his own book. The obvious question arises regarding their classification as a streamer at all, they certainly fall into that of a conventional wet fly by the mere fact that they were tied on wet fly hooks. It is obvious that Bates was grasping for material for his book. This is also evidenced with the number of steelhead patterns he attempted to classify as streamers. This confused a good number of fly tiers for decades.

The following is another variation of this pattern as others see it.

Bumblepuppy No. 2

Hooks: TMC5263 or DAI1720, sizes 4-6.
Thread: Black.
Tail: Red hackle barbs.
Body: White chenille.
Hackle: Red and white tied on as a collar mixed and tied back and down.
Wing: White bucktail tied over the body and extending slightly past the tail.
Shoulders: Four white tipped small turkey tail feathers tied in on each side. Feathers are overlaid with two per side.
Head: Black.

Campeona

Hooks: TMC9395 or DAI2220, sizes 4-8.
Thread: Red.
Tip: Oval silver tinsel.
Tail: Two narrow sections of red duck quill.
Butt: White chenille.
Ribbing: Flat silver tinsel.
Body: Dubbed with #15 insect green lambs wool. Body should be picked out for "shaggy" effect.
Hackle: Dark crimson red tied on as a collar and tied back and down.
Wing: Strands of peacock herl tied over the body and extending just past the tail.
Shoulders: Barred teal feathers tied in at each side and extending by one-third.
Head: Red.

This pattern originated in Chile, found its way to this country and has found favor with a number of anglers.

Cardinelle

Hooks: TMC5263 or DAI1720, sizes 2-10.
Thread: Fluorescent red.
Body: Dubbed with #52 fluorescent orange African Angora goat.
Wing: Fluorescent orange calf tail tied over the body with overwings of fluorescent orange marabou and then fluorescent hot pink marabou tied on top.
Hackle: Yellow tied on as a collar and tied back.
Head: Fluorescent red.

Originated by Paul Kukonen.

Plate 4 · Champ's Special

Hooks: TMC5263 or DAI1720, sizes 4-8.
Thread: Black.
Tag: Red floss.
Ribbing: Oval silver tinsel.
Body: Flat silver tinsel.
Throat: Strands of peacock herl with white bucktail tied over. Both should extend to bend of hook.
Wings: Small bunch of yellow bucktail tied over the body with an overwing of four grizzly saddles.
Head: Black.

Originated by Frank Congdon of Middletown, Connecticut.

Plate 5 · Champlain Special

Hooks: TMC5263 or DAI1720, sizes 4-8.
Thread: Black.
Ribbing: Flat gold tinsel.
Body: Yellow floss thinly tapered.
Throat: Red hackle barbs.
Wing: White bucktail tied over the body with an overwing of yellow bucktail.
Topping: Strands of peacock herl.
Head: Black.

Chief Needahbeh

Hooks: TMC9395 or DAI2220, sizes 2-6.
Thread: Black.
Tip: Flat silver tinsel.
Tail: Red goose quill section.
Ribbing: Flat silver tinsel.
Body: Red floss thinly tapered.
Wings: Yellow saddle hackle tied over the body with red saddle hackle tied on the sides.
Hackle: Red tied on as a collar in front of the wing.
Head: Black.

Originated by Chief Needahbeh of the Penobscot Indian tribe of Greenville, Maine.

Clouser Deep Minnows

Originated August 1988 by Bob Clouser of Middletown, Pennsylvania, for smallmouth bass. You will see this fly tied in many configurations. In fact, Bob Clouser himself would be overwhelmed to learn of the many patterns that bear his name. The patterns I have given here are Bob's original dressings. The only difference is the color of the eyes. Today they are painted as indicated. Eyes on any streamer gives the fish a good target to zero in on.

The lead eyes should always be positioned well back on the hook shank. This allows space for a proper head in front. The eyes are tied in on the top side of the hook first. Because of their weight, the fly will reverse itself in the water. With this in mind, tie in your bottom wing as if you were tying a normal wing on top of the fly. This wing is secured with your thread at both the front and rear of the eye. Now reverse your hook in the vise, turning it upside down, and tie in your remaining wing. Wing is secured in front of the eyes. Wing length should be equal to about three times the hook shank.

Lefty Kreh first brought this fly to our attention more than a decade ago. Lefty needed a particular tan shade of calf tail to tie the pattern he was calling the Clouser Minnow and was using it for bonefish and other saltwater species. He can be credited with popularizing the pattern for those purposes. Most have forgotten that the originals are good freshwater patterns.

There is an abundance of other variations that can be tied using this design. Just look at the Thunder Creek series in this chapter and you will soon discover other possibilities.

I would say that Bob Clouser's idea for a fly pattern has gone astray in many areas and become a style rather than a specific series of Clouser patterns.

Plate 5 Clouser Deep Minnow, Chartreuse

Hooks: TMC3761 or DAI1560, sizes 2-8.
Thread: White.
Bottom Wing: White bucktail.
Wing: Chartreuse bucktail with a sparse underwing of multi-colored or CH01 pearl Crystal Hair.
Lead Eyes: Red with black centers.

Plate 4 Clouser Deep Minnow, Golden Shiner

Hooks: TMC3761 or DAI1560, sizes 2-8.
Thread: Tan.
Bottom Wing: White bucktail.
Wing: Natural brown bucktail with a sparse underwing of CH31 gold Crystal Hair.
Lead Eyes: Red with black centers.

Plate 5 Clouser Deep Minnow, Sculpin

Hooks: TMC3761 or DAI1560, sizes 2-8.
Thread: Brown.
Bottom Wing: Orange bucktail.
Wing: Overdyed dark orange natural brown bucktail with an underwing of CH31 gold Crystal Hair.
Lead Eyes: Yellow with black centers.

Plate 4 Clouser Deep Minnow, Silver Shiner

Hooks: TMC3761 or DAI1560, sizes 2-8.
Thread: White.
Bottom Wing: White bucktail.
Top Wing: Dyed gray bucktail with a sparse underwing of sparse multi-colored Crystal Hair.
Lead Eyes: Red with black centers.

Also see Chapter 23 for other Clouser Minnow patterns.

Coachman

Hooks: TMC5263 or DAI1720, sizes 4-8.
Thread: Black.
Tip: Flat gold tinsel.
Body: Peacock herl over an underbody of olive yarn or floss. Body is reverse wrapped with fine gold wire.
Hackle: Brown tied on as a collar and tied back and down.
Wing: Four white saddles tied over the body.
Head: Black.

This pattern is a converted wet fly pattern. It is also tied with a wing of white bucktail.

Cock Robin

Hooks: TMC300, DAI2340 or DAI2370, sizes 4-8.
Thread: Black.
Tip: Flat silver tinsel.
Ribbing: Flat silver tinsel.
Body: Rear half, dubbed with #6 yellow lambs wool and the front half dubbed with #4 red lambs wool.
Throat: Red bucktail tied in and extending to hook point.
Wing: Fire orange bucktail tied over the body with an overwing of white bucktail and then another bunch of fire orange bucktail. Bucktail should be kept sparse and in equal portions.
Head: Black.

Originated by Joseph Kvitsky of Westfield, Massachusetts.

Colonel Bates

Hooks: TMC5263 or DAI1720, sizes 4-10.
Thread: Red.
Tail: Red duck quill section.
Body: Flat silver tinsel.
Hackle: Brown tied on as a collar and tied back and down.
Wings: Two yellow saddle hackles tied over the body with two slightly shorter white saddles tied to the sides.
Cheeks: J.C. or substitute.
Head: Red with a black band at the base of the wing.

Originated by Carrie G. Stevens.

Colonel Fuller

Hooks: TMC9395 or DAI2220, sizes 4-8.
Thread: Black.
Ribbing: Oval silver tinsel.
Body: Flat silver tinsel.
Throat: Small bunch of golden yellow hackle barbs.
Wings: Four golden yellow saddles tied over the body.
Shoulders: Red turkey flat tied in at each side.
Head: Black.

Wing variations include the use of either bucktail or marabou. This pattern was originated in 1894 by John Shields of Brookline, Massachusetts and named after Colonel Charles E. Fuller of Boston. The original pattern was a wet fly.

Colonel White

Hooks: TMC9395 or DAI2220, sizes 4-8.
Thread: Black.
Ribbing: Oval silver tinsel.
Body: Flat silver tinsel.
Throat: Small bunch of white hackle barbs.
Wing: Four white neck hackles tied over the body.
Shoulders: Tip of red turkey flat tied in at each side.
Head: Black.

Originated by William Burgess of Maine. This pattern is also know as Rooster's Regret.

Counterfitter

Hooks: TMC300, DAI2340 or DAI2370, sizes 2-10.
Thread: Black.
Body: Flat silver tinsel.
Hackle: Orange bucktail tied in at the throat and extending to the bend of the hook with white bucktail tied over and finishing with a golden pheasant crest.
Wing: Pink and purple bucktail tied over the body with an overwing of blue dun neck hackles.
Shoulders: Small barred lemon woodduck flank feathers tied in at each side.
Cheeks: J.C. or substitute.

Head: Black.

Plate 5   Crane Prairie

Hooks: TMC9395 or DAI2220, sizes 4-8.
Thread: Red.
Tail: Golden olive calf tail.
Butt: Oval gold tinsel.
Body: Peacock herl over and under body of olive floss or yarn. Reverse wrap the body with fine gold wire.
Wings: Dyed yellow natural brown bucktail tied over the body with overwings of two grizzly saddle hackles.
Head: Red.

This pattern was originated by A. A. "Tony" Whitney of Stockton, California, for Crane Prairie Reservoir in central Oregon. I have no idea when this fly originated but at some time over the years it found its way into my fly boxes. I have used it repeatedly through the years and find it to be one of the best stillwater streamer patterns that I have encountered.

Cosseboom Special

Hooks: TMC300, DAI2340 or DAI2370, sizes 2-10.
Thread: Red.
Tip: Flat silver tinsel.
Tag: Olive floss.
Ribbing: Flat silver tinsel.
Body: Olive floss thinly tapered.
Wing: Gray squirrel tied over the body and extending to end of tag.
Hackle: Chartreuse tied on as a collar.
Head: Red.

Originated by John C. Cosseboom of Providence, Rhode Island. This is thought to be the original dressing for this pattern.

Crystal Minnows

Blue Minnow

Hooks: TMC9395 or DAI2220, sizes 2-6.
Thread: White.
Belly: CH01 pearl Crystal Hair tied in at the head and folded back and tied in at the rear to form belly.
Back: CH13 blue Crystal Hair tied in at the head and folded back and tied in at the rear to form back.
Wing: Blue bucktail tied over the body and extending slightly past the end of the tail.
Head: Blue.
Eyes: White with red centers.

Golden Shadow

Hooks: TMC9395 or DAI2220, sizes 2-6.
Thread: White.
Belly: CH05 golden yellow Crystal Hair tied in at the head and folded back and tied in at the rear to form belly.
Back: CH31 gold Crystal Hair tied in at the head and folded back and tied in at the rear to form back.
Wing: Natural brown bucktail tied over the body and extending slightly past the end of the tail.
Head: Brown.
Eyes: Yellow with red centers.

Pearl Gray Minnow

Hooks: TMC9395 or DAI2220, sizes 2-6.
Thread: White.
Belly: CH01 pearl Crystal Hair tied in at the head and folded back and tied in at the rear to form belly.
Back: CH26 gray Crystal Hair tied in at the head and folded back and tied in at the rear to form back.
Wing: Dyed gray bucktail tied over the body and extending slightly past the tail.
Head: Gray.
Eyes: Black with white centers.

Silver Mint

Hooks: TMC9395 or DAI2220, sizes 2-6.
Thread: White.
Belly: CH30 silver Crystal Hair tied in at the head and folded back and tied in at the rear to form belly.
Back: CH23 chartreuse Crystal Hair tied in at the head and folded back and tied in at the rear to form back.
Wing: Green bucktail tied over the body and extending slightly past the tail.
Head: Green.
Eyes: Yellow with red centers.

Sun Fish

Hooks: TMC9395 or DAI2220, sizes 2-6.
Thread: White.
Belly: CH04 yellow Crystal Hair tied in at the head and folded back and tied in at the rear to form belly.
Back: CH15 olive Crystal Hair tied in at the head and folded back and tied in at the rear to form back.
Wing: Olive bucktail tied over the body and extending slightly past the tail.
Head: Olive.
Eyes: Black with white centers.

Teal N'Blue

Hooks: TMC9395 or DAI2220, sizes 2-6.
Thread: White.
Belly: CH12 light blue Crystal Hair tied in at the head and folded back and tied in at the rear to form belly.
Back: CH22 teal Crystal Hair tied in at the head and folded back and tied in at the rear to form back.
Wing: Teal blue bucktail tied over the body and extending slightly past the tail.
Head: Dark blue.
Eyes: White with black centers.

The Crystal Minnows were developed in 1988 by Mary Nashford of Lodi, California. An underbody of white floss or yarn is constructed as a first step in tying these minnow patterns. The folded back Crystal Hair is tied off independently of the hook and trimmed to the shape of a minnow tail. Finish head with clear epoxy.

Cupsuptic
Hooks: TMC9395 or DAI2220, sizes 4-8.
Thread: Black.
Tail: Yellow hackle barbs.
Butt: Peacock herl.
Rear Body: White floss.
Center Joint: Peacock herl.
Ribbing: Oval silver tinsel over red floss only.
Front Body: Red floss.
Throat: Small bunch of yellow hackle barbs.
Wings: Two crimson red saddle hackles tied over the body with furnace saddles tied in at the sides.
Shoulders: Grizzly neck hackle tips tied in at each side and extending one-third.
Cheeks: J.C. or substitute.
Head: Black.

Originated by Herbert Welch of Oquossoc, Maine.

Cut Lips
Hooks: TMC9395 or DAI2220, sizes 2-8.
Thread: Black.
Tail: Blue dun hackle barbs.
Ribbing: Flat silver tinsel.
Body: Dubbed with #30 purple lambs wool.
Throat: Small bunch of blue dun hackle barbs.
Wings: Two olive saddle hackles tied over the body with dark blue dun saddles tied in at the sides.
Cheeks: J.C. or substitute.
Head: Black.

Originated by Lew Oatman of Shushan, New York.

Dick's Killer
Hooks: TMC5263 or DAI1720, sizes 6-8.
Thread: Black.
Tip: Flat gold tinsel.
Tail: Golden pheasant tippet barbs.
Body: Peacock herl over an underbody of olive floss or yarn. Reverse wrap the body with fine gold wire.
Wing: Yellow bucktail tied over the body.
Topping: Barred lemon woodduck barbs.
Shoulders: Tip of red turkey flat tied in at each side.
Cheeks: J.C. or substitute.
Head: Black.

Originated in 1928 by Dick Eastman of Groveton, New Hampshire.

Dolly's Hat
Hooks: TMC5262 or DAI1280, sizes 2-6.
Thread: Black.
Tip: Oval silver tinsel.
Ribbing: Oval silver tinsel.
Body: Dark orange floss well tapered.
Throat: Golden pheasant crest tied in with white bucktail over, followed by strands of peacock herl.
Wings: Barred teal flank feather tied flat over the body.
Topping: Strands of peacock herl.
Head: Black.

Originated by Dick Brady.

Plate 4 Don's Delight
Hooks: TMC5263 or DAI1720, sizes 4-6.
Thread: Black.
Tail: Red hackle barbs.
Body: Flat gold tinsel.
Throat: White hackle barbs.
Wings: Four white saddle hackles tied over the body.
Shoulders: Golden pheasant tippet feather tied in at each side.
Cheeks: J.C. or substitute.
Head: Black with a red band at the base of the wing.

Originated by Carrie G. Stevens.

Down East Smelt
Hooks: TMC300, DAI2340 or DAI2370, sizes 2-8.
Thread: Black.
Body: Silver diamond braid.
Wings: White bucktail tied over the body with overwings of two dyed blue dun badger saddle hackle.
Shoulders: Dyed blue dun barred mallard breast feather tied in at each side.
Head: Black.
Eyes: Yellow with black centers.

Dr. Burke
Hooks: TMC5263 or DAI1720, sizes 4-6.
Thread: Black.
Tail: Several peacock sword feather barbs tied long.
Ribbing: Oval silver tinsel.

Body: Flat silver tinsel over an underbody of white floss.
Throat: Yellow bucktail tied in and extending to the bend of the hook.
Wings: Four white saddle hackles tied over the body.
Head: Black.

Originated in 1927 by Dr. Edgar Burke of Jersey City, New Jersey.

Dr. Milne
Hooks: TMC5263 or DAI1720, sizes 4-8.
Thread: Black.
Tip: Oval gold tinsel.
Tail: Golden pheasant crest.
Body: Yellow chenille.
Wing: Dyed black squirrel tail tied over the body with an overwing of four grizzly saddles that extend well past tail.
Topping: Narrow section (3 barbs) of red turkey quill.
Shoulders: Brown mallard breast feather tied in at each side.
Cheeks: J.C. or substitute.
Head: Black.

Originated by Bert Quimby of South Windham, Maine. It was named after Dr. Douglas M. Milne.

Dr. Oatman
Hooks: TMC5263 or DAI1720, sizes 2-6.
Thread: Black.
Tail: White hackle barbs.
Ribbing: Flat gold tinsel.
Body: Rear two-thirds, white floss and the front third red floss.
Throat: Small bunch of yellow hackle barbs.
Wings: Four white saddle hackles tied over the body.
Cheeks: J.C. or substitute.
Head: Black.

Plate 5   Dusty
Hooks: TMC5263 or DAI1720, sizes 4-6.
Thread: Black.
Tip: Flat silver tinsel.
Ribbing: Flat silver tinsel.
Body: Black floss thinly tapered.
Throat: White bucktail tied in with strand of peacock herl tied over. Both should extend to hook bend.

Wings: Four grizzly saddle hackles tied over the body.
Cheeks: J.C. or substitute.
Head: Black.

Originated by Bert Quimby of South Windham, Maine.

Edson Tiger, Dark
Hooks: TMC5263 or DAI1710, sizes 4-10.
Thread: Yellow.
Tip: Flat gold tinsel.
Tail: Two small yellow neck hackle tips tied in a V.
Body: Yellow chenille.
Hackle: Tie in the tips of two small red hackles. They should be spread in a V and look like a conventional throat hackle.
Wing: Dyed yellow natural brown bucktail tied over the body and extending just to the end of the hook.
Head: Yellow.

Edson Tiger, Light
Hooks: TMC5263 or DAI1720, sizes 4-10.
Thread: Black.
Tail: Black and white barred section of lemon woodduck.
Body: Peacock herl. Reverse wrap the body with fine gold wire.
Wing: Yellow bucktail tied over the body and extending just to the bend of the hook.
Head: Black.

You will often see the Edson Tiger patterns dressed with jungle cock. The original patterns had small gold metal cheeks and painted eyes. Today I find that short strips of wide Mylar tinsel make excellent cheeks on these patterns. These flies were originated in 1929 by William R. Edson of Portland, Maine.

Plate 5   Esopus Bucktail
Hooks: TMC9395 or DAI2220, sizes 4-10.
Thread: Black.
Tail: Red calf tail.
Body: Embossed silver tinsel.
Wing: White bucktail tied over the body with an overwing of black bucktail.
Cheeks: J.C. or substitute.
Head: Black.

Family Secret
Hooks: TMC5263 or DAI1720, sizes 4-6.
Thread: Black.
Tail: Peacock sword feather barbs.
Ribbing: Oval silver tinsel.
Body: Flat silver tinsel over an underbody of white floss.
Throat: Guinea fowl barbs.
Wings: Four white saddle hackles tied over the body.
Cheeks: J.C. or substitute.
Head: Black.

Originated by Edgar Burke.

F N'G Marabou, Black
Hooks: TMC9395 or DAI2220, sizes 8-10.
Thread: Black.
Tail: Red hackle barbs.
Ribbing: Flat silver tinsel.
Body: Black chenille.
Hackle: Red hackle barbs tied in at the throat.
Wing: Gray marabou tied over the body with an overwing of sparse black bucktail.
Shoulder: Grizzly hackle tip tied in at each side and extending half the length of the wing.
Head: Black.

F N'G Marabou, Brown
Hooks: TMC9395 or DAI2220, sizes 2-8.
Thread: Black.
Tail: Yellow hackle barbs.
Ribbing: Flat gold tinsel.
Body: Beige chenille.
Wing: Yellow marabou tied over the body with an overwing of sparse brown bucktail.
Shoulder: Dyed yellow grizzly hackle tip tied in at each side and extending half the length of the wing.
Hackle: Red hackle barbs tied in at the throat.
Head: Black.

F N'G Marabou, Green
Hooks: TMC9395 or DAI2220, sizes 2-8.
Thread: Black.
Tail: Yellow hackle barbs.
Ribbing: Flat gold chenille.
Body: Yellow chenille.
Wing: Green marabou tied over the body with an overwing of sparse green bucktail.
Shoulder: Dyed yellow grizzly hackle tip tied in at each side and extending half the length of the wing.
Hackle: Red hackle barbs tied in at the throat.
Head: Black.

F N'G Marabou, White
Hooks: TMC9395 or DAI2220, sizes 2-8.
Thread: Red.
Tail: Red hackle barbs.
Ribbing: Flat silver tinsel.
Body: White chenille.
Wing: White marabou tied over the body with an overwing of sparse black bucktail.
Shoulder: Grizzly hackle tip tied in at each side and extending half the length of the wing.
Hackle: Red hackle barbs tied in at the throat.
Head: Red.

Frank and Gay Lunstrom of Fresno, California, developed the F N'G series of streamers in 1980.

Fiery Brown
Hooks: TMC9395 or DAI2220, sizes 4-8.
Thread: Black.
Tail: Golden pheasant crest.
Ribbing: Oval gold tinsel.
Body: Flat gold tinsel.
Hackle: Red hackle barbs tied in at the throat.
Wing: Golden badger neck hackles tied over the body.
Cheeks: J.C. or substitute.
Head: Black.

Flagg's Smelt
Hooks: TMC9395 or DAI2220, sizes 2-6.
Thread: White.
Tail: Red calf tail.
Butt: Red thread which secures body at rear.
Body: Large silver Mylar piping pressed flat.
Throat: White bucktail tied in and extending to bend of hook.
Wing: Blue FisHair tied over the body.
Topping: Strands of peacock herl with a narrow barred mallard flank feather tip tied flat.

Head: White.
Eyes: Tiny red dots.
Originated by Rodney Flagg.

Fox Squirrel

Hooks: TMC5263 or DAI1710, sizes 4-14.
Thread: Black.
Ribbing: Oval silver tinsel.
Body: Flat silver tinsel.
Hackle: Crimson red hackle barbs tied in at the throat.
Wing: Fox squirrel tail tied over the body.
Head: Black.

Frank Smith Special

Hooks: TMC9395 or DAI2220, sizes 6-10.
Thread: Black.
Body: Flat silver tinsel.
Throat: White bucktail tied in and extending to bend of hook.
Wing: Orange calf tail tied over the body with an overwing of brown calf tail.
Head: Black.

Frost's Blue Smelt

Hooks: TMC300, DAI2340 or DAI2370, sizes 4-10.
Thread: White.
Butt: Blue thread which secures body at rear.
Body: Silver Mylar piping slipped over an underbody of white floss or yarn.
Wing: White bucktail tied over the body with overwings of strands of peacock herl, then blue bucktail tied on top.
Head: Blue.
Eyes: White with black centers.
Originated by Dick Frost.

Gasperaux

Hooks: TMC9395 or DAI2220, sizes 8-10.
Thread: Black.
Body: Embossed silver tinsel.
Wing: Yellow bucktail tied over the body with an overwing of red bucktail.
Cheeks: J.C. or substitute.
Head: Black.

Originated by George Richards and Charles Wetzel.

Gee-Beau

Hooks: TMC5263 or DAI1720, sizes 4-6.
Thread: Black.
Tail: Pair of orange goose quill sections tied together and curved upward.
Ribbing: Oval silver tinsel over entire body.
Body: Rear half, flat silver tinsel and front half, dubbed with #6 yellow lambs wool.
Throat: Small bunch of yellow hackle barbs.
Wings: Four white saddle hackles tied over the body.
Shoulders: Wide orange goose quill section tied in at each side with points down.
Cheeks: J.C. or substitute.
Head: Black.

Originated by Charles Phair of Presque Isle, Maine.

General MacArthur

Hooks: TMC9395 or DAI2220, sizes 4-6.
Thread: White.
Tail: Red hackle barbs.
Body: Flat silver tinsel.
Throat: Small bunches of red, white and blue hackle barbs stacked one on the other.
Wings: Light blue saddle hackle tied over the body with white and then grizzly saddles tied to the outsides.
Cheeks: J.C. or substitute.
Head: White with red and blue bands.

Originated by Carrie G. Stevens. Named in honor of General Douglas MacArthur. Although this pattern was originally tied as a patriotic gesture, it turned out to be an effective smelt imitation.

Ghost Shiner

Hooks: TMC9395 or DAI2220, sizes 8-10.
Thread: Tan.
Tail: Light green hackle barbs.
Ribbing: Flat silver tinsel.
Body: White floss well tapered.
Throat: Small bunch of white hackle barbs.
Wing: Natural tan rabbit tied over the body.
Cheeks: J.C. or substitute.
Head: Tan.

Wing material is taken from the longer back hair of a rabbit skin. Originated by Lew Oatman of Shushan, New York.

Golden Darter

Hooks: TMC300, DAI2340 or DAI2370, sizes 6-8.
Thread: Black.
Tail: Small section of mottled brown turkey quill tied short.
Ribbing: Flat gold tinsel.
Body: Yellow floss.
Throat: Grizzly hen hackle barbs.
Wings: Two golden badger saddle hackles tied over the body.
Cheeks: J.C. or substitute.
Head: Black.

Another Lew Oatman pattern. Throat hackle was originally jungle cock body feather barbs.

Golden Demon

Hooks: TMC5263 or DAI1720, sizes 4-10.
Thread: Black.
Tail: Golden pheasant crest.
Body: Gold diamond braid.
Hackle: Fire orange tied on as a collar and tied back and down.
Wings: Two bronze mallard flanks tied flat over each other and extending past bend of hook.
Head: Black.

Goldenhead

Hooks: TMC5263 or DAI1720, sizes 2-10.
Thread: Black.
Ribbing: Oval gold tinsel.
Body: Black floss thinly tapered.
Wings: White bucktail tied over the body with two brown saddle hackles tied flat on top with one golden pheasant tippet feather tied flat and extending one-third the wing length.
Head: Black.

Golden Minnow

Hooks: TMC9395 or DAI2220, sizes 4-10.
Thread: Red.
Butt: Red thread which secures body at rear.

Body: Gold Mylar piping slipped over an underbody of yellow floss or yarn.
Throat: Red hackle barbs.
Wings: White bucktail tied over the body with an overwing of yellow bucktail with dyed yellow mallard flank feathers tied at the sides.
Head: Painted gold.
Eyes: Red with black centers.

Golden Shiner

Hooks: TMC300, DAI2340 or DAI2370, sizes 6-10.
Thread: Black.
Tail: Tuft of orange marabou. This can be taken from the butt of orange saddle hackle.
Ribbing: Flat gold tinsel.
Body: White floss thinly tapered.
Throat: Another tuft of orange marabou with white bucktail tied over.
Wing: Yellow bucktail tied over the body with an overwing of peacock herl. A blue dun saddle is tied in at each side of wing.
Cheeks: J.C. or substitute.
Head: Black.

Golden Smelt

Hooks: TMC300, DAI2340 or DAI2370, sizes 2-6.
Thread: Black.
Tail: Golden pheasant tippets tied short.
Ribbing: Flat gold tinsel.
Body: Rear two-thirds, yellow floss and the front third, pink floss.
Throat: Small bunch of yellow hackle barbs.
Wings: Two light green saddle hackle tied over the body with golden badger saddle tied in at the sides.
Cheeks: J.C. or substitute.
Head: Black.

The two preceding patterns were originated by Lew Oatman of Shushan, New York.

Golden Witch

Hooks: TMC300, DAI2340 or DAI2370, sizes 4-8.
Thread: Black.
Tip: Flat silver tinsel.
Ribbing: Flat silver tinsel.
Body: Orange floss thinly tapered.

Throat: Grizzly hackle barbs tied in with white bucktail over and extending to bend of hook.
Wings: Strand of peacock herl tied over the body with an overwing of four grizzly saddle hackles.
Shoulders: Golden pheasant tippet feather tied in at each side.
Cheeks: J.C. or substitute.
Head: Black with a red band at the base of wing.

Originated by Carrie G. Stevens.

Governor Aiken

Hooks: TMC300, DAI2340 or DAI2370, sizes 4-8.
Thread: Black.
Tail: Section of black and white barred lemon woodduck.
Ribbing: Oval silver tinsel.
Body: Flat silver tinsel.
Throat: Narrow section of red goose quill tied in and extending back to the center of the body. White bucktail is tied over and extends to just past the hook.
Wing: Purple bucktail tied over the body.
Topping: Strands of peacock herl.
Cheeks: J.C. or substitute.
Head: Black.

There is some dispute as to proper wing color for this pattern. Some state that it should be a lavender. It has been explained to me that purple is the intended color. It is often washed out some with use and/or is faded by exposure to the sun leaving a faded purple or lavender shade.

This pattern was named after former Governor George D. Aiken of Vermont. Originator unknown.

Governor Brann

Hooks: TMC5263 or DAI1720, sizes 4-6.
Thread: Black.
Tail: Section of red duck quill.
Ribbing: Oval silver tinsel.
Body: Flat silver tinsel.
Throat: Small bunch of natural brown bucktail tied in and extending to end of hook.

Wings: Four olive saddle hackles tied over the body with furnace neck hackles tied in at each side.
Cheeks: J.C. or substitute.
Head: Black.

Originated by Bert Quimby of South Windham, Maine, and named after their former Governor.

Grand Laker

Hooks: TMC300, DAI2340 or DAI2370, sizes 4-6.
Thread: Black.
Tip: Flat gold tinsel.
Ribbing: Flat gold tinsel. Ribbing is tied in at the front and wrapped to the rear and returned to the front.
Body: Black floss thinly tapered.
Throat: Small bunch of natural brown bucktail tied in and extending to the end of the hook.
Wings: Four brown saddle hackles tied over the body.
Cheeks: J.C. or substitute.
Head: Black.

No one person can be given credit for this pattern. It is the product of many who were trying for that better fly for Grand Lake Stream in Maine. There are many variations.

Gravel Gertie

Hooks: TMC9395 or DAI2220, sizes 4-8.
Thread: Black.
Tag: Orange yarn.
Body: Alternating bands of black and white chenille.
Throat: Pink tag of yarn.
Wing: White calf tail tied over the body.
Half Collar: Fox squirrel tail tied on top and to the sides.
Head: Black.

Gray Ghost

Hooks: TMC300, DAI2340 or DAI2370, sizes 2-10.
Thread: Black.
Tip: Flat silver tinsel.
Ribbing: Flat silver tinsel.
Body: Orange floss.

Throat: Tie in a golden pheasant crest feather. The tip of the feather should extend to the tip of the hook and it should point upward. Tie in a sparse bunch of white bucktail along the bottom of the fly and extending just past the bend of the hook. Over this tie in strands of peacock herl to extend slightly past the bucktail.
Wings: Four olive dun saddle hackles tied over the body.
Shoulders: Silver pheasant body feather tied in at each side. They should extend only one-third the length of the wing.
Head: Black with a red band at the base of wing.
Note: The proper wing color is obtained by overdying light olive with #39 Rit dye.

This pattern has received universal acknowledgment since it was first introduced by Carrie G. Stevens in 1924. She developed this pattern to simulate a smelt, it was so successful it launched her into a career of professional fly tying. A memorial and plaque at the site of her home at Upper Dam, Mooselookmeguntic Lake, Maine, reads:

"Fishermen: Pause here a moment and pay your respects to Carrie Gertude Stevens. On July 1, 1924, while engaged in household tasks in her home across this portage road, she was inspired to create a new fish-fly pattern. With housework abandoned her nimble hands had soon completed her vision. In less than an hour the nearby Upper Dam Pool had yielded a 6 pound 13 ounce brook trout to the new fly that would become known throughout the world as the Gray Ghost Streamer."

Gray Prince

Hooks: TMC5263 or DAI1720, sizes 6-8.
Thread: Black.
Tail: Golden pheasant crest tied short.
Ribbing: Oval silver tinsel.
Body: Embossed silver tinsel.

Hackle: Badger tied on as a collar and tied back and down.
Wings: Four match tips of barred mallard flank tied over the body and extending to the end of the tail.
Cheeks: J.C. or substitute.
Head: Black.

Originated by B. A. Gulline of Montreal, Canada.

Gray Smelt

Hooks: TMC300, DAI2340 or DAI2370, sizes 4-8.
Thread: Gray.
Tail: Golden pheasant tippet barbs tied short.
Ribbing: Flat silver tinsel.
Body: White floss thinly tapered.
Wings: Two light olive saddle hackles tied over the body with a blue dun saddle tied in at each side. Wings should extend well past the end of the tail.
Cheeks: J.C. or substitute.
Head: Gray.

Originated by Lew Oatman of Shushan, New York.

Gray Squirrel

Hooks: TMC5263 or DAI1720, sizes 4-14.
Thread: Black.
Ribbing: Oval silver tinsel.
Body: Flat silver tinsel.
Hackle: Crimson red hackle barbs tied in at the throat.
Wing: Gray squirrel tail tied over the body.
Head: Black.

Gray Squirrel Silver

Hooks: TMC5263 or DAI1720, sizes 4-8.
Thread: Black.
Body: Embossed silver tinsel.
Throat: Dyed red golden pheasant crest.
Wings: Gray squirrel tied over the body with an overwing of two grizzly saddle hackles.

Cheeks: J.C. or substitute.
Head: Black.

This pattern was originated in 1933 by Ray Bergman.

Plate 5 ## Gray Tiger
Hooks: TMC9395 or DAI2220, sizes 4-10.
Thread: Black.
Tail: Black and white barred silver pheasant quill section.
Ribbing: Oval silver tinsel.
Body: Dubbed with #2 white African Angora goat. Pick out and make shaggy.
Throat: Red hackle barbs.
Wing: Gray squirrel tail tied over the body with a single barred mallard flank feather tied flat over the top.
Head: Black.

Green Beauty
Hooks: TMC300, DAI2340 or DAI2370, sizes 4-6.
Thread: Black.
Ribbing: Flat silver tinsel.
Body: Orange floss.
Throat: Golden pheasant crest tied in and extending to the center of the body. White bucktail tied over and extending to the bend of the hook.
Wings: Strands of peacock herl tied over the body with an overwing of four olive saddle hackles.
Shoulders: Barred lemon woodduck feathers tied in at each side.
Cheeks: J.C. or substitute.
Head: Black with a red band at the base of the wing.

Originated by Carrie G. Stevens.

Green Drake Streamer
Hooks: TMC300, DAI2340 or DAI2370, sizes 4-10.
Thread: Black.
Tip: Flat gold tinsel.
Tail: Black hackle barbs.
Butt: Peacock herl.
Ribbing: Heavy black thread.
Body: Tan floss.
Throat: Ginger hackle barbs.
Wings: Two olive saddle hackles tied over the body with a brown saddle tied in at each side.

Shoulders: Dyed yellow barred teal feather tied in at each side.
Cheeks: J.C. or substitute.
Head: Black.

Originated by Gardner Percy.

Green Ghost
Hooks: TMC300, DAI2340 or DAI2370, sizes 4-6.
Thread: Black.
Tip: Flat silver tinsel.
Ribbing: Flat silver tinsel.
Body: Orange floss thinly tapered.
Throat: Small bunch of white bucktail with strands of peacock herl tied over. Both should extend to bend of hook.
Wings: Four green saddle hackles tied over the body.
Topping: Golden pheasant crest.
Shoulders: Silver pheasant body feather tied in at each side.
Cheeks: J.C. or substitute.
Head: Black.

Originated by Bert Quimby.

Green King
Hooks: TMC9395 or DAI2220, sizes 4-6.
Thread: Black.
Body: Flat silver tinsel.
Wings: White bucktail tied over the body with an overwing of two grizzly neck hackles with olive neck hackles tied in at each side.
Cheeks: J.C. or substitute.
Head: Black.

Originated by Gardner Percy.

Green Wonder
Hooks: TMC300, DAI2340 or DAI2370, sizes 2-8.
Thread: Black.
Body: Flat silver tinsel.
Wings: White bucktail tied over the body with overwings of four dyed green grizzly saddles.
Topping: Strands of peacock herl.
Head: Black.

Greyhound
Hooks: TMC300, DAI2340 or DAI2370, sizes 4-6.
Thread: Red.
Tip: Flat silver tinsel.
Tail: Red hackle barbs.

Ribbing: Flat silver tinsel.
Body: Red floss thinly tapered.
Throat: Red hackle barbs tied in with white bucktail and strands of peacock herl tied over. Peacock and bucktail should extend to end of hook.
Wings: Four blue dun saddle hackles tied over the body.
Shoulders: Wide badger hen hackle tips tied in at each side.
Cheeks: J.C. or substitute.
Head: Red with a black band at the base of the wing.

Originated by Carrie G. Stevens. The shoulder material for the original dressing called for jungle cock body feathers.

Plate 5 **Grizzly King**
Hooks: TMC9395 or DAI2220, sizes 4-8.
Thread: Black.
Tip: Flat gold tinsel.
Tail: Red hackle barbs.
Ribbing: Flat gold tinsel.
Body: Green floss thinly tapered.
Hackle: Grizzly tied on as a collar and tied back and down.
Wings: Four grizzly saddle hackle tied over the body and extending just past the end of the tail.
Head: Black.

There have been a large number of variations on this pattern. Another has gray squirrel tail for the wing. This fly originated from a wet fly pattern.

Grizzly Prince
Hooks: TMC9395 or DAI2220, sizes 4-6.
Thread: Black.
Tail: Orange hackle barbs.
Body: Flat silver tinsel.
Throat: Orange hackle barbs tied in with white bucktail over and extending to the bend of the hook.
Wings: Four white saddle hackles tied over the body with two grizzly saddles tied in at each side. The barbs on the grizzly saddles are stripped off on the bottom side to allow the bottom half of the white to show through.

Shoulders: Barred lemon woodduck feathers tied in at each side.
Cheeks: J.C. or substitute.
Head: Black.

Originated by Austin Hogan of Fultonville, New York.

Harlequin
Hooks: TMC9395 or DAI2220, sizes 4-8.
Thread: Black.
Tail: Narrow section of red goose quill.
Ribbing: Oval silver tinsel.
Body: Flat silver tinsel.
Hackle: Badger tied on as a collar and tied back and down.
Wing: Black, dark blue and white bucktail mixed and tied over the body.
Head: Black.

This is a variation of the original which had swan quill section married for wings.

Plate 4 **Harris Special**
Hooks: TMC9395 or DAI2220, sizes 2-10.
Thread: Black.
Tail: Golden pheasant tippet barbs.
Body: Flat gold tinsel.
Throat: Red bucktail tied in and extending to hook point.
Wing: White bucktail tied on the body with an overwing of one barred lemon woodduck flank feather tied flat.
Head: Black.

Helen Bates
Hooks: TMC5263 or DAI1720, sizes 6-8.
Thread: Black.
Tip: Flat gold tinsel.
Tail: Golden pheasant crest.
Butt: Red floss.
Body Hackle: Brown tied palmer style over the body.
Body: Flat gold tinsel.

Wings: Four dark furnace saddle hackles tied over the body.
Topping: Golden pheasant crest.
Cheeks: J.C. or substitute.
Head: Black.

Originated by William Reynolds of Sturbridge, Massachusetts.

Herb's Ghost

Hooks: TMC300, DAI2340 or DAI2370, sizes 4-6.
Thread: Black.
Tip: Flat silver tinsel.
Tail: Golden pheasant crest tied short.
Ribbing: Flat silver tinsel.
Body: Orange floss thinly tapered.
Throat: Yellow hackle barbs.
Wings: White bucktail tied over the body with an overwing of natural brown bucktail. Add a yellow and then a fire orange saddle hackle to each side. The fire orange saddles should be cocked up slightly to expose some of the yellow behind them.
Cheeks: J.C. or substitute.
Head: Black.

Originated by Herbert Howard and Herbert Gerlach of Ossining, New York.

Plate 5   Hornberg Special

Hooks: TMC5263 or DAI1720, sizes 4-14.
Thread: Brown.
Body: Flat silver tinsel.
Wings: Pair yellow neck hackles tied on edge over the body with a well matched pair of barred mallard flank feathers tied in at each side.
Cheeks: J.C. or substitute.
Hackle: Brown and grizzly tied on as a collar mixed.
Head: Brown.

I don't want boredom to set in so I will make this brief. This is one of my all-time favorite flies. First off, it shouldn't work for me at all, it's one of those Eastern creations and everyone in the West knows they don't work out here.

I fish this fly as a streamer, wet fly, dry fly, emerger—you name it. It is even one of my favorites during hopper season.

The underwing is different, using yellow bucktail rather than hackle. This is a normal variation of this pattern and not of my own design. I do refrain from using calf tail however, it does not lay like I want it to.

I am not sure if the cheeks are an essential ingredient for this fly, I have never fished it without some sort of cheek. For my tastes it appears to be too undressed without cheeks, much like attending the opera in blue jeans.

Do not get hung up on jungle cock or anything that even simulates it for this pattern. I have been able to determine this after 40 or more years of fishing this fly. I either use a well marked pair of grizzly hackle tips or black and white barred lemon woodduck sections.

This fly can be tied on any number of hook models. Hooks with long or short shanks, heavy wire, etc., it just depends on what you are trying to accomplish.

When Frank Hornberg created this fly he should have named it the "Defiant One" rather than Hornberg Special. This fly resists fitting into any logic we fly fishermen come up with. It resembles nothing because it is nothing, nothing other than a damn good fly and fish will eat it on a regular basis.

Housatonic Special

Hooks: TMC9395 or DAI2220, sizes 4-10.
Thread: Black.
Tail: White calf tail.
Body: Dubbed with a blend of 1 part #1 black and 4 parts #13 light gray lambs wool.
Wing: Natural brown bucktail tied over the body.
Head: Black.

Originated by Walt Stockman.

Hurricane

Hooks: TMC9395 or DAI2220, sizes 4-8.
Thread: Black.
Tail: Yellow hackle barbs.
Ribbing: Oval silver tinsel.
Body: Flat silver tinsel.
Throat: Peacock sword feather barbs.
Wings: Red bucktail tied over the body with an overwing of white bucktail. Add a grizzly saddle to each side.
Head: Black.

Originated in 1925 by Fred Fowler of Oquossoc, Maine.

Integration Fly

Hooks: TMC300, DAI2340 or DAI2370, sizes 2-10.
Thread: Black.
Butt: Red thread which secures body at rear.
Body: Silver Mylar piping slipped over an underbody of white yarn or floss.
Throat: White bucktail tied in at the throat and tied one and one half the length of the body.
Wing: White bucktail tied over the body with an overwing of black bucktail. Wing should be equal in length to the throat.
Head: Black.
Eyes: Tiny red dots.

The Mylar on the body of this fly is tied down at the rear with red thread. I apply red enamel over the thread to give it even more seductiveness. This pattern was created by Ted Trueblood and is considered by many to be more productive for saltwater.

Jane Craig

Hooks: TMC9395 or DAI2220, sizes 4-6.
Thread: Black.
Body: Flat silver tinsel.
Throat: White hackle barbs.
Wings: Six white saddle hackles tied over the body.
Topping: Strands of peacock herl.
Cheeks: J.C. or substitute.
Head: Black.

Originated by Herbert Welch.

Joe's Smelt

Hooks: TMC9395 or DAI2220, sizes 2-10.
Thread: Black.
Tail: Red calf tail tied short.
Butt: Red thread which secures body at rear.
Body: Silver Mylar piping slipped over an underbody of white floss or yarn. The front of the body is secured with red thread.
Wing: Narrow tip of barred teal flank tied flat over the body.
Head: Black.
Eyes: Yellow with black centers.

Originated by Joe Sterling.

Jossy Special

Hooks: TMC9395 or DAI2220, sizes 6-10.
Thread: Black.
Ribbing: Peacock herl twisted on thread core.
Body: White chenille.
Wings: Natural brown bucktail tied over the body with white neck hackles tied in at the sides with concave sides out.
Head: Black.

The Jossy Special was originated by W. E. Jossy for Oregon's Deschutes River.

Kelly Bill

Hooks: TMC5263 or DAI1720, sizes 6-8.
Thread: Red.
Tag: Orange yarn tied thick.
Ribbing: Flat gold tinsel.
Body: Rear half, flat gold tinsel and the front half, dubbed with #9 orange lambs wool.
Hackle: Black tied on as a collar and tied back and down.
Wing: Gray squirrel tail tied over the body.
Cheeks: J.C. or substitute.
Head: Red.

Originated by Herbert Howard for the Adirondack Mountains in New York state.

Kennebago

Hooks: TMC300, DAI2340 or DAI2370, sizes 4-6.
Thread: Black.
Tail: Orange hackle barbs.
Butt: Peacock herl.

Body: Rear third, light blue floss with a peacock herl joint wrapped in front and the front two-thirds, flat gold tinsel.
Ribbing: Oval silver tinsel over gold tinsel only.
Throat: Orange hackle barbs.
Wings: Two crimson red saddle hackles tied over the body with a golden badger saddles tied in at each side.
Cheeks: J.C. or substitute.
Head: Black.

Originated by Herbert Welch.

King Smelt

Hooks: TMC300, DAI2340 or DAI2370, sizes 2-10.
Thread: Black.
Body: Silver diamond braid.
Wing: White bucktail tied over the body with overwings of purple bucktail, blue bucktail, green bucktail, and black bucktail.
Head: Black.
Eyes: White with red centers.

Kukonen Smelt

Hooks: TMC300, DAI2340 or DAI2370, sizes 2-10.
Thread: Red.
Ribbing: Heavy red thread.
Body: Pearlescent Mylar piping slipped over and tied in at the rear with red thread.
Hackle: White calf tail tied in at the throat and extending to end of body.
Wings: Dark blue dun neck hackles tied over the body.
Cheeks: J.C. or substitute.
Head: Red.

Lady Ghost

Hooks: TMC300, DAI2340 or DAI2370, sizes 2-6.
Thread: Black.
Ribbing: Oval silver tinsel.
Body: Flat silver tinsel.
Throat: Short gold pheasant crest feather curved up, small bunch of white bucktail and then strands of peacock herl.

Wings: Golden pheasant crest tied with curve up and extending the length of the hook with four golden badger saddle hackles tied over the body.
Shoulders: Silver pheasant body feather tied in at each side.
Cheeks: J.C. or substitute.
Head: Black.

Originated by Bert Quimby of South Windham, Maine.

Leitz Bucktail

Hooks: TMC9395 or DAI2220, sizes 2-8.
Thread: Black.
Tip: Flat gold tinsel.
Tail: Two red hackle tips tied on edge and split with concave sides outward.
Butt: Black chenille.
Body: Embossed silver tinsel with a black chenille joint at the front of the body.
Hackle: Red tied on as a collar and tied back and down.
Wing: White bucktail tied over the body with an overwing of red and black mixed bucktail.
Cheeks: J.C. or substitute.
Head: Black.

Originated by Earl Leitz of Sault St. Marie, Michigan.

Little Brook Trout

Hooks: TMC300, DAI2340 or DAI2370, sizes 4-12.
Thread: Black.
Tail: Green bucktail tied short.
Tag: Red floss tied over the tail.
Ribbing: Flat silver tinsel.
Body: Dubbed with #3 cream Bunny-Blend.
Hackle: Orange hackle barbs tied in at the throat.
Wing: White bucktail tied over the body with overwings of orange bucktail, then green bucktail with badger guard hair tied on top.
Head: Black.

Little Brown Trout

Hooks: TMC300, DAI2340 or DAI2370, sizes 4-12.
Thread: Black.
Tail: Small cock ringneck pheasant breast feather. The dark center is clipped out of the feather and mounted curved upward.

Ribbing: Copper wire.
Body: Dubbed with #2 white Bunny-Blend.
Wing: Yellow bucktail tied over the body with overwings of hot orange bucktail, then gray squirrel tail, then dark fox squirrel tail tied on top.
Head: Black.

Little Rainbow Trout

Hooks: TMC300, DAI2340 or DAI2370, sizes 4-12.
Thread: Black.
Tail: Green bucktail tied short.
Ribbing: Flat silver tinsel.
Body: Dubbed with #29 pale pink Bunny-Blend.
Wing: White bucktail tied over the body with overwings of pink bucktail, then green bucktail with badger guard hairs tied on top.
Head: Black.

These three Little Trout patterns were originated by Samuel Slaymaker, II of Gap, Pennsylvania. Fly tiers have repeatedly tried to improve upon these flies without success. Unfortunately, there was a period when some of the larger tackle companies tried to cash in on these patterns. As a result of their thoughtless substitutions of materials and other shortcomings in their dressings, these flies suffered a bum rap and were disfavored by many fly fishermen.

Llama

Hooks: TMC300, DAI2340 or DAI2370, sizes 2-10.
Thread: Black.
Tail: Grizzly hen hackle barbs.
Ribbing: Flat silver tinsel.
Body: Red floss.
Wing: Woodchuck hair tied over the body.
Hackle: Grizzly hen hackle tied on as a collar and tied back.
Cheeks: J.C. or substitute.
Head: Black.

Lord Denby

Hooks: TMC300, DAI2340 or DAI2370, sizes 4-6.
Thread: Black.
Tail: Golden pheasant tippet barbs.
Body: Flat silver tinsel.
Hackle: Red and light blue tied on as a collar and tied back and down.
Wings: Two light blue saddles tied over the body with a grizzly saddle tied in at each side.
Cheeks: J.C. or substitute.
Head: Black.

Originated by Robert E. Coulson of Buffalo, New York.

MacGregor

Hooks: TMC9395 or DAI2220, sizes 4-6.
Thread: Black.
Tip: Flat silver tinsel.
Tail: Golden pheasant crest.
Ribbing: Flat silver tinsel.
Body: Dark orange chenille.
Throat: Grizzly hackle barbs.
Wing: Gray squirrel tail tied over the body.
Cheeks: J.C. or substitute.
Head: Black.

This is an old pattern that immigrated from Edinburgh, Scotland. It was originated by George Fraser.

Magog Smelt

Hooks: TMC5263 or DAI1720, sizes 2-6.
Thread: Black.
Tail: Barred teal barbs.
Body: Flat silver tinsel.
Throat: Red hackle barbs.
Wing: White bucktail tied over the body with an overwing of yellow bucktail followed with a small bunch of red and purple mixed bucktail tied on top.
Topping: Strands of peacock herl.
Shoulders: Barred teal feather tied in at each side.
Head: Black.
Eyes: Yellow with black centers.

Originated by Frier Gulline.

Male Dace

Hooks: TMC9395 or DAI2220, sizes 4-10.
Thread: Black.
Ribbing: Flat gold tinsel.
Body: Cream floss thinly tapered.
Throat: Orange hackle barbs.
Wings: Olive saddle hackle tied over the body with golden badger saddles tied in at the sides.
Cheeks: J.C. or substitute.
Head: Black.

Originated by Lew Oatman of Shushan, New York.

Mallard Minnow

Hooks: TMC300, DAI2340 or DAI2370, sizes 4-8.
Thread: Red.
Butt: Red thread which secures body at rear.
Body: Silver Mylar piping slipped over an underbody of white yarn or floss.
Wings: Tie in a small bunch of orange bucktail followed with a well marked grizzly neck hackle tied in at each side with concave sides inward.
Shoulders: Barred mallard flank feather tied in at each side which extends back half the length of the grizzly.
Cheeks: Yellow hen hackle tips tied in at each side.
Hackle: Furnace tied on as a collar and tied back.
Head: Red.

This pattern was originally tied for northern California's Shasta Lake but has been found to be equally successful in other areas. It was developed by my father in 1967.

Mansfield

Hooks: TMC300 or DAI2220, sizes 2-10.
Thread: Black.
Body: Silver diamond braid.
Throat: Red bucktail tied in and extending to the bend of the hook.
Wings: White bucktail tied over the body with overwings of four fluorescent orange saddle hackles.
Cheeks: J.C. or substitute.

Head: Black.

Marabou, Black

Hooks: TMC5263 or DAI1720, sizes 2-8.
Thread: Black.
Tag: Red yarn.
Body: CC02 black Crystal Chenille.
Throat: Red bucktail tied in and extending past the bend of the hook.
Wing: Black bucktail tied over the body with an overwing of black marabou.
Topping: Strand of peacock herl.
Head: Black.

Marabou, Blue

Hooks: TMC5263 or DAI1720, sizes 2-8.
Thread: Black.
Tag: Red yarn.
Body: CC12 light blue Crystal Chenille.
Throat: White bucktail tied in and extending past the bend of the hook.
Wing: White bucktail tied over the body with an overwing of blue marabou.
Topping: Strands of peacock herl.
Head: Black.

Marabou, Brown

Hooks: TMC5263 or DAI1720, sizes 2-8.
Thread: Black.
Tag: Red yarn.
Body: CC25 copper brown Crystal Chenille.
Throat: White bucktail tied in and extending past the bend of the hook.
Wing: Black bucktail tied over the body with overwings of tan marabou and then brown marabou.
Topping: Strands of peacock herl.
Head: Black.

Marabou, Gray

Hooks: TMC5263 or DAI1720, sizes 2-8.
Thread: Black.
Body: CC01 pearl Crystal Chenille.
Throat: White bucktail tied in and extending past the bend of the hook.
Wing: White bucktail tied over the body with overwings of white marabou and then gray marabou.
Topping: Strands of natural gray ostrich herl.
Head: Black.

This pattern is one of the better flies used to simulate threadfin shad.

Marabou, Multi-Color

Hooks: TMC5263 or DAI1720, sizes 2-8.
Thread: Red.
Tag: Red yarn.
Body: CC01 pearl Crystal Chenille.
Throat: White bucktail tied in and extending past the bend of the hook.
Wing: Black bucktail tied over the body with overwings of yellow marabou, then olive marabou and then dark brown marabou.
Topping: Strands of peacock herl.
Cheeks: Grizzly hackle tips tied in at each side.
Head: Red.

Marabou, Olive

Hooks: TMC5263 or DAI1720, sizes 2-8.
Thread: Olive.
Tag: Yellow yarn.
Body: CC04 yellow Crystal Chenille.
Throat: Yellow bucktail tied in and extending past the bend of the hook.
Wing: Yellow bucktail tied over the body with an overwing of olive marabou.
Topping: Strands of peacock herl.
Head: Olive.

Marabou Perch

Hooks: TMC300, DAI2340 or DAI2370, sizes 2-6.
Thread: Yellow.
Butt: Yellow thread which secures body at rear.
Body: Pearlescent green Mylar piping slipped over an underbody of white yarn or floss.
Throat: Yellow marabou tied in and extending the length of the body.
Wing: Green bucktail tied over the body with overwings of yellow marabou and then dark olive marabou.
Topping: CH16 dark olive Crystal Hair.
Head: When completing the head the Crystal Hair should be pulled back over and secured at the back with yellow thread.

All too often we find that some of the better trout waters are infested with perch. I have resolved to make the best of the situation and give them some of what they are really accustomed to feeding on. You would be more than excited if you knew just how many big browns find refuge in such places. This is also an excellent bass-producing pattern.

Marabou, White

Hooks: TMC5263 or DAI1720, sizes 4-10.
Thread: Red.
Tag: Red yarn.
Body: CC01 pearl Crystal Chenille.
Throat: White bucktail tied in at and extending past the bend of the hook.
Wing: White bucktail tied over the body with white marabou tied on top.
Topping: Strands of peacock herl.
Head: Red.

Marabou, Yellow

Hooks: TMC5263 or DAI1720, sizes 2-8.
Thread: Olive.
Tag: Red yarn.
Body: CC01 pearl Crystal Chenille.
Throat: White bucktail tied in and extending past the bend of the hook.
Wing: Yellow bucktail tied over the body with an overwing of yellow marabou.
Topping: Strands of peacock herl.
Head: Olive.

Mascoma

Hooks: TMC9395 or DAI2220, sizes 4-10.
Thread: Black.
Tail: Golden pheasant crest tied short.
Ribbing: Oval gold tinsel.
Body: Flat gold tinsel wrapped over an underbody of yellow floss.
Throat: Orange hackle barbs.
Wings: Small bunches of red, blue and yellow bucktail mixed and tied over the body with a barred mallard section tied in at each side.
Cheeks: J.C. or substitute.
Head: Black.

This pattern is also successfully tied using either barred teal or bronze mallard in the wing.

Matuka, Blue Dun

Hooks: TMC9395 or DAI2220, sizes 4-10.
Thread: Black.
Ribbing: Oval silver tinsel.
Body: Dubbed with muskrat fur.
Wings: Four dyed blue dun badger neck hackles tied over the body.
Hackle: Dyed blue dun badger tied on as a collar and tied back.
Head: Black.

Plate 5 ## Matuka, Green Weeny

Hooks: TMC9395 or DAI2220, sizes 4-10.
Thread: Olive.
Ribbing: Oval gold tinsel.
Body: Dubbed with #21 golden olive African Angora goat.
Wings: Four dyed olive grizzly neck hackles tied over the body.
Hackle: Dyed olive grizzly tied on as a collar and tied back.
Head: Olive.

Matuka, Grizzly

Hooks: TMC9395 or DAI2220, sizes 4-10.
Thread: Black.
Ribbing: Oval silver tinsel.
Body: Dubbed with #12 light gray African Angora goat.
Wings: Four grizzly neck hackles tied over the body.
Hackle: Grizzly tied on as a collar and tied back.
Head: Black.

Matuka, Platte River Special

Hooks: TMC9395 or DAI2220, sizes 4-10.
Thread: Yellow.
Ribbing: Oval gold tinsel.
Body: Dubbed with #24 brown African Angora goat.
Wings: Two yellow neck hackles tied over the body with a brown neck hackle tied in at each side.
Hackle: Brown and yellow tied on as a collar mixed and tied back.
Head: Yellow.
See Platte River Special.

Matuka, Red Throat

Hooks: TMC9395 or DAI2220, sizes 4-10.
Thread: Black.
Ribbing: Oval silver tinsel.

Body: Rear three-quarters, dubbed with #2 white African Angora goat and the front quarter, dubbed with #4 red African Angora goat.
Wings: Four blue dun neck hackles tied over the body.
Hackle: Blue dun tied on as a collar and tied back.
Head: Black.

Matuka, Sculpin

Hooks: TMC9395 or DAI2220, sizes 4-10.
Thread: Brown.
Ribbing: Oval gold tinsel.
Body: Rear three-quarters, dubbed with #19 olive African Angora goat and the front quarter, dubbed with #4 red African Angora goat.
Wings: Four dyed brown grizzly neck hackles tied over the body Matuka style.
Pectoral Fins: Dyed olive mottled hen body feathers tied in at each side.
Collar: Dyed olive deer hair spun on as a half collar over the top.
Head: Dyed olive deer hair with strips of black deer hair spun on and clipped to shape.

Originated by Dave Whitlock.

Matuka, Spruce

Hooks: TMC9395 or DAI2220, sizes 4-10.
Thread: Black.
Ribbing: Oval silver tinsel.
Body: Rear third, dubbed with #4 red African Angora goat and the front two-thirds, peacock herl.
Wings: Four badger neck hackles tied over the body.
Hackle: Badger tied on as a collar and tied back.
Head: Black.

The Matuka flies originated in New Zealand. Although the fly design was known for at least three decades in this country they did not become popular until about 1975. Since that time they have been tied in just about any and every color combination one could fathom.

Mickey Finn

Hooks: TMC5263 or DAI1720, sizes 4-10.
Thread: Black.
Ribbing: Oval silver tinsel.
Body: Flat silver tinsel.
Wing: Small bunch of yellow bucktail tied over the body with another small bunch of red bucktail tied in as an overwing. Over these to smaller bunches tie a larger bunch of yellow bucktail. This bunch should equal the first two.
Head: Black.

This pattern is not on the top of my list to start out a day's fishing with. It has only been when I have seen others having success with it that I change over.

I have read some very intriguing accounts of this pattern for more than 40 years now and often wonder just how naive the writers of these articles believe we are. One such piece was in three monthly installments which read like one of today's soap operas on TV. This "master fly fisherman" was employed to rid the bass from Midwestern farm ponds and lakes which had become overpopulated. I am sure this was a real concern in the late 1950s when this article appeared. Well, this great master went from pond to pond, state by state, issue by issue and finally the climax came when his secret weapon was revealed, the Mickey Finn. If the youngsters of today read this, it would explain away their skepticism.

Miller's River Special

Hooks: TMC9395 or DAI2220, sizes 4-6.
Thread: Black.
Tail: Golden pheasant tippet barbs.
Ribbing: Oval gold tinsel.
Body: Flat gold tinsel.
Wing: Yellow bucktail tied over the body with an overwing of black bucktail.
Shoulders: Natural red golden pheasant body feather tied in at each side.
Cheeks: J.C. or substitute.

Head: Black.

Originated by Paul Kukonen and Henry Scarborough of Worcester, Massachusetts.

Minnow Streamer

Hooks: TMC5263 or DAI1720, sizes 6-8.
Thread: Black.
Tail: Ringneck pheasant tail feather barbs.
Ribbing: Flat silver tinsel.
Body: Claret floss thinly tapered.
Wings: Two section of ringneck pheasant tail tied on edge and extending to the end of the tail.
Head: Black.
Eyes: Tiny yellow dots.

This pattern originated in central Oregon and is regarded by some as a highly effective lake fly.

Miracle Minnows

Blacknose Dace

Hooks: TMC300, DAI2340 or DAI2370, sizes 2-6.
Thread: White.
Tail: Light ginger hackle barbs.
Body: Dubbed with #2 white Bunny-Blend.
Throat: Light ginger hackle barbs.
Wing: White marabou tied over the body with an overwing of olive-brown marabou.
Shoulders: Silver Mylar with black stripe on upper edge.
Topping: CH16 dark olive Crystal Hair.
Head: Brown with a white lower half.
Note: Upper wing color can be obtained by overdying olive with #16 Rit dye.

Blueback

Hooks: TMC300, DAI2340 or DAI2370, sizes 2-6.
Thread: White.
Tail: White hackle barbs.
Body: Dubbed with #2 white Bunny-Blend.

Throat: Light ginger hackle barbs.
Wing: White marabou tied over the body with overwings of light blue marabou and medium blue marabou.
Shoulders: Silver Mylar.
Topping: CH11 green Crystal Hair.
Head: Blue with a white lower half.

Golden Shiner

Hooks: TMC300, DAI2340 or DAI2370, sizes 2-6.
Thread: Pale yellow.
Tail: Pale yellow hackle barbs.
Body: Dubbed with #7 pale yellow Bunny-Blend.
Throat: Orange hackle barbs.
Wing: Pale yellow marabou tied over the body with an overwing of olive marabou.
Shoulders: Gold Mylar.
Topping: CH15 olive Crystal Hair.
Head: Pale yellow.

Longnose Dace

Hooks: TMC300, DAI2340 or DAI2370, sizes 2-6.
Thread: White.
Tail: Light ginger hackle barbs.
Body: Dubbed with a 50/50 blend of #2 white and #18 light olive Bunny-Blend.
Throat: Orange hackle barbs.
Wing: Pale yellow marabou tied over the body with an overwing of olive marabou.
Shoulders: Gold Mylar with black stripe on upper edge.
Topping: CH17 brown olive Crystal Hair.
Head: Olive with a white lower half.

Silver Shiner

Hooks: TMC300, DAI2340 or DAI2370, sizes 2-6.
Thread: White.
Tail: White and light olive hackle barbs mixed.
Body: Dubbed with #2 white Bunny-Blend.
Throat: White and light olive hackle barbs mixed.
Wing: White marabou tied over the body with an overwing of dark olive marabou.
Shoulders: Silver Mylar.
Topping: CH16 dark olive Crystal Hair.
Head: Olive with a white lower half.

Originated by Bob Zwirz and Kani Evans. I guess my interest in marabou as a fly tying material was just starting to peak when I learned of these flies in the March 1963 issue of *Field & Stream*. Combined with some new and interesting patterns was a new term not yet introduced into the world of fly tying—"Mylar." I didn't know how gimmicky it was, but this was supposed to be a new space age material that only those in the space industry had access to. That may have been true because I know that the material which we call Mylar today comes from the textile industry and is actually a polyester material; they have several trade names, none of which is Mylar.

This material drove fly tiers mad in their quest for it. It was only some time later that suitable material started appearing in isolated areas. Today it can be found in fly shops and through most mail order catalogs offering fly tying materials or lure-making components.

Miss Sharon

Hooks: TMC300, DAI2340 or DAI2370, sizes 2-10.
Thread: Black.
Ribbing: Flat silver tinsel.
Body: Red floss.
Wing: Very sparse bits of red, white, orange and black (top) bucktail tied over the body.
Head: Black.
Eyes: White with red centers.

Montreal

Hooks: TMC5263 or DAI1720, sizes 4-6.
Thread: Black.
Tail: Red duck quill section.
Ribbing: Oval silver tinsel.
Body: Flat silver tinsel.
Throat: Magenta hackle barbs.
Wings: Four magenta saddle hackle tied over the body.

Shoulders: Dark brown turkey tail feather section tied in at each side.
Head: Black.

Montreal Whore

Hooks: TMC300, DAI2340 or DAI2370, sizes 2-6.
Thread: Black.
Ribbing: Flat silver tinsel.
Body: Fluorescent fire orange yarn.
Wing: Blue bucktail tied over the body with overwings of white and red bucktail and white marabou tied on top. Bucktail underwings should be sparse.
Head: Black.

Moose River

Hooks: TMC5263 or DAI1720, sizes 4-6.
Thread: Black.
Body: Embossed silver tinsel.
Wings: White bucktail tied over the body with overwings of four golden badger neck hackles.
Topping: Strands of peacock herl.
Shoulders: Golden pheasant tippet feather tied in at each side.
Head: Black.

Originated by George Munster of Rockwood Station, Maine.

Muddler Minnow

Hooks: TMC9395 or DAI2220, sizes 2-12.
Thread: Brown.
Tail: Mottled brown turkey quill section.
Body: Embossed gold tinsel.
Wings: Fox squirrel tail tied over the body with a mottled brown turkey quill section tied in at each side.
Collar: Well marked coastal blacktail deer hair spun on.
Head: Natural deer hair spun on and clipped top shape.

Muddler Minnow, Black

Hooks: TMC9395 or DAI2220, sizes 4-10.
Thread: Black.
Tail: Barred teal section.
Ribbing: Oval silver tinsel.

Body: Dubbed with #1 black lambs wool.
Wings: Small bunch of CH02 black Crystal Hair tied over the body with an overwing of gray squirrel tail with a black goose quill section tied in at each side.
Collar: Dyed black elk hair spun on.
Head: Dyed black deer hair spun on and clipped to shape.

Muddler Minnow, Brown

Hooks: TMC9395 or DAI2220, sizes 4-10.
Thread: Brown.
Tail: Mottled brown turkey quill section.
Ribbing: Oval gold tinsel.
Body: Dubbed with #24 brown lambs wool.
Wings: Small bunch of CH25 copper brown Crystal Hair tied over the body with an overwing of fox squirrel tail with a brown goose quill section tied in at each side.
Collar: Dyed brown elk hair spun on.
Head: Dyed brown deer hair spun on and clipped to shape.

Muddler Minnow, Charlie's

Hooks: TMC9395 or DAI2220, sizes 2-4.
Thread: Brown.
Tail: Scarlet red hackle barbs.
Ribbing: Oval silver tinsel.
Body: Flat silver tinsel.
Wings: Four grizzly neck hackles tied over the body.
Head: Natural deer hair spun on and clipped flat on the bottom. Top and sides are left crude and scraggly.

Originated by Charlie Fulford of Chambly, Quebec, Canada, in the late 1960s. Although this pattern was originally conceived for use on trout in the St. Lawrence River, it has become a favorite for Atlantic salmon in Nova Scotia.

Muddler Minnow, Purple

Hooks: TMC9395 or DAI2220, sizes 4-10.
Thread: Black.
Tail: Dyed purple barred teal section.
Ribbing: Oval silver tinsel.
Body: Dubbed with #30 purple lambs wool.
Wings: Small bunch of CH19 purple Crystal Hair tied over the body with an overwing of dyed purple gray squirrel tail with mottled

brown turkey quill sections tied in at each side.

Collar: Dyed purple elk hair spun on.
Head: Dyed purple deer hair spun on and clipped to shape.

Plate 5 Muddler Minnow, White

Hooks: TMC9395 or DAI2220, sizes 4-10.
Thread: White.
Tail: Dyed red goose quill section.
Ribbing: Oval silver tinsel.
Body: Dubbed with #2 white lambs wool.
Wings: Small bunch of CH01 pearl Crystal Hair tied over the body with an overwing of barred mallard barbs with a light cast mottled brown turkey quill section tied in at each side.
Collar: Light gray elk hair spun on.
Head: Natural gray deer hair spun on and clipped to shape.

Muddler Minnow, Yellow

Hooks: TMC9395 or DAI2220, sizes 4-10.
Thread: Brown.
Tail: Dyed yellow mottled brown turkey quill section.
Ribbing: Oval gold tinsel.
Body: Dubbed with #7 pale yellow lambs wool.
Wings: Small bunch of CH05 golden yellow Crystal Hair tied over the body with an overwing of dyed yellow gray squirrel tail with a dyed yellow mottled brown turkey quill section tied in at each side.
Collar: Coastal blacktail deer hair spun on.
Head: Natural deer hair spun on and clipped to shape.

Muddler Minnow, Bulletheads

Any of the Muddler Minnow patterns can have the head and collar substituted with the Bullethead design. It is a simple matter of tying in either elk or deer hair by the butts, with tips forward, and then securing it with your thread up to the back of the eye of the hook. It is then folded back over the head, forming the collar, then it is secured with tying thread and a good whip finish knot. Some tiers mount a split shot concealed within the head.

Muddler Minnow, Black Marabou

Hooks: TMC9395 or DAI2220, sizes 4-10.
Thread: Black.
Tail: Red hackle barbs.
Body: CC02 black Crystal Chenille.
Wing: Dyed black bucktail tied over the body with an overwing of black marabou.
Topping: Strands of peacock herl.
Collar: Dyed black elk hair spun on.
Head: Dyed black deer hair spun on and clipped to shape.

Muddler Minnow, Brown Marabou

Hooks: TMC9395 or DAI2220, sizes 4-10.
Thread: Brown.
Tail: Orange hackle barbs.
Body: CC25 copper brown Crystal Chenille.
Wing: Natural brown bucktail tied over the body with an overwing of reddish brown marabou.
Topping: Strands of peacock herl.
Collar Coastal blacktail deer hair spun on.
Head: Natural deer hair spun on and clipped to shape.

Muddler Minnow, Gray Marabou

Hooks: TMC9395 or DAI2220, sizes 4-10.
Thread: Gray.
Tail: Red hackle barbs.
Body: CC01 pearl Crystal Chenille.
Wing: Dyed gray bucktail tied over the body with an overwing of gray marabou.
Topping: Strands of peacock herl.
Collar: Coastal blacktail deer hair spun on.
Head: Natural deer hair spun on and clipped to shape.

Muddler Minnow, Multi•Color Marabou

Hooks: TMC9395 or DAI2220, sizes 4-10.
Thread: Brown.
Tail: Yellow hackle barbs.
Body: CC01 pearl Crystal Chenille.
Wing: Yellow bucktail tied over the body with overwings of yellow, olive, brown and dark olive marabou.
Collar: White (bottom) and dyed brown natural well marked (top) deer hair spun on.
Head: Deer hair spun on with brown on top, yellow to the sides and white on bottom. This is clipped to shape.

Muddler Minnow, Olive Marabou

Hooks: TMC9395 or DAI2220, sizes 4-10.
Thread: Brown.
Tail: Yellow hackle barbs.
Body: CC25 copper brown Crystal Chenille.
Wing: Natural brown bucktail tied over the body with an overwing of golden olive marabou.
Topping: Strands of peacock herl.
Collar: Coastal blacktail deer hair spun on.
Head: Natural deer hair spun on and clipped to shape.

Plate 5 Muddler Minnow, Purple Marabou

Hooks: TMC9395 or DAI2220, sizes 4-10.
Thread: Black.
Tail: Grizzly hackle barbs.
Body: CC19 purple Crystal Chenille.
Wing: Black bucktail tied over the body with an overwing of purple marabou.
Topping: Strands of peacock herl.
Collar: Coastal blacktail deer hair spun on.
Head: Natural dark deer hair spun on and clipped to shape.

Muddler Minnow, White Marabou

Hooks: TMC9395 or DAI2220, sizes 4-10.
Thread: White.
Tail: Red hackle barbs.
Body: CC01 pearl Crystal Chenille.
Wing: White bucktail tied over the body with an overwing of white marabou.
Topping: Strands of peacock herl.
Collar: Light elk hair spun on.
Head: White deer hair spun on and clipped to shape.

Muddler Minnow, Yellow Marabou

Hooks: TMC9395 or DAI2220, sizes 4-10.
Thread: Brown.
Tail: Orange hackle barbs.
Body: CC04 yellow Crystal Chenille.
Wing: Natural brown bucktail tied over the body with an overwing of yellow marabou.
Topping: Strands of peacock herl.
Collar: Coastal blacktail deer hair spun on.
Head: Natural deer hair spun on and clipped to shape.

We have spent years crediting Don Gapen as the originator of the Muddler Minnow. In 1937 he devised a pattern in an attempt to simulate sculpins, however, this was a very crudely assembled affair. Dan Bailey of Livingston, Montana, picked up on the idea and developed it into a more realistic form. Dan went on, with the help of others, to develop a white pattern (Mizooulan Spook) and a yellow pattern (Gordon Dean).

From the Bailey patterns an endless list of variations have sprung up that include our sculpin patterns and others. He is probably responsible for giving us the first properly clipped (bullet shaped) deer hair head. Gapen's creation had the butts of the hair tied over the head much like an Elk Hair Caddis—only exaggerated.

Needle Smelt

Hooks: TMC300, DAI2340 or DAI2370, sizes 2-10.
Thread: Black.
Body: Silver diamond braid.
Wing: Golden yellow bucktail tied over the body with overwings of four gray saddle hackles.
Head: Black.
Eyes: White with black centers.

Neptune

Hooks: TMC300, DAI2340 or DAI2370, sizes 2-10.
Thread: Black.
Ribbing: Oval silver tinsel.

Body: Flat silver tinsel.
Wing: Four cree neck hackles tied over the body.
Hackle: Cree tied on as a heavy collar.
Head: Black.

This is a pattern I received from Mike Boudreau of Montreal, Canada. It was originated in 1962 by Yvon Gendron.

Nimrod Bucktail

Hooks: TMC5263 or DAI1720, sizes 4-6.
Thread: Black.
Ribbing: Oval silver tinsel.
Body: Flat silver tinsel.
Throat: Yellow bucktail tied in and extending to bend of hook.
Wing: Green bucktail tied over the body with an overwing of dyed black squirrel tail.
Cheeks: J.C. or substitute.
Head: Black.

Originated by Henry Beverage of Portland, Maine.

Nine•Three

Hooks: TMC9395 or DAI2220, sizes 4-6.
Thread: Black.
Wings: White bucktail tied over the body with overwings of three green saddle hackles tied flat and two black saddles tied on edge.
Cheeks: J.C. or substitute.
Head: Black.

Originated by Hubert Sanborn of Waterville, Maine.

Ordway

Hooks: TMC9395 or DAI2220, sizes 4-6.
Thread: Yellow.
Body: Flat silver tinsel.
Throat: White bucktail tied in and extending to bend of hook.
Wings: Four white neck hackles tied over the body with concave sides out.
Shoulders: Red turkey flat tied in at each side with concave side out.
Head: Yellow.

Originated by George Ordway of Franklin, New Hampshire.

Partridge Sculpin

Hooks: TMC9395 or DAI2220, sizes 2-4.
Thread: Brown.
Ribbing: Oval gold tinsel.
Body: Rear three-quarters, dubbed with #7 pale yellow African Angora goat and the front quarter, dubbed with #4 red Bunny-Blend.
Wings: Two Hungarian partridge tail feathers tied Matuka style over the body.
Pectoral Fins: Mottled brown hen body feather tied in at each side.
Head: Dyed brown deer hair spun on and clipped to shape.

Although the Hungarian partridge tail feathers are often hard to find this pattern is well worth the trouble. This is one pattern that I always tie well weighted.

Pink Lady Bucktail

Hooks: TMC300, DAI2340 or DAI2370, sizes 4-8.
Thread: Red.
Tip: Flat gold tinsel.
Tail: Golden pheasant tippet barbs.
Ribbing: Flat gold tinsel.
Body: Dubbed with #28 pink lambs wool.
Throat: Small bunch of yellow bucktail tied in and extending to bend of hook.
Wing: Small bunch of dark gray bucktail tied over the body with a larger amount of natural brown bucktail tied on top.
Head: Red.

Plate 5 Platte River Special

Hooks: TMC9395 or DAI2220, sizes 2-8.
Thread: Brown.
Ribbing: Oval gold tinsel.
Body: Dubbed with #24 brown African Angora goat.
Wings: Yellow saddles hackle tied over the body with a brown neck hackle tied in at each side. Tips of the yellow should protrude slightly past the brown.
Hackle: Brown and yellow tied on as a collar and tied back.
Head: Brown.

This fly was born on the North Platte River in Wyoming. With this and other patterns all being called the "Platte River Special" it would be extremely difficult to determine what this fly really is, the variations are without count. I first learned of this fly in Casper in the mid 1960s and have for some reason formed a sort of kinship with it. The ironic thing is that I seldom show it any favor while fishing the Platte. Other patterns work better for me there.

Here is where the name of a fly can stigmatize it because other fly fishermen think that it is only effective for the particular water it is named after. I fish the Platte River Special with confidence for browns in the Trinity River here in California. I am especially partial to the Matuka style for this pattern.

Plymouth

Hooks: TMC5263 or DAI1720, sizes 4-6.
Thread: Black.
Tail: Red goose quill section.
Ribbing: Oval silver tinsel.
Body: Flat silver tinsel.
Hackle: Grizzly tied on as a collar and tied back and down.
Wings: Four grizzly saddle hackles tied over the body.
Head: Black.

Pond Smelt

Hooks: TMC9395, DAI2220 or DAI2370, sizes 2-6.
Thread: Gray.
Butt: Gray thread which secures body at rear.
Body: Pearl Mylar piping slipped over an underbody of white floss or yarn.
Throat: White bucktail tied in and extending just past bend of hook.
Wing: Strip of natural gray rabbit tied Matuka style over the body.
Gills: Red hen hackle tip tied in at each side and kept very short.
Head: Gray.
Eyes: Tiny red dots.

Pond smelt *(Hypomesus olidus)* are an important forage fish for fly fishermen in northern California. They were brought here from the island of Hokkaido, Japan, as an experiment during the 1920s. They were only planted in Lake Almanor and the project was for the most part forgotten; I believe depression era budgets killed it.

They prospered and today can be found throughout the Feather River drainage which includes primarily Butt Valley Reservoir and Lake Oroville. The water carried from Lake Almanor by pipe to Butt Valley Reservoir and the spillway at Lake Oroville serves to grind up a good number of these small fish as they pass through the hydroelectric turbines. Large trout relish this opportunity and feed on the bits and pieces as well as the stunned fish which pass through the turbines. These moments can provide some real action for the fly fishing opportunist.

These fish are not to be confused with the threadfin shad that are more widespread in the freshwater impoundments of California.

The threadfin shad *(Dorosoma petenense)* have also been planted as a forage fish. These little guys probably get the most attention during the fall turnover of the lakes. Turnover is when the water cools on the surface and sinks, this brings the threadfins to the surface and with them some very nice fish. The threadfin has three distinctive spots on its sides that are easy to duplicate.

I am personally familiar only with the activity here in northern California, but I assume that there must be other areas in North America where similar occurrences take place.

Oh yes, there are a number of variations and opinions concerning these small forage fish. See Threadfin Shad in this chapter.

Quebec

Hooks: TMC5263 or DAI1720, sizes 4-8
Thread: Black.
Tail: Golden pheasant crest tied short.
Butt: Yellow floss.
Ribbing: Oval gold tinsel.
Body: Dubbed with #32 claret lambs wool.
Hackle: Claret tied on as a collar and tied back and down.
Wing: Purple bucktail tied over the body and extending to the end of the tail.
Cheeks: Black and white barred lemon woodduck section tied in at each side.
Head: Black.

Originated in 1931 by Alexander Learmonth of Montreal, Canada.

Queen Bee

Hooks: TMC5263 or DAI1720, sizes 4-6.
Thread: Black.
Body: Flat silver tinsel.
Throat: Red hackle barbs.
Wings: Yellow bucktail tied over the body with overwings of white bucktail and four brown saddle hackles.
Cheeks: J.C. or substitute.
Head: Black.

Originated by Dr. J. Hubert Sanborn of Waterville, Maine.

Raymond Streamer

Hooks: TMC5263 or DAI1720, sizes 6-8.
Thread: Black.
Tip: Flat gold tinsel.
Tail: Golden pheasant crest tied short.
Ribbing: Flat gold tinsel.
Body: Brown floss thinly tapered.
Throat: Natural red golden pheasant body feather barbs.
Wing: Natural brown bucktail tied over the body.
Shoulders: Bronze mallard section tied in at each side.
Cheeks: J.C. or substitute.
Head: Black.

Originated by William Reynolds of Sturbridge, Massachusetts, and named after Warren G. Raymond.

Red Fin

Hooks: TMC300, DAI2340 or DAI2370, sizes 6-8.
Thread: Black.
Tail: Tuft of red marabou.
Ribbing: Flat gold tinsel.
Body: Pink floss thinly tapered.
Throat: Tuft of red marabou.
Wings: Black saddle hackle tied over the body with golden badger saddles tied in at each side.
Cheeks: J.C. or substitute.
Head: Black.

Originated by Lew Oatman of Shushan, New York.

Redhead

Hooks: TMC9395 or DAI2220, sizes 8-12.
Thread: Red.
Tail: Red Amherst pheasant crest tied short.
Ribbing: Oval gold tinsel.
Body: Flat gold tinsel.
Wing: White calf tail tied over the body with an overwing of fox squirrel tail. Wing should be dressed sparse.
Head: Red.

Originated by A. I. Alexander, III of Andover, Massachusetts.

Redsided Shiner

Hooks: TMC9395 or DAI 2220, sizes 2-6.
Thread: White.
Body: Pearl diamond braid wrapped over a well tapered underbody of white floss or yarn.
Wing: Fire orange bucktail tied over the body with overwings of dark brown bucktail, yellow bucktail and natural black skunk tail tied on top. Each of the overwings extends a bit past the one under it creating a graduated taper.
Head: Apply black enamel over the top leaving a white throat.
Eyes: Yellow with black centers.

The western states are practically void of shiners as opposed to what is available east of us. The redsided shiner

(Richardsonius balteatus) is only found in Utah, Colorado, Wyoming, Idaho, and the Columbia River basin. They inhabit lakes and streams alike, however, in streams they seek out slow-moving pools.

When I first became aware of these colorful little guys in 1975 I immediately went through my library of fly fishing books in an attempt to find a pattern that would best simulate them. Nothing, so I started from scratch and tied a pattern using collected samples as a guide in determining the correct colors. At the time I was unaware that they were early summer spawners and I had captured the male in its spawning colors. I had success from the get go and the question of color disappeared years ago.

Should you locate a school of these shiners, fish your fly off to the side of them and be prepared for some real action. Large fish prey on the strays.

Red Squirrel Gold

Hooks: TMC5263 or DAI1720, sizes 6-8.
Thread: Black.
Body: Embossed gold tinsel.
Throat: Red hackle barbs.
Wings: Fox squirrel tail tied over the body with an overwing of two honey badger saddle hackles.
Cheeks: J.C. or substitute.
Head: Black.

Originated by Ray Bergman.

Rose of New England

Hooks: TMC300, DAI2340 or DAI2370, sizes 4-6.
Thread: Black.
Tip: Embossed silver tinsel.
Tail: Golden pheasant crest tied short.

Ribbing: Oval silver tinsel over tinsel portion of body only.
Butt: Dubbed with #4 red lambs wool.
Body: Embossed silver tinsel with a joint of #4 red lambs wool at the front.
Wing: Yellow bucktail tied over the body with overwings of red, yellow and natural brown bucktail. Keep wing sparse.
Cheeks: J.C. or substitute.
Head: Black.

Originated by Everett Price.

Roxy's Fox Squirrel

Hooks: TMC300, DAI2340 or DAI2370, sizes 2-8.
Thread: Black.
Tail: Dyed imitation barred lemon woodduck barbs.
Ribbing: Flat silver tinsel.
Body: Red floss thinly tapered.
Hackle: Brown tied on as a collar and tied back and down.
Wing: Fox squirrel tail tied over the body.
Shoulder: White duck breast feather tied in at each side.
Head: Black.

Roxy's Gray Squirrel

Hooks: TMC300, DAI2340 or DAI2370, sizes 2-8.
Thread: Black.
Tail: Dyed imitation barred lemon woodduck barbs.
Ribbing: Flat gold tinsel.
Body: Golden olive floss thinly tapered.
Throat: Narrow section of red goose quill.
Hackle: Grizzly tied on as a collar and tied back and down.
Wing: Gray squirrel tail tied over the body.
Shoulders: White duck breast feather tied in at each side.
Head: Black.

The Roxy patterns were originated by Roxy Roach of Tawas City, Michigan.

Royal Coachman

Hooks: TMC9395 or DAI2220, sizes 4-6.
Thread: Brown.
Tail: Golden pheasant tippets.
Butt: Peacock herl.

Body: Red floss with a peacock joint at the front.
Hackle: Brown tied on as a collar and tied back and down.
Wing: White bucktail tied over the body.
Head: Black.

This is a conversion from the wet fly version. See Chapter 8.

Russell's Fancy

Hooks: TMC5263 or DAI1720, sizes 4-6.
Thread: Black.
Tip: Embossed silver tinsel.
Tail: Golden pheasant crest.
Ribbing: Oval silver tinsel.
Body: Embossed silver tinsel.
Throat: White bucktail tied in and extending to the bend of the hook.
Wing: White bucktail tied over the body with an overwing of yellow bucktail.
Cheeks: J.C. or substitute.
Head: Black.

Originated by Jack Russell.

Saguenay

Hooks: TMC5263 or DAI1720, sizes 4-8.
Thread: Black.
Tail: Golden pheasant tippet barbs.
Body: Embossed silver tinsel.
Hackle: Yellow tied on as a collar and tied back and down.
Wing: Two yellow saddle hackles tied over the body with a grizzly saddle tied in at each side.
Cheeks: J.C. or substitute.
Head: Black.

Sandbar Smelt

Hooks: TMC9395 or DAI2220, sizes 4-6.
Thread: Black.
Ribbing: Flat silver tinsel.
Body: Orange floss.
Hackle: Yellow bucktail tied in at the throat and extending to hook bend with white bucktail tied on and followed by golden olive hackle barbs.
Wings: Strands of peacock tied over the body with four white saddle hackles tied over and a golden olive saddle hackle tied in at each side.
Shoulders: Barred lemon woodduck flank tied in at each side.

Cheeks: J.C. or substitute.
Head: Black.

Sanborn

Hooks: TMC9395 or DAI2220, sizes 4-6.
Thread: Black.
Ribbing: Flat gold tinsel.
Body: Black floss well tapered.
Throat: Yellow hackle barbs.
Wings: Four yellow neck hackles tied over the body.
Cheeks: J.C. or substitute.
Head: Black.

Originated by Fred Sanborn of Norway, Maine.

Sanders

Hooks: TMC9395 or DAI2220, sizes 4-8.
Thread: Black.
Body: Flat silver tinsel.
Wings: White bucktail tied over the body with overwings of four grizzly saddle hackles.
Cheeks: J.C. or substitute.
Head: Black.

Satin Fin

Hooks: TMC5263 or DAI1720, sizes 2-10.
Thread: Black.
Tail: Tuft of yellow marabou.
Ribbing: Flat silver tinsel.
Body: White floss thinly tapered.
Throat: Tuft of yellow marabou.
Wings: Two blue saddle hackles tied over the body with two magenta saddles tied to the sides.
Cheeks: J.C. or substitute.
Head: Black.

Originated by Keith Fulsher of Eastchester, New York.

St. Ignace

Hooks: TMC5263 or DAI1720, sizes 4-8.
Thread: Black.
Tail: Golden pheasant tippet barbs.
Body: Flat gold tinsel.
Hackle: Honey badger tied on as a collar and tied back and down.
Wings: Four honey badger saddle hackles tied over the body.
Cheeks: J.C. or substitute.
Head: Black.

The two preceding patterns were originated in 1924 by Robert Coulson of Buffalo, New York.

Plate 4 — Stayner Ducktail

Hooks: TMC5263 or DAI1720, sizes 4-10.
Thread: Black.
Tail: Fire orange hackle barbs.
Ribbing: Oval gold tinsel.
Body: Dark olive chenille.
Hackle: Fire orange hackle barbs tied beard style.
Wing: Tip of a barred mallard flank feather tied flat over the body and extending to the end of tail.
Head: Black.

Originated by Ruel Stayner of Twin Falls, Idaho. This pattern performs well as a forage fish in many lakes of the west and has done equally as well in such places as New Zealand.

Scaled Shiner

Hooks: TMC9395 or DAI2220, sizes 6-10.
Thread: Black.
Body: Dubbed with #19 olive Bunny-Blend.
Ribbing: Copper wire tied in at the front, wrapped to the rear and returned. Have wires cross each other on the sides of the body to simulate diamond (scale) effect.
Throat: Red hackle barbs tied short.
Wings: Four black saddles tied over the body.
Cheeks: J.C. or substitute.
Head: Black.

Originated by Don Shiner of Nescopeck, Pennsylvania.

Shang's Favorite

Hooks: TMC300, DAI2340 or DAI2370, sizes 4-6.
Thread: Black.
Ribbing: Flat silver tinsel.
Body: Red floss thinly tapered.
Throat: Grizzly hackle barbs tied in with white bucktail over and extending to bend of hook.
Wings: Strands of peacock herl tied over the body with two grizzly saddle hackles tied in at each side.
Shoulders: Red duck breast feather tied in at each side.
Head: Black with a red band at base of wings.

Originated by Carrie G. Stevens.

Shushan Postmaster

Hooks: TMC300, DAI2340 or DAI2370, sizes 6-10.
Thread: Black.
Tail: Small section of mottled brown turkey quill.
Ribbing: Flat gold tinsel.
Body: Pale yellow floss thinly tapered.
Throat: Red hackle barbs.
Wing: Fox squirrel tail tied over the body.
Cheeks: J.C. or substitute.
Head: Black.

Silver Darter

Hooks: TMC300, DAI2340 or DAI2370, sizes 4-10.
Thread: Black.
Tail: Silver pheasant quill section.
Ribbing: Flat silver tinsel.
Body: White floss thinly tapered.
Throat: Peacock sword feather barbs.
Wings: Two badger saddles tied over the body.
Cheeks: J.C. or substitute.
Head: Black.

The two preceding patterns were originated by Lew Oatman of Shushan, New York.

Silver Minnow

Hooks: TMC9395 or DAI2220, sizes 4-6.
Thread: White.
Butt: Red thread which secures body at rear.
Body: Silver Mylar piping slipped over an underbody of white floss or yarn.
Throat: White bucktail tied in and extending to bend of hook.
Wing: White bucktail tied over the body with overwings of gray and dark blue bucktail.
Head: Blue with white throat.
Eyes: Black with yellow centers.

Silver Salmon

Hooks: TMC5263 or DAI1720, sizes 2-6.
Thread: Black.
Tail: Yellow hackle barbs.
Ribbing: Flat silver tinsel.
Body: Yellow floss thinly tapered.
Hackle: Yellow tied on as a collar and tied back and down.
Wings: Four white saddle hackles tied over the body.
Cheeks: J.C. or substitute.
Head: Black.

Originated by Horace Bond, Bangor, Maine.

Slim Jim

Hooks: TMC5263 or DAI1720, sizes 4-10.
Thread: Black.
Tail: Red hackle barbs.
Ribbing: Flat silver tinsel.
Body: Black floss thinly tapered.
Wings: Grizzly neck hackle tips the in a V over the body with concave sides out.
Hackle: Grizzly tied on as a collar and tied back.
Head: black.

The Slim Jim and its cousins were popular in the Rocky Mountain area during the 40s and 50s. The variations consisted of simply changing body colors. The black served me well in my younger years. There is no doubt in my mind that this particular pattern influenced the design of the Silver Hilton, the steelhead pattern.

Spencer Bay Special

Hooks: TMC5263 or DAI1720, sizes 4-8.
Thread: Black.
Tail: Golden pheasant tippet barbs.
Ribbing: Oval silver tinsel.
Body: Flat silver tinsel.
Hackle: Light yellow tied on as a collar, followed by light blue which is also tied on as a collar in front. Both are then tied back and down.
Wings: Two light blue saddle hackles tied over the body with a badger saddle tied in at each side.
Cheeks: J.C. or substitute.
Head: Black.

Originated by Horace Bond of Bangor, Maine.

Spruce, Dark

Hooks: TMC5263 or DAI1720, sizes 4-10.
Thread: Black.
Tail: Peacock sword feather barbs.
Body: Rear third, red floss and the front two-thirds, peacock herl. Reverse wrap the peacock herl with fine gold wire.
Wings: Pair of furnace neck hackles tied on edge over the body with concave side out.
Hackle: Furnace tied on as a collar and tied back.
Head: Black.

Spruce, Light

Hooks: TMC5263 or DAI1720, sizes 4-10.
Thread: Black.
Tail: Peacock sword feather barbs.
Body: Rear third, red floss and the front two-thirds peacock herl. Reverse wrap the peacock herl with fine gold wire.
Wings: Pair badger neck hackles tied on edge over the body with concave side out.
Hackle: Badger tied on as a collar and tied back.
Head: Black.

The Spruce patterns originated on the West Coast. They gained popularity as streamers in the Rocky Mountain states. The Light Spruce or Spruce is the original and at one time was also known as the Godfrey Special.

Spuddler

Hooks: TMC9395 or DAI2220, sizes 2-6.
Thread: Brown.
Tail: Brown calf tail.
Body: Dubbed with #3 cream African Angora goat.
Gills: Dubbed with #4 red African Angora goat. This is a joint located in the space between the body and the head.

Wings: Brown bucktail tied over the body with overwings of four dyed reddish brown grizzly neck hackles.
Half Collar: Fox squirrel tail over the top and to each side.
Head: Dyed reddish brown deer hair spun on and clipped to shape. Finished head takes on the appearance of a smashed marshmallow.

This pattern was originated in Livingston, Montana by Red Monical and Don Williams.

Plate 4   Summers' Gold

Hooks: TMC300, DAI2340 or DAI2370, sizes 6-8.
Thread: Black.
Tail: Golden pheasant tippet barbs.
Body: Oval gold tinsel.
Hackle: Red tied on as a collar and tied back and down.
Wing: White bucktail tied over the body with an overwing of natural brown bucktail.
Head: Black.

Originated in 1912 by Dr. Orrin Summers of Boundbrook, New Jersey. On the surface this pattern may appear to be too old or too simple to tie. Don't let this delude you—it works everywhere.

Supervisor

Hooks: TMC300, DAI2340 or DAI2370, sizes 2-6.
Thread: Black.
Tag: Red yarn.
Ribbing: Oval silver tinsel.
Body: Flat silver tinsel.
Throat: White hackle barbs.
Wings: White bucktail tied over the body with overwings of four light blue saddle hackles.
Topping: Strands of peacock herl.
Shoulders: Pale green hen hackle tips tied in at each side and extending two-thirds the length of the wing.
Cheeks: J.C. or substitute.
Head: Black.

The Supervisor was originated in 1925 by Joseph Stickney of Saco, Maine.

The Thief

Hooks: TMC5263 or DAI1720, sizes 4-10.
Thread: Black.
Tail: Red section of duck quill.
Ribbing: Oval silver tinsel.
Body: Flat silver tinsel.
Wings: Gray squirrel tail tied over the body with overwings of mottled brown turkey quill sections.
Head: Black chenille.

Originated by Don Gapen of Anoka, Minnesota.

Plate 5   Threadfin Shad

Hooks: TMC9395, DAI2220 or DAI2370, sizes 4-10.
Thread: Gray.
Tail: Tuft of gray marabou.
Body: Pearl Mylar piping tied flattened over an underbody of plastic cut to shape.
Wing: Gray rabbit fur strip tied over the body and secured at rear.
Head: Gray.
Eyes: Yellow with black centers.
Sides: Three black spots.

The underbody can be made of any flat material, preferably one that is impervious to water. I suggest milk cartons, either plastic or cardboard, as they are readily available.

I have fabricated some small metal templates in varying sizes which allow me to be consistent when making these flies. They are made up quickly by using any sharp knife.

Threadfin shad can be observed schooled just under the surface. It is at times like this that opportunistic large trout display higher level intelligence. They will charge the school and bombast it with their tail, stunning a couple of the shad, then they return and feed at will on the stunned fish. Beats the hell out of expending a lot of energy trying to chase down each one individually.

Use an underbody of balsa wood or closed cell foam to simulate them in this condition. If possible, cast to the side of an active school and let your imitation lay helplessly for extended moments, then give it a twitch. Watch out! See Pond Smelt in this chapter.

Thunder Creek Bucktails

Blacknose Dace
Hook: TMC300, DAI2340 or DAI2370, sizes 6-12.
Thread: Red.
Body: Embossed silver tinsel.
Throat: White bucktail.
Wing: Black bucktail with an overwing of natural brown bucktail.

Step-by-step instructions for tying the Blacknose Dace:

Step 1. Complete the tinsel body with thread finishing up at the front of the fly. It is important that you leave more room at the head of the fly than normal.

Step 2. Tie in the brown overwing and the white throat. These two bunches of hair should be equal in length. When securing their butts to the hook shank, wrap your thread up snug to the base of the eye.

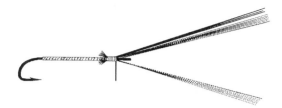

Step 3. Tie in a sparse underwing of black bucktail.

Step 4. Fold the throat under and secure and fold the wing back over the body and secure. The fly should be finished off with a good whip finish knot. Apply a generous amount of a deep penetrating cement to the head.

Apply a cream (pale yellow) eye with black centers. I usually apply a coat of bright red enamel over the band of thread to give the fly more gill flash. I allow the finished fly to cure overnight then apply a coat of epoxy to the head.

Emerald Shiner
Hook: TMC300, DAI2340 or DAI2370, sizes 6-12.
Thread: Red.
Ribbing: Flat silver tinsel.
Body: Fluorescent green floss.
Throat: White bucktail.
Wing: Natural brown bucktail.

For the body of this fly I often substitute pearlescent green diamond braid or Mylar piping.

Golden Shiner
Hook: TMC300, DAI2340 or DAI2370, sizes 6-12.
Thread: Red.
Body: Flat gold tinsel.
Throat: White bucktail.
Wing: Yellow bucktail with an overwing of natural brown bucktail.

Marabou Shiner

Hook: TMC300, DAI2340 or DAI2370, sizes 6-10.
Thread: Red.
Body: Embossed silver tinsel.
Throat: White marabou.
Wing: Dark brown marabou.

Rainbow Trout

Hook: TMC300, DAI2340 or DAI2370, sizes 6-12.
Thread: Red.
Body: Embossed silver tinsel.
Throat: White bucktail.
Wing: Pink bucktail with an overwing of dyed green natural brown bucktail.

Redfin Shiner

Hook: TMC300, DAI2340 or DAI2370, sizes 6-12.
Thread: Red.
Ribbing: Flat silver tinsel.
Body: Fluorescent red floss.
Throat: White bucktail.
Wing: Natural brown bucktail.

Redlip Shiner

Hook: TMC300, DAI2340 or DAI2370, sizes 6-12.
Thread: Red.
Tail: Black floss.
Ribbing: Flat gold tinsel.
Body: Black floss.
Fins: Orange floss.
Throat: Pale yellow bucktail.
Wing: Pale yellow bucktail with an overwing of black bucktail.

The fins consist of short strands of floss that trail out each side of the body. They are tied in about one third up from the rear of the body and extend back to the end of the body.

Silver Shiner

Hook: TMC300, DAI2340 or DAI2370, sizes 6-12.
Thread: Red.
Body: Embossed silver tinsel.
Throat: White bucktail.
Wing: Natural brown bucktail.

Smelt

Hook: TMC300, DAI2340 or DAI2370, sizes 6-12.
Thread: Red.
Body: Embossed silver tinsel.
Throat: White bucktail.
Wing: Hot pink bucktail with an overwing of natural brown bucktail.

Spottail Shiner

Hook: TMC300, DAI2340 or DAI2370, sizes 6-12.
Thread: Red.
Tag: Black floss.
Body: Embossed gold tinsel.
Throat: White bucktail.
Wing: Dyed green natural brown bucktail.

Steelcolor Shiner

Hook: TMC300, DAI2340 or DAI2370, sizes 6-12.
Thread: Red.
Ribbing: Flat silver tinsel.
Body: Fluorescent blue floss.
Throat: Pale yellow bucktail.
Wing: Dyed blue natural brown bucktail.

Strawcolor Shiner

Hook: TMC300, DAI2340 or DAI2370, sizes 6-12.
Thread: Red.
Body: Embossed silver tinsel.
Throat: White bucktail.
Wing: Blue bucktail with an overwing of dyed pink natural brown bucktail.

Striped Jumprock

Hook: TMC300, DAI2340 or DAI2370, sizes 6-12.
Thread: Red.
Body: Embossed gold tinsel.
Throat: Pale orange bucktail.
Wing: Pale orange bucktail with an overwing of dark brown bucktail.

Swamp Darter

Hook: TMC300, DAI2340 or DAI2370, sizes 6-12.
Thread: Red.
Body: Embossed silver tinsel.
Throat: White bucktail.
Wing: Two grizzly hackles with an overwing of natural brown bucktail.

Wedgespot Shiner
Hook: TMC300, DAI2340 or DAI2370, sizes 6-12.
Thread: Red.
Tag: Black floss.
Ribbing: Flat silver tinsel.
Body: Black floss.
Throat: White bucktail.
Wing: Two strands of brown floss with an overwing of natural brown bucktail.

This series of bucktails were originated by Keith Fulsher and were popularized through his 1973 book, *Tying and Fishing the Thunder Creek Series.* You should make note of the Marabou Shiner pattern that I have given here. Any number of marabou patterns are possible using this as an example. I personally like a black and white combination. Keith has tied all of these patterns with marabou at one time or another.

Today Keith uses a few strands of pearl Crystal Hair or other like materials mixed in with the throat material on these patterns.

It should be noted that this tying technique was first used by Carrie G. Stevens. The lady had talent.

Van DeCar
Hooks: TMC9395 or DAI2220, sizes 6-10.
Thread: Black.
Tail: Red hackle barbs.
Ribbing: Oval gold tinsel.
Body: Flat gold tinsel.
Hackle: Red tied on as a collar and tied back and down.
Wing: Fox squirrel tail tied over the body.
Cheeks: J.C. or substitute.
Head: Black.

Originated by Tom Van DeCar of Hutchinson, Kansas.

Warden's Worry
Hooks: TMC300, DAI2340 or DAI2370, sizes 2-6.
Thread: Black.

Tip: Flat gold tinsel.
Tail: Red duck quill section.
Ribbing: Oval gold tinsel.
Body: Dubbed with #8 golden yellow lambs wool.
Hackle: Yellow tied on as a collar and tied back and down.
Wing: Natural brown bucktail tied over the body.
Head: Black.

Originated around 1930 by Joseph Stickney of Saco, Maine. Stickney was a game warden, hence the name, and through the years many writers and commercial fly tiers have tried to play up this point. Heaven knows, a man in such a position certainly knows more about fly design than us mere mortals. One company went as far as stating that the fly was banned in the state of Maine because it was so good. They went on to say it got its name because anglers were afraid of being caught using the fly. They certainly got a lot of mileage out of the term "worry."

Wesley Special
Hooks: TMC300, DAI2340 or DAI2370, sizes 4-6.
Thread: Black.
Tail: Golden pheasant tippet barbs.
Ribbing: Oval silver tinsel.
Body: Flat silver tinsel.
Hackle: Black tied on as a collar and tied back and down.
Wing: White bucktail tied over the body with an overwing of blue dun bucktail.
Cheeks: J.C. or substitute.
Head: Black.

White Water
Hooks: TMC5263 or DAI1720, sizes 2-4.
Thread: Black.
Tag: Heavy red yarn.
Butt: Dubbed with #1 black lambs wool.
Body: Flat silver tinsel with a peacock herl joint tied at the front.
Throat: Black hackle barbs tied long.

Wing: Natural brown bucktail tied long over the body.
Head: Black. Build up large with thread to accommodate eyes.
Eyes: White with black centers.

The two preceding patterns were originated by Herbert Howard of New Rochelle, New York.

Whitlock Sculpin, Brown

Hooks: TMC9395 or DAI2220, sizes 2-8
Thread: Brown.
Ribbing: Oval gold tinsel.
Body: Dubbed with #31 tan African Angora goat with #4 red lambs wool dubbed in front for gills.
Wing: Four dyed brown grizzly neck hackles tied Matuka style.
Pectoral Fins: Mottled brown hen body feather tied in at each side.
Half Collar: Dyed brown natural deer hair tied over top and sides.
Head: Dyed brown natural deer hair spun on and clipped to shape.

Whitlock Sculpin, Olive

Hooks: TMC9395 or DAI2220, sizes 2-8.
Thread: Olive.
Ribbing: Oval gold tinsel.
Body: Dubbed with #21 golden olive African Angora goat with #4 red lambs wool dubbed in front for gills.
Wings: Four dyed olive grizzly neck hackles tied Matuka style.
Pectoral Fins: Dyed olive mottled hen body feather tied in at each side.
Half Collar: Dyed olive natural deer hair tied over top and sides.
Head: Dyed olive natural deer hair spun on and clipped to shape.

Originated by Dave Whitlock. These patterns demonstrate creative fly tying and the simplicity of what much of it is all about. What you are really looking at is a "Matuka Muddler." This can be carried even further with rabbit fur strips used for the wings.

Whitlock includes small black bunches of deer hair when spinning his heads to give tops a dark mottled effect as found on sculpins. This can also be accomplished with a black waterproof marker.

Wizard

Hooks: TMC300, DAI2340 or DAI2370, sizes 4-6.
Thread: Black.
Ribbing: Flat silver tinsel.
Body: Red floss thinly tapered.
Throat: White hackle barbs tied in with white bucktail, then strands of peacock herl tied over and extending to bend of hook.
Wings: Two black saddle hackles tied over the body with a yellow saddles tied in at each side.
Cheeks: J.C. or substitute.

Originated by Carrie G. Stevens.

Woolhead Sculpin, Black

Hooks: TMC9395 or DAI2220, sizes 4-10.
Thread: Black.
Ribbing: Clear monofilament.
Body: Dubbed with #12 light gray African Angora goat.
Underwing: Strands of CH01 black Crystal Hair.
Wing: Natural black rabbit fur strip tied Matuka style.
Head/Collar: Black wool fleece on top and gray on bottom.

⬤ Plate 5 Woolhead Sculpin, Brown

Hooks: TMC9395 or DAI2220, sizes 4-10.
Thread: Brown.
Ribbing: Clear monofilament.
Body: Dubbed with #31 tan African Angora goat.
Underwing: Strands CH25 copper brown Crystal Hair.
Wing: Natural brown rabbit fur strip tied Matuka style.
Head/Collar: Brown wool fleece on top and tan on bottom.

Woolhead Sculpin, Olive

Hooks: TMC9395 or DAI2220, sizes 4-10.
Thread: Olive.
Ribbing: Clear monofilament.
Body: Dubbed with #18 light olive African Angora goat.
Underwing: Strands of CH18 golden olive Crystal Hair.

Wing: Dyed olive rabbit fur strip tied Matuka style.
Head/Collar: Olive wool fleece on top and pale yellow on bottom.

Woolhead Sculpin, Multi-Color

Hooks: TMC9395 or DAI2220, sizes 4-10.
Thread: Brown.
Ribbing: Clear monofilament.
Body: Dubbed with #3 cream African Angora goat.
Underwing: Strands of CH01 pearl Crystal Hair.
Wing: Natural brown rabbit fur strip tied Matuka style.
Head: Brown wool fleece on top and cream on bottom.
Note: The head on these flies is very easy to fashion. It is tied in by small bunches and does not flare in every direction as deer hair does. Tease out some of the top of the head as a half collar before clipping.

The return to the use of natural wool in our flies is one of the best things that has happened since I started tying. Using wool instead of deer hair opens up new avenues in fly tying. With the buoyancy of deer hair gone our flies will certainly sink better and in a more natural manner.

Many refer to the wool used on these patterns as "lambs wool." This is very misleading. Lambs wool could never do the job that these patterns call for. Lambs wool is much finer in texture than the coarser wool needed. We want wool that compares to what is found on a fly patch on your vest or in a wet fly book. This wool grades out at about #20 where lambs wool is about #60 grade and finer.

Excuse the wool talk—but it is probably necessary if you are going to be able to use this book and understand these patterns as opposed to all others requiring lambs wool. So, what we are looking at in this book is three grades of sheep's wool, each different grade fills a different need.

If you take a moment to review the other Muddler type designs given I'll bet you can come up with other Woolheads on your own. More recently I have been using DAI2370 hooks for these patterns.

Yellow Breeches

Hooks: TMC5263 or DAI1720, sizes 6-8.
Thread: Yellow.
Body: Oval silver tinsel.
Throat: Red hackle tip.
Wing: Yellow marabou tied over the body with an overwing of light brown marabou and three strands of peacock herl tied in at each side.
Cheeks: J.C. or substitute.
Head: Yellow.

Originated by R. W. McCafferty and Charles Fox of Hershey, Pennsylvania.

Yellow Jane Craig

Hooks: TMC9395 or DAI2220, sizes 4-6.
Thread: Black.
Ribbing: Oval silver tinsel.
Body: Flat silver tinsel.
Wings: Four yellow saddle hackle tied over the body.
Topping: Strands of peacock herl.
Cheeks: J.C. or substitute.
Head: Black.

Originated by Herbert Welch of Mooselookmeguntic, Maine.

Yellow Perch

Hooks: TMC9395 or DAI2220, sizes 2-6.
Thread: Black.
Ribbing: Flat gold tinsel.
Body: Pale yellow floss thinly tapered.
Throat: Yellow hackle barbs with four or five orange hackle barbs tied in at each side.
Wings: Two dyed yellow grizzly saddle hackles tied over the body with a yellow saddle tied in at each side.
Topping: Strands of peacock herl.
Cheeks: J.C. or substitute.
Head: Black.

The Yellow Perch originated by Lew Oatman of Shushan, New York.

Yellow Squirrel

Hooks: TMC300, DAI2340 or DAI2370, sizes 2-6.
Thread: Black.
Tip: Flat gold tinsel.
Tail: Red hackle barbs.
Ribbing: Flat gold tinsel.
Body: Dubbed with #6 yellow lambs wool.
Throat: Red hackle barbs.
Wing: Dark blue bucktail tied over the body with an overwing of gray squirrel tail.
Cheeks: J.C. or substitute.
Head: Black.

Originated by Arthur Houle of Southbridge, Massachusetts.

Yerxa Bucktail

Hooks: TMC300, DAI2340 or DAI2370, sizes 4-6.
Thread: Black.
Tip: Flat gold tinsel.
Ribbing: Flat gold tinsel.
Body: Dubbed with #6 yellow lambs wool.
Hackle: Yellow tied on as a collar and tied back and down.
Wing: White bucktail tied over the body.
Cheeks: J.C. or substitute.
Head: Black.

Originated by Jack Yerxa or Square Lake, Maine.

York's Kennebago

Hooks: TMC9395 or DAI2220, sizes 4-6.
Thread: Black.
Tip: Flat silver tinsel.
Tail: Golden pheasant crest tied short.
Butt: Red floss.
Ribbing: Oval silver tinsel.
Body: Flat silver tinsel.
Throat: Red hackle barbs.

Wings: Four badger saddle hackles tied over the body.
Topping: Red hackle barbs.
Cheeks: J.C. or substitute.
Head: Black.

Originated by Bert Quimby of Kennebago Lake, Maine.

Zonker

Hooks: TMC9395 or DAI2220, sizes 2-8.
Thread: Black.
Butt: Red thread which secures body at rear.
Tail: Frayed end of Mylar piping from body.
Body: Silver Mylar piping slipped over a preshaped underbody of metal tape.
Wing: Natural gray rabbit fur strip tied Matuka style.
Hackle: Grizzly tied on as a collar and tied back.

Originated by Dan Byford. This is the original dressing as I have come to know it. This fly is tied using any number of configurations and material colors, some have eyes of all sorts. To lessen the weight factor use cut out pieces of milk carton to form the underbody.

Zonker, Cutthroat

Hooks: TMC9395 or DAI2220, sizes 2-8.
Thread: Olive.
Butt: Red thread which secures body at rear.
Tail: Frayed end of Mylar piping from body.
Body: Pearl Mylar piping slipped over an underbody of white floss or yarn.
Wing: Dyed olive rabbit fur strip tied Matuka style.
Hackle: Scarlet red hackle barbs tied on as a collar and tied back and down.
Head: Olive.

See Chapter 23.

Chapter 19

Shad Flies

After a long wet winter in northern California one can hardly wait to get out and feel the warmth of the sun and enjoy the new green that blankets the Sacramento Valley. One way to get a friend of yours interested in our sport of fly fishing is to take them out fly fishing for shad.

The American shad is occasionally referred to as the "poor man's" steelhead or tarpon. It is found on both the East and West Coasts. Their size ranges from two to eight pounds, with some very rare ones reported up to twelve pounds. A three to four pounder is average, nonetheless catching these fish on a fly rod is a kick in the pants no matter how you slice it.

Originally shad were native only to the Atlantic. These members of the herring family are now well established on the West Coast thanks to pioneering fish culturist, Seth Green. See Chapter 8 for a popular pattern named after Green. In 1871 he transported eight milk cans of newly-hatched fingerlings from Rochester, New York, to Tehama, California. Even with the long journey more than sixty-six percent (40,000) of them survived and were released in the Sacramento River.

By 1921 over one and a half million pounds of fish were being harvested in California annually and they had spread, being caught in Oregon's Umpqua and Columbia Rivers. Today they range from San Diego to southern Alaska. Their main concentration still remains in the Sacramento River drainage system. The Sacramento, Feather, American and Yuba Rivers are hosts to very good spring-runs annually.

Several anglers of the area take great pride in their knowledge of these scrappy game fish. Jim Fuji is one of these people. I witnessed Jim being drilled about shad one evening and when the question came up, "When will the run be in this year?" He thought for a moment and replied, "Just as the cherries are ripe and ready for picking." Jim lives in Yuba City and keeps a pretty good account of all runs, which include salmon, steelhead, stripers, and shad.

I too lived in Yuba City for a couple of years and had both the Feather and Yuba Rivers at my doorstep. I remember runs in the Yuba in 1969 that were so thick it made wading across the shallower riffles difficult due to the abundance of fish. At that time just about any fly thrown at the fish would work, especially if it was tied very bright and colorful. At least that was the popular line of thinking at that time.

Now this is no fish story, I promise. I started out one morning using a Timbuctoo, a fly of my own design, and fished well into the afternoon. In the fever of it all, after taking fish after fish, when the day was over the fly consisted of only the disrobed hook and bead chain eyes. I kept on fishing and continued to take fish regularly. Obviously it wasn't my great new fly pattern that was doing the trick, there was just one hell of a lot of shad.

Now after many years have passed and with the farmers dumping an enormous amount of pesticides into the drainage system the runs have thinned. At one time the Yuba was a magnet for fly fishermen from all parts of the West. Thanks to the shad's high rate of productivity which has been able to sustain the huge amounts of toxic waste that has been poured on them, these rivers still have reasonable runs. In fact, noticeable improvement is now being evidenced.

Eastern fly rodders have also seen a degradation in their shad fisheries due to dam building and other thoughtless encroachments made in the name of progress. They are also seeing a rebirth of their shad runs making this fish their largest anadromous species.

Generally speaking, shad can be found on the East Coast from southern Labrador to the St. Johns River in northern Florida. Some of the more prolific runs occur in the Connecticut and Delaware Rivers, to name a few. Fly fishermen on the East Coast will find that the patterns listed work equally as well in their rivers.

Because of the decline in shad population it is now taking more skill to catch a reasonable amount of fish each day. More and more fly fishermen have started getting as creative in their fly patterns for shad as they do for other game fish. Over the past thirty or more years I have been collecting many of these patterns and trying all of them. This is one area where no one single fly tier can truly take credit for most of the patterns. In most cases they are all very close cousins and share the same family name, "Shad Fly."

The era of the nickel-plated hook, once favored by some, has generally subsided with the advent of the superior Japanese hooks. Most anglers have come to realize the advantages of a good sharp hook and will unequivocally defend them over any of the old nickel-plated models. The TMC3769 and the DAI1530 in sizes 4 through 10 are now the most popular. It is a truth that has evolved on its own without any stimulation from the media. After reviewing the patterns used for shad as a whole one can readily see why nickel-plated hooks are no longer a player. The advent of Crystal Hair, Crystal Chenille and Fly Brite now dominate our dressings and has changed our thinking considerably.

Chain Size:	Hook Size:
Small (.0940")	8 and smaller
Medium (.1250")	6
Large (.1562")	4
X-Large (.1875")	2 and larger

Shad run early in the year while river flows are generally higher than normal. Bead chain eyes have been favored for many years to get the flies down where they need to be. I have provided as a guide the size comparison chart above. These are the sizes that I find are most often used with the hook models indicated above. This chart can be applied to other types of flies found elsewhere in this book. Even though I have included eyes on most patterns they should be considered optional.

 Plate 4

Abomination
Thread: White.
Tail: White calf tail.
Ribbing: Flat silver tinsel.
Body: White chenille.
Hackle: CH30 silver Crystal Hair spun on as a collar.
Eyes: Silver bead chain.

Ardin
Thread: Fluorescent red.
Tail: Tuft of red marabou.
Body: Dubbed with a blend of #57 fluorescent chartreuse lambs wool and FB23 chartreuse Fly Brite.
Hackle: Chartreuse hen hackle tied on as a collar and tied back.
Eyes: Gold bead chain.

Eric Sumpter of Rancho Cardova, California, has been using this pattern on the American River and he claims the tail should first be tied long and then pinched back until the fish find it to their liking.

Black Knight
Thread: Black.
Body: Black monofilament wrapped over a well tapered underbody of black floss.
Hackle: Black tied on as a collar and tied back.
Eyes: Silver bead chain.

Occasionally something not so bright and flashy is in order and this would be a good fly to use at those times.

Black N'Black
Thread: Black.
Tail: Black calf tail.
Body: Dubbed with a blend of #1 black lambs wool and FB02 black Fly Brite.

Hackle: Black hen hackle tied on as a collar and tied back.
Eyes: Silver bead chain.

Plate 4　Boomer

Thread: White.
Tail: Tuft of white marabou.
Body: Wrapped with silver diamond braid.
Wing: CH01 pearl Crystal Hair.
Hackle: White tied on as a collar and tied back.
Eyes: Silver bead chain.

Plate 4　Copper Shad

Thread: Orange.
Tail: CH32 copper Crystal Hair.
Body: Copper diamond braid.
Hackle: Fire orange tied on as a collar and tied back.
Eyes: Gold bead chain.

Delaware Special

Thread: Red.
Tail: Yellow marabou.
Body: Yellow mono over an underbody of flat silver tinsel.
Eyes: Silver bead chain.
Head: Red chenille wrapped through eyes.

Designated Hitter

Thread: Fluorescent fire orange.
Tail: CH23 chartreuse Crystal Hair.
Body: CH23 chartreuse Crystal Hair wrapped over an underbody of yellow floss.
Hackle: Fluorescent fire orange hen hackle tied on as a collar and tied back.
Eyes: Nickel plated lead eyes.
Head: Fluorescent green chenille wrapped through the eyes.

Echo

Thread: Red.
Tail: CH03 red Crystal Hair.
Body: Dubbed with FB03 red Fly Brite.
Hackle: Red tied on as a collar and tied back.
Eyes: Silver bead chain.

Executioner

Thread: Black.
Tail: FB07 fire orange Fly Bright.
Body: Dubbed with a blend of #9 orange lambs wool and FB06 orange Fly Brite.

Hackle: Black tied on as a collar and tied back.
Eyes: Gold bead chain.

Fitzgerald

Thread: Fluorescent blue.
Tail: CH13 blue Crystal Hair.
Body: Silver diamond braid.
Hackle: Blue hen hackle tied on as a collar and tied back.
Head: Silver bead.

Full Moon Fever

Tail: CH03 red Crystal Hair.
Body: CH02 black Crystal Hair wrapped over an underbody of black floss.
Thorax: Red Glo-Brite chenille.
Head: Black nickel bead.

Golden Girl

Thread: Yellow.
Tail: FB31 gold Fly Brite.
Body: Clear 20 pound monofilament over an underbody of gold diamond braid.
Hackle: Fluorescent fire orange hen hackle tied on as a collar.
Eyes: Gold bead chain.

Golden Shad

Thread: Orange.
Tail: CH31 gold Crystal Hair.
Body: Dubbed with FB31 gold Fly Brite.
Hackle: CH31 gold Crystal Hair spun on as a collar.

Green Death

Thread: Fluorescent green.
Tail: Frayed out silver Mylar piping from body.
Body: Fluorescent green 20 pound Amnesia over an underbody of silver Mylar piping.
Hackle: Frayed pearl Mylar piping.
Eyes: Silver bead chain.
Head: Fluorescent green chenille wrapped through eyes.

Plate 4　Howdy

Thread: Fluorescent orange.
Body: Fluorescent orange chenille.
Hackle: Fluorescent fire orange tied on as a collar and tied back.
Eyes: Gold bead chain.

Judge

Plate 4

Thread: Black.
Tail: CH02 black Crystal Hair.
Body: Black chenille.
Hackle: Black hen hackle tied on as a collar and tied back.
Eyes: Silver bead chain.

Juror

Thread: White.
Tail: FB01 pearl Fly Brite.
Body: White chenille.
Hackle: White hen hackle tied on as a collar and tied back.
Eyes: Silver bead chain.

Log Hole

Thread: Black.
Tail: Fluorescent pink glow in the dark Flashabou.
Body: Fluorescent pink glow in the dark Flashabou over an underbody of white floss.
Hackle: Blue dun tied on as a collar and tied back.
Head: Silver bead.

Lolo

Thread: Fluorescent chartreuse.
Tail: FB23 chartreuse Fly Brite.
Body: Fluorescent green chenille.
Hackle: Fluorescent chartreuse tied on as a collar and tied back.
Eyes: Gold bead chain.

Mac's Black

Thread: Black.
Tail: Black calf tail.
Body: Dubbed with a blend of #1 black lambs wool and FB01 pearl Fly Brite.
Hackle: Black hen hackle tied on as a collar and tied back.
Head: Large black.
Eyes: Red dots.

Marta

Thread: Yellow.
Tail: CH04 yellow Crystal Hair.
Body: Yellow chenille.
Hackle: Yellow tied on as a collar and tied back.
Eyes: Gold bead chain.

Orange Death

Thread: Fluorescent orange.

Tail: Frayed out pearl Mylar piping from body.
Body: Fluorescent orange 20 pound Amnesia over an underbody of silver tinsel.
Hackle: Frayed pearl Mylar piping.
Eyes: Silver bead chain.
Head: Fluorescent white chenille wrapped through eyes.

Paradise Beach

Thread: Red.
Tail: Dyed red grizzly marabou.
Body: Black diamond braid.
Eyes: Silver bead chain.

Designed to fish the early morning hours at Paradise Beach on the American River.

Pat's Prince

Plate 4

Thread: White.
Tail: Clear (white) Miclon or Z-Lon.
Body: Chartreuse plastic lace wrapped over an underbody of flat silver Mylar tinsel.
Hackle: White tied on as a collar and tied back.
Eyes: Silver bead chain.

This fly is also successful when tied with a red or orange body.

Porker

Thread: Yellow.
Body: Dubbed with #6 yellow African Angora Goat. Body is fat and full.
Hackle: Yellow tied on as a collar and tied back.
Eyes: Gold bead chain.

Princeton Plus

Thread: White.
Tail: White calf tail and FB01 pearl Fly Brite mixed.
Body: White chenille.
Hackle: Red tied on as a collar and tied back.
Eyes: Silver bead chain.

Royal Shad

Plate 4

Thread: Red.
Butt: Dark olive chenille.
Body: Red floss.
Hackle: Red tied on as a collar and tied back.
Eyes: Silver bead chain.

Rosy

Thread: Red.
Tail: Red calf tail.
Body: Dubbed with a blend of #4 red lambs wool and FB03 red Fly Brite.
Hackle: Red tied on as a collar and tied back.
Eyes: Silver bead chain.

Shad Buster

Thread: White.
Tail: White calf tail.
Body: Dubbed with a blend of #2 white lambs wool blended FB01 pearl Fly Brite.
Hackle: Orange tied on as a collar and tied back.
Eyes: Silver bead chain.

Silver Shad

Thread: White.
Tail: CH30 silver Crystal Hair.
Body: Silver diamond braid.
Hackle: CH30 silver Crystal Hair spun on as a collar.
Head: White.

Silverado

Thread: White.
Tail: CH30 silver Crystal Hair.
Body: Wrapped with fine silver Mylar piping.
Hackle: CH30 silver Crystal Hair spun on as a collar.
Eyes: Silver bead chain.

Stan's Orange

Thread: Fluorescent orange.
Tail: CH06 orange Crystal Hair.
Body: Fluorescent orange chenille.
Hackle: CH06 orange Crystal Hair spun on as a collar.
Eyes: Gold bead chain.

Timbuctoo

Thread: Chartreuse.
Tail: Clear (white) Miclon or Z-Lon.
Ribbing: Oval gold tinsel.
Body: Chartreuse chenille.
Hackle: Chartreuse tied on as a collar and tied back.
Eyes: Gold bead chain.

Ugo

Thread: Blue.
Tail: White marabou.
Body: Dubbed with a blend of #30 purple lambs wool and FB19 purple Fly Brite.
Hackle: Purple hen hackle tied on as a collar and tied back.
Eyes: Silver bead chain.

Verdict

Thread: Black.
Tail: FB11 green Fly Brite.
Body: Dubbed with FB21 claret Fly Brite.
Hackle: Black hen hackle tied on as a collar and tied back.
Eyes: Silver bead chain.

Plate 4

Verona Fly

Thread: Fluorescent green.
Tag: Fluorescent green yarn (flared).
Body: Well tapered fluorescent green yarn.
Hackle: White tied on as a collar and tied back.
Eyes: Gold bead chain.

Wet Pinky

Thread: Fluorescent pink.
Tail: White marabou.
Ribbing: Oval silver tinsel.
Body: Fluorescent white chenille.
Eyes: Gold bead chain.

Developed by Dave Howard of Roseville, California.

White's Light

Thread: White.
Tail: White marabou mix with CH01 pearl Crystal Hair.
Body: CH01 pearl Crystal Hair wrapped over an underbody of white floss.
Eyes: Silver bead chain.
Head: Fluorescent white chenille wrapped through eyes.

This fly was developed by Burke White of Sacramento, California.

Yuba Special

Thread: White.
Tail: Black marabou.
Body: Dubbed with FB02 black Fly Brite.
Hackle: White hen hackle tied on as a collar and tied back.
Eyes: Silver bead chain.

Do not discount the possibilities with a dry fly after the early flows in the rivers have subsided. Many anglers get too consumed with trout at this time of year and do not realize these fish are still reasonably available to them as late as August. Some of the more common patterns, i.e., Black Gnat and Coachman are successful. Shad are a real thrill on a three or four weight rod and you will enjoy sharpening your angling skills.

Chapter 20

Steelhead Flies

Now we get into a subject I have quite a fancy for. These particular fish are migratory rainbows. On the West Coast they go to the ocean and those immature and mature fish who return to the rivers within six months are known as spring and summer fish. Those which enter the rivers during December through May are known as winter fish. Then there are those streams which abide by no seasonal cycles, they hold big and little runs throughout the year, or every month of the year. The tampering of man has altered the gene pools in every river on the West Coast. You might say, "We have messed around with the guts of the clock." What once appeared to be a dependable seasonal run of fish can be altered in just a very short time.

Many of the coastal streams are vulnerable to seasonal weather conditions. Some years a stream can have too much water and others, simply not enough to bring the fish in. They are forced to stay in holding at the mouths of the streams awaiting the first big storm to clear away the tidal debris, this includes sand as well as other forms of rubbish which block the channels. When upper flows justify it, some states don't wait on Mother Nature to take her course and use appropriate equipment to free these channels.

There are several races within the rainbow trout species *(Salmo gairdneri),* but the steelhead is the most prized and is scattered over a wide range, genetically speaking of course. Take a trip to either New Zealand or Australia and let the locals know you are from California and you may be looked upon as some sort of nut. "Why have you traveled all these thousands of miles to fish?" This is a commonly asked question down under. Their fantastic fishing is attributed to stock taken from northern California's Russian River many years back; if only they could see what man has done to this river today. Anglers would certainly be thrilled to learn how well some species have prospered. Their growth rate has been marvelous in some of these new environments.

Right here in my own state of California I've had the opportunity to witness the genetic differences between the common hybrid rainbow that our fish people think to be so great, and steelhead. Round Valley Reservoir just north of Susanville was a prime example of this, for commercial purposes the name of this body of water has also been referred to as "High Prairie," but no one has influenced the map makers as yet to make an official change and it is doubtful they ever will. Although this water is on private and BLM leased ranch land the state got involved in some experimentation.

Initially they planted hybrid rainbows. After some seasons had past they dumped another strain, the steelhead. Whether this was done purposely or just another way for them to rid their hatcheries of surplus fish, I am not certain. The point is, it happened. When we fished it three seasons later it was phenomenal. Never have I witnessed such a contrast in a species. Even though the steelhead were only three years old and had reached two and a half to three pounds, they were dynamite fish in everyone's book, catching the earlier planted rainbows from seven to ten pounds was like hooking up with a carp in comparison. This fishery is nonexistent today due to the ranch management drawing it dry in 1991 for field irrigation purposes. It was a sickening experience to witness this, but it was also reassuring to realize that the steelhead is the undisputed "Monarch of Trout."

In the late 1800s civilization pressed further west in ever greater numbers. The steel rails had been laid and the quest for gold was not the first thing on everyone's mind anymore. A new color of riches had turned from gold to red, redwood lumber that is. Railroad spur lines pushed north opening up the West Coast even more. To put this time frame in better perspective, it should be remembered that it wasn't until October 1873, that the Modoc Indians surrendered. They were the last of the Indians in California to do so. Those who were left, about 100, were placed on the Klamath Reservation with fragments of other tribes. Because of their continued discontent these proud war-like people still give anglers who fish parts of the Klamath River some stories to bring home.

As a result of its more knowledgeable and sophisticated international populous, the San Francisco Bay Area developed a fly fishing interest in the local streams with their runs of both steelhead and salmon. Later this group started progressing north in their quest for these new-found fish.

Ships continued to come around the horn during this period for destinations other than San Francisco. Portland and the mighty Columbia River, Puget Sound and Seattle-Tacoma. British ships made their 9,000 nautical mile voyages from Liverpool, England, to Vancouver, British Columbia, and the Frazier River. Gold and other riches in Alaska drew people even further north. With these ships came new settlers not unlike those who arrived at San Francisco earlier.

Eventually this new California interest flowed over into southern Oregon and its Rogue River Valley. Zane Grey was largely responsible for bringing the Oregon fishery to our attention with his writings. With the publication in 1928 of his book, *Tales of Fresh-Water,* which contained exploits with the steelhead on Oregon's Rogue River, many anglers throughout the world realized he could write more than just fiction. It was during this period that steelhead came to be regarded as something other than a means of subsistence and sport fishing started to flourish on the West Coast.

In conjunction with this, eggs from wild Oregon steelhead were being introduced in 1870 by Michigan's fishery biologists into the Great Lakes area. Many readers will be interested to know that the Great Lakes steelhead territory of today spreads over a much wider piece of geography than that on the Pacific Coast. This is a lot of territory that includes literally hundreds of rivers. Of these, only about 60 rivers attract steelhead as suitable spawning runs and other waters have to be planted. The rivers in this region tend to be smaller, tamer and usually shorter than Pacific Coast streams, this favors the fisherman as fish are usually concentrated in greater numbers.

In 1966 plantings were again made in Michigan waters with 182,000 steelhead fry coming from eggs supplied by Oregon and Alaska. These fish did so well that by 1972 over a million steelhead eggs were planted annually in the state. Many other states have on-going programs to improve their steelhead fisheries.

The states of Michigan, Minnesota, New York, Ohio, Pennsylvania, Indiana and Wisconsin all have fair to good fisheries; Ontario, Canada, also shares in these productive inland freshwater-seas. Michigan definitely excels in this respect and is the undisputed pace setter.

I will always remember the fall trips down the Trinity River Canyon, with an overnight stop at Willow Creek, followed the next day by returning up the Klamath. Seeing steelhead and salmon laying in the large clear pools of the rivers like cord wood was an experience to remember. If I could love but one river it would be hard to select between these two. Memories of fish taken on the Ice Cream Riffle above Somes Bar on the Klamath would fill more than a dozen or so angler's logs. The Trinity River however holds more special remembrances for me: My father coming to the rescue and tailing my first large steelhead when I was twelve; the fish was eleven pounds, eight ounces, however, when telling of it in the years that followed, it was always twelve pounds taken when I was twelve. These were the years of structuring my personal philosophy that has continued to evolve into what it is today.

The run that year was skimpy, nonetheless as "canyon people" at the time we were known to always have meat for the table and my first big steelhead was shared with many. We returned to the Cabin Riffle the following day and I took one more smaller fish and my father took seven. These were all fish best to be caught another day. My father with his guiding business learned early the value of a well-bred wild steelhead. He was way out of step in the 1940s, marching to the beat of a different drummer, suggesting catch-and-release methods wasn't considered an option that would ultimately improve our fisheries. It was never a matter of denial at the kitchen table or saving fish for clients and others to enjoy, fish were generally always in abundance. A swing by the Weitchpec area most evenings during the season would yield an occasional gratuitous fresh salmon from my father's Indian friends. In fact, more were refused than taken home for our meager needs.

As any dedicated steelheader will tell you, this brand of fishing is strictly for the patient and hardy. In addition to many fishless days, one can always expect a cold penetrating mist in the morning hours which likely as not will turn into rain and last for days. It all becomes worthwhile when the day finally arrives when you fair hook one of the big thrillers. The sight of a nine pound silvery fish walking across the water on its tail brings with it an excitement like no other in fly fishing. The past days of what appeared to be nothing more than casting practice sessions and the loss of a few dozen flies are all erased from memory. The only thought that I have at moments like this are "Which way is he going—up or downstream? I wonder if I have enough backing? Can I get around those roots if he makes a run downstream? Where will I be able to beach him?" My last collective thought is "Oh, what the hell, at least I'll get to play him for awhile and really that is enough for me."

I have known a few gifted anglers who take and release a hundred or more steelhead per season. They are not just lucky either. These few may be rare, but it makes me try even harder, I feel I fish just as aggressively as they do, but my all-time high has only been twenty-one hefty fish in a season. This of course has always been supplemented with some good days when half-pounders were available. One gratifying factor is that no one ever gets upset with me when I say, "I'm going steelheading."

In my opinion there is no other fish more rewarding to catch on a fly rod than a nice fresh-run steelhead. Unfortunately, I would bet only about ten percent of the steelheaders today have ever experienced the ultimate thrill of beaching one of these beautiful fish while using a fly rod. One forms a great respect and develops a certain kinship with these migratory devils like no other game fish of its kind.

With the exception of "fully dressed" Atlantic salmon flies, I believe I would rather tie steelhead flies than any other. While tying commercially for so many years I had few opportunities to tie these flies, today I can get really engrossed in tying them when the opportunity arises. In those days I probably never tied more than fifty dozen per season, the demand just wasn't there. I always made sure there were a sufficient number of culls set aside on my tying bench for my own personal use.

In examining some of the fly patterns for steelhead and Atlantic salmon you may be able to detect only a very little difference. You will hear the term "classic" freely applied to both of them and for the most part both are now being tied on salmon fly hooks. Forty-plus years ago my steelhead fishing was confined mostly to northern California, at that time you might have gotten an argument from me had you inferred that these flies were influenced by old British patterns. I really didn't see any indication of this until I was in Bellingham, Washington, in the early 1960s. This is where I got my first real exposure to the fact that there are other approaches to this thing called "steelheading." There was some preference being shown the Blue Charm, Silver Doctor and other such patterns tied on the traditional salmon fly hook. Early rejection, you bet. That's just not the way things should be done, or was it?

A season later while fishing British Columbia for the first time I saw the influence this type of fly had on local fly fishermen. While visiting a shop in Vancouver I was waited on by a gentleman with the name, "Polly Peacock." Honest, that was his real given name, until then I thought the English only gave their fly patterns unusual names. He was a recent arrival from England, or at least that was the impression I was given, and well versed in salmon flies. He may well have known what he was talking about when he started in on their use for steelhead, but I didn't. Much of what he was trying to convince me of was just a bit over my head, both in the terms that he used and with the strong cockney dialect used to deliver the message. I cannot remember the name of the shop, but who could forget that guy's name? Thirty years later I learned his real name was "Collie."

During these past years more steelhead flies are being tied on salmon fly hooks, plus a revitalization of old British fly patterns have become popular with steelheaders. Especially the Spey type patterns being tied and used primarily in British Columbia, Washington and northern Oregon. They are probably used there more than any place in North America. These flies are slowly creeping their way down the coast to southern Oregon and northern California and I can see them taking more space in our fly boxes in the very near future. See Chapter 22.

I should mention the fact that there are even a few who are attempting to revisit the feather or strip wing variations. Darn, just when we think we have most of our breed well-taught in the prudence of hair wings some start back peddling. These flies may not be as durable as their hair wing cousins, however, I see value in their use. It was not too many years ago when this style was considered "old fashioned" and outmoded. Now maybe those advocates of yesterday are finally getting their message across.

With respect to the hooks, I can understand why we have had a slow transition into the use of salmon fly hooks for steelhead flies. Change inherently comes slowly to fly fishermen. Once it does though, natural stubbornness precludes any further changes for some time. This is evident in how history records the very slow transition in the demands of North American fly fishing.

It is my belief that this recent change in hook preference has come about for two reasons. First, these flies look classy when dressed on these hooks. They look great in catalogs and in color plates on the pages of books, I guess "photogenic" best describes them. Secondly, because of their superior sharpness at the time the change started taking place.

There is a growing interest in the British tackle designs, the two handed rods of twelve feet or longer are seeing considerable interest. One might be prone to think that this newborn interest in old British traditions might even surpass the traditions of the East Coast Atlantic salmon fly fishermen one day. Do you suppose we are coming full circle on this one?

Because of the close correlation between our steelhead flies and the Atlantic salmon flies as they are used today, I strongly recommend you refer to Chapter 21. You will find such patterns as the Rat series which are very adaptable to steelhead use. I doubt that you will want to jazz up more than just a few of these patterns, most of the patterns offered in that chapter are of the hair wing design and are well suited to Western fishing preferences.

The following patterns are what one might expect to find in the fly boxes of anglers who pursue the great steelhead in North America. Some are very old patterns. Some are new but tried and proven to be productive. There are a number of very effective stonefly and caddisfly patterns listed in their respective chapters which are very effective for steelhead. Also, there are a number of other references to steelhead producing patterns made elsewhere in this book. Chapter 21 has several patterns coded (**SH**). These are patterns which I recommend you either tie and use for steelhead or create variations thereof. The patterns in this chapter coded with an (**S**) are also recommended for Pacific salmon.

Plate 9 Adam's Rib

Hooks: AC80500BL, AC80501BL, TMC7999 or DAI2441, sizes 4-6.
Thread: Black.
Tail: Red hen hackle barbs.
Ribbing: Fine silver wire over peacock only.
Body: Rear half, embossed silver tinsel and the front half, peacock herl.
Center Joint Hackle: Grizzly hackle tied on as a collar and tied back.
Hackle: White bucktail tied in at the throat.
Wing: Dyed black bucktail tied over the body.
Cheeks: Grizzly hackle tips tied in at each side.
Head: Black.
Note: The wing and throat hackle are of equal proportions and of the same length. In other words, you have a wing on top and one on the bottom.

Originated by Russell Langston of Brown's Valley, California.

Acid Flashback

Hooks: AC80500BL, AC80501BL, TMC7999 or DAI2441, sizes 4-8.
Thread: Claret.
Tail: Scarlet red hackle barbs mixed with CH01 pearl Crystal Hair.
Ribbing: Flat silver tinsel.
Body: Purple chenille.
Hackle: Purple tied on as a collar and tied back and down.
Wing: Purple marabou tied over the body.
Topping: CH01 pearl Crystal Hair.
Head: Claret.

This pattern was conceived by Kevin Cooney.

Admiral

Hooks: AC80500BL, AC80501BL, TMC7999 or DAI2441, sizes 4-8.
Thread: Red.
Tail: Scarlet red hackle barbs.

Ribbing: Oval gold tinsel.
Body: Dubbed with red lambs wool.
Hackle: Brown tied on as a collar and tied back and down.
Wing: White calf tail tied over the body.
Head: Red.

This is a variation of an old American wet fly pattern we can safely assume was created around the turn of the century. Its originator, Rear Admiral Eustace Baron Rogers first dressed this attractor pattern for trout little realizing it would later be adapted through an adjustment in materials to a standard steelhead fly.

After Dinner Mint

Hooks: AC80500BL, AC80501BL, TMC7999 or DAI2441, sizes 4-8.
Thread: Fluorescent green.
Tail: Coachman brown hen hackle barbs.
Body: Fluorescent green chenille.
Wing: Dyed reddish-brown gray squirrel tail tied over the body.
Hackle: Coachman brown hen hackle tied on as a collar and tied back.
Head: Fluorescent green.

This was originally designed in 1969 for the Feather River. Carl Glisson named the fly and in later years reported it was first rate for the Rogue and Eel Rivers.

Plate 9 Aid's Marabou Spiders

Bob Aid of Seattle, Washington, developed these patterns and I believe they are flies you will want to give some attention to at your next session behind the vise. The prime points you should attend to in tying these patterns are first, the shoulder should be dominant enough to support the base of the hackle properly. Second, select blood marabou feathers and tie them in by their tips for the hackle. The shorter barbs of these feathers and the shoulder assist in keeping the marabou hackle from matting against the body of the fly. When wrapping the hackle, you may want to pack the stem with your thumbnail tightly against the shoulder to get it to seat better.

Note the abrupt taper at the front of the shoulder.

Black and Orange

Hooks: AC80500BL, AC80501BL, TMC7999 or DAI2441, sizes 2/0-6.
Thread: Black.
Body: Wrapped with fine gold braided Mylar piping.
Shoulder: Dubbed with #9 orange African Angora goat.
Hackle: First, wrap on a collar of black marabou, followed with fluorescent orange hen hackle and finally with dyed orange guinea fowl.
Head: Black.

Plate 10 ### Orange and Red

Hooks: AC80500BL, AC80501BL, TMC7999 or DAI2441, sizes 2/0-6.
Thread: Black.
Body: Wrapped with fine silver braided Mylar piping.
Shoulder: Dubbed with #9 orange African Angora goat.
Hackle: First, wrap on a collar of fluorescent orange marabou, followed with fluorescent red marabou and finally with dyed black pheasant rump.
Head: Black.

Pink and Red

Hooks: AC80500BL, AC80501BL, TMC7999 or DAI2441, sizes 2/0-6.
Thread: Fluorescent red.
Body: Wrapped with fine silver braided Mylar piping.
Shoulder: Dubbed with #28 pink African Angora goat.
Hackle: First, wrap on a collar of fluorescent hot pink marabou, followed with fluorescent red hen hackle and finally with dyed red guinea fowl.
Head: Fluorescent red.

Purple and Blue

Hooks: AC80500BL, AC80501BL, TMC7999 or DAI2441, sizes 2/0-6.
Thread: Fluorescent blue.
Body: Wrapped with fine silver braided Mylar piping.
Shoulder: Dubbed with purple African Angora goat.
Hackle: First, wrap on a collar of purple marabou followed with full turn of teal blue marabou.
Head: Fluorescent blue.

Skagit Special

Hooks: AC80500BL, AC80501BL, TMC7999 or DAI2441, sizes 2/0-6.
Thread: Fluorescent orange.
Body: Wrapped with fine braided silver Mylar piping.
Shoulder: Dubbed with #9 orange African Angora goat.
Hackle: First, wrap on a collar of yellow marabou followed with orange marabou and finally with dyed orange guinea fowl.
Head: Fluorescent orange.

Steelhead Pinkie

Hooks: AC80500BL, AC80501BL, TMC7999 or DAI2441, sizes 2/0-6.
Thread: Fluorescent blue.
Body: Flat silver tinsel.
Shoulder: Dubbed with #28 pink African Angora goat.
Hackle: First, wrap on a collar of fluorescent hot pink marabou followed with a full turn of kingfisher blue marabou.
Head: Fluorescent blue.

Guess what fly I'm going to have with me on my next trip to Alaska? Thank you, Bob, for some good ideas.

Alaska Mary Ann

Hooks: AC80500BL, AC80501BL, TMC7999 or DAI2441, sizes 1-4.
Thread: Black.
Tail: Crimson red hackle barbs.
Ribbing: Oval silver tinsel.
Body: White chenille.
Wing: White bucktail tied over the body.
Cheeks: J.C. or substitute.
Head: Black.

Created out of necessity in Alaska in 1929 by Frank Dufresne. For lack of anything else to work with, the first fly had a red tail, cream wool with a silver wire ribbing for the body and a polar bear hair wing.

Algan

Hooks: AC80500BL, AC80501BL, TMC7999 or DAI2441, sizes 2-8.
Thread: Black.
Tail: Fluorescent fire orange hackle barbs.
Ribbing: Oval silver tinsel.
Body: Black chenille.
Hackle: Black and claret tied on as a collar mixed and tied back.
Wing: Black bucktail tied over the body.
Head: Black.

Almvig

Hooks: AC80500BL, AC80501BL, TMC7999 or DAI2441, sizes 4-6.
Thread: Fluorescent fire orange.
Ribbing: Embossed silver tinsel.
Body: Dubbed with #53 fluorescent fire orange lambs wool.
Wing: White calf tail tied over the body with an overwing of fluorescent red calf tail.
Head: Fluorescent fire orange.

Both of the preceding patterns came into being about 50 years ago in Washington.

Al's Special

Hooks: AC80500BL, AC80501BL, TMC7999 or DAI2441, sizes 2-6.
Thread: Yellow.

Tip: Oval silver tinsel.
Tail: Crimson red hackle barbs.
Ribbing: Oval silver tinsel.
Body: Yellow chenille.
Hackle: Crimson red tied on as a collar and tied back and down.
Wing: White bucktail tied over the body.
Head: Yellow.

Al Knudson, father of the Wet Spider, and for that matter one of the leading fathers of steelheading with a fly, developed this pattern in the 1930s and it is still hanging in there.

Altima

Hooks: AC80500BL, AC80501BL, TMC7999 or DAI2441, sizes 2-8.
Thread: Red.
Tail: Red hen hackle barbs.
Body: Dubbed with FB01 pearl Fly Brite.
Hackle: White tied on as a collar and tied back.
Wing: Red bucktail tied over the body.
Head: Red.

This is one of many new patterns starting to show up since the advent of Fly Brite. Originated by Carter Moore of Oroville, California.

Plate 6   American River Special

Hooks: AC80500BL, AC80501BL, TMC7999 or DAI2441, sizes 6-10.
Thread: Black.
Tail: Brown hen hackle barbs.
Ribbing: Narrow strip of dyed dark brown raffia.
Body: Green chenille.
Hackle: Furnace hen hackle tied on as a collar and tied back.
Head: Black chenille.

This is one of several patterns developed for the American River and christened with the same name. Also see Chapter 9.

Plate 9   Assassin

Hooks: TMC7989 or DAI2421, sizes 8-10.
Thread: Olive.
Ribbing: Oval gold tinsel.

Body: Dubbed with a 50/50 blend of #19 olive and #24 brown African Angora goat.
Hackle: Brown tied on as a collar and tied back.
Wing: Dozen strands of CH17 brown olive Crystal Hair tied over the body.
Head: Olive.

Originated by Dale Lackey. This is a good late summer and fall pattern for the Yuba, Trinity and Klamath Rivers.

Atom Bomb

Hooks: AC80500BL, AC80501BL, TMC7999 or DAI2441, sizes 4-8.
Thread: Fluorescent yellow.
Tail: A pair of fluorescent yellow hen hackle tips tied on edge in a V with concave side out. Make a few wraps under so the tail cocks upward.
Body: Wrapped with fine silver braided Mylar piping.
Hackle: Ginger variant tied on as a collar and tied back and down.
Wing: White bucktail tied sparse over the body. Then, half dozen strands of CH01 pearl Crystal Hair followed with fluorescent yellow marabou tied on top.
Topping: CH03 red Crystal Hair.
Head: Fluorescent yellow.

Originated by George Voss. I picked up the original pattern in Portland, Oregon in 1961. Since then I have played with it some and now find it to be one of the better "yellow" patterns that I carry. Generally, yellow is not a color that fly fishermen come running after, but this fly has done the job many times over for me. This fly is also tied in a gray variation.

Babine Special

Hooks: AC80500BL, AC80501BL, TMC7999 or DAI2441, sizes 1-6.
Thread: Fluorescent fire orange.
Butt: Fluorescent red chenille.
Body: Black chenille.
Hackle: Fluorescent fire orange. Hackle should be tied long and reach to the end of the body.
Head: Fluorescent fire orange.

Babine Special Two

Hooks: AC80500BL, AC80501BL, TMC7999 or DAI2441, sizes 2/0-4.
Thread: Fluorescent pink.
Body: Fluorescent pink chenille. Chenille should be wrapped in two rather large distinctive lumps.
Center Hackle: Fluorescent red tied on as a collar and tied back slightly.
Hackle: White tied on as a collar and tied back slightly.
Head: Fluorescent pink.

Everyone that visits the Babine River for any period of time always comes away with their Babine Special. The two patterns above are what I have found to be the most consistent. The beauty of it is they produce elsewhere.

Badger Hackle Peacock

Hooks: AC80500BL, AC80501BL, TMC7999 or DAI2441, sizes 2-8.
Thread: Black.
Tip: Oval gold tinsel. Wrap five turns under the tail and one or two above, using the tinsel to cock the tail upward.
Tail: Amherst pheasant crest.
Body: Peacock herl. Wrap an underbody of olive yarn to give the peacock a plump appearance. Reverse wrap the body with fine gold wire.
Hackle: Well marked badger tied on as a collar and tied back.
Head: Black.

E. H. "Polly" Rosborough of Chiloquin, Oregon did not originate this pattern, but he sure is responsible for showing me how to improve upon it and convincing me just how effective it can be for steelhead. Polly likes the natural dead drift of the fly and never weights it.

Badger Palmer

Hooks: AC80500BL, AC80501BL, TMC7999 or DAI2441, sizes 4-6.
Thread: Black.
Tail: Scarlet red hackle barbs mixed with CH03 red Crystal Hair.
Body: Fluorescent yellow chenille.

Body Hackle: Badger tied palmer style over the body. Tie hackle in by the tip and wrap so concave is to the rear.
Head: Black.

This northern California pattern has been around since I was a small boy. I can say with conviction that it has been used in all of the streams there and in southern Oregon with a high degree of success.

Badger and Red

Hooks: AC80500BL, AC80501BL, TMC7999 or DAI2441, sizes 1-6.
Thread: Red.
Tail: Crimson red turkey quill section.
Ribbing: Oval silver tinsel.
Body: Dubbed with #4 red lambs wool. Body should be picked out and made "shaggy."
Wings: Badger hackle tips tied over the body and tied upward in a V with concave sides out.
Hackle: Badger tied on as a collar and tied back.
Head: Red.

Buz Buszek sent me this pattern in 1960 as a sample. It originated in British Columbia, but by its successful migration south one would think it was created for these waters.

Plate 6

Bair's Black

Hooks: AC80500BL, AC80501BL, TMC7999 or DAI2441, sizes 4-8.
Thread: Red.
Tip: Red floss.
Body: Black chenille.
Hackle: Black hen hackle tied on as a collar and tied back and down.
Wing: White calf tail tied over the body with an overwing of white (clear) Miclon or Z-Lon.
Topping: Single strand of red floss.
Head: Red.

Bair's Railbird

Hooks: AC80500BL, AC80501BL, TMC7999 or DAI2441, sizes 2-6.
Thread: Black.
Tail: Claret hackle barbs.
Body: Flat silver tinsel wrapped over a tapered white floss underbody.
Hackle: Yellow tied on as a collar and tied back and down.
Wing: Barred teal barbs tied over the body.
Cheeks: J.C. or substitute.
Head: Black.

These patterns were originated by Fred Bair of Klamath Lodge, California, around 1920. Bair collaborated with Jim Pray on his Railbird variation and added another to a long list of Railbirds of that period. He was instrumental in originating a number of other patterns, however, these two are the patterns that have lasted and not faded away into obscurity as many of his other patterns have.

Barber Pole

Hook: AC80501BL, sizes 2/0-8.
Thread: Red.
Tip: Embossed silver tinsel.
Tail: Scarlet red and white hackle barbs mixed.
Body: Alternating wraps of red and white chenille. Start with white at rear.
Hackle: Scarlet red and white mixed and tied on as a collar and tied back.
Eyes: Silver bead chain.

One of the many highly productive patterns developed in 1955 by Frederic Nicholas Kozy. Fred calls Happy Camp, California home but he can be found just about anyplace on the West Coast where steelhead are on the move, including Alaska. Fred prides himself on being able to forecast runs in more than a hundred streams throughout the year. He maintains finely detailed logs of his own activities, plus he relies strongly on weather patterns.

His research on weather movements dates back to the turn of the century. His long career as a chemical engineer and chemist specializing in adhesives has carried over into his second career, fly fishing. He has contributed his knowledge to some rather unique cements and finishes for the fly tier. He calls them his "Kozy Koats."

Plate 8 Bear's Flashback

Hook: AC80501BL, sizes 2/0-8.
Thread: Black.
Tail: Black hen hackle barbs.
Shellback: CH22 teal Crystal Hair.
Body: Dubbed with #1 black African Angora goat.
Hackle: Black hen hackle tied on as a collar and tied back.
Eyes: Silver bead chain.

This particular variation was created by Jeff "Bear" Andrews of Grand Ledge, Michigan. Coincidental to this another Jeff, Jeff Bowers of Crescent City, California, has been working on a very similar pattern since 1962 for the Eel River. The latter Jeff first used peacock herl for the shellback and was one of the first to make the change to Crystal Hair in 1984. He claims that the CH02 black Crystal Hair makes his Black Comet even more effective and is still experimenting with other patterns.

Bellamy

Hooks: AC80500BL, AC80501BL, TMC7999 or DAI2441, sizes 1-6.
Thread: Black.
Tail: Red calf tail.
Body: Copper wire.

Wing: White bucktail tied over the body with an overwing of dyed yellow natural brown bucktail.

This pattern is one of many designed by Pete Schwab in 1927 while he was residing in Yreka, California. Originally intended for the Klamath and Eel Rivers it gained favor in Oregon on the Rogue River.

Other wire body patterns of this era are the Brass Hat, Princess, Queen Bess, Paint Brush and the Bobbie Dunn. These are listed elsewhere in this chapter. All of these patterns have nicely finished black heads which often have small red dots on them for eyes. These dots are applied by using the head of a common straight pin as an applicator.

Bench Mark

Hooks: AC80500BL, AC80501BL, TMC7999 or DAI2441, sizes 1-6.
Thread: Fluorescent orange.
Tail: Fluorescent fire orange bucktail.
Ribbing: Silver embossed tinsel.
Body: Dubbed with #52 fluorescent orange lambs wool.
Hackle: Fluorescent fire orange tied on as a collar and tied back and down.
Wing: White calf tail tied over the body.
Head: Fluorescent orange.

Originated in British Columbia by Karl Mausser. The name resulted from its body being tied with orange surveyor's tape when it was first created.

Benn's Coachman

Hooks: AC80500BL, AC80501BL, TMC7999 or DAI2441, sizes 1-6.
Thread: Black.
Tail: Crimson red hackle barbs.
Body: Peacock herl. Reverse wrap with fine gold wire.
Hackle: Brown tied on as a collar and tied back and down.
Wing: White calf tail tied over the body with an overwing of red calf tail.
Head: Black.

This is possibly one of the earliest fly patterns ever designed specifically for steelhead. Its originator, John S. Benn of San Francisco, California, created it for the Eel River before the turn of the century. The original pattern had married red and white goose quill sections as wings. See Humboldt Railbird.

Big Henry

Hooks: AC80500BL, AC80501BL, TMC7999 or DAI2441, sizes 6-8.
Thread: Red.
Tail: Golden pheasant crest.
Ribbing: Oval gold tinsel.
Body: Rear two-thirds, dubbed with #13 gray lambs wool and the front third, dubbed with #32 claret Bunnytron.
Hackle: Dyed dark blue dun pheasant rump tied on as a collar and tied back with hackle tips extending to bend of hook.
Head: Red.

The Big Henry has been a proven fly for a number of years. One that knowledgeable steelheaders have few qualms in using. It was designed for the Trinity and Klamath Rivers by Jim Nelson of Klamath, California, in 1952. It was named for C. E. "Big Henry" Sainsbury of Santa Monica, California. This first variation of this pattern incorporated blue heron barbs for the rear body and hackle.

Obviously this was a short lived practice. Today, if you can get your hands on a natural blue dun hen saddle patch you can get extremely close to the very first one tied, not that it will be any more productive than the variation now being tied, just peace of mind in knowing you are close to Jim's first fly.

Black Ant

Tied the same as the Red Ant except wing is of black calf tail.

Black Bear

Hooks: AC80500BL, AC80501BL, TMC7999 or DAI2441, sizes 1-8.
Thread: Black.
Tail: Black and crimson red hackle barbs mixed.
Ribbing: Oval silver tinsel.
Body: Black chenille.
Hackle: Black and crimson red tied on as a collar mixed and tied back and down.
Wing: Black calf tail tied over the body.
Head: Black.

Developed in the early 1950s by Al Knudson while he was living in Everett, Washington. The original pattern had black bear hair for the wing.

Black Beauty

Hooks: AC80500BL, AC80501BL, TMC7999 or DAI2441, sizes 4-8.
Thread: Black.
Body: Fluorescent fire orange chenille.
Hackle: Black tied on as a collar and tied back.
Head: Black.

This simple pattern, proving simplicity still works, was originated in 1960 by Karl Mausser for British Columbia. It works and works well wherever steelhead run.

Black Bomber

Hooks: AC80500BL, AC80501BL, TMC7999 or DAI2441, sizes 4-8.
Thread: Black.
Tail: Fluorescent orange hackle barbs.
Body: Black chenille.
Wing: White bucktail tied over the body and extending to the center of the tail.
Head: Black.
Eyes: White ring eyes.

Created in 1957 by Warren Erholm of Anacortes, Washington. Many of you are probably not familiar with "ring eyes," they are made from the insulation off electrical wire. This tubing-like material is cut into little donuts or rings. Generally 8 or 10 gauge wire is used. These little rings can be applied by using clear head cement. I usually give them a couple of coats allowing each to dry for a short period. You end up with some great eyes that appear as if they have been meticulously hand painted.

Black Boss

See Boss.

Black Coachman

The Black Coachman is the same as the Coachman except the body is of black chenille rather than peacock herl.

Black Demon

Hooks: AC80500BL, AC80501BL, TMC7999 or DAI2441, sizes 2-6.
Thread: Black.
Tail: Black and white barred lemon woodduck section.
Body: Oval silver tinsel.
Hackle: Orange tied on as a collar and tied back and down.
Wing: Black bucktail tied over the body.
Head: Black.

A Jim Pray pattern which he originated in the mid 1930s. There is considerably more about Jim further on in this chapter.

Black Diamond

Hooks: TMC7989 or DAI2421, sizes 6-8.
Thread: Black.
Tip: Flat silver tinsel.
Ribbing: Flat silver tinsel.
Body: Dubbed with #1 black Bunny-Blend.
Wing: Gray squirrel tail tied sparse over the body with an overwing of four or five strands of CH01 pearl Crystal Hair tied in and four or five peacock sword feather barbs on the top.
Hackle: Guinea fowl tied on as a collar and tied back.
Head: Black.

This fly is generally tied reduced, hence the lighter wire hooks, and used for summer-runs. It was originated in 1969 by Harry Lemire of Black Diamond, Washington.

Plate 10　Black Ember

Hook: AC80501BL, sizes 2/0-8.
Thread: Orange.
Tail: Black squirrel tail tied equal to one and a half the body length.
Butt: Fluorescent fire orange chenille. Wrap one full turn only.
Ribbing: Oval gold tinsel. Ribbing is applied over the black chenille body area only.
Body: Black chenille.
Hackle: Black hen hackle tied on as a collar and tied back.
Eyes: Gold bead chain.

This is a hybrid taken from ideas of many patterns that I have used successfully. I do believe though that Darwin Atkin had some influence over me with his marabou patterns, at least in naming the pattern. I first used this fly in 1974 and have since had the opportunity to use it in many areas where it has performed very well for me. It's a good winter pattern.

Black Gnat Bucktail

Hooks: AC80500BL, AC80501BL, TMC7999 or DAI2441, sizes 4-8.
Thread: Black.
Tail: Crimson red hackle barbs.
Body: Black chenille.
Hackle: Black tied on as a collar and tied back and down.
Wing: Coastal blacktail deer body hair tied over the body.
Head: Black.

A long used pattern originally taken from an old English wet fly pattern. If you take the time and review the patterns in this chapter, then return to the fly, you will no doubt recognize the similarities to many of these other patterns. Can we say that the Black Gnat was "seed" for a number of them?

Black Gordon

Hooks: AC80500BL, AC80501BL, TMC7999 or DAI2441, sizes 4-8.
Thread: Black.
Tip: Oval gold tinsel, two full turns.
Ribbing: Oval gold tinsel.
Body: Rear third, dubbed with #4 red lambs wool and front two-thirds, dubbed with #1 black lambs wool.
Hackle: Black tied on as a collar and tied back.
Wing: Dyed black squirrel tail tied over the body.
Topping: CH02 black Crystal Hair.
Head: Black.

This fly has been successful from Alaska to California. It was created by Oregon fly tier and guide Clarence Gordon while he was working at the North Umpqua's Steamboat Lodge.

Plate 6
Black Joe

Hooks: AC80500BL, AC80501BL, TMC7999 or DAI2441, sizes 4-8.
Thread: Black.
Tail: Black hackle barbs.
Body: Black chenille.
Wing: White calf tail tied over the body with a sparse overwing of white (clear) Miclon or Z-Lon.
Hackle: Grizzly tied on as a collar and tied back.
Head: Black.

Please note that the hackle is tied on after the wing. This pattern was originated by Mary and Everett Bundt of Arlington, Washington.

Black Knight

Hooks: AC80500BL, AC80501BL, TMC7999 or DAI2441, sizes 2-8.
Thread: Fluorescent red.
Tip: Dubbed with #50 fluorescent red lambs wool.

Body: CC02 black Crystal Chenille.
Wing: Black marabou tied over the body.
Topping: CH02 black Crystal Hair.
Hackle: Black hen hackle tied on as a collar and tied back.
Head: Fluorescent red.

I created this pattern in 1986 as an inquisitive venture in determining just how effective both Crystal Hair and Crystal Chenille would produce on the heavily pounded northern California streams. It has been a success and at last report Oregon is now also enjoying this fly.

Black Magic

Hooks: AC80500BL, AC80501BL, TMC7999 or DAI2441, sizes 4-8.
Thread: Black.
Tip: Oval silver tinsel.
Ribbing: Oval silver tinsel.
Body: Dubbed with #1 black African goat. Body should be nice and full and then picked out for that "shaggy" effect.
Wing: Dyed black squirrel tail tied over the body.
Head: Black.

Tony Petrella of Lansing, Michigan, spun this Black Magic. A variation of this fly is also tied in all brown with a fox squirrel tail wing.

Black O'Lindsay

Hooks: AC80500BL, AC80501BL, TMC7999 or DAI2441, sizes 2-8.
Thread: Black.
Tail: Dyed blue barred teal and brown hackle barbs mixed.
Ribbing: Oval gold tinsel.
Body: Dubbed with #51 fluorescent yellow Bunnytron.
Hackle: Brown tied on as a collar and tied back and down with dyed blue barred teal tied in at the throat.

Wings: Four or five peacock sword feather barbs with dyed blue barred teal sections and natural barred teal sections tied over the body.
Cheeks: J.C. or substitute.
Head: Black.

I acquired this pattern in Vancouver, British Columbia, in the summer of 1962. It has been real productive in California on the south fork of the Eel River.

Black Optic
Hook: DAI2451, sizes 1-4.
Thread: Black.
Body: Oval gold tinsel.
Hackle: Black tied on as a collar and tied back and down.
Wing: Black bucktail tied over the body.
Head: Black over 1/4" hollow brass bead.
Eyes: Yellow with a black center.

More than any of the other Jim Pray patterns, the Optics touch home for me. These are some of the primary flies that my father tied while under his tutorship. Jim mentioned many times how the locals loved these flies. Jim told my dad, "it's about time they started using something other than a dead chicken with a six ounce bell sinker tied around its neck."

Jim had a monopoly on these flies as he was the only one who knew where to buy the split brass beads for the heads. Not only was he able to get ten cents a fly, he could sell the raw beads for two for a penny and make a big profit. You have to remember that the 1930s spelled hard times and even a job paying a dollar or two a day was hard to come by.

The laborious task of producing these flies in sufficient quantities would often run all night. First the tying of the basic fly, followed by hand painting a primer coat on the head and allowing to dry. This was followed by dipping the head in black paint and allowing that to dry. Since the flies were processed in lots of a couple hundred at a time it would take almost three days before they were ready for the eyes.

The final day came and several hundred flies were taken from the drying racks, the hook eyes cleaned to remove excess paint, and the eyes were put on. This was a job that Jim reserved for himself, he had his own private little nails with heads ideally suited for the "Pray Optic" flies. Jim considered this to be his own little trade secret and tried to keep it closely guarded.

The Black Optic was also known as the "Pray Optic" because of the following that it had gained as the result of being the most tied fly. The basic black materials were easiest to obtain and maintain since anything could be dyed black. By the mid 1940s all of the Pray optic patterns were referred to as "Pray Optics" and never a differentiation made between patterns. By this time others in Eureka were trying to steal Jim's thunder and further complicated matters.

Other optic patterns in this chapter by Jim Pray include the Cock Robin, Red Optic and the Eel River Optic.

Plate 9 ### Black Prince
Hooks: AC80500BL, AC80501BL, TMC7999 or DAI2441, sizes 4-8.
Thread: Black.
Tail: Amherst pheasant crest.
Ribbing: Oval silver tinsel.

Body: Rear third, dubbed with #6 yellow Bunny-Blend and the front two-thirds, black chenille.
Hackle: Black tied on as a collar and tied back.
Wing: Dyed black squirrel tail tied over the body.
Topping: CH02 black Crystal Hair.
Head: Black.

Black Rat

Hooks: AC80500BL, AC80501BL, TMC7999 or DAI2441, sizes 4-8.
Thread: Black.
Tip: Oval silver tinsel.
Tail: Yellow hackle barbs.
Ribbing: Oval silver tinsel.
Body: Dubbed with #1 black African Angora goat.
Wing: Gray squirrel tail tied over the body. Use hair from the base of the tail.
Hackle: Grizzly tied on as a collar and tied back.
Head: Black.

Black and Silver

Hooks: AC80500BL, AC80501BL, TMC7999 or DAI2441, sizes 2-6.
Thread: Black.
Tip: Oval silver tinsel.
Tail: Golden pheasant crest.
Ribbing: Oval silver tinsel.
Body: Rear half, flat silver tinsel and the front half, dubbed with #1 black lambs wool.
Hackle: Guinea fowl tied on as a collar and tied back and down.
Wings: Bronze mallard sections tied over the body.
Topping: Golden pheasant crest.
Cheeks: J.C. or substitute.
Head: Black.

This pattern was originated by Judge Black of Lindsay, California. He used it in British Columbia for many years for Kamloops trout. Buz Buszek sent me a sample pattern and I have been using it successfully for steelhead since 1963.

Black Spook

Plate 7

Hooks: AC80500BL, AC80501BL, TMC7999 or DAI2441, sizes 4-8.
Thread: Black.
Tail: Dyed black squirrel tail.
Ribbing: Oval gold tinsel.
Body: Dubbed with #4 red lambs wool.
Hackle: Black tied on as a collar and tied back and down.
Wing: White calf tail tied over the body.
Head: Black.

I have no idea where I came across this pattern other than it must have been one my father was keeping as a sample. I have never fished it and have no knowledge of anyone else doing so. All I have are wild claims made by some of my father's friends.

Blood on the Water

Hooks: AC80500BL, AC80501BL, TMC7999 or DAI2441, sizes 1-6.
Thread: Red.
Tail: Dyed red golden pheasant tippet barbs.
Butt: Dubbed with #50 fluorescent red lambs wool.
Center Band: Flat silver tinsel.
Body: Front quarter, dubbed with #50 fluorescent red African Angora goat.
First Wing: Fluorescent red calf tail tied over the body.
First Hackle: Fluorescent red marabou tied on as a collar and tied back.
Second Wing: Red marabou tied over the body.
Second Hackle: Dyed red grizzly tied on as a collar and tied back.
Cheeks: J.C. or substitute.
Head: Red.

This is a pattern created by Washington steelheader and fly tier Jimmy Hunnicutt.

Bloody Butcher

Hooks: AC80500BL, AC80501BL, TMC7999 or DAI2441, sizes 2-6.
Thread: Black.
Tail: Crimson red hackle barbs.
Body: Dubbed with #13 gray Bunnytron.

Body Hackle: Yellow and crimson red tied palmer style over the body.
Wing: Gray squirrel tail tied over the body.
Head: Black.

The Bloody Butch originated as a wet fly in England in 1838 and you might say that it has been butchered ever since. This is a steelhead version which has been in use for more than 50 years.

Blue Charm

Hooks: AC80500BL, AC80501BL, TMC7999 or DAI2441, sizes 2-6.
Thread: Black.
Tip: Oval silver tinsel.
Tail: Golden pheasant crest.
Ribbing: Oval silver tinsel.
Body: Finely tapered with dubbed #1 black lambs wool.
Hackle: Dark blue tied on as a collar and tied back and down.
Wing: Dyed dark brown calf tail tied over the body.
Head: Black.

This is a steelhead variation of this pattern. See Chapter 21.

Blue Max

Hooks: AC80500BL, AC80501BL, TMC7999 or DAI2441, sizes 2-6.
Thread: Black.
Tip: Copper wire.
Ribbing: Copper wire.
Body: Rear half, dubbed with #10 orange stone lambs wool and the front half, black chenille.
Hackle: Light blue tied on as a collar and tied back and down.
Wing: Black calf tail tied over the body with an overwing of sparse orange calf tail.
Head: Black.

This pattern was created by Mark Melody.

Blue Muther

Hooks: AC80500BL, AC80501BL, TMC7999 or DAI2441, sizes 4-8.
Thread: Red.
Body: Wrapped with fine pearl braided Mylar piping.

Wing: Blue calf tail tied over the body with six strands of CH14 dark blue Crystal Hair mixed in and tied the length of hook.
Hackle: Purple tied on as a collar and tied back.
Head: Red.

This fly was created by another one of Michigan's top fly tiers and guides, Al Doll. This fly is very successful on the Little Manistee River.

Blue Sky

Hook: DAI2151, sizes 1-10.
Thread: Black.
Tip: Oval silver tinsel, two full turns only.
Ribbing: Oval silver tinsel.
Body: Dubbed with #35 kingfisher blue lambs wool.
Wings: Two dyed kingfisher blue hackle tips tied in a V over the body and curved outward.
Hackle: Dyed kingfisher blue tied on as a collar and tied back.
Head: Black.

This pattern was created by Stanley Young of Bellevue, Washington.

Blue Thunder

Hook: DAI2151, sizes 6-10.
Thread: Black.
Ribbing: Oval silver tinsel.
Body: Flat silver tinsel.
Wing: White bucktail tied over the body with an overwing of CH19 purple Crystal Hair.
Head: Black.

Canadian fly tier and guide Ian James from Guelph, Ontario, originated this fly.

Blueberg

Hooks: AC80500BL, AC80501BL, TMC7999 or DAI2441, sizes 4-8.
Thread: Tan.
Body: Blue diamond braid.
Wing: White calf tail tied over the body with an overwing of one barred mallard flank feather tip tied flat.
Hackle: Ginger tied on as a collar and tied back.
Head: Tan.

Created by John Kluesing from Baldwin, Michigan.

Bobbie Dunn

Hooks: AC80500BL, AC80501BL, TMC7999 or DAI2441, sizes 1-6.
Thread: Black.
Tail: Red calf tail.
Body: Copper wire.
Hackle: Scarlet red tied on as a collar and tied back and down.
Wing: White bucktail tied over the body with an overwing of red bucktail which is topped with a sparse bunch of dyed dark brown bucktail.
Head: Black.

Named for Robert F. "Bobbie" Dunn of Stockton, California. See Bellamy.

Bosquito

Hooks: AC80500BL, AC80501BL, TMC7999 or DAI2441, sizes 4-8.
Thread: Black.
Tail: Pair of scarlet red hackle tips tied on edge in a V.
Ribbing: Oval silver tinsel.
Body: Yellow chenille.
Hackle: Black tied on as a collar and tied back and down.
Wing: White calf tail tied over the body.
Head: Black.

I don't know when this pattern creeped into my covey of dependables. It has been there forever and has always proved itself on half-pounders on both the Klamath and Rogue Rivers.

Plate 8   ### Boss Fly (S)

Hook: AC80501BL, sizes 2/0-8.
Thread: Fluorescent orange.
Tail: Dyed black bucktail tied one and a half the length of the body.
Ribbing: Oval silver tinsel.
Body: Black chenille.

Hackle: Fluorescent fire orange tied on as a collar and tied back.
Eyes: Silver bead chain.

Grant King, former owner of King's Western Angler, Santa Rosa, California, popularized this fly. No one really knows where it originated. It has not only been a good steelhead fly, but through the years has accounted for many of the bigger salmon as well. I have been tying this same fly since 1969 using a black hackle and it is known to me and my friends as the "Black Boss." I am sure there are others who have done likewise.

Boss Fly, Crystal (S)

Hook: AC80501BL, sizes 2/0-8.
Thread: Fluorescent fire orange.
Tail: Dyed black bucktail with six strands of CH02 black Crystal Hair mixed in. Tail should be equal to one and a half times the length of the body.
Body: CC02 black Crystal Chenille.
Hackle: CH07 fire orange Crystal Hair spun on as a collar and tied back.
Eyes: Silver bead chain

My son Stan developed this variation of the Boss in 1986. He sent a sample to Grant King for his approval and the telephone didn't stop ringing for a couple of days. At that time we had only just developed Crystal Hair and Crystal Chenille and Grant wanted to know all about it. He reportedly claimed that he used it on everything but his cereal in the morning. We sincerely miss you, Grant.

Boss Fly, Purple (S)

Hook: AC80501BL, sizes 2/0-8.
Thread: Black.
Tail: Dyed black bucktail tied equal to one and a half the length of the body.
Ribbing: Oval silver tinsel.
Body: Dubbed with #30 purple Bunnytron.
Hackle: Purple tied on as a collar and tied back.

Eyes: Silver bead chain.

This variation is the brainchild of Andy Puyans from Walnut Creek, California. Upon publication of this book this fly will be exactly 30 years old. This fly has proven to be a good fly when the water is high and roiled.

Brad's Brat (S)

Hooks: AC80500BL, AC80501BL, TMC7999 or DAI2441, sizes 2-8.
Thread: Black.
Tail: White and orange bucktail mixed with three or four strand of CH01 pearl Crystal Hair mixed in.
Ribbing: Flat gold tinsel.
Body: Rear half, dubbed with #52 fluorescent orange Bunnytron and front half, dubbed with #50 fluorescent red Bunnytron.
Hackle: Brown tied on as a collar and tied back.
Wing: White bucktail tied over the body with an overwing of orange bucktail with five or six strands of CH01 pearl Crystal Hair mixed in.

Originated by Enos Bradner of Seattle, Washington, more than 50 years ago. It remains popular for both summer and winter-runs.

Brass Hat

Hooks: AC80500BL, AC80501BL, TMC7999 or DAI2441, sizes 1-6.
Thread: Black.
Tail: Yellow calf tail.
Body: Copper wire.
Center Wing: White bucktail.
Wing: Yellow bucktail tied over the body with a sparse bunch of black bucktail tied in on top.

The original pattern called for brass wire, hence the name. See Bellamy.

Bright Delight

Hook: AC80501BL, sizes 2/0-8.
Thread: White.
Tail: White calf tail tied long with strands of CH19 purple Crystal Hair tied on top.
Ribbing: Oval silver tinsel wrapped closely with six wraps.

Body: White chenille with a full, fat taper.
Hackle: White tied on as a collar and tied back, follow with purple.
Eyes: Silver bead chain.

This is a fly that dear old dad came up with and used intensely on Oregon's Rogue River for over twenty years. I have substituted Crystal Hair for the purple hackle barbs in the tail and I am sure he would have approved.

Bright Ember

Hooks: AC80500BL, AC80501BL, TMC7999 or DAI2441, sizes 2-8.
Thread: Fluorescent red.
Tail: Fluorescent orange marabou with a small bunch of fluorescent yellow marabou tied in on top.
Body: Copper wire.
First Wing: Fluorescent yellow marabou.
Second Wing: Fluorescent orange marabou.
Third Wing: Black marabou.
Hackle: Small bunch of black marabou tied in at the throat.
Cheeks: Small bunch of fluorescent fire orange marabou tied in at each side.
Head: Fluorescent red.

The Bright Ember was originated by California fly tier Darwin Atkin. His use of marabou and wire bodies in his flies is a winning combination. It is a pleasure to watch Darwin tie his flies, it has always amazed me to see such large men do such tedious work. His flies stand as masterpieces. Some of his other creations I have included in this chapter are the Chiquita, Daisy, Dark Ember, Pole-Kat, Streaker, and the Sun Burst.

Plate 7   Brindle Bug

Hooks: AC80500BL, AC80501BL, TMC7999 or DAI2441, sizes 2-8.
Thread: Black.
Tail: Brown hackle tips tied on edge in a V.
Body: Black and yellow variegated chenille.

Hackle: Brown tied on as a collar and tied back.
Head: Black.

Developed in 1960 by Lloyd Silvius of Eureka, California. After the Silver Hilton, this stands as one of the more productive flies for both the Trinity and Klamath Rivers.

Brown Drake

Hooks: TMC7989 or DAI2421, sizes 6-10.
Thread: Black.
Tail: Barred teal barbs.
Ribbing: Single strand of waxed black floss.
Body: Dubbed thin with #18 light olive lambs wool.
Hackle: Furnace tied on as a collar and tied back and down
Wing: Barred teal barbs tied over the body with an overwing of sparse natural brown bucktail.
Head: Black.

A long dependable fly for summer-runs in the Yuba River and for the fall half-pounds on the Trinity and Klamath Rivers.

Brown Legged Shrimp

See Chapter 17.

Brunch

Hooks: AC80500BL, AC80501BL, TMC7999 or DAI2441, sizes 2-4.
Thread: Black.
Tail: Purple bucktail mixed with CH19 purple Crystal Hair.
Body: Fluorescent pink chenille.
Body Hackle: Purple tied palmer style over the body. Tie your hackle in by the tip and wrap with concave side to the rear.
Hackle: Dyed black pheasant rump is tied on as a collar, two full turns, and tied back and slightly down.
Wing: Purple bucktail tied over the body.
Topping: CH19 purple Crystal Hair.
Head: Black.

It was one of those nights in the winter of 1970 filled with great expectations. Carl Glisson and I had planned to leave early the following morning for the Rogue River. Here it was almost midnight and neither of us felt sleepy, Carl announced "What the hell, let's get our butts out of here." I didn't need any prodding. We arrived on the Rogue before daylight—drank a gallon of coffee in the rain—and finally got on the river.

After about an hour I saw Carl wading out upriver from me and heading back to the truck. I thought little of it. A bladder full of coffee and cold water makes one want to shuck waders rather often. After about two hours I got the "hungers" and headed for the camper myself, all of the time wondering where in the hell Carl had ducked to. Upon opening the door of the little camper I observed this big lug hunched over, tying flies. He was quick to explain, "I didn't have time to get anything tied and I know you would have been pissed had I asked you for flies. You always are." Carl made due with what was available in the camper. Frankly, I had little confidence in his new creations and had fully planned on letting him suffer for awhile before giving him something good to fish with.

We ate an early lunch and were back out on the river well before noon. It was wet and cold but after wading in to my crotch and working some line that was all forgotten. It hadn't been five minutes when Carl had the first fish of the day on. Probably a seven pounder. All I could hear after he had released it was, "See, that damn thing works. It really works, but we'll see," and see we did. About fifteen minutes later he had another fish on. It completed a few tail exercises on top and was history. That day Carl got into more than a dozen fish and landed three. I batted zero. "Zero" may be a poor choice of words in that I gained knowledge of a new pattern that I knew would work when nothing else would. More than twenty years later this fly has been tried and tried again, always proving its worth wherever we have used it. You might have guessed why Carl named his new fly "Brunch."

With the exception of adding some Crystal Hair, this fly has not been altered from the original dressings in any fashion.

Bucktail Coachman

See Coachman.

Bunny Leech, Hot Blaze

Hook: TMC9394, sizes 2-6.
Thread: Fluorescent orange.
Tail: Strip of dyed fluorescent orange rabbit. Over this is tied six strands of CH06 orange Crystal Hair.
Body: Strip of dyed fluorescent orange rabbit wrapped forward.
Topping: Six strands of CH06 orange Crystal Hair.
Head: Fluorescent orange.

Bunny Leech, Hot Fire

Hook: TMC9394, sizes 2-6.
Thread: Fluorescent fire orange.
Tail: Strip of dyed fluorescent fire orange rabbit. Over this is tied six strands of CH07 fire orange Crystal Hair.
Body: Strip of dyed fluorescent fire orange rabbit wrapped forward.
Topping: Six strands of CH07 fire orange Crystal Hair.
Head: Fluorescent fire orange.

Bunny Leech, Hot Flame

Hook: TMC9394, sizes 2-6.
Thread: Fluorescent red.
Tail: Strip of dyed fluorescent orange rabbit. Over this is tied six strands of CH03 red Crystal Hair.
Body: Strip of dyed fluorescent orange rabbit wrapped forward with a fluorescent red collar of rabbit spun on at the front.

Topping: Six strands of CH03 red Crystal Hair.
Head: Fluorescent red.

Bunny Leech, Hot Pink

Hook: TMC9394, sizes 2-6.
Thread: Fluorescent red.
Tail: Strip of dyed fluorescent hot pink rabbit. Over this is tied six strands of CH08 pink Crystal Hair.
Body: Strip of dyed fluorescent hot pink rabbit wrapped forward with a fluorescent red collar of rabbit spun on at the front.
Topping: Six strands of CH08 pink Crystal Hair.
Head: Fluorescent red.

Bunny Leech, Hot Torch

Hook: TMC9394, sizes 2-6.
Thread: Fluorescent red.
Tail: Strip of dyed fluorescent red rabbit. Over this is tied six strands of CH03 red Crystal Hair.
Body: Strip of dyed black rabbit wrapped forward with a fluorescent red collar of rabbit spun on at the front.
Topping: Six strands of CH03 red Crystal Hair.
Head: Fluorescent red.

We have experimented with all of the greens and blues and all proved to be less than successful. See Chapter 15 for other Bunny Leech patterns which do well for steelhead also.

Burlap

Plate 6

Hooks: DAI2151 or DAI2161, sizes 2-8.
Thread: Black.
Tail: Coastal blacktail deer body hair tied heavy.
Body: First wrap an underbody of lead wire, then wrap natural burlap strands over to form a full fat body. Rough up the burlap with a sharp object to create a "shaggy" effect.

Hackle: Grizzly tied on as a collar and tied back.
Head: Black.

The idea of the Burlap started with Arnold Arana of Dunsmuir, California, about 1942. Both my father and Wayne "Buz" Buszek were on the Klamath that following year when Arnold gave them samples to try out. My father put his in his fly box and never thought much more about it, not exotic enough I guess. Buz on the other hand started getting ideas and the results are what you see above. By thickening the tail material it gave the fly more buoyancy at the other end for a change, so much that the lead wire was added to the front of the underbody to give the fly a "rocking horse" effect in the water. Buz went on to popularize the fly, but Arnold was always given full credit for its origination. Today I see sparsely dressed Burlaps and I wonder what the tiers are thinking about. Apparently they have not fished them in their original form. Sure sounds like Abe Snake is in there fixing things again, things that in my eyes aren't broken.

Plate 8   Bush Master
Hooks: TMC7989 or DAI2421, sizes 6-10.
Thread: Brown.
Tail: Nutria fur.
Ribbing: Grizzly tied over the body palmer style then clipped short and tapering down towards the rear of the body.
Body: Dubbed with #24 brown lambs wool.
Hackle: Grizzly tied on as a collar and tied back.
Wing: Nutria fur tied over the body.
Head: Brown.

This is a summer-run pattern.

Caldwell
Hooks: AC80500BL, AC80501BL, TMC7999 or DAI2441, sizes 2-6.
Thread: Fluorescent red.

Tip: Flat silver tinsel.
Tail: Fluorescent red hackle barbs.
Ribbing: Flat silver tinsel.
Body: Dubbed with #54 fluorescent hot pink lambs wool.
Hackle: Fluorescent red tied on as a collar and tied back and down.
Wing: Red bucktail with an overwing of white bucktail, equally proportioned, and tied over the body.
Head: Fluorescent red.

Originated by Louie Caldwell.

Canary
Hooks: AC80500BL, AC80501BL, TMC7999 or DAI2441, sizes 2-8.
Thread: Yellow.
Tail: Small bunch of brown marabou.
Ribbing: Flat gold tinsel bordered with oval silver tinsel.
Body: Dubbed with #6 yellow Bunny-Blend.
Hackle: Dyed yellow barred mallard tied in at the throat.
Wing: Yellow marabou with an equal portion of brown marabou tied over the top and extending the length of the body.
Topping: CH25 copper brown Crystal Hair.
Head: Yellow.

This pattern is tied in a range of sizes and is used as an all-season fly. Reduced by twenty percent, minus the tail, and tied in a size 8 it will bring up the wariest of fish in late summer.

Plate 8   Carbon
Hooks: AC80500BL, AC80501BL, TMC7999 or DAI2441, sizes 2-6.
Thread: Black.
Tip: Oval silver tinsel.
Tail: Black hackle barbs.
Butt: Black ostrich herl.
Ribbing: Oval silver tinsel.
Body: Dubbed with #1 black lambs wool.
Body Hackle: Black tied palmer style over the body.
Hackle: Black tied in at the front and tied back.
Wing: Black bucktail tied over the body.
Topping: Fluorescent fire orange calf tail extending two-thirds the length of the wing.
Head: Black.

This pattern in its original form had a fluorescent fire orange band of thread tied in at the rear of the head. I reserve this band for identification purposes only on those flies that I have weighted.

Carson

Hooks: AC80500BL, AC80501BL, TMC7999 or DAI2441, sizes 2-8.
Thread: Black
Tail: Golden pheasant tippet barbs.
Body: Peacock herl with a red floss center band.
Hackle: Brown tied on as a collar and tied back and down.
Wing: White bucktail tied over the body.
Topping: Red bucktail.
Cheeks: J.C. or substitute.
Head: Black.

This variation of the Royal Coachman can be attributed to Sumner Carson of Eureka, California, around 1900. His first flies had sections of married white and red quills and were later change about 1935 to hair wings. This was a period, strongly influenced by Jim Pray, that a number of patterns were going through this process. Hair wings had finally been excepted and I strongly believe it was because "Jim said so."

Plate 6 ### Carter's Dixie

Hooks: DAI2151 or DAI2161, sizes 2-8.
Thread: Black.
Tail: Salmon yellow calf tail.
Body: Oval gold tinsel.
Hackle: Scarlet red tied on as a collar and tied back and down.
Wing: White bucktail tied over the body.
Head: Black.

Jim Pray originated this fly in 1934 and later named it after Harley Carter, one of his clients and a friend from Berkeley, California.

Plate 6 ### Carter Fly

Hooks: AC80500BL, AC80501BL, TMC7999 or DAI2441, sizes 4-8.
Thread: Black.
Tail: Golden pheasant crest.
Ribbing: Oval silver tinsel.
Body: Red chenille.
Hackle: Scarlet red tied on as a collar and tied back and down.
Wing: Black bucktail tied over the body.
Head: Black.

This fly of unknown origin was popularized by Harley Carter.

Chappie

Hooks: TMC7989 or DAI2421, sizes 6-8.
Thread: Orange.
Tail: Grizzly hackle tips tied in a V with their concave side out.
Body: Dubbed #9 orange Bunny-Blend.
Wings: Grizzly hackle tips tied in a V. Position the wings so they ride high and their concave side is out.
Hackle: Grizzly tied on as a collar and tied back.
Head: Orange.

This fly is best used for summer-runs and should be tied reduced. Previously I have stated that this was a good bass and trout fly for me and maybe it should be tied as a streamer, this still holds true, however, in recent years it has become more productive for me when tied and used as suggested. It was originated about 1945 by C. L. Franklin of Los Angeles, California.

Chappie, Donnelly's

This is a Roy Donnelly variation of the fly above which has a yellow body and oval silver ribbing.

Plate 9 ### Chaveney

Hooks: AC80500BL, AC80501BL, TMC7999 or DAI2441, sizes 2-8.
Thread: Black.
Tail: Golden pheasant tippet barbs.

Ribbing: Oval silver tinsel.
Body: Dubbed with muskrat fur.
Hackle: Grizzly tied on as a collar and tied back and down.
Wing: Natural brown bucktail tied over the body.
Head: Black.

This was one of my father's favorites for the Rogue River which he records as being originated around 1945. His notes read, "summer only" and "small fish" which I interpret to mean "half-pounders in the fall."

 ### Chief

Hooks: AC80500BL, AC80501BL, TMC7999 or DAI2441, sizes 4-8.
Thread: Black.
Tail: Scarlet red hackle barbs.
Ribbing: Oval gold tinsel.
Body: Dubbed with raccoon fur.
Wing: Dyed black squirrel tail tied over the body and extending the length of the hook.
Hackle: Natural black hen hackle tied on as a collar and tied back.
Head: Black.

This is a pattern from the family file which found its peak in popularity in northern California around 1950. Even today I carry it with me and find that it is well suited for summer-run fish. I usually fish it in a size 8.

Chiquita

Hooks: AC80500BL, AC80501BL, TMC7999 or DAI2441, sizes 2-8.
Thread: Fluorescent red.
Tail: White marabou with a small bunch of fluorescent yellow marabou tied in on top.
Body: Copper wire.
Hackle: Small bunch of fluorescent yellow marabou tied in at throat.
Wing: Fluorescent yellow.
Cheeks: Short bunch of fluorescent fire orange marabou tied in at each side.
Topping: CH03 red Crystal Hair.
Head: Fluorescent red.

A Darwin Atkin pattern. See Bright Ember.

Chub

Hooks: AC80500BL, AC80501BL, TMC7999 or DAI2441, sizes 4-8.
Thread: Red.
Ribbing: Embossed silver tinsel.
Body: White yarn with a fluorescent red strip of yarn woven along the belly.
Hackle: White tied on as a collar and tied back and down.
Wing: White calf tail tied over the body.
Topping: CH03 red Crystal Hair.
Head: Red.

This fly was originated by Larry Hicks of Tacoma, Washington.

Clear Creek Special

Hooks: AC80500BL, AC80501BL, TMC7999 or DAI2441, sizes 2-8.
Thread: Black.
Tail: Yellow hackle barbs.
Ribbing: Flat gold tinsel.
Body: Rear third, yellow floss and center third, black floss and the front third red floss.
Hackle: Grizzly tied on as a collar and tied back.
Wing: Gray squirrel tail tied over the body.
Head: Black.

Perfected by Bill Kennerly of Happy Camp, California, for use on the Klamath River.

This particular fly has significant meaning to me although not directly connected with fishing of any sort. It was where Clear Creek flows into the Klamath that my mother was killed by a logging truck in February, 1942. In October, 1975 I made a journey up Clear Creek itself for the first time just out of curiosity, I had been by the mouth a thousand times and that morning for some unexplainable reason I had to see just where it was coming from. To my amazement I discovered a mini Grand Canyon with no reasonable access, but you could look down into clear pools carved out of stone and see fish. I spent a good part of that morning just watching their activity and wondering just how they might spawn on the gravelless bottom. It was here that the ashes of my mother had been scattered.

Plate 6 ### Cliff's Special
Hooks: AC80500BL, AC80501BL, TMC7999 or DAI2441, sizes 1-4.
Thread: Orange.
Tail: Scarlet red hackle barbs.
Ribbing: Embossed silver tinsel.
Body: Orange chenille.
Hackle: Orange tied on as a collar and tied back and down.
Wing: White calf tail tied over the body.
Head: Orange.

I was given this fly on Washington's not so famous Green River by an old gentleman from Auburn who prided himself on the fact that he had just passed his twenty year mark, a mark he had set for himself after retiring from the banking business in Seattle. His promise to himself was to fish twenty years straight without missing a day before he died. This old Harris Carpenter did and then some. This is a fly he fished more than half of this period. The original pattern used goose or turkey quill sections for the wings and tail.

Coachman
Hooks: AC80500BL, AC80501BL, TMC7999 or DAI2441, sizes 4-8.
Thread: Black.
Tip: Embossed gold tinsel.
Body: Peacock herl. For a nice fat body, wrap an underbody of olive yarn. Reverse wrap the body with fine gold wire.
Hackle: Brown tied on as a collar and tied back and down.
Wing: White calf tail tied over the body.
Head: Black.

This fly has always been high on the list for all fly fishermen and has probably accounted for more trout and steelhead than any other fly today.

Coachman, Donnelly's
Hooks: AC80500BL, AC80501BL, TMC7999 or DAI2441, sizes 4-6.
Thread: Black.
Tip: Orange floss.
Tail: Crimson red hackle barbs.
Body: Peacock with a red floss center band. Reverse wrap the body with fine gold wire.
Hackle: Orange tied on as a collar and tied back and down.
Wing: A small bunch of yellow bucktail tied over the body with an overwing of white bucktail.
Head: Black.

Another of the Roy Donnelly variations.

Plate 9 ### Coal Car
Hooks: AC80500BL, AC80501BL, TMC7999 or DAI2441, sizes 2-6.
Thread: Black.
Tail: Black hen hackle barbs.
Ribbing: Oval silver tinsel.
Body: Rear first quarter, #53 fluorescent fire orange lambs wool, second quarter, #50 fluorescent red lambs wool and front half black chenille.
Hackle: Black hen hackle tied on as a collar and tied back.
Wing: Dyed black squirrel tail mixed and tied in over the body.
Head: Black.

Originated by Randall Kaufmann of Portland, Oregon.

Coal Car
Hooks: AC80500BL, AC80501BL, TMC7999 or DAI2441, sizes 2/0-6.
Tip: Lower half, flat silver tinsel and the upper half, fluorescent fire orange floss.
Tail: Black marabou.
Ribbing: Flat silver tinsel.
Body: Dubbed thin with #1 black lambs wool.

First Wing: CH02 black Crystal Hair tied over the body with an overwing of black marabou.
First Hackle: Black tied in at the throat.
Second Wing: Black marabou tied over the body with an overwing of more black marabou.
Second Hackle: Black tied on as a collar and tied back.
Head: Black.

This is Trey Combs' variation of the Coal Car dressed in marabou.

Cock Robin
Hook: DAI2451, sizes 1-4.
Thread: Black
Body: Oval silver tinsel.
Hackle: Orange tied on as a collar and tied back and down.
Wing: Badger hair.
Head: Black over 1/4" hollow brass bead.
Eyes: Yellow with a black center.

Another of the Jim Pray patterns. See Black Optic.

Columbia River Special
Hooks: AC80500BL, AC80501BL, TMC7999 or DAI2441, sizes 2-6.
Thread: Black.
Tip: Flat silver tinsel.
Tail: Crimson red hackle barbs.
Ribbing: Flat silver tinsel.
Body: Dubbed with #4 red lambs wool.
Hackle: Crimson red tied on as a collar and tied back and down.
Wing: White bucktail tied over the body.
Head: Black.

Originated by Frank Headrick around 1950.

 ## Comet
Hook: AC80501BL, sizes 2/0-8.
Thread: Fluorescent fire orange.
Tail: Fluorescent fire orange bucktail tied equal to one and one half the length of the body.
Body: Oval silver tinsel over and underbody of white floss or yarn.
Hackle: Fluorescent fire orange tied on as a collar and tied back.
Eyes: Silver bead chain.

The original design of this fly did not have the bead chain eyes. The eyes were added later starting a new era in the development of steelhead flies. Both the Comet and Boss series of flies were offspring of this idea. This pattern was originated by Lloyd Silvius and a host of others from Eureka, California. These flies were generally known as the "pop-eyed" patterns up until the early 1960s when the term "Russian River" flies was coined.

Lloyd you could say filled the gap that Jim Pray left behind in northern California. It would take a very unique person to fill the shoes of either of these men. Lloyd's little shop in Eureka at one time held the record for selling the most shooting heads on the West Coast for the Cortland Line Company. Obviously, he believed in them.

Comet, Cole's
Hook: AC80501BL, sizes 2/0-8.
Thread: Orange.
Tail: Orange calf tail tied equal to one and one half the length of the body.
Body: Oval gold tinsel. Wrap an underbody of yellow floss to give the body a tapered fullness.
Hackle: Fluorescent yellow and fluorescent fire orange tied on as a collar and tied back mixed.
Eyes: Brass bead chain.

Comet, Crystal
Hook: AC80501BL, sizes 2/0-8.
Thread: Fluorescent fire orange.
Tail: Fluorescent fire orange bucktail with four or five strands of CH07 fire orange Crystal Hair mixed. Tie the tail equal to one and one half times the length of the body.
Body: Oval silver tinsel.
Hackle: A sparse collar of CH06 orange Crystal Hair spun on, followed by fluorescent fire orange hackle tied on as a collar and tied back.
Eyes: Silver bead chain.

I came up with this variation after the development of Crystal Hair. The Comet was a natural for this evolutionary upgrade.

Comet, Crystal Black
Hook: AC80501BL, sizes 2/0-8.
Thread: Black.
Tail: Natural black hen hackle barbs.
Ribbing: Fine silver wire.
Shellback: CH01 pearl Crystal Hair pulled over the back of the entire body.
Body: Dubbed with #1 black Bunny-Blend.
Hackle: Black tied on as a collar and tied back.
Eyes: Silver bead chain.

This is another one of the many Comet variations. It was created by Al Doll of Lansing, Michigan. I have made a modification in the ribbing on this pattern by substituting fine silver wire for added durability. See Bear's Flashback.

Comet, Gary's Crystal
Hook: AC80501BL, sizes 2/0-8.
Thread: Fluorescent fire orange.
Tail: Fluorescent fire orange bucktail tied equal to one and one half the length of the body.
Butt: Band of fluorescent fire orange tying thread or floss.
Body: Rear third, flat silver tinsel and front two-thirds, extra large CC07 fire orange Crystal Chenille.
Hackle: Fluorescent fire orange tied on as a collar and tied back.
Eyes: Silver bead chain.

Developed by commercial fly tier Gary Selig of Mertztown, Pennsylvania.

Comet, Gold (S)
Hook: AC80501BL, sizes 2/0-8.
Thread: Yellow.
Tail: Fluorescent fire orange bucktail tied equal to one and one half the length of the body.
Body: Embossed gold tinsel.

Hackle: Fluorescent yellow and fluorescent fire orange mixed and wrapped on as a collar and tied back.
Eyes: Silver bead chain.

Comet, Orange (S)
Hook: AC80501BL, sizes 2/0-8.
Thread: White.
Tail: Fluorescent orange bucktail tied equal to one and one half the length of the body.
Body: Oval silver tinsel.
Hackle: Fluorescent orange tied on as a collar and tied back.
Eyes: Silver bead chain.

Comet, P. M.
Hook: AC80501BL, sizes 2/0-8.
Thread: Fluorescent red.
Tail: White calf tail tied equal to the length of the body.
Body: Oval silver tinsel. When wrapping the body make a few turns under the tail.
Hackle: Fluorescent hot pink and white mixed and wrapped on as a collar and tied back.
Eyes: Silver bead chain.

When I first got this pattern it was tied on a nickel silver short shank bait hook with a turned up eye. After pondering this for a time, I got to experimenting and have made the hook change to suit my type of fishing. This fly was originated by Paul Goodman and John Maxi of Farmington, Michigan, for use on the Pere Marquette River.

Comet, Prichard's (S)
Hooks: AC80500BL, AC80501BL, TMC7999 or DAI2441, sizes 2-6.
Thread: Red.
Tail: Fluorescent fire orange bucktail.
Body: Oval silver tinsel.
Hackle: Yellow and scarlet red mixed and tied on as a collar and tied back.
Head: Red.

Developed by Al Prichard. Also see Prichard's Rocket.

Comet, Purple (S)

A variation also designed by Andy Puyans. Same as the Purple Boss except the body is of oval silver tinsel.

Comet, Silver (S)

Hook: AC80501BL, sizes 2/0-8.
Thread: White.
Tail: Fluorescent orange bucktail tied equal to one and one half the length of the body.
Body: Embossed silver tinsel.
Hackle: Fluorescent orange tied on as a collar and tied back.
Eyes: Silver bead chain.

It would be extremely difficult to give credit, or blame, to the originator of any specific comet pattern other than those indicated. This bead chain idea started in the early 1940s and by the 1950s caught on strongly and there has been a repeated number of flies that have had bead chain eyes added which christened them as "Comets" in the minds of most. Also see Norton's Special.

Conway Special

Hooks: AC80500BL, AC80501BL, TMC7999 or DAI2441, sizes 4-8.
Thread: Red.
Tip: Oval gold tinsel.
Tail: Crimson red and white hackle barbs mixed.
Ribbing: Oval gold tinsel.
Body: Dubbed with #6 yellow lambs wool.
Body Hackle: Yellow tied palmer style over the body.
Hackle: Yellow and crimson red hackle tied on as a collar mixed and tied back.
Wing: White bucktail tied over the body.
Topping: Small bunch of red bucktail.
Head: Red.

Originated in 1934 by Dan Conway of Seattle, Washington. At the time this one-armed commercial tier created this fly he had a peacock head and white quill wings with married narrow red strips incorporated in the pattern.

Plate 6 Copper Demon Plate 9

Hooks: AC80500BL, AC80501BL, TMC7999, DAI2441, sizes 2-6.
Thread: Orange.
Tail: Small bunch of fluorescent fire orange marabou.
Body: Oval copper tinsel over an underbody of light brown floss or yarn.
Hackle: Fluorescent orange tied on as a collar and tied back.
Wing: Fluorescent orange calf tail tied over the body.
Head: Orange.

I cannot say too much for this pattern. When tied in a wide range of sizes and fished religiously throughout the winter, as many do, it produces fish after fish.

Coquihalla Orange

Hooks: AC80500BL, AC80501BL, TMC7999 or DAI2441, sizes 2-6.
Thread: Orange.
Tip: Lower half, oval gold tinsel and the upper half, orange floss.
Tail: Golden pheasant crest.
Butt: Black ostrich herl.
Ribbing: Oval silver tinsel.
Body: Rear half, orange floss and the front half, dubbed with #52 fluorescent orange African Angora goat. Dubbing should be picked out and made "shaggy."
Hackle: Orange tied on as a collar and tied back and down.
Wing: Orange calf tail tied over the body with an overwing of white calf tail.
Head: Orange.

Coquihalla Orange, Dark

Hooks: AC80500BL, AC80501BL, TMC7999 or DAI2441, sizes 2-6.
Thread: Orange.
Tip: Oval silver tinsel.
Tail: Golden pheasant crest. An additional pair of short orange hackle tips are tied on edge at each side of the crest feather.
Butt: Black ostrich herl.

Ribbing: Flat silver tinsel overwrapped with a narrower oval silver tinsel.
Body: Rear half, orange floss and the front half, dubbed with #52 fluorescent orange African Angora goat. Dubbing should be picked out and made "shaggy."
Wing: Sparse orange calf tail tied over the body with narrow strips of bronze mallard tied along the base and parallel to the wing.
Topping: Golden pheasant crest.
Cheeks: J.C. or substitute.
Head: Orange.

Coquihalla Red

Hooks: AC80500BL, AC80501BL, TMC7999 or DAI2441, sizes 2-6.
Thread: Black.
Tip: Oval silver tinsel.
Tail: Short scarlet red hackle tip.
Butt: Black ostrich herl.
Ribbing: Oval silver tinsel.
Body: Rear half, orange floss and the front half, dubbed with #50 fluorescent red African Angora goat. Dubbing should be picked out and made "shaggy."
Hackle: Scarlet red tied on as a collar and tied back and down.
Wing: Peacock sword feather barbs tied over the body with barred mallard barbs tied on top.
Head: Black.

Plate 6   Coquihalla Silver

Hooks: AC80500BL, AC80501BL, TMC7999 or DAI2441, sizes 2-6.
Thread: Black.
Tail: Golden pheasant tippet barbs.
Butt: Dubbed with #4 red lambs wool.
Ribbing: Oval silver tinsel.
Body: Flat silver tinsel.
Hackle: Scarlet red tied on as a collar and tied back and down.
Wing: White calf tail tied over the body with an overwing of orange calf tail.
Head: Black.

The Coquihalla series was named after one of Tommy Brayshaw's favored streams in British Columbia. His skillful designs not only express his artistic talents, but reflect his practical side as well.

Crick

Hooks: AC80500BL, AC80501BL, TMC7999 or DAI2441, sizes 2-6.
Thread: Black.
Tail: Black calf tail.
Body: Rear third, fluorescent pink chenille and the front two-thirds, black chenille.
Hackle: Dyed black calf tail tied in at the throat and kept sparse.
Wing: White calf tail tied over the body with an overwing of black calf tail mixed with CH02 black Crystal Hair.
Head: Black.

Originated by George Richey of Honor, Michigan, in the 1970s.

Crystal Shrimp

See Chapter 17.

Crystal Woolly Bugger (s)

See Chapter 15.

Crystal Woolly Worm

See Chapter 8.

Cuenin's Advice

Hooks: AC80500BL, AC80501BL, TMC7999 or DAI2441, sizes 4-8.
Thread: Black.
Tip: Flat silver tinsel.
Tail: Orange hackle barbs.
Body: Oval silver tinsel wrapped over a tapered underbody of white floss.
Wing: Natural brown bucktail tied over the body.
Head: Black.

Originated in 1933 by J. P. Cuenin of San Francisco, California.

Cummings

This pattern is tied same as the Cummings Special except it is without cheeks.

Cummings Special

Hooks: AC80500BL, AC80501BL, TMC7999 or DAI2441, sizes 4-8.
Thread: Black.
Ribbing: Oval silver tinsel.
Body: Rear third, yellow floss and front two-thirds dubbed with #32 claret Bunny-Blend.
Hackle: Claret tied on as a collar and tied back.
Wing: Natural brown bucktail tied over the body.
Cheeks: J.C. or substitute.
Head: Black.

This pattern was developed in the 1930s by Ward Cummings and Clarence Gordon for the Umpqua River in Oregon. It is still a favorite of many along the West Coast.

Curt's Special

Hooks: AC80500BL, AC80501BL, TMC7999 or DAI2441, sizes 4-8.
Thread: Black.
Tail: Yellow hackle barbs.
Butt: Dark orange chenille.
Body: Embossed silver tinsel.
Hackle: Orange tied on as a collar and tied back and down.
Wing: Natural brown bucktail tied over the body.
Head: Black.

I am not certain where this pattern originated. I suspect that it must have been on the Rogue River as some of the descriptions I have read of the wing indicate an upright and divided wing.

Cutthroat

Hooks: AC80500BL, AC80501BL, TMC7999 or DAI2441, sizes 4-8.
Thread: Black.

Tail: Black hackle barbs.
Body: Dubbed with #32 claret Bunnytron.
Hackle: Black tied on as a collar and tied back and down.
Wing: White bucktail tied over the body.
Head: Black.

Cutthroat, Red

Same as Cutthroat with the exception of the body which is #4 red Bunnytron.

Cutthroat, Yellow

Hooks: AC80500BL, AC80501BL, TMC7999 or DAI2441, sizes 4-8.
Thread: Red.
Tail: Scarlet red hackle barbs.
Body: Dubbed with #6 yellow lambs wool.
Body Hackle: Yellow tied palmer style over the body.
Hackle: Scarlet red tied in as a collar and tied back.
Wing: White bucktail tied over the body.
Head: Red.

Cutthroat No. 2

Hooks: AC80500BL, AC80501BL, TMC7999 or DAI2441, sizes 4-8.
Thread: Red.
Tip: Oval silver tinsel.
Tail: Scarlet red hackle barbs.
Ribbing: Oval silver tinsel.
Body: Dubbed with #6 yellow lambs wool.
Hackle: Scarlet red tied on as a collar and tied back and down.
Wing: Red bucktail tied over the body with an overwing of white bucktail.
Head: Red.

While visiting with Ted Bentz, of the former Bentz Fly and Tackle in Tacoma, Washington, during the 1960s he was kind enough to show me what some of the many Cutthroat patterns consisted of. He supplied many of these patterns for Alaska tied in sizes 2/0. His unique little operation also shipped Mosquitoes and Black Gnats in a size 12 by the thousands. He claimed that he could never get enough flies to satisfy the large demand.

In the Puget Sound area just about everyone has a Cutthroat pattern and few are the same. Although originally tied for sea-run cutthroats many have been adapted for steelhead use in the larger sizes.

Daisy

Hooks: AC80500BL, AC80501BL, TMC7999 or DAI2441, sizes 2-8.
Thread: Fluorescent red.
Tail: White marabou with a small bunch of fluorescent yellow tied in on top.
Body: Gold diamond braid.
Hackle: Small bunch of fluorescent yellow marabou tied in at throat.
Wing: White marabou tied over the body with a small bunch of fluorescent yellow marabou tied in on top.
Cheeks: Short bunch of fluorescent fire orange marabou tied in at each side.
Topping: CH04 yellow Crystal Hair.
Head: Fluorescent red.

Dark Ember

Hooks: AC80500BL, AC80501BL, TMC7999 or DAI2441, sizes 2-8.
Thread: Fluorescent red.
Tail: Small bunch of fluorescent orange marabou with CH07 fire orange Crystal Hair mixed.
Body: Copper wire.
Hackle: Small bunch of black marabou tied in at throat.
Wing: Fluorescent orange marabou tied over the body with an equal portion of black marabou tied on top. Then a small final overwing of fluorescent orange marabou is tied on the top.
Cheeks: Short bunch of fluorescent fire orange marabou tied in at each side.
Topping: CH02 black Crystal Hair.
Head: Fluorescent red.

The two preceding patterns were originated by Darwin Atkin pattern. See Bright Ember.

Dave's Favorite

Hooks: AC80500BL, AC80501BL, TMC7999 or DAI2441, sizes 4-8.

Thread: Fluorescent fire orange.
Tail: Salmon yellow calf tail.
Body: Fluorescent orange chenille.
Hackle: Salmon yellow calf tail tied in at throat.
Wing: Red calf tail tied over the body with an overwing of salmon yellow calf tail.
Head: Fluorescent fire orange.

Developed in 1967 by George Richey of Honor, Michigan. Named after his fishing companion, his brother Dave.

Dead Chicken

Hooks: AC80500BL, AC80501BL, TMC7999 or DAI2441, sizes 2-6.
Thread: Black.
Tail: Scarlet red hackle barbs.
Ribbing: Flat silver tinsel.
Body: Yellow chenille.
Hackle: Grizzly hen hackle tied on as a collar and tied back.
Head: Black.

This is a pattern sent to me by Robert Shallenberger of Klamath Falls, Oregon. He says it is the one fly he uses on a regular basis on the Rogue River and is his top producer.

Plate 8 Dean River Lantern, Green

Hooks: AC80500BL, AC80501BL, TMC7999 or DAI2441, sizes 2-8.
Thread: Fluorescent green.
Tail: Dyed black squirrel tail tied equal the length of body.
Body: Dyed bright green flat monofilament wrapped over an underbody of fluorescent green floss.
Hackle: Black tied on as a collar and tied back.
Head: Fluorescent green.

Dean River Lantern, Orange

Hooks: AC80500BL, AC80501BL, TMC7999 or DAI2441, sizes 2-8.
Thread: Fluorescent fire orange.
Tail: Dyed black squirrel tail tied equal the length of body.
Body: Dyed orange flat monofilament wrapped over and underbody of fluorescent orange floss.

Hackle: Dyed fluorescent fire orange grizzly tied on as a collar and tied back.
Head: Fluorescent fire orange.

Dean River Lantern, Purple
Hooks: AC80500BL, AC80501BL, TMC7999 or DAI2441, sizes 2-8.
Thread: Black.
Tail: Dyed black squirrel tail tied equal the length of body.
Body: Dyed purple flat monofilament wrapped over an underbody of blue floss.
Hackle: Dyed purple grizzly tied on as a collar and tied back.
Head: Black.

Dean River Lantern, Red
Hooks: AC80500BL, AC80501BL, TMC7999 or DAI2441, sizes 2-8.
Thread: Fluorescent red.
Tail: Dyed black squirrel tail tied equal the length of body.
Body: Dyed red flat monofilament wrapped over an underbody of fluorescent red floss.
Hackle: Fluorescent red tied on as a collar and tied back.
Head: Fluorescent red.

Dean River Lantern, Yellow
Hooks: AC80500BL, AC80501BL, TMC7999 or DAI2441, sizes 2-8.
Thread: Fluorescent yellow.
Tail: Dyed yellow gray squirrel tail tied equal the length of body.
Body: Dyed yellow flat monofilament wrapped over an underbody of white floss.
Hackle: Dyed fluorescent yellow grizzly tied on as a collar and tied back.
Head: Fluorescent yellow.

Developed by Dr. Arthur Cohen of San Francisco, California, for the Dean River in British Columbia. Since that time there have been a number of variations developed. There was also an orange pattern which used orange bow string for the body.

Dean River Special
Hooks: AC80500BL, AC80501BL, TMC7999 or DAI2441, sizes 2-8.
Thread: Black.
Tail: CH14 dark blue Crystal Hair.

Body: Dubbed with #19 purple Fly Brite.
Wing: Black marabou tied over the body.
Topping: CH14 dark blue Crystal Hair.
Hackle: Black hen saddle tied on as a collar and tied back.
Head: Black.

Every good river has its own specials. Of the many Dean River Specials I have had experience with, this is by far the best I have found. Don't let the name fool you as it is more than just a B.C. pattern. It has taken fish from northern California to Alaska. We are still waiting on reports from Michigan.

Deer Creek
Hooks: AC80500BL, AC80501BL, TMC7999 or DAI2441, sizes 2/0-4.
Thread: Black.
Tail: Scarlet red hackle barbs.
Ribbing: Oval silver tinsel.
Body: Flat silver tinsel.
Wing: Purple marabou.
Hackle: Purple marabou tied in at the throat with silver doctor blue hackle tied on as a collar and tied back.
Head: Black.

Created by Bob Arnold of Seattle, Washington for winter-run steelhead. This fly is intended to be used in larger sizes to get the attention of fish holding deep.

Del Cooper
Hooks: AC80500BL, AC80501BL, TMC7999 or DAI2441, sizes 4-6.
Thread: Black.
Tip: Flat silver tinsel.
Tail: Scarlet red hackle barbs.
Ribbing: Flat silver tinsel.
Body: Dubbed with #30 purple lambs wool.
Hackle: Scarlet red tied on as a collar and tied back.
Wing: White bucktail tied over the body.
Head: Black.

Developed by Mike Kennedy of Lake Oswego, Oregon.

Plate 9　　Dependable
Hook: AC80500BL, AC80501BL, TMC7999 or DAI2441, sizes 2-6.
Thread: Orange.
Tip: Flat silver tinsel.
Tail: Orange hackle barbs.
Ribbing: Oval silver tinsel.
Body: Rear third, dubbed with #9 orange Bunny-Blend and front two-thirds, dubbed with #1 black Bunny-Blend.
Hackle: Dyed black pheasant rump tied in at the front as a collar and tied back followed with barred teal flank tied in front.
Wing: White calf tail tied over the body with an over wing of orange calf tail.
Head: Orange.

This fly was created by Henry Simpson of Menlo Park, California. While Henry originally intended this fly for use in Oregon, he has found it very effective since he moved to California in 1982. This pattern is normally tied in larger sizes and weighted.

Deschutes Demon
Hooks: AC80500BL, AC80501BL, TMC7999 or DAI2441, sizes 2-6.
Thread: Black.
Tail: Fluorescent fire orange hackle barbs.
Ribbing: Embossed gold tinsel.
Body: Dubbed with #23 golden stone lambs wool.
Hackle: Fluorescent fire orange tied on as a collar and tied back and down.
Wing: Deer body hair with a white bucktail overwing tied over the body.
Head: Black.

Designed by Don and Lola McClain of Portland, Oregon.

Deschutes Madness
Hooks: AC80500BL, AC80501BL, TMC7999 or DAI2441, sizes 4-6.
Thread: Fluorescent red.
Tip: Flat gold tinsel.
Butt: Fluorescent red floss.
Tag: Fluorescent red floss.
Ribbing: CC19 purple Crystal Chenille.
Body: Fluorescent red floss.

Hackle: Purple tied on as a collar and tied back.
Wing: Purple calf tail tied over the body.
Topping: CH01 pearl Crystal Hair.
Head: Fluorescent red.

This pattern, as I understand it, is the result of a number of fly tiers experimenting with Crystal Chenille in their development of patterns for the Deschutes River in Oregon. After a number of variations were attempted, this is the fly they felt most confident with.

Plate 7　　Deschutes Skunk
Hooks: AC80500BL, AC80501BL, TMC7999 or DAI2441, sizes 2-6.
Thread: Black.
Tail: Scarlet red hackle barbs.
Ribbing: Embossed silver tinsel.
Body: Dubbed with #1 black lambs wool.
Hackle: Black hen hackle tied on as a collar and tied back and down.
Wing: Deer body hair with a white bucktail overwing tied over the body.
Head: Black.

Another pattern designed by Don and Lola McClain of Portland, Oregon.

Deschutes Special
Hooks: AC80500BL, AC80501BL, TMC7999 or DAI2441, sizes 2-6.
Thread: Black.
Tail: Scarlet red hackle barbs.
Ribbing: Oval silver tinsel.
Body: Dubbed with #57 fluorescent chartreuse lambs wool.
Hackle: Blue dun hen hackle tied on as a collar and tied back and down.
Wing: Gray squirrel tail tied over the body.
Head: Black.

Originated by Mike Kennedy.

Dillon Creek Special

Hooks: AC80500BL, AC80501BL, TMC7999 or DAI2441, sizes 4-8.
Thread: Fluorescent red.
Tail: Guinea fowl barbs.
Butt: Fluorescent red chenille.
Ribbing: Oval silver tinsel.
Body: Black chenille.
Wings: Golden badger hackle tips tied cocked upward in a V over the body with concave side out.
Hackle: Guinea fowl tied on as a collar and tied back.
Head: Fluorescent red.

This pattern was originated in 1989 by Austin McWithey of Happy Camp, California.

Dingbat

Hooks: TMC7989 or DAI2421, sizes 6-10.
Thread: Black.
Tip: Oval silver tinsel.
Tail: Golden pheasant tippet barbs.
Ribbing: Oval silver tinsel.
Body: Fluorescent orange chenille.
Hackle: Furnace tied on as a collar and tied back.
Wing: Fox squirrel tail tied over the body.
Head: Black.

Originated by Mike Kennedy and should be dressed sparse. This is a popular pattern for the Rogue River half-pounders when using a floating line.

Doll's Steelhead Spruce

Hooks: AC80500BL, AC80501BL, TMC7999 or DAI2441, sizes 4-8.
Thread: Black.
Body: Dubbed with #4 red lambs wool.
Wings: Badger hackle tips tied in a V over the body with concave side out. A second wing of black marabou is tied on top reaching only half of the first wing length.
Hackle: Badger tied on as a collar and tied back.
Head: Black.

This is a Michigan variation of the Spruce. It is one of many patterns created by Al Doll of Lansing. See Spruce.

Donnelly's Partridge

Hooks: AC80500BL, AC80501BL, TMC7999 or DAI2441, sizes 8-10.
Thread: Black.
Tail: Golden pheasant tippet barbs.
Ribbing: Embossed gold tinsel.
Body: Dubbed with #6 yellow lambs wool.
Body Hackle: Brown partridge tied palmer style over the body.
Wings: Brown partridge hackle tips tied over the body.
Head: Black.

This is a creation of Roy Donnelly of San Pedro, California. He also tied this pattern with an olive body. Another variation of this pattern which has become popular more recently has the hackle tied on as a collar and tied back with a natural brown bucktail wing. Roy was one of northern California's pioneer steelheaders and was found seasonally on the Klamath River. He was also an addicted dry fly fisherman. See Donnelly's Variant, Chapter 16.

Double Flame Egg

See Babine Special Two. There are a number of variations on this style with a number of names. A novice tier can spend many enjoyable evenings experimenting with their own designs.

Doc Spratley

Hooks: TMC7989 or DAI2421, sizes 4-10.
Thread: Black.
Tail: Barred mallard barbs.
Ribbing: Oval silver tinsel.
Body: Dubbed with black lambs wool.
Hackle: Grizzly tied on as a collar and tied back and down.
Wing: Bunch of ringneck pheasant center tail barbs.
Head: Black.

Occasionally you will see this pattern tied with a peacock head. It was originated for British Columbia by Dick Prankard of Mt. Vernon, Washington. I got my first taste of fishing with the Doc Spratley on northern Washington's Ross Lake. The fishing was good and the fly worked every day for the week we were there. I left with the thought "that's one hell of a good wet fly I have found." It was only in later years I realized it was originally tied for steelhead as well as a caddis imitation. It is now considered one of the better summer-run flies. The Doc Spratley still comes out however when I hit a lake that is untried.

Drain's 20

Hooks: AC80500BL, AC80501BL, TMC7999 or DAI2441, sizes 2-6.
Thread: Black.
Tip: Flat silver tinsel.
Tail: Golden pheasant tippet barbs tie short.
Butt: Fluorescent yellow floss.
Ribbing: Flat silver tinsel.
Body: Dubbed with #50 fluorescent red lambs wool.
Hackle: Purple tied on as a collar and tied back and down.
Wing: Dyed red pheasant rump barbs tied the length of the body. Then an overwing of gray squirrel tail.
Head: Black.

Designed by Wes Drain of Seattle, Washington. He named this pattern after taking a fish over 20 pounds on the Skagit River which set a Washington state record. This fly is normally tied reduced.

Durham Ranger

Hooks: AC80500BL, AC80501BL, TMC7999 or DAI2441, sizes 2-6.
Thread: Black.
Tail: Golden pheasant tippet barbs.
Butt: Peacock herl.
Ribbing: Oval gold tinsel.
Body: Dubbed with #4 red lambs wool.
Hackle: Scarlet red tied on as a collar and tied back and down.
Wings: Golden pheasant tippet feathers tied on edge over the body.
Cheeks: J.C. or substitute.

Head: Black.

This is a popular steelhead variation of an Atlantic salmon pattern. See Chapter 21 for another good hairwing version of this fly.

Plate 8 — Dusk

Hooks: AC80500BL, AC80501BL, TMC7999 or DAI2441, sizes 2-6.
Thread: Red.
Tip: Oval silver tinsel.
Tail: Golden pheasant tippet barbs.
Ribbing: Flat silver tinsel, reversed.
Body: Red and white chenille. The white chenille is wrapped first, then the red chenille is overwrapped so it is the predominant color yet allowing much of the white to show through.
Hackle: White tied on as a collar and tied back with one full turn of scarlet red tied in front. Keep hackle sparse.
Wing: Bunch of barred mallard barbs tied over the body.
Head: Red.

A British Columbia pattern by Tommy Brayshaw.

Plate 8 — Dusty Miller

Hooks: AC80500BL, AC80501BL, TMC7999 or DAI2441, sizes 4-8.
Thread: Black.
Tail: Amherst pheasant crest.
Body: Embossed silver tinsel wrapped over a tapered underbody of white floss.
Hackle: Dyed brown guinea fowl tied on as a collar and tied back.
Wing: Brown calf tail tied over the body.
Head: Black.

This is a steelhead pattern adapted from an Atlantic salmon fly. There are a number of variations which crop up now and again, this particular one has been around considerably longer than I have.

Eel Beauty

Hooks: AC80500BL, AC80501BL, TMC7999 or DAI2441, sizes 2-6.
Thread: Black.
Tip: Oval silver tinsel.
Tail: Crimson red hackle barbs.
Ribbing: Oval silver tinsel.

Body: Dubbed with a blend of #50 fluorescent red African Angora goat and FB03 red Fly Brite.
Wings: Dyed scarlet red badger hackle tips tied cocked up in a V over the body with concave side out.
Hackle: Dyed scarlet red badger tied on as a collar and tied back.
Head: Black.

This pattern was created in 1954 by my father to use for the winter-run in Eel River. I've jazzed it up with Fly Brite.

Eel River Optic

Hook: DAI2451, sizes 1-4.
Thread: Red.
Body: Oval silver tinsel.
Wing: Red bucktail tied over the body with an overwing of yellow bucktail.
Head: White over 1/4" hollow brass bead.
Eyes: Red with black centers.

This pattern was encouraged by a Rick Eggstorm from San Pablo, California, who traditionally spent his winter vacation on the Eel. He had some success on the Mickey Finn and felt that the optic approach would better enhance his chances. Jim Pray tied very few of these flies and tried to play them down whenever he could. The white heads just didn't fit into his production process since they often needed two coats of paint to come out looking right.

Later Lloyd Silvius started tying this fly with a black head and white eyes with red centers and it is the most accepted variation. In the start there were a number of other colors tried for the head before black was finally settled upon. This pattern came to be known by many as either the "Mickey Optic" or the "Red and Yellow Optic." See Black Optic.

Egg Head (S)

Hook: AC80501BL, sizes 2/0-8.
Thread: Fluorescent fire orange.
Tip: Dubbed with #53 fluorescent fire orange lambs wool.
Tail: Black squirrel tail tied equal to one and one half the length of the body.
Ribbing: Oval gold tinsel.
Body: Dubbed with #52 fluorescent orange African Angora goat.
Hackle: Fluorescent orange tied on as collar and tied back.
Eyes: Silver bead chain.
Head: Fluorescent fire orange chenille. This is wrapped with a figure eight around the eyes.

Egg Sac (S)

Hooks: AC80500BL, AC80501BL, TMC7999 or DAI2441, sizes 2/0-6.
Thread: Fluorescent fire orange.
Tail: Black squirrel tail tied equal to one and one half the length of the body.
Body: Rear two-thirds, dubbed with #1 black Bunnytron and the front third, fluorescent fire orange chenille.
Hackle: Black tied on as a collar and tied back.
Head: Fluorescent fire orange.

The two above patterns are examples of an endless variety of such flies which have evolved in northern California. The Egg Sac can be found tied all black or with fluorescent red, orange, green or pink chenille in place of the fluorescent fire orange.

Plate 9 Egg Sucking Leech

Hooks: TMC9395, DAI1750 or DAI2220, sizes 4-10.
Thread: White.
Tail: Black marabou tied equal to the length of the hook.
Body Hackle: Black tied palmer style over the body. Tie hackle in by the tip and wrap with concave side to the rear.
Body: Black chenille.
Head: Egg yarn. Selection includes your choice of red, green, orange, fire orange, pink, etc.

This design idea was first brought to my attention by Art Redmond of Fairfield, California. Art spends a month in Alaska every year and picked up the idea. He brought it back to California and it has been working wonders on the entire West Coast since at least 1983. These flies are also tied with either large bead chain or lead eyes. Identical flies coming from individual tiers will often have different names attached to them, like the Woolly Worm, there is a list for the lists of names of the many variations.

Let's get back to the subject of the heads for these flies. In view of the fact that chenille is much more expedient for less talented tiers than egg yarn some resort to it. My personal preference is one made much like the Glo Bug type bodies. Whether it makes this pattern more productive is certainly another unmeasurable factor we have to contend with. I like it because it does make a nicer looking fly in the eye of the angler. It also gives the fly tier more flexibility in sizing his head. It probably breathes in the water better than chenille, depending on how compact the material is tied. To make one further point in favor of this head design I will concede that Glo Bugs do take more than their share of fish each year. There are many who will not believe these words came from me since I place the Glo Bug on a very thin edge as an instrument of fly fishing. I know that this is a minority opinion in some circles and I hope that it does not come off making me sounding like a snob, but where do we draw the line?

Egg patterns tend to dominate the colors we select for our steelhead flies.

Here is some further food for thought regarding color.

Lynn Austin of Belleview, Washington, has been using the gray scale for salmon and steelhead for more than a twenty years. He ties Glo Bugs in varying shades of gray. He states they are far more effective than the colors we normally see.

Electric Blue
Hooks: AC80500BL, AC80501BL, TMC7999 or DAI2441, sizes 2-8.
Thread: Red.
Ribbing: Oval silver tinsel.
Body: Flat silver tinsel.
First Hackle: Kingfisher blue marabou tied on as a collar and tied back. This hackle should be tied long and extend beyond the bend of hook.
Second Hackle: CH01 pearl Crystal Hair spun on as a collar. Use material sparsely, only a dozen strands extending the same length as the marabou.
Third Hackle: Fluorescent red tied on as a collar and tied back.
Forth Hackle: Purple tied on as a collar and tied back.
Head: Red.

This pattern was designed for winter-run steelhead and is credited to Sean Gallagher.

Enchantress
Hooks: AC80500BL, AC80501BL, TMC7999 or DAI2441, sizes 4-8.
Thread: Black.
Tail: A short tuft of scarlet red marabou stripped from the base of a saddle or neck hackle.
Butt: Dubbed with #57 fluorescent chartreuse African Angora goat.
Ribbing: Flat gold tinsel.
Body: Dubbed with a blend of #1 black African Angora goat and FB02 black Fly Brite.
Body Hackle: Gray tied palmer style from the first full turn of tinsel ribbing.
Wings: White turkey quill sections tied low over the body.

Roger Turner of Vancouver, B.C. originated this pattern. It is a steady producer in most of their rivers.

Plate 7 **Espos, Black**
Hook: DAI2451, sizes 1-8.
Thread: Black.
Body: Black diamond braid.
Wing: Gray squirrel tail tied over the body.
Head: Black.
Eyes: Tiny red dots.

Plate 7 **Espos, Copper**
Hook: DAI2451, sizes 1-8.
Thread: Black.
Body: Copper diamond braid.
Wing: Fox squirrel tail tied over the body.
Head: Black.
Eyes: Tiny orange dots.

Plate 7 **Espos, Green**
Hook: DAI2451, sizes 1-8.
Thread: Black.
Body: Green diamond braid.
Wing: Dyed green gray squirrel tail tied over the body.
Head: Black.
Eyes: Tiny orange dots.

Espos, Hot Pink
Hook: DAI2451, sizes 1-8.
Thread: Black.
Body: Pink diamond braid.
Wing: Fluorescent hot pink bucktail tied over the body.
Head: Black.
Eyes: Tiny red dots.

Espos, Orange
Hook: DAI2451, sizes 1-8.
Thread: Black.
Body: Orange diamond braid.
Wing: Dyed orange gray squirrel tail tied over the body.
Head: Black.
Eyes: Tiny red dots.

Espos, Red
Hook: DAI2451, sizes 1-8.
Thread: Black.
Body: Red diamond braid.
Wing: Dyed red gray squirrel tail tied over the body.
Head: Black.
Eyes: Tiny red dots.

Plate 7 **Espos, Silver**
Hook: DAI2451, sizes 1-8.
Thread: Black.
Body: Silver diamond braid.
Wing: White calf tail tied over the body.
Head: Black.
Eyes: Tiny red dots.

The body of these flies is wrapped well down on the bend of the hook. The wing is cocked upward. The head is built up rather large to accommodate the eyes.

The Espos series was started by Eric Larson of San Jose, California, in the early 1970s. They were created out of his wanting something lighter in weight than the Pray Optics yet with similar features.

Estuary Shrimp
See Chapter 17.

Evening Coachman
Hooks: AC80500BL, AC80501BL, TMC7999 or DAI2441, sizes 6-10.
Thread: Fluorescent fire orange.
Tip: Flat silver tinsel.
Tail: Golden pheasant crest.
Body: Peacock herl with a fluorescent red floss center band.
Hackle: Grizzly hen hackle tied on as a collar and tied back.

Originated by Walt Johnson. His earlier variation was tied on light wire hooks for fishing in the surface film.

Plate 8 **Fall Favorite** (S)
Hooks: AC80500BL, AC80501BL, TMC7999 or DAI2441, sizes 2-8.
Thread: Red.
Body: Silver embossed tinsel. For best effect, wrap a tapered underbody of white

floss. Wrap tinsel from head to rear and return.

Hackle: Red tied on as a collar and tied back.

Wing: Orange calf tail tied over the body.

Head: Red.

This is another one of Lloyd Silvius's contributions and probably his most important one. This fly can be found just about any place steelhead are found. Created in the mid 1940s.

Fall Favorite, Optic (S)

Hook: DAI2451, sizes 1-4.

Thread: Black.

Body: Embossed silver tinsel.

Hackle: Fluorescent red tied on as a collar and tied back and down.

Wing: Fluorescent orange calf tail tied over the body.

Head: Black over 1/4" hollow brass bead.

Eyes: White with red centers.

Lloyd Silvius not only extended his original pattern into the realm of the Optics but tied this pattern with brass bead chain eyes as well.

Farrar Marabou

Hooks: AC80500BL, AC80501BL, TMC7999 or DAI2441, sizes 4-8.

Thread: Red.

Ribbing: Flat silver tinsel.

Body: Dubbed with a blend of #30 purple African Angora goat and FB19 purple Fly Brite.

First Hackle: Purple marabou spun on using a hair spinner.

Wing: About a dozen strands of CH19 purple Crystal Hair tied over the body.

Second Hackle: Natural red golden pheasant body plumage. Wrap one full turn.

Third Hackle: One full turn of barred teal.

Topping: Natural red golden pheasant body plumage barbs.

Head: Red.

Originated by John Farrar of Seattle, Washington.

 Faulk

Hooks: AC80500BL, AC80501BL, TMC7999 or DAI2441, sizes 2-8.

Thread: Red.

Tail: Scarlet red hackle barbs.

Ribbing: Oval gold tinsel.

Body: Dubbed with #9 orange lambs wool.

Hackle: Scarlet red tied on as a collar and tie back and down.

Wing: White bucktail tied over the body. Leave butts of wing flared out over the eye of the hook.

Head: Red.

The Faulk was a 1923 pattern designed by Washingtonian Emil Faulk.

Feather Merchant

Hooks: AC80500BL, AC80501BL, TMC7999 or DAI2441, sizes 2-6.

Thread: Black.

Tail: Golden pheasant tippet barbs.

Butt: Dubbed with #4 red lambs wool.

Ribbing: Oval silver tinsel over peacock only.

Body: Peacock herl.

Hackle: Orange tied on as a collar and tied back and down.

Wing: Red calf tail tied over the body.

Cheeks: J.C. or substitute.

Head: Black.

Originated by Ted Trueblood. To my knowledge this is the only steelhead pattern that Ted designed and used with regularity.

Ferry Canyon

Hooks: AC80500BL, AC80501BL, TMC7999 or DAI2441, sizes 4-8.

Thread: Black.

Tail: Scarlet red hackle barbs.

Ribbing: Oval silver tinsel.

Butt: Dubbed with #53 fluorescent fire orange lambs wool.

Body: Purple chenille.

Wing: Six strands each of CH03 red, CH13 blue and CH21 claret Crystal Hair. Over this is tied purple marabou.

Hackle: Purple tied on as a collar and tied back.

Head: Black.

Created by Randall Kaufmann of Portland, Oregon.

Fiery Brown

Hooks: TMC7989 or DAI2421, sizes 6-10.
Thread: Brown.
Tip: Flat gold tinsel.
Body: Dubbed with dyed fluorescent fire orange blended hare's mask fur.
Wing: Fiery brown woodchuck guard hair tied sparse and short.
Head: Brown.

This pattern was originated by Mike Brooks of Veneta, Oregon.

Firefly

Hooks: AC80500BL, AC80501BL, TMC7999 or DAI2441, sizes 2-8.
Thread: Fluorescent fire orange.
Tail: Fluorescent orange hackle barbs.
Ribbing: Flat silver tinsel.
Body: Fluorescent orange chenille.
Hackle: Fluorescent orange tied on as a collar and tied back and down.
Wing: White bucktail tied over the body with an overwing of white marabou.
Topping: Six strands of CH01 pearl Crystal Hair.
Cheeks: J.C. or substitute.
Head: Fluorescent fire orange.

This pattern was developed by Bill Yonge of Vancouver, British Columbia.

 ### Flame (S)

Hook: AC80501BL, sizes 2/0-8.
Thread: Fluorescent orange.
Tail: Black bucktail tied equal to one and one half the length of the body.
Ribbing: Oval silver tinsel.
Body: Dubbed with #53 fluorescent fire orange lambs wool.
Hackle: Fluorescent fire orange tied on as a collar and tied back.
Eyes: Silver bead chain.

Originated in 1960 for the Russian River by Ralph Stone.

Flame Chappie

Tied same as the Chappie except the body is fluorescent fire orange chenille with an oval silver tinsel ribbing.

Flame Squirrel Tail (S)

Hooks: AC80500BL, AC80501BL, TMC7999 or DAI2441, sizes 2-6.
Thread: Black.
Tail: Red goose quill section.
Ribbing: Embossed silver tinsel.
Body: Fluorescent fire orange chenille.
Hackle: Orange tied on as a collar and tied back and down.
Wing: Fox squirrel tail tied over the body.
Head: Black.

Created by Victor Moore of Smithers, British Columbia.

Flat Car

Hooks: AC80500BL, AC80501BL, TMC7999 or DAI2441, sizes 4-8.
Thread: Black.
Tail: Black hackle barbs.
Butt: Dubbed with #57 fluorescent chartreuse lambs wool.
Ribbing: Oval silver tinsel.
Body: Black chenille.
Wing: Six strands each of CH01 pearl and CH02 black Crystal Hair tied over the body with an overwing of black marabou.
Hackle: Black tied on as a collar and tied back.
Head: Black.

This is another of Randall Kaufmann's patterns.

Flirt

Hooks: AC80500BL, AC80501BL, TMC7999 or DAI2441, sizes 2-6.
Thread: Black.
Tip: Flat silver tinsel.
Tail: Purple hackle barbs.
Body: Fluorescent fire orange floss with two full turns of fluorescent orange chenille at the front.
Hackle: Purple tied on as a collar and tied back and down.
Wing: Natural brown bucktail.
Head: Black.

Fool's Gold

Hooks: AC80500BL, AC80501BL, TMC7999 or DAI2441, sizes 2-6.
Thread: Black.
Tail: Golden pheasant tippet barbs.
Butt: Peacock herl.
Body: Oval gold tinsel.
Hackle: Brown tied on as a collar and tied back and down.
Wing: Fox squirrel tail tied over the body.
Head: Black.

Both of the preceding patterns can be attributed to Mike Kennedy.

 ## Forrester

Hooks: AC80500BL, AC80501BL, TMC7999 or DAI2441, sizes 4-8.
Thread: Fluorescent fire orange.
Tail: Orange calf tail.
Body: Rear two-thirds, fluorescent orange chenille and the front third, black chenille.
Hackle: Orange calf tail tied in at throat.
Wing: Orange calf tail tied over the body.
Head: Fluorescent fire orange.

Originated in 1979 by George Richey for Michigan's spring fishing.

Frank's Fly (S)

Hooks: AC80500BL, AC80501BL, TMC7999 or DAI2441, sizes 2/0-6.
Thread: Fluorescent orange.
Body: Fluorescent orange chenille.
Body Hackle: Fluorescent orange tied palmer style over the body.
Wing: White calf tail tied over the body.
Topping: Six strands of CH01 pearl Crystal Hair.
Head: Fluorescent orange.

This pattern was originated by Frank Moore of Anchorage, Alaska. It is now proving itself on steelhead waters everywhere.

Freight Train

Hooks: AC80500BL, AC80501BL, TMC7999 or DAI2441, sizes 4-8.
Thread: Black.
Tail: Purple hackle barbs.
Ribbing: Oval silver tinsel.

Body: Rear half, dubbed with #53 fluorescent fire orange lambs wool and front half, black chenille.
Hackle: Purple tied on as a collar and tied back and down.
Wing: White calf tail tied over the body.
Head: Black.

Freight Train, Crystal

Tied same as the preceding pattern except the wing is constructed with about twenty strands of CH01 pearl Crystal Hair.

The Freight Train was originated by Randall Kaufmann of Portland, Oregon. This is without a doubt one of his best steelhead patterns.

Garth

Hooks: AC80500BL, AC80501BL, TMC7999 or DAI2441, sizes 4-6.
Thread: Black.
Tail: Scarlet red hackle barbs.
Body: Fluorescent orange chenille.
Body Hackle: Grizzly tied palmer style over the body.
Hackle: Grizzly tied in as a collar and tied back.
Wing: Black moose mane tied over the body.
Head: Black.

Developed in 1960 by Bob Arnold.

Gary's Assassin

Hooks: AC80500BL, AC80501BL, TMC7999 or DAI2441, sizes 4-8.
Thread: Fluorescent red.
Tail: Dyed black squirrel tail tied equal to one and one half the length of the body.
Butt: Fluorescent red floss tied as a narrow band.
Body: Dubbed with #57 fluorescent chartreuse lambs wool.
Hackle: Black tied on as a collar and tied back.
Head: Fluorescent red.

This is a Canadian pattern which has been redesigned for steelhead by Gary Selig of Mertztown, Pennsylvania.

Gary's Smurf
Hook: AC80501BL, sizes 2/0-8.
Thread: Black.
Body: None.
Wing: Black squirrel tail.
Hackle: Grizzly tied on as a collar and tied back.
Eyes: Silver bead chain.

This is another of Gary Selig's patterns.

General Money I
Hooks: AC80500BL, AC80501BL, TMC7999 or DAI2441, sizes 2/0-6.
Thread: Black.
Tail: Natural red golden pheasant breast barbs.
Ribbing: Oval silver tinsel over the dubbed portion of the body.
Body: Rear two-fifths, oval silver tinsel and the front three-fifths, dubbed with #1 black lambs wool.
Hackle: Claret tied on as a collar and tied back and down.
Wing: Orange bucktail tied over the body.
Cheeks: J.C. or substitute.
Head: Black.

General Money II
Hooks: AC80500BL, AC80501BL, TMC7999 or DAI2441, sizes 2/0-6.
Thread: Black.
Tip: Oval gold tinsel.
Tail: Golden pheasant crest.
Ribbing: Oval gold tinsel.
Body: Dubbed with #1 black lambs wool.
Wing: Red bucktail tied over the body.
Hackle: Yellow tied on as a collar and tied back. Note that the hackle goes on after the wing.
Head: Black.

Both of the preceding patterns were originated by General Noel Money for British Columbia. These flies originally sported goose quill wings that were clipped over fifty years ago here in northern California and replaced with bucktail.

George's Green (S)
Hook: AC80501BL, sizes 2/0-8.
Thread: Black.
Tail: Black hackle barbs.
Body: Dubbed with #57 fluorescent chartreuse African Angora goat.
Hackle: Black tied on as a collar and tied back.
Wing: Sparse black squirrel tail tied over the body.
Eyes: Silver bead chain.
Head: Black chenille. The chenille is wrapped figure eight through the eyes.

No one can tell me who George is, however, there have been reports on this fly throughout northern California and southern Oregon. Proportion this fly a bit differently when you tie it. The body is kept rather short to compensate for the larger head.

Ghost Leech
Hook: AC80501BL, sizes 2/0-8.
Thread: Fluorescent red.
Tail: Small bunch of CH01 pearl Crystal Hair.
Ribbing: Oval gold tinsel.
Body: Flat gold tinsel.
Wing: Strip of white rabbit tied Matuka style.
Hackle: Collar of black rabbit fur.
Eyes: Brass bead chain.

This is a Gary Miltenberger pattern.

Giant Killer
Plate 10
Hooks: AC80500BL, AC80501BL, TMC7999 or DAI2441, sizes 2-6.
Thread: Black.
Tail: Purple hackle barbs.
Body: Dubbed with #57 fluorescent chartreuse lambs wool. Body should be kept a narrow taper.
Hackle: Purple tied on as a collar and tied back.
Wing: White bucktail tied over the body.
Head: Black.

This is an old pattern which stood the test of time. It was originated by Don Larson of Seattle, Washington. It was first designed for British Columbia waters but has since reached up into Alaska where it is highly regarded by many.

Gladiator

Hooks: AC80500BL, AC80501BL, TMC7999 or DAI2441, sizes 4-8.
Thread: Black.
Tail: Scarlet red hackle barbs.
Ribbing: Peacock herl.
Body: Green floss.
Hackle: Grizzly tied on as a collar and tied back and down.
Wing: Gray squirrel tail.
Head: Black.

I know when you were reading this recipe you were turned off by the fragile peacock ribbing. Don't be. Here is how it is done.

Tie in two strands of peacock herl by their tips along with a piece of black tying thread. Grasp the three ends with your hackle pliers and twist into a rope. Wrap, and you have a good reinforced ribbing material. This fly was developed by Nick Gayeski.

Goblin

Hooks: AC80500BL, AC80501BL, TMC7999 or DAI2441, sizes 4-8.
Thread: Black.
Tail: Red goose quill section.
Body: Wrapped with fine gold braided Mylar piping.
Wing: Orange bucktail tied over the body with an overwing of black bucktail.
Head: Black.
Eyes: White ring eyes.

This pattern was originated in 1961 by Warren Erholm of Anacortes, Washington. See Black Bomber for how to apply eyes.

Gold Demon

Hooks: AC80500BL, AC80501BL, TMC7999 or DAI2441, sizes 2-6.
Thread: Orange.
Tail: Golden pheasant crest.
Body: Oval gold tinsel.

Hackle: Orange tied on as a collar and tied down and back.
Wing: Fox squirrel tail tied over the body.
Head: Orange.

This fly is thought to have been brought into this country from New Zealand as a streamer fly sometime during the 1930s. Jim Pray is largely responsible for popularizing it out of his little shop in Eureka, California. Also see Silver Demon.

This period in American history was very grim for many. The country was in the midst of the great depression. My grandfather left Wisconsin in a two ton truck with his wife and eleven children. They ended up in the Owens Valley in southern California. This is where my father got his first real taste of fly fishing. At the same time my grandfather was taking advantage of everyone with their misfortune brought on by the times. He made several large land purchases for pennies and thought he had captured most of the water rights to the Owens River.

The City of Los Angeles had beat him to it in the courts, prior to his purchases, so the family again sold out and loaded up. They headed north and ended up in Ontario, Oregon. It was here that my father completed high school.

My grandfather got restless after a couple of years and wanted to return to California. On the way, while passing through Bonanza, Oregon, my father and uncle John decided they had had enough and jumped ship. My uncle John stayed in Oregon and homesteaded a ranch in the Langell Valley. He is still there today.

After some months my father decided it was time to move on and landed in Eureka, California. Here he met Jim Pray. Jim took him in and treated him like a son. He put my father up on a cot in his back room and here is where he learned to tie flies. Looking back today, it was more like an indentured apprenticeship than a relationship.

Jim was a thoughtful old gentleman and he and my father went through some real hard times together. Shellfish and salmon were always on the menu. Jim's little shop had very little to offer. He was the western distributor for both Orvis and Leonard. He had six rods. They sustained themselves however with the flies they tied. During the winter months they never had enough of anything. All of their summers long hours of tying was depleted in a very short time. This meant working even longer hours in the winter months. After a couple of years of this my father decided it was time to go. He had heard that there were guiding opportunities on the Klamath and he made his way to Happy Camp taking a few of Jim's clients with him.

Gold Spider

Hooks: DAI2151 or DAI2161, sizes 1-6.
Thread: Black.
Butt: Peacock herl.
Body: Rear half, flat silver tinsel and the front half, dubbed with #23 golden stone Bunny-Blend.
Hackle: One full turn of golden pheasant flank, two full turns of dyed brown pheasant rump and one full turn of dyed imitation barred lemon woodduck.
Head: Black.

This pattern was created by Karl Hauffler and later named by Trey Combs for identification purposes.

Golden Bear

Hooks: AC80500BL, AC80501BL, TMC7999 or DAI2441, sizes 1-6.
Thread: Brown.
Tail: Crimson red hackle barbs.
Body: Rear half, reddish-brown floss and the front half, dubbed with FB31 gold Fly Brite.
Hackle: Coachman brown tied on as a collar and tied back and down.
Wing: Dark brown calf tail tied over the body.
Topping: Small bunch of CH25 copper brown Crystal Hair.
Head: Brown.

I don't like to speak of the good old days all of the time, but we received three bear hides from Kodiak Island, Alaska in 1955 which to this day I doubt could ever be duplicated. The hair on two of the hides was of such superior fly tying quality that one would just as soon hang these large carpets of hair on the wall to be admired by all. This is when my father developed one of his other patterns into the Golden Bear. He tied thousands of flies from this supply and still had choice pieces around in 1970. Since that time I have tied the wing with calf tail and found it equally effective on the fish but quite damaging to my psyche.

Golden Demon

Hooks: AC80500BL, AC80501BL, TMC7999 or DAI2441, sizes 1-6.
Thread: Black.
Tail: Golden pheasant crest.
Body: Oval gold tinsel wrapped over a tapered underbody of yellow floss.
Hackle: Orange tied on as a collar and tied back and down.
Wing: Well marked coastal blacktail deer body hair tied over the body.
Cheeks: J.C. or substitute.
Head: Black.

See Gold Demon.

Golden Demon II

Hooks: AC80500BL, AC80501BL, TMC7999 or DAI2441, sizes 2-6.
Thread: Black.
Tip: Flat silver tinsel.
Tail: Golden pheasant crest.
Ribbing: Oval silver tinsel.
Body: Flat gold tinsel.
Hackle: Long fluorescent fire orange tied palmer style from the center of the body and tied back. Tie in by the tip and wrap with concave side to the rear.
Wings: Furnace hackle tips tied over the body with concave side inward. An overwing of bronze mallard sections are then tied over the hackle tips.
Topping: Six or eight golden pheasant crest feathers.
Cheeks: J.C. or substitute.
Head: Black.

This is one of the innovative dressings of Dave McNeese of Salem, Oregon.

Golden Edge, Orange

Hooks: AC80500BL, AC80501BL, TMC7999 or DAI2441, sizes 2-8.
Thread: Orange.
Tip: Flat silver tinsel.
Tail: Golden pheasant crest tied equal to half the length of the body.
Ribbing: Flat silver tinsel.
Body: Dubbed with a blend of #9 orange African Angora goat and FB06 orange Fly Brite.
Hackle: Guinea fowl tied in at the throat. Material should be only half the length as normal.
Wing: Gray squirrel tail tied sparse with a section of bronze mallard tied flat on the top.
Topping: Golden pheasant crest.
Head: Orange.

Golden Edge, Yellow

This pattern is tied same as the above pattern except the body is #6 yellow African Angora goat and FB04 yellow Fly Brite.

The Golden Edge patterns were developed by Harry Lemire of Black Diamond, Washington. They are flies for all seasons. The larger sizes are used for winter-runs and the smaller sizes are used for summer-runs. Some anglers tie them reduced rather than going to smaller hooks.

Golden Girl

Hooks: AC80500BL, AC80501BL, TMC7999 or DAI2441, sizes 2-6.
Thread: Black.
Tail: Orange hackle barbs tied short.
Body: Flat gold tinsel.
Hackle: Orange tied on as a collar and tied back and down.
Wings: First tie in sparse orange bucktail, then tie golden pheasant tippets in at each side of the bucktail.
Head: Black.

Originated by Roderick L. Haig-Brown for British Columbia's Campbell River. This man was a very prolific writer and most of us are familiar with his books that pertain to fishing. Others I have collected and enjoy are *On The Highest Hill, The Living Land*, and *The Whale People*. The last book is a great children's attention-getter. There are other titles that I have not been able to obtain.

Golden Goose (S)

Hook: AC80501BL, sizes 2/0-8.
Thread: Black.
Tail: Natural brown bucktail tied equal to one and one half the length of the body.
Body: Oval gold tinsel.
Hackle: Scarlet red and yellow tied on as a collar and tied back mixed.
Eyes: Gold bead chain.

Originated by Bill Schaadt for the Smith and Eel Rivers.

Golden Heron

Hooks: DAI2151 or DAI2161, sizes 1-6.
Thread: Black.
Tip: Flat silver tinsel.
Ribbing: Oval silver tinsel.
Body: Flat gold tinsel.
Hackle: Dyed black pheasant rump tied on as a collar and tied back.
Wings: Four dyed salmon yellow hen hackle tips tied over the body.
Overwing: Narrow section of bronze mallard tied flat over the hen hackle tips.
Cheeks: J.C. or substitute.
Head: Black.

This is a variation of the Gold Heron as tied by Dave McNeese of Salem, Oregon.

Golden Pheasant

Hooks: AC80500BL, AC80501BL, TMC7999 or DAI2441, sizes 4-8.
Thread: Black.
Tail: Golden pheasant tippet barbs.
Ribbing: Flat gold tinsel.
Body: Orange floss.
Hackle: Orange tied on as a collar and tied back and down.
Wings: Matched pair of golden pheasant tippets feathers tied on edge over the body.
Head: Black.

Origin unknown. This pattern was popular on the Eel, Mad and Rogue Rivers during the 1920s.

Golden Rogue

Hooks: AC80500BL, AC80501BL, TMC7999 or DAI2441, sizes 4-8.
Thread: Brown.
Tail: Two small golden pheasant tippet feathers tied together on edge.
Body: Oval gold tinsel.
Body Hackle: Brown tied palmer style over the body.
Wing: Fox squirrel tail tied over the body.

Originated by J. Duckett owner of the former Cascade Tackle Company in Medford, Oregon. He also had a Silver Rogue which was the same except it had an oval silver tinsel body. Although my father was not real good friends with Mr. Duckett, they did considerable business together. Duckett published his *Fly-Tying Dictionary* in the early 1940s and it was rather remarkable for the time. I still have a copy of this fifty-six page guide which I enjoy bringing down every couple of years and browsing through. Here is how he lists the Golden Rogue: "Oval gold tinsel body, golden pheasant tippet tail, brown hackle tied palmer, red squirrel hair wings."

From this one would surmise that he was speaking of golden pheasant tippet barbs for the tail. Not true. The samples my father had obtained from him were as described above. Others in trying to interpret this tail material went for golden pheasant crest.

To give you some idea of the times I am going to take the liberty of quoting other excerpts from this work which are taken from his "Helpful Hints" section.

"Keep your rod in a dry cool place between trips." Remember this was the age of bamboo. "Trout will keep better and it is more merciful if their necks are broken upon being caught." How times have changed. It won't be long until this younger generation will be shed of those who were raised in the era of subsistence fishing.

I don't want to end here though, I have more. "Vanishing cream or cold cream borrowed from the wife's dressing table is as good as the best patented preparation on the market for floating dry flies." Mr. Duckett might have been surprised to know that some enterprising individuals were packaging his recommended floatant up until the late 1970s and calling it "Fly Cream." Little messy but a reasonably good floatant.

A thought that could fit more into today's way of thinking. "A newspaper carried along in winter fishing and a page torn off at intervals, crumpled and lit will provide considerable warmth especially when changing leaders or flies." Then he ends his little book of fly patterns with, "In case the description in the dictionary is not plain enough on any of the flies, we will be glad to ty [sic] and ship one or more postpaid for 35 cents each." Damn, I must be getting old, I can remember the three cent stamp.

Goldsmith (S)

Hook: AC80501BL, sizes 2/0-8.
Thread: Orange.
Tail: Fluorescent orange bucktail with black bucktail tied on top and tied equal to one and one half the length of the body.
Body: Gold Mylar piping. After the piping is slipped over the body, tie in at rear and fray out the ends so they extend a quarter of the tail.
Hackle: Fluorescent orange and yellow tied on as a collar and tied back mixed.
Eyes: Gold bead chain.

An alternate pattern to this one is the Silversmith. It is the same except it uses silver Mylar piping and silver bead chain. Originated by Ed Given for northern California and southern Oregon. Ed's original flies used nickel and gold plated hooks which made them more attractive in the angler's eye but I believe the fish don't give a hoot.

Gray Drake

Hooks: TMC7989 or DAI2421, sizes 6-10.
Thread: Black.
Tail: Barred mallard barbs.
Ribbing: Heavy black thread.
Body: Dubbed with #2 white lambs wool.
Wing: Gray squirrel tail tied over the body.
Hackle: Grizzly tied on as a collar and tied back.
Head: Black.

Little did I know as a boy of fifteen that someday I would be writing about the Gray and Green Drakes. The wing on the Gray Drake was originally silver monkey. When that was in short supply we reverted to California gray squirrel. Then in later years as they became more available we used Eastern gray squirrel but only using the lower part of the tail where the barring was finer. The Green Drake posed a smaller problem. The original tail called for black monkey and that was easily procured by dying squirrel tails black. The hair on the black monkey was too long and thick to be practical in the first place. Just another one of those exotic materials that we can do better without.

I have no record where these patterns came from or who was responsible for bringing them to old dads attention. I do know they played a major role in his fishing as far back as the mid 1930s. They were fished on well greased silk lines and always produced fish on the Trinity and Klamath Rivers in the late summer and fall. Today they are still recognized as good flies for the half-pounders on these rivers. See Green Drake.

⬤Plate 6 Gray Hackle Yellow

Hooks: AC80500BL, AC80501BL, TMC7999 or DAI2441, sizes 4-8.
Thread: Black.
Tip: Oval gold tinsel.
Tail: Amherst pheasant crest.
Ribbing: Oval gold tinsel.
Body: Yellow floss.
Body Hackle: Grizzly tied palmer style over the body at the edge of the ribbing.
Hackle: Grizzly tied on as a collar and tied back.
Head: Black.

It is reasonable to assume that this pattern was taken from an early American pattern. We originated grizzly or the Plymouth Rock chicken in this country. This pattern should not be sold short, it was not too many years ago when it could be rated amongst the top ten in northern California. It still has some fairly dedicated followers who add bead chain eyes when conditions warrant.

Green Butt

`Plate 8`

Hooks: AC80500BL, AC80501BL, TMC7999 or DAI2441, sizes 4-8.
Thread: Black.
Butt: Fluorescent green yarn.
Ribbing: Flat silver tinsel.
Body: Dubbed with #1 black Bunnytron.
Hackle: Black tied on as a collar and tied back and down.
Wing: Fox squirrel tail tied over the body.
Head: Black

This pattern obviously evolved from the Atlantic salmon pattern, Green Butt Black Bear. See Chapter 21.

Green Butt Spider

`Plate 7`

Hooks: AC80500BL, AC80501BL, TMC7999 or DAI2441, sizes 1-6.
Thread: Fluorescent red.
Butt: Fluorescent green chenille.
Ribbing: Oval silver tinsel.
Body: Dubbed with #1 black African Angora goat.
Hackle: Dyed black pheasant rump tied on as a collar and tied back.
Head: Fluorescent red.

Every time I look at this pattern I think "Why didn't I think of that?" Many of us are always searching for the Holy Grail of flies. The basic colors, the silhouette, everything one could ask for in a basic steelhead fly. The creator of this simple to tie pattern, Frederic Nicholas Kozy, has successfully demonstrated its productivity since 1960

on most West Coast streams. Fred favors this pattern only second to the Wet Spider that Al Knudson gave us.

Green Dean (S)

Hooks: AC80500BL, AC80501BL, TMC7999 or DAI2441, sizes 2/0-4
Thread: Red.
Tip: Flat silver tinsel.
Tail: Red calf tail.
Ribbing: Flat silver tinsel.
Body: Dubbed with #57 fluorescent chartreuse lambs wool.
Wing: Red bucktail tied over the body.
Hackle: Scarlet red tied on as a collar. Do not tie back.
Head: Red.

All I can determine about this pattern is that it was originated for the Dean River in British Columbia.

Green Drake

Hooks: TMC7989 or DAI2421, sizes 6-10.
Thread: Black.
Tail: Barred teal barbs.
Ribbing: Heavy black thread.
Body: Dubbed with #19 olive lambs wool.
Wing: Dyed black squirrel tail tied over the body.
Hackle: Brown tied on as a collar and tied back.
Head: Black.

See Gray Drake.

Green Head (S)

Hook: AC80501BL, sizes 2/0-8.
Thread: Fluorescent green.
Tip: Dubbed with #57 fluorescent chartreuse lambs wool.
Tail: Black squirrel tail tied equal to one and one half the length of the body.
Ribbing: Oval gold tinsel.
Body: Dubbed with #53 fluorescent fire orange lambs wool.
Hackle: Orange tied on as a collar and tied back.

Eyes: Gold bead chain.
Head: Fluorescent green chenille. The chenille should be wrapped figure eight through the eyes.

Originated in 1980 by Rex Collingsworth.

Green Lady

Plate 9

Hooks: AC80500BL, AC80501BL, TMC7999 or DAI2441, sizes 2-6.
Thread: Fluorescent green.
Tail: Yellow hen hackle barbs.
Ribbing: Oval silver tinsel.
Body: Rear half, flat silver tinsel and the front half, dubbed with #57 fluorescent chartreuse Bunny-Blend.
Center Joint Hackle: Chartreuse hackle tied on as a collar and tied back.
Hackle: White bucktail tied in at the throat.
Wing: Natural brown bucktail tied over the body.
Cheeks: Chartreuse hen hackle tips (lacquered) tied in at each side.
Head: Fluorescent green.
Note: The wing and throat hackle are of equal proportions and of the same length. In other words, you have a wing on top and one on the bottom.

Originated by Russell Langston of Brown's Valley, California.

Green Weanie (S)

Hook: AC80501BL, sizes 2/0-8.
Thread: Black.
Tail: Black squirrel tail tied equal to one and one half the length of the body.
Body: Rear half, silver diamond braid and the front half, fluorescent green chenille.
Hackle: Fluorescent green tied on as a collar and tied back.
Eyes: Silver bead chain.

Grizzly King

Hooks: AC80500BL, AC80501BL, TMC7999 or DAI2441, sizes 4-8.
Thread: Black.
Tip: Oval gold tinsel.
Tail: Scarlet red hackle barbs.
Ribbing: Oval gold tinsel.
Body: Green floss.
Hackle: Grizzly tied on as a collar and tied back.

Wing: Gray squirrel tail tied over the body.
Head: Black.

This was adapted from one of our older wet fly patterns.

Haile Selassie

Hooks: AC80500BL, AC80501BL, TMC7999 or DAI2441, sizes 2-6.
Thread: Black.
Tip: Flat silver tinsel.
Tail: Fluorescent orange hackle barbs.
Ribbing: Flat silver tinsel.
Body: Dubbed with #1 black lambs wool.
Hackle: Fluorescent orange tied on as a collar and tied back and down.
Wing: Black bucktail tied over the body.
Topping: Two strands of fluorescent orange yarn.
Head: Black.

"King of the Blacks" was what Frank Headrick of Seattle, Washington, chose to call his new creation when he named it in 1965.

Half N' Half

Hooks: AC80500BL, AC80501BL, TMC7999 or DAI2441, sizes 2-6.
Thread: Fluorescent fire orange.
Tail: Amherst pheasant tippet.
Ribbing: Oval silver tinsel.
Body: Rear half, dubbed with #6 yellow lambs wool and the front half, dubbed with #9 orange lambs wool.
Body Hackle: Dyed red grizzly tied palmer style over the front half of the body.
Wing: White calf tail tied over the body.
Topping: Small bunch of CH03 red Crystal Hair.
Head: Fluorescent fire orange.

Originated in 1983 by Wes Gage of Turlock, California.

Hardy's Favorite

Hooks: AC80500BL, AC80501BL, TMC7999 or DAI2441, sizes 4-8.
Thread: Black.
Tip: Red floss.
Tail: Orange hackle and guinea fowl barbs mixed.
Ribbing: Red floss.
Body: Peacock herl.

Hackle: Guinea fowl tied on as a collar and tied back and parted at the top.
Wing: Ringneck pheasant tail barbs tied over the body.
Head: Black.

Adapted from an English wet fly as tied by J. J. Hardy of Hardy Brothers, Alnwick, England. It is believed that this transformation took place in northern California around the mid 1920s.

Hairy Mary
Hooks: AC80500BL, AC80501BL, TMC7999 or DAI2441, sizes 2-6.
Thread: Black.
Tip: Flat gold tinsel.
Tail: Fluorescent orange hackle barbs.
Ribbing: Oval gold tinsel.
Body: Dubbed with #1 black lambs wool.
Hackle: Kingfisher blue tied on as a collar and tied back and down.
Wing: Gray squirrel tail tied over the body.
Head: Black.

This is a variation of a British Atlantic salmon fly pattern that my father obtained in 1940. Because of its similarity to the Blue Charm it has gone unrecognized by many. I have found this to be a very good winter pattern wherever it is used.

Harry Hari Bucktail
Hooks: AC80500BL, AC80501BL, TMC7999 or DAI2441, sizes 2-8.
Thread: Black.
Tail: Red marabou tied short. This is taken from the base of a red neck or saddle hackle.
Ribbing: X-Fine black chenille.
Body: Yellow chenille.
Hackle: Green-gray plumage taken from the back of a ringneck pheasant and tied on as a collar and tied back.
Wing: Black bucktail tied over the body.
Head: Black.

Originated in 1957 by Harry Lemire of Black Diamond, Washington.

Hellcat
Hooks: AC80500BL, AC80501BL, TMC7999 or DAI2441, sizes 2-6.
Thread: Black.
Tip: Flat silver tinsel.
Tail: Golden pheasant crest.
Ribbing: Flat silver tinsel.
Body: Fluorescent pink chenille.
Hackle: Purple tied on as a collar and tied back and down.
Wing: White bucktail tied over the body.
Head: Black.

The Hellcat was developed in the 1950s by Frank Headrick of Seattle, Washington.

Herniator
Hooks: AC80500BL, AC80501BL, TMC7999 or DAI2441, sizes 4-6.
Thread: Black.
Body: First wrap a thin tapered underbody of olive floss, then overwrap with CH15 olive Crystal Hair.
Thorax: Peacock herl.
Wing: About twenty strands of CH15 olive Crystal Hair.
Hackle: Guinea fowl tied on as a collar and tied back.

Originated by Bill Geise for California's Klamath and Trinity Rivers. As the story goes, Bill was hospitalized with a hernia shortly after creating this pattern. He told everyone that he was in the hospital because of having to lift so many big fish on his new pattern. Sounds fishy wouldn't you say?

Hilton Spider
Hooks: DAI2151 or DAI2161, sizes 1-6.
Thread: Black.
Tip: Flat silver tinsel.
Ribbing: Oval silver tinsel.
Body: Black chenille.
Wings: Grizzly hackle tips tied in a V and cocked upward with their concave side out.
Hackle: Speckled guinea fowl tied on as a collar and tied back.
Head: Black.

This is an alternative pattern that Fredric Nicholas Kozy developed in 1961 for his home river, the Klamath.

Hopeful Hare

Hooks: AC80500BL, AC80501BL, TMC7999 or DAI2441, sizes 2-6.
Thread: Orange.
Tag: Orange floss.
Ribbing: Oval gold tinsel.
Body Hackle: Grizzly saddle hackle tied palmer style. Wrap between ribs.
Body: Dubbed with hare's mask fur.
Head: Orange.

Horner's Silver Shrimp

See Chapter 17.

Horny Shrimp

See Chapter 17.

Horrible Matuka

Hooks: AC80500BL, AC80501BL, TMC7999 or DAI2441, sizes 2-6.
Thread: Black.
Ribbing: Oval silver tinsel.
Body: Fluorescent orange chenille.
Wing: Four dyed fluorescent orange neck hackles tied Matuka style.
Hackle: Badger dyed fluorescent orange tied on as a collar and tied back.
Head: Black.

This fly was developed by Harry Darbee of Livingston Manor, New York, for Atlantic salmon. While collecting patterns for my first book in 1972 Harry sent me a sample of this pattern. I really did not have a chance to see how effective it was until 1974. It proved to be a winner. Harry called in 1977 and thanked me for including it in *Popular Fly Patterns*. He was proud of the fact that he, as an Easterner, would have the first Matuka style steelhead pattern introduced with success on the West Coast. I am sure there might have been others but it wasn't in me to tell him so. It works and works well.

Hot Orange

Hooks: AC80500BL, AC80501BL, TMC7999 or DAI2441, sizes 2-6.
Thread: Red.
Tip: Lower half, flat silver tinsel and the upper half, fluorescent fire orange floss.
Tail: Amherst pheasant crest.
Body: Rear half, oval silver tinsel and the front half, #53 fluorescent fire orange Bunny-Blend.
Body Hackle: Fluorescent orange tied palmer style over the front half of the body.
Wing: White calf tail tied over the body.
Topping: Amherst pheasant crest.
Head: Red.

There are a good number of Hot Orange patterns associated with steelhead flies. According to Eric Moorsie of Gerber, California, he was always the one his friends looked upon to furnish the flies whenever they went fishing. They always asked for the "hot orange" one and the generic name has stuck since he first started using it on the Feather River in 1961.

Hot Orange Champ

Hook: DAI2451, sizes 1-4.
Thread: Fluorescent fire orange.
Tail: Six strands of fluorescent fire orange floss.
Ribbing: Flat silver tinsel.
Body: Dubbed with #53 fluorescent fire orange lambs wool.
Wing: Six strands of fluorescent fire orange floss.
Head: Fluorescent fire orange.

Hot Shot I

Hooks: AC80500BL, AC80501BL, TMC7999 or DAI2441, sizes 2-6.
Thread: Fluorescent fire orange.
Tail: Scarlet red hackle barbs.
Ribbing: Flat silver tinsel.
Body: Fluorescent fire orange chenille.
Hackle: Fluorescent orange tied on as a collar and tied back and down.
Wing: White bucktail tied over the body.
Head: Fluorescent fire orange.

Both of the preceding patterns were developed by Al Knudson.

Hot Shot II

Hooks: AC80500BL, AC80501BL, TMC7999 or DAI2441, sizes 2-6.
Thread: Black.
Tip: Flat silver tinsel.
Tail: Golden pheasant crest.
Ribbing: Flat silver tinsel.
Body: Fluorescent fire orange chenille.
Hackle: Fluorescent orange tied on as a collar and tied back and down.
Wing: White bucktail tied over the body.
Topping: Golden pheasant crest.
Head: Black.

This Hot Shot pattern was created by Frank Headrick of Seattle, Washington.

Plate 7

Hoyt's Killer

Hooks: AC80500BL, AC80501BL, TMC7999 or DAI2441, sizes 6-8.
Thread: Black.
Tail: Scarlet red hackle barbs.
Ribbing: Embossed silver tinsel.
Body: Black chenille.
Hackle: Grizzly tied on as a collar and tied back.
Wing: Coastal blacktail deer hair tied over the body.
Head: Black.

This pattern is also known as Hoyt's Special. Originated in 1940 by Clyde Hoyt for summer-run steelhead.

Humboldt Railbird

Hooks: AC80500BL, AC80501BL, TMC7999 or DAI2441, sizes 2-6.
Thread: Black.
Tail: Amherst pheasant crest.
Body: Dubbed with #32 claret lambs wool.
Body Hackle: Claret tied palmer style over the body.

Hackle: Yellow hackle tied on as a collar and tied back.
Wing: Gray squirrel tail tied long and extending beyond the tail.
Cheeks: J.C. or substitute.
Head: Black.

The original of this well known northern California fly was created by John S. Benn, an Irish fly tier. He was born in Malta, County Cork, Ireland in 1838, moved to San Francisco around 1855, where he died in 1907. Taken from my father's notes: *"The original pattern was from feathers of the bird whose name the fly bears. It was dressed with a black head, dark claret wool body, yellow throat palmer tied with claret, yellow tail, and a gray mallard wing. Another one of his patterns was the Martha, named after his favorite daughter, a constant companion."*

Ice Berg

Hooks: AC80500BL, AC80501BL, TMC7999 or DAI2441, sizes 4-8.
Thread: Black.
Tail: Scarlet red hackle barbs.
Ribbing: Flat silver tinsel.
Body: CC01 pearl Crystal Chenille.
Wing: Dyed blue gray squirrel tail tied over the body.
Hackle: Kingfisher blue hen hackle tied on as a collar and tied back.
Head: Black.

Originated by Keith Stonebreaker of Lewiston, Idaho.

Ice N' Fire

Hooks: AC80500BL, AC80501BL, TMC7999 or DAI2441, sizes 4-8.
Thread: Fluorescent fire orange.
Tail: Dyed black squirrel tail tied equal to the length of the body.
Body: CC12 light blue Crystal Chenille.
Hackle: Fluorescent fire orange tied on as a collar and tied back and down.
Wing: Dyed black squirrel tail tied over the body.
Head: Fluorescent fire orange.

I put this pattern together during the winter of 1986 for the Feather and Yuba Rivers and I keep getting good reports on the fly for all steelhead waters. This is a real good pattern when the water is running an off color.

Improved Governor

Hooks: AC80500BL, AC80501BL, TMC7999 or DAI2441, sizes 2-6.
Thread: Black.
Ribbing: Oval gold tinsel over rear third only.
Rear Body: Red floss over the rear third.
Tail: Crimson red hackle barbs. The tail is tied in front of the red floss portion of the body.
Front Body: Peacock herl over front two-thirds.
Hackle: Coachman brown tied on as a collar and tied back and down.
Wing: Dyed brown fox squirrel tail tied over the body.
Cheeks: J.C. or substitute.
Head: Black.

This fly was adapted for steelhead use by Martha Benn of San Francisco, California, in 1915 from an old English wet fly pattern. Her earlier variation called for bronze mallard wings. Around 1930 Jim Pray replaced the wing with squirrel tail. See Governor, Chapter 8. Also see Humbolt Railbird in this chapter.

Improvised Practitioner

Hooks: AC80500BL, AC80501BL, TMC7999 or DAI2441, sizes 2/0-4.
Thread: Black.
Tail: Orange bucktail with two matching natural red golden pheasant body feathers.
Ribbing: Flat silver tinsel.
Body: Dubbed with #52 fluorescent orange lambs wool.
Center Body: Tie in one golden pheasant tippet in the Practitioner style and hackle forward palmer style with dyed orange pheasant rump.

Wing: Two matching dyed orange pheasant rump feathers with a single natural red golden pheasant body feather tied on top.
Hackle: Dyed orange barred teal tied long as a collar and tied back.
Head: Black.

This shrimp simulation is one of the patterns Mike Kenny popularized.

Indian Fly

Hooks: AC80500BL, AC80501BL, TMC7999 or DAI2441, sizes 4-8.
Thread: Brown.
Tail: Yellow calf tail.
Body: Rear half, dubbed with #6 yellow lambs wool and the front half, dubbed with #4 red lambs wool.
Hackle: Dark ginger tied on as a collar and tied back.
Wing: Fox squirrel tied over the body.
Head: Brown.

This pattern was given to me by a well meaning fellow fly fisherman while I was fishing the Yuba River in 1969. It is allegedly one that accounted for numerous fish the previous year on the Bella Coola River in British Columbia. The exact origin of the fly is not known. I have found it to be a good late summer and fall pattern in northern California.

Indian Girl

Hooks: AC80500BL, AC80501BL, TMC7999 or DAI2441, sizes 4-8.
Thread: Black.
Tail: Black hen hackle barbs.
Ribbing: Oval gold tinsel.
Body: Fluorescent fire orange chenille.
Hackle: Natural black hen hackle tied on as a collar and tied back and down.
Wing: Gray squirrel tied over the body.
Head: Black.

Indian Summer

Hooks: AC80500BL, AC80501BL, TMC7999 or DAI2441, sizes 2-6.
Thread: Red.
Tip: CH32 copper Crystal Hair.
Tail: Crimson red hackle barbs.
Butt: Red chenille.
Ribbing: Flat copper tinsel.

Body: Dubbed with #52 fluorescent orange African Angora goat.
Hackle: Crimson red tied on as a collar and tied back and down.
Wing: Pink bucktail tied over the body.
Head: Red.

Originated in 1963 by Walt Johnson of Seattle, Washington. For copper tinsel ribbing you can fray out diamond braid.

Plate 6   Ive's Green

Hooks: AC80500BL, AC80501BL, TMC7999 or DAI2441, sizes 4-8.
Thread: Red.
Tail: Scarlet red hackle barbs.
Ribbing: Flat silver tinsel.
Body: Fluorescent green chenille.
Hackle: Grizzly tied on as a collar and tied back and down.
Wing: Red bucktail tied over the body.
Head: Red.

Nobody knows who "Ive" is or was, at least not one that takes credit for this pattern. I first saw this pattern being used on the Mad River about 1956 and went crazy over it because of the body color. Fluorescent chenille wasn't a common material at that time. Oh yes, it was catching fish for everyone. As far as I can tell it may have been originated for the North Umpqua River in Oregon in the mid 1940s.

Jean Bucktail

Hooks: AC80500BL, AC80501BL, TMC7999 or DAI2441, sizes 2-6.
Thread: Black.
Tail: Orange hackle barbs.
Body: Flat gold tinsel.
Hackle: Yellow tied on as a collar and tied back and down.
Wing: Gray bucktail with an overwing of orange bucktail with gray bucktail tied on top. Each of the three wing portions should be equal.
Cheeks: J.C. or substitute.
Head: Black.

This is a British Columbia pattern which found its way to northern California in the mid 1940s.

Jennie Lind

Hooks: AC80500BL, AC80501BL, TMC7999 or DAI2441, sizes 4-8.
Thread: Fluorescent red.
Tail: Purple hen hackle barbs.
Ribbing: Oval gold tinsel.
Body: Dubbed with #51 fluorescent yellow Bunnytron.
Wing: Purple marabou tied over the body with strands of CH03 red Crystal Hair tied in at each side. Crystal Hair should extend the length of the wing.
Hackle: Fluorescent red tied on as a collar and tied back.
Head: Fluorescent red.

I developed this pattern in 1961 from an old English wet fly pattern of the same name. In 1984 I upgraded it using a touch of Crystal Hair. Whether it is by chance or there was more that went into their thinking than given credit for when the old English patterns were created, I don't know. They certainly deserve praise for this one. I do know that my variation does very well for winter-run fish. I just wish there was more time to use it.

Jock Scott

Hooks: AC80500BL, AC80501BL, TMC7999 or DAI2441, sizes 2-6.
Thread: Black.
Tail: Golden pheasant crest.
Ribbing: Flat silver tinsel.
Body: Rear half, yellow floss and the front half, black floss.
Hackle: Speckled guinea fowl tied in at the throat.
Wing: Dark brown bucktail tied over the body.
Topping: Peacock sword feather barbs.
Cheeks: J.C. or substitute.
Head: Black.

This is a steelhead variation of a very complex British pattern originally intended for Atlantic salmon. See Chapter 21 for still another variation.

Joe O'Donnell

Hooks: AC80500BL, AC80501BL, TMC7999 or DAI2441, sizes 4-6.
Thread: Red.
Tail: Scarlet red and yellow hackle barbs mixed.
Body: Cream (off white) chenille.
Wings: Pair of well marked badger hackle tips tied upward in a V over the body with concave side out.
Hackle: Scarlet red and yellow mixed and tied on as a collar and tied only slightly back.
Head: Red.

Originally tied for the Klamath River by Joe O'Donnell of Orleans, California. It is now considered a good winter pattern for the Eel and Rogue Rivers.

Juicy Bug

Hooks: AC80500BL, AC80501BL, TMC7999 or DAI2441, sizes 2-6.
Thread: Black.
Tail: Scarlet red hackle barbs.
Butt: Black chenille.
Ribbing: Oval silver tinsel.
Body: Red chenille.
Wings: White bucktail tied upward in a V over the body.
Cheeks: J.C. or substitute.
Head: Black.

Originated for the Rogue River by Ike Tower and Ben Chandler. When I think of this fly I invariably flash back to an article of about June 1926, by Zane Grey where he so eloquently expressed his inner-feelings for these fish, entitled *Rocky Riffle on the Rogue River*. This description of a hookup is one of my favorites:

"Beyond the flat, by a submerged stone was a deep channel with a ragged break in the ledge. Here the water swirled smoothly. To reach it meant a long cast for me, fully sixty feet, even to the outer edge of that likely spot. Wading deeper, I performed as strenuously as possible, and missed the spot by a couple of yards. My fly alighted below. But the water exploded, and the straightened rod jerked almost out of my hand.

"My whoop antedated the leap of that Rogue River beauty. After I saw him high in the air—long, broad, heavy, pink as a rose, mouth gaping wide—I was too paralyzed to whoop. I had established contact with another big steelhead. Like lightning he left that place. He ran up the river, making four jumps, one of them a greyhound leap—long, high, curved. I had to turn so my back was downstream, something new in even that ever-varying sport.

"When he felt the taut line again, he made such a tremendous lunge that I lost control of the click, and could not prevent him from jerking my rod partly under water. I was up to my waist, and that depth and the current augmented my difficulties. The fish changed his course, swerving back between me and the shore, and he leaped abreast of me, so close that the flying drops of water wet my face. As I saw him then I will never forget him.

"The slack line did not seem to aid him in any way, for he could not shake the hook. I anticipated his downstream rush, and was wading out, all ready when he made it. He leaped once more, a heavy, limber fish, tiring from the furious speed. I follow him so well that he never got more than half of the line. He took me down the channel, through the rapids, along the gravel bar below,

down the narrow green curve into the rough water below, where I could neither follow nor hold him.

"That fight gave me more of an understanding of the game fish and the marvelous sport they afford. As I wearily plodded back, nearly a half mile, I felt sick, and yet I had to rejoice at that unconquerable fish. My tackle was too light, but I would not have exchanged it for my heavy one, with that magnificent fish again fast to my line."

Most fly fishermen will find this tantamount to poetry of the highest measure. Some may even equate it to scripture.

Jungle Dragon
Hooks: AC80500BL, AC80501BL, TMC7999 or DAI2441, sizes 2-6.
Thread: Black.
Tip: Embossed silver tinsel.
Tail: Golden pheasant tippet barbs.
Ribbing: Embossed silver tinsel over front half only.
Body: Rear half, embossed silver tinsel and the front half, dubbed with #50 fluorescent red Bunnytron.
Hackle: Badger tied on as a collar and tied back and down.
Wing: Gray squirrel tail.
Cheeks: J.C. or substitute.
Head: Black.

Originated in 1943 by William Hosie.

Kalama Special
Hooks: TMC7989 or DAI2421, sizes 6-8.
Thread: Black.
Tail: Scarlet red hackle barbs.
Body: Dubbed with #51 fluorescent yellow African Angora goat.
Body Hackle: Badger tied palmer style over the body.
Wing: White calf tail tied over the body.
Hackle: Badger tied on as a collar and tied back.
Head: Black.

This fly was originated by Mooch Adams (I can guess where his name came from) of Portland, Oregon. Mike Kennedy popularized the fly for summer-runs and because he was so involved it became known as the Kennedy Special in some circles. Mike corresponded with my father frequently and influenced him to use it on the Klamath. California fly fishermen have been sleeping at the switch for years as this pattern is a sound producer from early summer until late fall. It will take fish just about any time of the year on the Yuba River. Use a floating line and fish just under the surface. You will see the take.

Kaleidoscope
Hooks: AC80500BL, AC80501BL, TMC7999 or DAI2441, sizes 2-6.
Thread: Fluorescent red.
Tail: Scarlet red hackle barbs.
Body: Dyed purple flat monofilament wrapped over and under body of blue floss.
Underwing: Dozen strands of CH01 pearl Crystal Hair.
Wing: White calf tail tied over the body.
Topping: Dozen strands of CH19 purple Crystal Hair.
Hackle: Purple tied on as a collar and tied back.
Head: Fluorescent red.

This fly was originally created by Walt Balek of Spokane, Washington. Evaluation has carried it a few steps further and it has become a very effective winter-run pattern.

Kate
Hooks: AC80500BL, AC80501BL, TMC7999 or DAI2441, sizes 4-6.
Thread: Red.
Tail: Golden pheasant crest.
Ribbing: Oval gold tinsel.
Body: Dubbed with #50 fluorescent red Bunnytron.
Hackle: Yellow.

Wing: CH03 red, CH04 yellow and CH14 dark blue Crystal Hair mixed with an overwing of barred mallard barbs tied over the body.
Cheeks: J.C. or substitute.
Head: Red.

This is a steelhead variation of this Atlantic salmon pattern which has been in use on the West Coast since the early 1900s. See Chapter 21.

Killer
Hooks: AC80500BL, AC80501BL, TMC7999 or DAI2441, sizes 2-6.
Thread: Black.
Tail: Scarlet red hackle barbs.
Ribbing: Oval silver tinsel.
Body: Dubbed with #50 fluorescent red Bunny-Blend.
Hackle: Scarlet red tied on as a collar and tied back and down.
Wing: Black calf tail tied over the body.
Cheeks: J.C. or substitute.
Head: Black.

Originated in Washington state around 1940.

Kispiox Bright
Hooks: AC80500BL, AC80501BL, TMC7999 or DAI2441, sizes 1-6.
Thread: Fluorescent fire orange.
Tail: Red calf tail mixed with a few strands of CH04 yellow Crystal Hair.
Ribbing: Flat silver tinsel.
Body: Purple chenille.
First Wing: White bucktail.
Second Wing: Salmon yellow bucktail mixed with strands of CH04 yellow Crystal Hair.
Hackle: Fluorescent fire orange tied on as a collar and tied back.
Head: Fluorescent fire orange.

Kispiox Dark
Hooks: AC80500BL, AC80501BL, TMC7999 or DAI2441, sizes 1-6.

Thread: Black.
Tail: Black bucktail mixed with CH02 black Crystal Hair.
Ribbing: Oval gold tinsel.
Body: Green floss.
Hackle: Grizzly tied on as a collar and tied back and down.
Wing: Black bucktail mixed with CH02 black Crystal Hair.
Head: Black.

The two patterns above were originated by Bob York for British Columbia waters and are now used with success up and down the West Coast. The dark is a welcome pattern in northern California for fall-run fish in the Trinity and Klamath Rivers.

Kispiox Shrimp
See Chapter 17.

Kispiox Special
Hooks: AC80500BL, AC80501BL, TMC7999 or DAI2441, sizes 1-6.
Thread: Red.
Tail: Red calf tail.
Body: Fluorescent orange chenille.
Hackle: Red tied on as a collar and tied back and down.
Wing: White calf tail tied over the body.
Head: Red.

This fly was originally created for the Kispiox River in British Columbia by Karl Mausser and Roy Pitts where it has accounted for some record catches. Since its origination in 1957 and due to its popularity, it is now used as far south as northern California.

Klickitat
Hooks: AC80500BL, AC80501BL, TMC7999 or DAI2441, sizes 4-8.
Thread: Fluorescent pink.
Body: Fluorescent pink chenille tied with a fat full taper.
Wing: White bucktail tied over the body.
Head: Fluorescent pink.

This pattern was created for Washington's Klickitat River.

Knudson's Spider
See Wet Spider.

Lady Caroline
Hooks: TMC7989 or DAI2421, sizes 6-8.
Thread: Claret.
Tail: Natural red golden pheasant body feather barbs.
Ribbing: Oval silver tinsel.
Body: Dubbed with a blend of two parts #19 olive and one part #24 brown African Angora goat.
Hackle: Natural red golden pheasant breast barbs tied in at the throat.
Wings: Sections of bronze mallard tied over the body.
Head: Claret.

This is a dressed down version of a British Atlantic salmon fly pattern which has been adapted for summer-runs.

Lady Claret
Hooks: AC80500BL, AC80501BL, TMC7999 or DAI2441, sizes 2-6.
Thread: Claret.
Tail: Blue dun hackle barbs.
Ribbing: Oval silver tinsel.
Body: Dubbed with #32 claret lambs wool.
Hackle: Blue dun tied on as a collar and tied back and down.
Wing: Coastal blacktail deer body hair tied over the body.
Head: Claret.

Lady Coachman
Hooks: TMC7989 or DAI2421, sizes 6-8.
Thread: Fluorescent red.
Tip: Lower half, flat silver tinsel and the upper half, fluorescent red floss.
Tail: Fluorescent red hackle barbs.
Ribbing: Fine silver wire wrapped in reverse over the body after it has been completed.
Butt: Peacock herl.
Center Body: Dubbed with #54 fluorescent hot pink lambs wool.
Thorax: Peacock herl.
Hackle: Fluorescent hot pink hen hackle barbs tied in at the throat.
Wing: White rabbit tied over the body.
Topping: Golden pheasant crest.
Cheeks: Kingfisher blue hen hackle tips tied in at each side.

Head: Fluorescent red.

An early season summer-run pattern created by Walt Johnson.

Lady Godiva
Hooks: AC80500BL, AC80501BL, TMC7999 or DAI2441, sizes 4-6.
Thread: Red.
Tip: Flat silver tinsel.
Tail: Scarlet red and yellow hackle barbs mixed.
Butt: Red chenille.
Ribbing: Flat silver tinsel.
Body: Dubbed with #2 white African Angora goat.
Wing: White bucktail tied over the body with an overwing of red bucktail.
Head: Red.

Lady Godiva, Orange
Hooks: AC80500BL, AC80501BL, TMC7999 or DAI2441, sizes 4-6.
Thread: Orange.
Tail: Orange hackle barbs.
Butt: Orange chenille.
Ribbing: Flat silver tinsel.
Body: Dubbed with #52 fluorescent orange African Angora goat.
Wing: White bucktail tied over the body with an overwing of orange bucktail.
Cheeks: J.C. or substitute
Head: Orange.

The two previous patterns were originated by Ralph Olson of Bellingham, Washington. The second pattern is also known as Orange Wing.

Lady Hamilton (s)
Hooks: AC80500BL, AC80501BL, TMC7999 or DAI2441, sizes 2-6.
Thread: Black.
Tail: Section of red goose quill.
Ribbing: Embossed silver tinsel.
Body: Red floss.
Wing: White bucktail tied over the body with an overwing of orange bucktail.
Head: Black.
Eyes: White with black centers.

Originated in the 1940s by Ralph Wahl of Bellingham, Washington.

Plate 8 — Langston

Hooks: AC80500BL, AC80501BL, TMC7999 or DAI2441, sizes 4-6.
Thread: Fluorescent orange.
Tail: Golden pheasant tippet barbs.
Ribbing: Oval gold tinsel.
Body: Rear half, flat gold tinsel and the front half, dubbed with #53 fire orange Bunny-Blend.
Center Joint Hackle: Fire orange hackle tied on as a collar and tied back.
Hackle: Natural brown bucktail tied in at the throat.
Wing: Dyed dark brown bucktail tied over the body.
Cheeks: Fire orange hen hackle tips tied in at each side.
Head: Fluorescent orange.
Note: The wing and throat hackle are of equal proportions and of the same length. In other words, you have a wing on top and one on the bottom.

Originated by Russell Langston of Brown's Valley, California.

Lead Eyed Leech

Hooks: AC80500BL, AC80501BL, TMC7999 or DAI2441, sizes 2-6.
Thread: Select color to match overall color of the fly.
Tail: Marabou.
Body: Chenille.
Body Hackle: Saddle tied palmer style over the body.
Eyes: Lead.

This type of fly is tied in basic black, dark brown, reddish brown and olive. The eyes are either chrome plated or painted white with either black or red centers. They are intended to reach fish in deep swift water where normal flies will not reach. With the added weight of lead they are probably better candidates for the ultra-light spin fisherman than they are for fly fishermen.

Lemire's Winter Fly

Hooks: AC80500BL, AC80501BL, TMC7999 or DAI2441, sizes 2/0-4.
Thread: Red.
Tip: Flat silver tinsel.
Tail: Scarlet red and yellow hackle barbs mixed.
Ribbing: Flat silver tinsel overwrapped with a narrower embossed silver tinsel. The embossed tinsel is then overwrapped with a single strand of red floss and FLI-BOND cement is applied to the floss.
Body: Dubbed with #11 salmon Bunnytron.
Hackle: Yellow tied on as a collar and tied back and down.
Wing: Sparse white monga ringtail tied over the body.
Head: Red.

Credit for this pattern goes to Harry Lemire. Due to the non-existence of red embossed tinsel I have had to get a bit creative with the ribbing on this pattern.

Lisa Bell

Hooks: AC80500BL, AC80501BL, TMC7999 or DAI2441, sizes 4-8.
Thread: Red.
Tip: Flat gold tinsel.
Tail: Golden pheasant crest.
Ribbing: Flat gold tinsel.
Body: Dubbed with #4 red lambs wool.
Hackle: Dyed orange guinea fowl tied in as a collar and tied back and down.
Wings: Barred teal sections tied low over the body.
Head: Red.

Lively Shrimp

See Chapter 17.

Lord Hamilton (S)

Hooks: AC80500BL, AC80501BL, TMC7999 or DAI2441, sizes 2-6.
Thread: Black.
Tail: Section of red goose quill.
Ribbing: Embossed silver tinsel.
Body: Dubbed with #6 yellow lambs wool.
Wing: White bucktail tied over the body with an overwing of red bucktail.
Head: Black.
Eyes: White with black centers.

Originated in the 1940s by Ralph Wahl of Bellingham, Washington.

Low Water Green
Hooks: TMC7989 or DAI2421, sizes 4-8.
Thread: Black.
Body: Dubbed thin with #15 insect green lambs wool.
Hackle: Furnace tied on as a collar and tied back and down.
Wing: White calf tail tied over the body.
Head: Black.

This simple tie is kept sparse, even reduced in some cases, to meet the low water conditions of many streams. This is a Bob York pattern designed for the Kispiox River. Like others of his design, this fly is useful in a wide range of areas. As an example, the Low Water Green is a major asset to fly fishermen on California's American River.

Mad River
Hooks: AC80500BL, AC80501BL, TMC7999 or DAI2441, sizes 2/0-8.
Thread: Black.
Tip: Oval silver tinsel.
Tail: Amherst pheasant crest.
Ribbing: Oval silver tinsel.
Shellback: Dyed black turkey quill section.
Body: Dubbed with #6 yellow lambs wool.
Hackle: Black tied on as a collar and tied back and down.
Wing: White calf tail tied over the body.
Topping: CH03 red Crystal Hair.
Head: Black.

Named for the river in which it was designed by my father in 1952. The original topping was a red Amherst pheasant crest.

Magenta Spider
Hooks: AC80500BL, AC80501BL, TMC7999 or DAI2441, sizes 2-6.
Thread: Black.
Tail: Yellow hackle barbs mixed with CH04 yellow Crystal Hair.
Body: Dubbed with #33 magenta lambs wool.
Wing: CH04 yellow Crystal Hair.
Hackle: Barred mallard tied on as a collar and tied back.

Topping: Red bucktail. Keep narrow and sparse.
Head: Black.

This is a pattern designed after Al Knudson's Wet Spider and was originated by Bob Betzig, Sr. of Snohomish, Washington.

March Brown
Hooks: TMC7989 or DAI2421, sizes 6-8.
Thread: Brown.
Tip: Four turns of oval gold tinsel.
Tail: Brown Hungarian partridge barbs.
Ribbing: Oval gold tinsel.
Body: Dubbed with blended English hare's mask fur.
Hackle: Brown Hungarian partridge barbs tied in at the throat.
Wings: Golden pheasant tail feather sections tied low over the body.
Head: Brown.

This is my variation of the old English wet fly pattern. I tie it for summer-run fish about twenty percent reduced. In late summer I often reduce it even further.

March Brown, Kennedy's
Hooks: AC80500BL, AC80501BL, TMC7999 or DAI2441, sizes 4-8.
Thread: Brown.
Tail: Golden pheasant tippet barbs.
Ribbing: Flat gold tinsel.
Body: Dubbed with #24 brown lambs wool.
Hackle: Furnace tied on as a collar and tied back and down.
Wing: Natural brown bucktail tied over the body.
Head: Brown.

This is a summer-run pattern designed by Mike Kennedy.

Margot
Hooks: AC80500BL, AC80501BL, TMC7999 or DAI2441, sizes 4-8.
Thread: Orange.
Tip: Oval gold tinsel.
Butt: Fluorescent orange yarn.
Body: Peacock herl. Reverse wrap with fine gold wire.

Wing: Dyed black squirrel tied over the body.
Hackle: Natural black hen hackle tied on as a collar and tied back.
Head: Orange.

This is a pattern I adapted from an Atlantic salmon fly which was originated in Canada by Roger Pelletier.

Marrietta

Hooks: AC80500BL, AC80501BL, TMC7999 or DAI2441, sizes 2/0-6.
Thread: Orange.
Tip: Flat silver tinsel.
Tail: Scarlet red hackle barbs.
Body: Fluorescent fire orange chenille.
Hackle: Fluorescent orange tied on as a collar and tied back and down.
Wing: Natural brown bucktail tied over the body.

Created during the mid 1950s by Don Redfern for British Columbia waters.

Martha

Hooks: AC80500BL, AC80501BL, TMC7999 or DAI2441, sizes 2-6.
Thread: Black.
Tail: Crimson red hackle barbs.
Ribbing: Oval gold tinsel.
Body: Rear half, red floss and the front half, yellow floss.
Hackle: Brown tied on as a collar and tied back and down.
Wing: Barred mallard barbs tied over the body.
Cheeks: J.C. or substitute.
Head: Black.

Originated about 1900 by John S. Benn of San Francisco, California. The fly was named after his daughter who in her own right was an excellent fly tier. See Humbolt Railbird.

Maverick

Hooks: AC80500BL, AC80501BL, TMC7999 or DAI2441, sizes 2-6.
Thread: Black.
Tail: Amherst pheasant tippet barbs.
Body: CC02 black Crystal Chenille.

Hackle: Badger tied on as a collar and tied back and down.
Wing: Gray squirrel tail tied over the body.
Head: Black.

Designed for the Rogue River in 1961 by Mike Kennedy.

Max Canyon

Hooks: AC80500BL, AC80501BL, TMC7999 or DAI2441, sizes 2-6.
Thread: Black.
Tail: Orange and white hackle barbs mixed.
Ribbing: Flat silver tinsel over entire body.
Body: Rear third, dubbed with #9 orange Bunny-Blend and the front two-thirds, black chenille.
Hackle: Black tied on as a collar and tied back and down.
Wing: White calf tail tied over the body.
Topping: Orange bucktail mixed with CH09 salmon Crystal Hair.
Head: Black.

Originated in 1972 by Doug Stewart of Gresham, Oregon.

Max Canyon, Dark

Hooks: AC80500BL, AC80501BL, TMC7999 or DAI2441, sizes 1-4.
Thread: Black.
Tail: CH07 fire orange Crystal Hair.
Ribbing: Oval gold tinsel.
Body: Rear third, dubbed #52 fluorescent orange Bunnytron and the front two thirds, dubbed with #1 black Bunnytron.
Wing: Black calf tail tied over the body.
Topping: CH02 black Crystal Hair.
Hackle: Black hen hackle tied on as a collar and tied back.
Head: Black.

This is a variation of the Max Canyon, origin unknown, that works well for winter-runs on most of the larger rivers on the West Coast.

Maxwell Purple

Hook: DAI2151, sizes 1-8.
Thread: Black.
Tip: Flat silver tinsel.
Ribbing: Oval silver tinsel.
Body: Dubbed with #58 fluorescent purple African Angora goat.

Wing: Purple neck hackle tied Matuka style.
Hackle: Purple tied on as a collar and tied back.
Head: Black.

This particular pattern was originated in the 1970s by Forrest Maxwell of Salem, Oregon. This was during a period when many Matuka style patterns were re-introduced. Few have been able to hold their popularity up to now. Another good variation of this fly is tied using dyed purple grizzly neck hackle. Frankly., it is hard for me to measure which of the two is better.

McClain's Fancy

Hooks: TMC7989 or DAI2421, sizes 6-10.
Thread: Brown.
Tail: Coastal blacktail deer body hair.
Ribbing: Single strand of brown yarn.
Body: Dubbed with #6 yellow lambs wool.
Wing: Coastal blacktail deer body hair tied over the body.
Head: Brown.

This summer-run pattern was originated by Don McClain. Tie this pattern sparsely and fish it with a floating line in the surface film.

McGinty

Hooks: AC80500BL, AC80501BL, TMC7999 or DAI2441, sizes 2-8.
Thread: Black.
Tail: Scarlet red hackle and speckled guinea fowl barbs mixed.
Body: Alternating bands of black and yellow chenille. Start at the rear with black first.
Hackle: Brown tied on as a collar and tied back and down.
Wing: Gray squirrel tail tied over the body.
Head: Black.

A variation of the wet fly pattern and first used for steelheading on the Klamath River way back when. It is an on again and off again popular fly in both southern Oregon and northern California, it just depends on who you talk to.

McKenzie Sapphire

Hooks: AC80500BL, AC80501BL, TMC7999 or DAI2441, sizes 2/0-4.
Thread: Black.
Tip: Oval silver tinsel.
Butt: Yellow floss with an underwrap of flat silver tinsel.
Ribbing: Flat silver tinsel.
Body: Dubbed with #1 black African Angora goat.
Body Hackle: Kingfisher blue tied palmer style over the body, starting with the second turn of ribbing, with two full turns at the front.
Wing: Four strands each of **l.** light blue, **2.** red, **3.** yellow and **4.** green bucktail mixed with an overwing of sparse white monga ringtail tied over the body.
Head: Black.

Originated by Mike Brooks of Veneta, Oregon. I like his use of monga ringtail in the wing of his flies. Many tiers miss out using this material as it is not always on the general menu of most suppliers. These are beautiful tails collected from furs of what is better known to some as the "miner's cat." They come from the Southwest and are usually available; at least I have been able to have them around at will since the 1940s. A softer textured material than most and well worth a try on your favorite pattern. Mike has another pattern called the McKenzie Sapphire No. 2 tied the same as above but with black squirrel tail for the wing.

McLeod's Bucktail

Hooks: AC80500BL, AC80501BL, TMC7999 or DAI2441, sizes 2-6.
Thread: Black.
Tail: Scarlet red hackle barbs.
Body: Black chenille tied fat.
Body Hackle: Fluorescent orange tied palmer style over the body.
Hackle: Grizzly hackle tied on as a collar and tied back.
Wing: Black calf tail tied over the body.
Head: Black.

Plate 6 — McLeod's Ugly

Hooks: AC80500BL, AC80501BL, TMC7999 or DAI2441, sizes 1-8.
Thread: Black.
Tail: Scarlet red tuft of marabou. This can be taken from the base of a neck or saddle hackle.
Body: Black chenille tied fat.
Hackle: Grizzly tied palmer style over the body.
Wing: Black calf tail tied over the body.
Head: Black.

These flies were originated in 1962 by Ken and George McLeod of Seattle, Washington. The patterns came about during the time I was living in Tacoma and there was little stir over it until I returned to California a few years later. I had samples from Roy Patrick's shop and have been tying them periodically ever since. The restrictions on the use of bear parts here in California has had little or no effect on the original patterns which called for a black bear hair wing.

McLeod's Shrimp

Hooks: AC80500BL, AC80501BL, TMC7999 or DAI2441, sizes 4-6.
Thread: Black.
Tail: Yellow hen hackle barbs.
Ribbing: Oval silver tinsel.
Body: Rear half, flat silver tinsel and the front half, dubbed with #1 black African Angora goat.
Center Joint Hackle: Orange tied on as a collar and tied back.
Hackle: Dyed black bucktail tied in at the throat.
Wing: Dyed black bucktail tied over the body.
Cheeks: J.C. or substitute.
Head: Black.

Note: The wing and throat hackle are of equal proportions and of the same length. In other words, you have a wing on top and one on the bottom.

This is a variation of a Scottish pattern which was originated by Robin McLeod of Inverness, Scotland.

McNeese Madness

Hooks: AC80500BL, AC80501BL, TMC7999 or DAI2441, sizes 2-6.
Thread: Black.
Tip: Flat silver tinsel.
Tail: Single strand of fluorescent orange floss.
Ribbing: CC19 purple Crystal Chenille.
Body: Fully tapered with fluorescent orange floss. Reverse wrap the body with fine silver wire after the ribbing is in place.
Hackle: Purple tied on as a collar and CH08 pink Crystal Hair spun on as a collar and both tied back and down.
Wing: Purple calf tail mixed with CH19 purple Crystal Hair tied over the body.
Head: Black.

"Creative Fly Tier" best describes Dave McNeese of Salem, Oregon, the originator of this pattern.

McReynolds

Hooks: AC80500BL, AC80501BL, TMC7999 or DAI2441, sizes 4-8.
Thread: Black.
Tail: Black hackle barbs.
Ribbing: Heavy black thread.
Body: Dubbed with #9 orange lambs wool.
Hackle: Grizzly tied on as a collar and tied back.
Head: Black.

Originated in 1940 by Clarence McReynolds of Eureka, California.

Plate 7 ### Mead

Hooks: AC80500BL, AC80501BL, TMC7999 or DAI2441, sizes 4-8.
Thread: Black.
Tail: Brown hackle barbs.
Body: Black and yellow variegated chenille.
Body Hackle: Brown tied palmer style over the body.
Head: Black.

Family files show this pattern was in use in northern California around 1940. The original body was of black and yellow chenille twisted together before they were wrapped, after the arrival of variegated chenille the change was made. It is strongly believed that the Brindle Bug sprang from this pattern.

Mickey Finn

Hooks: AC80500BL, AC80501BL, TMC7999 or DAI2441, sizes 4-6.
Thread: Red.
Body: Silver Mylar piping slipped over the body and tied down in the rear with red thread which in turn produces a red butt.
Wing: Yellow calf tail first, red calf tail in the middle with yellow calf tail tied on top. Each part of the wing should be proportions equal to each other.
Head: Red.

This pattern is a variation of the famous streamer fly which was adapted for use in northern California in 1942. This fly can also be successfully tied with a marabou wing. Every time someone makes mention of a Mickey Finn around my son Stan or his generation I detect a dubious snickering in the air. Snicker on, young men and after you wet one of these your attitude is sure to change. Also see Chapter 18.

Plate 7 ### Midnight Sun (S)

Hooks: AC80500BL, AC80501BL, TMC7999 or DAI2441, sizes 2/0-6.
Thread: Fluorescent red.
Tip: Flat silver tinsel.
Tail: Orange hackle barbs.
Ribbing: Flat silver tinsel.
Body: Fluorescent orange floss wrapped sparsely over an underbody of flat silver tinsel.
First Wing: CH01 pearl Crystal Hair tied over the body with an overwing of white marabou.
First Hackle: Orange and yellow marabou tied in at the throat.
Second Wing: White marabou tied over the body with marabou overwings of first yellow and then orange.
Hackle: Scarlet red tied on as a collar and tied back.
Head: Fluorescent red.

This is a pattern given us by angling author Trey Combs who has contributed much to steelhead fishing with his books and articles on the subject.

Plate 10 ### Midnite Sun

Hooks: AC80500BL, AC80501BL, TMC7999 or DAI2441, sizes 1/0-6.
Thread: Black.
Tip: Oval gold tinsel.
Tail: Orange hackle and guinea fowl barbs mixed.
Ribbing: Oval gold tinsel.
Body: Orange chenille.
Hackle: Guinea fowl tied on as a collar and tied back.
Wing: Black bucktail tied sparse over the body.
Head: Black.

This is an old reliable pattern originated by Mike Frith of Renton, Washington.

Migrant Orange

Hooks: AC80500BL, AC80501BL, TMC7999 or DAI2441, sizes 2-6.
Thread: Fluorescent fire orange.

Tip: Lower half, flat gold tinsel and the upper half, dubbed with #53 fluorescent fire orange lambs wool.
Tail: Fluorescent fire orange hackle barbs.
Ribbing: Flat gold tinsel.
Body: Dubbed with #53 fluorescent fire orange lambs wool.
Hackle: Fluorescent fire orange tied on as a collar and tied back and down.
Wing: Fluorescent orange bucktail.
Topping: Strand of fluorescent fire orange yarn.
Head: Fluorescent fire orange.

Originated by veteran steelheader Walt Johnson. Another variation has a flat copper tinsel tip and rib.

Montreal

Hooks: AC80500BL, AC80501BL, TMC7999 or DAI2441, sizes 4-8.
Thread: Claret.
Tip: Oval gold tinsel.
Tail: Scarlet red hackle barbs.
Ribbing: Oval gold tinsel.
Body: Dubbed with #32 claret lambs wool.
Hackle: Claret tied on as a collar and tied back and down.
Wing: Natural brown bucktail tied over the body.

This is the steelhead version of this pattern. It was adapted from a Canadian wet fly which dates back to 1840. See Chapter 8.

Plate 7 | Morning Glory

Hooks: AC80500BL, AC80501BL, TMC7999 or DAI2441, sizes 4-8.
Thread: Fluorescent orange.
Tail: Scarlet red hackle barbs.
Body: Rear third, dubbed with #57 fluorescent chartreuse lambs wool and the front two-thirds, fluorescent fire orange chenille.
Hackle: Fluorescent fire orange tied on as a collar and tied back and down.
Wing: White bucktail tied over the body.
Head: Fluorescent orange.

Originated by Paul Anderson of Kent, Washington.

Mossback

Hooks: AC80500BL, AC80501BL, TMC7999 or DAI2441, sizes 4-8.
Thread: Black.
Tail: Brown hackle tips tied on edge in a V.
Body: Black and green variegated chenille.
Hackle: Brown tied on as a collar and tied back.
Head: Black.

This is obviously a spin off of the Brindle Bug. It was given a good name, gets a lot of attention, and has caught some good fish on both the Trinity and Klamath Rivers where it is primarily used.

Mover

Hooks: TMC7989 or DAI2421, sizes 6-8.
Thread: Claret.
Tip: Oval gold tinsel.
Ribbing: Oval gold tinsel.
Body: Dubbed with #32 claret lambs wool.
Wing: Fox squirrel tail tied over the body.
Hackle: Dyed imitation barred lemon woodduck tied on as a collar one full turn and tied back. In front of this wrap dyed claret speckled guinea fowl one full turn. The guinea fowl should be slightly shorter than the woodduck.
Head: Claret.

The Mover is one of several experiments by Tim Coleman of Lynnwood, Washington. This particular pattern is fruitful when used for summer-runs.

Muddled Skunk

Hooks: AC80500BL, AC80501BL, TMC7999 or DAI2441, sizes 2/0-6.
Thread: Black.
Tail: Black bucktail.
Body: Wrapped with fine pearl braided Mylar piping.
Wing: Black bucktail tied over the body with an overwing of clear (white) Miclon topped with black bucktail. Each of the three wing portions should be equal.

Head: Dyed black deer hair spun on and clipped Muddler style. The collar is omitted, leaving a sparsely dressed fly.

This pattern was originally created in 1978 by Gene Parmeter for Alaska. It has since been proven in the lower forty-eight for steelhead and other freshwater species.

Muddler, Black Crystal
Hooks: AC80500BL, AC80501BL, TMC7999 or DAI2441, sizes 2-6.
Thread: Black.
Body: CC02 black Crystal Chenille.
First Wing: Dyed black squirrel tail with six strands of CH02 black Crystal Hair tied in on top.
Second Wing: Mottled brown turkey quill sections tied on edge over the body.
Collar: Dyed black coastal blacktail deer body hair spun on as a collar.
Head: Dyed black deer body hair spun on and clipped to shape.

See Chapter 18 for other Muddler Minnow variations. I am guilty of creating this pattern in view of how well other such patterns succeed. It has been useful for both summer and winter-run fish. I weight the underbody with lead wire for sizes 1 and 2.

Muddler, Coon
Hooks: AC80500BL, AC80501BL, TMC7999 or DAI2441, sizes 2-8.
Thread: Black.
Body: Embossed gold tinsel.
Wing: Black and white barred lemon woodduck sections tied on edge over the body with raccoon guard hair tied on top.
Collar: Coastal blacktail deer body hair spun on as a collar.
Head: Deer body hair spun on and clipped to shape.

This is a pattern by Joe Howell of Idleyld Park, Oregon. I have substituted the collar material on this pattern as explained in Chapter 18.

Muddy Waters
Hooks: AC80500BL, AC80501BL, TMC7999 or DAI2441, sizes 2-6.
Thread: Fluorescent fire orange.
Tail: Black hackle barbs.
Ribbing: Flat silver tinsel.
Body: Fluorescent fire orange yarn.
Wing: White bucktail tied over the body with an overwing of natural brown bucktail.
Topping: Four strands of fluorescent fire orange yarn.
Head: Fluorescent fire orange.

This pattern was developed in 1950 by Wes Drain of Seattle, Washington.

Naknek Demon
Hooks: AC80500BL, AC80501BL, TMC7999 or DAI2441, sizes 2-6.
Thread: Fluorescent orange.
Tip: Flat silver tinsel.
Tail: Single strand of fluorescent orange floss.
Body: Flat silver tinsel.
Hackle: Fluorescent orange tied on as a collar and tied back and down.
Wing: White bucktail tied over the body with a single strand of fluorescent orange floss tied over the top with an overwing of fluorescent orange bucktail.
Head: Fluorescent orange.

Developed in 1968 by angling author Trey Combs.

Nation's Fancy
Hooks: AC80500BL, AC80501BL, TMC7999 or DAI2441, sizes 4-8.
Thread: Black.
Tail: Golden pheasant tippet barbs.
Ribbing: Oval silver tinsel.
Body: Rear third, flat silver tinsel and the front two-thirds, dubbed with #1 black lambs wool.
Wings: Golden pheasant tippet barbs tied over the body with barred teal sections tied in on the sides.
Hackle: Badger tied on as a collar and tied back.
Head: Black.

Nation's Red

Hooks: AC80500BL, AC80501BL, TMC7999 or DAI2441, sizes 4-8.
Thread: Black.
Tail: Barred mallard barbs.
Ribbing: Oval silver tinsel.
Body: Rear half, flat silver tinsel and the front half, dubbed with #4 red lambs wool.
Wings: Bronze mallard sections tied low over the body.
Hackle: Badger tied on as a collar and tied back.
Head: Black.

The two previous patterns were developed in British Columbia by Bill Nation around 1930. He had another pattern called Nation's Silver Tip which is the same as Nation's Fancy except the wings consist of mottled brown turkey quill sections with narrow sections of red goose quill tied down the sides.

Many years ago Roy Patrick got me onto using the Nation's Fancy for summer-run fish. That one little piece of advice will stay with me forever as this pattern has been very good to me.

Neon

Hook: AC80501BL, sizes 2/0-8.
Thread: Fluorescent fire orange.
Tail: Fluorescent orange bucktail.
Body: Fluorescent fire orange chenille.
Wing: Fluorescent orange bucktail tied over the body and extending to the end of the tail.
Hackle: Fluorescent red tied on as a collar and tied back.
Eyes: Silver bead chain.

Take note that the wing is mounted prior to the hackle. This fly was developed in the early 1960s for the Russian River.

Nicomekyl

Hooks: AC80500BL, AC80501BL, TMC7999 or DAI2441, sizes 4-8.
Thread: Black.
Tail: Golden pheasant crest with a small short section of red duck quill tied flat on top.

Ribbing: Oval gold tinsel.
Body: Rear half, orange floss and the front half, dubbed with #32 claret lambs wool.
Hackle: Claret tied on as a collar and tied back and down.
Wings: Bronze mallard sections tied low over the body.
Head: Black.

Originated by W. Brougham of Vancouver, British Columbia.

Night Dancer

Hooks: DAI2151 or DAI2161, sizes 1-6.
Thread: Black.
Tail: Scarlet red hackle barbs.
Ribbing: Flat silver tinsel.
Body: Dubbed with #1 black lambs wool.
Hackle: Purple tied on as a collar and tied back and down.
Wing: Black bucktail tied over the body.
Head: Black.

This fly was originated by Frank Amato of Portland, Oregon. In addition to Frank's flourishing publishing business he has a generous amount of time to spend steelheading. I believe it is referred to as R and D. All I know is that he is never in his office.

Night Owl

Hooks: AC80500BL, AC80501BL, TMC7999 or DAI2441, sizes 1-4.
Thread: Fluorescent fire orange.
Tail: Salmon yellow hackle barbs.
Butt: Red chenille.
Body: Oval silver tinsel.
Wing: White bucktail tied over the body.
Hackle: Fluorescent fire orange tied on as a collar and tied back.

Another of Lloyd Silvius's great successes. I can remember spending an afternoon with Lloyd in his shop in Eureka, California. It had been raining a couple of days and all of the streams were totally out of shape. This happened to be the fly he was tying to pass away the doldrums of the day. He always was one to share and show the utmost respect to other fly tiers, especially if he knew you were trying to also make some money to support a fishing habit. He explained how he liked this as a winter pattern, but "on days like today, you need to get bead chain eyes on this one and get it down deep." A couple of days later we did and it worked.

Nix's Woolly Special

Hooks: AC80500BL, AC80501BL, TMC7999 or DAI2441, sizes 2-6.
Thread: Black.
Body: Rear half, fluorescent green chenille and front half, fluorescent pink chenille.
Body Hackle: Grizzly tied palmer style over the body.

This is a simple enough fly to tie and I am not sure of its origin. East Coast steelheader Ron Nix is responsible for its popularity and it bears his name.

Norton's Special (S)

Hook: AC80501BL, sizes 2/0-8.
Thread: White.
Tail: Fluorescent orange calf tail tied equal to one and one half the length of the body.
Ribbing: Embossed silver tinsel.
Body: Fluorescent orange chenille.
Hackle: Fluorescent orange tied on as a collar and tied back.
Eyes: Silver bead chain.

This fly of the Comet design was originated by Howard Norton of Sebastopol, California. See Comets.

Norwegian Moustache

Hooks: AC80500BL, AC80501BL, TMC7999 or DAI2441, sizes 4-6.
Thread: Black.
Tail: Golden pheasant tippet barbs.
Ribbing: Oval gold tinsel.
Body: Flat gold tinsel.
Hackle: Orange tied on as a collar and tied back and down.

Wings: Bucktail tied over the body and tied cocked upward in a V approximately 30 degree to each other. Wing color consists of one side white and the other side natural brown.
Head: Black.

Originated in 1942 by Morley Griswold, former governor of Nevada, for the North Umpqua River in Oregon. The Norwegian Moustache was named for the governor's Norwegian gardener who sported a tobacco stained mustache. This fly can get some fairly wide grins from those who first see it. In 1946 Governor Griswold won the annual *Field & Stream* contest with a 28 pounder taken on this fly from the lower Deschutes River. The fish was a world record.

Old English Iron Blue Dun

Hooks: AC80500BL, AC80501BL, TMC7999 or DAI2441, sizes 4-8.
Thread: Black.
Tail: Natural red golden pheasant breast barbs.
Ribbing: Oval silver tinsel.
Body: Dubbed with muskrat fur.
Hackle: Natural black hen hackle tied on as a collar and tied back and down.
Wing: Gray squirrel tail tied over the body.
Head: Black.

This has proven to be a good summer-run pattern. It is believed that it was adapted from an English wet fly pattern.

Old Mare

Hooks: AC80500BL, AC80501BL, TMC7999 or DAI2441, sizes 2-6.
Thread: Black.
Tail: Orange hackle barbs.
Butt: Dark olive chenille.
Ribbing: Oval silver tinsel.
Body: Dubbed with #4 red lambs wool.
Hackle: Brown tied on as a collar and tied back and down.
Wings: White bucktail tied over the body and tied upward in a V.

Head: Black.

This is an old classic which is a variation of the Rogue River Special.

Olive Breadcrust

Hooks: AC80500BL, AC80501BL, TMC7999 or DAI2441, sizes 4-8.
Thread: Olive.
Tip: Flat gold tinsel.
Tail: Mottled ringneck pheasant body feather barbs.
Body Hackle: Brown tied palmer style over the body.
Body: Olive tinsel core chenille.
Hackle: Mottled greenish ringneck pheasant saddle tied on as a collar and tied back.
Head: Olive.

The term "riverkeeper" is one we often find intertwined with the more common "fishing bum." However, I know of no term other than riverkeeper to best describe Herb Burton of Lewiston, California. The river is the Trinity and here is where Herb makes his living caring for his wife and children, plus the river for twenty-five years. Herb guides approximately 1,000 miles per season out of his little shop. A writer, naturalist, conservationist and avid fly fisherman wrapped into one package, he has been successful in many projects which have been for the betterment of our sport. If you want to talk "Trinity River" and what may or may not be ailing it, speak with Herb.

He came up with the Olive Breadcrust in 1986 after years of experimentation. It is used for both summer and winter-run fish.

Orange Bucktail (S)

Hooks: AC80500BL, AC80501BL, TMC7999 or DAI2441, sizes 2-8.
Thread: Fluorescent orange.
Tail: Scarlet red hackle barbs and CH01 pearl Crystal Hair mixed.
Ribbing: Fluorescent orange thread.
Shellback: White bucktail mixed with CH01 pearl Crystal Hair.
Body: Dubbed with #52 fluorescent orange African Angora goat.
Wing: White bucktail tied over the body.
Cheeks: Short strand of fluorescent fire orange yarn. Yarn should be frayed out.
Topping: CH06 orange Crystal Hair.
Head: Fluorescent orange.

My father originated this pattern in the winter of 1950 for the Eel and Mad Rivers. I have updated it material wise using some of today's contemporary materials. It was intended for use as a winter pattern and often tied in sizes up to 2/0 and well weighted.

Orange Carey

Hooks: AC80500BL, AC80501BL, TMC7999 or DAI2441, sizes 2-6.
Thread: Black.
Tip: Yellow floss.
Tail: Red duck quill section.
Ribbing: Oval silver tinsel.
Body: Dubbed with #6 yellow lambs wool.
Hackle: Grizzly tied on as a collar and tied back and down.
Wing: Orange bucktail tied over the body with white goose quill sections tied over the top.
Head: Black.

Orange Demon

Hooks: AC80500BL, AC80501BL, TMC7999 or DAI2441, sizes 4-8.
Thread: Black.
Tail: Fluorescent orange hackle barbs.
Ribbing: Oval gold tinsel.
Body: Dubbed with #57 fluorescent chartreuse Bunnytron.
Hackle: Fluorescent orange tied on as a collar and tied back and down.
Wing: Dyed black deer body hair tied over the body.
Head: Black.

This fly was taken from an original idea of Jim Pray's for a pattern which never really succeeded. The original body had orange yarn. In later years when fluorescents were introduced to steelhead flies my father took the pattern and experimented with a variety of body colors for the Klamath River. From all of the colors, this is the one that was most productive. The fluorescent green body color stuck and so did the name, Orange Demon.

Orange Optic

Hooks: DAI2451, sizes 1-4.
Thread: Orange.
Body: Oval silver tinsel.
Wing: Orange bucktail tied over the body.
Head: Black over 1/4" hollow brass bead.
Eyes: White with red center.

This pattern was originated for the Eel River and was patterned after the Jim Pray designs.

Orange Scooter

Hooks: TMC7989 or DAI2421, sizes 4-8.
Thread: Black.
Tail: CH06 orange Crystal Hair.
Body: Dubbed with #52 fluorescent orange lambs wool.
Wing: CH06 orange Crystal Hair tied over the body with an overwing of sparse black bucktail.
Head: Dyed black deer hair spun on and clipped to shape.

This pattern was originated by Joe Howell.

Plate 7   Orange Shrimp

Hooks: AC80500BL, AC80501BL, TMC7999 or DAI2441, sizes 2-8.
Thread: Black.
Tip: Flat gold tinsel.
Tail: Scarlet red hackle barbs.
Body: Orange chenille.
Hackle: Orange tied on as a collar and tied back and down.
Wing: White calf tail tied over the body.
Cheeks: J.C. or substitute.

It is my belief that this single pattern is the model from which all other orange steelhead patterns have been formulated for the past fifty years or more. My own Orange Shrimp Spey will certainly attest

to this. See Chapter 22. Because of its extensive record of productivity, any steelheader not carrying the Orange Shrimp in its original dressing probably is working with a handicap. Some of our new fancifully dressed patterns are works of the fly tiers art, however, just how productive are they when compared to those of thirty or more years ago?

Plate 8   Orange Shrimp Cocktail

Hooks: AC80500BL, AC80501BL, TMC7999 or DAI2441, sizes 4-8.
Thread: Red.
Tail: Red hen hackle barbs.
Ribbing: Oval silver tinsel.
Body: Rear half, flat silver tinsel and the front half, dubbed with #6 orange Bunny-Blend.
Center Joint Hackle: Orange tied on as a collar and tied back.
Hackle: White bucktail tied in at the throat.
Wing: White bucktail tied over the body.
Cheeks: Red hen hackle tips (lacquered) tied in at each side.
Head: Red.
Note: The wing and throat hackle are of equal proportions and of the same length. In other words, you have a wing on top and one on the bottom.

Originated by Russell Langston of Brown's Valley, California.

Orange Steelheader

Hook: DAIJ101, size 6.
Thread: Black.
Tail: Fluorescent fire orange bucktail.
Body: Copper wire.
Middle Wing: Fluorescent fire orange bucktail.
Front Wing: Fluorescent fire orange bucktail.
Head: Black.
Eyes: Tiny red dots.

The Orange Steelheader was created by Fred A. Reed of Nevada City, California. All accounts of the dressing for this fly state that the wings are of polar bear hair and the body is of silver wire. In all of these years I have yet to see it dressed in this fashion. It must be assumed that this pattern was inspired by the Pete Schwab design. See Bellamy.

Orleans
Hooks: AC80500BL, AC80501BL, TMC7999 or DAI2441, sizes 2/0-8.
Thread: Orange.
Tag: Short strand of orange yarn well frayed out.
Body: Dubbed with #25 reddish brown Bunny-Blend.
Body Hackle: Furnace tied palmer style over the body.
Hackle: Dyed brown barred mallard tied on as a collar, one full turn and tied back and down.
Wing: Dyed brown coastal blacktail deer hair tied sparsely over the body.
Head: Orange.

Should you be unfamiliar with my definition of a "tag" refer to Chapters 6 or 21. This is truly a pattern for all seasons. I can still remember the night my father first tied this fly; he may have been ahead of his time because up until that time, 1950, I had never seen a steelhead fly with anything other than a black head. He used orange silk from a project he had underway to restore a bamboo rod. I had also never seen many materials overdyed such as the deer hair and barred mallard used. Two weeks later, after he returned from the Klamath, "Orleans" became a standard household word.

Plate 6   Orleans Barber
Hooks: DAI2151 or DAI2161, sizes 4-8.
Thread: Black.
Tail: Black and white barred section of lemon woodduck.
Body: Red chenille.
Hackle: Grizzly tied on as a collar and tied back.
Head: Black.

This pattern was created in 1934 by the local barber, name not of record, of Orleans, California, for use on the Klamath River. For identification as well as commercial purposes, Jim Pray named this fly which has become somewhat of a classic in northern California.

Plate 10   Orphan
Hooks: AC80500BL, AC80501BL, TMC7989 or DAI2421, sizes 6-10.
Thread: Black.
Tail: Dyed imitation barred lemon woodduck barbs.
Ribbing: Oval gold tinsel.
Body: Dark olive chenille.
Hackle: Grizzly tied on as a collar and tied back.
Wing: Coastal blacktail deer hair tied sparse over the body.
Head: Black.

This fly was originated by Myron Sprague of Palo Alto, California. Family records indicate that it was first tied with a peacock body but after a short time chenille took its place because it is so much more durable. The change doesn't make a difference, however, I still favor the peacock. This fly was intended for the fall-run on the Klamath River using a floating fly line with a well greased nine foot leader. From my experience it is a real good fly on all of the streams of northern California and southern Oregon.

Oso Special

Hooks: AC80500BL, AC80501BL, TMC7999 or DAI2441, sizes 2-6.
Thread: Black.
Tail: Single strand of fluorescent fire orange floss.
Body: Rear three-quarters, fluorescent fire orange chenille and the front quarter, black chenille.
Hackle: Natural black hen hackle tied on as a collar and tied back and down.
Wing: Natural black moose mane tied over the body and tied sparse and long.
Head: Black.

This pattern is a product of Charles Gearheart.

Otter Bar Purple

Hooks: AC80500BL, AC80501BL, TMC7999 or DAI2441, sizes 4-8.
Thread: Claret.
Tail: Purple hackle barbs.
Ribbing: Flat silver tinsel.
Body: Dubbed with #30 purple African Angora goat.
Hackle: Purple tied on as a collar and tied back and down.
Wing: Ringneck pheasant tail feather barbs.
Head: Claret.

This is one of Marty Sherman's patterns, he named it after Otter Bar Lodge while fishing northern California's Salmon River. Marty, I wish you hadn't let this one out. I keep telling everyone that the Salmon River is in Idaho, especially, the brushy North Fork.

Paint Brush

Hooks: AC80500BL, AC80501BL, TMC7999 or DAI2441, sizes 1-6.
Thread: Black.
Tail: Red calf tail.
Body: Copper wire.
Center Wing: Red bucktail.
Wing: Yellow bucktail with an overwing of red bucktail which is topped with dyed brown bucktail.
Head: Black.

The body on the original pattern called for brass wire. See Bellamy.

Paint Pot

Hooks: AC80500BL, AC80501BL, TMC7999 or DAI2441, sizes 2-6.
Thread: Black.
Tail: Scarlet red hackle barbs.
Body: Flat silver tinsel wrapped over an underbody of well tapered white floss.
Hackle: Scarlet red tied on as a collar and tied back and down.
Wing: Dyed yellow gray squirrel tail tied over the body.
Head: Black.

Painted Lady

Hooks: AC80500BL, AC80501BL, TMC7999 or DAI2441, sizes 2-6.
Thread: Black.
Tail: Orange goose quill section.
Body: Flat silver tinsel wrapped over an underbody of well tapered white floss.
Side stripes: The body of this unusual fly is pin-striped on the sides. Before completing the body tie in four strands each of fluorescent red floss to be pulled up the sides after the body is completed. After the strips are in place, apply two consecutive coats of FLI-BOND cement to the entire body which will secure your work in place.
Top of Body: Fill in the area on top of the body with fluorescent yellow enamel.
Wing: White bucktail tied over the body with an overwing of orange bucktail. The Painted Lady's body must dry some before mounting the wing.
Head: Black. The head should be constructed rather large.
Eyes: White with black centers.

The winters in Bellingham, Washington, can be very long, very wet and very cold. The last time I was there it was seven below with a forty mile an hour wind, the wind chill factor was undetermined. I can only assume that it was at a time like this that Ralph Wahl found time to develop the two patterns above. His knowledge of winter steelheading told him that he needed something that would get down to the fish. I wonder if he felt as I did the first time I constructed a Painted Lady? Remembrances of my youth when I completed a model car given to me at Christmas time will always come to mind when I see this fly.

Park
Hooks: AC80500BL, AC80501BL, TMC7999 or DAI2441, sizes 4-6.
Thread: Black.
Tip: Flat silver tinsel.
Ribbing: Oval silver tinsel.
Body: Black chenille.
Hackle: Yellow tied on as a collar and tied back and down.
Wing: Natural black monga ringtail tied over the body.
Head: Black.

This is a variation of an Atlantic salmon fly which Mike Kennedy tied and popularized. See Chapter 21.

Parmachene Belle
Hooks: AC80500BL, AC80501BL, TMC7999 or DAI2441, sizes 4-6.
Thread: Red.
Tail: Scarlet red and yellow hackle barbs mixed.
Ribbing: Oval gold tinsel.
Body: Dubbed with #51 fluorescent yellow Bunny-Blend.
Wing: White bucktail tied over the body with an overwing of red bucktail and CH03 red Crystal Hair mixed.
Head: Red.

This is a steelhead variation of an old American wet fly. See Chapter 8.

Patricia
Hooks: AC80500BL, AC80501BL, TMC7999 or DAI2441, sizes 4-8.
Thread: Claret.
Tip: Oval gold tinsel.
Tail: Claret hackle barbs.
Ribbing: Oval gold tinsel.
Body: Dubbed with #32 claret Bunny-Blend.

Hackle: Claret tied on as a collar and tied back and down.
Wing: Sparse white bucktail tied over the body.
Cheeks: J.C. or substitute.
Head: Claret.

Originated in 1985 by Randy Stetzer.

Pete's Lady Bug
Hooks: AC80500BL, AC80501BL, TMC7999 or DAI2441, sizes 2-6.
Thread: Fluorescent fire orange.
Tail: Fox squirrel tail.
Ribbing: Oval gold tinsel.
Shellback: Fluorescent pink chenille.
Body: Brown chenille.
Body Hackle: Fluorescent fire orange tied palmer style over the body.
Head: Fluorescent fire orange.

This productive fly was originated by Pete Peterson of Vancouver, British Columbia. This contrast in colors would certainly upset me if one of my daughters were to dress in this fashion, however, the excitement it arouses with fish on the other hand is pleasing.

Pete's Shrimp
Hooks: AC80500BL, AC80501BL, TMC7999 or DAI2441, sizes 2-6.
Thread: Fluorescent fire orange.
Tail: Fluorescent orange bucktail.
Butt: Black chenille.
Body: Fluorescent fire orange chenille.
Body Hackle: Fluorescent orange tied palmer style over the body.
Wing: Bunch of golden pheasant tippet barbs tied over the body with an overwing of a single natural red golden pheasant breast feather tied flat.
Head: Fluorescent fire orange.

Originated by Pete McVey of Merritt, British Columbia.

Pete's Special
Hooks: AC80500BL, AC80501BL, TMC7999 or DAI2441, sizes 2-6.
Thread: Fluorescent red.
Tail: Scarlet red hackle barbs.

Body: Rear third, fluorescent green chenille and the front two-thirds, fluorescent red chenille.
Hackle: Orange tied on as a collar and tied back and down.
Wing: White bucktail tied over the body.
Head: Fluorescent red.

Pink Lady

Hooks: AC80500BL, AC80501BL, TMC7999 or DAI2441, sizes 4-8.
Thread: Fluorescent pink.
Tip: Oval gold tinsel.
Tail: Amherst pheasant tippet barbs.
Ribbing: Oval gold tinsel.
Body: Dubbed with #28 pink Bunny-Blend.
Hackle: Ginger tied on as a collar and tied back and down.
Wing: Natural deer body hair tied over the body.
Head: Fluorescent pink.

This is a variation of an American wet fly pattern. See Chapter 8.

Pink Lady (S)

Hook: AC80500BL, AC80501BL, TMC7999 or DAI2441, sizes 4-6.
Thread: Fluorescent red.
Tail: Red bucktail.
Ribbing: Flat silver tinsel.
Body: Fluorescent pink chenille.
Hackle: Fluorescent red tied on as a collar and tied back and down.
Wing: Red bucktail tied over the body.
Head: Fluorescent red.

This is a pattern from the family file with little or no information. It is certain that it was not inspired by the wet fly version. Or was it? The reason I bothered including this pattern is because of how well it seems to go in and out of favor every three or four years. One group I know carry only this pattern with them to Alaska each year. I also know of others who rely on it heavily for the Eel River.

Pink Mambo

Hooks: AC80500BL, AC80501BL, TMC7999 or DAI2441, sizes 2-6.
Thread: Red.
Tail: Scarlet red hackle barbs.
Body: Rear half, dubbed with #54 fluorescent hot pink lambs wool and the front half, black chenille.
Wing: Pink bucktail tied over the body.
Hackle: Scarlet red tied on as a collar and tied back.
Head: Red.

Originated in 1960 by Victor Moore of Smithers, British Columbia.

Pink Pearl

Hooks: AC80500BL, AC80501BL, TMC7999 or DAI2441, sizes 2/0-6.
Thread: Fluorescent red.
Tip: Flat silver tinsel.
Tail: Fluorescent red hackle barbs.
Ribbing: Flat silver tinsel.
Body: Sparsely wrapped fluorescent red floss over an underbody of flat silver tinsel.
First Wing: CH01 pearl Crystal Hair tied over the body with an overwing of white marabou.
First Hackle: Fluorescent hot pink marabou tied in at the throat.
Second Wing: White marabou tied over the body with an overwing of fluorescent hot pink marabou.
Second Hackle: Fluorescent red tied on as a collar and tied back.
Head: Fluorescent red.

Originated by Trey Combs.

Pink Rat

Hooks: AC80500BL, AC80501BL, TMC7999 or DAI2441, sizes 4-8.
Thread: Red.
Tip: Oval silver tinsel.
Tail: Amherst pheasant crest.
Ribbing: Oval silver tinsel.
Body: Dubbed with #54 fluorescent hot pink African Angora goat.
Wing: Gray squirrel tail tied over the body. Use hair from the base of the tail.
Hackle: Grizzly tied on as a collar and tied back.
Head: Red.

Pink Salmon

Hook: AC80501BL, sizes 2/0-8.
Thread: Fluorescent red.
Tail: Fluorescent hot pink marabou with CH08 pink Crystal Hair mixed.
Body: CC20 fuchsia Crystal Chenille.
Body Hackle: Fluorescent hot pink tied palmer style over the body.
Hackle: Fluorescent fire orange tied on as a collar and tied back.
Eyes: Silver bead chain.

This extraordinary pattern is the product of Mike Mercer of Redding, California. I use the term "extraordinary" because of its higher than average results for winter-run fish.

Polar Shrimp (S)

Hooks: AC80500BL, AC80501BL, TMC7999 or DAI2441, sizes 2/0-6.
Thread: Fluorescent fire orange.
Tail: Scarlet red hackle barbs.
Body: Fluorescent orange chenille.
Hackle: Fluorescent orange tied on as a collar and tied back and down.
Wing: White bucktail tied over the body.
Topping: CH01 pearl Crystal Hair.
Head: Fluorescent fire orange.

Thought to have been originated in Washington state. This fly was first used on the Eel River in 1936. Some credit Clarence Shoff as the originator. This is also a good Pacific salmon pattern. When tied for salmon the wing should be tied longer than normal.

Polar Shrimp

Hooks: AC80500BL, AC80501BL, TMC7999 or DAI2441, sizes 2-6.
Thread: Fluorescent red.
Tip: Oval gold tinsel.
Ribbing: Oval gold tinsel.
Body: Dubbed with #53 fluorescent fire orange Bunnytron.
Hackle: Orange tied on as a collar and tied back and partially down.
Wing: White calf tail.
Topping: CH01 pearl Crystal Hair.
Head: Fluorescent red.

This pattern is a variation created by Ed Haas of Forks of the Salmon, California. At one time Ed supplied my father with a good number of flies. Every time he visited us in Redding it was an all day, all night affair. Each time I don't know who came out ahead, my father or Ed. He seemed to always leave with more than he came with. Ed was our main source at that time for coastal blacktail deer hides. We sold them to some Easterners who tacked fancy names and prices to them.

Pink Shrimp (S)

See Chapter 17.

Polar Shrimp, Crystal (S)

Hooks: AC80500BL, AC80501BL, TMC7999 or DAI2441, sizes 4-8.
Thread: Fluorescent orange.
Tail: Scarlet red hackle barbs mixed with a few strands of CH03 red Crystal Hair.
Body: CC07 fire orange Crystal Chenille.
Hackle: Fluorescent orange tied on as a collar and tied back.
Wing: White monga ringtail tied over the body.
Topping: Six strands of CH01 pearl Crystal Hair.
Head: Fluorescent orange.

A sign of taking your fly patterns too seriously is when you feel like I initially did about this one. A moment of guilt came over me when calling this a Polar Shrimp. Having such respect for the original pattern and the multitude of good days it rendered caused me to have temporary second thoughts. I am not looking for credit for this pattern, just blame for possibly altering the original in some positive manner. Now, after fishing with this fly for five years I pass it off as an act of evolution. The fly works real well and is endorsed by many.

Pole-Kat

Hooks: AC80500BL, AC80501BL, TMC7999 or DAI2441, sizes 2-8.
Thread: Black.
Tail: Small bunch of white marabou mixed with CH01 pearl Crystal Hair.
Body: Wrapped with fine silver braided Mylar piping.
Hackle: Small bunch of black marabou tied in at throat.
Wing: White marabou tied over the body with an equal portion of black marabou tied on top.
Cheeks: Short bunch of fluorescent fire orange marabou tied in at each side.
Topping: CH02 black Crystal Hair.
Head: Black.

Another of the Darwin Atkin patterns. See Bright Ember.

Polly's Pride (s)

Hooks: AC80500BL, AC80501BL, TMC7999 or DAI2441, sizes 1-6.
Thread: Black.
Tail: Scarlet red hackle barbs.
Ribbing: Flat silver tinsel.
Body: Dubbed with #4 fluorescent red lambs wool.
Hackle: Fluorescent red hen hackle tied on as a collar and tied back and down.
Wing: White marabou.
Topping: Six strands of black ostrich herl.
Head: Black.

Originated by E. H. "Polly" Rosborough of Chiloquin, Oregon. He proclaimed this fly his trademark. I know that Polly, wherever he is, will never forgive me for recommending these hooks. His real work centered around his nymphs.

Poodle Dog

Hooks: AC80500BL, AC80501BL, TMC7999 or DAI2441, sizes 4-6.
Thread: Black.
Tail: Scarlet red hackle barbs.
Body: Black chenille with a flat silver tinsel center band.
Hackle: White tied on as a collar and tied back and down.

Wing: White bucktail tied over the body.
Head: Black.

Originated in the 1950s by Robert Wesson of Marysville, Washington.

Poor Man's G.P.

Hooks: DAI2151 or DAI2161, sizes 1-4.
Thread: Fluorescent red.
Body: Flat gold tinsel.
First Hackle: Fluorescent orange hackle tied on as a collar and tied back.
Second Hackle: Fluorescent fire orange marabou tied on as a collar and tied back.
Wings: Two natural red golden pheasant body feathers placed on top of each other and tied flat over the body.
Third Hackle: Bronze mallard tied on as a collar using one full turn and tied back.
Head: Fluorescent red.

This variation of the General Practitioner is far quicker to tie and by some reports can be just as effective. It is an innovation from Russ Miller of Arlington, Washington.

Pritchard's Rocket

Hooks: AC80500BL, AC80501BL, TMC7999 or DAI2441, sizes 2-4.
Thread: Black.
Tail: Fluorescent fire orange bucktail.
Ribbing: Embossed gold tinsel.
Body: Dubbed with #1 black African Angora goat.
Wing: Fluorescent fire orange bucktail tied over the body.
Head: Black.

The original of this pattern had a black yarn body. It was created by Al Pritchard and kept very simple. See Pritchard's Comet in this chapter.

Princess

Hooks: AC80500BL, AC80501BL, TMC7999 or DAI2441, sizes 1-6.
Thread: Black.
Tail: Orange bucktail.
Body: Copper wire.
Wing: Gray squirrel tied over the body with an overwing of yellow bucktail.
Head: Black.

This is a Pete Schwab design that was inspired by Charles H. Conrad of San Francisco, California. See Bellamy.

Professor
Hooks: AC80500BL, AC80501BL, TMC7999 or DAI2441, sizes 4-6.
Thread: Black.
Tip: Flat gold tinsel.
Tail: Amherst pheasant crest.
Ribbing: Flat gold tinsel.
Body: Dubbed with #6 yellow lambs wool.
Hackle: Brown tied on as collar and tied back and down.
Wing: Gray squirrel tail tied over the body.
Head: Black.

This is a steelhead variation of an old Scottish wet fly pattern which dates back to about 1830. I have fished both the wet and dry fly versions of this pattern with very little success, however, this particular dressing seems to have something that the others do not offer. I have caught some good fish on it, and not just steelhead. See Chapter 8.

Purple Angel
Hooks: AC80500BL, AC80501BL, TMC7999 or DAI2441, sizes 2-6.
Thread: Fluorescent fire orange.
Tail: Tuft of purple marabou. Use butt portion of purple neck or saddle hackle.
Butt: Fluorescent fire orange chenille.
Ribbing: Oval silver tinsel.
Body: Purple chenille.
Hackle: Claret tied on as a collar and tied back and down.
Wing: White bucktail tied over the body.
Head: Fluorescent fire orange.

This pattern was originated by Bob Strobel.

Purple Bad Habit (S)
Hooks: AC80500BL, AC80501BL, TMC7999 or DAI2441, sizes 2/0-6.
Thread: Fluorescent fire orange.
Tail: Purple marabou. Use tip from a marabou short.
Body: Silver braided Mylar piping.
Wing: Purple marabou.

Topping: CH20 fuchsia Crystal Hair.
First Hackle: Purple marabou tied in at the throat.
Remaining Hackles: One full turn each of red, purple and magenta tied on as a collar and tied back.
Head: Fluorescent fire orange.

An Alaskan pattern designed primarily for silvers by Don Hathaway. This fly will take fish from northern California north. Some very good results with steelhead in the Mad River have been reported in the last couple of years.

Purple Brat
Hooks: AC80500BL, AC80501BL, TMC7999 or DAI2441, sizes 4-8.
Thread: Black.
Tip: Lower half, flat gold tinsel and the upper half, fluorescent orange floss.
Tail: Dyed orange golden pheasant crest.
Ribbing: Oval gold tinsel.
Body: Dubbed with #52 fluorescent orange African Angora goat over the rear third and #58 fluorescent purple African Angora goat over the front two-thirds.
Hackle: Purple tied on as a collar and tied back and down.
Wing: White bucktail tied over the body with an overwing of purple bucktail.
Cheeks: J.C. or substitute.
Head: Black.

This is a variation of the Brad's Brat as tied by Dave McNeese of Salem, Oregon.

Purple Flame Hilton
Hooks: AC80500BL, AC80501BL, TMC7999 or DAI2441, sizes 4-8.
Thread: Claret.
Tip: Lower half, flat silver tinsel and the upper half, fluorescent red floss.
Tag: Single strand of fluorescent red floss. Tag should be no longer than half the length of the body.
Ribbing: Oval silver tinsel.
Body: Dubbed with a 50/50 blend of #50 fluorescent red and #52 fluorescent orange African Angora goat over the rear third and

#58 fluorescent purple African Angora goat over the front two-thirds.
Wings: Dyed purple grizzly hackle tips tied in a V over the body and extending to end of tag. Hackle tips should be tied with concave side out for better action.
Hackle: Dyed purple guinea fowl wrapped two turns as a collar and tied back.
Head: Claret.

This is another of Dave McNeese's variations and is again taken from one of the established classics, the Silver Hilton. Dave's drive for improvement in our patterns is to be commended. We must keep looking and trying innovative methods and designs.

Purple Flash

Hooks: AC80500BL, AC80501BL, TMC7999 or DAI2441, sizes 2-6.
Thread: Black.
Tail: Purple hackle barbs.
Ribbing: Oval silver tinsel.
Body: Purple chenille.
Hackle: Purple tied on as a collar and tied back and down.
Wing: Strands of CH21 claret, CH01 pearl, CH10 light green and CH19 purple Crystal Hair mixed and tied over the body with an overwing of purple marabou.
Head: Black.

This pattern was originated by Randall Kaufmann of Portland, Oregon.

Purple Hilton

Hooks: AC80500BL, AC80501BL, TMC7999 or DAI2441, sizes 2/0-6.
Thread: Black.
Tip: Flat silver tinsel.
Tail: Dyed red golden pheasant crest.
Ribbing: Oval silver tinsel.
Body: Rear third, divided with fluorescent orange floss in the rear and dubbed with #53 fluorescent fire orange African Angora goat in the front. The front two-thirds, dubbed with #30 purple African Angora goat.
Hackle: Dyed purple barred mallard tied on as a collar and tied back.
Wings: Four dyed purple grizzly hackle tips tied over the body.

Head: Black.

Dave McNeese created this pattern in 1985.

Purple Jesus (S)

Hooks: AC80500BL, AC80501BL, TMC7999 or DAI2441, sizes 2/0-6.
Thread: Red.
Tail: Purple bucktail with CH20 fuchsia Crystal Hair tied on top.
Body: Dubbed with #54 fluorescent hot pink lambs wool.
Body Hackle: Purple tied palmer style over the body.
Hackle: Purple tied on as a collar and tied back.
Wing: Purple bucktail tied over the body.
Head: Red.

Originated by Gary Miltenberger for Alaska, he also ties variations of this pattern. Possibly in a future edition I will be able to give you more established dressings for them. There is another fly which is close to this one. See Brunch.

Purple Joe

Hooks: AC80500BL, AC80501BL, TMC7999 or DAI2441, sizes 2-6.
Thread: Black.
Tail: Scarlet red hackle barbs.
Butt: Fluorescent fire orange yarn.
Ribbing: Oval silver tinsel over chenille only.
Body: Purple chenille.
Wings: Two badger neck hackles tied over the body with tips curved out.
Hackle: Badger tied on as a collar and tied back.
Head: Black.

Purple Matuka

Hooks: AC80500BL, AC80501BL, TMC7999 or DAI2441, sizes 1/0-6.
Thread: Black.
Ribbing: Oval silver tinsel.

Body: Dubbed with #58 fluorescent purple Bunnytron.
Wing: Dyed purple grizzly neck hackles tied Matuka style.
Hackle: Dyed purple grizzly tied on as a collar and tied back.
Head: Black.

There is a considerable number of variations on this pattern. This particular variation however is the one that is most favored by steelhead anglers. Do not hesitate though to try this in either orange, brown or olive—they work also.

Purple Peril

Hooks: AC80500BL, AC80501BL, TMC7999 or DAI2441, sizes 2-6.
Thread: Black.
Tip: Embossed silver tinsel.
Tail: Purple hen hackle barbs.
Ribbing: Embossed silver tinsel.
Body: Purple chenille.
Hackle: Purple hen hackle tied on as a collar and tied back.
Wing: Natural brown bucktail tied over the body.
Head: Black.

This pattern was originated in 1934 by Ken McLeod.

Purple Porcupine

See Egg Sucking Leech.

Purple Red-Butt

Hooks: AC80500BL, AC80501BL, TMC7999 or DAI2441, sizes 4-6.
Thread: Black.
Tip: Flat silver tinsel.
Butt: Fluorescent red floss.
Tail: Scarlet red hackle barbs. The tail is tied in over the tip and butt and should be only half the length of the body.
Ribbing: Oval silver tinsel.
Body: Dubbed with #30 purple Bunny-Blend.
Hackle: Purple hen hackle tied on as a collar and tied back and down.
Wings: Purple hen hackle tips tied in a V over the body.
Head: Black.

This is one of the patterns that I let myself really get into. Although it is a rather simple tie, materials, color and form are what I look for in steelhead flies. Originated by Al Buhr of Keizer, Oregon.

Purple Rat

Hooks: AC80500BL, AC80501BL, TMC7999 or DAI2441, sizes 4-8.
Thread: Red.
Tip: Oval silver tinsel.
Tail: Peacock sword feather barbs.
Ribbing: Oval silver tinsel.
Body: Rear half, purple floss and the front half, peacock herl. Reverse wrap with fine silver wire.
Wing: Gray fox guard hair tied low over the body.
Cheeks: Dyed purple hen hackle tips (lacquered) tied in at each side.
Hackle: Grizzly tied on as a collar and tied back.
Head: Red.

This is one pattern that I keep going back to—a great producer.

Purple Skunk

Hooks: AC80500BL, AC80501BL, TMC7999 or DAI2441, sizes 2-8.
Thread: Black.
Tail: Gray squirrel tail.
Butt: Fluorescent green chenille.
Ribbing: Oval silver tinsel.
Body: Purple chenille.
Wing: Gray squirrel tail tied over the body.
Hackle: Purple tied on as a collar and tied back.
Head: Black.

Originated by Keith Stonebreaker of Lewiston, Idaho.

Purple Spider

Hooks: DAI2151 or DAI2161, sizes 1-6.
Thread: Claret.
Tail: Small tuft of purple marabou. This is taken from the base of the purple hackle you are using to tie this pattern with.
Body: Rear half, flat silver tinsel and the front half, dubbed with #30 purple African Angora goat.

Hackle: Two full turns of long purple hackle, finished up with dyed black pheasant rump.
Head: Claret.

This pattern was created by Karl Hauffler and later named by Trey Combs for identification purposes.

Purple Sunrise

Hooks: AC80500BL, AC80501BL, TMC7999 or DAI2441, sizes 1-6.
Thread: Black.
Tail: Fluorescent red and fluorescent fire orange hackle barbs mixed.
Body: CC19 purple Crystal Chenille.
Body Hackle: Fluorescent red tied palmer style over the body.
Hackle: Fluorescent fire orange tied on as a collar and tied back and down.
Wing: Purple bucktail tied over the body.
Head: Black.

This fly pattern is a creation of Dave Hall for British Columbia waters.

Purple Ugly

Hook: AC80501BL, sizes 2/0-8.
Thread: Red.
Tail: Claret calf tail.
Ribbing: Flat silver tinsel.
Body: Dubbed with #30 purple Bunny-Blend.
Hackle: Fluorescent red tied on as a collar and tied back.
Eyes: Silver bead chain.

Another British Columbia pattern, this time originated by Gary Miltenberger.

Plate 9   Queen Bess

Hooks: AC80500BL, AC80501BL, TMC7999 or DAI2441, sizes 1-6.
Thread: Black.
Tail: Gray squirrel tail.
Body: Oval silver tinsel.
Hackle: Golden pheasant tippet barbs tied in at throat.
Wing: Yellow bucktail tied over the body with an overwing of gray squirrel tail.
Head: Black.

The original pattern called for silver wire for the body. See Bellamy.

Quinsam Hackle

Hooks: AC80500BL, AC80501BL, TMC7999 or DAI2441, sizes 2-4.
Thread: Black.
Tip: Yellow floss.
Ribbing: Flat gold tinsel.
Body: Dubbed with #1 black lambs wool.
Body Hackle: Yellow tied palmer style over the body starting from the center.
Hackle: Scarlet red tied on as a collar and tied back.
Head: Black.

This pattern was developed by Brigadier General Noel Money of Qualicum Beach, British Columbia. Also known locally as the Shrimp Fly.

Rajah

Hooks: AC80500BL, AC80501BL, TMC7999 or DAI2441, sizes 4-8.
Thread: Fluorescent pink.
Tail: Fluorescent hot pink bucktail.
Ribbing: Two turns of flat silver tinsel over the chenille portion of the body. Ribbing is then overwrapped with a single strand of fluorescent pink floss.
Body: Rear two-thirds, embossed silver tinsel and the front third, fluorescent pink chenille.
Wing: White bucktail tied sparsely over the body.
Hackle: Fluorescent hot pink hen hackle tied on as a collar and tied back. Hackle should be extra long.
Head: Fluorescent pink.

Originated in 1967 by Arthur Solomon of Spokane, Washington.

Plate 6   Red Ant

Hooks: AC80500BL, AC80501BL, TMC7999 or DAI2441, sizes 4-8.
Thread: Black.
Tail: Scarlet red hackle barbs.
Butt: Peacock herl.
Body: Red floss.
Hackle: Brown tied on as a collar and tied back and down.
Wing: Natural brown bucktail tied over the body.
Head: Black.

The wing (wings) on this fly are often tied divided and cocked upward over the body. This is a variation of an earlier English wet fly pattern, when it was first adapted to steelhead is unknown. Patrick Hoisington from San Francisco had my father tying an assortment of these each season for use on the Eel, Klamath and Rogue Rivers. Patrick was one of my father's early "sugar daddies" that nurtured our lifestyle for a good many years. My father first guided him on the Smith River in the 1930s and a great friendship was born.

Red•Butted Rhesus

Hooks: AC80500BL, AC80501BL, TMC7999 or DAI2441, sizes 2-6.
Thread: Black.
Butt: Red chenille.
Body: Black chenille.
Body Hackle: Black tied palmer style over the body.
Wing: White bucktail tied over the body.
Head: Black.

Originated in 1948 by Ken McLeod.

Red Dragon

Hooks: AC80500BL, AC80501BL, TMC7999 or DAI2441, sizes 2-8.
Thread: Red.
Tail: Red calf tail.
Body: Rear two-thirds, embossed silver tinsel and the front third, dubbed with #4 red African Angora goat.
Hackle: Badger tied on as a collar and tied back and down.
Wing: Gray squirrel tail tied over the body.
Cheeks: Short strand of scarlet red yarn tied in at each side and frayed out.

Originated by Carl Glisson in 1969 for use on the Feather River. Its productivity on the Feather has been almost nil, however, it has been used on other rivers with considerable success.

Red Fox

Plate 8

Hooks: AC80500BL, AC80501BL, TMC7999 or DAI2441, sizes 2-6.
Thread: Black.
Ribbing: Silver embossed tinsel overwrapped with a narrower oval silver tinsel.
Body: Red floss.
Hackle: Speckled guinea fowl tied on as a collar and tied back.
Wing: Fox squirrel tail tied over the body.
Head: Black.

Variation originated by Tom Darling of Seattle, Washington.

Red Fox

Hooks: AC80500BL, AC80501BL, TMC7999 or DAI2441, sizes 2-6.
Thread: Black.
Tail: Golden pheasant tippet barbs.
Ribbing: Oval gold tinsel.
Body: Dubbed with #4 red lambs wool.
Hackle: Brown tied on as a collar and tied back and down.
Wing: Fox squirrel tail tied over the body.
Head: Black.

This is a Mike Kennedy variation.

Red Optic

Hook: DAI2451, sizes 1-4.
Thread: Black.
Body: Oval silver tinsel.
Wing: Red bucktail.
Head: Black over 1/4" hollow brass bead.
Eyes: Yellow with black centers.

This is another of the Jim Pray patterns. Some outdoor writers focused on this pattern and twisted the name into *"Owl Eyed Optic."* Rather than seek out their true names they also just attached numbers to the Pray Optic patterns on occasion. See Black Optic.

Red Rat

Hooks: AC80500BL, AC80501BL, TMC7999 or DAI2441, sizes 4-8.
Thread: Red.
Tip: Oval silver tinsel.
Tail: Golden pheasant crest.
Ribbing: Oval silver tinsel.

Body: Dubbed with #4 red African Angora goat.
Wing: Gray squirrel tail tied over the body. Use hair from the base of the tail.
Hackle: Grizzly tied on as a collar and tied back.
Head: Red.

Redwing

Hooks: DAI2151 or DAI2161, sizes 1-4.
Thread: Fluorescent red.
Tip: Flat silver tinsel.
Tail: Golden pheasant crest.
Ribbing: Fine silver wire wrapped over floss portion of body only.
Body: Rear half, orange floss and front half, loosely dubbed fluorescent red marabou. This is marabou taken from the base of a hen hackle stem.
Wings: Pair of golden pheasant tippets tied together on edge over the body.
Cheeks: J.C. or substitute. Small fluorescent red hackle tip, or breast if you have them, tied in at each side and extending just about quarter way past the cheeks.
Topping: Golden pheasant crest.
Head: Red.

Originated by Dave McNeese of Salem, Oregon. This may or may not be a version of what Dave intended but I believe it to be very close.

Plate 6 ## Redwing Blackbird

Hooks: AC80500BL, AC80501BL, TMC7999 or DAI2441, sizes 4-8.
Thread: Fluorescent red.
Tail: Fluorescent red hackle barbs.
Ribbing: Oval silver tinsel.
Body: Black chenille.
Hackle: Dyed red guinea fowl tied on as a collar and tied back.
Wing: Fluorescent red calf tail tied over the body.
Head: Red.

Ray Baker of Eugene, Oregon, developed this spider design in 1985.

Reiff's Shrimp

See Chapter 17.

Rick's Revenge

Hooks: DAI2151 or DAI2161, sizes 1-6.
Thread: Red.
Tip: Flat silver tinsel.
Tail: A single strand of fluorescent pink floss equal in length to that of the floss portion of the body.
Rear Body Half: Fluorescent pink floss.
Trailer: A single strand of fluorescent pink floss tied over the floss portion of the body and extending to end of tip.
Front Body Half: Dubbed with #30 purple Bunny-Blend.
First Hackle: Purple tied on as a collar and tied back and down.
Wing: White bucktail tied over the body with a sparse overwing of purple bucktail.
Topping: A few strands of CH19 purple Crystal Hair.
Second Hackle: Dyed purple guinea fowl tied on as a collar and tied back and down. The guinea should be slightly longer than the first hackle.
Cheeks: J.C. or substitute.
Head: Red.

This project was undertaken by Rick Wren and John Shewey and was completed in 1986. Frankly, when I first saw this fly my mind clicked back to the mid 1950s. Blue suede shoes, an old girl friend by the name of Beverly Portersmith and most of all, a friend's 1955 Ford Crown Victoria which sported colors not unlike those used in this fly. After some moments of reminiscing I thought, "why revenge and not regret?" Oh, how I regret now, if I had only…

Rick and John did a good job on this fly and I am not poking fun, just being honest about my aimless train of thought. Their use of the "trailer" is seldom seen in steelhead flies and is one that follows along with my own line of thinking. I have been known on occasion to incorporate this design feature into some of my own patterns. Using the correct material, as they have, might surprise you with what happens in the water.

Plate 7   Ringold (s)

Hooks: AC80500BL, AC80501BL, TMC7999 or DAI2441, sizes 2/0-4.
Thread: Red.
Tail: Scarlet red hackle barbs.
Ribbing: Oval gold tinsel.
Body: White chenille.
Hackle: Scarlet red tied on as a collar and tied back and down.
Wing: White calf tail tied over the body.
Tipping: Clear (white) Miclon or Z-Lon.
Head: Red.

Originated in 1984 by Josh Ringold for fishing the tidal waters of the Russian River. He often uses brass bead chain eyes on the fly when fishing further inland. This fly has taken some serious fish, both steelhead and salmon.

Richey's Golden Girl

Hooks: AC80500BL, AC80501BL, TMC7999 or DAI2441, sizes 6-10.
Thread: Red.
Tail: Salmon yellow calf tail.
Body: CC24 gold Crystal Chenille.
Hackle: Salmon yellow calf tail tied in at the throat.
Wing: Salmon yellow calf tail tied over the body.
Head: Red.

Collaboration between George Richey and Chuck Lunn of Flint, Michigan, brought us this pattern.

Richey's Platte River Pink

Hooks: AC80500BL, AC80501BL, TMC7999 or DAI2441, sizes 2-6.
Thread: Red.
Tag: Flared pale pink egg yarn.
Ribbing: Flat silver tinsel.
Body: Fluorescent pink chenille.
Hackle: Flared pale pink egg yarn tied in at the throat.
Wing: White calf tail tied over the body.
Topping: CH01 pearl Crystal Hair.

Head: Red.

This is another George Richey pattern that he came up with in 1973.

Rio Grande King

Hooks: AC80500BL, AC80501BL, TMC7999 or DAI2441, sizes 4-6.
Thread: Black.
Tip: Oval gold tinsel.
Tail: Golden pheasant crest.
Body: Black chenille.
Wing: White calf tail tied over the body.
Hackle: Brown hen hackle tied on as a collar and tied back.
Head: Black.

This is a steelhead version of an American trout fly and enjoys a considerable following. See Chapter 8.

Rippa's Revenge

Hooks: AC80500BL, AC80501BL, TMC7999 or DAI2441, sizes 2-6.
Thread: Red.
Tail: Scarlet red hackle barbs.
Ribbing: Flat silver tinsel.
Body: Rear third, dubbed with #58 fluorescent hot pink African Angora goat and the front two-thirds, dubbed with #1 black African Angora goat.
Hackle: Black tied on as a collar and tied back and down.
Wing: White calf tail tied over the body with an overwing of CH14 dark blue Crystal Hair.
Head: Red.

Originated in 1979 by Stew Wallace of Portland, Oregon. He named the fly in honor of Bob Rippa.

Roe Fly

Hook: DAI2451, sizes 6-8.
Thread: Fluorescent pink.
Tail: Single strand of white floss.
Body: Roe chenille tied fat and round.
Hackle: White marabou tied on as collar one full turn.
Head: Fluorescent pink.

Not a real big accomplishment considering, but this is a fly I put together some time back using some very unusual chenille given to me as a sample. Aside from the real thing, this is the closest material I have found to simulate a chunk of roe with parts of membrane still attached. Surprisingly it has also been found effective for inland trout in the Rockies and Middle West as well.

Rogue River

Hooks: AC80500BL, AC80501BL, TMC7999 or DAI2441, sizes 2-6.
Thread: Black.
Tail: Crimson red hackle barbs.
Butt: Dark olive chenille.
Ribbing: Silver embossed tinsel.
Body: Red floss.
Wings: Gray squirrel tail tied over the body and tied upward and divided.
Cheeks: J.C. or substitute.
Head: Black.
Eyes: White with black centers.

This fly was first tied on a double hook, a practice I hope we have seen the last of. Our forefathers were "meat fishermen" and measured their catch in the "pounds" rather than number beached and released. Not just this pattern, but many were tied on a double hook. This pattern is well over fifty years old, but there are other patterns which are younger. Over the past century the "Mighty Rogue River" has hosted countless fishermen, many of them coming away with their own "special" patterns. The list of patterns is long and varied. I share just a few with you here.

Rogue River Special I

Hooks: AC80500BL, AC80501BL, TMC7999 or DAI2441, sizes 2-8.
Thread: Black.
Tip: Yellow floss.
Tail: Salmon yellow hackle barbs.
Ribbing: Gold embossed tinsel.
Body: Red floss.
Wings: Salmon yellow bucktail tied over the body and tied upward and divided.
Cheeks: J.C. or substitute.
Head: Black.

Rogue River Special II

Hooks: AC80500BL, AC80501BL, TMC7999 or DAI2441, sizes 2-8.
Thread: Black.
Tip: Dubbed with #4 red lambs wool.
Tail: Red and white bucktail mixed.
Ribbing: Silver embossed tinsel.
Body: Dubbed with #4 red lambs wool.
Hackle: Brown tied on as a collar and tied back and down.
Wing: Red and white bucktail mixed and tied over the body.
Head: Red.

Royal Coachman

Hooks: AC80500BL, AC80501BL, TMC7999 or DAI2441, sizes 4-8.
Thread: Black.
Tail: Golden pheasant tippet tied equal in length to the floss center of the fly.
Body: Peacock herl with a center band of red floss.
Hackle: Brown tied on as a collar and tied back and down.
Wing: White bucktail tied over the body.
Head: Black.

Always reverse wrap the entire body with fine gold wire. I don't know when, where, why or who started using this pattern as a steelhead fly. I have tied literally thousands of these commercially and the demand never seems to diminish. See Chapter 7 for more information. I have never caught a fish on this fly.

Royal Coachman, Waiting (s)

Tied same as above except has a white hackle. Also used for Pacific salmon with the wing tied twice the length of the hook shank. This is a variation by Al Allard.

Rusty Squirrel (s)

Hook: AC80501BL, sizes 2/0-8.
Thread: Orange.
Tip: Silver diamond braid.
Tail: Dyed black squirrel tail. Wrap under the tail so that it cocks upward.
Body: Silver diamond braid.
Hackle: Fluorescent fire orange tied on as a collar and tied back.
Wing: Fox squirrel tail tied over the body.
Head: Fluorescent orange chenille tied on as a collar just behind the eyes.
Eyes: Silver bead chain.

This pattern was created by Jim Victorine of Loomis, California. I have known Jim for a very long time and he seems to be playing with a variety of flies that he calls the "Rusty Squirrel." This has been going on now for a decade or more so I believe that this pattern he shares with us has all of the *"bugs"* out of it. Used for both salmon and steelhead wherever they might swim.

Plate 8   ### Salmo Le Sac

Hooks: AC80500BL, AC80501BL, TMC7999 or DAI2441, sizes 6-8.
Thread: Black.
Tail: Peacock sword feather barbs.
Ribbing: Oval gold tinsel.
Body: Dubbed with #11 salmon Bunny-Blend.
Hackle: Furnace hen hackle tied on as a collar and tied back.
Wing: Fox squirrel tail tied over the body.
Head: Black.

This pattern was originated by Mike Kennedy.

Salmon Fly (s)

Hook: AC80501BL, sizes 2/0-8.
Thread: White.

Tail: White bucktail tied equal to one and one half the body length.
Body: Silver embossed tinsel.
Hackle: Scarlet red tied on as a collar and tied back.
Eyes: Silver bead chain.

This is another of the Russian River or "Pop-Eyed" type flies which started emerging during the 1940s.

Salmon River Spring Wiggler

See Chapter 17.

Samson

Hooks: TMC5263 or DAI1720, sizes 4-6.
Thread: Red.
Body: Dubbed with #53 fluorescent fire orange African Angora goat. The body is divided into four equal segments: **1.** body with white hackle at front, **2.** body with white hackle at front, **3.** body with white hackle at front, and **4.** body with scarlet red hackle at front.
Head: Red.

If you have been able to follow these unusual instructions chances are you may catch a fish or two on this one. Originated by Darrell Arnold of Novato, California.

Salmon River Seducer

Hooks: AC80500BL, AC80501BL, TMC7999 or DAI2441, sizes 2-8.
Thread: Fluorescent green.
Tail: Fluorescent chartreuse marabou with a few strands of CH01 pearl Crystal Hair mixed.
Body: Fluorescent green chenille.
Wing: White bucktail tied over the body with an overwing of fluorescent chartreuse marabou.
Topping: CH01 pearl Crystal Hair.
Hackle: White tied on as a collar and tied back.
Head: Fluorescent green.

San Juan Spider

Hooks: DAI2151 or DAI2161, sizes 1-6.
Thread: Fluorescent orange.
Tip: Flat silver tinsel.
Body: Fluorescent orange chenille.

Hackle: Two full turns of long fluorescent yellow with dyed yellow barred mallard flank tied in front and tied on as a collar and tied back.
Topping: Sparse red bucktail.

The San Juan Spider is a product of Bob Bettzig. I have omitted the tail of fluorescent yellow hackle barbs and used a hook of my personal liking. Sorry Bob, I just have more faith in these minor adjustments.

Sarp's Seducer (S)
Hook: AC80501BL, sizes 2/0-8.
Thread: Red.
Tail: CH01 pearl Crystal Hair.
Wing: Fluorescent red marabou tied over the body with an equal portion of black marabou tied in as an overwing.
Topping: Several strands of CH14 dark blue Crystal Hair.
Eyes: Silver bead chain.

This fly was designed by Tony Sarp for Alaska. It is also called Tony's Seducer or "TS" for short.

Sauk River Shrimp
Hooks: TMC5263 or DAI1720, sizes 2-6.
Thread: Red.
Tail: Orange bucktail tied long.
Body: Red ostrich herl twisted onto your tying thread and wrapped as if you were using chenille. As with the Samson above, this body is also divided into four segments. The only difference is that you have hackle tied at the rear of the body also.
Hackle: An orange hackle tied in at the front and rear of the body (that's two) and a orange hackle tied between each segment (that's three). Two plus three equals five. Simple—right?
Head: Red.

This is a creation for winter-runs which Alec Jackson uses. His Sauk River Grub is the same pattern except it has no tail.

Sawtooth
Hooks: AC80500BL, AC80501BL, TMC7999 or DAI2441, sizes 4-6.
Thread: Black.
Tail: Guinea fowl barbs.
Ribbing: Flat gold tinsel.
Body: Orange chenille.
Hackle: Guinea fowl tied on as a collar and tied back and down.
Wing: Fox squirrel tail tied over the body.
Cheeks: J.C. or substitute.
Head: Black.

Scarlet Ibis
Hooks: AC80500BL, AC80501BL, TMC7999 or DAI2441, sizes 4-8.
Thread: Red.
Tail: Scarlet red hackle barbs.
Ribbing: Gold embossed tinsel.
Body: Dubbed with #4 red lambs wool.
Hackle: Scarlet red tied on as a collar and tied back and down.
Wing: Red bucktail tied over the body.
Head: Red.

This is the steelhead version of a Northeastern wet fly pattern. See Chapter 8.

Scarlet Woman
Hooks: AC80500BL, AC80501BL, TMC7999 or DAI2441, sizes 4-6.
Thread: Black.
Body: Oval silver tinsel.
Hackle: Orange tied on as a collar and tied back and down.
Wings: J.C. tied together on edge over the body with shorter red goose quill sections tied in at each side.
Head: Black.

Originated in 1968 by Martin Tolley of Vancouver, British Columbia.

Plate 10 Schweitzer's Wateck

Hooks: AC80500BL, AC80501BL, TMC7999 or DAI2441, sizes 6-8.
Thread: Fluorescent green.
Tail: Ringneck pheasant tail barbs.
Ribbing: Oval silver tinsel.
Body: Dubbed with #19 olive Bunny-Blend.
Hackle: Brown hen hackle tied on as a collar and tied back.
Wing: Dyed yellow gray squirrel tail tied over the body.
Head: Fluorescent green.

This pattern was developed by Eugene W. Schweitzer of Salinas, California. It was first tied using both dark and medium olive chenille for the body. Fly fishermen have shown more interest in the dubbed body in more recent years.

Semi-Respectable

Hooks: AC80500BL, AC80501BL, TMC7999 or DAI2441, sizes 2/0-4.
Thread: Fluorescent fire orange.
Tip: Flat silver tinsel.
Tail: Pink bucktail tied long.
Ribbing: Flat silver tinsel.
Body: Fluorescent orange chenille.
Hackle: Pink tied on as a collar and tied back.
Wings: Pair of scarlet red marabou feathers tied over the body. Wings should be twice the length of the hook.
Head: Fluorescent fire orange.

This pattern was designed by Dan Reiff.

Shammy Bee

Hooks: AC80500BL, AC80501BL, TMC7999 or DAI2441, sizes 4-6.
Thread: Red.
Tip: Flat silver tinsel.
Tail: Narrow strip of chamois skin.
Body: Yellow and red alternating bands of chenille. Start at the rear with yellow first.
Hackle: Scarlet red and yellow mixed tied on as a collar and tied back.
Wing: White bucktail tied long over the body.
Head: Red.

Shammy Royal

Hooks: AC80500BL, AC80501BL, TMC7999 or DAI2441, sizes 4-6.
Thread: Black.
Tip: Flat silver tinsel.
Tail: Narrow strip of chamois skin.
Body: Black chenille with a flat silver tinsel center band.
Hackle: Furnace tied on as a collar and tied back.
Wing: White bucktail tied long over the body.
Head: Black.

I was first introduced to these flies when I was bass fishing on some private timber property in Washington state. The only other person on the lake that day besides myself was one of the locals. He was hammering the fish and my efforts with poppers were getting no place. I guess he took pity on me because he ended up giving me ten or more of the two Shammy patterns. Made my day. It was seven years before I discovered these flies were originally intended for steelhead.

Sicilian Gold

Hooks: AC80500BL, AC80501BL, TMC7999 or DAI2441, sizes 4-6.
Thread: Orange.
Tip: Silver embossed tinsel.
Tail: Scarlet red hackle barbs.
Ribbing: Embossed silver tinsel.
Body: Yellow floss.
Wing: Orange bucktail tied over the body.
Head: Orange

Dress this pattern sparse. Originated in 1968 by publisher and fly fisherman, Frank Amato of Portland, Oregon.

Signal Light

Hooks: AC80500BL, AC80501BL, TMC7999 or DAI2441, sizes 4-8.
Thread: Black.
Tail: Purple hackle barbs tied short and only equaling half the length of the body.
Ribbing: Oval silver tinsel.

Body: Rear quarter, dubbed with #53 fluorescent fire orange lambs wool and second quarter, dubbed with #57 fluorescent chartreuse lambs wool and the front half, black chenille.
Wing: Strands of CH13 blue, CH01 pearl, CH21 claret, and CH11 green Crystal Hair mixed and tied over the body. An overwing of black marabou is then tied in.
Hackle: Purple tied on as a collar and tied back.
Head: Black.

Along many canyon floors in the West it is not uncommon to see some of the better rivers along with railroad tracks sharing the same space. The Deschutes River is one of these and it is where Randall Kaufmann coined the name for his pattern. On an overcast day the signal lights along the tracks are brightly displayed.

Silly Stilly

Hooks: AC80500BL, AC80501BL, TMC7999 or DAI2441, sizes 4-6.
Thread: Black.
Tail: Fluorescent orange hackle barbs.
Butt: Fluorescent fire orange chenille.
Body: Dubbed with #52 fluorescent orange lambs wool.
Wing: White bucktail tied over the body with an overwing of orange bucktail.
Head: Black.
Eyes: White ring eyes.

Originated in 1958 by Warren Erholm. See Black Bomber for how to apply eyes.

Silver Ant

Hooks: AC80500BL, AC80501BL, TMC7999 or DAI2441, sizes 2-8.
Thread: Black.
Tail: Crimson red hackle barbs.
Butt: Black chenille.
Body: Oval silver tinsel.
Wings: White bucktail tied upright and divided.
Cheeks: J.C. or substitute.
Hackle: Black tied on as a collar and tied back.

Head: Black.

There is no question in my mind who originated this pattern. I.R. "Ike" Towers of Coos Bay, Oregon. This pattern was devised from a variety of old, and I mean old, English wet fly patterns in the mid 1920s. If any fly qualifies, this is a true "Rogue River classic."

Plate 10 ## Silver Bell

Hooks: AC80500BL, AC80501BL, TMC7999 or DAI2441, sizes 4-8.
Thread: Red.
Tail: White calf tail.
Butt: Peacock herl.
Body: Silver embossed tinsel.
Hackle: Scarlet red tied on as a collar and tied back.
Wing: Red calf tail tied over the body.
Head: Red.

Originated by a gentleman by the name of Soul from Eureka, California. Red goose quill sections were used for the wings when it was first used in the early 1920s.

Silver Blue

Hooks: AC80500BL, AC80501BL, TMC7999 or DAI2441, sizes 4-8.
Thread: Black.
Tip: Fine silver wire.
Tail: Golden pheasant crest.
Ribbing: Oval silver tinsel.
Body: Flat silver tinsel.
Hackle: Light blue tied on as a collar and tied back and down.
Wings: Barred teal barbs tied over the body.
Head: Black.

Silver Brown

Hooks: AC80500BL, AC80501BL, TMC7999 or DAI2441, sizes 4-8.
Thread: Black.
Tail: Red hen hackle barbs.
Body: Flat silver tinsel.
Hackle: Brown tied on as a collar and tied back and down.
Wing: Golden pheasant tail feather sections tied low over the body.

Head: Black.

Originated by Roderick Haig-Brown. The original pattern called for red Indian crow breast barbs for the tail.

Silver Brown Bucktail
Hooks: AC80500BL, AC80501BL, TMC7999 or DAI2441, sizes 2-6.
Thread: White.
Body: Flat silver tinsel.
Hackle: Coachman brown tied on as a collar and tied back and down.
Wing: Natural brown bucktail tied over the body.
Head: White.

This is a variation of a hair wing streamer pattern.

Silver Demon
Hooks: AC80500BL, AC80501BL, TMC7999 or DAI2441, sizes 2-8.
Thread: Black.
Tip: Oval silver tinsel.
Tail: Black and white barred section of lemon woodduck.
Body: Oval silver tinsel. Wrap an underbody of white floss to give the body a full taper.
Hackle: Orange tied on as a collar and tied back and down.
Wing: Gray squirrel tail tied over the body.
Head: Black.

This is another of the Demon patterns Jim Pray developed in 1935. See Gold Demon.

Silver Doctor
Hooks: AC80500BL, AC80501BL, TMC7999 or DAI2441, sizes 4-8.
Thread: Red.
Tip: Flat silver tinsel.
Tail: Golden pheasant crest.
Butt: Dubbed with #4 red lambs wool.
Body: Flat silver tinsel.
Hackle: Light blue tied on as a collar and tied back and down.
Wing: Natural brown bucktail tied over the body with an overwing of mixed red, yellow and blue bucktail.
Cheeks: J.C. or substitute.
Head: Red.

This is a variation of a British pattern. See Chapter 21.

Plate 6 — Silver Hilton
Hooks: AC80500BL, AC80501BL, TMC7999 or DAI2441, sizes 2-8.
Thread: Black.
Tail: Barred mallard tied short and sparse.
Ribbing: Oval silver tinsel.
Body: Black chenille.
Wings: Grizzly hackle tips tied in an upright V over the body with the concave side outward.
Hackle: Grizzly tied on as a collar and tied back.
Head: Black.

I cringe every time I see the majority of the dressings advocated for this fly today. Here I go again, taking my fly patterns too seriously. Some clarification must be given for this particular pattern. The fly itself was created by Art McGee of Whiskeytown, California. His homesite today is under many feet of water at the bottom of Whiskeytown Lake.

Art was a private contractor and specialized as a "powder monkey" blasting holes for the Pacific Gas and Electric Company. During and after the Shasta Dam Project the need for large towers to transport the newly acquired hydroelectric power over rocky terrain was necessary. Both Art and California gained economically from this project. Being one-of-a-kind made him into a real independent individual, combining this with his love for fly fishing resulted in a unique person.

I found Art and my father out in the back graphiting a fly line one afternoon. In 1947 powdered graphite applied to a fly line was the only way, it not only resisted any line drag on the guides better, but it cut down on the so-called visibility of the line. And for some reason, yet to be explained to me today, it made the line sink better. Who it was that came up with the idea is a mystery to me. They never were able to justify the graphite residue left on the hands.

It was a real hot "Redding" afternoon, and we all went inside where the fly boxes (Prince Albert cans) started coming out. Art was showing my father some of the flies he wanted him to tie. Although Art was a fairly good tier in his own right, he would rather fish and there was not enough time left for him to mess with tying. Art left, leaving some patterns behind as samples of the flies he wanted, they were all flies that he had created and found to be successful on the Trinity River. From the samples left behind there was one that I found a record of in my father notes.

"August 2, 1947. Black Beauty—wisp of barred mallard for tail, black chenille body with silver rib, wings of grey hackle (tie these Rogue fashion), grey hackle."

Black Beauty was the name my father attached to the pattern for identification purposes. I really don't know when Art came up with the "Silver Hilton." I do know that by late summer of 1954 it was the Silver Hilton and was widely recognized by that name up and down both the Trinity and Klamath River Canyons.

Without reservation, I can say that this single fly has taken more big fish on these rivers than any other. It is used so assiduously that the competing patterns are all just runners-up. So, when tying the Silver Hilton keep the tail sparse and short. Tail length should only be two-thirds the length of the body. Oval tinsel ribbing has always been the accepted material, regardless of my father's description as "silver rib." The wings are always tied in an upright position over the body with their concave side outward. The hackle is tied on as a collar with four or five full turns and tied back. Saddle hackle has always been the best for this because of the narrower stem.

I don't know of a single place where steelhead are pursued that a seasoned steelheader is unable to give a brief description of the Silver Hilton. Maybe it is this verbal communication that has led us astray at times.

Silver Hilton, Peacock
A variation of Art McGee's. He also used red, yellow and orange chenille bodies which never really took off.

A peacock variation is tied same as the Silver Hilton except peacock is substituted for body material. This variation has really proven to be a good one. Like I have always said, "put peacock on it and it will catch fish." I really wish that were true, but it's close and close counts in fly fishing.

Andy Puyans of Pleasant Hills, California has a similar pattern with barred teal barbs used for the tail that is referred to as Peacock Hilton. As you can see from what little I have covered, there is a never ending chain of "Hiltons."

Silver Lady
Hooks: AC80500BL, AC80501BL, TMC7999 or DAI2441, sizes 4-8.
Thread: Black.
Tail: Pair of small golden pheasant tippet feathers tied together on edge.
Body: Flat silver tinsel.

Hackle: Badger tied on as a collar and tied back and down.
Wings: Pair of badger neck hackles tied over the body with an overwing of peacock sword feather barbs followed by barred teal barbs.
Topping: Golden pheasant crest.
Head: Black.

Originated by Roderick Haig-Brown for summer-runs in British Columbia.

Silver N'Mallard

Hooks: AC80500BL, AC80501BL, TMC7999 or DAI2441, sizes 4-8.
Thread: Black.
Tail: Golden pheasant tippet barbs.
Ribbing: Oval silver tinsel.
Body: Rear two-thirds, flat silver tinsel and the front third, dubbed with #1 black lambs wool.
Hackle: Badger tied on as a collar and tied back and down.
Wing: Barred mallard barbs tied over the body.
Head: Black.

A British Columbia pattern most favored for summer-runs.

Silver Minnow

Hooks: AC80500BL, AC80501BL, TMC7999 or DAI2441, sizes 4-6.
Thread: Black.
Body: Flat silver tinsel.
Wing: Barred mallard barbs tied over the body.
Head: Olive chenille.

A British Columbia pattern tied to simulate salmon fry.

Silver Orange

Hooks: DAI2151 or DAI2161, sizes 2-4.
Thread: Orange.
Body: Embossed silver tinsel.
Hackle: Orange hen hackle tied on as a collar and tied back.

Wing: Yellow calf tail tied short over the body.
Head: Orange.

Originated by Fred A. Reed of Nevada City, California. This is an effective winter-run pattern in most of the larger northern California rivers.

Silvius Demon

Hooks: AC80500BL, AC80501BL, TMC7999 or DAI2441, sizes 1/0-6.
Thread: Black.
Tail: Yellow hackle barbs.
Butt: Red chenille.
Body: Oval gold tinsel.
Hackle: Orange tied on as a collar and tied back and down.
Wing: Dyed black squirrel tail tied over the body.
Head: Black.

This is a Lloyd Silvius pattern which he originally brought out in the 1930s for use on the Eel River. Since that time it has been used on countless streams on the West Coast.

Simmy Special

Hooks: AC80500BL, AC80501BL, TMC7999 or DAI2441, sizes 4-8.
Thread: Black.
Body: Olive chenille.
Body Hackle: Brown tied palmer style over the body.
Wing: Barred mallard barbs tied over the body and extending to the bend of the hook.
Head: Black.

Created many years ago by Michigan river guide Simmy Nolf. One point that took many years for me to grasp was that experienced guides, no matter where they are, always keep their flies sweet and simple. Remember now, this is how they make their living. I guess a good sign of a guide who is hopelessly doomed is when they start bringing out intricately dressed flies with unheard of claims that would make even

Abe Snake blush. This has happened to me more than once.

Skagit Cutthroat

Hooks: AC80500BL, AC80501BL, TMC7999 or DAI2441, sizes 2-6.
Thread: Red.
Tail: Fluorescent red and orange hackle barbs mixed.
Butt: Fluorescent orange chenille.
Body: Wrapped with fine silver Mylar piping.
Wing: White calf tail tied over the body.
Cheeks: Short sections of red goose quill.
Head: Red.
Eyes: White ring eyes.

See Black Bomber for how to apply eyes.

Skeena Nymph (S)

Hooks: AC80500BL, AC80501BL, TMC7999 or DAI2441, sizes 2/0-6.
Thread: Black.
Tail: Black bucktail.
Body: CC02 black Crystal Chenille.
Body Hackle: Black tied palmer style over the body.
Throat: Black bucktail tied in at the bottom and extending the length of the hook.

This fly was originated by Stew Wallace of Portland, Oregon. It is used here in northern California as a shrimp pattern in the estuaries, however, it is very productive clear to Alaska as its name suggests.

Skeena Woolly Bugger

Hooks: AC80500BL, AC80501BL, TMC7999 or DAI2441, sizes 2/0-6.
Thread: Fluorescent fire orange.
Tail: Golden pheasant tippet barbs.
Body: Dubbed with #1 black lambs wool.
Body Hackle: Grizzly tied palmer style over the body.
Wing: CH02 black Crystal Hair tied sparsely over the body.
Hackle: Fluorescent fire orange tied on as a collar and tied back.
Head: Fluorescent fire orange.

This pattern was created by Bob York.

Skunk

Hooks: AC80500BL, AC80501BL, TMC7999 or DAI2441, sizes 1-8.
Thread: Black.
Tail: Crimson red hackle barbs.
Ribbing: Oval silver tinsel.
Body: Black chenille.
Hackle: Black tied on as a collar and tied back.
Wing: White calf tail tied over the body.
Head: Black.

The earliest versions of the Skunk were tied with white skunk tail hair, hence the name. Another old classic that many want credit for but none can truly be given. Unlike the many Atlantic salmon flies which are hued in stone, steelheading is still in its conception and much will never be known. In a nutshell, this is a West Coast pattern which has given anglers great rewards time and time again.

The dressing I cite above is from a family sample obtained from Jim Pray around 1934.

Plate 9　Skunk, Green Butt

Hooks: AC80500BL, AC80501BL, TMC7999 or DAI2441, sizes 1-8.
Thread: Black.
Tail: Scarlet red hackle barbs.
Butt: Dubbed with #57 fluorescent chartreuse lambs wool.
Ribbing: Oval silver tinsel.
Body: Black chenille.
Hackle: Black tied on as a collar and tied back and down.
Wing: White calf tail tied over the body.
Head: Black.

This bastard pattern has found a foster home with a good many of us and definitely has some added qualities that its alleged parent doesn't. This pattern stands tall among steelheaders from one end of the West Coast to the other, here in northern California it reached the top ten long ago. Amazing what a little green will do.

Skunk, Red Butt

Dressed the same as the Green Butt Skunk except the butt material is substituted with #50 fluorescent red lambs wool.

Skykomish Sunrise

Hooks: AC80500BL, AC80501BL, TMC7999 or DAI2441, sizes 2-8.
Thread: Red.
Tip: Oval silver tinsel.
Tail: Scarlet red and yellow hackle barbs mixed.
Ribbing: Oval silver tinsel.
Body: Red chenille.
Hackle: Scarlet red and yellow mixed and tied on as a collar and tied back and down.
Wing: White calf tail tied over the body.
Head: Red.

This is another of Ken and George McLeod's creations created in the 1940s.

Skykomish Sunrise

Hooks: AC80500BL, AC80501BL, TMC7999 or DAI2441, sizes 2/0-6.
Thread: Red.
Tip: Flat silver tinsel.
Tail: Scarlet red and yellow hackle barbs mixed.
Ribbing: Flat silver tinsel.
Body: Sparsely wrapped fluorescent red floss over an underbody of flat silver tinsel.
First Wing: CH01 pearl Crystal Hair tied over the body with an overwing of white marabou.
First Hackle: Fluorescent red marabou tied in at the throat.
Second Wing: White marabou tied over the body with overwings of first yellow and then fluorescent red marabou.
Second Hackle: Fluorescent red tied on as a collar and tied back.
Head: Red.

This is another of Trey Combs' variations which he chooses to dress in marabou.

Skykomish Yellow

Tied the same as the Skykomish Sunrise except yellow chenille is substituted for the body.

Plate 8   Spade (S)

Hooks: DAI2151 or DAI2161, sizes 6-10.
Thread: Black.
Tail: Coastal blacktail deer body hair.
Body: Black chenille.
Hackle: Grizzly hen hackle tied on as a collar and tied back. This hackle should be long enough to reach the tip of the hook point.
Head: Black.

Bob Arnold of Seattle, Washington, created this pattern in 1964. Since that time there has been an endless string of variations created. I will list just some of them.

Spade, Claret Guinea

Hooks: AC80500BL, AC80501BL, TMC7999 or DAI2441, sizes 4-10.
Thread: Fluorescent red.
Tail: Coastal blacktail deer body hair.
Butt: Dubbed with #50 fluorescent red lambs wool.
Body: Black ostrich herl. Strands of ostrich herl are twisted around fine silver oval tinsel before wrapping.
Hackle: First, grizzly tied on as a collar and tied back, then dyed claret guinea fowl tied on as a collar and tied back.
Head: Fluorescent red.

Originated by Alec Jackson of Kenmore, Washington.

Spade, Dean

Hooks: TMC7989 or DAI2421, sizes 4-8.
Thread: Black.
Tip: Flat silver tinsel.
Butt: Dubbed with #53 fluorescent orange African Angora goat.
Body: Dubbed with #1 black African Angora goat.

Hackle: Grizzly tied on as a collar and tied back.

Head: Black.

Originated in 1988 by Bruce McNae and tied to be fished with a floating line just under the surface film.

Spade, Fancy

Hooks: AC80500BL, AC80501BL, TMC7999 or DAI2441, sizes 4-10.

Thread: Fluorescent red.

Tail: Coastal blacktail deer body hair.

Body: Rear third, fine peacock herl and the front half, black ostrich herl. Strands of ostrich herl twisted around fine silver oval tinsel before wrapping.

Hackle: Grizzly tied on as a collar and tied back.

Head: Fluorescent red.

Spade, Plain

Hooks: AC80500BL, AC80501BL, TMC7999 or DAI2441, sizes 4-10.

Thread: Fluorescent red.

Tail: Coastal blacktail deer body hair.

Body: Peacock herl. Strands of peacock herl twisted around fine silver oval tinsel before wrapping.

Hackle: Grizzly tied on as a collar and tied back.

Head: Fluorescent red.

Spade, Purple

Hooks: AC80500BL, AC80501BL, TMC7999 or DAI2441, sizes 4-10.

Thread: Fluorescent red.

Tail: Coastal blacktail deer body hair.

Butt: Dubbed with #50 fluorescent red lambs wool.

Body: Black ostrich herl. Strands of ostrich herl are twisted around fine silver oval tinsel before wrapping.

Hackle: First, grizzly tied on as a collar and tied back, then dyed claret guinea fowl tied on as a collar and tied back.

Head: Fluorescent red.

The three preceding patterns were originated by Alec Jackson.

Plate 10 Spade, Spider

Hooks: AC80500BL, AC80501BL, TMC7999 or DAI2441, sizes 4-10.

Thread: Black.

Tip: Flat silver tinsel.

Butt: Dubbed with #9 orange African Angora goat.

Body: Dubbed with #1 black African Angora goat.

Hackle: Grizzly tied on as a collar and tied back with an additional collar of speckled guinea tied in front.

Head: Black.

Originated by Chris Matthew of Oakland, California.

Spade, Yellow

Hooks: AC80500BL, AC80501BL, TMC7999 or DAI2441, sizes 6-10.

Thread: Yellow.

Tail: Coastal blacktail deer body hair.

Butt: Dubbed with #51 fluorescent yellow lambs wool.

Body: Black ostrich herl. Strands of ostrich herl twisted around fine silver oval tinsel before wrapping.

Hackle: First, grizzly tied on as a collar and tied back, then dyed yellow guinea fowl tied on as a collar and tied back.

Head: Yellow.

Spade, Whaka Blonde

Hooks: AC80500BL, AC80501BL, TMC7999 or DAI2441, sizes 6-10.

Thread: Fluorescent red.

Tail: Purple hen hackle barbs.

Body: Purple ostrich herl. Strands of ostrich herl are twisted around fine silver oval tinsel before wrapping.

Hackle: Purple hen hackle tied on as a collar and tied back.

Head: Fluorescent red.

The two preceding patterns are creations of Alec Jackson.

Spectral Spider

Hooks: DAI2151 or DAI2161, sizes 1-6.

Thread: Gray.

Tag: Short strand of frayed yellow synthetic yarn.

Body: Flat silver tinsel.

Wing: Single strands of frayed red, orange, green and blue synthetic yarn. These frayed fibers should be married to give the spectral effect. A light badger hackle tip is tied in at each side and extending half the first wing length.
Hackle: Barred mallard tied on as a collar and tied back extending the length of the hook.
Cheeks: Dyed kingfisher blue hen hackle tips.
Head: Gray.

Created in the 1970s by Walt Johnson. I have never fished this fly but the numerous variations of it, or ones like it, lead me to believe that it is a good one. Holding this fly in the natural sunlight certainly brings out the sought after spectral effect of the wing.

Spring Favorite

Hooks: AC80500BL, AC80501BL, TMC7999 or DAI2441, sizes 2/0-6.
Thread: Red.
Tail: Red calf tail.
Butt: Dubbed with #57 fluorescent chartreuse lambs wool.
Body: Red chenille.
Hackle: Scarlet red tied on as a collar and tied back and down.
Wing: Orange calf tail tied over the body.
Topping: CH06 orange Crystal Hair.
Head: Red.

This is a Bob York pattern.

Spring's Wiggler, Green

Hooks: AC80500BL, AC80501BL, TMC7999 or DAI2441, sizes 4-6.
Thread: Fluorescent green.
Tail: Dyed fluorescent green gray squirrel tail.
Shellback: Dyed fluorescent green gray squirrel tail.
Body Hackle: Fluorescent green tied palmer style over the body.
Body: Fluorescent green chenille.
Head: Fluorescent green.

Spring's Wiggler, Orange

Hooks: AC80500BL, AC80501BL, TMC7999 or DAI2441, sizes 4-6.
Thread: Fluorescent orange.
Tail: Dyed orange gray squirrel tail.
Shellback: Dyed orange gray squirrel tail.
Body Hackle: Fluorescent orange tied palmer style over the body.
Body: Orange chenille.
Head: Fluorescent orange.

Ron and Frank Spring of Muskegon, Michigan, developed the Wiggler patterns.

Springer Green

Hooks: DAI2151 or DAI2161, sizes 1-6.
Thread: Fluorescent green.
Tip: Lower half, flat silver tinsel and the upper half, fluorescent green floss.
Tail: Salmon yellow hackle barbs.
Ribbing: Flat silver tinsel.
Body: Rear half, dubbed with #51 fluorescent yellow Bunny-Blend and the front half, dubbed with #57 fluorescent chartreuse Bunny-Blend.
Hackle: Salmon yellow tied on as a collar and tied back. Barred lemon woodduck barbs are tied in at the throat.
Wing: Beige rabbit tied over the body.
Cheeks: Fluorescent green hen hackle tips.
Head: Fluorescent green.

Walt Johnson created this pattern for spring-runs, hence the name "Springer."

Spruce

Hooks: AC80500BL, AC80501BL, TMC7999 or DAI2441, sizes 4-8.
Thread: Black.
Tail: Peacock sword feather barbs.
Body: Rear third, red floss and the front two-thirds, peacock herl. Reverse wrap the peacock with fine gold wire.
Wings: Badger hackle tips tied in a high V over the body and extending to the end of the tail. Hackle tips should be tied with concave side outward.
Hackle: Badger tied on as a collar and tied back.
Head: Black.

Nice light cast badger with good center markings will give you a fly to be proud of. This fly was originated in the 1930s for sea-run cutthroat but has since been found good for steelhead and other freshwater game fish. It was first known as the Godfrey Special, so with no one else to blame, let's assume that "Godfrey" is responsible for bringing it into the world. See Chapter 18.

Spruce Matuka

Hooks: AC80500BL, AC80501BL, TMC7999 or DAI2441, sizes 2-6.
Thread: Black.
Ribbing: Oval silver tinsel.
Body: Rear third, dubbed with #50 fluorescent red lambs wool and the front two-thirds, peacock herl.
Wing: Four badger hackles tied Matuka style.
Topping: CH01 pearl Crystal Hair.
Hackle: Badger tied on as a collar and tied back.
Head: Black.

This is my variation (not unlike many others) of the Spruce which I tie with six wraps of .035" lead wire as an underbody for the peacock when tying sizes 2 and 4.

Squirrel and Teal

Hooks: AC80500BL, AC80501BL, TMC7999 or DAI2441, sizes 6-8.
Thread: Black.
Tip: Oval gold tinsel.
Tail: Golden pheasant crest.
Ribbing: Oval gold tinsel.
Body: Dubbed with beaver fur.
Hackle: Blue dun tied on with three wraps and tied back and down.
Wing: Gray squirrel tail and barred teal barbs mixed and tied over the body.
Cheeks: J.C. or substitute.
Head: Black.

This is a summer-run pattern developed by Harry Lemire in 1969.

Stan Ogden

Hooks: AC80500BL, AC80501BL, TMC7999 or DAI2441, sizes 6-8.
Thread: Yellow.
Ribbing: Flat silver tinsel with six turns.
Body Hackle: Black saddle wrapped over the body between the ribs and clipped to a pencil shape.
Body: Dubbed with #1 black lambs wool.
Wing: Natural red golden pheasant body feather tied flat over the body.
Head: Yellow.

A summer-run pattern created by Stan Ogden of Vancouver, British Columbia.

Steel Woolly, Black (S)

Hooks: TMC300 or DAI2220, sizes 2-8.
Thread: Red.
Tag: Red yarn frayed.
Body: Black chenille.
Body Hackle: Black tied palmer style over the body.
Hackle: Red marabou tied on one full turn as a collar.
Head: Red.

Steel Woolly, Orange (S)

Hooks: TMC300 or DAI2220, sizes 2-8.
Thread: Orange.
Tag: Orange yarn frayed.
Body: Orange chenille.
Body Hackle: Brown tied palmer style over the body.
Hackle: Orange marabou tied on one full turn as a collar.
Head: Orange.

Steel Woolly, Purple (S)

Hooks: TMC300 or DAI2220, sizes 2-8.
Thread: Black.
Tag: Purple yarn frayed.
Body: Purple chenille.
Body Hackle: White tied palmer style over the body.
Hackle: Black marabou tied on one full turn as a collar.
Head: Black.

Plate 10   Steel Woolly, Red (S)

Hooks: TMC300 or DAI2220, sizes 2-8.
Thread: Red.
Tag: Red yarn frayed.
Body: Red chenille.
Body Hackle: Grizzly tied palmer style over the body.
Hackle: Red marabou tied on one full turn as a collar.
Head: Red.

The Steel Woolly patterns were created by Howard Kizell of Chicago, Illinois. They have proven to be productive in both the Great Lakes region and on the West Coast. Howard tied his first Steel Woolly in 1989 while working as a welder in Alaska. After running out of any fishable flies, he spent an evening putting together whatever he could with the materials he had available, by the end of the season he had narrowed his selection down to those patterns above. In his enthusiasm he spent that winter in Chicago tying up several dozen of his patterns and sent them out to steelheaders for their approval. The following year he found that he had gained an endorsement from all who had used them.

Hats off to Mr. Kizell for his willingness to share his new approach to the Woolly Worm. Isn't that what this is all about?

Steelhead Bloody Mary

Hooks: AC80500BL, AC80501BL, TMC7999 or DAI2441, sizes 1-6.
Thread: White.
Body: Silver diamond braid over a tapered underbody of white floss.
Hackle: Small tuft of red marabou tied in at the throat.
Wing: Orange bucktail with a center wing of yellow bucktail and topped with white bucktail. All three colors of bucktail are tied in equal proportions.
Topping: CH01 Pearl Crystal Hair.

Head: White.
Eyes: Tiny black dots.

Steelhead Caddis

Hooks: AC80500BL, AC80501BL, TMC7999 or DAI2441, sizes 6-8.
Thread: Black.
Ribbing: Oval gold tinsel.
Body: Dubbed with #10 orange stone Bunny-Blend.
Wing: Brown deer hair tied over the body.
Head: Brown clipped lambs wool.

Originated for the Klamath River by Henry Long of Stockton, California.

Plate 10   Steelhead Carey

Hooks: AC80500BL, AC80501BL, TMC7999 or DAI2441, sizes 1-6.
Thread: Orange.
Tip: Lower half, flat silver tinsel and the upper half, fluorescent green floss.
Ribbing: Oval gold tinsel.
Body: Rear half, flat silver tinsel and the front half, #19 olive African Angora goat.
Hackle: Greenish-brown pheasant rump tied on as a collar and tied back.
Head: Orange.

It would be extremely difficult, if not totally impossible, to give credit or for a fly tier to take credit for any pattern labeled "Carey." Years back while visiting Patrick's Fly Shop in Seattle I came to realize just how many of these flies could be generated from a single idea. If it was hackled with any feather from a ringneck pheasant body, and not just the familiar rump hackle, it had Carey attached to it. This pattern is one of hundreds that I have singled out as a very good one, one which I personally use with success. I am sure that opinions will run feverishly in a different direction within certain circles in western Washington. See Chapter 9.

Plate 1

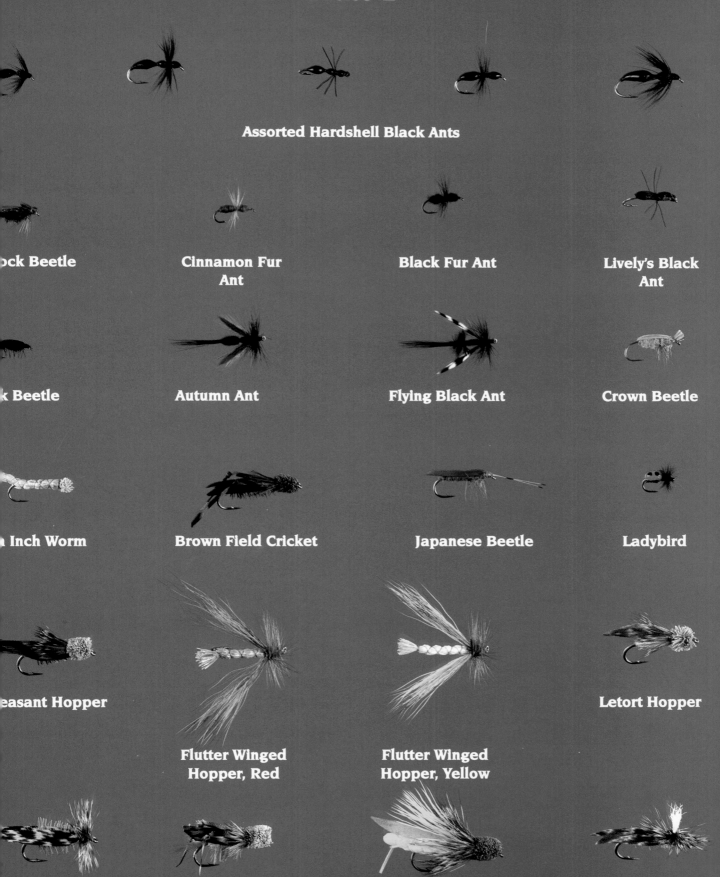

Assorted Hardshell Black Ants

...ck Beetle   **Cinnamon Fur Ant**   **Black Fur Ant**   **Lively's Black Ant**

...k Beetle   **Autumn Ant**   **Flying Black Ant**   **Crown Beetle**

...Inch Worm   **Brown Field Cricket**   **Japanese Beetle**   **Ladybird**

...easant Hopper   **Flutter Winged Hopper, Red**   **Flutter Winged Hopper, Yellow**   **Letort Hopper**

...Joe's Hopper   **Dave's Hopper**   **MacHopper**   **Parahopper**

Plate 2

June Damsel

Aspen Damsel, Light

Marabou Damsel, Kafmann

Zygo Dam Nymph, Da

Peacock Dragon

Lake Dragon

Giant Green Dragon

Beaverpe

Crystal Damsel, Blue

Deer Hair Dragon

Parachute Blue Damsel

Henry's Lake Leech

Black Woolly Bugger

Bunny Leech, Olive

Howell's Leech

Ozark Leech, Brown

Davis Leech, Black

Mini Leech, Gray

Mohair Leech, Brown

Articulated Leech Style 1

Articulated Leech Style 2

Plate 3

d Bent
merger

Hair Quill,
Midge

Cain's Fur
Midge

Gray Bent
Emerger

ckMidge
Pupa

Dark Mosquito
Larva

Dark Mosquito
Pupa

Dark Adult
Mosquito

omino
ge, Dark
Pupa

Griffith's Gnat,
Sparkle

Mosquito Larva

Palomino
Midge, Dark
Adult

Mosquito Larva
Peacock

ntor Shrimp

Werner Shrimp

Salmon River
Spring Wiggler

Terry's Scud

rystal Shrimp,
Black

Lively Shrimp,
Gray

Bodega Shrimp, Brown

Barbied Shrimp

Baby Crawfish

Jim's Crayfish

Whitlock's Crayfish

Skip's Dad

Plate 4

Boomer

Royal Shad

Abomination

Judge

Howdy

Pat's Prince

Verona Fly

Copper Sh

AA Special

Alexandra

**Black Nose
Dace**

Black Ghost

Anson Special

Don's Delight

Champ's Special

Clouser Deep Minnow, Gold Shiner

Harris Special

Stayner Ducktail

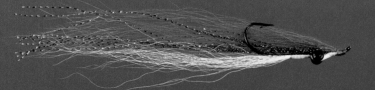

Clouser Deep Minnow, Silver Shrimp

Summer's Gold

Plate 5

Baby Smelt

Dusty

Champlain Special

Crane Prairie

Esopus Bucktail

Gray Tiger

atuka, Green Weeny

Bauman

Muddler Minnow, White

Muddler Minnow, Purple Marabou

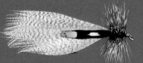

Hornberg Special

Platte River Special

Bucktail, Silver

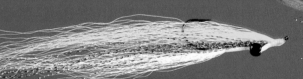

Clouser Deep Minnow, Chartreuse

Woolhead Sculpin, Brown

Threadfin Shad

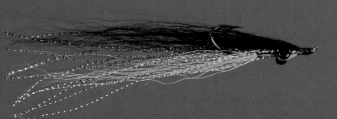

Clouser Deep Minnow, Sculpin

Grizzly King

Plate 6

Orleans Barber

Burlap

Gray Hackle Yellow

Cliff's Special

Carter Fly

Ive's Green

McLeod's Ugly

Red Ant

Redwing Blackbird

American River Special

Bair's Black

Coquihalla Silver

Black Joe

Carter's Dixie

Chub

Copper Demon

Ally's Shrimp

Silver Hilton

Plate 7

Espos Black

Orange Shrimp

Espos Silver

Green Butt Spider

Deschutes Skunk

Forrester

Black Spook

Brindle Bug

Mead

Morning Glory

Ringold

Hoyt's Killer

Midnight Sun

Dillon Creek Special

Clear Creek Special

Espos Copper

Flame

Espos Green

Plate 8

Chief

Red Fox

Spade

Bush Master

Salmo **Le Sac**

Bear's Flashback

Dean River Lantern, Green

Orange Shrimp Cocktail

Del Cooper

Flirt

Carbon

Dusty Miller

Dusk

Langston

Green Butt

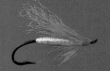

Fall Favorite

Boss Fly

Ringold

Plate 9

Assassin

Queen Bess

Chaveney

Coal Car

Adam's Rib

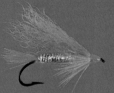

Copper Demon

Faulk

Comet

Egg Sucking Leech

Curt's Special

Green Lady

Dingbat

Black Prince

Dependable

Wet Spider

Thor

Aid's Black & Orange Spider

Skunk, Green Butt

Plate 10

Trinity Torch

Weitchpec Witch

Black Ember

Freight Train

Hot Orange

Giant Killer

Hopeful Hare

X-Long

Spade, Spider

Midnight Sun

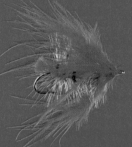

Steel Woolly, Red

Trinity

Orphan

Pole-Kat

Silver Bell

Steelhead Carey

Aid's Orange and Red Spider

Schweitzer's Wateck

Plate 11

Cains Copper

Patty Green

March Brown

range Bucktail

Bondatti's Killer

Margot

Nuit Blanche

Moore's Fancy

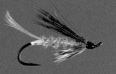

Nipisguit Gray

Midnight

Quick Silver

Blue Opal

Maurice

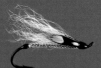

Gouffre

Black Silver Tip

Publicover

Foxfire

Echo Beach

Plate 12

Onset

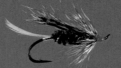

Rat

Hilda Special

Miramichi Special

Bloody Mary

Hairy Mary

Tobique

Tide Water

Yellow Montreal

Bandit

Black Reynard

Brenda's Delight

Dunkeld

Blackville

Gold Fever

Tarnished Silver

Veever's Fancy

Sunny Day

Plate 13

Black Spey

Wanda

Special Delivery

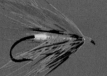

Morning Break

Gled Wing

Klamath Prancer

Gray Heron

Yarrow's Purple

Ian's Silver Spey

Trinity Teal

Jock "O" Dee

Della

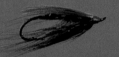

Skykomish Purple

Crane

Super Spey

Linda

Spawning Silver

Curtis Lee

Plate 14

Situk Special

Black Amos

Copper Cousin

Acxkerlund Humpy Fly

Anchovy

Blue Smolt

Coho, Russian River

Silver Minnow

Sand Lance

Point Arena Streamer

Giloth Salmon Streamer

Bodega Bay, Green

Chief Fat Dog

Frisco Streamer

Cameron Baitfish

Plate 15

Anchovy Streamer

Candlefish, Lambuth

Silversides

Fire Cracker

Candlefish Fly

Coho

Coho, Blue (Tube Style)

Tillamook Bay Shiner, Blue

Tillamook Bay Shiner, Red

Bodega Bay, Blue

Lefty's Deceiver, Blue

Lefty's Deceiver, Green

King's Explorer, Black

Alevin

Alevin, Brent's

Crystal Euphausid

King's Explorer, Red

Plate 16

Beetle Bug Coachman

MacIntosh

Boxcar

Black Bee

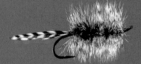

Whiskey and Soda

Cigar Butt

Moose Turd

Disco Mouse

Grease Liner

Waller Walker

Muddler, Orange After Dinner Mint

Wulff, October

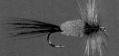

Speed Skater Orange

Speed Skater, Black

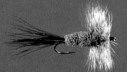

Speed Skater, Gray

Rusty Bomber

Bomber

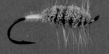

Green Machine

Steelhead Charlie, Blue

Hooks: TMC800S or DAI2546, sizes 4-6.
Thread: Fluorescent blue.
Body: Dyed medium blue flat monofilament wrapped over an underbody of fluorescent blue floss.
Wing: Dyed fluorescent blue gray squirrel tail.
Eyes: Silver bead chain.

Steelhead Charlie, Chartreuse

Hooks: TMC800S or DAI2546, sizes 4-6.
Thread: Fluorescent green.
Body: Dyed chartreuse flat monofilament over an underbody of fluorescent green floss.
Wing: Dyed fluorescent green gray squirrel tail.
Eyes: Gold bead chain.

Steelhead Charlie, Green

Hooks: TMC800S or DAI2546, sizes 4-6.
Thread: Green.
Body: Dyed green flat monofilament over an underbody of fluorescent green floss.
Wing: Dyed green gray squirrel tail.
Eyes: Gold bead chain.

Steelhead Charlie, Orange

Hooks: TMC800S or DAI2546, sizes 4-6.
Thread: Fluorescent orange.
Body: Dyed orange flat monofilament over an underbody of fluorescent orange floss.
Wing: Dyed fluorescent fire orange fox squirrel tail.
Eyes: Gold bead chain.

Steelhead Charlie, Purple

Hooks: TMC800S or DAI2546, sizes 4-6.
Thread: Black.
Body: Dyed purple flat monofilament over an underbody of light blue floss.
Wing: Dyed black squirrel tail.
Eyes: Silver bead chain.

Steelhead Charlie, Red

Hooks: TMC800S or DAI2546, sizes 4-6.
Thread: Fluorescent red.

Body: Dyed red flat monofilament over an underbody of fluorescent red floss.
Wing: Dyed fluorescent red gray squirrel tail.
Eyes: Silver bead chain.

The Steelhead Charlie's are patterned after Bob Nauheim's saltwater Crazy Charlie fly intended for bonefish. Michael Villanti, Gordy Carroll and Charlie Lovelette of Vermont have developed similar variations for the Great Lakes region. Of all the colors, the purple in a size 6 has been the most productive in northern California and southern Oregon. The fact that it was developed there is probably the reason for it getting the most attention.

Steelhead Kelly

Hooks: AC80500BL, AC80501BL, TMC7999 or DAI2441, sizes 4-6.
Thread: Black.
Tail: Scarlet red hackle barbs.
Ribbing: Oval silver tinsel.
Body: Fluorescent green chenille.
Hackle: Black tied on as a collar and tied back and down.
Wing: Gray squirrel tied over the body.
Head: Black.

This pattern was created by Wes Drain.

Steelhead Sunset

Hooks: DAI2151 or DAI2161, sizes 1-6.
Thread: Fluorescent orange.
Body: Flat silver tinsel.
First Hackles: Red, yellow and orange, in that order, each tied on individually as a collar and tied back. This hackle should extend back about the length of the body.
Second Hackle: Dyed purple pheasant rump tied on as a collar and tied back, extending just past the bend of the hook.
Wings: Dyed purple narrow turkey quill sections tied low of the body.
Head: Fluorescent orange.

This promising looking pattern is a creation of Bob Veverka. Even though

Bob resides in Vermont, his obvious insight into steelhead flies merits our attention.

Stevenson Special

Hooks: AC80500BL, AC80501BL, TMC7999 or DAI2441, sizes 4-6.
Thread: Black.
Tail: Guinea fowl barbs.
Ribbing: Oval gold tinsel. Apply to rear portion only.
Body: Rear two-thirds, yellow floss and the front third, black ostrich herl.
Hackle: Grizzly tied on as a collar and tied back and down. One full turn of guinea is added at the front.
Wing: Mottled brown turkey quill sections tied over the body.
Head: Black.

Created in the early 1940s by C. N. Stevenson.

Stillaguamish Belle

Hooks: AC80500BL, AC80501BL, TMC7999 or DAI2441, sizes 4-8.
Thread: Black.
Tail: Golden pheasant tippet barbs.
Butt: White chenille.
Body: Black floss with yellow chenille tied in at the front.
Hackle: Brown tied on as a collar and tied back and down.
Wings: Natural gray duck or goose quill sections tied over the body.
Head: Black.

This is an old Al Knudson pattern which he created around 1930.

Stillaguamish Special

Hooks: AC80500BL, AC80501BL, TMC7999 or DAI2441, sizes 4-6.
Thread: Red.
Tip: Flat silver tinsel.
Tail: Scarlet red and white hackle barbs mixed.
Ribbing: Flat silver tinsel.
Body: Dubbed with #6 yellow lambs wool.
Body Hackle: Yellow tied palmer style over the body.
Hackle: Scarlet red tied on as a collar and tied back.

Wing: Red and white bucktail mixed and tied over the body.
Topping: CH01 pearl and CH03 red Crystal Hair mixed.
Head: Red.

Stillaguamish Sunrise

Hooks: AC80500BL, AC80501BL, TMC7999 or DAI2441, sizes 4-6.
Thread: Orange.
Tail: Scarlet red and yellow hackle barbs mixed.
Ribbing: Oval silver tinsel.
Body: Yellow chenille.
Hackle: Orange tied on as a collar and tied back and down.
Wing: White calf tail tied over the body.
Head: Orange.

Stillaguamish Sunset

Hooks: AC80500BL, AC80501BL, TMC7999 or DAI2441, sizes 2-8.
Thread: Orange.
Tail: Scarlet red hackle barbs.
Ribbing: Oval silver tinsel.
Body: Orange chenille.
Hackle: Orange tied on as a collar and tied back and down.
Wing: White bucktail tied over the body.
Head: Orange.

This pattern obviously borrows heavily from the Polar Shrimp or Orange Shrimp patterns with silver ribbing added. There are other variations that use different fluorescent materials. Also, the addition of bead chain eyes is not uncommon in some areas.

Streaker

Hooks: AC80500BL, AC80501BL, TMC7999 or DAI2441, sizes 2-8.
Thread: Fluorescent red.
Tail: White marabou with a small bunch of fluorescent yellow tied in on top.
Body: Wrapped with fine gold braided Mylar piping.
Hackle: Small bunch of white marabou tied in at throat.
Wing: White marabou tied over the body.

Cheeks: Small bunch of fluorescent orange marabou tied in at each side.
Topping: CH06 orange Crystal Hair.
Head: Fluorescent red.

Another of the Darwin Atkin patterns. See Bright Ember.

Street Walker

Hooks: AC80500BL, AC80501BL, TMC7999 or DAI2441, sizes 2-8.
Thread: Black.
Tail: Purple hackle barbs.
Ribbing: Oval silver tinsel.
Body: Purple chenille.
Hackle: Purple hen hackle tied on as a collar and tied back.
Wing: CH19 purple Crystal Hair tied sparsely over the body.
Head: Black.

Originated in the 1980s by Oregon fishing guide Ogden Nash. A reasonably simple fly to construct, but I doubt if that has anything to do with its popularity, or does it?

Sun Burst

Hooks: AC80500BL, AC80501BL, TMC7999 or DAI2441, sizes 2-8.
Thread: Fluorescent red.
Tail: Fluorescent yellow and orange marabou mixed.
Body: Copper wire.
Hackle: Fluorescent yellow and orange marabou mixed and tied in at throat.
Wing: Fluorescent yellow and orange marabou mixed and tied over the body with a small bunch of fluorescent orange marabou tied in on top.
Cheeks: Short bunch of fluorescent yellow marabou tied in at each side.
Topping: CH07 fire orange Crystal Hair.
Head: Fluorescent red.

Another of the Darwin Atkin patterns. See Bright Ember.

Sundowner, Black

Hooks: AC80500BL, AC80501BL, TMC7999 or DAI2441, sizes 4-8.
Thread: Black.
Tail: Fluorescent fire orange hackle barbs.
Butt: Oval silver tinsel.

Body: Dubbed with #57 fluorescent chartreuse lambs wool.
Body Hackle: Black tied palmer style over the body.
Hackle: Black tied on as a collar and tied back.
Wing: CH07 fire orange Crystal Hair tied over the body.
Head: Black.

Sundowner, Orange

Hooks: AC80500BL, AC80501BL, TMC7999 or DAI2441, sizes 4-8.
Thread: Orange.
Tail: Black hackle barbs.
Butt: Oval silver tinsel.
Body: Dubbed with #57 fluorescent chartreuse lambs wool.
Body Hackle: Fluorescent orange tied palmer style over the body.
Hackle: Fluorescent orange tied on as a collar and tied back.
Wing: CH02 black Crystal Hair tied over the body.
Head: Orange.

Sundowner, Pink

Hooks: AC80500BL, AC80501BL, TMC7999 or DAI2441, sizes 4-8.
Thread: Fluorescent pink.
Tail: Fluorescent pink hackle barbs.
Butt: Oval silver tinsel.
Body: Dubbed with #50 fluorescent red lambs wool.
Body Hackle: Fluorescent pink tied palmer style over the body.
Hackle: Fluorescent pink tied on as a collar and tied back.
Wing: CH08 pink Crystal Hair tied over the body.
Head: Fluorescent pink.

Sundowner, Purple

Hooks: AC80500BL, AC80501BL, TMC7999 or DAI2441, sizes 4-8.
Thread: Black.
Tail: Purple hackle barbs.
Butt: Oval silver tinsel.
Body: Dubbed with #52 fluorescent orange lambs wool.
Body Hackle: Purple tied palmer style over the body.

Hackle: Purple tied on as a collar and tied back.
Wing: CH19 purple Crystal Hair tied over the body.
Head: Black.

Sundowner, Red
Hooks: AC80500BL, AC80501BL, TMC7999 or DAI2441, sizes 4-8.
Thread: Red.
Tail: Scarlet red hackle barbs.
Butt: Oval silver tinsel.
Body: Dubbed with #50 fluorescent red lambs wool.
Body Hackle: Scarlet red hackle tied palmer style over the body.
Hackle: Scarlet red tied on as a collar and tied back.
Wing: CH03 red Crystal Hair tied over the body.
Head: Red.

A number of people take credit for this series of flies. I personally like these flies. I use silver diamond braid for the butt material and wrap a couple of turns under the tail so that it cocks upward.

Surgeon General, Dark
Hooks: AC80500BL, AC80501BL, TMC7999 or DAI2441, sizes 4-8.
Thread: Black.
Tip: Oval silver tinsel.
Tail: Scarlet red hackle barbs.
Ribbing: Oval silver tinsel.
Body: Dubbed with #30 purple lambs wool.
First Hackle: Guinea fowl barbs tied in at the throat.
Wing: White bucktail tied over the body.
Topping: CH01 pearl Crystal Hair.
Second Hackle: Scarlet red tied on as a collar and tied back.
Head: Black.

Surgeon General, Green
Hooks: AC80500BL, AC80501BL, TMC7999 or DAI2441, sizes 4-8.
Thread: Black.
Tip: Oval silver tinsel.
Tail: Scarlet red hackle barbs.
Ribbing: Oval silver tinsel.
Shellback: Fluorescent green chenille.

Body: Dubbed with #30 purple Bunny-Blend.
First Hackle: Guinea fowl barbs tied in at the throat.
Wing: Yellow bucktail tied over the body with an overwing of white bucktail.
Topping: CH01 pearl Crystal Hair.
Second Hackle: Scarlet red tied on as a collar and tied back.
Head: Black.

Surgeon General, Light
Hooks: AC80500BL, AC80501BL, TMC7999 or DAI2441, sizes 4-8.
Thread: Black.
Tip: Oval silver tinsel.
Tail: Scarlet red hackle barbs.
Ribbing: Oval silver tinsel.
Body: Dubbed with 50/50 blend of #36 blue and #30 purple lambs wool.
First Hackle: Guinea fowl barbs tied in at the throat.
Wing: White bucktail tied over the body.
Topping: CH01 pearl Crystal Hair.
Second Hackle: Scarlet red tied on as a collar and tied back.
Head: Black.

Surgeon General, Yellow
Hooks: AC80500BL, AC80501BL, TMC7999 or DAI2441, sizes 4-8.
Thread: Black.
Tip: Oval silver tinsel.
Tail: Scarlet red hackle barbs.
Ribbing: Oval silver tinsel.
Shellback: White chenille.
Body: Dubbed with #30 purple lambs wool.
First Hackle: Guinea fowl barbs tied in at the throat.
Wing: Yellow bucktail tied over the body with an overwing of white bucktail.
Topping: CH01 pearl Crystal Hair.
Second Hackle: Scarlet red tied on as a collar and tied back.
Head: Black.

Credit for the Surgeon General goes to Dr. Robert P. Terrill of Gleneden Beach, Oregon. It is believed that the "dark" pattern is the original, however, the pattern met with such success that a good number of variations were created from it.

Surveyor

Hooks: AC80500BL, AC80501BL, TMC7999 or DAI2441, sizes 4-6.
Thread: Black.
Tail: White bucktail with a small bunch of natural brown bucktail tied over the top.
Body: Rear half, red diamond braid and the front half, yellow chenille.
Hackle: Grizzly and brown mixed (Adams style) and tied on as a collar and tied back and down.
Wing: White bucktail tied over the body with CH03 red Crystal Hair tied in at each side.
Head: Black.

Sustut Boss

Hook: AC80501BL, sizes 2/0-8.
Thread: Red.
Tag: Egg yarn tied short and thick. Reds, oranges and pinks are the most commonly used colors.
Ribbing: Flat gold tinsel.
Body: Black chenille.
Wing: Black calf tail tied over the body.
Topping: CH01 pearl Crystal Hair.
Eyes: Gold bead chain.

Sustut Sunrise

Hooks: AC80500BL, AC80501BL, TMC7999 or DAI2441, sizes 2/0-4.
Thread: Red.
Tail: Orange calf tail with CH19 purple Crystal Hair tied on top.
Ribbing: Flat gold tinsel.
Body: Fluorescent fire orange chenille.
Hackle: Purple tied on as a collar and tied back and down.
Wing: Orange calf tail tied over the body.
Topping: CH19 purple Crystal Hair.
Head: Red.

Both of the above Sustut River patterns were originated by Gary Miltenberger.

Sweet Loretta

Hooks: DAI2151 or DAI2161, sizes 1-6.
Thread: Black.
Tag: Fluorescent fire orange yarn tied short.

Body: Dubbed with #1 black African Angora goat. The body should be constructed so that it is plump and shaggy.
Hackle: Long and soft black tied on as a collar and tied back.
Head: Black.

This fly was created by Jimmy Hunnicutt. People that I know who use this pattern prefer to tie it well weighted and bounce it along the bottom. A body of FB02 black Fly Brite is also used with considerable success.

Teal N'Teal

Hook: DAI2151, sizes 2-8.
Thread: Black.
Tip: Oval silver tinsel.
Body: CC22 teal Crystal Chenille.
Wing: Gray squirrel tail.
First Hackle: Black hen hackle tied on as a collar and tied back.
Second Hackle: Barred teal tied on as a collar with one full turn and tied back.
Head: Black.

I have gotten a good response from this fly from a number of areas and felt compelled to share it with you. It is one of my own. When tying it use X-large Crystal Chenille for sizes 2 and 4.

Thompson River

Hooks: AC80500BL, AC80501BL, TMC7999 or DAI2441, sizes 2-6.
Thread: Black.
Tail: Scarlet red and orange hackle barbs mixed.
Body: Flat gold tinsel.
Hackle: Scarlet red and orange mixed and tied on as a collar and tied back and down.
Wing: Red bucktail tied over the body with a sparse overwing of natural brown bucktail.
Head: Black.

This pattern has a number of variations and there is speculation by some as to the true pattern. This is the pattern that I find most often used, it was originated in the 1960s by Walt Johnson.

Thompson Special

Hooks: AC80500BL, AC80501BL, TMC7999 or DAI2441, sizes 2-6.
Thread: Orange.
Tail: Brown calf tail.
Ribbing: Oval silver tinsel.
Body: Dubbed with #1 black lambs wool.
Hackle: Grizzly tied on as a collar and tied back and down.
Wing: Brown calf tail tied over the body.
Topping: CH02 black Crystal Hair.
Head: Orange.

This pattern was originated by Bob York. The body should be tied thin and the wing and hackle should be kept sparse.

Plate 9   Thor

Hooks: DAI2151 or DAI2161, sizes 2-8.
Thread: Black.
Tail: Orange hackle barbs.
Body: Red chenille.
Hackle: Brown tied on as a collar and tied back and down.
Wing: White calf tail tied over the body.
Head: Black.

I think the first steelhead flies that I ever tied were the Thor and the Orleans Barber. When your upbringing has the continual presence of Jim Pray included, you learn to tie the Thor and tie it correctly. Bucktail was used for the wing on the early flies. If you wanted Polar bear hair you paid an extra ten cents, although legal, it was at a premium even in the 1930s and 1940s.

It would have been sacrilegious for me to even think of using calf tail for the wing. Looking back though I can understand why. The calf tail that was available to the Western fly tier at that time was from local sources and in most cases was classed as "cow tail." A couple times a year I would see the premium stuff from Chicago, but it was always set aside for special flies of other designs. In later years as fly fishermen became more knowledgeable they started wanting calf tail. The fly was used religiously, especially on the Eel River where Jim Pray had developed it in 1936. Bucktail wings were not holding up to their satisfaction and a harder hair was demanded.

Thunder and Lightning, Polly's

Hooks: AC80500BL, AC80501BL, TMC7999 or DAI2441, sizes 4-6.
Thread: Black.
Tail: Golden pheasant crest.
Ribbing: Oval gold tinsel.
Body: Dubbed with #1 black lambs wool.
Hackle: Fluorescent fire orange tied on as a collar and tied back and down.
Wing: Dyed dark brown bucktail tied over the body.
Cheeks: J.C. or substitute.
Head: Black.

This is a dressed down version of a popular Atlantic salmon fly pattern that Polly Rosborough created for steelhead. This is another of Polly's patterns that has apparently been suppressed by his "fuzzy nymph" popularity.

Thunder Mountain

Hooks: AC80500BL, AC80501BL, TMC7999 or DAI2441, sizes 4-6.
Thread: Black.
Tail: Crimson red hackle barbs.
Ribbing: Oval silver tinsel.
Body: Red floss.
Hackle: Crimson red and black tied on as a collar mixed and tied back and down.
Wing: White bucktail tied over the body.
Head: Black.

Tiger

Hooks: AC80500BL, AC80501BL,
TMC7999 or DAI2441, sizes 4-8.
Thread: Orange.
Tail: CH07 fire orange Crystal Hair.
Body: Black chenille.
Hackle: Dyed black pheasant rump tied on
as a collar and tied back.
Wing: Sparse orange calf tail.
Head: Orange.

This simple pattern has proven to be successful throughout northern California. In addition to being on the steelhead menu, it has become an excellent shad fly.

Tranquilizer

Hooks: AC80500BL, AC80501BL,
TMC7999 or DAI2441, sizes 4-8.
Thread: Black.
Tail: Yellow hackle barbs.
Ribbing: Oval gold tinsel. Wrap two or three
turns under the tail so it cocks upward.
Body: Dubbed with #30 purple lambs wool.
Hackle: Purple tied on as a collar and tied
back and down.
Wing: Gray squirrel tail tied over the body.
Head: Black.

This is an old pattern of Mike Kennedy's, or is it? Mike was a well traveled steelheader that thrived on his sport, I have been told that it was doubtful there was a stream left untouched by him. As active as he was, there is a fine line in trying to determine if he originated a pattern or just liked it and let everyone, wherever he went, know of its qualities. For an individual to give credibility to a pattern certainly does not make them the creator.

Plate 10 Trinity

Hooks: AC80500BL, AC80501BL,
TMC7999 or DAI2441, sizes 4-8.
Thread: Black.
Tail: Black calf tail.
Body: Rear half, dubbed FB32 copper Fly
Brite and the front half, dubbed with #1 black
African Angora goat.
Hackle: Natural black hen saddle tied on as
a collar and tied back.
Wing: Black calf tail tied over the body.
Head: Black.

This pattern was developed in 1990 by Wilson Rudd of San Jose, California.

Trinity Brown

Hooks: AC80500BL, AC80501BL,
TMC7999 or DAI2441, sizes 6-8.
Thread: Brown.
Tail: Brown hackle tips tied on edge in an
upward V.
Ribbing: Oval silver tinsel.
Body: Dubbed with #24 brown African
Angora goat.
Hackle: Brown tied on as a collar and tied
back and down.
Head: Brown.

Trinity Gray

Hooks: AC80500BL, AC80501BL,
TMC7999 or DAI2441, sizes 6-8.
Thread: Black.
Tail: Grizzly hackle tips tied in an upward V.
Ribbing: Oval silver tinsel.
Body: Dubbed with #13 gray African Angora
goat.
Hackle: Grizzly tied on as a collar and tied
back.
Head: Black.

Both of the previous patterns emerged from the fly boxes of some uncelebrated fly fisherman more than forty years ago. These two are but a few of the many color combinations I have seen tied in this style over the years, but as the others have fallen, these continue to hang in there season after season.

Trinity Golden Olive

Hook: AC80501BL, sizes 2/0-8.
Thread: Orange.
Tail: Brown hackle barbs.
Body: Dubbed with #21 golden olive Bunny-Blend.
Hackle: Brown tied on as a collar and tied back.
Eyes: Gold bead chain.

The Trinity Golden Olive, the Trinity River and Edward Hutton are tantamount with having an excellent outing for steelhead. Ed knows the river, fishes only one pattern—you don't have to ask, and is one hell of a guy to be with when you find yourself on the way home "pooped and skunked." Never a dull moment hearing about the one that got away.

Trinity Hilton

Hooks: AC80500BL, AC80501BL, TMC7999 or DAI2441, sizes 4-10.
Thread: Orange.
Tail: Brown hen hackle barbs.
Ribbing: Oval gold tinsel.
Body: Black chenille.
Wing: Furnace hackle tips tied over the body with concave side out.
Hackle: Brown tied on as a collar and tied back.
Head: Orange.

The Trinity Hilton was originated in 1987 by Dave DeMoss of Lewiston, California. Dave is a guide and works with Herb Burton on the Trinity. He created this pattern to deal with the low summer water conditions and since that time it has been accepted as a fly for all seasons.

Trinity Special

Hooks: AC80500BL, AC80501BL, TMC7999 or DAI2441, sizes 4-8.
Thread: Black.
Tail: Amherst pheasant crest.
Butt: Natural gray ostrich herl.
Ribbing: Oval silver tinsel.

Body: Dubbed with muskrat fur.
Hackle: Black tied on as a collar and tied back and down.
Wing: Gray squirrel tail tied over the body.
Topping: CH02 black Crystal Hair.
Head: Black.

Earl Dombroski of San Francisco, California, originated this pattern in 1963. He states that between four people, it accounted for over 200 steelhead during the 1990 season.

Plate 10 Trinity Torch

Hooks: AC80500BL, AC80501BL, TMC7999 or DAI2441, sizes 2-6.
Thread: Black.
Tail: Fluorescent fire orange hackle barbs.
Ribbing: Oval gold tinsel.
Body: Dubbed with #25 reddish brown African Angora goat. Pick out the body and make "shaggy" after the ribbing is wrapped.
Wing: Dyed orange fox squirrel tail tied over the body and cocked upward.
Hackle: Brown tied on as a collar and tied back.
Head: Black.

Arthur Wellington of Truckee, California, came up with this pattern for the Trinity River in 1986. It has been used with success in all of the streams in northern California.

Today I hear many who make statements about the Trinity, saying, "It isn't like it used to be." Nothing is or ever will be again, and in most cases those making these statements are not old enough or experienced enough to make a comparison, had they been around before the dams were put in they would realize the contribution they have made. With the upper river alterations and the inception of Trinity and Lewiston Dams in 1963, the Trinity River is at this time a uniquely rich and fertile tailwater fishery that supports both resident and anadromous fish populations. These include spring and summer-run steelhead, Chinook salmon, fall-run steelhead, silver salmon and winter-run steelhead. Lesser populations of resident rainbows and browns play an important role in this fishery, with sea-run browns now returning to the lower Klamath and the entire Trinity River system.

The Trinity is not for everyone, nature has seen to that. With its steep canyon walls carved from stone, it provides sanctuary for the fish like few rivers can. Anglers come away displaying contempt for natural things that they fail to understand.

The controlled water releases have reflected a somewhat stabilized habitat that has nurtured a rich ecosystem teaming with a broad spectrum of aquatics. Returning "native" steelhead often express aggressive receptiveness towards a variety of well presented fly patterns. As you can see from the patterns listed in this chapter, success often tends to be with those patterns that are dark and drab in their appearance.

With a better understanding of the river and good management practices we could see the birth of one of America's leading fisheries. Bureaucrats, they should all be fly fishermen.

Ultimate Leech
Hook: AC80501BL, sizes 2/0-8.
Thread: Fluorescent red.
Tail: Small bunch of CH01 pearl Crystal Hair.
Ribbing: Oval gold tinsel.
Body: Flat gold tinsel.
Wing: Strip of black rabbit tied Matuka style.
Hackle: Black rabbit fur tied in at the throat.
Eyes: Brass bead chain.

This pattern was created by Gary Miltenberger. Also see his Ghost Leech.

Umpqua
See Umpqua Special. It seems that this pattern became "special" when the cheeks were added. Without the cheeks it is just a "plain Jane" Umpqua.

Umpqua Dredger
Hook: AC80501BL, sizes 2/0-8.
Thread: Black.
Tail: Purple marabou.
Body: Purple chenille.
Side Trailers: CH01 pearl Crystal Hair is tied in at the head and extending down each side of the body to the end of the tail. This is accomplished prior to the hackle being wrapped.
Body Hackle: Purple tied palmer style over the body.
Eyes: Silver bead chain.

This is a variation of Mike Mercer's of Redding, California. With the exception of the eyes, this is what Stan Hellekson, my son, developed in 1985 for freshwater use. See Chapter 10. This will give you other ideas along this line and all you have to do is add the eyes.

Umpqua Pearly•Bou
Hooks: AC80500BL, AC80501BL, TMC7999 or DAI2441, sizes 2/0-4.
Thread: Fluorescent fire orange.
Tail: Fluorescent fire orange hen hackle barbs.
Body: Wrapped with fine pearl braided Mylar piping.
Wing: White marabou tied over the body.
Hackle: Fluorescent fire orange hen hackle. This hackle should be long and extend to the point of the hook.
Head: Fluorescent fire orange.

This a Joe Howell pattern.

Umpqua Special
Hooks: AC80500BL, AC80501BL, TMC7999 or DAI2441, sizes 2-8.
Thread: Red.
Tail: White hackle barbs.
Ribbing: Oval silver tinsel.
Body: Rear third, yellow chenille and the front two thirds, red chenille.

Wing: Sparse white bucktail tied over the body with even sparser amounts of red bucktail tied in at the sides of the white.
Cheeks: J.C. or substitute.
Hackle: Brown tied on as a collar and tied back.
Head: Red.

I have tried to keep this pattern in its "virgin state" for you, at least the pattern that I have known all of my life. Today, many add a few strands of CH01 pearl Crystal Hair to either the tail or the wing, or both, and claim there is an improvement. This pattern was created in or around 1935 by either Vic O'Byrne or Don Harter, take your pick. This is another of the patterns that has passed the test of time and is worth tying and trying. You don't have to be headed for Oregon's North Umpqua River either. It works equally well in a number of other streams.

Van Duzen Devil

Hooks: AC80500BL, AC80501BL, TMC7999 or DAI2441, sizes 6-8.
Thread: Fluorescent red.
Tip: Oval silver tinsel.
Ribbing: Oval silver tinsel.
Body: Fluorescent red chenille.
Wings: White hen hackle tips tied in a V over the body with the concave side outward.
Hackle: Fluorescent red tied on as a collar and tied back.
Head: Fluorescent red.

Once while fishing the Eel River in 1969 we suffered two days of rejection. That night in Fortuna I got to playing around with the materials I had with me and came up with this pattern. As it turned out, the fish in the Van Duzen River took a liking to it the following day and it was christened the Van Duzen Devil. I haven't had a chance to try it in the Eel as I had originally intended.

Van Luven

Hooks: AC80500BL, AC80501BL, TMC7999 or DAI2441, sizes 2/0-8.
Thread: Red.
Tail: Scarlet red hackle barbs.
Ribbing: Flat silver tinsel.
Body: Dubbed with #4 red lambs wool.
Hackle: Brown tied on as a collar and tied back and down.
Wing: White bucktail tied over the body.
Head: Red.

A Rogue River classic originated by Harry Van Luven of Portland, Oregon. This pattern was developed in the 1920s in an attempt to improve on the Royal Coachman. As you can see it did. It is used wherever steelhead are found on the West Coast.

Van Zandt

Hooks: AC80500BL, AC80501BL, TMC7999 or DAI2441, sizes 2-6.
Thread: Red.
Tail: Crimson red hackle barbs.
Body: Peacock herl. Reverse wrap the body with fine silver wire.
Hackle: Crimson red tied on as a collar and tied back and down.
Wings: Crimson red duck or goose quill sections tied over the body.
Head: Red.

This pattern appeared around the turn of the century and is credited to Josh Van Zandt of Eureka, California. Obviously this pattern was strongly influenced by the then-popular Scarlet Ibis wet fly pattern. Should you decide to substitute the wing with red bucktail or calf tail you will have a more durable fly.

Wahlflower

Hooks: TMC7989 or DAI2421, sizes 8-12.
Thread: Black.
Tip: Flat silver tinsel.
Butt: Fluorescent orange floss.
Tail: Golden pheasant crest.
Ribbing: Oval silver tinsel.
Body: Fluorescent green floss.
Hackle: Golden pheasant crest tied in at the throat.
Wing: Sparse dyed salmon yellow gray squirrel tail tied over the body.
Head: Black.

While visiting the Bellingham area in 1964 I was introduced to this fly. I was checking out the local sporting goods stores and ran into someone who was very helpful in Ira Yeager's store. I was on an exploration trip seeking out new hot fishing spots, I had reports of some good areas around Birch Bay and here is where I got straightened out. I was given directions to a small estuary just south of Blaine might be holding fish. The kind gentleman and I exchanged some fly patterns and other information. He expressed amazement seeing someone as young and so far from home, as I was, so involved with fly fishing. He introduced himself as Ralph Wahl.

I did as he instructed and watched for any seal activity on the water and sure enough it paid off. I caught some small silvers and sea-run cutthroat. I had some memorable days on the water and in fact I may have overstayed my welcome. I did not bring home any fish, but I did bring home something even better—a newborn baby, our third daughter Linda, who had the privilege of being a guest in a Bellingham hospital for three days.

Later that fall I realized that I had come home with one of the Wahlflowers. Today as I look back at that adventure to the north I realize that I returned to California with two "flowers" and appreciate them both.

This pattern was intended as a summer-run fly and I have treated it as such. It has taken more than steelhead. I have had reasonably good success with native trout as well. For me, it should be called "Feather River Special."

Washougal Olive

Hooks: AC80500BL, AC80501BL, TMC7999 or DAI2441, sizes 6-8.
Thread: Black.
Tip: Flat gold tinsel.
Tail: Golden olive calf tail.
Body: Flat gold tinsel.
Hackle: Golden olive calf tail tied in at the throat.
Wing: White calf tail tied over the body.
Head: Black.

A favored spring-run fly created in 1968 by Bill McMillan of Washougal, Washington.

Weekend Warrior

Hooks: AC80500BL, AC80501BL, TMC7999 or DAI2441, sizes 6-8.
Thread: Black.
Tail: Scarlet red hackle barbs.
Body: Flat silver tinsel.
Wing: Sparse white calf tail with a pair of J.C. or substitute feathers tied tent style over the wing.
Hackle: Fluorescent green tied on as a collar and tied back.
Head: Black.

This pattern was originated in 1971 by Eugene Sunday of Flushing, Michigan.

Plate 10 Weitchpec Witch

Hooks: AC80500BL, AC80501BL, TMC7999 or DAI2441, sizes 2-8.
Thread: Black.
Tail: Golden pheasant tippet barbs.
Body: Black chenille.
Hackle: Black tied on as a collar and tied back and down.
Wing: Orange calf tail tied over the body.
Head: Black.

Originated in the winter of 1945 by Angus Barnet of Anderson, California. Named after the small town of Weitchpec which is located at the edge of Hoopa Valley Indian Reservation and the juncture of the Trinity and Klamath Rivers.

Wells' Special

Hooks: AC80500BL, AC80501BL, TMC7999 or DAI2441, sizes 4-8.
Thread: Black.
Tip: Flat gold tinsel.
Tail: Claret hackle barbs.
Body: Peacock herl. Reverse wrap the body with fine silver wire.
Hackle: Salmon yellow tied on as a collar and tied back.
Wing: Coastal blacktail deer body hair tied over the body.
Head: Black.

Originated in 1920 by Sam Wells of Eureka, California. The original pattern had wings of natural gray goose quill sections which often had red, yellow and blue strips married and either tied on top or along the sides. The deer hair wing came into vogue around 1945. Although given little attention today, this fly still produces fish for those who use it regularly.

Plate 9 Wet Spider

Hooks: AC80501BL, sizes 2/0-8.
Thread: Black.
Tail: Barred mallard barbs tied short and sparse.
Body: Yellow chenille.

Hackle: Barred mallard flank tied on as a collar and tied back.
Head: Black.

Al Knudson first tied the pattern for the Rogue River in the 1930s. Because of its great success a series of Spider type flies started coming from the vises of tiers throughout southern Oregon and northern California. By the early 1940s the original pattern was almost lost in the maze of creations. In my father's frustration he was able to contact Al and get a sample of his "Yellow Spider."

This is essentially what I have given you here. Questions always arise with regard to the sparse tail. Minute maybe, however, many considered this an essential part of the original design which has proven itself time and time again. Bearing this in mind, the tail specification was later incorporated into the Silver Hilton.

Whitesel's Wine

Hooks: AC80500BL, AC80501BL, TMC7999 or DAI2441, sizes 4-8.
Thread: Red.
Tail: Black hackle barbs.
Ribbing: Oval silver tinsel.
Body: Dubbed with #32 claret lambs wool.
Hackle: Black tied on as a collar and tied back.
Wing: White bucktail tied over the body with an overwing of red bucktail.
Head: Red.

Originated by Mike Kennedy and named in honor of Jack Whitesel.

Whopper

Hook: AC80500BL, AC80501BL, TMC7999 or DAI2441, sizes 2-8.
Thread: Black.
Tail: Dyed black pheasant rump barbs.
Body: Dubbed with a blend of #1 black African Angora goat and FB02 black Fly Brite.
Hackle: Dyed black pheasant rump tied on as a collar and tied back.

Wing: Black marabou tied over the body.
Head: Black.

This is one of Herb Lawson's patterns. Herb fishes this fly religiously on the South Fork of the Eel. He states that he never changes patterns, just sizes.

Willow
Hooks: AC80500BL, AC80501BL, TMC7999 or DAI2441, sizes 4-6.
Thread: Black.
Tail: Amherst pheasant tippet barbs.
Ribbing: Oval silver tinsel.
Body: Dubbed with #2 white lambs wool.
Hackle: Badger tied on as a collar and tied back and down.
Wing: Gray squirrel tail tied over the body.
Head: Black.

This is another of the Mike Kennedy patterns.

Wind River
Hooks: AC80500BL, AC80501BL, TMC7999 or DAI2441, sizes 4-6.
Thread: Orange.
Tail: Golden pheasant crest.
Body: Silver diamond braid. Wrap a couple of turns under the tail.
Hackle: Brown tied on as a collar and tied back and down.
Wing: Dyed orange natural brown bucktail tied over the body.
Head: Orange.

This is a pattern I obtained while in Portland, Oregon, a few years back. You will note that some of the materials correspond with those of the Wind River Optic below.

Wind River Optic
Hook: DAI2451, sizes 1-4.
Thread: Black.
Body: Oval silver tinsel.

Wing: Dyed orange natural brown bucktail tied over the body.
Head: Black over 1/4" hollow brass bead.
Eyes: Red with a black center.

This pattern was originated in Washington state and named after its Wind River. The design is the same as the Pray Optics'. A more recent version of this fly has a wing of dyed fluorescent fire orange squirrel tail.

Wind River Witch
Hooks: AC80500BL, AC80501BL, TMC7999 or DAI2441, sizes 4-6.
Thread: Black.
Tail: Amherst pheasant tippet barbs.
Ribbing: Flat gold tinsel.
Body: Dubbed with #57 fluorescent chartreuse lambs wool.
Hackle: Black tied on as a collar and tied back and down.
Wing: White calf tail tied over the body.
Head: Black.

This is another pattern that was originated for the Wind River.

Winter Fly
Hooks: AC80500BL, AC80501BL, TMC7999 or DAI2441, sizes 1/0-6.
Thread: Black.
Body: Silver diamond braid wrapped over an underbody of white floss.
Wing: Dyed black squirrel tail tied over the body.
Hackle: Fluorescent fire orange tied on as a collar and made full.
Head: Black.

Developed in 1965 by Ralph Wahl of Bellingham, Washington. Ralph has taken many good fish with this fly—one of which was a record.

Winter Orange
Hooks: AC80500BL, AC80501BL, TMC7999 or DAI2441, sizes 2/0-6.
Thread: Fluorescent fire orange.
Tip: Flat silver tinsel.
Tail: Orange hackle barbs.
Ribbing: Flat silver tinsel.

Body: Fluorescent orange floss over an underbody of flat silver tinsel.
First Wing: CH06 orange Crystal Hair tied over the body with an overwing of orange marabou.
First Hackle: Orange marabou tied in at the throat.
Second Wing: Orange marabou tied over the body with a sparse overwing of red marabou.
Second Hackle: Scarlet red tied on as a collar and tied back.
Head: Fluorescent fire orange.

Winter Red

Hook: AC80500BL, AC80501BL, TMC7999 or DAI2441, sizes 2/0-6.
Thread: Red.
Tip: Flat silver tinsel.
Tail: Scarlet red hackle barbs.
Ribbing: Flat silver tinsel.
Body: Fluorescent red floss over an underbody of flat silver tinsel.
First Wing: CH03 red Crystal Hair tied over the body with an overwing of fluorescent red marabou.
First Hackle: Fluorescent red marabou tied in at the throat.
Second Wing: Fluorescent red marabou tied over the body with an overwing of crimson red marabou.
Second Hackle: Crimson red tied on as a collar and tied back.
Head: Red.

Winter Rose

Hooks: AC80500BL, AC80501BL, TMC7999 or DAI2441, sizes 2/0-6.
Thread: Fluorescent pink.
Tip: Flat silver tinsel.
Tail: Pink hackle barbs.
Ribbing: Flat silver tinsel.
Body: Pink floss over an underbody of flat silver tinsel.
First Wing: CH08 pink Crystal Hair tied over the body with an overwing of pink marabou.
First Hackle: Pink marabou tied in at the throat.
Second Wing: Pink marabou tied over the body with an overwing of fluorescent hot pink marabou.

Second Hackle: Magenta tied on as a collar and tied back.
Head: Fluorescent pink.

The previous patterns are part of what Trey Combs refers to as his winter series. Other patterns can be found elsewhere in this chapter.

Winter Shrimp

Hooks: AC80500BL, AC80501BL, TMC7999 or DAI2441, sizes 2/0-4.
Thread: Fluorescent fire orange.
Tip: Flat silver tinsel.
Tail: CH06 orange Crystal Hair.
Ribbing: CC07 fire orange Crystal Chenille.
Body: Dubbed with #52 fluorescent orange lambs wool.
Wing: White calf tail tied sparse over the body with an overwing of CH01 pearl Crystal Hair.
Hackle: Fluorescent orange tied on as a collar and tied back.

Originated in 1986 by John Shewey of Bend, Oregon.

Winter's Hope (S)

Hooks: DAI2151 or DAI2161, sizes 3/0-2.
Thread: Claret.
Body: Flat silver tinsel.
Hackle: Teal blue and then purple tied on as a collar and tied back.
Wings: Two yellow hackle tips with two fluorescent fire orange hackle tips tied on the outside and extending over the body.
Head: Claret.

Originated in 1971 by Bill McMillan of Grande Ronde, Oregon.

Winter's Hope (S)

Hooks: AC80500BL, AC80501BL, TMC7999 or DAI2441, sizes 2/0-6.
Thread: Black.
Tip: Flat silver tinsel.
Tail: Orange hackle barbs.
Ribbing: Flat silver tinsel.
Body: Fluorescent orange over an underbody of flat silver tinsel.
First Wing: Yellow marabou tied over the body.
First Hackle: Orange marabou tied in at the throat.

Second Wing: Orange marabou tied over the body with an overwing of more orange marabou.
Second Hackle: Purple and then kingfisher blue tied on as a collar and tied back.
Head: Black.

This is a variation of the original pattern that Trey Combs ties.

Witch
Hooks: AC80500BL, AC80501BL, TMC7999 or DAI2441, sizes 2-8.
Thread: Black.
Tail: Black hackle barbs.
Ribbing: Oval gold tinsel.
Body: Dubbed with #6 yellow lambs wool.
Hackle: Black tied on as a collar and tied back and down.
Wing: Gray squirrel tail tied over the body.
Head: Black.

Witch, Black
Hooks: AC80500BL, AC80501BL, TMC7999 or DAI2441, sizes 2-8.
Thread: Black.
Tail: Scarlet red hackle barbs.
Ribbing: Oval silver tinsel.
Body: Dubbed with #1 black lambs wool.
Hackle: Black tied on as a collar and tied back and down.
Wing: Dyed black squirrel tail tied over the body.
Head: Black.

Witch, Orange
Hooks: AC80500BL, AC80501BL, TMC7999 or DAI2441, sizes 2-8.
Thread: Black.
Tail: Black hackle barbs.
Ribbing: Oval gold tinsel.
Body: Dubbed with #9 orange lambs wool.
Hackle: Black tied on as a collar and tied back and down.

Wing: Dyed orange fox squirrel tail tied over the body.
Head: Black.

Witch, Purple
Hooks: AC80500BL, AC80501BL, TMC7999 or DAI2441, sizes 2-8.
Thread: Black.
Tail: Purple hackle barbs.
Ribbing: Oval silver tinsel.
Body: Dubbed with #30 purple lambs wool.
Hackle: Black tied on as a collar and tied back and down.
Wing: Dyed purple gray squirrel tail tied over the body.
Head: Black.

The original Witch pattern was a product of Mike Kennedy of Lake Oswego, Oregon. The other three patterns listed were devised later by tiers in southern Oregon.

Yellow Hammer
Hooks: AC80500BL, AC80501BL, TMC7999 or DAI2441, sizes 2-6.
Thread: Red.
Tip: Flat silver tinsel.
Body: Yellow chenille.
Hackle: Scarlet red tied on as a collar and tied back and down.
Wing: White bucktail tied over the body.
Head: Red.

Yellow Hammer
Hooks: AC80500BL, AC80501BL, TMC7999 or DAI2441, sizes 2-6.
Thread: Red.
Tip: Flat gold tinsel.
Tail: Scarlet red and white hackle barbs mixed.
Ribbing: Flat gold tinsel.
Body: Dubbed with #6 yellow lambs wool.
Hackle: Scarlet red and yellow mixed and tied on as a collar and tied back and down.
Wing: White bucktail tied over the body with red bucktail tied in at each side.
Head: Red.

There are a number of Yellow Hammer variations. The previous two are as Al Kundson originally conceived them.

Plate 10   **X•Long**
Hooks: AC80500BL, AC80501BL, TMC7999 or DAI2441, sizes 2-6.
Thread: Black.
Tag: Fluorescent green yarn.
Rear Body: Orange chenille.

Center Wing: Dyed red gray squirrel tied short over the body. Keep sparse.
Front Body: Red chenille.
Hackle: Dyed red guinea fowl tied on as a collar and tied back.
Head: Black.

The X-long has always produced fish for me. Possibly some other pattern might have done equally as well had it been fished with the dedication and the confidence that I do this one. The only variation I make in this pattern is in the wing. I occasionally substitute natural brown rabbit hair for the squirrel.

Not too many years ago I was visiting with my good friend, Ned Long, at North Shore on Lake Tahoe. Ned is a gentleman that I find interesting to be around, he gets overly-enthused about every new fly tying material that comes to his attention. He just has to have it, whatever it is, for his inexhaustible supply. His extremely innovative mind allows him to always develop new applications for any material, regardless of its original intended use.

Being somewhat of a father figure to me, I always find that he is worth listening to. Before starting out on a three day adventure to Hot Creek with him, we spent the evening going over his collection of tackle and fly tying materials. One large room of his home is devoted exclusively to fly fishing.

After a number of tying demonstrations and the like, I finally found myself alone; I forget where Ned had wondered off to. Going through his library is always an interesting experience, this night however proved to be more rewarding than I had ever anticipated. There it was, *Steelhead* by Claude M. Kreider, a book I had been trying to get my hands on for years. First published in 1948, it was the first book dedicated to the subject. It had in its time been the steelheader's bible.

Frankly, I had expected something a bit bigger, say 1,000 pages, but there it was. Growing up in northern California and hearing quotation after quotation from this work had led me to believe that I would never be an accomplished steelheader until I had the opportunity to study the text of this book thoroughly. The book is mine now and I am still waiting for something to happen. That is, in the area of improved angling skills.

It is a great little book which has served to confirm many pieces of information for me that I had previously classified as mythology, plus many other points. Thanks Ned, little did you know that your $3.50 investment in the 1940s would bring such gratification to another fly fisherman today. From this visit came the inspiration to give this pattern the name of an *"eXtra"* special man named *"Long."*

Chapter 21

Atlantic Salmon Flies

Some of the first written records on Atlantic salmon flies come from Charles Bowlker's book, *The Art of Angling*, 1747. His statement, *"made just as the painter pleases"* undoubtedly set into motion some of the early salmon fly designs which lasted for many years. Originally taken from trout flies of the time, tied in larger sizes, they did not take on their extremely flamboyant appearance until the end of the nineteenth century.

In this chapter the majority of patterns are North American hair wing Atlantic salmon flies. I have also included some of the simpler strip feather winged patterns. You will also find some of the older as well as some of the more recent Scottish patterns that have proven their worth in North America. I have tried to stick with "fishing flies" only, there are many good books for those who want to indulge in the beautifully dressed more complex feather winged varieties. These exquisite coffee table style books deal with this type of fly in varied ways and the patterns differ from region to region as patterns do most everywhere. One book that I particularly like and recommend is *Classic Salmon Flies*, 1991, by Swedish author Mikael Frodin. It deals very well with patterns for 165 flies, most of which are the fully dressed classics. You will also find that it has an extensive bibliography that gives other references.

I am speaking of art now and not fishing flies. I feel that the greatest achievement of any fly tier is when he can produce true fully dressed feather winged Atlantic salmon flies in their full splendor. Flies tied off with small black heads. The British incidentally often used black tar to secure the heads of their earlier flies and this is believed to be what started the popularity of black heads on flies. The tying of these flies is no doubt a self-inflicted addiction which may well border on artistic expression. There is no other area in fly tying where one can express themselves as artistically as they can with Atlantic salmon flies. When the naysayers challenge me as to whether fly tying is either an art or a craft, I just show them a fully dressed salmon fly. No further discussion is necessary.

Judith Dunham's book, *The Atlantic Salmon Fly,* 1991, also showcases a good sampling of these flies and it is filled with the level of interest our contemporary fly tiers are exhibiting today.

I have known a number of people who spend months pursuing materials, and then days constructing some of these flies. Flies never to be fished with, just enjoyed. There have been accusations that I too have created bait for shadow boxes—I'm guilty, what can I say? As I have been told, "there are flies for fishin' and flies for lookin'."

Fishing for Atlantic salmon is just a fantasy for most of us who live in the West. For those of us who have an occasional opportunity to go after these fish it becomes an obsession which can never quite be fulfilled. The pursuit of these fish in Europe long ago generated down to having to pay an access fee to have the opportunity to enjoy them. The proliferation of dams and pollution in the U.S. has gradually destroyed our salmon habitats to the point that they have become almost nonexistent. Maine today has the last of the waters where these fish make any notable appearance. This water is highly regulated and bidding for a place to stand while waiting your turn at a small piece of water can be a circus.

The Maritime Provinces of eastern Canada however do act as a pressure release valve for this fishery to some extent. Canada has a large number of salmon rivers and they rate as some of the greatest in the world. I should add that since the dissolving of the Soviet Union a whole new unexplored frontier is opening up to the western world, some speculate that this fishery will one day be more important to the fly fisherman than Alaska.

For the most part, both Maine and Canada restrict their salmon rivers to "fly fishing only." That point alone excites many, however, I believe the opportunity to potentially take the largest fish that can be taken in eastern freshwater on a fly is what encourages most.

As a young man serving in the United States Air Force I had the opportunity of pulling a tour at Presque Isle, Maine. Arriving in January, little did I know that I was about to experience the hardest winter that I had ever seen. Northern California was a long ways away and certainly nothing like this new environment. After getting settled in I came to realize that there were no opportunities for even a glimpse of night life, so I wrote home and had some books and fly tying materials sent along to help pass the winter months.

Other than feeding fuel to the furnaces that winter, you can probably guess what I did until spring arrived. Tied flies, lots of flies. I also learned many new terms that winter, like, "cabin fever" and "snow bound" to name a few. I acquired a host of new friends who knew the area and a few were fly fishermen. They were impressed with the fact that I could tie flies and coached me on brookie and salmon patterns. When the maples started turning green in spring, I had amassed an enormous amount of flies. I never did have a chance to meet those friendly local girls the old-timers kept mentioning and bragging about.

This was my first opportunity at the Atlantic salmon. At that time, the mid fifties, I had had very little experience with the migratory steelhead and salmon on the West Coast. This more than made up for it. Circumstance created the chance for me to fish to my heart's content in both the U.S. and Canada. I learned the size of a real New England pond as opposed to our Western puddles, caught my very first "big" brook trout that year and had my first real good sampling of Atlantic salmon on a fly. Both experiences gave me a taste that I will always savor. That was a year of many firsts for me—I had my first fly rod jerked from my hands as a fish took the fly on the swing, caught my first salmon on a dry fly, and was befriended by my first true "old school dedicated salmon fly fisherman," Olef Olsen.

Olef Olsen was from the old school, having fished all of the Maritime Provinces of Canada, and most of Europe. Olie, as it turned out had roots in Sweden, coming from the same area as my mother's side of the family had. Fortunately for me he took me under his wing that year and we became the best of friends. As a tutor of sorts, Olie inevitably talked over my head, compounding this even further, in his excitement he would switch into his broken English mode and there were times when I understood nothing. It took very little to get Olie's blood running at high speed when it came to the pursuit of Atlantic salmon, he thoroughly enjoyed having someone to listen to his yarns. He was a worldly person and a true gentleman of the highest caliber. When you showed interest in his love, he would go all out to impart any knowledge that he could. He stored so much in his head that you often felt you were with a walking library, name any salmon fly pattern and the detailed dressing and background of the fly would be forthcoming.

Evenings with Olie meant one thing, fly tying. He was always willing to go into the early hours with tying instructions and demonstrations. There was no question of him not being fully appreciative of any interest shown in his sport—a sport that he would have liked to have shared with the whole world. His fly tying skills were as good as any I have ever seen. I only wish that I could have had more time to learn even more from him. Up until that time I often became frustrated trying to maintain small heads on salmon flies. With feathers it was easy, but now Olie had me tying hair wing patterns. His philosophy was to not be too concerned with the size and concentrate on durability. He was fascinated with the squirrel tails that were available in America and he had started using them on most of the patterns he tied. It was comforting to realize this was something that was also a little new to him. It was different from what he had been practicing and he concluded that because of the harder hair of the squirrel, it required a head almost twice the size as found on feather winged patterns.

His fishing skills were fair to maybe good. He never had his line in the water enough. He spent more time worrying about and helping those who were with him than he did fishing. His first chore upon arriving at the river was to see that we had some sort of fire going. A "gill knocker," he would say, "Who can fish if they get a gill?" Then there were the lunches by Olie, lunch was always a splendid affair. It started about ten in the morning and lasted well into the afternoon. You learned to fish in between bites or risk the chance of offending Olie. He was always asking if you had had enough, yet I believe we always took home as much as we had brought.

I felt grossly under-rodded with my eight foot, six weight rod when Olie would line up his ten and half foot, ten weight plus Hardy. He could turn the fish better than I could, but I believe my experiences with the lighter rod that season were more rewarding. This was also the first time I had seen a fly line thrown such a great distance and with such precise accuracy.

After tagging along with Olie that season, I too felt that there might be some sort of future for me as a fishing bum. I often wondered where Olie obtained his wealth which enabled him to live his envied lifestyle. In those days I thought hard about the possibility that maybe even I could be of the same caliber that I had admired and tried to emulate in the shadow of Olie.

We talked of more destinations in New Brunswick and Nova Scotia for the following season. This never came to be. Olie was lost in a small plane in the Lake of the Woods area north of Warroad, Minnesota, that following spring. Subsequent trips to the Maritime Provinces of Canada through the years have always been shrouded with the memorable unique space on the rivers left by the "gentleman angler."

Without a doubt these earlier experiences were part of a learning process that helped later on. In retrospect, what young man could have asked for anything more enlightening? When I was later asked to tie specific Atlantic salmon fly patterns commercially it was not new territory, I was able to differentiate between the traditional and the functional. Yes, there does exist two different schools of thought and I will address these as we go along.

The frustration in fishing for Atlantic salmon, as with most migratory fish, lies in the fact that they are not a feeder when in freshwater. After years in the boundless ocean, they find freshwater streams a strange environment. The fly fisherman must take this into account. Working in his favor, however, is the fact that as a young parr, the salmon was an insect feeder, if the right fly and a delicate cast can stir the salmon's memory, a rise and a strike is sure to follow. The fish has no intention of eating, but he will mouth an insect, as he did in his earlier days in the river, and then spit it out. This adult response to a habit fixed in youth gives the fly fisherman some chance.

The fly used to tempt an Atlantic salmon can be any of the thousands in regular everyday use. There are almost no standard salmon fly patterns that make any sense, since they in no way resemble living insects in either color or form. The wet fly tradition used is a carry-over from centuries of salmon fishing in Scotland and England. In Dr. T. E. Pryce-Tannatt's book, *How to Dress Salmon Flies,* 1914, he spells out the procedures for tying the old traditional flies and gives dressings for 100 patterns. Most of their flies called for heavily dressed, bulky bundles of bright feathers from many parts of the world. These flies were laced with tinsels of all types. Many of the older patterns require up to two dozen or more different materials.

Hugh Falkus writes in his book, *Salmon Fishing (A Practical Guide)*, 1984, that: *"During the second half of the 19th century, these new, vividly-hued patterns, which had originated in Ireland some years earlier, started to push the duller, more simple flies into the background.*

"This invasion of gaudy Irish patterns did not occur without some local resistance, notably on Tweedside where the salmon fishers - according to a contemporary writer - not only held what was called the "Irish Fly" in ridicule, but actually forbade the use of it on those parts of the river they individually rented. This was not because they thought it too deadly for everyday use, but solely because it was considered: "a kind of bugbear to the fish, scaring them from their accustomed haunts and resting spots."

"It was no good. Once started, the new fashion in salmon flies quickly climbed to unprecedented heights of fancy. Whatever their effect on the fish, these new lures certainly hooked the fishermen. And so started the Victorian era of lavish attention to detail. Every fibre of every exotic feather, every twist of silk, every turn of tinsel had to be exact." This is a very good book and I recommend it for your personal library.

We will never see many of these materials incorporated in flies again. It is reasonable to assume that these materials were a by-product of the millinery trade of that period. Affluent ladies demanded large feathery hats at any cost. The resourceful fly tiers acquired the leavings and put them into their flies. From some of the ancient patterns that have been recorded in literature it is also reasonable to assume that many of these patterns were the result of those tiers who had the most materials on their tying bench. Possibly the display of these gaudy feather dusters to fellow anglers played some significant role, or maybe they were a status symbol of sorts.

North American salmon flies are more sedate. The trend is toward more modest hues with less flash and gingerbread. Some areas in Canada attest to this fact and say that, "Any pattern is good, but it must be black." Naturally there are other areas which gravitate to other colors such as orange, etc. The confusion in fly selection arises from the fact that all of these patterns, in a wide range of sizes, will raise fish. It all depends on where you are and at what time of the year, and oddly enough, some say, "how you hold your mouth." Do you suppose they are suggesting that we always smile?

When the British salmon fly patterns arrived in North America they were highly prized. The materials needed for tying them were not available here. When these flies were not available direct from the mother country, fly fishermen had to improvise. Somewhere around the turn of the century hair wing flies began to appear. The leavings of the hunters, trappers, and fur dealers were good pickings for the fly tier.

It is thought by many that the North American hair winged salmon flies evolved due to the steelhead patterns on the West Coast. These flies too were creations of necessity as the steelheaders were developing their patterns. The point will never be made clear, who copied who? I believe that there has always been a mutual exchange of ideas, most revolving around and being developed from original trout patterns which had already proven to be a success. No doubt historians will credit fly tiers on both coasts with developing the hair winged patterns simultaneously.

Most students of the "greased line" techniques know that they were developed by A.H.E. Wood, an Englishman, when fishing for Atlantic salmon on the Cairnton stretch of the Aberdeenshire Dee. It was here that he recorded catches of 3,540 salmon from 1913 to 1934. Wood did not embellish the end of his line with a large assortment of fly patterns, instead he was a strong believer in size and presentation and basically used only the Blue Charm and March Brown.

These flies were first tied in different sizes using different sized hooks. Here is where Wood became more adventurous, at least for an Englishman of that period, maybe it had something to do with the intoxicating air of the Scottish countryside. He started tying his flies smaller, yet maintained the same hook size. These he called his "short dressed" flies. Later when making reference to these flies he stated, *"I do not use a smaller hook than I can help, but you must remember that the fly proper, the body, wings, etc., is smaller than the hook."*

Today we refer to this as "reduced" or "low water" style. I have briefly touched on this in Chapter 8 and suggest this practice when tying some other flies. It is reasonable to assume that fish sometimes ignore that which is rather obvious to us. This is a good thing or how else would we ever be able to catch them? Let's discuss the reduced or low water designs along with conventional standard or high water style of tying. In view of the fact that no matter which methodology I outline there will be some disagreement, I will try and keep it in the simplest form. This is one of the most "over-discussed" subjects in Atlantic salmon fly tying.

Low Water Style. This style is probably the most complex. Low water hooks are used for these flies. They are made of finer wire and you will often find them listed in American catalogs as *"salmon dry fly"* hooks. Along with low water hooks comes the low water style of tying, these flies should be tied smaller and sparser. Included in this style we find three different basic levels:

◆ **Level 1.** This is the three-quarter low water style with the rear of the body starting slightly in front of the hook point.

◆ **Level 2.** This is the full low water style with the rear of the body starting halfway between the point and the eye of the hook. This level is also expressed as "reduced 50%." Some others carry this even further and produce flies reduced in increments of ten percent, i.e., 30% or 40%.

◆ **Level 3.** The medium water flies are tied in the standard style with the rear of the body starting either at the point of the hook or halfway between the point and the barb. This largely depends on the particular hook style being used and of course the desires of the individual fly tier.

High Water Style. These flies are tied on the heavier or regular wire hooks. They are tied in the same style as the level 3 style and are probably the most commonly used type of salmon fly. As a casual tier you can see the many varied possibilities you have when tying these flies, you are not bound by any set rules as are many of the professional tiers who shackle themselves to fanciful fantasies of the past.

You would do well to inquire when planning a trip to any Atlantic salmon waters in Canada, learn which fly patterns to bring and the specific styles, low or high water, and sizes. You may find that some areas have a way of thinking that you interpret as eccentric or bizarre. For example, it is considered by some to be both inefficient and unethical to fish large flies, with their larger hooks, in low water conditions, it is felt that your chances of accidentally snagging a fish are increased with the possibility of mortally wounding it.

You will find, as I have, "too large" is interpreted with uncertainty and in so many different ways. Also, when I speak with those who regularly fish in both Canada and Europe I am told that the Canadians are decades behind the British who use what they regard as a more practical approach. The British idea of a low water fly is one that is tied in smaller sizes, mostly 10-14 doubles and trebles. They do this in the interest of not spooking fish in low water. Obviously with their use of multiple pointed hooks they are not concerned with the possibility of snagging one.

Some tiers feel salmon flies can only be tied on hand-made hooks. They feel they offer more sizes and styles and include a variety of wire weights and other features. They go on to point out that because these hooks are hand-made their quality will vary greatly, and then express considerable dissatisfaction with the higher cost for these hooks.

While doing research for this chapter it quickly became evident that there is a very broad range of opinions, probably more far reaching than for any other type of fly. Fly tiers as a whole are generally quick to give an opinion. There is no general consensus of opinion with respect to salmon flies, just lots of opinions. You almost have to divide salmon fly tiers into two categories: One would be those who only tie the traditional classic feather winged designs; some of these tiers don't even fish, they simply find satisfaction in tying flies which replicate those of the Victorian era. These tiers perform on an international level and have no general geographical location where they congregate. In fact, even though the Irish are credited with starting this movement, one would seriously question any influence they might have today. British salmon flies for the most part now consist of hair wing creations tied on long shank double and treble hooks, some comment that the British may have taken a few steps back. They are happy so what the heck.

The second category would be those who tie the more functional hair wing designs. These two categories of tiers share some common characteristics, they are generally very good tiers and often appear to be incommunicable and reserved which can be frustrating to someone trying to gain information. I try to reject any thoughts of them being snobbish, but with some, a degree of pretension is often involved. It is much like trying to solicit brain donors rather than picking an individual's brain for information. The fact remains that generally they are not forthcoming with any information about their flies or other matters pertaining to flies. One is forced to pick this information up piece by piece and try to put it all together and make some meaning out of it all.

There could possibly be a third group in all of this: Fly fishermen who are more down to earth, living in close proximity to their fishery and knowing what catches fish. They have a wealth of knowledge that pertains to flies, flies that they use, but histories and the like are uncertain. Some label these anglers as an unsophisticated bunch of knownothings, well whatever they might be called, they are for me. They could care less about the proper length of "horns" as found on a classic salmon fly. These are the type of fly fishermen that I found to be the most willing to provide information for this chapter, they are not preoccupied with inflexible views and are well within the mainstream. A little ego stroking goes a long way.

If you remember, I stated in *Volume I* that I would not include any flies that called for materials which were not generally available. This chapter is the exception due to the region where these flies are primarily tied and fished—Canada. The Canadians have different laws to abide by and can obtain many of the materials we find restricted in this country. Some experienced salmon fly tiers in America insist they can obtain any and all materials that I have offered substitutes for. When questioned where, all at once it becomes a big secret. I never get a straight answer, which leads me to believe they are trying to make fish soup from the shadow of a fish that swam by yesterday.

There has always been a certain amount of discussion regarding the conversion of fly patterns from the feather wing style to hair wing variations. I have had the pleasure of meeting with a few of these highly enlightened gurus and found little or no reasoning behind their complex theories—their theories have no foundation. *Hair-Wing Atlantic Salmon Flies,* 1973, by Keith Fulsher and Charles Krom deals with these conversions better than any book that I am aware of at this time. I have been able to include much of their work in this chapter plus other updated information from them. Keith wrote to me saying, *"I'm content now, Terry, in fishing with existing patterns."*

Many salmon fly patterns have indeed evolved here in North America, coming from known productive wet flies and streamers. Many may not concur with some of the specifications given, there are certainly variations that may be better known to them. With no true standards to rely on and creative talent in abundance we must give credence to Bowlkers's words, *"made just as the painter pleases."* Those patterns coded with **(SH)** are also recommended for steelhead or at least deserve thoughts leading to conversion.

The following patterns are those I have been able to acquire over the years. Many are variations of other flies, but I believe many are cousins of the feather winged designs. In my personal collection I have more variations of the Blue Charm alone than the law probably allows. I have not listed recommended hook models and sizes with the individual patterns as I have in other chapters. There are many sources for hooks. Refer to Chapter 4 for guidance.

Before trying to tie any of these patterns I strongly recommend you refer to Chapter 6 and review the definitions of fly parts. Some Atlantic salmon fly tiers are certain to become confused and/or disgruntled, especially when they realize how I define the fly parts "tips" and "tags." My decision to use Webster over a Chambers English Dictionary apparently destroys a bit of the nostalgic mysticism for some. It certainly substantiates the fact that we are indeed two countries divided by a common language. Nevertheless some still want to hold on to the more traditional complex definitions set forth by the British in the feather winged designs of yesterday.

I believe that all fly tying books should be instructive in nature and give the reader an unquestioned direction to follow. While writing this chapter and reviewing how others approach this, it became obvious that I needed to go into more detail and not brush over the little things that have always been either senselessly argued over or ignored. If you do not fully understand the fly parts described, then how in the dickens are you going to be able to tie the flies properly? I will go back and give some background so you understand where my roots in fly tying are anchored.

My first reference to fly parts came by reading the 1941 edition of George Leonard Herter's, *Fly Tying and Tackle Making.* Now, good old George was far from being a modest character, in retrospect, I would say that much of what he might have been trying to tell us was destroyed because of his approach. Herter's, Inc., George's company, pioneered mail-order fly tying material in this country. Herter's, Inc. enjoyed being the source of sources for many decades, in their marketing they used the term "World's Best" in connection with every product they sold. When you received something from them that wasn't even "good" you start questioning "best." As you can see this diminished George's credibility to some extent.

Later I read, *Fishing Flies and Fly Tying*, 1951, by William F. Blades and it went along reasonably well with what George had to say, except when making reference to the tip Blades stated: *"The tag or tip, composed of a few turns of tinsel and silk floss."* This was probably my first encounter with waffling or lack of specificity, and I was not convinced that Blades knew what a cheek or shoulder was either. I had to stick with the terms George had given. They made the most sense.

Through the years my library has grown and I always try to figure out what the individual author is trying to say with respect to fly parts. It is rather obvious that all have had some problems, especially when they attempt to describe a pattern for an Atlantic salmon fly. Ninety-five percent of what they say is in agreement with George, however, tips and tags go astray. I attribute this to our obsession with trying to use terms that we are unaccustomed to—terms listed in foreign dictionaries.

Let me outline the fly parts we have the most problems with so you can better understand the approach I use.

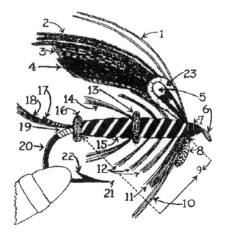

Herter's fly parts.

Tip. This is #19 on Herter's illustration and is much like what I use. It does fail to recognize that this part can be tied in more than one part—it often becomes two. Atlantic salmon flies often utilize two materials, i.e., tinsel at the bottom and floss at the top. This is why I use the terms "lower" and "upper." Should there be a third material, which is rare, I identify it as "center." As a rule of thumb, and unless I specify otherwise, the lower portion of the tip, when it is tinsel, will occupy approximately twenty percent of the space and the floss or other material will be the other eighty percent.

Butt. This is #16 and can be confusing when it is a material, i.e., tinsel, floss or yarn. This is especially true when the upper portion of the tip is of the same material as the butt.

Tag. No matter how you slice it, a tag always has one loose end. George identifies this as #17. Some argue that this is a "tail tag," then the question has to be asked, "What is it if the tail is not included in the dressing?" In this case it could only be a tag.

Abbey

Thread: Black.
Tip: Oval gold tinsel.
Tail: Golden pheasant crest.
Ribbing: Flat gold tinsel.
Body: Red floss.
Hackle: Brown tied on as a collar and tied back and down.
Wing: Gray squirrel tail tied low over the body.
Head: Black.

This pattern was converted from a trout wet fly. Also see Red Abbey.

Abe Munn Killer

Thread: Black.
Tail: Two narrow sections of mottled brown turkey quill.
Ribbing: Oval gold tinsel.
Body: Buttercup yellow floss.
Hackle: Brown tied on as a collar and tied back and down with sparse bunch of mottled brown turkey quill barbs tied in at the throat.
Wings: Mottled brown turkey quill sections tied low over the body or substitute.
Head: Black.

Originated by Abe Munn of Boyston, New Brunswick. Munn was a guide on the Miramichi during the early 1920s. Since that time there have been a number of variations including Ira Gruber's "Abe Mohn" and John Atherton's "Abe Munn Upriver."

Afternoon Delight

Thread: Black.
Tip: Flat silver tinsel.
Tail: Golden pheasant crest.
Ribbing: Oval silver tinsel.
Center Joint: Fluorescent green yarn.
Body: Rear half, flat silver tinsel and the front half, peacock herl.
Wing: Dyed yellow gray squirrel tail tied over the body and extending to the hook end.
Hackle: Yellow hen hackle tied on as a collar and tied back.
Head: Black.

Originated in the mid 1970s by Mike Crosby of Halifax, Nova Scotia.

Aguanus

Thread: Black.
Tip: Lower, flat silver tinsel and the upper, yellow floss.
Butt: Black ostrich herl.
Ribbing: Oval gold tinsel.
Body: Dark orange floss.
First Wing: Small bunch of golden pheasant tippet barbs tied over the body with an overwing of a dyed yellow hackle tip tied flat.
First Hackle: Bright blue tied on as a collar and tied back.
Second Wing: Small bunch of golden pheasant tippet barbs.
Second Hackle: Natural black hen hackle tied on as a collar and tied back.
Head: Black.

Originated by Francois Barnard of Sept-Isle, Quebec.

Allot Fly, Blue

Thread: Black.
Tip: Flat silver tinsel.
Tail: Single strand of fluorescent blue yarn.
Ribbing: Oval silver tinsel.
Body: Flat silver tinsel.
Hackle: White tied on as a collar and tied back and down.
Wing: Gray squirrel tail tied low over the body.
Cheeks: J.C. or substitute.
Head: Black.

Allot Fly, Orange

Thread: Black.
Tail: Single strand of fluorescent orange yarn.
Ribbing: Oval silver tinsel.
Body: Flat silver tinsel.
Hackle: White tied on as a collar and tied back and down.
Wing: Dyed orange gray squirrel tail tied low over the body.
Cheeks: J.C. or substitute.
Head: Black.

Plate 6   Ally's Shrimp (SH)

Thread: Red.
Tail: Orange bucktail tied two and one half times the length of the body with sparse strands of clear (white) Miclon tied on top.
Ribbing: Oval gold tinsel.
Body: Rear half, red floss and the front half, black floss.
Wing: Sparse gray squirrel tail tied over the body with an overwing of a golden pheasant tippet feather tied flat.
Hackle: Orange tied on as a collar and tied back.
Head: Red.

This pattern was sent to me from Scotland and was originated in 1989 by Alistair Gowans. Since its inception, this has become one of the most popular salmon fly patterns in the U.K. There are at least a half dozen variations of the pattern and they are collectively thought to be responsible for taking over half of the salmon each season.

Amsel Amherst

Thread: Black.
Tip: Oval silver tinsel.
Tail: Amherst pheasant tippet barbs.
Ribbing: Oval silver tinsel.
Body: Rear half, embossed silver tinsel and the front half, black floss.
Hackle: Black tied on as a collar and tied back and down.
Wing: Dyed black squirrel tail tied low over the body.
Cheeks: Amherst pheasant tippet sections tied in on each side.
Head: Black.

Anthea Fly

Thread: Black.
Tip: Lower, oval gold tinsel and the upper, fluorescent orange yarn.
Tail: Light ginger hackle barbs.
Ribbing: Oval gold tinsel.
Body: Light rust colored yarn.
Hackle: Light ginger variant tied on as a collar and tied back and down.
Wing: Ginger mink tail tied low over the body.
Head: Black.

Originated in 1978 by Keith Fulsher. The wing material for his original pattern used hair from his favorite dog.

Arndilly Fancy I

Thread: Black.
Tip: Oval silver tinsel.
Tail: Golden pheasant crest.
Ribbing: Oval silver tinsel.
Body: Dubbed with yellow seal fur or substitute.
Hackle: Light blue tied on as a collar and tied back and down.
Wing: Dyed black squirrel tail tied low over the body.

Cheeks: J.C. or substitute.

Head: Red ostrich herl. First tie in the ostrich herl and partially finish head without wrapping the ostrich herl. Apply a narrow band of red lacquer at the base of the head and while still wet wrap two turns of the ostrich herl and finish the front portion of the head off with the black tying thread.

Arndilly Fancy II

Thread: Black.

Tip: Flat silver tinsel.

Tail: Golden pheasant crest.

Ribbing: Flat silver tinsel.

Body: Dubbed with yellow seal fur or substitute.

Hackle: Kingfisher blue tied on as a collar and tied back and down.

Wing: Dark brown mink tail tied low over the body.

Head: Black.

As De Pique

Thread: Black.

Tip: Oval silver tinsel.

Tail: Golden pheasant crest.

Ribbing: Oval silver tinsel.

Body: Dubbed with chartreuse seal fur or substitute.

Hackle: Yellow tied on as a collar and tied back and down.

Wing: Dyed black squirrel tail tied low over the body.

Cheeks: J.C. or substitute.

Head: Black.

Originated by Yves Demers of Trois-Rivieres, Quebec.

Babcock

Thread: Black.

Tail: Dyed yellow gray squirrel tail.

Ribbing: Flat gold tinsel.

Body: Dubbed with red seal fur or substitute.

Hackle: Black tied on as a collar and tied back and down.

Wing: Dyed yellow gray squirrel tail tied low over the body.

Head: Black.

 ## Bandit

Thread: Black.

Tip: Lower, flat silver tinsel and the upper, white floss.

Tail: Black hackle barbs.

Butt: Black ostrich herl.

Ribbing: Flat silver tinsel.

Body: White floss.

Wing: Dyed black squirrel tail tied low over the body.

Hackle: Black hackle barbs tied in at the throat with white tied on as a collar and tied back.

Head: Black.

Bats

Thread: Black.

Tip: Flat gold tinsel.

Tail: Golden pheasant crest.

Ribbing: Flat gold tinsel.

Body: Dubbed with green seal fur or substitute.

Hackle: Guinea fowl barbs tied in at the throat.

Wing: Red fox guard hair tied low over the body.

Topping: Peacock sword with dyed orange golden pheasant crest tied on top.

Head: Black.

Beadle Red

Thread: Black.

Tail: Golden pheasant crest.

Ribbing: Flat gold tinsel.

Body: Dubbed with #1 black lambs wool.

Body Hackle: Tie palmer style over the body 1. rear third, scarlet red, 2. center third, purple, and 3. front third, deep dark blue.

Wing: Red bucktail tied over the body.

Head: Black.

Bear Paw

Thread: Black.

Tip: Lower, oval gold tinsel and the upper fluorescent orange floss.

Tail: Natural red golden pheasant breast barbs.

Ribbing: Oval gold tinsel.

Body: Dubbed with #1 black lambs wool.

Hackle: Brown tied on as a collar and tied back and down.

Wing: Golden pheasant crest barbs with an overwing of a small bunch of brown bear hair.
Head: Black.

The original pattern for this fly called for bear paw hair for use in the wing.

Bette Jane

Thread: Black.
Tip: Oval gold tinsel.
Tail: Scarlet red hackle barbs.
Butt: Fluorescent green floss.
Ribbing: Oval gold tinsel over rear half of body only.
Body: Rear half, green floss and the front half, peacock herl.
Body Hackle: Bright green tied palmer style over the peacock portion of the body.
Wing: Peacock sword barbs tied over the body with an overwing of badger hair.
Hackle: Yellow tied on as a collar and tied back.
Head: Black.

Bette Jane

Thread: Black.
Tip: Oval gold tinsel.
Tail: Scarlet red hackle barbs.
Butt: Fluorescent green yarn.
Ribbing: Oval gold tinsel.
Body: Rear half, green floss and the front half, peacock herl.
Hackle: Bright green tied in at the throat with a bunch yellow tied over.
Wing: Badger hair tied low over the body.
Head: Black.

These are two versions of this pattern. The later was originated by Dave Goulet of New Hartford, Connecticut, in 1979. The first variation is of unknown origin.

Big Intervale Blue

Thread: Black.
Tip: Oval gold tinsel.
Tail: Golden pheasant crest.
Ribbing: Oval gold tinsel.
Body: Fluorescent blue floss tied with a nice full taper.

Wing: White calf tail tied over the body with a sparse overwing of clear (white) Miclon.
Hackle: Silver doctor blue tied on as a collar and tied back.
Head: Black.

Originated in 1987 by Len Rich, author of *Newfoundland Salmon Flies*.

Big Three

Thread: Red.
Tip: Oval gold tinsel.
Ribbing: Oval gold tinsel.
Body: Orange floss.
Hackle: Deep dark blue tied on as a collar and tied back and down.
Wing: Black moose hair.
Head: Red.

Bill's Badger

Thread: Black.
Ribbing: Flat silver tinsel.
Body: Black floss.
Hackle: Kingfisher blue hackle barbs tied in at the throat.
Wing: Black-tipped badger hair tied low over the body.
Head: Black.

Black and Blue

Thread: Black.
Tip: Oval gold tinsel.
Tail: Golden pheasant crest.
Ribbing: Oval gold tinsel.
Body: Flat silver tinsel.
Wing: Dyed black squirrel tail tied low over the body.
Hackle: Kingfisher blue tied on as a collar and tied back.
Head: Black.

Black Bear (SH)

Thread: Black.
Tip: Oval gold tinsel.
Tail: Black hackle barbs.
Ribbing: Oval gold tinsel.
Body: Dubbed with #1 black lambs wool.
Hackle: Black tied on as a collar and tied back and down.
Wing: Black moose hair tied low over the body.
Head: Black.

Black Bear, Green Butt (SH)

Tied same as the Black Bear except has a fluorescent chartreuse yarn butt added. It is not uncommon to see other colors of butts on this pattern, i.e., red or orange.

Black Beard

Thread: Black.
Tail: Crimson red hackle barbs.
Ribbing: Oval silver tinsel over dubbed portion of body only.
Body: Rear half, flat silver tinsel and the front half, dubbed with black seal fur or substitute.
Hackle: Black calf tail with claret calf tail in front and tied in at the throat.
Wing: Dyed black squirrel tail tied low over the body.
Head: Black.

The original pattern for this fly called for black lab or spaniel for the wing.

Black Bomber (SH)

Thread: Black.
Tip: Lower, oval silver tinsel and the upper, yellow floss.
Tail: Golden pheasant crest.
Ribbing: Oval silver tinsel.
Body: Dubbed with #1 black lambs wool.
Hackle: Black tied on as a collar and tied back and down.
Wing: Dyed black squirrel tail tied low over the body.
Topping: Golden pheasant crest.
Cheeks: J.C. or substitute.
Head: Black.

See Brown Bomber.

Black Brahan

Thread: Red.
Tip: Oval silver tinsel.
Tail: Black squirrel tail tied equal to one and one half the length of the body.

Ribbing: Oval silver tinsel.
Body: Red floss.
Hackle: Black tied on as a collar and tied back and down.
Wing: Dyed black squirrel tail tied low over the body and extending the length of the tail.
Head: Red.

Black Bucktail

Thread: Black.
Tail: Golden pheasant crest.
Body: Flat silver tinsel.
Hackle: Coachman brown tied on as a collar and tied back and down.
Wing: Dyed black bucktail tied over the body.
Topping: CH03 red Crystal Hair.
Cheeks: J.C. or substitute.
Head: Black.

Black Cosseboom

Thread: Red.
Tip: Flat silver tinsel.
Tag: Single strand of black floss kept short.
Ribbing: Flat silver tinsel.
Body: Black floss.
Wing: Gray squirrel tail tied low over the body.
Cheeks: J.C. or substitute.
Hackle: Black tied on as a collar and tied back.
Head: Red.

Black Domino

Thread: Red.
Tip: Oval silver tinsel.
Tail: White hen hackle barbs.
Ribbing: Oval gold tinsel.
Body: Black floss.
Wing: White calf tail tied over the body with a sparse overwing of clear (white) Miclon.
Cheeks: J.C. or substitute.
Hackle: Guinea fowl tied on as a collar and tied back.
Head: Red.

Originated by Paul LeBlanc of Montreal, Canada, in 1977. Also see Silver Domino.

Black Dose

Thread: Black.
Tip: Lower, oval silver tinsel and the upper, orange floss.
Tail: Golden pheasant crest.
Ribbing: Oval silver tinsel.
Body Hackle: Black tied palmer style over the body.
Body: Rear fourth, fluorescent blue floss and the front three-fourths, dubbed with #1 black lambs wool.
Wing: CH03 red, CH06 orange and CH11 green Crystal Hair mixed and tied over the body with an overwing of dyed black squirrel tail.
Head: Black.

The Black Dose is an old British pattern. This is a dressed down variation of the feather wing design.

Black Dose, Restigouche

Thread: Black.
Tip: lower, oval silver tinsel and the upper, burnt orange floss.
Tail: Golden pheasant crest.
Ribbing: Oval silver tinsel.
Body Hackle: Black tied palmer style from the second rib.
Body: Black floss.
Hackle: Black tied on as a collar and tied back and down.
Wing: Peacock sword feather barbs tied over the body with an overwing of sparse black bear hair.
Head: Black.

This is a variation of the Black Dose which was developed for the Restigouche and Tobique areas of New Brunswick.

Black Dragon

Thread: Black.
Tail: Black bucktail tied sparse and long.
Ribbing: Embossed silver tinsel.
Body: Fine black chenille.
Hackle: Black tied on as a collar and tied back.
Wing: Dyed black bucktail tied sparse and extending to the end of the tail.
Head: Black.

Black Fairy

Thread: Black.
Tip: Lower, oval gold tinsel and the upper, yellow floss.
Tail: Golden pheasant crest.
Butt: Black ostrich herl.
Ribbing: Oval gold tinsel.
Body: Dubbed with black seal fur or substitute.
Hackle: Black tied on as a collar and tied back and down.
Wing: Bronze mallard sections tied low over the body.
Head: Black.

A Scottish classic with many versions. The hair wing version of this pattern is tied with red pine squirrel tail.

Black Fitch Tail

Thread: Black.
Tip: Lower, flat silver tinsel and the upper, fluorescent orange floss.
Tail: Golden pheasant crest.
Ribbing: Flat silver tinsel.
Body: Black floss.
Hackle: Black tied on as a collar and tied back and down.
Wing: Black fitch tail tied low over the body. Dyed black squirrel tail is a suitable substitute.
Head: Black.

Black Ghost

Thread: Black.
Tip: Oval silver tinsel.
Tail: Golden pheasant tippet barbs.
Ribbing: Oval silver tinsel.
Body: Black floss.
Wing: White calf tail tied low over the body with a sparse overwing of clear (white) Miclon.
Hackle: Yellow hen hackle tied on as a collar and tied back.
Head: Black.

This pattern was adapted from the classic streamer pattern. See Chapter 18.

Black Goldfinch

Thread: Black.
Tip: Lower, oval silver tinsel and the upper, orange floss.
Tail: CH03 red and CH04 yellow Crystal Hair mixed.
Butt: Black ostrich herl.
Ribbing: Oval gold tinsel.
Body: Black floss.
Hackle: Dyed blue guinea fowl tied in at the throat.
Wing: Dyed orange gray squirrel tail tied low over the body.
Head: Black.

Black Heron

Thread: Black.
Tip: Oval gold tinsel.
Body: Peacock herl. The body is reverse wrapped with fine silver wire.
Wing: Dyed black squirrel tail tied low over the body.
Hackle: Grizzly tied on as a collar and tied back.
Head: Black.

Black J.C. Nymph

Thread: Black.
Tip: Lower, oval silver tinsel and the upper, yellow floss.
Tail: Golden pheasant crest.
Ribbing: Oval silver tinsel.
Body: Dubbed with black seal fur or substitute.
Hackle: Black tied on as a collar and tied back and down.
Wing: Natural brown bucktail tied low over the body.
Cheeks: J.C. or substitute.
Head: Black.

Black Maria

Tip: Oval silver tinsel.
Tail: Golden pheasant crest.
Ribbing: Oval silver tinsel.
Body: Rear half, yellow floss and the front half, black floss.
Hackle: Guinea fowl tied in at the throat.
Wing: Dyed black bucktail tied low over the body.
Head: Black.

Black Marie

Thread: Black.
Tip: Flat gold tinsel.
Tail: Golden pheasant crest.
Ribbing: Oval silver tinsel.
Body: Black floss.
Wing: Black bear hair tied low over the body.
Head: Black.

Black Maw Maw

Thread: Black.
Tip: Oval silver tinsel.
Tail: Orange hackle barbs.
Ribbing: Oval silver tinsel.
Body: Dubbed with #1 black lambs wool.
Wing: Black bear hair tied low over the body.
Cheeks: J.C. or substitute.
Hackle: Black tied on as a collar and tied back.
Head: Black.

Black Mike

Thread: Black.
Tip: Flat gold tinsel.
Tail: Golden pheasant crest.
Ribbing: Flat silver tinsel.
Body: Black yarn. Pick out after applying ribbing.
Wing: Gray squirrel tail tied over the body.
Hackle: Orange tied on as a collar and tied back.
Head: Black.

Originated by Michael Brislain of New Brunswick.

Black Monarch

Thread: Black.
Tip: Oval silver tinsel.
Tag: Single strand of black floss tied short.
Butt: White ostrich herl.
Ribbing: Oval silver tinsel.
Body: Dubbed with #1 black lambs wool.
Hackle: Badger tied on as a collar and tied back and down.
Wing: Two single strands of yellow floss with an overwing of gray squirrel tail tied low over the body.
Head: Black.

Black Paradise

Thread: Black.
Tip: Lower, oval gold tinsel and the upper, fluorescent orange floss.
Tail: Scarlet red hackle barbs.
Ribbing: Oval gold tinsel wrapped over entire butt and body.
Butt: Blue floss.
Body: Dubbed with black seal fur or substitute.
Hackle: Grizzly tied on as a collar and tied back and down with guinea fowl barbs tied in at the throat.
Wing: Dyed black squirrel tail tied low over the body.
Cheeks: Dyed kingfisher blue hen hackle tips tied in at each side.
Head: Black.

Originated by Charles DeFeo.

Black Rat (SH)

Thread: Black.
Tip: Oval silver tinsel.
Tail: Golden pheasant crest.
Ribbing: Oval silver tinsel.
Body: Dubbed with black seal fur or substitute.
Wing: Gray fox guard hair tied low over the body.
Hackle: Grizzly tied on as a collar and tied back.
Head: Black.

See Rat.

Plate 12   Black Reynard

Thread: Black.
Tip: Lower, oval silver tinsel and the upper, black floss.
Tail: Guinea fowl barbs.
Ribbing: Oval silver tinsel.
Body: Dubbed with #1 black lambs wool.
Wing: Fox squirrel tail tied low over the body.
Hackle: Black tied on as a collar and tied back.
Head: Black.

Originated by Keith Fulsher in 1982.

Plate 11   Black Silver Tip

Thread: Black.
Tip: Flat silver tinsel wrapped wide in a reduced form.
Tail: Golden pheasant crest.
Ribbing: Oval silver tinsel.
Body: Black floss.
Wing: Dark moose hair tied over the body.
Head: Black.

Originated by Rocky Schulstad of Corner Brook, Newfoundland, in 1951.

Black Spider

Thread: Black.
Tail: Dyed black squirrel tail.
Butt: Fluorescent orange yarn.
Ribbing: Oval silver tinsel.
Body: Dubbed with #1 black lambs wool.
Hackle: Black tied on as a collar and tied back and down. Hackle should reach bend of hook.
Wing: Dyed black squirrel tail tied low over the body.
Head: Black.

Black Squirrel

Thread: Black.
Tail: Golden pheasant tippet barbs.
Ribbing: Oval gold tinsel.
Body: Dubbed with black seal fur or substitute.
Hackle: Natural dark dun hen hackle barbs tied in at the throat.
Cheeks: J.C. or substitute.
Head: Black.

Black Standard

Thread: Black.
Tip: Lower, fine silver wire and the upper, orange floss.
Tail: Golden pheasant crest.
Butt: Fluorescent red yarn.
Ribbing: Flat silver tinsel.
Body: Dubbed with black seal fur or substitute.
Hackle: Badger tied on as a collar and tied back and down.
Wing: Black bear hair tied low over the body.
Cheeks: Small section of golden pheasant tippet tied in at each side.
Head: Black.

Black Star

Thread: Black.
Tip: Lower, oval silver tinsel and the upper, yellow floss.
Tail: Golden pheasant crest.
Ribbing: Oval silver tinsel.
Body: Dubbed with #1 black lambs wool.
Hackle: Black tied on as a collar and tied back and down.
Wing: Black moose hair tied low over the body.
Cheeks: J.C. or substitute.
Head: Black.

 Plate 12   # Blackville

Thread: Black.
Tip: Lower, silver wire and the upper, yellow floss.
Tail: Golden pheasant crest.
Butt: Peacock herl.
Ribbing: Oval silver tinsel.
Body: Embossed silver tinsel.
Hackle: Orange tied on as a collar and tied back and down with a small bunch of guinea fowl barbs tied in at the throat.
Wing: Gray squirrel tail tied over the body and extending to the tail.
Head: Black.

Originated by Bert Miner of Doaktown, New Brunswick, in the 1940s. The original pattern called for barred mallard sections for wings.

Black Wulff

Thread: Black.
Tip: Flat silver tinsel.
Tail: Golden pheasant crest.
Body: Black floss.
Hackle: White deer hair tied in at the throat.
Wing: Black moose hair tied low over the body.
Head: Black.

Plate 12   # Bloody Mary

Thread: Black.
Tip: Oval gold tinsel.
Tail: Amherst pheasant crest.
Ribbing: Oval gold tinsel.
Body: Dubbed with #1 black lambs wool.
Hackle: Scarlet red tied on as a collar and tied back and down.

Wing: Red calf tail tied low over the body.
Topping: Golden pheasant crest.
Cheeks: J.C. or substitute.
Head: Black.

Blue Beard

Thread: Black.
Tail: Pale yellow calf tail.
Ribbing: Oval silver tinsel wrapped over the front half of body.
Body: Rear half, flat silver tinsel and the front half, dubbed with black seal fur or substitute.
Hackle: Blue calf tail tied in at the throat.
Wing: Blue and gray mixed calf tail tied low over the body.
Topping: Pale yellow calf tail.
Head: Black.

Blue Boy

Thread: Black.
Tip: Lower, flat silver tinsel and the upper, white floss.
Tail: Amherst pheasant tippet barbs.
Butt: Black yarn.
Ribbing: Flat silver tinsel.
Body: Blue floss.
Hackle: Grizzly tied on as a collar and tied back and down.
Wing: Gray squirrel tail tied low over the body.
Head: Black.

Blue Charm (SH)

Thread: Black.
Tip: Lower, oval silver tinsel and the upper, yellow floss.
Tail: Golden pheasant crest.
Butt: Black ostrich herl.
Ribbing: Oval silver tinsel.
Body: Black floss.
Hackle: Dark blue tied on as a collar and tied back and down.
Wing: Gray squirrel tail tied low over the body.
Cheeks: J.C. or substitute.
Head: Black.

The Blue Charm can be seen in any number of versions. There have been discussions about the color of the hackle for as long as I can remember. My most trusted sources stick by the dark (deeper) blue as opposed to lighter shades. My experiences have always been with the darker blue and it has proven successful.

Blue Doctor
Thread: Red.
Tip: Lower, oval silver tinsel and the upper, yellow floss.
Tail: Golden pheasant crest.
Butt: Red yarn.
Ribbing: Oval silver tinsel.
Body Hackle: Light blue tied palmer style over the body.
Body: Light blue floss.
Hackle: Dyed blue guinea tied in at the throat.
Wing: CH03 red, CH04 yellow and CH13 blue Crystal Hair tied over the body with an overwing of gray squirrel tail.
Head: Red.

Another popular versions of this pattern calls for light blue hackle.

Blue Fox
Thread: Red.
Tip: Oval gold tinsel.
Tail: Golden pheasant crest.
Ribbing: Oval gold tinsel.
Body: Flat silver tinsel.
Hackle: Grizzly tied on as a collar and tied back and down.
Wing: Gray fox guard hair tied over the body.
Cheeks: J.C. or substitute.
Head: Red.

Originated by Gary Anderson in 1980.

Blue Goblin
Thread: Black.
Tip: Embossed silver tinsel.
Tail: Golden pheasant crest.
Ribbing: Oval silver tinsel wrapped over butt and body.
Butt: Fluorescent chartreuse yarn.

Body: Embossed silver tinsel.
Hackle: Grizzly tied on as a collar and tied back and down.
Wing: Dyed black squirrel tail tied low over the body.
Topping: Several strands CH16 dark blue Crystal Hair.
Head: Black.

Blue Lady
Thread: Black.
Tail: Yellow calf tail tied short.
Ribbing: Oval silver tinsel.
Body: Dubbed with #1 black lambs wool.
Hackle: Medium blue tied on as a collar and tied back and down.
Wing: Dyed blue gray squirrel tail tied low over the body.
Cheeks: J.C. or substitute.
Head: Black.

Plate 11 — Blue Opal
Thread: Black.
Tip: Flat silver tinsel.
Tail: Golden pheasant tippet barbs.
Butt: Dark blue ostrich herl.
Ribbing: Oval silver tinsel.
Body: Fluorescent blue floss with dark blue ostrich herl tied in at the front shoulder.
Hackle: Grizzly tied on as a collar and tied back and down.
Wing: Gray squirrel tail tied low over the body.
Topping: Peacock sword feather barbs.
Head: Black.

Blue Rat
Thread: Red.
Tip: Oval gold tinsel.
Tail: Peacock sword feather barbs.
Ribbing: Oval gold tinsel.
Body: Rear half, medium blue floss and the front half, peacock herl.
Trailer: Single strand of medium blue floss from top center and extending to the end of the body.
Wing: Gray fox guard hair tied low over the body.
Cheeks: Dyed kingfisher blue hen hackle tips tied in at each side.
Hackle: Grizzly tied on as a collar and tied back.
Head: Red.

Blue Reynard

Thread: Black.
Tip: Lower, oval silver tinsel and the upper, fluorescent blue floss.
Tail: Guinea fowl barbs.
Ribbing: Oval gold tinsel.
Body: Flat silver tinsel.
Wing: Fox squirrel tail tied low over the body.
Hackle: Bright blue tied on as a collar and tied back.
Head: Black.

Originated by Keith Fulsher in 1982.

Blue Sapphire

Thread: Black.
Tip: Lower, oval gold tinsel and the upper, yellow floss.
Tail: Golden pheasant crest with mixed blue and red hackle barbs tied on top.
Ribbing: Oval gold tinsel.
Body Hackle: Black and dark blue wrapped together palmer style over the body.
Body: Black floss.
Hackle: Dark blue hackle barbs tied in at the throat.
Wing: Sparse blue bucktail tied over the body with an overwing of red pine squirrel.
Head: Black.

Blue Vulture

Thread: Black.
Tip: Fine silver wire.
Ribbing: Oval silver tinsel.
Body: Dubbed with black seal fur or substitute.
Wing: Gray squirrel tail tied low over the body with an overwing of brown mink tail.
Hackle: Medium blue tied on as a collar and tied back.
Head: Black with a red center band.

Plate 11   Bondatti's Killer

Thread: Black.
Tip: Flat silver tinsel.
Tail: Golden pheasant crest.
Ribbing: Flat silver tinsel.
Body: Rear half, fluorescent green floss and the front half, fluorescent orange floss.

Hackle: Black tied on as a collar and tied back and down.
Wing: Gray squirrel tail tied low over the body.
Head: Black.

Originated by Keith Fulsher in 1969.

Plate 12   Brenda's Delight

Thread: Black.
Tip: Oval silver tinsel.
Tail: Golden pheasant crest.
Ribbing: Oval silver tinsel.
Body: Flat silver tinsel.
Wing: Sparse black calf tail tied over the body.
Hackle: Scarlet red tied on as a collar and kept sparse.
Head: Black.

Originated by Mike Boudreau of Montreal, Canada. The pattern was named after his sister-in-law after she landed the first fish on the Miramichi River in New Brunswick.

Mike is a professional fly tier and much of the material you will find in this chapter is a direct result of his efforts.

Bronson's Barrister

Thread: Black.
Tip: Oval silver tinsel.
Tail: Golden pheasant crest.
Ribbing: Oval silver tinsel.
Body: Dubbed with #1 black lambs wool.
Wing: Dyed black squirrel tail tied low over the body.
Topping: Golden pheasant crest.
Hackle: Black and white mixed and tied on as a collar and tied back.
Head: Black.

Brown Bomber

Thread: Black.
Tip: Lower, oval silver tinsel and the upper, yellow floss.
Tail: Golden pheasant crest.
Ribbing: Oval silver tinsel.
Body: Brown floss.
Hackle: Brown tied on as a collar and tied back and down.

Wing: Red pine squirrel tail tied low over the body.
Topping: Golden pheasant crest.
Cheeks: J.C. or substitute.
Head: Black.

The Bomber patterns were originated right after the turn of the century by Joe Aucoin of New Waterford, Nova Scotia.

Brown Fairy

Thread: Black.
Tip: Oval gold tinsel.
Tail: Fox squirrel tail.
Ribbing: Oval gold tinsel.
Body: Brown floss.
Hackle: Brown tied on as a collar and tied back and down.
Wing: Red pine squirrel tail tied low over the body.
Cheeks: J.C. or substitute.
Head: Black.

Brown Mystery

Thread: Black.
Tip: Oval gold tinsel.
Tail: Yellow hackle barbs.
Butt: Black ostrich herl.
Ribbing: Oval gold tinsel.
Body: Fluorescent orange floss.
Hackle: Guinea fowl tied in at the throat. Keep short and sparse—just a wisp.
Wing: Red pine squirrel tail tied low over the body.
Head: Black.

When tying the two patterns above try and select the hair from the fox squirrel tail that has a minimal amount of black barring.

Brown Rat

Thread: Red.
Tip: Flat silver tinsel.
Ribbing: Flat silver tinsel.
Body: Dubbed with brown seal fur or substitute.

Wing: Gray fox guard hair tied low over the body.
Hackle: Grizzly tied on as a collar and tied back.
Head: Red.
See Rat.

Brown Samson Special

Thread: Yellow.
Tip: Heavy yellow thread.
Ribbing: Heavy yellow thread.
Body: Flat silver tinsel.
Wing: Brown calf tail.
Head: Yellow.

Brush Pile

Thread: Black.
Tail: Peacock sword feather barbs.
Ribbing: Embossed gold tinsel.
Body: Dubbed with reddish-brown seal fur or substitute.
Hackle: Brown tied on as a collar and tied back and down.
Wing: White bucktail tied over the body with an overwing of black bucktail and topped with natural brown bucktail.
Head: Black.

Bucktail and Gold

Thread: Black.
Tip: Oval gold tinsel.
Tail: Golden pheasant crest.
Ribbing: Oval gold tinsel.
Body: Flat gold tinsel.
Hackle: Kingfisher blue hen hackle barbs tied in at the throat and tied long.
Wing: Natural brown bucktail tied low over the body.
Topping: Strands of CH13 blue Crystal Hair.
Head: Black.

Bucktail Doctor

Tip: Lower, flat silver tinsel and the upper, yellow floss.
Tail: Golden pheasant crest.
Butt: Red ostrich herl.
Ribbing: Oval silver tinsel.
Body: Dubbed with #1 black lambs wool.
Hackle: Guinea fowl barbs tied in at the throat.
Head: Black.

Wing: Natural brown bucktail tied low over the body.
Head: Black.

Buttercup

Thread: Black.
Tip: Lower, oval silver tinsel and the upper, fluorescent orange floss.
Tail: Golden pheasant crest with golden pheasant tippet barbs tied on top.
Butt: Black chenille.
Ribbing: Oval gold tinsel.
Body: Buttercup yellow floss.
Hackle: Bright yellow hackle barbs tied in at the throat.
Wing: Dyed green gray squirrel tail tied over the body.
Head: Black with a red band at base.

Originated by Robert W. Baker of Bathurt, New Brunswick.

Butterfly, Ingalls

Thread: Black.
Tail: Red hackle barbs.
Body: Peacock herl. Body is reverse wrapped with fine gold wire.
Wings: White calf tail tied in a divided downwing V (delta wing style) over the body. Wings should extend to the end of the hook.
Hackle: Brown wrapped with two turns under the wings and three in front as a collar.
Head: Black.

Originated in 1956 by Maurice Ingalls of Fort Lauderdale, Florida, for fishing on the Miramichi River in New Brunswick. This uncommon pattern has enjoyed success on most Canadian salmon rivers.

Cabin Fever

Thread: Black.
Tail: Light ginger hackle barbs.
Ribbing: Oval silver tinsel.
Body: Dubbed with a 50/50 blend of cream and red seal fur or substitute.
Hackle: Light ginger tied on as a collar and tied back and down.
Wing: Dyed black squirrel tail tied low over the body.
Head: Black.

Originated in 1969 by Keith Fulsher and Charles Krom.

Plate 11 ## Cains Copper

Tip: Copper wire.
Tail: Scarlet red hackle barbs.
Butt: Fine black chenille.
Ribbing: Copper wire.
Body: Flat copper tinsel.
Wing: Orange bucktail tied low over the body with an overwing of gray squirrel tail.
Hackle: Black tied on as a collar and tied back.
Head: Black.

Originated by Matthew Vinciguerra of Livingston, New York, in 1969.

Cains River Special

Thread: Black.
Tip: Oval silver tinsel.
Tag: Single strand of fluorescent green yarn.
Ribbing: Oval silver tinsel.
Body: Rear half, fluorescent chartreuse yarn and the front half, peacock herl.
Hackle: Black tied on as a collar and tied back and down with peacock sword feather barbs tied in at the throat.
Wing: Dyed black squirrel tail tied low over the body.
Head: Black.

This pattern is also known as the Rutledge.

Captain

Thread: Black.
Tip: Flat gold tinsel.
Tail: Golden pheasant tippet barbs.
Ribbing: Flat gold tinsel.
Body: Dubbed with #1 black lambs wool.
Hackle: Brown tied on as a collar and tied back and down.
Wing: White calf body hair tied low over the body.
Head: Black.

Carr's Special

Thread: Black.
Tip: Flat silver tinsel.
Tail: Golden pheasant crest.
Butt: Fine red chenille.
Ribbing: Oval silver tinsel.

Body: Rear half, green floss and the front half, yellow floss.
Hackle: Yellow tied on as a collar and tied back and down.
Wing: Yellow bucktail tied low over the body with an overwing of white bucktail. Keep both colors in equal proportions and sparse.
Cheeks: J.C. or substitute.
Head: Black.

Cerf Noir

Thread: Black.
Tip: Flat gold tinsel.
Tag: Red yarn.
Ribbing: Oval gold tinsel.
Body: Peacock herl.
Wing: Well marked coastal blacktail deer hair tied over the body.
Hackle: Grizzly tied on as a collar and tied back.
Head: Black.

Originated by Marc LeBlanc of Maria, Quebec, in 1979.

Chamon

Thread: Black.
Tip: Flat silver tinsel.
Tag: Fluorescent green floss.
Ribbing: Oval silver tinsel.
Body: Fluorescent green floss.
Hackle: Bright green tied on as a collar and tied back and down.
Wing: Sparse dyed black squirrel tail tied low over the body.
Head: Black.

Charbell

Thread: Black.
Body: Dubbed with #1 black lambs wool with a flat silver tinsel center band.
Wing: Dark moose hair tied long and flat over the body.
Head: Black.

Charlie O

Thread: Red.
Tip: Lower, oval silver tinsel and the upper, orange floss.

Tail: Golden pheasant crest.
Ribbing: Oval gold tinsel.
Body: Royal blue yarn.
Hackle: Teal blue tied on as a collar and tied back and down with guinea fowl barbs tied in at the throat.
Wing: Red bucktail tied low over the body with an overwing of natural brown bucktail.
Cheeks: J.C. or substitute.
Head: Red.

Charlie's Muddler

See Chapter 18.

Ches's Black Fly

Thread: Black.
Tip: Flat silver tinsel.
Tail: Golden pheasant crest.
Body: Black floss.
Hackle: Cream hackle barbs tied in at the throat.
Wing: Black moose body hair tied thick and flared over the body.
Head: Black.

Originated by Ches Traverse of Corner Brook, Newfoundland, in 1970.

Chipper Lodge

Thread: Black.
Tip: Flat gold tinsel.
Butt: Fluorescent orange floss.
Tail: Golden pheasant tippet barbs tied short.
Ribbing: Oval gold tinsel.
Body: Dubbed with black seal fur or substitute.
Hackle: Purple hen hackle tied on as a collar and tied back and down.
Wing: Woodchuck guard hair tied over the body.
Topping: Orange hackle barbs extending one-third the wing length.
Cheeks: J.C. or substitute.
Head: Black.

Originated by Dave Goulet of New Hartford, Connecticut.

Chorus Girl

Thread: Black.
Tip: Flat gold tinsel.
Tail: Brown mink tail.
Ribbing: Flat gold tinsel.

Body: Light pink floss.
Hackle: Brown mink tail tied in at the throat.
Head: Black.

Cinnamon Turkey

Thread: Black.
Tip: Lower, oval silver tinsel and the upper, yellow floss.
Tail: Golden pheasant crest.
Tag: Short strand red yarn.
Ribbing: Oval silver tinsel.
Butt: Rear half, yellow floss and the front half, red floss.
Body: Dubbed with black seal fur or substitute.
Hackle: Dark blue dun tied on as a collar and tied back and down.
Wing: Woodchuck hair tied low over the body.
Head: Black.

Claret and Grizzly

Thread: Black.
Tip: Oval silver tinsel.
Tail: Golden pheasant crest.
Ribbing: Oval silver tinsel.
Body: Dubbed with claret seal fur or substitute.
Body Hackle: Grizzly tied palmer style over the body. Hackle barbs should only extend just past the hook point.
Wing: Gray squirrel tail tied low over the body.
Cheeks: J.C. or substitute.
Head: Black.

Colburn, Blue

Thread: Black.
Tip: Oval silver tinsel.
Tail: Dyed blue gray squirrel tail.
Body: Medium blue floss with a black ostrich herl center joint.
Wing: Dyed blue gray squirrel tail tied low over the body.
Hackle: Black tied on as a collar and tied back.
Head: Black.

Colburn, Claret

Thread: Black.
Tip: Oval silver tinsel.
Tail: Dyed claret gray squirrel tail.

Body: Claret floss with a black ostrich herl center joint.
Wing: Dyed claret gray squirrel tail tied low over the body.
Hackle: Black tied on as a collar and tied back.
Head: Black.

Colburn, Orange

Thread: Black.
Tip: Oval silver tinsel.
Tag: Single strand of fluorescent orange yarn.
Body: Fluorescent orange floss with a black ostrich herl center joint.
Wing: Dyed orange gray squirrel tail tied low over the body.
Hackle: Orange tied on as a collar and tied back.
Head: Black.

Colburn Special

Thread: Black.
Tip: Oval silver tinsel.
Tail: Green hackle barbs with black hackle barbs tied on top.
Body: Fluorescent green floss with a black ostrich herl center joint.
Wing: Green bucktail tied low over the body with an overwing of black bucktail.
Hackle: Yellow tied on as a collar and tied back.
Head: Black.

Originated by Walter Colburn of Bangor, Maine. All of the bodies on the Colburn patterns should be well tapered into a cigar shape.

Cold Turkey

Thread: Black.
Tail: Light ginger hackle barbs.
Butt: Fluorescent chartreuse yarn.
Body: Embossed gold tinsel.
Hackle: Light ginger tied on as a collar and tied back and down.
Wing: Dyed black squirrel tail tied low over the body.
Topping: Metallic turkey or duck barbs.
Head: Black.

Conrad

Thread: Black.
Tip: Oval silver tinsel..

Tail: Black hackle barbs.
Ribbing: Oval silver tinsel **Butt:** Fluorescent chartreuse yarn.
Body: Dubbed with #1 black lambs wool.
Hackle: Black tied on as a collar and tied back and down.
Wing: Black moose hair tied low over the body.
Head: Black.

This pattern is often tied with other fluorescent colors for the butt.

Copper Killer

Thread: Red.
Tip: Copper wire.
Tail: Fox squirrel tail.
Butt: Red floss.
Ribbing: Copper wire.
Body: Flat copper tinsel.
Hackle: Fluorescent orange tied on as a collar and tied back and down.
Wing: Red pine squirrel tail tied low over the body.
Head: Red.

Copper Rat (SH)

Thread: Red.
Tip: Copper wire.
Tail: Peacock sword feather barbs.
Ribbing: Copper wire.
Body: Flat copper tinsel.
Wing: Gray fox guard hair tied low over the body.
Hackle: Grizzly tied on as a collar and tied back.
Head: Red.

See Rat.

Cosseboom Special

Thread: Red.
Tip: Embossed silver tinsel wrapped well down the bend of hook.
Tail: Strand of light olive floss.
Ribbing: Embossed silver tinsel.
Body: Light olive floss.
Wing: Gray squirrel tail tied over the body and extending to the end of tail.
Hackle: Yellow hen hackle tied on as a collar and tied slightly back.
Head: Red.

Also see Chapter 18.

Cotes Bleues

Thread: Red.
Tip: Red plastic tubing.
Tail: Golden pheasant crest.
Ribbing: Blue plastic tubing.
Body: Flat silver tinsel.
Wing: Gray fox guard hair tied over the body.
Hackle: Dark blue hen hackle tied on as a collar and tied back.
Cheeks: J.C. or substitute.
Head: Red.

Originated by Denys Poirier of Montreal, Canada, in 1985. The plastic tubing used is insulation from electrical wire.

Covey Special

Thread: Black.
Tip: Oval silver tinsel.
Tail: Golden pheasant crest.
Ribbing: Oval gold tinsel.
Body: Peacock herl.
Wing: Red pine squirrel tied over the body.
Hackle: Orange and yellow, one full turn each, tied on as a collar and tied back.
Head: Black.

Crosfield

Thread: Black.
Tip: Oval silver tinsel.
Tail: Golden pheasant crest.
Body: Embossed silver tinsel.
Hackle: Kingfisher blue tied on as a collar and tied back and down.
Wing: Gray squirrel tail tied low over the body.
Head: Black.

This is a variation of a British pattern that was originated by Ernest M. Crosfield.

Cullman's Choice

Thread: Black.
Ribbing: Oval silver tinsel.
Body: Insect green floss.
Hackle: White hen hackle barbs tied in at the throat.
Wing: Black moose hair tied low over the body.
Topping: Golden pheasant crest.
Head: Black.

C.Z. Special

Thread: Black.
Tip: Lower, flat silver tinsel and the upper, fluorescent green floss.
Tail: Black hackle barbs with fluorescent green hackle barbs tied on top.
Butt: Black ostrich herl.
Ribbing: Oval gold tinsel over floss portion of body only.
Body: Rear half, black floss and the front half, peacock herl.
Wing: Dyed green gray squirrel tail tied over the body with an overwing of peacock sword feather barbs.
Hackle: Fluorescent green tied on as a collar and tied back.
Head: Black.

Originated by Claude Westfall of Orono, Maine.

Darbee's Spate Fly (SH)

Thread: Red.
Tip: Oval gold tinsel.
Tail: Golden pheasant crest.
Ribbing: Oval gold tinsel.
Body: Dubbed with dark brown seal fur or substitute.
Hackle: Black tied on as a collar and tied back and down. Hackle should extend to hook point.
Wing: Natural brown bucktail tied low over the body and extending to the end of the tail.
Cheeks: Sections of black and white barred lemon woodduck tied in at each side.
Topping: Two golden pheasant crests.
Head: Red.

Originated in 1946 by Harry Darbee of Livingston Manor, New York. He devised this fly to meet the high water conditions that often exist during the fall run of salmon on the Margaree River on Cape Breton Island, Nova Scotia. It is now gaining popularity as a steelhead pattern on the West Coast.

Dark Mystery

Thread: Black.
Tip: Lower, oval gold tinsel and the upper, fluorescent orange floss.
Tail: Blue dun hackle barbs.
Butt: Black ostrich herl.
Ribbing: Oval gold tinsel.
Body: Brown floss.
Hackle: Guinea fowl tied in at the throat. The guinea is often kept sparse (only six barbs) and separated with three barbs pulled to each side.
Wing: CH03 red and CH06 orange Crystal Hair mixed and tied over the body with an overwing of red pine squirrel tail.
Head: Black.

Dartmouth

Thread: Black.
Tip: Oval silver tinsel.
Tail: Golden pheasant crest.
Ribbing: Oval silver tinsel. .
Body: Dark orange floss.
Wing: Yellow monga ringtail tied over the body.
Topping: Golden pheasant crest.
Hackle: Olive green tied on as a collar and tied back.
Head: Black.

Originated by John Vuco of Montreal, Canada.

Deer Lake Special

Thread: Black.
Tip: Flat silver tinsel.
Tail: Golden pheasant crest.
Butt: Black ostrich herl.
Ribbing: Flat silver tinsel.
Body: Rear half, yellow floss and the front half, dark green floss.
Hackle: Yellow tied on as a collar and tied back and down.
Wing: Black moose hair tied low over the body.
Head: Black.

DeFeo's Black Diamond
Thread: Black.
Tip: Lower, flat silver tinsel and the upper, fluorescent orange floss.
Tail: Golden pheasant crest.
Butt: Black yarn.
Ribbing: Oval silver tinsel.
Body: Flat silver tinsel.
Hackle: Brown tied on as a collar and tied back and down.
Wing: CH03 red Crystal Hair tied over the body with an overwing of dyed black squirrel tail.
Cheeks: J.C. or substitute.
Head: Black.

DeFeo's Evening Fly
Thread: Black.
Tip: Oval gold tinsel.
Tail: Brown hackle barbs.
Ribbing: Oval gold tinsel.
Body: Fluorescent white yarn.
Hackle: Brown tied on as a collar and tied back and down.
Wing: Sparse white calf tail tied low over the body with an overwing of sparse clear (white) Miclon.
Head: Black.

DeFeo's Royal
Thread: Red.
Tip: Oval silver tinsel.
Tag: Single strand red floss.
Ribbing: Oval silver tinsel.
Body: Rear one-fourth, red floss and the front three-fourths, medium green floss.
Wing: Dyed black squirrel tail tied over the body.
Hackle: Yellow tied on as a collar and tied back.
Head: Red.

The preceding patterns are just a few of the many which were originated by Charles DeFeo of New York City.

Dick's Demon
Thread: Black.
Tip: Oval silver tinsel.
Tail: Golden pheasant tippet.
Butt: Black yarn.
Ribbing: Oval silver tinsel.
Body: Embossed silver tinsel.

Hackle: Orange tied on as a collar and tied back and down.
Wing: Dyed black squirrel tail tied low over the body.
Head: Black.

Dixon Bear
Thread: Black.
Tip: Lower, oval silver tinsel and the upper, fluorescent green floss.
Tag: Single strand of fluorescent green floss.
Ribbing: Oval silver tinsel.
Body: Black floss.
Hackle: Insect green tied on as a collar and tied back.
Wing: Dyed black squirrel tail tied low over the body.
Head: Black.

Dr. Hale
Thread: Black.
Tip: Oval gold tinsel.
Tail: Golden pheasant crest.
Ribbing: Oval gold tinsel.
Body: Rear third, yellow floss and the front two-thirds, black floss.
Hackle: Blue dun tied on as a collar and tied back and down.
Wing: Red pine squirrel tail tied low over the body.
Topping: Golden pheasant crest.
Cheeks: J.C. or substitute.
Head: Black.

Donnie
Thread: Orange.
Tip: Flat silver tinsel wrapped well down the bend of the hook.
Tail: Dyed hot orange golden pheasant crest.
Ribbing: Oval silver tinsel over dubbed portion of body between ostrich herl joints.
Body: Rear third, embossed silver tinsel and the front two-thirds, dubbed with fluorescent orange seal fur or substitute. A black ostrich herl joint is tied in at the front and rear of the dubbed portion of the body.
Wing: Fox squirrel tail tied over the body with an overwing of blue calf tail which is topped with black monga ringtail. Each color of wing should be in equal portions.

Hackle: Black tied on as a collar and tied back.
Head: Orange.

Down East

Thread: Black.
Tip: Flat silver tinsel.
Tail: Golden pheasant crest.
Butt: Black ostrich herl.
Body: Dubbed with muskrat fur.
Wing: Reddish-brown mink tail tied low over the body.
Hackle: Orange tied on as a collar and tied back.
Head: Black.

Downeaster

Thread: Black.
Tip: Lower, oval silver tinsel and the upper, fluorescent red floss.
Tail: Golden pheasant crest.
Butt: Black ostrich herl.
Ribbing: Oval silver tinsel.
Body: Silver gray floss.
Hackle: Orange tied on as a collar and tied back and down.
Wing: Black moose hair tied low over the body.
Head: Black.

Dumond

Thread: Black.
Tip: Lower, oval silver tinsel and the upper, yellow floss.
Tail: Golden pheasant crest.
Butt: Black ostrich herl.
Ribbing: Oval silver tinsel.
Body: Flat silver tinsel.
Hackle: Black tied on as a collar and tied back and down.
Wing: Black moose hair tied low over the body.
Cheeks: J.C. or substitute.
Head: Black.

Dungarvon

Thread: Black.
Tip: Oval gold tinsel.
Tail: Four guinea fowl barbs tied long.
Butt: Black ostrich herl.
Ribbing: Flat gold tinsel.
Body: Red floss.
Hackle: Guinea fowl tied in at the throat.

Wing: Red pine squirrel tail tied low over the body.
Head: Black.

Plate 12 · Dunkeld

Thread: Black.
Tip: Flat gold tinsel.
Tail: Golden pheasant crest with scarlet red hackle barbs tied on top.
Butt: Black ostrich herl.
Ribbing: Oval gold tinsel.
Body: Flat gold tinsel.
Wing: Dyed orange gray squirrel tail tied over the body and extending to the end of tail.
Hackle: Orange tied on as a collar and tied back.
Head: Black.

This is a variation of a very old British pattern.

Durham Ranger

Thread: Black.
Tip: Oval silver tinsel.
Tail: Scarlet red hackle barbs.
Ribbing: Flat silver tinsel which is over wrapped with a narrower oval silver tinsel.
Body Hackle: Dyed yellow badger tied palmer style over the body.
Body: Rear two-thirds, dark orange floss and the front third, dubbed with #1 black lambs wool.
Hackle: Light blue tied on as a collar and tied back and down.
Wing: CH07 fire orange Crystal Hair and gray squirrel tail mixed and tied low over the body.
Topping: Golden pheasant crest.
Cheeks: J.C. or substitute.
Head: Black.

Dusty Black

Thread: Black.
Tip: Lower, flat silver tinsel and the upper, fluorescent red floss.
Tail: Dyed orange golden pheasant crest.
Butt: Black yarn.
Ribbing: Oval silver tinsel.
Body: Rear two-thirds, embossed silver tinsel and the front third, orange floss.
Hackle: Guinea fowl barbs tied in at the throat with orange hackle barbs tied on front.

Wing: Gray bucktail tied low over the body with an overwing of black bucktail.
Topping: Golden pheasant crest.
Cheeks: J.C. or substitute.
Head: Black.

Dusty Miller (SH)

Thread: Black.
Tip: Lower, oval silver tinsel and the upper, fluorescent orange floss.
Tail: Scarlet red hackle barbs.
Butt: Fine black chenille.
Ribbing: Oval silver tinsel.
Body Hackle: Golden olive tied palmer style over front third of body.
Body: Rear two-thirds, embossed silver tinsel and the front third, fluorescent orange floss.
Hackle: Guinea fowl tied on as a collar and tied back and down.
Wing: CH03 red, CH04 yellow and CH06 orange Crystal Hair mixed and tied over the body with an overwing of gray squirrel tail.
Head: Black.

Dutot Blue Charm

Thread: Black.
Tip: Flat silver tinsel.
Tail: Yellow hackle barbs.
Ribbing: Flat silver tinsel.
Body: Black chenille.
Wing: Dark red pine squirrel tail tied over the body.
Hackle: Teal blue tied on as a collar and tied back.
Head: Black.

This variation of the Blue Charm was originated by Bill Dutot of Port-aux-Basque, Newfoundland, in the 1960s.

 ### Echo Beach

Thread: Black.
Tip: Oval silver tinsel.
Tail: Golden pheasant crest.
Butt: Rear half, fluorescent orange floss and the front half, red yarn.
Ribbing: Oval silver tinsel.
Body: Embossed silver tinsel.
Hackle: Brown tied on as a collar and tied back and down.
Wing: White calf tail tied over the body with an overwing of black calf tail which is topped

with yellow calf tail. All the colors are in three equal portions.
Head: Black.

Emerald Tail

Thread: Black.
Tip: Oval gold tinsel.
Tail: Dyed insect green golden pheasant crest.
Butt: Black yarn.
Ribbing: Oval gold tinsel over front half of body.
Body: Rear half, flat gold tinsel and the front half, dubbed with #1 black lambs wool.
Hackle: Natural brown bucktail tied in at the throat.
Wing: Natural brown bucktail tied low over the body with an overwing of gray squirrel tail.
Topping: Dyed red golden pheasant crest with an additional natural golden pheasant crest tied on top.
Head: Black.

Englehardt Special

Thread: Black.
Tip: Oval gold tinsel.
Ribbing: Oval gold tinsel.
Body: Bronze peacock herl.
Hackle: Black tied on as a collar and tied back and down.
Wing: Black moose hair tied low over the body.
Cheeks: J.C. or substitute.
Head: Black.

Eo River

Tip: Oval gold tinsel.
Tail: Golden pheasant crest.
Butt: Red yarn.
Ribbing: Oval gold tinsel.
Body: Rear three-quarters, embossed gold tinsel and the front quarter, fine yellow chenille.
Hackle: Pink tied on as a collar and tied back and down with guinea fowl barbs tied in at the throat.
Wing: Pink, yellow and red bucktail mixed and tied over the body with an overwing of peacock sword feather barbs, then topped with natural brown bucktail.
Cheeks: J.C. or substitute.
Head: Black.

Esau

Thread: Black.
Tail: Light yellow calf tail.
Ribbing: Oval silver tinsel over the dubbed portion of the body.
Body: Rear half, flat silver tinsel and the front half, dubbed with claret seal fur or substitute.
Hackle: Claret hen hackle barbs tied in at the throat with natural black hen hackle barbs tied in front.
Wing: Dark brown calf tail tied low over the body with an overwing of light yellow calf tail.
Head: Black.

Fahie

Thread: Black.
Tip: Fine gold wire.
Tail: Golden pheasant crest.
Butt: Black ostrich herl.
Ribbing: Oval gold tinsel.
Body: Dark green floss.
Hackle: Yellow hen hackle barbs tied in at the throat.
Wing: Yellow hen hackle barbs tied over the body with an overwing of dyed black squirrel tail.
Cheeks: J.C. or substitute.
Head: Black.

Fiery Brown

Thread: Black.
Tip: Oval gold tinsel.
Tail: Golden pheasant crest.
Ribbing: Oval gold tinsel.
Body Hackle: Brown tied palmer style from the second rib.
Body: Dubbed with brown seal fur or substitute.
Wing: Bronze mallard sections tied low over the body.
Head: Black.

This is a variation of a classic Scottish dressing.

Plate 11 ## Foxfire

Thread: Black.
Tip: Lower, flat silver tinsel and the upper, fluorescent orange floss.
Tail: Black squirrel tail tied short with very sparse fluorescent orange hackle barbs tied on top.

Butt: Black ostrich herl.
Ribbing: Oval silver tinsel.
Body: Black floss (lacquer after ribbing).
Wing: Black squirrel tail tied over the body with an overwing of peacock sword feather barbs.
Hackle: Fluorescent orange tied on as a collar and tied back.
Head: Black.

Originated by Claude Westfall of Orono, Maine, in 1984.

Frazer Special

Thread: Red.
Tip: Oval silver tinsel.
Tag: Single strand of yellow yarn.
Ribbing: Oval silver tinsel.
Body: Divided in three parts: rear third, yellow yarn the center third, dark olive yarn and the front third, black yarn.
Wing: Green bucktail (25%) tied over the body with an overwing of fox squirrel tail (25%) which is topped with gray squirrel tail (50%).
Cheeks: J.C. or substitute.
Hackle: Black hen hackle tied on as a collar and tied back.
Head: Red.

Originated in the 1920s by Andrew Frazer.

Fulkro

Thread: Black.
Tip: Lower, oval silver tinsel and the upper, fluorescent orange floss.
Tail: Red calf tail.
Ribbing: Oval silver tinsel.
Body: Dubbed with #1 black lambs wool.
Hackle: Brown tied on as a collar and tied back and down.
Wing: Red pine squirrel tail tied low over the body.
Head: Black.

Originated in 1967 by Keith Fulsher and Charles Krom.

Gadabout Special

Thread: Black.
Tip: Fine silver wire.
Tail: Grizzly hackle barbs.
Butt: Fluorescent orange floss ribbed with fine silver wire.
Ribbing: Oval silver tinsel.
Body: Dark olive floss.
Wing: Gray squirrel tail tied low over the body.
Hackle: Olive tied on as a collar and tied back.
Head: Black.

Garrison

Thread: Black.
Tip: Flat silver tinsel.
Ribbing: Reverse wrapped with heavy black thread.
Body: Peacock herl.
Wing: Black moose hair tied heavy and flared over the body.
Head: Black.

Garry

See Munroe Killer.

George's Fly

Thread: Black.
Tip: Lower, flat silver tinsel and the upper, fluorescent green floss.
Tail: Black hen hackle barbs.
Ribbing: Oval silver tinsel.
Body: Black floss.
Hackle: Black hen hackle barbs tied in at the throat.
Wing: Two strands each of fluorescent green and blue floss. Over this is tied a sparse bunch of green monga ringtail with overwings of mixed green and black monga ringtail with overdyed green black monga ringtail tied on top.
Head: Black.

Originated by George Hayes.

Ghost

Thread: Black.
Tip: Lower, flat gold tinsel and the upper, fluorescent red floss.
Tail: Fluorescent hot pink hen hackle barbs.
Butt: Fluorescent hot pink ostrich herl.
Ribbing: Oval gold tinsel.

Body: Peacock herl.
Wing: Dyed black squirrel tail tied over the body.
Hackle: Fluorescent hot pink hen hackle tied on as a collar and tied back.
Head: Black.

Originated by Gayland Hachey of Veazie, Maine, in 1988.

Giggler

Thread: Black.
Tip: Lower, oval silver tinsel and the upper, fluorescent red floss.
Tail: Golden pheasant crest.
Butt: Black ostrich herl.
Ribbing: Oval gold tinsel reverse wrapped.
Body: Peacock herl.
Wing: Green monga ringtail.
Head: Black.

Gold Cosseboom

Thread: Black.
Tip: Oval gold tinsel.
Tail: Peacock sword feather barbs.
Butt: Fluorescent green floss.
Ribbing: Oval gold tinsel.
Body: Flat gold tinsel.
Wing: Dyed brown red pine squirrel tied over the body.
Hackle: Yellow tied on as a collar and tied back.
Head: Black.

Plate 12   Gold Fever

Thread: Black.
Tip: Lower, flat gold tinsel and the upper, yellow floss.
Tail: Black hackle barbs.
Butt: Black yarn.
Ribbing: Oval gold tinsel.
Body: Flat gold tinsel.
Hackle: Guinea fowl barbs tied in at the throat.
Wing: Dyed yellow gray squirrel tail tied low over the body with an overwing of gray squirrel tail.
Head: Black.

Originated in the mid 1970s by Charles Krom.

Gold Mongrel

Thread: Black.
Tip: Lower, oval gold tinsel and the upper, fluorescent orange floss.
Tail: Brown hackle barbs.
Butt: Peacock herl.
Ribbing: Oval gold tinsel.
Body: Flat gold tinsel.
Hackle: Brown tied on as a collar and tied back and down.
Wing: Dyed gold gray squirrel tail tied low over the body.
Topping: CH31 gold Crystal Hair.
Head: Black.

Gold Rat (SH)

Thread: Red.
Tip: Flat silver tinsel.
Tail: Amherst pheasant crest.
Ribbing: Oval silver tinsel.
Body: Flat gold tinsel.
Wing: Gray fox guard hair tied low over the body.
Hackle: Grizzly tied on as a collar and tied back.
Head: Red.

See Rat.

Gold Squirrel Tail

Thread: Black.
Ribbing: Oval gold tinsel.
Body: Flat gold tinsel.
Hackle: Natural blue dun hen hackle barbs tied in at the throat.
Wing: CH31 gold Crystal Hair tied over the body with an overwing of gray squirrel tail.
Head: Black.

Golden Girl

Thread: Black.
Tip: Lower, flat gold tinsel and the upper, fluorescent green floss.
Tail: Golden pheasant tippet barbs.
Ribbing: Oval gold tinsel.
Body: Black floss.
Hackle: Natural black hen hackle tied on as a collar and tied back and down.
Wing: Dyed black squirrel tail tied low over the body.
Cheeks: J.C. or substitute.
Head: Black.

Originated by Dave Goulet of New Hartford, Connecticut.

Golden Hope

Thread: Black.
Tip: Fine gold wire.
Tail: Golden pheasant crest.
Butt: Fine black chenille.
Ribbing: Oval gold tinsel.
Body: Fluorescent orange floss.
Wing: Red pine squirrel tail tied low over the body.
Hackle: Furnace tied on as a collar and tied back.
Head: Black.

Golden Sprite

Thread: Red.
Tip: Lower, flat gold tinsel and the upper, fluorescent red floss.
Tail: Golden pheasant crest.
Ribbing: Oval gold tinsel.
Body: Flat gold tinsel.
Hackle: Burnt orange hen hackle barbs tied in at the throat.
Wing: Fox squirrel tail tied low over the body. Use hair without black markings.
Topping: Golden pheasant crest.
Cheeks: J.C. or substitute.
Head: Red.

Originated in 1960 by Ron Bielli.

Gorgeous George

Thread: Black.
Tip: Fine silver wire.
Ribbing: Fine silver wire.
Body: Black floss.
Hackle: Orange tied on as a collar and tied back.
Head: Black.

Gorilla

Thread: Black.
Ribbing: Oval silver tinsel wrapped close.
Body: Black floss.
Hackle: Black tied on as a collar and tied back and down.
Wing: Woodchuck hair tied low over the body.
Head: Black.

Plate 11

Gouffre

Thread: Black.
Body: Silver Mylar piping slipped over the hook shank and secured at the rear with black thread.
Wing: White calf tail tied over the body with overwings of red and then white calf tail.
Cheeks: J.C. or substitute.
Head: Black ostrich herl.

Originated by Daniel Bradet.

Gray Beard

Thread: Black.
Tip: Flat silver tinsel.
Tail: Ginger hackle barbs and CH24 gold Crystal Hair mixed.
Ribbing: Oval silver tinsel.
Body: Dubbed with pale green seal fur or substitute.
Hackle: Light olive hen hackle barbs tied in at the throat.
Wing: Gray bucktail tail tied long over the body.
Topping: CH04 yellow Crystal Hair.
Head: Black.

Gray Buck

Thread: Black.
Tip: Oval silver tinsel.
Tail: Light blue dun hackle barbs.
Ribbing: Oval silver tinsel.
Body: Dubbed with light green seal fur or substitute.
Hackle: Light blue dun tied on as a collar and tied back and down.
Wing: Badger hair tied low over the body.
Head: Black.

Gray Rat

Thread: Black.
Tip: Oval silver tinsel.
Body: Dubbed with muskrat fur.
Wing: Gray fox guard hair tied low over the body.
Hackle: Grizzly tied on as a collar and tied back.
Head: Black.

See Rat.

Green Betty

Thread: Black.
Tip: Green floss.
Tail: Golden pheasant crest.
Butt: Dark olive ostrich herl.
Ribbing: Oval silver tinsel.
Body Hackle: Light olive tied palmer style over dubbed portion of the body.
Body: Rear half, dark olive floss and the front half, dubbed with dark olive seal fur or substitute.
Wing: Green bucktail mixed with CH11 green Crystal Hair tied over the body with an overwing of natural brown bucktail.
Head: Black.

Green Butt

This refers to almost any pattern which has a green butt.

Green Charm

Thread: Black.
Tip: Oval silver tinsel.
Tail: Yellow hackle barbs.
Ribbing: Oval silver tinsel.
Body: Green floss.
Hackle: Yellow hen hackle barbs tied in at the throat.
Wing: Dyed green gray squirrel tail tied low over the body.
Head: Black.

Green Conrad

Thread: Black.
Tail: Golden pheasant crest.
Butt: Bronze peacock herl.
Ribbing: Oval gold tinsel.
Body: Embossed gold tinsel.
Wing: Mixed green bucktail and CH11 green Crystal Hair and tied low over the body.
Hackle: Fluorescent green hen hackle tied on as a collar and tied back.
Head: Black.

Green Cross

Thread: Black.
Tip: Oval silver tinsel.
Ribbing: Oval silver tinsel.
Trailer: Single strand of fluorescent green floss from center top to end of body.
Body: Rear half, fluorescent green floss and the front half, peacock herl.

Hackle: Black tied on as a collar and tied back and down.
Wing: Black squirrel tail tied low over the body.
Head: Black.

Originated by Tom Corcoran.

Green Dose

Thread: Black.
Tip: Lower, oval silver tinsel and the upper, yellow floss.
Tail: Golden pheasant crest with red hackle barbs tied on top.
Butt: Black ostrich herl.
Ribbing: Oval silver tinsel.
Body: Green floss.
Hackle: Green hen hackle barbs tied in at the throat.
Wing: Dyed black squirrel tail tied low over the body.
Topping: Peacock sword feather barbs.
Cheeks: J.C. or substitute.
Head: Black.

This variation of the many Dose patterns was created by Bill Taylor.

Green Drake

Thread: Black.
Tip: Oval gold tinsel.
Tail: Natural yellow golden pheasant body feather barbs.
Ribbing: Heavy black thread.
Body: Yellow floss.
Hackle: Brown tied on as a collar and tied back and down.
Wings: Dyed light yellowish olive barred mallard flank sections tied over the body.
Head: Black.

Originated by D.A. and L.A. LaPointe of Matapedia, Quebec, in the 1930s. The original body material was yellow floss with a greenish cast.

Green Highlander

Thread: Black.
Tip: Oval silver tinsel.
Tail: Barred lemon woodduck barbs.
Butt: Black ostrich herl.
Ribbing: Oval silver tinsel.
Body Hackle: Bright green tied palmer style over the dubbed portion of the body.

Body: Rear fourth, golden yellow floss and the front three-fourths, dubbed with fluorescent chartreuse seal fur or substitute.
Hackle: Yellow tied on as a collar and tied back and down.
Wing: CH04 yellow and CH11 green Crystal Hair mixed and tied over the body with an overwing of dyed orange gray squirrel.
Head: Black.

This is a variation as tied and proven by Warren Collins of Pittsburgh, Pennsylvania. The original pattern is an old British pattern which enjoys most of its popularity in North America and has been tied using countless variations. Originally known as Highlander.

Green Hornet

Thread: Green.
Tip: Oval silver tinsel.
Butt: Fluorescent red floss.
Body: Dubbed with fluorescent chartreuse seal fur or substitute.
Wing: Yellow bucktail tied over the body with an overwing of green bucktail.
Head: Dyed green deer hair spun on and trimmed to form collar and head (Muddler style.)

Green "A" Hornet

Thread: Black.
Tail: CH03 red Crystal Hair.
Ribbing: Oval silver tinsel.
Butt: Fluorescent chartreuse yarn.
Body: Dubbed with #1 black lambs wool.
Wing: Golden pheasant tippet barbs and CH06 orange Crystal Hair mixed and tied over the body with an overwing of dyed black squirrel tail.
Hackle: Blue dun tied on as a collar and tied back.
Head: Black.

Green Peacock
Thread: Black.
Tip: Lower, oval silver tinsel and the upper, yellow floss.
Tail: Golden pheasant crest.
Ribbing: Oval silver tinsel.
Body: Light blue floss.
Hackle: Light blue tied on as a collar and tied back and down.
Wing: Peacock sword feather barbs tied over the body.
Cheeks: J.C. or substitute.
Head: Black.

Green Plume
Thread: Red.
Tip: Flat silver tinsel.
Tail: Golden pheasant tippet barbs.
Butt: Insect green ostrich herl.
Body: Fluorescent green floss with a joint of insect green ostrich herl tied at the front.
Hackle: Grizzly hen hackle barbs tied in at the throat.
Wing: Dyed green gray squirrel tail tied low over the body.
Head: Red.

Green Reynard
Thread: Black.
Tip: Lower, oval gold tinsel and the upper, fluorescent green floss.
Tail: Guinea fowl barbs.
Ribbing: Oval silver tinsel.
Body: Flat gold tinsel.
Wing: Fox squirrel tail tied low over the body.
Hackle: Bright green tied on as a collar and tied back.
Head: Black.

Originated by Keith Fulsher in 1982.

Green Widow
Thread: Black.
Ribbing: Oval silver tinsel.
Body: Flat silver tinsel.
Wing: Black moose hair tied low over the body.
Hackle: Green tied on as a collar and tied back.
Head: Black.

Green-Winged Squirrel
Thread: Black.
Tip: Gold wire.
Tail: Golden pheasant crest.
Butt: Fluorescent orange floss.
Body: Peacock herl. Reverse wrap the body with fine gold wire.
Hackle: Orange tied on as a collar and tied back and down.
Wing: Dyed green gray squirrel tail tied low over the body.
Topping: CH11 green Crystal Hair.
Head: Black.

Grenade
Thread: Yellow.
Tail: White calf tail.
Ribbing: Oval gold tinsel.
Body: Flat silver tinsel.
Wing: Dyed yellow gray squirrel tail tied over the body with overwings of red pine squirrel tail and black squirrel tail.
Topping: Peacock sword feather barbs.
Cheeks: J.C. or substitute.
Head: Yellow.

Originated by Claude Bernard.

Haggis
Thread: Black.
Tip: Flat silver tinsel.
Ribbing: Flat silver tinsel.
Body: Black floss.
Hackle: Dyed yellow hen hackle barbs tied in at the throat.
Wing: Black bear hair tied low over the body.
Head: Black.

Originated by Lee Wulff in 1962.

Plate 12 — Hairy Mary
Thread: Black.
Tip: Oval gold tinsel.
Tail: Golden pheasant crest.
Ribbing: Oval gold tinsel.
Body: Black floss.
Hackle: Kingfisher blue tied on as a collar and tied back and down.
Wing: Red pine squirrel tied low over the body.
Head: Black.

This Scottish pattern is also tied with a gray squirrel tail wing. It emerged as a hair wing pattern in the mid 1930s and still enjoys a large following on the Scottish West Coast and in the Hebrides. Others have written that it came into being in the 1960s, however, it was being used here on the West Coast for steelhead as early as 1940. See Chapter 20.

Half and Half

Thread: Black.
Tip: Oval silver tinsel.
Ribbing: Oval silver tinsel.
Body: Rear half, fluorescent chartreuse yarn and the front half, fine black chenille.
Wing: Black bear hair tied low over the body.
Hackle: Black tied on as a collar and tied back.
Head: Black.

Half Stone

Thread: Black.
Tip: Oval silver tinsel.
Tail: Golden pheasant crest.
Ribbing: Oval gold tinsel.
Body: Rear third, dubbed with yellow seal fur and the front two-thirds, dubbed with black seal fur or substitute.
Hackle: Black tied on as a collar and tied back and down.
Wing: Fox squirrel tail tied low over the body. Select hair from the base of the tail.
Head: Black.

Harding Special

Thread: Black.
Tip: Lower, oval silver tinsel and the upper, yellow floss.
Tail: Golden pheasant crest.
Butt: Black ostrich herl.
Ribbing: Oval silver tinsel.
Body: Flat silver tinsel.
Hackle: White tied on as a collar and tied back and down.
Wing: Red pine squirrel tail tied low over the body.
Cheeks: J.C. or substitute.
Head: Black.

Hilda Special

Thread: Black.
Tip: Oval silver tinsel.
Tail: Orange hackle barbs.
Butt: Red floss.
Body: Embossed silver tinsel.
Wing: Red pine squirrel tail tied low over the body.
Hackle: Orange tied on as a collar and tied back.
Head: Black.

Hoot Smith Special (SH)

Thread: Black.
Tip: Oval silver tinsel.
Ribbing: Oval silver tinsel.
Body: Fluorescent pink yarn.
Wing: Dyed black squirrel tail tied low over the body.
Head: Black.

Horton

Thread: Black.
Tip: Fluorescent blue floss.
Tail: Golden pheasant crest.
Ribbing: Flat silver tinsel.
Body: Black floss.
Hackle: Black tied on as a collar and tied back and down.
Wing: Fox squirrel tail tied low over the body.
Cheeks: J.C. or substitute.
Head: Black.

Hosmer Horror

Thread: Orange.
Tail: Orange hackle barbs.
Body: Peacock herl wrapped over an underbody of tapered olive yarn. The body should be reverse wrapped with fine gold wire.
Wing: White monga ringtail tied low over the body.
Hackle: Yellow and orange tied mix as a collar and tied back.
Head: Orange.

Hot Orange I (SH)

Thread: Black.
Tip: Lower, flat gold tinsel and the upper, yellow floss.
Tail: Golden pheasant crest.
Ribbing: Flat gold tinsel.

Body: Black floss.
Hackle: Hot orange tied on as a collar and tied back and down.
Wing: Black squirrel tail tied low over the body.
Head: Black.

Hot Orange II (SH)

Thread: Fluorescent red.
Tip: Oval silver tinsel.
Tag: Single strand of fluorescent orange yarn.
Body: Dubbed with fluorescent orange seal fur or substitute.
Hackle: Orange tied on as a collar and tied back and down.
Wing: Dyed orange gray squirrel tail tied low over the body.
Head: Fluorescent red.

Humber Orange

Thread: Black.
Tip: Oval silver tinsel.
Tail: Orange hackle barbs.
Ribbing: Oval silver tinsel.
Body: Flat silver tinsel.
Wing: Sparse dyed black squirrel tail tied over the body.
Hackle: Orange tied on (two turns) as a collar. Hackle should be undersized.
Head: Orange chenille.

Originated in 1983 by Rob Solo of Corner Brook, Newfoundland.

Icy Blue

Thread: Black.
Tip: Lower, flat silver tinsel and the upper, fluorescent blue floss.
Tail: Golden pheasant crest.
Ribbing: Oval silver tinsel.
Body: Flat silver tinsel.
Hackle: Medium blue tied on as a collar and tied back and down.
Wing: White bucktail tied low over the body with an overwing of dyed blue gray squirrel tail.
Head: Black.

Originated in the mid 1970s by Charles Krom.

Inconnue

Thread: Black.
Tip: Lower, oval gold tinsel and upper, yellow floss.
Ribbing: Oval gold tinsel.
Body: Bright green chenille.
Hackle: Kingfisher blue hen hackle barbs tied in at the throat.
Wing: Dyed green gray squirrel tail tied low over the body.
Topping: Golden pheasant crest.
Head: Black.

The Inconnue was created in 1981 by Gilles Aubert of Levis, Quebec.

Interceptor

Thread: Black.
Tip: Flat silver tinsel.
Ribbing: Oval silver tinsel.
Body: Black floss.
Hackle: Natural black hen hackle tied on as a collar and tied back and down.
Wing: Red pine squirrel tied over the body.
Head: Black.

Iris Lullaby

Thread: Black.
Tip: Lower, flat silver tinsel and the upper, fluorescent orange floss.
Tail: Golden pheasant crest.
Butt: Red yarn.
Ribbing: Copper wire.
Body: Rear half, fluorescent green floss and the front half, peacock herl.
Hackle: Guinea fowl barbs tied in at the throat.
Wing: Red pine squirrel tail tied low over the body.
Cheeks: J.C. or substitute.
Head: Black.

Irritator

Thread: Black.
Tip: Oval silver tinsel.
Tag: Single strand of black floss.
Ribbing: Oval silver tinsel.
Body: Black floss.
Wing: Red pine squirrel tail tied over the body with an overwing of black squirrel tail.
Hackle: White tied on as a collar and tied back.
Head: Black.

Irwin's Special

Thread: Black.
Tip: Oval gold tinsel.
Tail: Golden pheasant crest.
Ribbing: Oval gold tinsel.
Body: Dubbed with fluorescent chartreuse seal fur or substitute.
Hackle: Black tied on as a collar and tied back and down.
Wing: Black moose hair tied low over the body.
Head: Black.

Jeannie

Thread: Black.
Tip: Oval silver tinsel.
Tail: Golden pheasant crest.
Ribbing: Oval silver tinsel.
Body: Rear half, yellow floss and the front, dubbed with black seal fur or substitute.
Hackle: Black tied on as a collar and tied back and down.
Wing: Red pine squirrel tail tied low over the body.
Topping: CH05 golden yellow Crystal Hair.
Head: Black.

Jerram's Fancy

Thread: Black.
Tip: Flat silver tinsel.
Tag: Single strand dark blue yarn.
Ribbing: Oval silver tinsel.
Body: Rear half, red floss and the front half, black floss.
Hackle: Dark blue tied on as a collar and tied back and down.
Wing: Black bear hair tied low over the body.
Head: Black.

Jock Scott

Thread: Black.
Tip: Lower, fine silver wire and the upper, yellow floss.
Tail: Golden pheasant crest.
Tag: Single strand fluorescent fire orange yarn tied over the tail.
Butt: Black ostrich herl.
Ribbing: Rear half, oval silver tinsel and front half, flat silver tinsel.
Body Hackle: Black tied palmer style over front half of body.

Body: Rear half, yellow floss and the front half, black floss. A center joint of black ostrich herl is tied in between the two colors of floss.
Trailers: Single strands of fluorescent orange floss tied in at the center, top and bottom and extending to end of hook.
Hackle: Guinea fowl barbs tied in at the throat.
Wing: CH03 red, CH04 yellow and CH13 blue Crystal Hair mixed and tied over the body with an overwing of peacock sword feather barbs and sparse gray squirrel tail tied on top.
Topping: Golden pheasant crest.
Cheeks: J.C. or substitute.
Head: Black.

The original feather wing dressing for this British pattern dates back to the mid 1800s and John (Jock) Scott is given credit.

Joe Joe (SH)

Thread: Black.
Tip: Embossed silver tinsel.
Tail: Golden pheasant crest.
Ribbing: Embossed silver tinsel.
Body: Dubbed with reddish-brown seal fur or substitute.
Wing: Gray squirrel tail tied low over the body.
Hackle: Black tied on as a collar and tied back.
Head: Black.

Jordan Special

Thread: Black.
Tip: Fluorescent red yarn.
Butt: Black ostrich herl.
Ribbing: Flat gold tinsel.
Body: Rear half, light orange floss and the front half, black floss.
Hackle: Orange tied on as a collar and tied back and down.
Wing: Fox squirrel tail tied low over the body.
Head: Black.

Kate

Thread: Black.
Tip: Lower, oval silver tinsel and the upper, yellow floss.
Tail: Golden pheasant crest topped with medium blue hen hackle barbs which extend half the length of the tail.
Butt: Black ostrich herl.
Ribbing: Oval silver tinsel.
Body Hackle: Crimson red tied palmer style over the body.
Body: Dubbed with red seal fur or substitute.
Hackle: Yellow tied on as a collar and tied back and down.
Wing: CH03 red, CH05 golden yellow and CH06 orange Crystal Hair mixed and tied over the body with an overwing of gray squirrel tail with red pine squirrel tied on top.
Head: Black.

King Rat

Thread: Black.
Tip: Oval silver tinsel.
Tail: Single strand of yellow floss with peacock herl tied on top.
Ribbing: Flat silver tinsel overwrapped with a narrower oval gold tinsel.
Body: Rear half, flat silver tinsel and the front half, bronze peacock herl.
Trailers: Single strands of yellow floss tied in at the center, top and bottom and extending to the end of hook.
Wing: Gray fox guard hair tied low over the body.
Hackle: Grizzly tied on as a collar and tied back.
Head: Black.
    See Rat.

King of Waters

Thread: Black.
Ribbing: Oval silver tinsel.
Body: Red floss.
Body Hackle: Brown tied palmer style over the body.
Wing: Gray fox hair tied low over the body.
Head: Black.

Kinsey Special

Thread: Brown.
Tail: Golden pheasant tippet barbs.
Ribbing: Oval gold tinsel.
Body: Dubbed with red squirrel belly.
Hackle: Brown tied on as a collar and tied back and down.
Wing: Dark fine deer hair tied low and over the body.
Head: Brown.

Kitson

Thread: Black.
Tip: Flat gold tinsel.
Tail: Black hackle barbs.
Ribbing: Oval gold tinsel.
Body: Dubbed with yellow seal fur or substitute.
Hackle: Claret tied on as a collar and tied back and down.
Wing: Dyed yellow gray squirrel tail tied low over the body.
Cheeks: Kingfisher blue hen hackle tips tied in at each side.
Head: Black.

Lady Amherst

Thread: Black.
Tip: Lower, oval silver tinsel and the upper, yellow floss.
Tail: Golden pheasant crest.
Butt: Black ostrich herl.
Ribbing: Oval silver tinsel.
Body Hackle: Badger tied palmer style over the body.
Body: Flat silver tinsel.
Hackle: Grizzly tied on as a collar and tied back and down.
Wing: Gray squirrel tail tied low over the body.
Cheeks: Kingfisher blue hen hackle tips tied in at each side.
Head: Black.

Lady Atherton

Thread: Black.
Tip: Lower, oval silver tinsel and the upper, fluorescent orange floss.
Ribbing: Oval silver tinsel.
Body: Dubbed with #1 black lambs wool.
Hackle: Black tied on as a collar and tied back and down.

Wing: Black moose hair tied low over the body.
Topping: CH02 black Crystal Hair.
Cheeks: J.C. or substitute.
Head: Black.

Lady Clairol

Thread: Black.
Tip: Lower, embossed silver tinsel and the upper, fluorescent pink floss.
Tail: Section of red duck quill.
Ribbing: Embossed silver tinsel.
Body: Yellow floss.
Hackle: Red tied on as a collar and tied back and down.
Wing: Bleached light tan gray squirrel tail tied low over the body.
Topping: CH04 yellow Crystal Hair.
Cheeks: J.C. or substitute.
Head: Black.

Lady Ellen

Thread: Black.
Tip: Oval silver tinsel.
Body: Fine Mylar piping slipped over the hook shank and tied down at the rear with fluorescent red thread.
Hackle: Fluorescent blue tied on as a collar and tied back and down.
Wing: Dyed black squirrel tail tied low over the body.
Head: Black.

Lady Joan

Thread: Black.
Tip: Oval gold tinsel.
Ribbing: Oval gold tinsel.
Body: Orange floss.
Hackle: Yellow hen hackle barbs tied in at the throat.
Wing: Dyed black squirrel tail tied low over the body with an overwing of gray squirrel tail.
Head: Black.

Originated by Lee Wulff and named after his wife.

Lady Step

Thread: Black.
Tip: Lower, oval silver tinsel and the upper, dark orange floss.
Tail: Golden pheasant crest with green hackle barbs tied on top.

Butt: Black ostrich herl.
Ribbing: Oval gold tinsel.
Body: Rear third, black floss and the front two-thirds, dubbed with black seal fur or substitute.
Wing: Bunch of golden pheasant tippet barbs tied over the body with an overwing of red pine squirrel tail.
Cheeks: J.C. or substitute.
Hackle: Green tied on as a collar and tied back.
Head: Black.

Originated by Paul LeBlanc of Montreal, Canada, in 1984.

Lanctot

Thread: Black.
Tip: Lower, oval gold tinsel and the upper, yellow floss.
Tail: Golden pheasant crest.
Butt: Black ostrich herl.
Ribbing: Oval gold tinsel.
Body: Rear half, yellow floss and the front half, dubbed with black seal fur or substitute.
Hackle: Yellow tied on as a collar and tied back.
Wing: Red and blue mixed calf tail tied over the body with an overwing of yellow calf tail.
Head: Black.

This is a variation of a feather wing Canadian pattern originated in 1920 by Ivers S. Adams.

Laxa Blue

Thread: Black.
Tip: Lower, flat silver tinsel and upper, fluorescent orange floss.
Ribbing: Flat silver tinsel.
Body: Dubbed with #1 black lambs wool.
Hackle: Medium blue tied on as a collar and tied back and down.
Wing: Blue bucktail tied low over the body.
Head: Black.

Leeman's Fancy

Thread: Black.
Tip: Lower, oval silver tinsel and the upper, dubbed with orange lambs wool.
Tail: Golden pheasant crest.
Butt: Black ostrich herl.
Ribbing: Oval silver tinsel.
Body: Light green floss.

Hackle: Black tied on as a collar and tied back and down.
Wing: Dyed orange fox squirrel tail tied low over the body.
Head: Black.

Lefrancois Special

Thread: Black.
Tip: Oval gold tinsel.
Tail: Golden pheasant tippet barbs.
Ribbing: Oval gold tinsel.
Body: Dubbed with #1 black lambs wool.
Wing: White monga ringtail tied low over the body.
Hackle: Yellow tied on as a collar and tied back.
Head: Black.

Lemac

Thread: Black.
Tail: Woodchuck hair.
Ribbing: Oval silver tinsel.
Body: Dubbed with #1 black lambs wool.
Hackle: Grizzly tied on as a collar and tied back and down.
Wing: White calf tail tied low over the body with an overwing of woodchuck hair.
Head: Black.

Lemon Gray

Thread: Black.
Tip: Lower, flat silver tinsel and the upper, yellow floss.
Tail: Golden pheasant crest.
Butt: Black ostrich herl.
Ribbing: Oval silver tinsel.
Body: Dubbed with muskrat fur.
Hackle: Blue dun and yellow mixed and tied on as a collar and tied back and down.
Wing: Gray squirrel tail tied low over the body with an overwing of yellow monga ringtail tail.
Topping: CH05 golden yellow Crystal Hair.
Head: Black.

Levoy

Thread: Orange.
Tail: Scarlet red hackle barbs.
Body: Medium green chenille.
Wing: Red pine squirrel tail tied low over the body.
Hackle: Orange tied on as a collar and tied back.

Head: Orange.

Lightning Bug

Thread: Black.
Tip: Oval gold tinsel.
Tag: Single strand of fluorescent red yarn.
Ribbing: Oval gold tinsel wrapped over front two-thirds of body.
Body: Rear third, fluorescent chartreuse yarn and the front two-thirds, peacock herl.
Hackle: Black tied on as a collar and tied back and down.
Wing: Dyed black squirrel tail tied low over the body.
Head: Black.

Lister's Gold

Thread: Black.
Tip: Flat gold tinsel.
Tail: Yellow hackle barbs.
Ribbing: Oval gold tinsel.
Body: Rear two-thirds, flat gold tinsel and the front third, dubbed with claret seal fur or substitute.
Hackle: Orange tied on as a collar and tied back and down.
Wing: Gray fox hair tied low over the body.
Head: Black.

Little Red Wing

Thread: Black.
Tip: Lower, flat silver tinsel and the upper, fluorescent red floss.
Tail: Golden pheasant crest.
Butt: Black ostrich herl.
Ribbing: Oval silver tinsel.
Body: Flat silver tinsel.
Hackle: Black tied on as a collar and tied back and down.
Wing: CH03 red Crystal Hair and red monga ringtail mixed and tied low over the body with an overwing of dyed black squirrel tail.
Head: Black.

Originated by Charles Krom in 1973.

Logie

Thread: Black.
Tip: Flat silver tinsel.
Tail: Golden pheasant crest.
Ribbing: Oval silver tinsel.
Body: Rear third, pale yellow floss and the front two-thirds, red floss.
Hackle: Light blue tied on as a collar and tied back and down.
Wing: Yellow monga ringtail tied over the body with an overwing of red pine squirrel.
Head: Black.

The Logie is another of the patterns from Scotland which was originally tied for their Dee River.

Lord Baltimore

Thread: Black.
Tail: CH02 black Crystal Hair.
Ribbing: Black floss.
Body: Orange floss.
Wing: Dyed black squirrel tail tied low over the body.
Cheeks: Dyed salmon yellow hen hackle tips tied in at each side.
Hackle: Black hen hackle tied on as a collar and tied back.
Head: Black.

Major Griggs

Thread: Black.
Body: Peacock herl. Reverse wrap the body with fine gold wire.
Hackle: White tied on as a collar and tied back and down.
Wing: Black monga ringtail tied low over the body with an overwing of white monga ringtail.
Cheeks: J.C. or substitute.
Head: Black.

Mar Lodge

Thread: Black.
Tip: Oval silver tinsel.
Tail: Golden pheasant crest.
Butt: Black ostrich herl.
Ribbing: Oval silver tinsel.
Body: Flat silver tinsel jointed in the center with black yarn.
Hackle: Guinea fowl barbs tied in at the throat.

Wing: CH01 pearl and CH07 fire orange Crystal Hair tied over the body with an overwing of sparse gray squirrel tail and topped with red pine squirrel tail.
Cheeks: J.C. or substitute.
Head: Black.

Marauder

Thread: Black.
Tip: Lower, oval gold tinsel and the upper, fluorescent red floss.
Tail: Golden pheasant crest.
Ribbing: Oval gold tinsel.
Body: Embossed gold tinsel.
Wing: Gray fox hair tied low over the body.
Topping: CH04 yellow Crystal Hair.
Hackle: Scarlet red tied on as a collar and tied back.
Head: Black.

 March Brown (SH)

Thread: Black.
Tip: Oval gold tinsel.
Tail: Golden pheasant crest.
Ribbing: Oval gold tinsel.
Body: Dubbed with hare's mask fur.
Hackle: Brown Hungarian partridge tied in at the throat.
Wing: Fox squirrel tail tied low over the body. Select hair from the base of the tail.
Head: Black.

This pattern is also successfully tied using mottled brown turkey quill wings. There are any number of variations. As previously stated, this was one of the patterns A.H.E. Wood used in Scotland. George M. Kelson listed the pattern as: *"Tag: Gold twist, Tail: A topping, Body: Silver monkey's fur and a little dirty-orange seal's fur mixed together, Ribs: Gold tinsel (oval), Throat: Partridge hackle, Wings: Sections from hen pheasant tail (in large sizes turkey)"*

Plate II **Margot** (SH)

Thread: Black.
Tip: Oval gold tinsel.
Butt: Fluorescent orange floss.
Ribbing: Fine gold wire reverse wrapped.
Body: Peacock herl.

Wing: Dyed black squirrel tail tied over the body.
Cheeks: J.C. or substitute tied short.
Hackle: Natural black hen hackle tied on as a collar and tied back.
Head: Black.

Originated by Roger Pelletier in 1980.

Martin

Thread: Black.
Tail: Golden pheasant crest with CH02 black Crystal Hair tied on top.
Ribbing: Oval gold tinsel.
Body: Yellow floss.
Hackle: Yellow tied on as a collar and tied back and down.
Wing: Woodchuck hair tied low over the body.
Head: Black.

Mattie's Mistake

Thread: Black.
Tip: Oval gold tinsel.
Tail: Golden pheasant tippet barbs.
Butt: Fine fluorescent fire orange chenille.
Ribbing: Oval gold tinsel.
Body: Dubbed with fluorescent chartreuse seal fur or substitute.
Wing: Black squirrel tail.
Hackle: Orange tied on as a collar and tied back.
Thread: Black.

Plate 11
Maurice

Thread: Black.
Tip: Flat gold tinsel.
Tail: Amherst pheasant crest.
Ribbing: Oval gold tinsel.
Body: Rear third, red floss and the front two-thirds, black floss.
Hackle: Yellow tied on as a collar and tied back and down.
Wing: Gray fox hair tied low over the body.
Head: Black.

McAlpin

Thread: Black.
Tip: Flat gold tinsel.
Tail: Barred lemon woodduck barbs and CH03 red Crystal Hair mixed.
Ribbing: Oval gold tinsel.

Body: Dubbed with claret seal fur or substitute.
Hackle: Guinea fowl barbs tied in at the throat.
Wing: Dyed red gray squirrel tied low over the body.
Topping: Peacock sword feather barbs.
Head: Black.

McLeod's Shrimp (SH)

Thread: Black.
Tail: Golden pheasant crest.
Ribbing: Oval silver tinsel.
Body: Rear half, flat silver tinsel and the front half, black floss.
Center Joint Hackle: Orange tied on as a collar and tied back.
Hackle: Dyed black bucktail tied in at the throat.
Wing: Dyed black bucktail tied over the body.
Cheeks: J.C. or substitute.
Head: Black.
Note: The wing and hackle are of equal proportions and of the same length. In other words, you have a wing on top and one on the bottom.

Originated in 1960 by Robin McLeod. This fly was originally designed for the River Conon in Scotland. He designed the fly, taking the more favored aspects from a number of flies and putting them all together into one pattern. With its long, flowing wings flickering in the water and the Jungle Cock cheeks providing a certain amount of contrasting flash and an aiming point for the fish, Robin took twelve fish on the first day it was used. It works as well today and is a standard pattern on most Scottish salmon rivers.

For the past sixteen years he has been head gillie on the prestigious Dochfour beat of the River Ness in Scotland. He is a very accomplished fly fisher, equally familiar in habitat fishing for salmon, trout or sea-trout. Since arriving at Dochfour he has taken a total of 565 salmon from the Ness and he says, *"I am only the gillie."* Robin is on the river every day during the season, January through October, giving the fishing guests the benefit of his vast experience and encyclopedic knowledge of the river.

Robin has been fishing since the age of seven when he cut his teeth on the Allan Water at Dunblane. The fishing bug bit him hard and angling became a lifelong passion. He helped pay his way through school by tying flies, making up gut leaders, and repairing split-cane rods. After graduating with a degree in Economics, he spent the next few years working as a gillie. First at Skeabost on the Isle of Skye, then on Loch Baa on the Isle of Mull. Moving to the mainland, he worked on Loch Maree for three seasons in its heyday as the prime sea-trout loch in Scotland.

When offered a chance of promotion from gillie to managing a fishing hotel, he grabbed it. He became manager of the Cluanie Inn in Inverness-shire, a job which enabled him to combine his love of angling with building a career. Over the next twenty years he managed several hotels, including the Simmer Isles Hotel at Achiltibuie and the famous Tomdoun Hotel in Inverness-shire. The later, arguably the best fishing hotel in Scotland.

During this time he was fishing as intense as ever, on the Conon, Findhorn, Garry, Shiel, Moriston and Polly Rivers. As a very competent fly caster, he has instructed beginners and has given demonstrations on the tournament field. On one occasion he managed a one-hundred-and-sixty-six-foot-plus cast, on grass, at the Lochinver Highland Games. He has instructed fly fishing courses on the world famous River Tweed and wrote the chapter on loch fishing for the *Hardy Guide to Angling.*

During a fifty year salmon fishing career Robin has invented seven salmon flies, a lesson to many of us who might claim to invent. The big difference, of course, is that Robin has had more experience and more opportunities to fish for salmon than most of us would have in several lifetimes. His patterns have been tried, tested and proven over many, many seasons.

The move back from being general manager of a large hotel group to being a full-time gillie came when he was offered the position of head gillie at Dochfour, where he remains today.

Menard

Thread: Black.
Tail: Golden pheasant crest.
Ribbing: Oval gold tinsel.
Body: Dubbed with olive seal fur or substitute.
Wing: Dyed yellow natural brown bucktail tied low over the body.
Hackle: Black hen hackle tied on as a collar and tied back.
Head: Black.

Micmac Moose

Thread: Brown.
Tag: Single strand red yarn.
Body: Light orange floss.
Wing: Black skunk tail tied low over the body.
Head: Brown.

 ### Midnight

Thread: Black.
Tail: Natural yellow golden pheasant body feather barbs.
Body: Oval silver tinsel.
Wing: Black bear hair tied low over the body and extending to the end of the hook.

Hackle: Natural black hen hackle tied on as a collar and tied back.
Head: Black.

Originated by Marc Pontbriand in 1983.

Mill Pool Special

Thread: Black.
Tip: Lower, oval silver tinsel and the upper, fluorescent green floss.
Tail: Golden pheasant crest.
Butt: Fluorescent red floss.
Ribbing: Oval silver tinsel.
Body: Dubbed with #1 black lambs wool.
Wing: Red pine squirrel tail low over the body.
Hackle: Brown tied on as a collar and tied back.
Head: Black.

Mink Tail

Thread: Black.
Tip: Flat silver tinsel.
Tail: Dark brown mink tail hair.
Ribbing: Oval silver tinsel.
Body: Dubbed with black seal fur or substitute.
Hackle: Natural black hen hackle tied on as a collar and tied back and down.
Wing: Dark brown mink tail tied low over the body.
Head: Black.

There are any number of Mink Tail patterns. John Atherton and others are probably the most responsible for popularizing the use of mink in many of their patterns.

Minktail

Thread: Black.
Tip: Lower, flat silver tinsel and the upper, yellow floss.
Tail: Golden pheasant crest.
Ribbing: Flat silver tinsel.
Body: Dubbed with black seal fur or substitute.
Hackle: Dark blue dun tied on as a collar and tied back and down.
Wing: Light brown mink tail tied low over the body.
Head: Black.

Miramichi

Thread: Black.
Ribbing: Oval silver tinsel.
Body: Dubbed with black seal fur or substitute.
Wing: Red pine squirrel tail and CH25 copper brown Crystal Hair mixed and tied low over the body.
Head: Black.

Miramichi Cosseboom

Thread: Black.
Tip: Oval gold tinsel.
Tail: Green hackle barbs.
Ribbing: Oval gold tinsel.
Body: Green floss.
Wing: Gray squirrel tail tied over the body.
Hackle: Yellow tied on as a collar and tied back.
Head: Black.

Plate 12   Miramichi Special

Thread: Black.
Tip: Oval silver tinsel.
Butt: Black floss.
Body: Embossed silver tinsel.
Hackle: Orange tied on as a collar and tied back and down.
Wing: Black bear hair tied low over the body.
Head: Black.

Miramichi Wildcat

Thread: Black.
Tip: Fine gold wire.
Ribbing: Fine gold wire.
Body Hackle: Black tied palmer style over front half of body.
Body: Rear half, red floss and the front half, peacock herl.
Wing: Dyed black squirrel tail tied low over the body.
Cheeks: J.C. or substitute.
Head: Black.

There are at least a dozen variations of this pattern.

Montreal

Thread: Black.
Tip: Flat gold tinsel.
Tail: Golden pheasant crest.
Ribbing: Flat gold tinsel.

Body: Dubbed with claret seal fur or substitute.
Hackle: Claret tied on as a collar and tied back and down.
Wing: Red pine squirrel tail tied low over the body.
Head: Black.

Plate II Moore's Fancy

Thread: Black.
Tip: Oval silver tinsel.
Tail: Single strand of fluorescent red floss.
Butt: Dubbed with #1 black lambs wool.
Body: Embossed silver tinsel.
Wing: Dyed red gray squirrel tail tied low over the body.
Cheeks: J.C. or substitute.
Hackle: Grizzly hen hackle tied on as a collar and tied back.
Head: Black.

Moose

Thread: Black.
Tail: Golden pheasant crest.
Body: Flat silver tinsel.
Hackle: Yellow hen hackle tied in at the throat with kingfisher blue hen hackle barbs tied in at the front.
Wing: Bleached amber moose hair tied low over the body.
Head: Black.

Morning Sunrise (SH)

Thread: Orange.
Tip: Oval silver tinsel.
Tail: Golden pheasant crest.
Butt: Fluorescent orange yarn.
Ribbing: Oval silver tinsel.
Body: Dubbed with fluorescent hot pink seal fur or substitute.
Hackle: White and fluorescent hot pink mix and tied on as a collar and tied back and down.
Wing: Dyed orange gray squirrel tail tied low over the body with an overwing of dyed blue gray squirrel tail.
Cheeks: J.C. or substitute.

Head: Orange.

Moufette De Waterloo

Thread: Black
Tip: Flat silver tinsel.
Butt: Black ostrich herl.
Ribbing: Oval silver tinsel.
Body: Flat silver tinsel.
Wing: Black skunk hair tied over the body with overwings of white and then black skunk hair tied on top.
Cheeks: J.C. or substitute.
Head: Black.

Originated by Michel Duranleau of Waterloo, Quebec.

Munroe's Killer

Thread: Black.
Tip: Lower, oval silver tinsel and the upper, yellow floss.
Tail: Golden pheasant crest topped with three barbs of red goose or turkey quill tied on top.
Ribbing: Oval silver tinsel.
Body: Black floss.
Hackle: Dyed blue guinea fowl barbs tied in at the throat.
Wing: Orange bucktail tied over the body with overwings of yellow and then black bucktail tied on top.
Head: Black.

MV

Thread: Black.
Tip: Oval gold tinsel.
Butt: Yellow yarn
Body: Fine fluorescent red chenille with four turns of oval silver tinsel tied in at the front.
Wing: CH07 fire orange Crystal Hair tied over the body with an overwing of dyed black squirrel tail.
Head: Black.

Mystery I

Thread: Black.
Tip: Lower, oval silver tinsel and the upper, yellow floss.
Tail: Golden pheasant crest.
Ribbing: Oval gold tinsel.
Body: Flat silver tinsel.
Hackle: Brown tied on as a collar and tied back and down.

Wing: Natural brown bucktail tied low over the body.
Topping: Golden pheasant crest.
Cheeks: J.C. or substitute.
Head: Black.

Mystery II

Thread: Black.
Tip: Lower, flat silver tinsel and the upper, yellow floss.
Tail: Golden pheasant crest.
Butt: Fine black chenille.
Body: Flat silver tinsel.
Hackle: Brown tied on as a collar and tied back and down.
Wing: Fox squirrel tail tied low over the body.
Cheeks: J.C. or substitute.
Head: Black.

Nicholson

Thread: Black.
Tip: Flat gold tinsel.
Tail: Barred mallard and natural red golden pheasant breast barbs mixed.
Ribbing: Oval gold tinsel.
Body: Dubbed with red seal fur or substitute.
Body Hackle: Blue and crimson red tied palmer style over the body with extra turns of blue at the front.
Wing: Bronze mallard sections tied low over the body.
Head: Black with a black ostrich herl collar at the base.

Nick's Tan Seal Bug

Thread: Orange.
Tip: Lower, flat gold tinsel and the upper, fluorescent green yarn.
Butt: Fluorescent red yarn.
Body Hackle: Light ginger tied palmer style over the body.
Body: Dubbed with tan seal fur or substitute.
Head: Orange.

Originated by Gordon Nicholson.

Night Hawk

Thread: Black.
Tip: Flat silver tinsel.
Tail: Golden pheasant crest.
Butt: Red yarn.
Ribbing: Oval silver tinsel.

Body: Flat silver tinsel.
Hackle: Black tied on as a collar and tied back and down.
Wing: Dyed black squirrel tail.
Topping: Golden pheasant crest.
Cheeks: J.C. or substitute.
Head: Black with a red band at the base of the wing.

This variation was derived from a pattern originated by Stanford White in about 1900.

Plate II — Nipisiguit Gray

Thread: Black.
Tip: Lower, oval silver tinsel and the upper, yellow floss.
Tail: Golden pheasant crest.
Butt: Peacock herl.
Ribbing: Oval silver tinsel.
Body: Dubbed with muskrat belly fur.
Hackle: Grizzly tied on as a collar and tied back and down.
Wing: Black moose hair tied low over the body.
Head: Black.

Nipisiguit Green

Thread: Black.
Tip: Fine gold wire.
Tail: Fluorescent yellow hackle barbs.
Ribbing: Oval gold tinsel.
Butt: Fluorescent orange floss.
Body: Fine black chenille.
Hackle: Fluorescent orange tied on as a collar and tied back and down.
Wing: Dyed green gray squirrel tail tied low over the body.
Head: Black.

Nocturne

Thread: Black.
Tip: Flat silver tinsel.
Ribbing: Narrow strand of red yarn.
Body: Dubbed with #1 black lambs wool.
Hackle: Speckled guinea fowl barbs tied in at the throat.
Wing: Dyed black squirrel tail tied low over the body.
Head: Black.

Nova Scotia

Thread: Black.
Tip: Lower, oval silver tinsel and the upper, yellow floss.
Tail: Golden pheasant crest.
Butt: Black ostrich herl.
Ribbing: Oval silver tinsel.
Body: Rear third, embossed silver tinsel, center third, black floss, and the front third, embossed silver tinsel.
Hackle: Yellow tied on as a collar and tied back and down.
Wing: Black moose hair tied low over the body.
Cheeks: J.C. or substitute.
Head: Black.

Plate 11   Nuit Blanche

Thread: Black.
Tip: Lower, oval gold tinsel and upper, fluorescent orange floss.
Ribbing: Oval gold tinsel.
Body: Black chenille.
Hackle: Guinea fowl tied on as a collar and tied back and down.
Wing: White calf tail tied low over the body.
Cheeks: J.C. or substitute.
Head: Black.

Originated by Raymond Dussault in 1984.

Old Charlie

Thread: Red.
Tip: Flat gold tinsel.
Tail: Golden pheasant crest.
Ribbing: Oval gold tinsel.
Body: Claret floss.
Hackle: Hot orange tied on as a collar and tied back and down.
Wing: Dyed brown deer hair with black tips tied low over the body.
Cheeks: J.C. or substitute.
Head: Red.

Old Swampwater's Shrimp

Thread: Green.
Tip: Embossed silver tinsel.
Tail: Dyed green gray squirrel.
Ribbing: Embossed silver tinsel.
Body Hackle: Badger dyed olive and tied palmer style over the body.
Body: Dubbed with fluorescent hot pink seal fur or substitute.
Wing: Dyed green gray squirrel tail tied low over the body.
Head: Green.

Plate 12   Onset

Thread: Black.
Tip: Lower, flat silver tinsel and the upper, yellow floss.
Tail: Golden pheasant crest.
Ribbing: Flat silver tinsel.
Body: Rear half, yellow floss and the front half, orange floss.
Hackle: Blue dun tied on as a collar and tied back and down.
Wing: Gray squirrel tail tied low over the body.
Head: Black.

Orange Blossom (SH)

Thread: Black.
Tip: Lower, oval silver tinsel and the upper, yellow floss.
Tail: Golden pheasant crest.
Butt: Black ostrich herl.
Ribbing: Oval silver tinsel.
Body Hackle: Yellow tied palmer style over the front half of the body.
Body: Rear half, embossed silver tinsel and the front half, dubbed with yellow seal fur or substitute.
Wing: Natural brown and white bucktail mixed and tied low over the body.
Cheeks: J.C. or substitute.
Hackle: Orange tied on as a collar and tied back.
Head: Black.

Plate 11   Orange Bucktail (SH)

Thread: Black.
Tip: Lower, flat silver tinsel and the upper, fluorescent red floss.
Ribbing: Flat silver tinsel.
Body: Black floss.

Hackle: Natural black hen hackle barbs tied in at the throat.
Wing: Orange bucktail tied over the body and extending to the end of hook.
Cheeks: J.C. or substitute.
Head: Black.

Orange Charm (SH)

Thread: Black.
Tip: Lower, flat silver tinsel and the upper, yellow floss.
Tail: Golden pheasant crest.
Ribbing: Flat silver tinsel.
Body: Black floss.
Hackle: Orange tied on as a collar and tied back and down.
Wing: Red pine squirrel tail tied low over the body.
Head: Black.

Orange Cosseboom

Thread: Black.
Tip: Oval silver tinsel.
Tag: Single strand orange floss.
Ribbing: Flat silver tinsel.
Body: Orange floss.
Wing: Gray squirrel tail tied low over the body.
Cheeks: J.C. or substitute.
Hackle: Orange tied on as a collar and tied back.
Head: Black.

Orange Parson

Thread: Black.
Tip: Lower, oval silver tinsel and the upper, blue floss.
Tail: Golden pheasant crest.
Ribbing: Oval silver tinsel.
Body Hackle: Yellow tied palmer style over the body.
Body: Dubbed with fluorescent orange seal fur or substitute.
Hackle: Orange tied on as a collar and tied back and down.
Wing: Dyed orange gray squirrel tail tied low over the body.
Cheeks: Kingfisher blue hen hackle tips tied in at each side.
Head: Black.

Orange Puppy

Thread: Black.
Tip: Embossed silver tinsel.
Tail: Hot orange hackle barbs.
Body: Fine black chenille.
Hackle: Hot orange tied on as a collar and tied back and down.
Wing: Gray squirrel tail tied low over the body.
Head: One turn of fine orange chenille and the base of the wing and then finished off with black thread.

Orange Reynard

Thread: Black.
Tip: Lower, oval silver tinsel and the upper, fluorescent orange floss.
Tail: Guinea fowl barbs.
Ribbing: Oval gold tinsel.
Body: Flat silver tinsel.
Wing: Fox squirrel tail tied low over the body.
Hackle: Orange tied on as a collar and tied back.
Head: Black.

Originated by Keith Fulsher in 1982.

Orange Tip

Thread: Black.
Tip: Fine silver wire.
Tag: Single strand of fluorescent orange yarn.
Body: Fine black chenille.
Trailer: Single strand of fluorescent orange yarn tied in center top of body and extending to the end of the hook.
Wing: Dyed orange woodchuck hair tied low over the body.
Head: Black.

Oriole Hairwing

Thread: Black.
Tip: Oval gold tinsel.
Tail: Natural red golden pheasant breast barbs.

Ribbing: Oval gold tinsel.
Body: Dubbed with #1 black lambs wool.
Hackle: Brown tied on as a collar and tied back and down.
Wing: Dyed yellow gray squirrel tail tied low over the body.
Head: Black.

Oscar

Thread: Black.
Tip: Lower, oval gold tinsel and the upper, fluorescent orange floss.
Tail: Dyed orange golden pheasant crest.
Ribbing: Oval gold tinsel.
Body: Tan floss.
Hackle: Brown tied on as a collar and tied back and down.
Wing: Bleached gray squirrel tail tied low over the body.
Topping: Dyed orange golden pheasant crest.
Head: Black.

Originated by Keith Fulsher in 1978.

Pack Rat

Thread: Red.
Tip: Flat silver tinsel.
Butt: Fluorescent pink yarn.
Body: Dubbed with dark olive seal fur or substitute.
Hackle: Dyed olive grizzly tied on as a collar and tied back.
Wing: Gray fox guard hair tied low over the body.
Head: Red.

See Rat.

Park (SH)

Thread: Black.
Tip: Oval silver tinsel.
Ribbing: Oval silver tinsel.
Body: Black ostrich herl.
Hackle: Yellow tied on as a collar and tied back and down.
Wing: Black bear hair tied low over the body.
Cheeks: J.C. or substitute.
Head: Black.

Parmachene Belle (SH)

Thread: Red.
Tip: Lower, oval silver tinsel and the upper, fluorescent red floss.
Tail: White hackle barbs.
Butt: Peacock herl.
Ribbing: Oval silver tinsel.
Body: Yellow floss.
Hackle: Scarlet red and white mixed and tied on as a collar and tied back and down.
Wing: White bucktail tied over the body with an overwing of sparse red bucktail.
Head: Red.

Pass Lake

Thread: Black.
Tail: Brown hackle barbs.
Body: Black chenille.
Hackle: Brown tied on as a collar and tied back and down.
Wing: White calf tail tied over the body with an overwing of sparse clear (white) Miclon.
Head: Black.

Patate

Thread: Black.
Tip: Oval silver tinsel.
Ribbing: Oval silver tinsel.
Body: Light blue floss.
Wing: Sparse white calf tail tied over the body.
Hackle: Yellow tied on as a collar and tied back.
Head: Black.

Pat's Invincible (SH)

Thread: Black.
Tail: Gray squirrel tail. The tail is mounted one-fourth of the way up in the body giving the body the appearance of having a nice wide butt.
Body: Silver diamond braid.
Hackle: Brown tied on as a collar and tied back and down.
Wing: Gray squirrel tail tied low over the body.
Head: Black.

Plate 11   Patty Green

Thread: Black.
Tip: Oval silver tinsel.
Tail: Golden pheasant crest.
Ribbing: Oval silver tinsel wrapped closely.

Body: Chartreuse yarn.
Hackle: Brown tied on as a collar and tied back and down.
Wing: Dyed black squirrel tail tied low over the body.
Head: Black.

Peacock Cosseboom
Thread: Red.
Tip: Embossed silver tinsel.
Tail: Peacock sword feather barbs.
Ribbing: Oval silver tinsel.
Body: Rear half, embossed gold tinsel and the front half, peacock herl.
Wing: Gray squirrel tail tied low over the body.
Topping: Peacock sword feather barbs.
Hackle: Peacock sword feather barbs tied in at the throat.
Cheeks: J.C. or substitute.
Head: Red.

Parson
Thread: Black.
Tip: Flat silver tinsel.
Tail: Golden pheasant crest.
Ribbing: Oval gold tinsel.
Body Hackle: Black tied palmer style over the body.
Body: Dubbed with muskrat fur.
Wing: Woodchuck hair tied low over the body.
Head: Black.

Pelletier
Thread: Black.
Tip: Oval gold tinsel.
Tail: Golden pheasant crest.
Butt: Yellow ostrich herl.
Ribbing: Oval gold tinsel.
Body: Dubbed with #1 black lambs wool.
Wing: White calf tail tied over the body with a sparse overwing of clear (white) Miclon.
Cheeks: J.C. or substitute.
Hackle: Grizzly hen hackle tied on as a collar and tied slightly back.

Head: Black.

Originated by Raymond Pelletier of Matane, Quebec, Canada, in 1974.

Petite
Thread: Black.
Tip: Lower, oval silver tinsel and the upper, yellow floss.
Tail: Golden pheasant crest.
Ribbing: Oval silver tinsel.
Body: Thinly tapered black floss.
Hackle: Sparse teal blue hackle barbs tied in at the throat.
Wing: Yellow bucktail tied over the body with overwings of red and then yellow tied on top. The wing should be kept very, very sparse.
Head: Black.

Picasse
Thread: Black.
Body: Clear flat mono or lace wrapped over an underbody of black thread or floss.
Hackle: Gray pheasant rump tied on as a collar and tied back.
Shoulder: Small Amherst tippet feather tied in at each side.
Cheeks: J.C. or substitute.
Head: Black with a yellow band.

Originated by Marc LeBlanc.

Pompier
Thread: Red.
Tip: Oval gold tinsel.
Tail: Natural yellow golden pheasant rump barbs.
Ribbing: Oval gold tinsel.
Body: Black chenille.
Wing: Yellow calf tail tied low over the body.
Cheeks: J.C. or substitute.
Hackle: Bright green hen hackle tied long.
Head: Red.

Originated by Michel Beaudin of Montreal, Canada, in 1980.

Pot Scrubber (SH)
Thread: Black.
Tip: Oval silver tinsel.
Tail: Golden pheasant crest.
Ribbing: Oval silver tinsel.
Body: Wrapped with CH32 copper Crystal Hair.

Hackle: Brown tied on as a collar and tied back and down.
Wing: Gray squirrel tail tied low over the body.
Topping: CH32 copper Crystal Hair.
Head: Black.

Potato Fly

Thread: Black.
Ribbing: Flat silver tinsel.
Body: Light blue floss.
Wing: White monga ringtail tied low over the body.
Hackle: Yellow tied on as a collar and tied back.
Head: Black.

Preacher

Thread: Black.
Tip: Fluorescent orange floss.
Tail: Golden pheasant crest.
Butt: Fluorescent red floss.
Ribbing: Oval silver tinsel.
Body: Dubbed with #1 black lambs wool.
Wing: Dyed black squirrel tail tied low over the body.
Hackle: Black tied on as a collar and tied back.
Head: Black.

Presbyterian Killer

Thread: Black.
Tail: Scarlet red hackle barbs.
Ribbing: Oval gold tinsel.
Body: Dubbed with yellow seal fur or substitute.
Hackle: White tied on as a collar and tied back and down.
Wing: Gray squirrel tail tied low over the body.
Head: Black.

Priest

Thread: White.
Tip: Oval silver tinsel.
Tail: Light blue dun hackle barbs.
Ribbing: Oval silver tinsel.

Body: Dubbed with white rabbit.
Wing: White calf tail tied low over the body.
Hackle: Light blue dun tied on as a collar and tied back.
Head: White.

Prince Edward

Thread: Black.
Tip: Lower, oval silver tinsel and the upper, fluorescent red floss.
Tail: Golden pheasant crest.
Tag: Short strand of fluorescent orange floss tied on top of tail.
Butt: Peacock herl.
Ribbing: Oval silver tinsel.
Body: Flat silver tinsel.
Hackle: Badger tied on as a collar and tied back and down.
Wing: CH11 green and CH07 fire orange Crystal Hair mixed and tied over the body with an overwing of fox squirrel tail.
Topping: Peacock sword feather barbs.
Head: Black.

Professor

Thread: Black.
Tip: Oval gold tinsel.
Tail: Amherst pheasant crest.
Ribbing: Flat gold tinsel.
Body: Dubbed with yellow seal fur or substitute.
Hackle: Brown tied on as a collar and tied back and down.
Wing: Gray fox hair tied low over the body.
Head: Black.

Prouses

Thread: Red.
Tip: Embossed silver tinsel.
Tail: Dyed red golden pheasant crest.
Ribbing: Fine silver wire.
Body: Dubbed with black seal fur or substitute.
Wing: Red pine squirrel tail tied low over the body.
Hackle: Black tied on as a collar and tied back.
Head: Red.

Publicover

Plate 11

Thread: Black.
Tip: Fine silver wire wrapped closely.
Tail: Golden pheasant crest.
Ribbing: Oval silver tinsel.
Body: Dubbed with red seal fur or substitute.
Wing: Fox squirrel tail tied low over the body.
Hackle: White tied on as a collar and tied back.
Head: Black.

Pumpkin

Thread: Black.
Tip: Oval gold tinsel.
Tail: Golden pheasant crest.
Butt: Black ostrich herl.
Body: Dubbed with fluorescent chartreuse seal fur or substitute.
Wing: Tan calf tail tied low over the body.
Hackle: Orange tied on as a collar and tied back.
Head: Black.

Purple Passion

Thread: Black.
Tip: Lower, oval silver tinsel and the upper, purple floss.
Tail: Golden pheasant crest.
Butt: Black ostrich herl.
Ribbing: Oval silver tinsel.
Body: Rear half, variegated Mylar thread and the front half, dubbed with black seal fur or substitute.
Hackle: Purple tied on as a collar and tied back and down.
Wing: Dyed black squirrel tail tied low over the body.
Cheeks: J.C. or substitute.
Head: Black.

Originated by Buddy MacIntyre.

Queen of Waters

Thread: Black.
Ribbing: Oval gold tinsel.
Body Hackle: Brown tied palmer style over the body.
Body: Fluorescent orange floss.
Wing: Fox squirrel tail tied low over the body.
Head: Black.

Q.O.T.W.

Thread: Black.
Tail: Golden pheasant crest.
Ribbing: Gold embossed tinsel.
Body: Dubbed with orange seal fur or substitute.
Hackle: Coachman brown tied on as a collar and tied back and down.
Wing: Gray squirrel tail tied low over the body.
Head: Black.

Quick Silver

Plate 11

Thread: Black.
Tip: Oval silver tinsel.
Tail: Golden pheasant crest.
Butt: Yellow yarn.
Ribbing: Oval silver tinsel.
Body: Embossed silver tinsel.
Hackle: Medium blue tied on as a collar and tied back and down. Keep sparse.
Wing: Woodchuck hair tied low over the body.
Head: Black.

Rainbow

Thread: Black.
Tip: Oval silver tinsel.
Tail: Guinea fowl barbs.
Ribbing: Oval silver tinsel.
Body: Divided into four equal parts from rear: **1.** fluorescent green floss, **2.** fluorescent red floss, **3.** fluorescent blue floss and **4.** fluorescent orange floss.
Hackle: Guinea flow barbs tied in at the throat.
Wing: Gray squirrel tail tied low over the body.
Head: Black.

Randall

Thread: Black.
Tip: Oval silver tinsel.
Butt: Fluorescent orange floss.
Ribbing: Oval silver tinsel over front half of body only.
Body: Rear half, oval silver tinsel and the front half, black floss.
Wing: Dyed black squirrel tail tied low over the body.

Hackle: Fire orange tied on as a collar and tied back.
Head: Black.

Originated by Harry Kelly of Musquodoboit, Nova Scotia.

Plate 12   **Rat (SH)**

Thread: Red.
Tip: Flat silver tinsel.
Tail: Golden pheasant crest.
Ribbing: Oval silver tinsel.
Body: Peacock herl. Reverse wrap the body with fine gold wire.
Wing: Gray fox guard hair tied low over the body.
Hackle: Grizzly tied on as a collar and tied back.
Head: Red.

Originated in 1911 by Roy Angus Thompson (R.A.T.) This single fly, according to those still around and keeping score, helped trigger into being the use of hair wing patterns today. There are at least a dozen Rat patterns in existence today, although not created by the same individual.

See the other Rat patterns listed in this chapter. The wing material I have given is thought to be the original, however, we did go through a long period where silver monkey was available and it was preferred until the supply was exhausted. Many then switched to gray squirrel tail never knowing what the original material had been. My preference for a Rat pattern is the finely barred hair found at the base of the gray squirrel tail.

Ray's Red

Thread: Fluorescent red.
Tip: Fluorescent red yarn.
Tag: Single strand of fluorescent orange floss.
Ribbing: Embossed silver tinsel.
Body: Fluorescent orange floss.

Wing: Dyed fluorescent orange gray squirrel tail tied low over the body.
Head: Fluorescent red.

Red Abbey

Thread: Black.
Tip: Flat silver tinsel.
Tail: Red turkey quill section.
Ribbing: Flat silver tinsel.
Body: Dubbed with red seal fur.
Wing: Red pine squirrel tied low over the body.
Hackle: Brown tied on as a collar and tied back.
Head: Black.

Red Baron

Thread: Black.
Tip: Flat gold tinsel.
Ribbing: Oval gold tinsel.
Body: Dubbed with #1 black lambs wool.
Hackle: Black tied on as a collar and tied back and down.
Wing: Dyed red gray squirrel tail.
Cheeks: J.C. or substitute.
Head: Black.

Red Beard

Thread: Black.
Tail: Light yellow calf tail.
Ribbing: Oval gold tinsel tied over front half of body.
Body: Rear half, flat gold tinsel and the front half, dubbed with claret seal fur or substitute.
Hackle: Claret tied on as a collar and tied back and down with dyed blue guinea fowl tied in at the throat.
Wing: Dyed reddish-brown monga ringtail tied low over the body with a sparse overwing of light yellow calf tail.
Head: Black.

Red Butt Miramichi

Thread: Black.
Butt: Fluorescent red yarn.
Ribbing: Oval gold tinsel.
Body: Dubbed with #1 black lambs wool.
Hackle: Black tied on as a collar and tied back and down.
Wing: Light brown mink tail tied low over the body.
Head: Black.

Red Cosseboom

Thread: Red.
Tip: Embossed silver tinsel.
Tag: Single strand red yarn.
Ribbing: Embossed gold tinsel.
Body: Red floss.
Wing: Gray squirrel tail tied low over the body.
Cheeks: J.C. or substitute.
Hackle: Black tied on as a collar and tied back.
Head: Red.

Red Cow Fly

Thread: Red.
Tip: Flat silver tinsel.
Tail: Golden pheasant crest.
Ribbing: Flat silver tinsel.
Body: Dubbed with reddish-brown seal fur or substitute.
Hackle: Brown tied on as a collar and tied back and down.
Wing: Reddish-brown calf tail tied low over the body.
Head: Red.

Red Dog

Thread: Black.
Tip: Lower, oval silver tinsel and the upper, yellow floss.
Tail: Golden pheasant crest.
Ribbing: Oval silver tinsel.
Body Hackle: Yellow tied palmer style over the body.
Body: Flat silver tinsel.
Wing: Reddish-brown bucktail tied long and low over the body.
Hackle: Scarlet red tied on as a collar and tied back.
Head: Black.

Red Rat

Thread: Red.
Tip: Oval silver tinsel.
Tail: Two sections of black and white barred lemon woodduck tied back to back.
Ribbing: Flat gold tinsel.
Body: Dubbed with red seal fur or substitute.
Wing: Gray fox guard hair tied low over the body.
Hackle: Grizzly tied on as a collar and tied back.
Head: Red.
See Rat.

Red Sandy

Thread: Black.
Tip: Flat silver tinsel.
Tail: Golden pheasant crest.
Butt: Red yarn.
Body Hackle: Red tied palmer style over front half of body.
Body: Flat silver tinsel with a center joint of red yarn.
Trailer: Single strand of red yarn tied in at the center top and extending to the end of the body.
Wing: Golden pheasant tippet barbs tied over the body with an overwing of dyed red gray squirrel tail.
Topping: Golden pheasant crest.
Head: Black with a red band at the base of the wing.

Red Tail

Thread: Black.
Tip: Oval silver tinsel.
Tail: Three strands of yellow bucktail with a section of red turkey quill tied on top.
Ribbing: Oval silver tinsel.
Body: Dubbed with #1 black lambs wool.
Hackle: Black moose hair tied in at the throat.
Wing: Black bear hair tied low over the body.
Head: Black.

Redeemer

Thread: Black.
Tip: Lower, oval silver tinsel and the upper, yellow floss.
Tail: Yellow hackle barbs.
Butt: Fluorescent blue floss.
Body: Gold embossed tinsel.
Hackle: Guinea fowl barbs tied in at the throat.
Wing: Gray fox hair tied low over the body.
Head: Black.

Reliable

Thread: Black.
Tail: Natural red golden pheasant body feather barbs.
Ribbing: Oval silver tinsel. Make two turns under tail before wrapping forward.
Body: Rear third, yellow floss and the front two-thirds, black floss.
Hackle: Natural black hen hackle tied on as a collar and tied back and down.
Wings: Bronze mallard sections tied low over the body.
Head: Black.

Originated by Ira Gruber.

Rimouski

Thread: Black.
Tip: Oval gold tinsel.
Tail: Red hackle barbs.
Ribbing: Oval gold tinsel.
Body: Green floss.
Hackle: Yellow hen hackle tied on as a collar and tied back and down.
Wing: White calf tail tied low over the body.
Cheeks: J.C. or substitute.
Head: Black.

Originated by Claude Desrosiers of Rimouski, Quebec, in 1979.

Roger's Fancy

Thread: Black.
Tip: Oval silver tinsel.
Butt: Fluorescent yellow floss.
Tail: Peacock sword feather barbs.
Ribbing: Oval silver tinsel.
Body: Green floss.
Hackle: Yellow hen hackle barbs tied in at the throat with green hackle barbs tied in front.
Wing: Gray fox guard hair tied low over the body.
Cheeks: J.C. or substitute.
Head: Black.

Originated by Shirley E. Woods in 1973. Please note that the butt is not part of the tip and is predominant, yet the tail is tied in after.

Ross Special

Thread: Black.
Tip: Oval silver tinsel.

Tail: Golden pheasant crest.
Ribbing: Oval silver tinsel.
Body: Dubbed with red seal fur or substitute.
Hackle: Yellow tied on as a collar and tied back and down.
Wing: Red pine squirrel tail tied low over the body.
Cheeks: J.C. or substitute.
Head: Black.

Rough Going

Thread: Black.
Tip: Oval silver tinsel.
Ribbing: Oval silver tinsel.
Body: Tying thread.
Hackle: Hungarian partridge barbs tied in at the throat.
Wing: Gray squirrel tail tied low over the body.
Head: Black.

Rube Wood

Thread: Black.
Tip: Lower, oval silver tinsel and the upper, red floss.
Tail: Barred teal barbs.
Ribbing: Oval silver tinsel.
Body: Dubbed with white rabbit fur.
Wing: Gray squirrel tail tied low over the body.
Hackle: Brown tied on as a collar and tied back.
Head: Black.

Ruelland Special

Thread: Black.
Tip: Lower, oval silver tinsel and the upper, fluorescent green floss.
Butt: Peacock herl.
Ribbing: Fine black chenille.
Body: Fluorescent green floss.
Wing: Black bear hair tied low over the body.
Hackle: Two narrow grizzly hackle tips tied in a V at the throat with grizzly tied on as a collar and tied back.
Head: Black.

Ruhlin's Riot

Thread: Black.
Tip: Oval silver tinsel.
Ribbing: Flat silver tinsel.

Body: Fluorescent chartreuse yarn.
Wing: Gray squirrel tail tied low over the body.
Hackle: Black tied on as a collar and tied back.
Head: Black.

O. Russell
Thread: Black.
Tip: Fine silver wire.
Tail: Golden pheasant crest.
Butt: Peacock herl.
Ribbing: Oval silver tinsel.
Body: Embossed silver tinsel.
Hackle: Yellow tied on as a collar and tied back and down.
Wing: Yellow calf tail tied low over the body with an overwing of natural brown bucktail.
Head: Black.

Rust and Gold
Thread: Black.
Tip: Oval gold tinsel.
Tail: Golden pheasant crest.
Ribbing: Oval gold tinsel.
Body: Rust colored yarn.
Hackle: Yellow tied on as a collar and tied back and down.
Wing: Red pine squirrel tail tied low over the body.
Cheeks: J.C. or substitute.
Head: Black.

Originated by Keith Fulsher in 1963. Keith states he had lots of help from his friends.

Rusty Rat (SH)
Thread: Red.
Tip: Oval gold tinsel.
Tail: Peacock sword feather barbs.
Ribbing: Oval gold tinsel.
Body: Rear half, fluorescent orange floss and the front half, bronze peacock herl.
Trailer: Single strand of fluorescent orange floss tied in at center top and extending to the end of the hook.
Wing: Gray fox guard hair tied low over the body.
Hackle: Grizzly tied on as a collar and tied back.
Head: Red.

Well, no listing of Atlantic salmon flies is worth a hoot without telling how the Rusty Rat got its name. According to the late J.C. Arsenault, who was a supplier of flies and tackle to the elite salmon anglers of Quebec and New Brunswick, he tied the first Rusty Rat in 1949. He was asked by a client to duplicate exactly a fly that he had found to be successful. The fly in question, possibly just a simple Rat, was made with an underbody which had become stained by the hook rusting and had also begun to unravel. Arsenault trying to be faithful to his client's request duplicated both the rusty orange color and the loose strand of floss producing one of the most easily recognized Atlantic salmon flies in existence.

See Rat.

Rutledge
See Cains River Special.

Saint Mary's River
Thread: Black.
Tip: Oval silver tinsel.
Tail: Golden pheasant crest.
Ribbing: Oval silver tinsel.
Body: Flat silver tinsel.
Hackle: Brown tied on as a collar and tied back and down.
Wing: Fox squirrel tail tied low over the body.
Cheeks: J.C. or substitute.
Head: Black.

Sampson Special
Thread: Yellow.
Tip: Yellow floss.
Ribbing: Heavy yellow thread.
Body: Flat silver tinsel.
Wing: Brown moose body hair tied low over the body.
Head: Yellow.

Originated by Reuben Sampson of River of Ponds, Newfoundland.

Scarlet Monarch

Thread: Black.
Tip: Oval silver tinsel.
Tag: Single strand of red floss.
Butt: Yellow ostrich herl.
Ribbing: Oval silver tinsel.
Body: Red floss.
Hackle: Yellow tied on as a collar and tied back and down.
Wing: CH04 yellow Crystal Hair tied over the body with an overwing of gray squirrel tail.
Head: Black.

Secret

Thread: Black.
Tip: Lower, oval gold tinsel and the upper, red floss.
Tail: Scarlet red hackle barbs.
Butt: Black ostrich herl.
Body: Oval gold tinsel.
Hackle: Scarlet red tied on as a collar and tied back and down.
Wing: Red pine squirrel tied low over the body.
Head: Black.

Seductrice

Thread: Black.
Tip: Lower, oval gold tinsel and the upper, fluorescent green floss.
Tail: Peacock sword feather barbs tied equal to the length of the hook gap.
Butt: Black ostrich herl.
Ribbing: Oval gold tinsel.
Body: Strands of CH11 green Crystal Hair wrapped over the body.
Hackle: Dyed yellow guinea fowl tied on as a collar and tied back and down.
Wing: Dyed green bucktail tied over the body with an overwing of a slightly larger bunch of fluorescent yellow bucktail.
Topping: Strands of peacock herl.
Cheeks: J.C. or substitute.
Head: Black.

Originated in 1987 by Claude Bedard.

Shaggy Dog

Thread: Black.
Tail: Pale yellow calf tail.
Ribbing: Oval gold tinsel wrapped over dubbed portion of body.
Body: Rear half, flat gold tinsel and the front half, dubbed with brown seal fur or substitute.
Hackle: Brown tied on as a collar and tied back and down with CH01 pearl Crystal Hair tied in at the throat.
Wing: Brown calf tail tied low over the body.
Topping: CH04 yellow Crystal Hair.
Head: Black.

Sheepscot Special ⊕2

Thread: Black.
Tip: Oval gold tinsel.
Tag: Single strand orange floss.
Ribbing: Oval gold tinsel.
Body: Dubbed with orange seal fur or substitute.
Wing: Fox squirrel tail tied low over the body.
Hackle: Furnace tied on as a collar and tied back.
Head: Black.

Shrimp

Thread: Black.
Tip: Lower, oval gold tinsel and the upper, pale yellow floss.
Tail: Golden pheasant crest.
Ribbing: Flat gold tinsel.
Body: Fluorescent pink yarn.
First hackle: Yellow tied on as a collar and tied back and down.
Wing: Woodchuck hair tied low over the body with an overwing of natural brown and white mixed bucktail.
Second Hackle: Olive tied on as a collar and tied back.
Head: Black.

Skookum

Tip: Flat silver tinsel.
Tail: Dyed red golden pheasant crest.
Body: Dubbed with fluorescent red seal fur or substitute with a flat silver tinsel center joint.

Hackle: Bright green and scarlet red hackle mix and tied on as a collar and tied down and back.
Wing: Gray fox hair tied low over the body.
Head: Black.

Silver Betsy

Thread: Black.
Tip: Oval silver tinsel.
Tail: Scarlet red hackle barbs.
Ribbing: Oval silver tinsel.
Body: Flat silver tinsel.
Wing: Gray squirrel tail tied low over the body.
Hackle: Grizzly tied on as a collar and tied back.
Head: Black.

Also known as Silver Abbey.

Silver Blue

Thread: Black.
Tip: Flat silver tinsel.
Tail: Yellow hackle barbs.
Ribbing: Oval silver tinsel.
Body: Flat silver tinsel.
Hackle: Medium blue tied on as a collar and tied back and down.
Wing: Gray squirrel tail tied low over the body.
Head: Black.

Silver Cosseboom

Thread: Red.
Ribbing: Oval silver tinsel.
Body: Flat silver tinsel.
Wing: Gray squirrel tail tied low over the body.
Hackle: Yellow tied on as a collar and tied back.
Head: Red.

Silver Doctor

Thread: Red.
Tip: Lower, oval silver tinsel and the upper, yellow floss.
Tail: Golden pheasant crest with kingfisher blue hen hackle barbs tied over the top.
Butt: Red yarn.
Ribbing: Oval silver tinsel.
Body: Flat silver tinsel.
Hackle: Light blue tied on as a collar and tied back and down with barred teal tied in at the throat.

Wing: Fox squirrel tail tied low over the body with CH03 red and CH14 dark blue Crystal Hair tied in at each side.
Head: Red.

Silver Domino

Thread: Red.
Tip: Oval silver tinsel.
Tail: White hen hackle barbs.
Ribbing: Oval silver tinsel.
Body: Flat silver tinsel.
Wing: White calf tail tied over the body with a sparse overwing of clear (white) Miclon.
Cheeks: J.C. or substitute.
Hackle: Guinea fowl tied on as a collar and tied back.
Head: Red.

Originated in 1977 by Paul LeBlanc of Montreal, Canada.

Silver Downeaster

Thread: Black.
Tip: Oval silver tinsel.
Tail: Golden pheasant crest.
Butt: Black ostrich herl.
Ribbing: Oval silver tinsel.
Body: Flat silver tinsel.
Hackle: Orange tied on as a collar and tied back and down.
Wing: Dyed black squirrel tail tied low over the body.
Head: Black.

Silver Gray

Thread: Black.
Tip: Lower, oval silver tinsel and the upper, yellow floss.
Tail: Golden pheasant crest.
Butt: Black ostrich herl.
Ribbing: Oval silver tinsel.
Body: Flat silver tinsel.
Wing: CH01 pearl and CH11 green Crystal Hair tied over the body with an overwing of gray squirrel tail.
Cheeks: J.C. or substitute.
Hackle: Badger tied on as a collar and tied back.
Head: Black.

Silver Gray Bomber

Thread: Black.
Tip: Lower, oval silver tinsel and the upper, yellow floss.
Tail: Golden pheasant crest.
Butt: Fine black chenille.
Ribbing: Oval silver tinsel.
Body: Flat silver tinsel.
Hackle: Guinea fowl barbs tied in at the throat.
Wing: Natural brown and white mixed bucktail tied low over the body.
Head: Black.

Silver Prince

Thread: Black.
Tip: Oval silver tinsel.
Tail: Peacock sword feather barbs.
Ribbing: Oval silver tinsel.
Body: Flat silver tinsel.
Hackle: Black tied on as a collar and tied back and down.
Wing: Red pine squirrel tied low over the body.
Head: Black.

Silver Ranger

Thread: Black.
Tip: Lower, oval silver tinsel and the upper, yellow floss.
Tail: Golden pheasant crest.
Butt: Red yarn.
Ribbing: Oval silver tinsel.
Body: Flat silver tinsel.
Hackle: Scarlet red tied on as a collar and tied back and down.
Wing: Dyed orange gray squirrel tail tied over the body.
Head: Black.

Silver Rat

Thread: Red.
Tip: Oval gold tinsel.
Ribbing: Oval gold tinsel.
Body: Flat silver tinsel.
Wing: Gray fox guard hair tied low over the body.
Hackle: Grizzly tied on as a collar and tied back.
Head: Red.
  See Rat.

Silver Satan

Thread: Red.
Tip: Lower, flat silver tinsel and the upper, fluorescent orange floss.
Tail: Golden pheasant crest.
Butt: Bronze peacock herl.
Ribbing: Oval silver tinsel.
Body: Rear two-thirds, flat silver tinsel and front third, black floss.
Wing: Bunch of golden pheasant tippet barbs tied over the body with an overwing of gray squirrel tail.
Cheeks: J.C. or substitute.
Head: Red.

Silver Squirrel Tail

Thread: Black.
Ribbing: Oval silver tinsel.
Body: Flat silver tinsel.
Hackle: Natural blue dun hen hackle barbs tied in at the throat.
Wing: Gray squirrel tail tied low over the body.
Head: Black.

Silver Standard

Thread: Black.
Tip: Lower, fine silver wire and the upper, orange floss.
Tail: Golden pheasant crest.
Butt: Fluorescent red yarn.
Ribbing: Flat silver tinsel.
Body: Dubbed with black seal fur or substitute.
Hackle: Badger tied on as a collar and tied back and down.
Wing: Gray fox hair tied low over the body.
Cheeks: Golden pheasant tippet sections tied in at each side.
Head: Black.

Silver Tip I

Thread: Black.
Tip: Oval gold tinsel.
Tag: Single strand of red yarn.
Body: Oval gold tinsel.
Wing: Gray squirrel tail tied low over the body.
Hackle: Yellow tied on as a collar and tied back.
Head: Black with a red center band and the base of the wing.

The original pattern called for silver tip grizzly hair for the wing.

Silver Tip II
Thread: Black.
Tip: Flat silver tinsel.
Ribbing: Flat silver tinsel.
Body: Black floss.
Wing: Black moose hair.
Head: Black.

The silver tinsel ribbing on this pattern should be wrapped so there are equal portions of both black and silver showing. Originated by Keith Fulsher in 1960.

Silver Vulture
Thread: Black.
Tip: Fine gold wire.
Ribbing: Oval gold tinsel.
Body: Flat silver tinsel.
Wing: Gray squirrel tail tied low over the body with an overwing of brown mink hair. Keep sparse.
Cheeks: J.C. or substitute.
Hackle: Medium blue hen hackle tied on as a collar and tied back.
Head: Black with a red center band.

Silver Wilkinson
Thread: Black.
Tip: Lower, oval silver tinsel and the upper, yellow floss.
Tail: Kingfisher blue hackle barbs.
Butt: Red yarn.
Ribbing: Oval silver tinsel.
Body: Flat silver tinsel.
Hackle: Magenta tied on as a collar and tied back and down with barred teal barbs tied in at the throat.
Wing: CH03 red, CH04 yellow, CH07 fire orange and CH14 dark blue Crystal Hair mixed and tied over the body with an overwing of sparse gray squirrel tail topped with red pine squirrel tail.
Head: Black.

Sir Richard
Thread: Black.
Tip: Lower, flat silver tinsel and the upper, dark orange floss.
Tail: Burnt orange hackle barbs.

Butt: Black ostrich herl.
Body Hackle: Black tied palmer style over the body.
Body: Dubbed with #1 black lambs wool.
Hackle: Guinea fowl tied in at the throat.
Wing: Gray fox hair tied low over the body with an overwing of sparse red pine squirrel tail and CH03 red, CH07 fire orange, CH14 dark blue Crystal Hair mixed and tied in at each side.
Head: Black.

Skunk
See Chapter 20.

Smitty's Secret
Thread: Black.
Tip: Flat silver tinsel.
Ribbing: Oval silver tinsel.
Body: Black floss.
Hackle: Fluorescent orange tied on as a collar and tied back and down.
Wing: White monga ringtail tied low over the body.
Head: Black with a band of orange chenille at the base.

Originated by Wendell Smith of Pasadena, Newfoundland.

Sneaky
Thread: Red.
Tail: Orange bucktail and CH06 orange Crystal Hair.
Ribbing: Oval gold tinsel.
Body: Dubbed with fluorescent orange seal fur or substitute.
Hackle: Natural black hen hackle barbs tied in at the throat and extending to the hook point.
Wing: Sparse orange bucktail tied over the body with an underwing of a few strands of CH06 orange Crystal Hair.
Topping: Peacock herl.
Head: Red.

This pattern was jointly developed by Mike and Bob Boudreau in 1992. They have used it in most of the Canadian provinces with success. In fact Mike states *"The fly has proven to be a great success (actually a bit too successful, you can be off the river early with this one if you are not careful)."*

Because of the lower waters conditions they have suffered in Canada over the past few season the larger patterns have been unsuccessful. This fly is tied on fine wire (low water) hooks in sizes 8-12.

Squirrel Tail

Thread: Black.
Tip: Oval silver tinsel.
Tail: Scarlet red hackle barbs.
Ribbing: Oval silver tinsel.
Body: Dubbed with #1 black lambs wool.
Hackle: Brown tied on as a collar and tied back and down.
Wing: Red pine squirrel tail tied low over the body.
Head: Black.

There is no standard pattern for this fly. There is an endless list of variations which often appear as variations of other patterns.

Squirrel Tail, Red

Thread: Black.
Tip: Lower, oval gold tinsel and the upper, fluorescent red floss.
Tail: Scarlet red hackle barbs.
Ribbing: Oval gold tinsel.
Body: Black floss.
Hackle: Black tied on as a collar and tied back and down.
Wing: Red pine squirrel tail tied low over the body.
Head: Black.

This fly is also known as the Red Butt Squirrel Tail and was originated in New Brunswick. It was first tied with a yellow butt and then later W. W. Doak and Sons started selling it with a red, orange or green butt. Jerry Doak says, *"On the Miramichi they like to put a fluorescent butt on everything."*

Stacy's Fancy

Thread: Black.
Tip: Oval gold tinsel.
Tail: Golden pheasant crest.
Butt: Pink ostrich herl.
Ribbing: Oval gold tinsel.
Body: Dubbed with orange seal fur or substitute.
Wing: Golden pheasant tippet barbs tied over the body with raccoon hair tied in at each side.
Hackle: Orange tied on as a collar and tied back.
Head: Black.

Star Fly

Thread: Black.
Tip: Oval silver tinsel.
Tail: Grizzly hackle barbs.
Butt: Fluorescent green floss.
Ribbing: Oval silver tinsel.
Body: Embossed silver tinsel.
Wing: Dyed black squirrel tail.
Hackle: Grizzly tied on as a collar and tied back.
Head: Black.

Stewiacke Special

Thread: Red.
Tail: Yellow hackle barbs.
Ribbing: Oval gold tinsel.
Body: Black floss.
Hackle: Scarlet red hen hackle barbs tied in at the throat.
Wing: Dyed black squirrel tail tied low over the body.
Head: Red.

Stoat Tail

Thread: Black.
Tip: Oval silver tinsel.
Tail: Golden pheasant crest.
Ribbing: Oval silver tinsel.
Body: Black floss.
Hackle: Black tied on as a collar and tied back and down.
Wing: Black moose hair tied low over the body.
Head: Black.

As the name suggests, the original dressing for this pattern called for stout tail for the wing.

Summer Deer

Thread: Black.
Ribbing: Oval gold tinsel.
Body: Fluorescent orange yarn.
Wing: Fine textured deer hair tied low over the body.
Head: Black.

Summer Quill

Thread: Black.
Tip: Flat copper tinsel.
Tail: Bronze mallard barbs tied long.
Ribbing: Single strand white moose mane.
Body: Black floss.
Hackle: Bronze mallard barbs tied in at the throat.
Wing: Red pine squirrel tied low over the body and extending only half way.
Head: Black.

Apply a coat of FLI-BOND cement to the body of the finished fly to increase the durability of the ribbing.

Sunday Special

Thread: Black.
Body: Black floss.
Wing: Red pine squirrel tied low over the body.
Head: Black.

 ## Sunny Day

Thread: Black.
Tip: Oval gold tinsel.
Ribbing: Oval gold tinsel.
Body: Dubbed with orange seal fur or substitute.
Hackle: Yellow tied on as a collar and tied back and down.
Wing: Gray squirrel tail tied low over the body.
Head: Black.

Sweep

Thread: Black.
Tip: Flat gold tinsel.

Tail: Golden pheasant crest.
Ribbing: Flat gold tinsel.
Body: Dubbed with #1 black lambs wool.
Hackle: Black hen hackle barbs tied in at the throat and extending to the point of hook.
Wing: Dyed black squirrel tail tied low over the body.
Cheeks: Kingfisher blue hen hackle tips tied in at each side.
Head: Black.

Tangi

Thread: Red.
Tip: Embossed gold tinsel.
Tail: Peacock sword feather barbs.
Ribbing: Embossed gold tinsel.
Body: Dubbed with red seal fur or substitute.
Wing: Dyed orange gray squirrel tail tied low over the body.
Hackle: Grizzly tied on as a collar and tied back.
Head: Red.

Plate 12 Tarnished Silver

Thread: Black.
Tip: Flat silver tinsel.
Tail: Golden pheasant crest.
Ribbing: Oval gold tinsel.
Body: Rear half, wrapped with flat copper tinsel and the front half, oval silver tinsel.
Hackle: Black tied on as a collar and tied back and down.
Wing: Red pine squirrel tied low over the body.
Head: Black.

Originated in the mid 1970s by Charles Krom.

Taylor Special

Thread: Black.
Tip: Oval silver tinsel.
Tail: Peacock sword feather barbs.
Ribbing: Oval silver tinsel over front half of body only.
Trailer: Single strand of fluorescent green floss tied in at center top and extending to end of body.
Body: Rear half, fluorescent green floss and the front half, peacock herl.
Wing: Dyed fluorescent green gray squirrel tail tied low over the body.

Hackle: Salmon yellow tied on as a collar and tied back.
Head: Black.

Originated by Arthur Taylor of Lee, Maine, in 1986.

Teagle Bee

Thread: Black.
Tip: Flat gold tinsel.
Tail: Red section of turkey quill.
Body: Yellow and black chenille wrapped together.
Wing: Natural brown bucktail tied low over the body.
Hackle: Brown tied on as a collar and tied back.
Head: Black.

Teddy Baseball

Thread: Red.
Tail: Golden pheasant crest.
Butt: Yellow yarn.
Ribbing: Oval silver tinsel.
Body: Dubbed with #1 black lambs wool.
Hackle: Black tied on as a collar and tied back and down.
Wing: CH03 red and CH05 golden yellow Crystal Hair mixed and tied over the body with an overwing of woodchuck hair.
Cheeks: J.C. or substitute.
Head: Red.

Texas Jack

Thread: Black.
Tip: Lower, oval silver tinsel and the upper, fluorescent red floss.
Tail: Golden pheasant crest.
Ribbing: Oval silver tinsel.
Body: Dubbed with gray seal fur or substitute.
Hackle: Guinea fowl tied on as a collar and tied back. Wrap one full turn only.
Wing: Black bear hair tied low over the body.
Head: Black.

Texas Jim Stonefly

Thread: Black.
Body Hackle: Black tied palmer style over the front third of the body. Hackle barbs should extend no further than the point of the hook.

Body: Rear two-thirds, dubbed with cream seal fur and the front third, dubbed with black seal fur or substitute.
Wing: Natural brown bucktail tied low over the body.
Head: Black.

The St. Laurent

Thread: Black.
Ribbing: Oval silver tinsel.
Body: Flat silver tinsel.
Wing: Bright green calf tail tied low over the body with overwings of red and then bright green. All wing portions should be equal.
Cheeks: J.C. or substitute.
Head: Black.

Originated by Roch St. Laurent of Thetford Mines, Quebec.

Thunder and Lightning

Thread: Black.
Tip: Lower, oval silver tinsel and the upper, yellow floss.
Tail: Fluorescent fire orange hackle barbs.
Butt: Black ostrich herl.
Ribbing: Oval gold tinsel.
Body Hackle: Burnt orange tied palmer style over the body.
Body: Dubbed with #1 black lambs wool.
Hackle: Dyed blue guinea fowl tied in at the throat.
Wing: Red pine squirrel tied low over the body.
Head: Black.

Thunder Stoat

Thread: Black.
Tip: Oval silver tinsel.
Tail: Golden pheasant crest.
Butt: Black ostrich herl.
Ribbing: Oval silver tinsel.
Body: Black floss.
Hackle: Medium blue tied on as a collar and tied back and down.
Wing: Dyed black squirrel tail tied low over the body.
Cheeks: J.C. or substitute.
Head: Black.

Plate 12   ### Tide Water

Thread: Black.
Tip: Flat silver tinsel.
Tail: Golden pheasant crest.
Ribbing: Flat silver tinsel.
Body: Brown floss.
Hackle: Bronze mallard barbs tied in at the throat.
Wing: Natural brown bucktail tied low over the body.
Head: Black.

Plate 12   ### Tobique

Thread: Black.
Tip: Oval silver tinsel.
Tail: Golden pheasant tippet barbs.
Ribbing: Oval silver tinsel.
Body: Rear third, chartreuse yarn and the front two-thirds, black yarn.
Hackle: Yellow tied on as a collar and tied back and down.
Wing: Red pine squirrel tied over the body.
Head: Black.

Tom's Favorite

Thread: Black.
Tip: Oval silver tinsel.
Tail: Golden pheasant tippet barbs.
Ribbing: Oval silver tinsel.
Body: Dubbed with brown seal fur or substitute.
Wing: Dyed black squirrel tail tied low over the body.
Head: Black.

Originated by Keith Fulsher in 1963. Keith gives much credit to suggestions from his guide.

Torpille

Thread: Black.
Tip: Oval silver tinsel.
Tail: Natural red golden pheasant body feather barbs.
Butt: Black ostrich herl.
Ribbing: Oval silver tinsel.
Body: Light gray floss.
Wing: Dyed black squirrel tail tied low over the body.
Topping: Golden pheasant crest.
Hackle: Light cast grizzly hen hackle tied on as a collar and tied back.
Head: Black.

Originated by Claude Bernard of Waterloo, Quebec, in 1981.

Torrent River Special

Thread: White.
Tip: Oval silver tinsel.
Ribbing: Oval silver tinsel.
Body: Fluorescent white floss.
Wing: White calf tail tied low over the body.
Hackle: Sparse furnace hen hackle tied on as a collar and tied back.
Head: White.

Originated by Len Rich of Clarenville, Newfoundland.

Torrish Yellow

Thread: Black.
Tip: Lower, flat silver tinsel and the upper, yellow floss.
Tail: Salmon yellow hackle barbs mixed with CH05 golden yellow Crystal Hair.
Butt: Dark brown ostrich herl.
Body: Flat silver tinsel with a center joint of red yarn.
Hackle: Yellow tied on as a collar and tied back and down.
Wing: Dyed yellow gray squirrel tail tied low over the body.
Topping: CH05 golden yellow Crystal Hair.
Cheeks: J.C. or substitute.
Head: Black.

Traffic Ticket

Thread: Black.
Tip: Oval gold tinsel.
Tail: Barred lemon woodduck barbs.
Body: Peacock herl. Reverse wrap with fine gold wire.
Hackle: Badger tied on as a collar and tied back and down.
Wing: Barred lemon woodduck tied over the body.
Head: Black.

Originated by David Ledlie of Buckfield, Maine.

Turk's Red Butt

Thread: Black.
Tip: Lower, oval gold tinsel and the upper, fluorescent red yarn.
Tail: Golden pheasant crest.

Ribbing: Oval gold tinsel
Body: Peacock herl.
Hackle: Sparse black bear hair tied in at the throat.
Wing: Sparse black bear hair tied low over the body.
Head: Black.

Uncaged Woman

Thread: Black.
Tip: Flat gold tinsel.
Tail: Orange hackle barbs.
Ribbing: Flat gold tinsel.
Body Hackle: Yellow tied palmer style over the body.
Body: White floss.
Hackle: Orange tied on as a collar and tied back and down.
Wing: CH01 pearl and CH05 golden yellow Crystal Hair tied over the body with an overwing of orange monga ringtail.
Cheeks: J.C. or substitute.
Head: Black.

Originated in 1980 by Charles Krom and named for his friend Judith Bowman.

Undertaker

Thread: Black.
Tip: Rear third, flat gold tinsel, center third, fluorescent green floss, and the front third, fluorescent orange floss.
Ribbing: Oval gold tinsel.
Body: Peacock herl.
Hackle: Black tied on as a collar and tied back and down.
Wing: Black bear hair tied low over the body.
Cheeks: J.C. or substitute.
Head: Black.

The originator of this pattern is unknown. In recent years Warren Duncan of St. John, New Brunswick, has been one of its biggest advocates. He was given a sample of the fly by Chris Russell who thought the fly had originated in the late 1960s and was named after Henry Bradford who owned a fish camp on the Miramichi at Boisetown.

Ungava

Thread: Black.
Tip: Silver wire.
Tail: Golden pheasant crest.
Ribbing: Oval silver tinsel.
Body: Dark blue floss.
Wing: White calf tail tied low over the body.
Hackle: Yellow hen hackle tied on as a collar and tied back.
Head: Black.

Originated by André Bellemare.

Upsalquitch Special

Thread: Black.
Tip: Flat silver tinsel.
Tail: Two red duck quill sections tied on edge together.
Ribbing: Oval silver tinsel.
Body: Flat silver tinsel.
Wing: Dyed black squirrel tail tied low over the body.
Hackle: Yellow tied on as a collar and tied back.
Head: Black.

Plate 12 ## Veever's Fancy

Thread: Black.
Tail: Golden pheasant crest.
Ribbing: Oval silver tinsel.
Body: Flat silver tinsel.
Hackle: Yellow tied on as a collar and tied back and down.
Wing: Gray squirrel tail tied low over the body.
Cheeks: J.C. or substitute.
Head: Black.

Verdict

Thread: Black.
Tip: Flat gold tinsel.
Butt: Fluorescent hot pink yarn.
Tail: Golden pheasant crest.
Ribbing: Flat gold tinsel.
Body: Black floss.
Wing: Dyed black squirrel tail tied over the body and extending to the end of the hook.
Hackle: Fire orange tied on as a collar and tied back.
Head: Black.

Originated by Jerry Clapp in 1980.

Wagstaff Special

Thread: Black.
Tip: Oval gold tinsel.
Tail: Peacock sword feather barbs.
Body: Rear half, orange floss and the front half, bronze peacock herl.
Trailer: Single strand of orange floss tied in at the center top of the body and extending to the end of the hook.
Wing: Natural brown bucktail tied low over the body.
Hackle: Brown tied on as a collar and tied back.
Head: Black.

Warden Watcher

Thread: Black.
Tip: Lower, flat gold tinsel and the upper, yellow floss.
Tail: Golden pheasant crest.
Butt: Peacock herl.
Ribbing: Flat gold tinsel.
Body: Yellow floss.
Hackle: Orange tied on as a collar and tied back and down.
Wing: Black bear hair tied low over the body.
Cheeks: J.C. or substitute.
Head: Black.

Watson's Fancy

Thread: Black.
Tip: Oval silver tinsel.
Tail: Golden pheasant crest.
Ribbing: Oval silver tinsel.
Body: Rear half, red floss and the front half, black floss.
Hackle: Black tied on as a collar and tied back and down.
Wing: Dyed black squirrel tail tied low over the body.
Cheeks: J.C. or substitute.
Head: Black.

Whale River Rat

Thread: Black.
Tail: Peacock herl tips.
Body: Peacock herl. Reverse wrap with fine gold wire.
Wing: Gray squirrel tail tied over the body and extending to end of hook.

Hackle: Grizzly hen hackle tied on as a collar and tied back.
Head: Black.

Whalin Galen

Thread: Yellow.
Tip: Oval silver tinsel.
Ribbing: Flat silver tinsel.
Body: Dubbed with muskrat fur.
Wing: Gray squirrel tail tied low over the body.
Hackle: Light blue tied on as a collar and tied back.
Head: Yellow.

White Thunder

Thread: Black.
Tip: Lower, oval silver tinsel and the upper, yellow floss.
Tail: Yellow hackle barbs.
Butt: Black ostrich herl.
Ribbing: Oval gold tinsel.
Body: Dubbed with #1 black lambs wool.
Hackle: Dyed orange guinea fowl tied in at the throat with dyed blue guinea fowl tied in front.
Wing: Fine textured white deer hair tied low over the body.
Head: Black.

White Wing

Thread: Black.
Tail: Golden pheasant crest.
Ribbing: Oval silver tinsel.
Body: This is a body divided into four equal parts: **1.** yellow, **2.** orange, **3.** red and **4.** black yarn.
Hackle: Medium blue tied on as a collar and tied back and down.
Wing: White monga ringtail tied low over the body.
Head: Black.

Woodchuck

Thread: Black.
Tip: Oval silver tinsel.
Tail: Orange hackle barbs.
Ribbing: Oval silver tinsel.

Body: Dubbed with #1 black lambs wool.
Wing: Woodchuck hair tied low over the body.
Hackle: Orange tied on as a collar and tied back.
Head: Black.

Originated by Keith Fulsher in 1964.

Wringer

Thread: Black.
Tip: Lower, flat silver tinsel and the upper, yellow floss.
Tail: Golden pheasant crest.
Butt: Black ostrich herl.
Ribbing: Oval silver tinsel.
Body: Dubbed with #1 black lambs wool.
Hackle: Blue charm tied on as a collar and tied back and down.
Wing: Dyed red gray squirrel tail tied low over the body with an overwing of dyed yellow gray squirrel tail.
Head: Black.

Yellow Bucktail

Thread: Black.
Tail: Golden pheasant crest.
Ribbing: Oval silver tinsel.
Body: Flat silver tinsel.
Hackle: Yellow tied on as a collar and tied back and down.
Wing: Yellow bucktail tied low over the body.
Head: Black.

Yellow Canary

Thread: Black.
Tip: Oval gold tinsel.
Tail: Dyed orange golden pheasant crest.
Tail Topping: Short strand of fluorescent orange floss tied over the tail.
Butt: Black yarn.
Ribbing: Oval silver tinsel.
Body: Flat silver tinsel.
Hackle: Orange tied on as a collar and tied back and down.
Wing: Dyed yellow gray squirrel tail tied low over the body.
Topping: Dyed orange golden pheasant crest.
Head: Black.

This is the hair wing version of the classic Canary as conceived by Charles Krom in 1965.

Yellow Cosseboom I

Thread: Red.
Tip: Embossed silver tinsel.
Tag: Single strand of yellow yarn.
Ribbing: Embossed silver tinsel.
Body: Yellow floss.
Wing: Gray squirrel tail tied low over the body.
Hackle: Grizzly tied on as a collar and tied back.
Head: Red.

Yellow Cosseboom II

Thread: Red.
Tip: Flat silver tinsel.
Tail: Golden pheasant crest.
Butt: Fine red chenille.
Ribbing: Oval silver tinsel.
Body: Olive green floss.
Hackle: Yellow tied on as a collar and tied back and down.
Wing: Yellow calf tail tied low over the body.
Head: Red.

Yellow Duce

Thread: Black.
Tail: Three black hairs tied long.
Ribbing: Heavy black thread.
Body: Pale yellow floss.
Hackle: Yellow tied on as a collar and tied back and down.
Wing: CH11 green Crystal Hair tied over the body with an overwing of dyed yellow gray squirrel tail.
Head: Black.

Yellow Killer

Thread: Black.
Tip: Flat silver tinsel.
Tail: Orange hackle barbs.
Body: Black chenille.
Hackle: Orange hackle barbs tied in at the throat.
Wing: Dyed yellow monga ringtail tied over the body and extending to end of hook.
Cheeks: J.C. or substitute.
Head: Black.

Originated by Ches Loughlin of Corner Brook, Newfoundland, in 1971.

Plate 12   **Yellow Montreal**

Thread: Black.
Tip: Oval gold tinsel.
Tail: Scarlet red hackle barbs.
Ribbing: Oval gold tinsel.
Body: Claret floss.
Wing: Yellow calf tail tied over the body.
Hackle: Yellow tied on as a collar and tied back.
Head: Black.

Yellow Reynard

Thread: Black.
Tip: Lower, oval gold tinsel and the upper, fluorescent yellow floss.
Tail: Guinea fowl barbs.
Ribbing: Oval silver tinsel.
Body: Flat gold tinsel.
Wing: Fox squirrel tail tied low over the body.
Hackle: Yellow tied on as a collar and tied back.
Head: Black.

Originated by Keith Fulsher in 1982.

Chapter 22

Spey Fly Evolution

The original Spey fly patterns are believed to have been originated in the Strathspey area of Scotland in the mid 1700s. From my observations it is apparent that not too many fly fishermen are familiar with the Spey fly and its design. A. E. Knox in his book, *Autumns on the Spey,* 1872, provided for us some of the earliest accounts of the Spey flies. Then George M. Kelson wrote, *The Salmon Fly*, 1895, and further elaborated on these flies. Spey flies and Dee flies are often confused with one another by fly tiers internationally. Aside from the wings and other ornamentation of the Dee design, the original Spey design had much longer hackle than the Dee.

My father took a great deal of interest in these flies. Information at that time was certainly hard to obtain. Let me quote some of the notes he made regarding Spey flies in the early 1940s:

"Tied on long hooks. No tip, tag, tail or butt. Slim bodies with ribs. Palmered hackle, should be long reaching far beyond hook. Many have no wings - with wings should be wet type. Tied tight over top of body. Cheeks left off and tops on just a few flies."

Then from other notes he made about the Dee style flies:

"Tied similar to Spey but hackle woolly worm type and not as long. Tails, tips, tags, butts, cheeks and topping are often used. Some only have hackle on front half of body. Wings are wet and tied in narrow V flat on top. Should be droopy at end. Scotland (DEE), England (MONOPLANE)."

My father's collection of different types of flies and patterns from the fly fishing community was from all parts of the world and was rather extensive. The specifics that were not scrolled in his extensive fly pattern log of notes were well inlaid in his head. The Spey flies were always one of his first considerations for use on the Trinity River here in northern California. My father's *"Autumns on the Spey"* were actually on the Madison River in Montana, he proved time and time again just how effective these flies were on our western rivers. His frustrations soared when fellow anglers passed off the Spey fly as just a variation of the Woolly Worm. Women and children had to leave the area when hearing him express his dissatisfaction with those unsophisticated $%&*@$.

In my early years I became involved (captivated) in the feather wing designs of Atlantic salmon flies and except for a few of the Rat series patterns I never considered the possibility of tying these flies any other way. As I kept reading and obtaining samples from all parts of the world myself, I came to the conclusion that the Americans and English were not singing off the same sheet of music. For that matter, neither were most others in the world of fly tying when it came to their designs.

This is when I finally realized that the world of fly tying was not as perfect and straight laced as I had thought and I started getting a better overall picture of how some of our flies probably should be tied. This got me to thinking. Being an American and living in the so-called melting pot of the world, why not tie American style? Who really cares if I put a tip, tag or tail on a Spey fly? It certainly isn't going to be entered into one of the traditional European fly exhibits where exotic materials are flaunted and ridiculous standards are imposed. However, I still had a lot to learn—I'm still learning.

If you, as a novice, were to start trying to research Spey flies and determine the exact meaning of *"Spey"* you would certainly run into some contradictory interpretations of the flies, and the word *"Spey"* itself. You might find that it not only applies to a fly design, but fly rods and fly lines as well. The word *"Spey"* and the flies came to us from the Spey River which flows through the Spey Valley in Scotland.

The composition of the original typical Scottish Spey fly consisted of a 2X or 3X long curved shank salmon fly hook in sizes 6 and 8. They were tied with down wings which were tied lower down on the shoulder so they laid closer to the body. Their wings were usually of regular turkey and barred or bronze mallard. They had no tail, tag or butt and their

Typical Spey Fly.

bodies were usually slim or with a medium taper. They most often had some tinsel ribbing on them. The hackles were brown (red game), gray (dun) or black and were originally taken from Spey roosters. These were a type of capon chickens which were raised in the Spey Valley at the time. Marabou was also used for hackle. These hackles had their barbs stripped off on one side of the stem to enhance sparseness and were wound palmer style over the body. The hackle was tied in by the butt so that the longest barbs were to the rear of the fly. The overall color of an original typical Scottish Spey fly was generally drab or somber in tone, with the exception of the Carron and the Orange Heaven, both having orange bodies.

I guess my knowledge of Spey flies came with my involvement in the classic salmon flies. The rods held very little interest for me until graphite started making a name for itself. These two-handed rods were also initially designed for use on the Spey and Dee Rivers. These rivers required rather long distance casts and the angler was hindered by the excessive growth of vegetation along their banks. The Scots perfected fly rod designs which allowed them to make long modified roll casts effortlessly. These rods were cumbersome twelve to fifteen foot long poles (not rods). Most of what I have read about fly lines of that time has been in metrics, a system that I have yet to learn. The *"old dog, new tricks"* syndrome I suppose.

A good majority (probably most) of the fly fishermen in North America relate Spey flies to the Spey fly rods, thinking you cannot take advantage of one without the other. This is not the case. You can cast a Spey fly with most any fly rod capable of handling larger flies. By the same token you can cast most any fly design, wet or dry, with a Spey rod. Literally dozens of the individuals I have spoken with agree that there is a need for better information about the Spey fly. That we need to better define what a Spey fly rod is and what type of fly line designs are appropriate.

The Spey fly gives you an additional design for your arsenal of flies. One should not think just in terms of salmon and steelhead either, these flies can also be effective for most of our other native resident fish. The Spey rod, because of its length and design, gives you the ability to make fantastically long modified roll type casts (Spey casts) which you normally cannot perform with a conventional nine foot rod. They also give you better line control and the ability to mend your fly line more easily. There are dozens of rivers where a Spey rod is heaven sent. Just having the ability to work a large stonefly nymph in the Box Canyon on the Henry's Fork makes having a Spey rod worthwhile for me. Think for a moment, just how much additional water could you cover with one of these longer fly rods? For this type of fishing I believe a six weight, twelve foot rod is the most appropriate.

Today some of the rod companies are sitting up and paying attention to a method of fly casting that they chose to ignore not too many years ago. This is understandable because until the advent of today's graphite fabricating methods these longer two-handed rods would not have been practical by our standards. During these past couple of years I have been in contact with some of the companies I know make the longer rods. It didn't take much to determine who made just *"long rods"* and who understood the Spey rod design.

I am the most impressed with what Sage and Scott are doing in the West. The East draws somewhat of a disappointing, negative response. They simply didn't understand or were not interested in our market here in this country at all. Their limited productions are going mostly to Europe. They have problems sorting out *"Spey fly fishing"* from *"old world salmon fly fishing."* One leading company told me to write a letter with my questions and it would be forwarded to England for a reply, not being particularly interested in how the Brits were faring I dropped the matter with them. My interest revolves around applications here in the U.S.

Due to there being a small market for the fly rod manufacturers, it can be projected that because Sage and Scott are doing their development quite meticulously, they are sure to be out there as the leaders in this area for some time to come. In Canada you will find Gold-N-West Flyfishers in Vancouver, British Columbia, which specializes in custom Spey fly rods. They have a somewhat different approach than you will hear from others, but I figure it doesn't hurt to consider all the views, and there are many. I believe some are unintentionally making this too complicated for all of us.

When selecting a Spey rod do not choose one on the basis of length alone. There are long rods and there are long Spey rods. The Spey rod has the ability to perform these longer casts because of its design. The ordinary long rods will perform, but not as effectively. A Spey rod is much like a *"buggy whip"* and flexes more freely throughout the length of the rod due to its softer butt and heavier tip.

In this country the Cortland Line Company was the first to put double tapered Spey fly lines on the market. Thinking back, it is interesting to note that Cortland was also instrumental in helping to develop some of the first shooting heads. They picked up the slack where Sunset left off. 3M's Scientific Anglers are also now making their versions of Spey lines. It should not be too long before there will be a good selection of both fly rods and lines available to us. At this time it appears that our new lines will be approximately 160 feet long to accommodate the longer casts and we will also be wanting larger capacity reels.

I personally like the early "basic" Scottish Spey fly design. These shrimp-like flies have an action in the water like no other fly design. Some say, *"these flies talk to the fish."* Their hooks with a longer curved shank, made from a round wire and looped eyes complement their simplistic dressings. With their long flowing hackle and yielding wings these flies hold their own under any critical fly tier's eye. Of all the feather wing salmon fly designs that have come from Europe, the Spey design certainly makes more sense than the others. These are truly *"fishing flies."*

Further on I give you a quote from Kelson's book. He recommended changing hackle lengths with the seasons. Kelson must have been a real theorist or armchair expert, because I find no validity in his reasoning. I have used Spey flies in all classifications of water, including lakes, and find that the longer flowing hackles are what makes these flies so effective.

Joseph D. Bates, Jr. devoted three pages of text in his 1970 book, *Atlantic Salmon Flies and Fishing*, to the Spey fly. It consisted of a quote from an article written in August 1969 by English angling-author Geoffrey Bucknall. This article reeked of Victorian era fly tying methods and without a doubt influenced the thinking of many North Americans. For lack of anything better, some have followed these guidelines rather blindly. It is not uncommon to find the serious tier reverently following some of the eccentric practices that Bucknall suggested, probably never realizing that they were his personal ideology and stiffly influenced by the Irish methods.

Now let us discuss some of the other people in Europe who have lent a hand in trying to recreate the wheel (Spey fly.) The drabness of the originals is often forgotten and they produce gaudy globs of feathers which for all practical purposes serve none. Some English writers have fed the world useless verbalizations that totally distort the original designs, and even exceed the so-called eccentric whims of Kelson. Naturally they go on to explain that others throughout the U.K. have expanded on the original idea due to its effectiveness. Most of this material should have been published in Repulsive Magazine rather than something connected with fly fishing.

I have visited stores in London and seen size 6/0 flies they called Spey flies that were closer to the Scottish Dee design. Possibly the tier had some other fantasy in mind. The hackles hardly reached past the barb of the hook and their wings simulated some sort of V. Believe me, early on, this kept me in a state of confusion for some time until I became a little better informed by, believe it or not, a transplanted Englishman.

My passion for these flies did not end there and I had to know even more. One would think that by personally visiting Scotland and inquiring with some who might know, i.e., members of the Stormont Angling Club or Aberfeldy Angling Club, that any questions would be resolved. Well that is a futile consideration. You have to go to the grass roots and pick the minds of the real fishermen to get real answers. Our angling literature paints an entirely different picture than what is factual. You will not see the Scots standing on the banks of the Spey River throwing anything that even resembles the original Spey flies. Upon close examination you might, if your are lucky, detect *hints* of some of the original design features.

Learning this took the wind out of my sails. It became hard for me to visualize how I could defend the merits of such a design when the Scots themselves had deserted it long ago in favor of hair winged patterns.

In view of the fact that I might be contradicting so many other writings laid down over the past decades I went to the extreme to verify my information. I got in contact with Neil McIntosh in Scotland. Neil, living in close proximity to the Spey, is a knowledgeable fly fisherman, fifteen foot rod and all, and was able to get opinions from the older Spey River gillies themselves. I felt that this was essential because it appeared that there were generations of Scots who had lost sight of some of their heritage.

From left: Bill Friedman and Neil McIntosh on the banks of Nairn River, Inverness, Scotland.

Access was gained to possibly one of the best collections of antique fly fishing tackle of this kind in the world. When you can document statements based on fly collections that are at least two hundred years old, tackle that A.H.E. Wood himself used and other treasures, it has a humbling effect. The myths of yesterday are soon forgotten and new perspectives are developed. I would like to call this a rebirth of knowledge, however, the knowledge has always been there and no one has particularly cared to take the time for discovery.

When I started exploring the subject of Spey flies and their origins I found that I knew as much as most of the Scots themselves. We just needed to fit some small pieces into the historical puzzle before a clearer picture was there for us. My project had special meaning to the Scots, rediscovering some of their own heritage was unique and it became a more meaningful effort for all of us. Collectively, the older gillies in Scotland have accumulated very valuable collections of both tackle and knowledge, taking great pride in their profession and making attempts to preserve their past. For security reasons involving their treasures and other sound reasons, it would not be proper to mention names or specific locations—this I must honor.

There are not more than a few hundred living fly tiers in the U.S. that have ever tied one of these flies in their true form. For something as simple as these flies are, the fly tiers of the world can certainly get them mixed up with the misinformation they have been provided about these unadorned little creatures.

As you might suspect, what is practiced in such places as England or the Scandinavian countries is often a totally different style from here. They have an assortment of so-called *"traditional"* designs which differ from each other. Kelson is probably the first to break with tradition, at least of notable record. This is what has generated some of the problems for many of us in our understanding of what these flies are about. My constant daily contact with fly fishermen leads me to believe that only about five percent, or maybe less, are informed enough to know what a Spey fly actually is.

Fly tiers on both coasts and in the Great Lakes region have been creating variations of the Spey fly design for some time now. We need not be restricted entirely to the patterns obtained from Europe and should dress our flies using materials and color combinations proven for our fishing conditions. The hooks that were most commonly used in the recent past are referred to in Europe as *"Dee"* style. Dee coming from a similar fly design mentioned earlier which was originally for Scotland's Aberdeenshire Dee salmon river. These designs came after the Spey design. This was thought to be an advancement in fly design of the time—more gingerbread and other accouterments. The Dee design was tied on hooks that were 3X to 4X long. Some tiers in this country have a preference for these longer shanked hooks for their Spey flies. They even go a couple of steps further and have them made from fine wire in odd numbered sizes, such as 3 and 5.

I find that these finer wire hooks have no advantage under normal fishing conditions, nor do the longer shanks. The odd hook sizes are not appreciably different from the even sizes of 2 and 4 when you get into these smaller sizes and you might say, *"it all hinges on a degree of eccentric reasoning."* Spey flies tied on finer wire is baffling to me. Some argue that the finer wire produces a sharper hook than heavier wires. A Spey fly on these hooks does not sink as well and in faster currents fails to stay in an upright position. Until someone convinces me differently, I'll stick with the heavier wire hooks with shorter shanks. By staying away from the longer shank hooks my body hackle also becomes a lesser problem on larger sizes.

At one time I used only English hooks for these flies—then Mustad made some great strides in the design of some of their hooks. The Mustad model numbers 80500BL 80501BL caught my eye and I have stuck with them since. These are rugged hooks and if they were any sharper you would probably have to get a *"use permit."* Well that may be stretching it a bit, but they are very serviceable. They have a good platform to display any and all materials one would want to put into a Spey fly. And I tie my Spey flies to fish with, not for color plates or shadow boxes.

Kelson wrote, *"The claret (or fiery brown) body and cinnamon wings is, however, a typical pattern on the Spey for porter-coloured water; and until summer season, when Cock's hackles take the place of Heron's, an almost universal system in the selection of flies prevails for conditions of weather and water. That is to say, the Rough Grouse is invariably reserved for a dark drizzly day; the Brown Dog for a bright day in dull water; whilt the Purple King is estimated as being the best general pattern on the river."*

I have quoted this for you not only so you can see the extent that Kelson went to in an attempt to better inform his fellow anglers, but also to demonstrate some of the first recorded references made to the use of heron feathers for hackle. I have also listed some of Kelson's Spey fly patterns alphabetically throughout the pattern section of this chapter. They are in his words and you can interpret them as you wish, but again I want to bring to your attention his mention of heron feathers. I feel that we need to go back a good ways before all of this fits in properly.

Kelson's book covered approximately 200 salmon fly patterns and was a major work for its time. Kelson drew some heavy criticism from some quarters and was called a snob, extravagant and other less-than-favorable comments were made by his fellow anglers. After reading some of these negative comments one has to wonder who the real snobs might have been. Some have concluded that he was a bit before his time. This worked in Dr. T. E. Pryce-Tannatt's favor when his book, *How to Dress Salmon Flies,* came out in 1914. Many wanted to forget the influences of Kelson and would have endorsed any reasonable work dealing with salmon flies.

Although my father was never able to get his hands on a copy of Kelson's book, in our house the name Kelson was a household word. My father had a friend in Wisconsin that sent him many hand-written excerpts from that book and others, and this was basically his bible for Spey flies. Apparently some copies of the book made there way to this country. One of the key factors to capture the fancy of the North American fly tiers was the use of heron feathers for hackle. It was not uncommon for my father to spend the morning along the banks of the Sacramento River plunking birds for their feathers. The day came when a warden kindly reminded him that these particular birds were protected and he should seek other sources. His attentions were then directed to England where small quantities were occasionally available up until about 1950 when they too could no longer supply feathers.

I bring this up in an attempt to clarify some misconceptions many fly tiers have today. Heron hackles were never used in any great quantity either here or in Europe. Spey flies lost much of their appeal at the turn of the century when more gaudy creations came into being. With the upheaval caused by a couple of world wars in Europe and the rethinking by many countries, they were forced to take a second look at their place in the world and a new order was suddenly in fashion. Treaties between countries also included international protection of certain species of wildlife which were previously unprotected. And yes, this included the heron.

The color plates of some fly tying books thoughtlessly portray Spey flies sporting heron hackles which sets the new fly tier wondering where on earth these feathers come from. To tell you that they must be from birds raised on a farm some place, or the feathers were gathered from road kills would be bull. They are illegal in every sense of the word. Possession of the feathers in any form is illegal even if they are recovered from molted feathers at the local zoo.

Now that I am finished being a party pooper let us look at the positive side. The original feathers used were those collected in Scotland from capon chickens. These feathers were desirable because of their longer barbs. Some have written that the cock side tail feathers were used. This is only partially true and infers that the other feathers were ignored. I had to be reminded that this was a naive assumption—thrifty Scots used all of the feathers. Granted, patterns, i.e., the Culdran, Dallas and Gold Riach were often tied using the tail feathers. The use of these particular feathers was never very popular and other feathers from the capon were often considered more desirable. There are large neck hackles available today which are equal to, or even better than, those used on the original patterns and if we want to go for something even longer there are other feathers to look at. Pheasant rump and large duck flank feathers, natural and dyed, do wonders on a Spey fly. And when they are available, large flank feathers from a goose also do the trick.

As stated elsewhere, creativity in your fly tying is strongly encouraged. There are a good number of Atlantic salmon patterns listed in Chapter 21 which are adaptable to Spey fly designs. It is reasonable to assume that some of these patterns could very well have evolved from an original Spey fly pattern. From the patterns given in this chapter you will notice that some do not have their long hackles wrapped the full length of the body which deviates from the true original design, these are flies that came in the succeeding Kelson era. I can go along with the desire for larger hooks which are not compatible with the hackle nature has provided us, thus leaving us in a position whereby we can only palmer a portion of the body. I cannot however agree that long hackles tied on as a collar justify classification as a Spey fly. You will see the term *"simplified Spey"* used in this fashion when it should really be *"spider."* For the life of me, I cannot envision anything more simplified than a true Spey fly. There is no need to keep analyzing and reanalyzing innocent beauty.

In the patterns I have listed there are also some other minor deviations which the purist among you may detect. I believe that many of the Spey patterns tied in the world today are hybridized creations taken from both the Dee and Spey designs. I guess we could call these designs contemporary or semi-Speys. Because of the confusion, I felt it essential to include these in this chapter rather than some obscure corner of my basic chapters on Atlantic salmon or steelhead flies. Their designers deserve the benefit of the doubt and proper recognition. I do this hoping that some effort will be made to make corrections in future designs of *"Spey"* patterns. I make this statement knowing it is possibly falling on deaf ears, there will always be those who will elect to follow other worldly directions. That is what fly tying is all about—a personal declaration.

Although it may be stretching it even more, I believe that hair wings on these flies are very practical. Because it is a pliable and more flowing material, I recommend bucktail in most cases when creating new patterns or when making substitutes. I also keep the hair wing rather sparse and long. This is only following a trend that the Scots themselves have embraced. I have come to respect much of their wisdom in these matters.

The use of feather types for wings rather than the traditional mallard and turkey strips is also encouraged. Many patterns are now using hackle tip wings which brings some life to the fly. In view of the fact that we have learned considerably more about fly design it would not be considered sacrilegious to add a few strands of Crystal Hair or Fly Brite to our wings also.

North American fly fishermen can take sanctuary in knowing that when Kelson introduced his theories the Scots themselves started being much more creative. Some of the patterns created just prior to the turn of the century were known as *"modern"* Spey flies. Neil McIntosh has written me that, *"There was apparently a wide variation in the tyings of Spey fly patterns—both in the sense that a single pattern would have many local variants, and also that the same tier might tie the same pattern with a fair amount of inconsistency, so there may not be, in fact there is almost certainly not any definitive dressings for the individual patterns—the ones that we have are presumably just some of the variations which happen to have been documented."*

I believe that this holds even more significance when we are dealing with all salmon flies in general and for that matter, all flies tied any place. However, in this particular context it is rewarding to have a Scot remind us.

In selecting patterns I based it on the hook used, the long Spey type body hackle and sparseness of dress. I have given fly patterns that fish have approved of, believing that is what this is all about. Now you can see why I included the term *"evolution"* in the title of this chapter.

Akroyd

Hooks: AC80500BL or AC80501BL, sizes 4-8.
Thread: Black.
Tip: Oval silver tinsel.
Ribbing: Flat silver tinsel overwrapped with a narrower oval silver tinsel.
Tail: Golden pheasant tippet.
Butt: Black ostrich.
Body: Rear half, fluorescent orange floss and the front half, black floss.
Center Joint: Black ostrich.
Body Hackle: Rear half, yellow tied palmer style over the body and the front half, black pheasant rump tied palmer style over the body.
Hackle: Barred teal tied on as a collar and tied back and down, one turn only.
Wing: Natural brown bucktail tied sparse and low over the body.
Head: Black.

Originated in Scotland by Charles Akroyd. This is one of many versions of this fly. The original pattern, as far as I can tell, had cinnamon turkey tail strips for the wings and jungle cock cheeks. Some body variations call for either wool or seal fur.

Alfa

Hooks: AC80500BL or AC80501BL, sizes 4-8.
Thread: Orange.
Ribbing: Heavy orange thread.
Body Hackle: Brown tied palmer style over the body.
Body: Orange floss.
Hackle: Dyed orange barred teal tied on as a collar and tied back.
Wing: Mottled brown turkey quill sections tied low over the body.
Head: Orange.

Originated by Ralph Emery.

Amethyst

Hooks: AC80500BL or AC80501BL, sizes 4-8.
Thread: Black.
Tip: Oval silver tinsel.
Butt: Red floss.
Ribbing: Oval silver tinsel.
Body Hackle: Dyed blue pheasant rump tied palmer style over the body.
Body: Peacock sword feather barbs wrapped over the body.
Wing: Dyed purple gray squirrel tail tied low over the body.
Head: Black.

Amethyst

Hooks: AC80500BL or AC80501BL, sizes 1-6.
Thread: Black.
Tip: Flat silver tinsel.
Butt: Red floss.
Ribbing: Oval silver tinsel.
Body: Peacock sword feather barbs wrapped over the body.
Hackle: Purple hackle barbs tied in at the throat with a second bunch of scarlet red hackle barbs tied over the first.
Wings: Dyed purple barred mallard sections tied low over the body.
Head: Black.

This variation is the work of Jimmy LeMert of Seattle, Washington.

Apple Maggot Spey

Hooks: AC80500BL or AC80501BL, sizes 2-6.
Thread: Yellow.
Tip: Copper wire.
Ribbing: Copper wire.
Body Hackle: Brown tied palmer style over front third of the body.
Body: Rear two-thirds, yellow floss and the front third, dubbed #6 yellow African Angora goat.
Hackle: Dyed yellow guinea fowl tied on as a collar and tied back and down.
Wings: Four burnt orange hackle tips tied over the body.
Head: Yellow.

Originated by Scott O'Donnell.

Balmoral

Hooks: AC80500BL or AC80501BL, sizes 4-8.
Thread: Black.
Tip: Oval silver tinsel.
Tail: Golden pheasant crest.
Butt: Black ostrich.
Ribbing: Flat silver tinsel overwrapped with a narrow oval silver tinsel.
Body Hackle: Black tied palmer style over front half of the body.
Body: Rear half, dubbed with #17 green highlander lambs wool and the front half, dubbed #36 blue charm lambs wool.
Hackle: Barred teal tied on as a collar and tied back.
Wing: Natural brown bucktail tied sparse and low over the body.
Head: Black.

Beauly Snow Fly

Hooks: AC80500BL or AC80501BL, sizes 1-6.
Thread: Fluorescent fire orange.
Ribbing: Flat silver tinsel overwrapped with narrower oval gold tinsel.
Body: Dubbed with #55 fluorescent blue African Angora goat and kept rather thin.
Body Hackle: Dyed black pheasant rump tied palmer style from the third turn of

ribbing. Reverse wrap the body with fine gold wire over the hackle.

Wing: Several strands of peacock herl tied over the body.

Hackle: Dyed black pheasant rump tied on as a collar and tied back. Hackle barbs should reach the bend of the hook.

Head: Fluorescent fire orange rabbit spun on as a collar.

This is a steelhead variation of an old establish British Atlantic salmon fly pattern.

Bedspring Spey

Hooks: AC80500BL or AC80501BL, sizes 1/0-6.

Thread: Fluorescent fire orange.

Tip: Flat gold tinsel.

Tail: Dyed orange golden pheasant crest.

Ribbing: Flat gold tinsel overwrapped with a narrower oval gold tinsel.

Body Hackle: Black tied palmer style over the front half of the body.

Body: Rear half, dubbed with #52 fluorescent orange and front half, dubbed with #25 reddish-brown African Angora goat.

Hackle: Dyed brown barred teal tied on as a collar and tied back.

Wings: Bronze mallard sections tied low over the body.

Head: Fluorescent fire orange.

This fly was created for use on the Deschutes by John Shewey of Bend, Oregon.

Belvedere

Hooks: AC80500BL or AC80501BL, sizes 2-6.

Thread: Claret.

Tail: Dyed red golden pheasant crest.

Ribbing: Flat red Mylar tinsel overwrapped with a narrow oval silver tinsel.

Body Hackle: Black tied palmer style over front two-thirds of the body.

Body: Rear third, flat red Mylar tinsel and the front two-thirds, dubbed #1 black African Angora goat.

Hackle: Dyed claret guinea fowl barbs tied in at the throat.

Wings: Dyed black goose quill sections tied low over the body.

Cheeks: Small J.C. or substitute.

Head: Claret.

Originated by Dec Hogan of Mt. Vernon, Washington.

Best Yet

Hooks: AC80500BL or AC80501BL, sizes 4-8.

Thread: Black.

Tip: Oval silver tinsel.

Ribbing: Oval silver tinsel.

Body Hackle: Purple tied palmer style over the body.

Body: Purple floss.

Hackle: Dyed purple guinea fowl tied on as a collar and tied back.

Wing: Dyed black goose quill sections tied low over the body.

Head: Black.

Originated by Reggie Malstrom.

Black Buck

Hooks: AC80500BL or AC80501BL, sizes 1-8.

Thread: Black.

Tip: Flat silver tinsel.

Tail: Golden Pheasant crest.

Ribbing: Flat silver tinsel.

Body Hackle: Black tied palmer style over the body.

Body: Dubbed with #1 black African Angora goat.

Wing: Gray squirrel tail tied low over the body.

Head: Black.

This pattern was originally developed for Eastern Atlantic salmon and now finds a home on steelhead waters.

Black Deceiver

Hooks: AC80500BL or AC80501BL, sizes 1-6.
Thread: Black.
Ribbing: Flat silver tinsel which is overwrapped with a narrower oval silver tinsel.
Body Hackle: Gray tied palmer style over the body.
Body: Natural gray ostrich herl.
Hackle: Guinea fowl tied on as a collar and tied back.
Wing: Black squirrel tail tied low over the body.
Head: Black.

Black Dog

Hooks: AC80500BL or AC80501BL, sizes 4-8.
Thread: Black.
Tip: Flat silver tinsel.
Tail: Golden pheasant crest.
Butt: Black ostrich.
Ribbing: Oval silver tinsel.
Body Hackle: Black tied palmer style over the body.
Body: Black floss.
Hackle: Blue tied on as a collar and tied back.
Wing: Dyed black bucktail tied sparse and long over the body.
Head: Black.

This is a variation of an old pattern of the Victorian era. The original had a very complex wing. It is believed that the "modern" version was taken from an even earlier version.

Black Heron

Hooks: AC80500BL or AC80501BL, sizes 1-8.
Thread: Black.
Tip: Flat silver tinsel.
Tail: Golden pheasant crest tied short.
Butt: Two full turns of yellow floss.
Ribbing: Oval silver tinsel.
Body Hackle: Black tied palmer style over the body.
Body: Black floss kept thin.
Hackle: Guinea fowl barbs tied in at the throat with tips touching point of hook.
Wings: Natural gray goose quill sections tied low over the body.
Head: Black.

This is a British variation of this pattern.

Black Heron

Hooks: AC80500BL or AC80501BL, sizes 1-4.
Thread: Black.
Ribbing: Oval silver tinsel over entire body.
Body Hackle: Dyed black tied palmer style over dubbed area only.
Body: Rear two-thirds, flat silver tinsel and front third, dubbed with #1 black African Angora goat.
Hackle: Guinea fowl tied on as a collar and tied back.
Wings: Dyed black narrow sections of either goose or turkey quill tied low over the body.
Head: Black.

This is one of the many Syd Glasso variations of Spey fly patterns which you will find in this chapter. Syd is undisputedly recognized as the tier who introduced and promoted these flies in the Pacific Northwest for steelhead and salmon.

Syd was able to take some of the British dressings and apply them to his kind of fishing. Syd was a great fly tier and we all miss his interpretive talents. He would often substitute fluorescent materials or change a floss portion of a body to dubbed material, but he basically stuck to the original colors. Syd tied the majority of his flies on size one and two hooks.

Black Jack

Hooks: AC80500BL or AC80501BL, sizes 2/0-4.
Thread: Black.
Tip: Flat gold tinsel.
Ribbing: Oval gold tinsel.
Body Hackle: Gray tied palmer style over the body from second rib.
Body: Black floss.

Hackle: Guinea fowl tied on as a collar and tied back.
Wing: Golden pheasant tail feather sections low over the body.
Cheeks: J.C. tied drooped.
Head: Black.

Originated by Joe Howell of Idleyld Park, Oregon. The original pattern calls for Argus pheasant tail for the wings. Use it if available. This is one of the few patterns that I do not recommend making a substitute for the cheeks. They are tied drooped and any other material would destroy the character of the fly.

Black King

(From Kelson's book)
"Body - Orange Berlin wool (three turns) followed by black wool (short).
Ribs - From far side gold tinsel (narrow), from near side silver tinsel (same size) both wound the reverse way, an equal distance apart.
Hackle - From end of body, a black Spey-cock hackle, but wound from the root instead of the point, in the usual direction, thus crossing over the ribs at each turn given.
Throat - Teal, one turn only.
Wings - Two strips of light brown mottled Mallard.
(Special Note - This is one of the standard flies on the Spey. For full particulars see the "Green King")"

Black Krahe Spey

Hooks: AC80500BL or AC80501BL, sizes 1-4.
Thread: Black.
Ribbing: Oval silver tinsel.
Body Hackle: Black tied palmer style over the body.
Body: Dubbed with #1 black Bunny-Blend.
Hackle: Guinea fowl tied in at the throat.
Wing: Silver pheasant wing quill sections tied low over the body.
Head: Black.

Tim Krahe from Manistee, Michigan, created this fly for his area. It will most likely work any place there are steelhead and salmon.

Black Phase Spey

Hooks: AC80500BL or AC80501BL, sizes 2-8.
Thread: Black.
Ribbing: Oval gold tinsel.
Body Hackle: Black tied palmer style over the body.
Trailer: Short strand of fluorescent orange yarn tied in the center of the body on top and frayed out.
Body: Rear half, flat gold tinsel and the front half, black floss.
Wing: Dyed orange monga ringtail tied low over the body.
Head: Black.

This is a Joe Howell pattern.

Plate 13   Black Spey

Hooks: AC80500BL or AC80501BL, sizes 4-8.
Thread: Black.
Tip: Oval silver tinsel.
Ribbing: Oval silver tinsel.
Body Hackle: Black tied palmer style over the body.
Body: Dubbed with #1 black African Angora goat.
Wing: Dyed black bucktail tied over the body and extending just past the hook.
Head: Black.

This has been a meat and potatoes pattern for many years.

Blue Dependable

Hooks: AC80500BL or AC80501BL, sizes 1-4.
Thread: Black.
Tip: Oval silver tinsel.
Tail: Natural red golden pheasant body feather barbs.

Ribbing: Flat silver tinsel with a narrower oval silver tinsel wrapped in as a border.
Body Hackle: Barred mallard tied palmer style over the body from the second turn of ribbing. A second hackle of teal blue marabou is then wrapped in front of each turn of the mallard.
 Body: Rear third, #1 black and the front two-thirds, #35 kingfisher blue Bunnytron.
Hackle: Black marabou tied on as a collar and tied back with an additional hackle of one full turn of barred teal.
Wings: Dark brown mottled turkey tail sections tied low over the body.
Head: Black.

I have tied some of these up and I am very pleased with them. For now they just sit there to be admired, but I hope to get them wet soon. This is my variation of a variation. This is taken from a design by Joe Rossano of Seattle, Washington. He got his idea from a Scottish pattern. Joe ties his fly on an 8X long shank hook which is substituted on my fly. Joe's choice of hooks has long been a jinx to me, or at least I feel so.

I can remember years ago the conversations that surrounded these hooks and considering the strong opposition towards them by my elders, I stayed away from them up until 1960. The old argument against them insisted that longer shanked hooks allowed the fish to have much more leverage when hooked and were better able to throw them. While fishing Henry's Lake in Idaho I decided to fish a Duck Lake Woolly Worm. By the end of that afternoon I had hooked as many fish as everyone else, but I had boated only four. You be the judge, is it leverage or a jinx?

Boulder Creek

Hooks: AC80500BL or AC80501BL, sizes 1-4.
Thread: Black.
Ribbing: Flat silver tinsel overwrapped with a single strand of fluorescent green floss.
Body Hackle: Black tied palmer style over the body.
Body: Black floss.
Hackle: Kingfisher blue hen hackle barbs tied in at the throat with guinea fowl barbs tied in front.
Wings: Pair of golden pheasant flanks tied low over the body.
Topping: Pair of golden pheasant crests.
Head: Black.

Developed by Mike Kenney of Oso, Washington, for the Skagit and Stillaguamish Rivers.

You may see this fly described with a chartreuse Mylar tinsel ribbing. Your first reaction is going to be, *"Now where in the hell am I going to find that stuff?"* Chances are it is right on your tying bench. See Mylar tinsel, Chapter 5.

Brad's Brat Spey

Hooks: AC80500BL or AC80501BL, sizes 2-6.
Thread: Black.
Tip: Flat gold tinsel.
Tail: Dyed orange golden pheasant crest.
Ribbing: Oval gold tinsel.
Body Hackle: Gray tied palmer style over front half of the body.
Body: Rear half, orange floss and the front half, dubbed #4 red African Angora goat.
Hackle: Dyed brown barred teal tied on as a collar and tied back.
Wing: Four white hackle tips tied over the body.
Head: Black.

A variation of the original pattern. See Chapter 20.

Brown Heron

Hooks: AC80500BL or AC80501BL, sizes 1-4.
Thread: Red.
Ribbing: Flat silver tinsel bordered with oval silver tinsel.
Body Hackle: Gray tied palmer style over the body at the edge of the ribbing.
Body: Rear two-thirds, orange floss and the front third, dubbed with 50/50 mixed #50 fluorescent red and #52 fluorescent orange African Angora goat.
Hackle: Barred teal tied on as a collar and tied back and down.
Wings: Bronze mallard sections tied low over the body.
Head: Red.

This is another of the Syd Glasso variations. His patterns in all of their beauty have given the fly tiers of today and the future real high standards to replicate. This version of the Brown Heron varies but very little from the European version.

Black Demon Spey

Hooks: AC80500BL or AC80501BL, sizes 3/0-4.
Thread: Black.
Ribbing: Flat silver tinsel overwrapped with a narrow oval silver tinsel.
Body Hackle: Black tied palmer style over front half of the body.
Body: Rear half, flat silver tinsel and the front half, dubbed #1 black African Angora goat.
Hackle: Dyed red guinea fowl tied on as a collar and tied back.
Wing: Four dyed scarlet red hackle tips tied over the body.
Head: Black.

Originated by Kent Helvie. Kent is the author of *Steelhead Fly Tying Guide* which I recommend highly. He puts a different slant on the subject. Good chap and deserves much credit for his work.

Car Body

Hooks: AC80500BL or AC80501BL, sizes 2-6.
Thread: Black.
Ribbing: Flat silver tinsel with an overwrap of a single strand of fluorescent green floss.
Body Hackle: Dark pheasant rump overdyed purple and tied palmer style over the body.
Body: Dubbed with #1 black Bunny-Blend.
Hackle: Kingfisher blue hen hackle barbs tied in at the throat.
Wings: Pair of dark pheasant rump feathers overdyed purple and tied low over the body.
Head: Black.

This is another of the Mike Kinney patterns. See Boulder Creek.

Carron

Hooks: AC80500BL or AC80501BL, sizes 1-8.
Thread: Black.
Ribbing: Red floss which is wrapped reversed then overwapped in with flat silver tinsel.
Body Hackle: Black tied palmer style from the second turn of ribbing.
Body: Dubbed with #9 orange lambs wool.
Hackle: Barred teal tied on as a collar with one full turn and tied back and down.
Wings: Bronze mallard sections tied low over the body.
Head: Black.

This is one of many variations of this pattern.

Carron

Hooks: AC80500BL or AC80501BL, sizes 1-4.
Thread: Black.
Ribbing: Oval silver tinsel. Reverse wrap the entire body with fine gold wire after the hackle is wrapped.
Body Hackle: Black tied palmer style over the body.
Body: Alternating wraps of red and orange floss.
Hackle: Barred teal tied in at the throat.
Wings: Bronze mallard sections tied low over the body.
Head: Black.

This is a variation of the pattern as tied by Washington *"fly artist"* Steve Gobin.

Charlatan

Hooks: AC80500BL or AC80501BL, sizes 4-8.
Thread: Black.
Ribbing: Oval silver tinsel.
Body Hackle: Gray tied palmer style over the body.
Body: Dubbed with muskrat fur.
Hackle: Dyed black pheasant rump tied on as a collar and tied back.
Wing: Barred teal sections tied low over the body.

Originated by Dan Townsend.

Claret N'Guinea

Hooks: AC80500BL or AC80501BL, sizes 4-8.
Thread: Red.
Tip: Flat gold tinsel.
Ribbing: Oval gold tinsel.
Body Hackle: Purple tied palmer style over the body, along the ribbing, starting from the second turn.
Body: Dubbed with #32 claret Bunny-Blend.
Hackle: Dyed claret pheasant rump hackle followed by one full turn of finely speckled guinea fowl.
Head: Red.

Created by Mike McCoy of Bothell, Washington. Basically this is a summer-run pattern. Tie it full in the spring and as the waters clear and subside, reduce the fly accordingly.

Claret Spey

Hooks: AC80500BL or AC80501BL, sizes 1-4.
Thread: Black.
Tag: Small tuft of yellow yarn.
Ribbing: Flat silver tinsel bordered with oval silver tinsel.

Body Hackle: Black tied palmer style over the body at the edge of oval tinsel.
Body: Dubbed with #32 claret Bunny-Blend.
Wings: Dyed black turkey quill section tied low over the body.
Head: Black.

This is a variation tied by Fredric Nicholas Kozy of Happy Camp, California.

Courtesan

Hooks: AC80500BL or AC80501BL, sizes 1-4.
Thread: Fluorescent orange.
Ribbing: Flat silver tinsel.
Body Hackle: Brown tied palmer style over the body.
Body: Fluorescent orange floss.
Wings: Four long narrow fluorescent fire orange hackle tips tied over the body.
Head: Fluorescent orange.

Originated in 1965 by Syd Glasso.

Plate 13 — Crane

Hooks: AC80500BL or AC80501BL, sizes 4-8.
Thread: Red.
Tip: Oval silver tinsel.
Butt: Dubbed with #4 red lambs wool.
Ribbing: Oval silver tinsel.
Body Hackle: Gray tied palmer style over the body.
Body: Medium blue floss.
Wings: Two grizzly hen hackle tips tied on edge over the body with concave side out.
Head: Dubbed with #4 red lambs wool.

This is a variation of the original which was featured in *A Book on Angling,* 1867, by Francis Francis.

Culdrain Fly
(From Kelson's book)

"Body - Black Berlin wool.
Rib - Bars of silver tinsel, rather far apart, and between each bar two threads of silk, one orange and one yellow.
Hackle - Jet black cock.
Wing - Grey mallard."

Plate 13 — Curtis Lee

Hooks: AC80500BL or AC80501BL, sizes 4-8.
Thread: Red.
Ribbing: Heavy red thread.
Body Hackle: Gray tied palmer style over the body.
Body: Orange floss.
Hackle: Barred mallard tied on as a collar and tied back.
Wing: Dyed orange gray squirrel tail tied low over the body.
Head: Red.

Originated by Mike Lee of South San Francisco, California, and named after his son.

Dallas Fly

(From Kelson's book)

"Body - Three turns of yellow Berlin wool, followed by black wool.

Ribs - Silver tinsel, gold tinsel (oval, narrow), red thread and blue thread, all running an equal distance apart.

Hackle - A black Spey-cock hackle, from end of body, but wound the reverse way so crossing over ribs.

Throat - A red hackle from the Golden Pheasant.

Wings - Two strips of cinnamon Turkey.

Head - Orange wool, picked out.

"(Special note: Like other local patterns, the body is short and begins a full 1/8 of an inch front of the point of the hook.)"

Dandy Touch

Hooks: AC80500BL or AC80501BL, sizes 4-8.
Thread: Black.
Ribbing: Flat gold tinsel.
Body Hackle: Olive tied palmer style over the body.
Body: Olive floss.
Hackle: Dyed olive barred mallard tied on as a collar and tied back.
Wing: Natural brown bucktail tied low over the body.
Head: Black.

Dark Daze

Hooks: AC80500BL or AC80501BL, sizes 1-4.
Thread: Black.
Ribbing: Flat silver tinsel overwrapped with a single strand of fluorescent green floss.
Body Hackle: Black tied palmer style over the body.
Body: Dubbed with #1 black Bunny-Blend.
Hackle: Highlander green hackle barbs tied in at the throat.
Wing: Dyed black pheasant flank tied low over the body.
Head: Black.

Another of the Mike Kinney patterns. See Boulder Creek.

Deep Purple Spey

Hooks: AC80500BL or AC80501BL, sizes 1-6.
Thread: Black.
Ribbing: Flat silver tinsel.
Body Hackle: Dark brown pheasant rump hackle tied palmer over the body from the second turn of ribbing.
Body: Dubbed with #58 fluorescent purple African Angora goat.
Hackle: Dyed purple pheasant rump tied on as a collar and tied back.
Wing: A pair of natural red golden pheasant body feathers tied low over the body and extending the length of the hook.
Head: Black.

Created by Syd Glasso and popularized by Walt Johnson of Arlington, Washington.

Plate 13 — Della

Hooks: AC80500BL or AC80501BL, sizes 4-8.
Thread: Claret.
Tail: Amherst pheasant crest tied short.
Ribbing: Oval silver tinsel.
Body Hackle: Black tied palmer style over the body.

Body: Dubbed with #32 claret lambs wool.
Hackle: Dyed black mallard flank tied on as a collar and tied back.
Wing: Pair grizzly hackle tips tied over the body cocked upward.
Head: Claret.

Originated by Dan Townsend.

Dragon's Tooth
Hooks: AC80500BL or AC80501BL, sizes 1-4.
Thread: Black.
Tip: Oval silver tinsel.
Ribbing: Flat silver tinsel bordered with a narrower oval silver tinsel.
Body: Dubbed with #30 purple Bunny-Blend.
Hackle: Barred teal tied on as a collar and tied back and down.
Body Hackle: Purple tied palmer style over the body.
Wings: Natural red golden pheasant body feathers tied over the body with overwings of natural yellow golden pheasant body feathers.
Head: Black.

Another of the Mike Kinney patterns. See Boulder Creek.

Dunt
Hooks: AC80500BL or AC80501BL, sizes 4-8.
Thread: Black.
Tip: Oval silver tinsel.
Tail: Golden pheasant crest with a small bunch of barred teal barbs tied on top and extending half way.
Ribbing: Flat silver tinsel overwrapped with a narrower oval silver tinsel.
Body Hackle: Black tied palmer style over front third of body.
Body: Rear third, dubbed with #6 yellow lambs wool, center third, dubbed with #9 orange lambs wool and the front third, dubbed with #32 claret lambs wool.
Hackle: Barred teal barbs tied in at the throat.
Wings: White tipped turkey tail feather sections tied low over the body.
Head: Black.

This is a variation of a Scottish pattern which was originated for the Dee. It is not uncommon to find this pattern tied with drooping jungle cock cheeks. It was originated by a Mr. Murdoch in the early 1800s.

Evening Break
Hooks: AC80500BL or AC80501BL, sizes 4-8.
Thread: Yellow.
Ribbing: Flat gold tinsel.
Body Hackle: Yellow tied palmer style over the body.
Body: Yellow floss.
Hackle: Dyed yellow guinea fowl tied on as a collar and tied back.
Wing: Fire orange bucktail tied over the body.
Head: Yellow.

Originated by Warren Becker.

Feather Wing Spey
Hooks: AC80500BL or AC80501BL, sizes 4-6.
Thread: Black.
Body: Rear half, embossed silver tinsel and the front half, dubbed with #32 claret African Angora goat.
Body Hackle: Black tied palmer style over the body.
Wings: Bronze mallard sections tied low over the body with outer sections of mottled brown turkey.
Head: Black.

This is a Joe Howell pattern.

Finishing Touch
Hooks: AC80500BL or AC80501BL, sizes 4-8.
Thread: Black.
Tip: Flat silver tinsel.
Ribbing: Flat silver tinsel.
Body Hackle: Brown tied palmer style over front half of body.
Body: Rear half, orange floss and the front half, peacock herl.
Hackle: Dyed orange barred mallard tied on as a collar and tied back.
Wing: Bronze mallard sections tied low over the body.

Head: Black.

Originated by Danna Lamb.

First Offering

Hooks: AC80500BL or AC80501BL, sizes 4-8.
Thread: Black.
Ribbing: Oval silver tinsel over front half of body.
Body Hackle: Black tied palmer style over front half of body.
Body: Rear half, flat silver tinsel and the front half, red floss.
Hackle: Dyed black pheasant rump tied on as a collar and tied back.
Wing: Pair black hackle tips tied over the body.
Head: Black.

Formal Offering

Hooks: AC80500BL or AC80501BL, sizes 4-8.
Thread: Black.
Ribbing: Oval silver tinsel over front half of body.
Body Hackle: Black tied palmer style over front half of body.
Body: Rear half, flat silver tinsel and the front half, black floss.
Hackle: Speckled guinea fowl tied on as a collar and tied back.
Wing: Pair white hackle tips tied over the body.
Head: Black.

The two preceding patterns were originated by Warren Becker.

Gambit

Hooks: AC80500BL or AC80501BL, sizes 4-8.
Thread: Black.
Tip: Oval gold tinsel.
Ribbing: Black floss.
Body Hackle: Brown tied palmer style over the body.
Body: Yellow floss.
Hackle: Dyed brown barred teal tied on as a collar and tied back.
Wing: Natural brown bucktail tied low over the body.
Head: Black.

This is a variation of a Scottish pattern.

Gardener

Hooks: AC80500BL or AC80501BL, sizes 4-8.
Thread: Black.
Tip: Oval gold tinsel.
Tail: Golden pheasant crest with a small bunch of golden pheasant tippet barbs tied over and extending half way.
Ribbing: Oval silver tinsel.
Body Hackle: Black tied palmer style over the front half of body.
Body: Rear half, dubbed with #57 fluorescent chartreuse lambs wool and the front half, dubbed with #36 blue charm lambs wool.
Wings: Cinnamon turkey sections tied low over the body.
Head: Black.

This is a Scottish pattern also developed for the Dee.

Plate 13 Gled Wing

Hooks: AC80500BL or AC80501BL, sizes 2-8.
Thread: Black.
Tip: Flat silver tinsel.
Tail: Natural red golden pheasant body feather barbs.
Ribbing: Flat silver tinsel.
Body Hackle: Black tied palmer style over front two-thirds of body.
Body: Rear third, dubbed with #52 fluorescent orange Bunny-Blend and the front two-thirds, dubbed with #30 purple African Angora goat.
Hackle: Barred teal tied on as a collar and tied back.
Wing: Natural brown bucktail tied sparse and low over the body.
Head: Black.

This is a hair wing variation of the original Scottish pattern. The original pattern had two strips of the swallow-tailed gled or red dun turkey for the wings.

Glen Grant

(From Kelson's book)

"Tail - Golden Pheasant yellow rump (point).

Body - Yellow wool, three turns, and black wool.

Ribs - Silver lace and silver tinsel (usual way).

Hackle - A black Spey-cock hackle from end of body, but wound from root the reverse way crossing over ribs.

Throat - Teal.

Wings - Two large Jungle Cock (back to back), two reaching halfway, two still shorter, and Teal.

Head - Yellow wool. (Special note: An old standard on the Spey)"

Glentana

Hooks: AC80500BL or AC80501BL, sizes 2-8.
Thread: Orange.
Tip: Oval silver tinsel.
Tail: Natural red golden pheasant body feather barbs.
Ribbing: Flat silver tinsel overwrapped with a narrower oval silver tinsel.
Body Hackle: Black tied palmer style over the front two-thirds of the body.
Body: Rear third, dubbed with #9 orange African Angora goat and the front two-thirds, dubbed with #32 claret African Angora goat.
Hackle: Barred mallard tied on as a collar and tied back and down.
Wing: Natural brown bucktail tied sparse and low over the body.
Head: Orange.

A variation of a Scottish pattern. Original wings were of cinnamon turkey strips.

Gold Deceiver

Hooks: AC80500BL or AC80501BL, sizes 1-6.
Thread: Yellow.
Ribbing: Flat silver tinsel which is overwrapped with a narrower oval silver tinsel.
Body Hackle: Salmon yellow tied palmer style over the body.
Body: Yellow ostrich herl.
Wing: Dyed gold natural brown bucktail tied low over the body.
Head: Yellow.

Gold Heron

Hooks: AC80500BL or AC80501BL, sizes 1-8.
Thread: Fluorescent orange.
Ribbing: Oval gold tinsel.
Body Hackle: Gray tied palmer style over the front third of body.
Body: Rear two-thirds, flat gold tinsel and front third, dubbed with #52 fluorescent orange African Angora goat.
Hackle: Barred teal tied on as a collar and tied back. Wrap one full turn only.
Wings: Bronze mallard sections tied low over the body.
Head: Fluorescent orange.

This pattern was created for winter-run fish by Syd Glasso of Forks, Washington.

Gold Reeach

Hooks: AC80500BL or AC80501BL, sizes 4-8.
Thread: Black.
Tip: Orange floss.
Ribbing: Flat gold tinsel overwrapped with a narrower oval gold tinsel.
Body Hackle: Ginger tied palmer style over the body.
Body: Dubbed with #1 black African Angora goat.
Hackle: Barred teal barbs tied in at the throat.
Wings: Bronze mallard sections tied low over the body.
Head: Black.

This pattern was first recorded in Knox's book, *Autumns on the Spey,* in 1872, however, there is evidence that there were earlier variations.

Gold Riach

Hooks: AC80500BL or AC80501BL, sizes 1-8.
Thread: Black.
Ribbing: Flat gold tinsel which is overwrapped with a narrower oval gold tinsel. The body is then reverse wrapped with fine silver wire.
Body Hackle: Reddish-brown tied palmer style over the body.
Body: Rear one-fourth, dubbed with #9 orange lambs wool and the front three-fourths, dubbed with #1 black lambs wool.
Wings: Bronze mallard sections tied low over the body.
Head: Black.

Gold Riach

(From Kelson's book)

"Body - Orange Berlin wool, three turns, followed by black wool.
Ribs - From different starting points, of gold tinsel (narrow), gold twist and silver twist, not wound as usual, but in the reverse way (towards head) and placed an equal distance apart.
Hackle - A red Spey-cock, from end of body, wound from the root of the feather instead of from the point of it, and crossing over the ribs the whole way.
Throat - Teal, two turns.
Wings - Two strips of Mallard with brown mottled points and grey mottled roots."

Golden Purple Spey

Hooks: AC80500BL or AC80501BL, sizes 4-8.
Thread: Black.
Tip: Lower half, flat gold tinsel and the upper half, fluorescent fire orange floss.
Ribbing: Oval gold tinsel.
Body: Dubbed with #30 purple Bunny-Blend.
Body Hackle: Reddish-brown golden pheasant body feather tied palmer style over the body.
Hackle: Guinea fowl tied on as a collar and tied back.

Wings: Reddish-brown golden pheasant body feather tips tied low over the body.
Head: Black.

This pattern was originated by Gary Alger.

Plate 13

Gray Heron

Hooks: AC80500BL or AC80501BL, sizes 1-8.
Thread: Black.
Ribbing: Flat silver tinsel which is overwapped with a narrower oval gold tinsel. Then reverse wrap with fine silver wire over the hackle.
Body Hackle: Black tied palmer style over the body.
Body: Rear third, dubbed with #6 yellow and the front two-thirds, #1 black lambs wool.
Hackle: Guinea fowl tied on as a collar and tied back and down.
Wings: Bronze mallard sections tied low over the body.
Head: Black.

This is a British variation of this pattern.

Green Butt Spey

Hooks: AC80500BL or AC80501BL, sizes 1-6.
Thread: Black.
Tip: Oval gold tinsel.
Butt: Fluorescent green floss wrapped over an underbody of flat silver tinsel.
Ribbing: Oval gold tinsel.
Body Hackle: Black tied palmer style over the dubbed portion of the body.
Body: Rear third, flat gold tinsel and the front two-thirds, dubbed thinly with #1 black Bunny-Blend.
Hackle: Dyed black pheasant rump tied on as a collar and tied back.
Wing: Sparse dyed black bucktail tied low over the body.
Topping: Small bunch of CH02 black Crystal Hair.
Head: Black.

This variation was originated in 1971 by C. S. Townsend of Fort Bragg, California, where he devotes all of his fishing hours to the Eel and Mad Rivers.

He states that this particular pattern is effective for him any time there are fish in and he simply adjusts the fly size to meet the water conditions.

Green King
(From Kelson's book)

"Body - A dull shade of green, composed of a mixture of light and dark green, brown, and a little yellow Berlin wools. Ribs - From separate starting points of gold tinsel (narrow), silver tinsel (narrow) and light olive-green sewing thread. These are all wound the reverse way an equal distance apart, but the sewing thread is left until the hackle is put on. The two metal ribs run under the hackle, the sewing thread is put over it, between the fibers.

Hackle - From end of body, a red Spey-cock hackle, but wound from the root instead of from the point, in the usual direction, thus crossing over the metal ribs.

Throat - Teal, two turns only.

Wings - Two strips of Mallard, having brown mottled points and grey mottled roots.

"(Note: The old standard Spey flies, like this one, are dressed upon long shanked hooks. The bodies start from a point as much before the direct line of the point of the hook as the work in ordinary standard flies starts behind it; that is equal to saying the bodies are comparatively very short. The wings are also very short, in fact, no longer than the bodies, if so long. In preparing the Spey-cock's hackle, do not remove all the fluffy fibers at the root, but leave about three on each side of the quill.)"

Green Queen
Hooks: AC80500BL or AC80501BL, sizes 4-8.
Thread: Black.
Tip: Oval gold tinsel.
Tail: Natural yellow golden pheasant body feather barbs.
Ribbing: Oval gold tinsel.
Body Hackle: Gray tied palmer style over the body.
Body: Dubbed with #15 insect green lambs wool.
Hackle: Dyed yellow guinea fowl barbs tied in at the throat.
Wings: Dark cinnamon turkey tail sections tied low over the body.
Head: Black.

Where there is a Green King there has to be a Green Queen. Kelson created this pattern and named it to fill this void. This variation of the Kelson pattern is slightly different in body only. Kelson's pattern had the same body as the King. This pattern is a good one for conversion to a hair wing design. I recommend natural brown bucktail that has been overdyed a few shades darker.

Grey Heron
Hooks: AC80500BL or AC80501BL, sizes 1-6.
Thread: Black.
Ribbing: Flat silver tinsel which is overwrapped with a narrower oval silver tinsel.
Body Hackle: Gray tied palmer style over the body.
Body: Rear third, yellow floss and the front two-thirds, black floss.
Hackle: Guinea fowl tied on as a collar and tied back and down.
Wings: Bronze mallard sections tied low over the body.
Head: Black.

Another of the Steve Gobin variations.

Gusto

Hooks: AC80500BL or AC80501BL, sizes 4-8.
Thread: Black
Tip: Flat silver tinsel.
Ribbing: Flat silver tinsel.
Body Hackle: Black tied palmer style over the body.
Body: Dubbed with #32 claret Bunny-Blend.
Hackle: Dyed claret barred mallard tied on as a collar and tied back.
Wing: Dyed black goose quill sections tied low over the body.
Head: Black.

Hairwing Spectrum Spey

Hooks: AC80500BL or AC80501BL, sizes 1-6.
Thread: Gray.
Tip: Flat silver tinsel.
Ribbing: Oval silver tinsel.
Body Hackle: Black tied palmer style over the claret and purple portions of the body.
Body: The body is a spectrum of color and divided in equal bands of dubbing fur starting from the rear as follows: **1.** yellow, **2.** orange, **3.** dark orange, **4.** scarlet red, **5.** crimson red, **6.** claret, and **7.** purple.
Wing: Fluorescent fire orange calf tail tied low over the body with an overwing of sparse purple calf tail.
Hackle: Purple with dyed purple teal tied in front. Hackle is tied long.
Head: Gray.

If you want to test your dexterity one evening and need some new steelhead flies, and all of us do, knock out a couple dozen of these. This pattern is the brainchild of John Shewey of Bend, Oregon.

High Tide

Hooks: AC80500BL or AC80501BL, sizes 1-6.
Thread: Fluorescent fire orange.
Tip: Flat gold tinsel.
Tail: Dyed orange golden pheasant crest.
Butt: Black ostrich herl.
Ribbing: Oval gold tinsel. Wrap over dubbed area only.
Body Hackle: Dyed orange pheasant rump wrapped palmer style over dubbed area.
Body: Make an additional six turns of flat gold tinsel proportioned same as tip. Dubbed with a blend of 50/50 mixed #50 fluorescent red and #52 fluorescent orange African Angora goat.
Hackle: Dyed orange barred teal tied in at throat.
Wings: Two dyed orange barred hen pheasant body plumes tied low and on edge over the body.
Cheeks: Dyed salmon yellow hen hackle tips.
Topping: Dyed orange golden pheasant crest.
Head: Fluorescent fire orange.

This pattern was created by Mark Waslick for use in British Columbia waters. More recently we have had good reports from the Rogue River. It did wonders after a good storm in the area. This pattern was given to me by three different sources. All three were slightly different, however, the one offered above is the pattern that I know is a producer.

Hot Peacock Spey

Hooks: AC80500BL or AC80501BL, sizes 1/0-4.
Thread: Black.
Tip: Oval silver tinsel.
Ribbing: Oval silver tinsel.
Body Hackle: Gray tied palmer style over front two-thirds of the body.
Body: Rear third, fluorescent red floss and the front two-thirds, peacock herl.
Hackle: Barred teal tied on as a collar and tied back.

Wing: Bronze mallard sections tied low over the body.
Head: Black.

Originated by Brad Burden.

Plate 13 ### Ian's Silver Spey
Hooks: AC80500BL or AC80501BL, sizes 2-6.
Thread: Black.
Ribbing: Oval gold tinsel with three turns at rear.
Body Hackle: Black tied palmer style over the body.
Body: Flat silver tinsel.
Hackle: Guinea fowl, one full turn, tied on as a collar and tied back.
Wings: Bronze mallard sections tied low over the body.
Head: Black.

This pattern was originated by Ian James of Guelph, Ontario. It was developed for the Great Lakes rivers in Ontario where they enjoy great fishing.

Imposter
Hooks: AC80500BL or AC80501BL, sizes 4-8.
Thread: Orange.
Tip: Flat gold tinsel.
Ribbing: Flat gold tinsel.
Body Hackle: Brown tied palmer style over the body.
Body: Brown floss.
Hackle: Dyed orange barred teal tied on as a collar and tied back.
Wing: Four dyed orange grizzly hackle tips tied over the body.
Head: Orange.

Originated by Mike Learner.

Plate 13 ### Jock "O" Dee
Hooks: AC80500BL or AC80501BL, sizes 1-6.
Thread: Black.
Tip: Lower half, oval silver tinsel and the upper half, orange floss.
Ribbing: Oval silver tinsel.
Body Hackle: Gray tied palmer style over the front two-thirds of the body.
Body: Rear third, yellow floss and the front two-thirds, dubbed with #1 black African Angora goat.

Hackle: Barred teal tied on as a collar and tied back.
Wing: Dyed yellow natural brown bucktail tied over the body.
Head: Black.

This pattern is a variation of a classic Scottish Dee style fly.

Kingfisher Blue Spey
Hooks: AC80500BL or AC80501BL, sizes 1-4.
Thread: White.
Ribbing: Flat silver tinsel.
Body Hackle: White hackle with a black tip tied palmer style over the body.
Body: Light blue floss.
Hackle: Light blue hen hackle tied on as a collar and tied back. Then barred silver pheasant is tied in at the throat.
Wings: Two white hen hackle tips. Then over this two light blue hen hackle tips. These hackle tips should be tied low over the body.
Topping: Dyed black Amherst pheasant crest.
Head: White.

When preparing the materials for this pattern select proper white hackle for the palmered area, using a waterproof black marker, color the tips of the hackle prior to wrapping. This is a Walt Johnson pattern. Walt has become a legend in Washington steelheading. When this pattern is tied correctly with the proper materials it is a beautiful piece of fly tying art.

Plate 13 ### Klamath Prancer
Hooks: AC80500BL or AC80501BL, sizes 4-8.
Thread: Black.
Ribbing: Copper wire.
Body Hackle: Orange tied palmer style over the body.
Body: Fluorescent orange floss.
Hackle: Dyed claret speckled guinea fowl tied on as a collar and tied back.
Wing: Dyed orange natural brown bucktail tied over the body.
Head: Black.

The Klamath Prancer was originated in 1960 by Herman Hellekson, my father. He often used this fly in the lower part of the Klamath and Trinity Rivers for salmon and steelhead.

Lady Caroline

Hooks: AC80500BL or AC80501BL, sizes 2-8.
Thread: Black.
Tail: Natural red golden pheasant breast barbs.
Ribbing: Flat gold tinsel overwrapped with oval silver tinsel. The body is then reverse wrapped with fine gold wire.
Body Hackle: Gray tied palmer style over the body.
Body: Dubbed with a blend of 1 part #19 olive lambs wool and 2 parts #24 brown lambs wool.
Hackle: Natural red golden pheasant tied on as a collar, two turns, and tied back.
Wings: Bronze mallard sections tied low over the body.
Head: Black.

This is one of the oldest Spey fly patterns known.

Lady Karen

Hooks: AC80500BL or AC80501BL, sizes 1-4.
Thread: Black.
Tip: Flat silver tinsel.
Tail: Scarlet red hackle barbs tied two-thirds the length of the body.
Ribbing: Oval silver tinsel.
Body Hackle: Black tied palmer style from the center of the body forward.
Body: Dubbed with #1 black African Angora goat.
Wing: Black marabou tied over the body.
Topping: CH02 black Crystal Hair.
Hackle: Barred teal tied on as a collar with one full turn and tied back.
Head: Black.

Named after Karen Gobin of Marysville, Washington. Originated in 1975 by Russ Miller of Arlington, Washington. This pattern is normally tied in larger sizes and used for winter-runs.

Plate 13 Linda

Hooks: AC80500BL or AC80501BL, sizes 4-8.
Thread: Orange.
Ribbing: Oval gold tinsel.
Body Hackle: Orange tied palmer style over the body.
Body: Embossed silver tinsel.
Hackle: Dyed tan barred mallard tied on as a collar and tied back.
Wing: Dyed orange natural brown bucktail tied over the body.
Head: Orange.

Named for one of my daughters.

Meager Offering

Hooks: AC80500BL or AC80501BL, sizes 4-8.
Thread: Black.
Tip: Flat silver tinsel.
Ribbing: Flat silver tinsel.
Body Hackle: Black tied palmer style over the body.
Body: Dubbed with #1 black Bunny-Blend.
Hackle: Barred teal barbs tied in at the throat.
Wing: Sparse black squirrel tail tied over the body.
Head: Black.
Note: This pattern is reduced by one-third.

Originated by Warren Becker.

Midnight Spey

Hooks: AC80500BL or AC80501BL, sizes 1-6.
Thread: Fluorescent fire orange.
Ribbing: Flat silver tinsel. Make three full turns behind the body before wrapping forward, thus creating a tip.
Body Hackle: Dyed purple pheasant flank tied palmer style from the second turn of ribbing.

Body: Rear half, purple floss and the front half, dubbed with #30 purple African Angora goat.

Hackle: Blue schlappen hackle tied on as a collar with two full turns and tied back and down.

Wing: Goose quill sections as follows: **1.** purple tied short, **2.** seven or eight barbs of purple, **3.** five barbs of blue, **4.** five barbs of green tied on top.

Head: Fluorescent fire orange.

This is a beautiful creation of Scott Noble.

Miss Grant
(From Kelson's book)

"Tag - Silver twist.
Tail - Teal, in strands.
Body - Two turns of orange silk followed by olive green Berlin wool.
Ribs - Silver tinsel.
Hackle - Grey Heron, from second turn.
Wings - Two strips from Golden Pheasant tail.
(Special note: A modern Spey pattern) (1895!)"

Plate 13 Morning Break

Hooks: AC80500BL or AC80501BL, sizes 4-8.

Thread: Orange.

Ribbing: Oval gold tinsel.

Butt: Yellow floss.

Body Hackle: Orange tied palmer style over the body.

Body: Dubbed with #9 orange lambs wool.

Hackle: Dyed orange guinea fowl tied on as a collar and tied back.

Wings: Pair of red hackle tips tied over the body.

Head: Orange.

Originated by Warren Becker.

Mrs. Grant
(From Kelson's book)

"Tag - Silver twist and yellow silk.
Tail - A topping and Indian Crow.
Butt - Black herl.
Body - Copper tinselled Chenille.

Hackle - A red Spey-cock hackle, from centre.
Throat - Jay.
Wings - Tippet strands, Bustard, Golden Pheasant tail, light mottled Turkey, grey Mallard, and a topping.
Horns - Red Macaw.
Head - Black herl.
(Special note: A modern standard on the Spey.)(1895!)"

Nola's Pink Spey

Hook: AC80500BL or AC80501BL, sizes 2-6.

Thread: Black.

Tip: Flat silver tinsel.

Body Hackle: Black tied palmer style over the body.

Body: Fluorescent pink chenille.

Hackle: Dyed black pheasant rump tied on as a collar and tied back.

Wings: Pink turkey quill sections tied low over the body.

Head: Black.

I received this pattern in a couple of variations. This is the one that looked most promising to me. Named after the originator's wife, Nola Krahe of Manistee, Michigan.

October Spey

Hooks: AC80500BL or AC80501BL, sizes 2/0-4.

Thread: Black.

Ribbing: Oval gold tinsel.

Body Hackle: Dyed dark gray pheasant rump tied palmer style over the body. Reverse wrap the body with fine gold wire after hackle is wrapped.

Body: Dubbed with #10 orange stone African Angora goat.

Hackle: Dyed orange barred teal tied in at the throat.

Wing: Bronze mallard sections tied low over the body.

Head: Black.

Originated by Randy Stetzer of Portland, Oregon.

Orange Blossom

Hooks: AC80500BL or AC80501BL, sizes 1-6.
Thread: Orange.
Tip: Lower half, oval silver tinsel and the upper half, yellow floss.
Tail: Golden pheasant crest.
Butt: Black ostrich herl.
Ribbing: Oval silver tinsel.
Body Hackle: Yellow tied palmer style over the body.
Body: Rear third, flat silver tinsel and the front two-thirds, dubbed with #51 fluorescent yellow African Angora goat.
Wing: Woodchuck guard hair tied over the body.
Cheeks: J.C. or substitute.
Hackle: Fluorescent orange tied on as a collar and tied back. This hackle should be tied long.
Head: Orange.

This pattern was created by Mike Brooks of Veneta, Oregon.

Orange Egret Spey

Hooks: AC80500BL or AC80501BL, sizes 1-4.
Thread: Red.
Tip: Flat silver tinsel.
Ribbing: Fine silver wire over the rear third and oval silver tinsel over the front two-thirds.
Body Hackle: One orange and one fluorescent fire orange wrapped palmer style over the dubbed portions of the body.
Body: Rear third, orange floss and the front two-thirds, dubbed with #52 fluorescent orange African Angora goat.
Wings: Two fluorescent red hackle tips tied low and on edge over the body.
Hackle: Fluorescent fire orange tied on as a collar and tied back.
Head: Red.

This is a beautiful orange creation that looks almost too good to get wet. Being suggestive of egg mass as most of the orange patterns are, it has done well in the Rogue River for winter-run fish. It is another brilliant idea of John Shewey from Bend, Oregon.

Orange Heaven

Hooks: AC80500BL or AC80501BL, sizes 1-6.
Thread: Fluorescent fire orange.
Ribbing: Flat silver tinsel which is overwrapped with a narrower oval silver tinsel.
Body Hackle: Gray tied palmer style from the second turn of ribbing.
Body: Rear two-thirds, orange floss and the front third, dubbed with #9 orange African Angora goat.
Hackle: Barred teal tied on as a collar and tied back.
Wings: Four fluorescent fire orange hackles tied low over the body.
Head: Fluorescent fire orange.

This is one of the more current Spey fly patterns to come about, it emerged in Scotland during the early part of this century.

Orange Heron

Hooks: AC80500BL or AC80501BL, sizes 1-6.
Thread: Red.
Tip: Flat silver tinsel.
Ribbing: Oval silver tinsel.
Body Hackle: Gray pheasant rump tied palmer style over the body.
Body: Rear half, fluorescent fire orange floss and the front half, dubbed with #53 fluorescent fire orange African Angora goat.
Hackle: Barred mallard tied on as a collar, one full turn, and tied back and down.
Wings: Four fluorescent fire orange hackle tips tied low and together over the body.
Head: Red.

This is a Syd Glasso version of this pattern.

Orange Shrimp Spey

Hooks: AC80500BL or AC80501BL, sizes 1-6.
Thread: Fluorescent orange.
Tip: Flat gold tinsel.
Butt: Red ostrich herl.

Body Hackle: Fluorescent orange tied palmer style over the body.
Body: Dubbed with #52 fluorescent orange African Angora goat.
Hackle: Fluorescent orange hen hackle tied on as a collar and tied back.
Wing: White bucktail tied sparse over the body.
Topping: CH06 orange Crystal Hair.
Head: Fluorescent orange.

I created this pattern in the fall of 1969 with the whimsical notion of "why not." From all I had learned at that point from Syd Glasso's patterns, it had to be a winner.

Orange Spey
Hooks: AC80500BL or AC80501BL, sizes 4-8.
Thread: Orange.
Tip: Oval silver tinsel.
Ribbing: Oval silver tinsel.
Body Hackle: Orange tied palmer style over the body.
Body: Dubbed with #52 fluorescent orange African Angora goat.
Wing: Dyed orange fox squirrel tail tied low over the body.
Head: Orange.

Paint Brush
Hooks: AC80500BL or AC80501BL, sizes 2-6.
Thread: Fluorescent red.
Body Hackle: Fluorescent fire orange tied palmer style over the body.
Body: Flat gold tinsel.
First Hackle: Purple tied on as a collar and tied back.
Second Hackle: Teal blue tied on as a collar and tied back. This hackle should be rather sparse as opposed to the first hackle.
Head: Fluorescent red.

Developed in 1973 by Bill McMillan and named after the wildflower, Indian Paint Brush.

Pheasant Spey
Hooks: AC80500BL or AC80501BL, sizes 1-6.
Thread: Black.
Body Hackle: Pheasant rump hackle tied palmer style over the dubbed portion of the body. This hackle should be selected using the gray with a greenish cast.
Body: Rear two-thirds, flat silver tinsel wrapped well down the bend of the hook. Front third, dubbed with #32 claret Bunnytron.
Hackle: Golden pheasant rump tied on as a collar and tied back and down.
Wings: Two natural red golden pheasant body feathers placed on top of each other and tied flat over the body.
Head: Black.

Originated by Cliff Baker of Bellevue, Washington. Although this pattern has gained attention as a winter pattern I suggest you also try it for summer-runs in the smaller sizes. Often reduced dressings make a big difference.

Pink Thrill
Hooks: AC80500BL or AC80501BL, sizes 4-8.
Thread: Fluorescent pink.
Ribbing: Oval silver tinsel.
Body Hackle: Hot pink tied palmer style over the body.
Body: Dubbed with #28 pink lambs wool.
Hackle: Barred mallard tied on as a collar and tied back.
Wing: Four white hackle tips tied over the body.
Head: Fluorescent pink.

Originated by Paul Lambert.

Polar Shrimp Spey
Hooks: AC80500BL or AC80501BL, sizes 1-6.
Thread: Red.
Tip: Oval silver tinsel.
Tail: Scarlet red hackle barbs.

Ribbing: Flat silver tinsel followed by narrower oval silver tinsel wrapped along the edged of the flat.
Body Hackle: Scarlet red tied palmer style over the dubbed portion of the body.
Body: Rear half, fluorescent orange floss and the front half, dubbed with #52 fluorescent orange Bunnytron.
Hackle: Fluorescent hot pink tied on as a collar and tied back and down.
Wing: White marabou tied sparse over the body.
Head: Red.

This is a Syd Glasso pattern. Just one of many patterns that he strengthened our arsenal of steelhead and salmon patterns with. This pattern can also be effectively tied with a sparse white bucktail wing.

Prawn Fly

Hooks: AC80500BL or AC80501BL, sizes 1-6.
Thread: Fluorescent pink.
Tip: Oval silver tinsel.
Ribbing: Oval silver tinsel.
Body Hackle: Dark gray pheasant rump tied palmer style over the front half of the body.
Body: Rear half, fluorescent pink floss and the front half, dubbed with #28 pink African Angora goat.
Hackle: Dyed fluorescent hot pink hen hackle tied on as a collar and tied back and slightly parted at the top.
Wing: Blue bucktail mixed with CH13 blue Crystal Hair tied sparsely over the body.
Head: Fluorescent pink.

This is one of my patterns which began evolving in Tacoma, Washington, in 1964. With initial guidance from Roy Patrick and a considerable amount of trial and error I have been able to develop a real *"working"* pattern.

Pretender

Hooks: AC80500BL or AC80501BL, sizes 4-8.
Thread: Fluorescent fire orange.
Tip: Oval gold tinsel.
Ribbing: Fluorescent orange floss.

Body Hackle: Orange tied palmer style over the body.
Body: White floss.
Hackle: Dyed light olive barred mallard tied on as a collar and tied back.
Wing: Four dyed orange grizzly hackle tips tied over the body.
Head: Fluorescent fire orange.

Originated by Emery Singleton of Eureka, California.

Prismatic Spey

Hooks: AC80500BL or AC80501BL, sizes 1-6.
Thread: Fluorescent fire orange.
Tip: Flat gold tinsel.
Ribbing: Flat gold tinsel.
Body Hackle: Dyed yellow schlappen tied palmer style over the body. One side of hackle is stripped of barbs prior to wrapping.
Body: Rear half, fluorescent orange floss and the front half, dubbed with a 50/50 mix of #4 red and #9 orange African Angora goat.
Wings: Goose quill sections from bottom to top, **1.** one fluorescent orange tied short (used as support), **2.** three barbs magenta, **3.** two barbs purple, **4.** two barbs green, **5.** two barbs blue, **6.** two barbs yellow, and **7.** two barbs orange. A single section of red is tied flat on top.
Head: Fluorescent fire orange.

This is a Scott Noble pattern. It is not as complicated as it appears. Once you get into it the process runs smoothly. Here is where it is important to have your materials well laid out in advance, then just sit back and enjoy.

Purple King

Hooks: AC80500BL or AC80501BL, sizes 1-8.
Thread: Black.
Ribbing: Flat gold tinsel with fine gold wire wrapped reversed.
Body Hackle: Black tied palmer style over the body.
Body: Dubbed with #30 purple African Angora goat.
Hackle: Barred teal barbs tied in at the throat.

Wings: Bronze mallard sections tied low over the body.
Head: Black.

This is the Scottish variation of this pattern and with only minor changes over these many years has remained well in tack.

Purple King

Hooks: AC80500BL or AC80501BL, sizes 1-6.
Thread: Black.
Ribbing: Oval silver tinsel. Make one full turn at the rear before wrapping forward.
Body Hackle: Black schlappen tied palmer style over the body at the leading edge of the ribbing. Reverse wrap the body with fine gold wire.
Body: Purple floss.
Hackle: Guinea fowl tied on as a collar and tied back and down.
Wings: Bronze mallard sections tied low over the body.
Head: Black.

Purple Marabou

Hooks: AC80500BL or AC80501BL, sizes 1-6.
Thread: Black.
Ribbing: Oval silver tinsel. Make one full turn at the rear before wrapping forward.
Body Hackle: Scarlet red schlappen tied palmer style over the body at the leading edge of the ribbing. Reverse wrap the body with fine gold wire.
Body: Dubbed with #30 purple African Angora goat.
Wing: Purple marabou tied over the body and tied long.
Hackle: Guinea fowl tied on as a collar, two full turns, and tied back.
Head: Black.

The preceding two patterns are creations of Steve Gobin.

Purple Phase Spey

Hooks: AC80500BL or AC80501BL, sizes 4-8.
Thread: Black.
Ribbing: Oval silver tinsel.
Body Hackle: Black tied palmer style over the body.

Body: Rear half, flat silver tinsel and the front half, purple floss.
Wing: Dyed purple monga ringtail tied low over the body.
Head: Black.

This pattern was originated by Joe Howell.

Purple Spey

Hooks: AC80500BL or AC80501BL, sizes 4-8.
Thread: Black.
Ribbing: Flat silver tinsel.
Body Hackle: Black tied palmer style over the body.
Body: Rear half, orange floss and the front half, dubbed with #30 purple African Angora goat.
Wings: Purple hackle tips tied low over the body.
Head: Black.

This is the original dressing for this pattern by Keith Mootry.

Purple Spey

Hooks: AC80500BL or AC80501BL, sizes 1-6.
Thread: Black.
Tip: Flat silver tinsel.
Ribbing: Oval silver tinsel.
Body Hackle: Dyed black pheasant rump tied palmer style over the body.
Body: Rear third, fluorescent orange floss and the front two-thirds, dubbed with #30 purple African Angora goat.
Hackle: Barred teal barbs tied in at the throat.
Wing: Dyed purple golden pheasant flank tied low over the body.
Topping: Two or three dyed purple golden pheasant crests.
Cheeks: J. C. or substitute.
Head: Black.

This is a variation originated by Dave McNeese of Salem, Oregon.

Quilceda

Hooks: AC80500BL or AC80501BL, sizes 1-6.
Thread: Claret.

Ribbing: Flat silver tinsel. When wrapping the ribbing, wrap one full turn at the rear prior to wrapping forward.
Body Hackle: Dyed crimson red pheasant rump.
Body: Rear fourth, dubbed with #13 gray and the front three-fourths, #22 amber stone African Angora goat.
Head: Claret.

This is a pattern designed by Karen Gobin of Marysville, Washington.

Quillayute

Hooks: AC80500BL or AC80501BL, sizes 1-6.
Thread: Black.
Tail: Scarlet red hackle barbs.
Ribbing: Flat silver tinsel.
Body Hackle: Barred teal tied palmer style from the second turn of ribbing.
Body: Rear half, orange floss and the front half, dubbed with #53 fluorescent fire orange African Angora goat.
Hackle: Dyed black pheasant rump tied on as a collar and tied back.
Wings: Two pairs of matched natural red golden pheasant body feathers tied low over the body.
Head: Black.

This pattern was originated for the Olympic Peninsula streams in Washington. This beautiful area had to be inspiration Dick Wentworth of Forks, who is credited with its creation.

Red Dog

Hooks: AC80500BL or AC80501BL, sizes 1-6.
Thread: Black.
Tip: Flat silver tinsel.
Ribbing: Flat silver tinsel.
Body Hackle: Brown pheasant rump tied palmer style over the body.
Body: Dubbed with #50 fluorescent red Bunnytron.
Hackle: Barred teal tied on as a collar and tied back and down.
Wings: Bronze mallard sections tied low over the body.
Head: Black.

Originated by Trey Combs.

Red King
(From Kelson's book)

"*Body - Red Berlin wool (brick colour). Ribs - Gold from far side, silver tinsel (narrow) from near side, wound the reverse way an equal distance apart. Hackle - A red Spey-cock hackle from end of body, but wound in the usual direction from the root instead of from the point, thus crossing over the ribs at each turn given.*
Throat - Teal, one turn only.
Wings - Two strips of Mallard, showing brown points and light roots.
(Special note: An old standard Spey fly)"

Red Phase Spey

Hooks: AC80500BL or AC80501BL, sizes 4-8.
Thread: Black.
Ribbing: Oval silver tinsel.
Body Hackle: Black tied palmer style over the body.
Body: Rear half, flat silver tinsel and the front half, red floss.
Wing: Dyed red monga ringtail tied low over the body.
Head: Black.

Originated by Joe Howell.

Red Shrimp

Hooks: AC80500BL or AC80501BL, sizes 1-8.
Thread: Red.
Ribbing: Flat silver tinsel. Before wrapping the ribbing wrap one full turn at the rear of the body.
Body Hackle: Gray pheasant rump tied palmer style over the body starting at the center.
Body: First wrap a finely tapered underbody with fluorescent orange floss. Then dub with #50 fluorescent red African Angora goat sparsely over the underbody. Your dubbing should be done in such a manner as to reveal at least forty percent of the underbody.

Hackle: Fluorescent red hen hackle tied on as a collar and tied back.
Wings: Fluorescent red hen hackle tips tied over the body.
Topping: Golden pheasant crest.
Head: Red.

Originated in the 1950s by Walt Johnson. It resembles roe more than many shrimp patterns and has been so successful that a number of other flies have been patterned after it.

Rose Petal

Hooks: AC80500BL or AC80501BL, sizes 1-6.
Thread: Black.
Tip: Flat silver tinsel.
Butt: Fluorescent pink floss ribbed with fine flat silver tinsel.
Tail: Dyed claret golden pheasant tippet barbs.
Ribbing: Flat silver tinsel.
Body Hackle: Claret tied palmer style over the body.
Body: Dubbed with #32 claret Bunnytron.
Wing: Sparse white bucktail tied over the body.
Hackle: Guinea fowl tied on as a collar one full turn and tied back.
Head: Black.

This is a beautiful creation of Steve Gobin of Marysville, Washington.

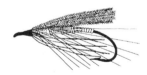

Royal Spey

Hooks: AC80500BL or AC80501BL, sizes 4-8.
Thread: Black
Tip: Oval silver tinsel.
Ribbing: Oval silver tinsel.
Body Hackle: Brown tied palmer style over the body from second rib.
Body: Red floss.
Hackle: Dyed brown pheasant rump tied on as a collar and tied back.

Wing: Strands of peacock herl tied over the body.
Head: Black.

This is one of the many variations of this pattern. Another has a peacock herl butt.

Rough Grouse
(From Kelson's book)

"Tail - A few fibers of yellow Macaw's hackle.
Body - Black Berlin wool (short).
Ribs - Silver tinsel.
Hackle - Grey heron from the third turn.
Throat - Black and white speckled Turkey.
Wings - Black and white speckled Turkey (strips).
(Special note: A splendid fly on the Spey in dull wet weather.)"

R.V.I.

Hooks: AC80500BL or AC80501BL, sizes 1-8.
Thread: Fluorescent red.
Tip: Flat silver tinsel.
Tail: Golden pheasant crest.
Ribbing: Oval silver tinsel.
Body Hackle: Barred teal tied palmer style over the dubbed portion of the body.
Body: Rear third, flat silver tinsel and front two-thirds, dubbed with #52 fluorescent orange African Angora goat.
Wings: Two pair of natural red golden pheasant body feathers placed together and tied low over the body.
Head: Fluorescent red.

Robert Van Iderstine of Springfield, Oregon, originated this pattern and created the name after his initials.

Santiam Spectrum

Hooks: AC80500BL or AC80501BL, sizes 1-6.
Thread: Gray.
Tip: Flat silver tinsel.
Ribbing: Oval gold tinsel. After the Spey hackle has been wrapped, then a second

ribbing of fine gold wire is reverse wrapped over the body.

Body Hackle: Purple tied palmer style over the dubbed portion of the body.

Body: Rear half, fluorescent red floss and front half, dubbed with #30 purple Bunnytron.

Hackle: Barred teal tied on as a collar with one full turn and tied back.

First Wing: A single strand of fluorescent red, orange and pink floss.

Overwings: Sections of bronze mallard tied low over the body.

Head: Gray.

This is yet another pattern from the prolific John Shewey.

Schmidt's Woolly Spey

Hooks: AC80500BL or AC80501BL, sizes 1-6.

Thread: Black.

Butt: Fluorescent red yarn.

Body Hackle: Black tied palmer style over the body.

Body: CH02 black Crystal Chenille.

Hackle: Dyed black pheasant rump tied on as a collar and tied back.

Head: Black.

As with all successful flies there are a number of variations on this pattern. It was created by Ray Schmidt of Wellston, Michigan.

Silver Hare

Hooks: AC80500BL or AC80501BL, sizes 4-8.

Thread: Black.

Tip: Oval silver tinsel.

Ribbing: Oval silver tinsel.

Body Hackle: Brown tied palmer style over dubbed portion of body.

Body: Rear third, flat silver tinsel and the front two-thirds, dubbed with hare's mask fur.

Hackle: Dyed brown barred mallard tied on as a collar and tied back.

Wings: Mottled brown turkey quill sections tied low over the body.

Head: Black.

Silver Hare, Olive

Hooks: AC80500BL or AC80501BL, sizes 4-8.

Thread: Black.

Tip: Oval silver tinsel.

Ribbing: Oval silver tinsel.

Body Hackle: Brown tied palmer style over dubbed portion of body.

Body: Rear third, flat silver tinsel and the front two-thirds, dubbed with dyed olive hare's mask fur.

Hackle: Dyed olive barred mallard tied on as a collar and tied back.

Wings: Mottled brown turkey quill sections tied low over the body.

Head: Black.

The two preceding flies were originated in 1952 by Herman Hellekson, my father.

Silver Heron

Hooks: AC80500BL or AC80501BL, sizes 1-6.

Thread: Black.

Ribbing: Oval silver tinsel over dubbed portion of body.

Body Hackle: Gray pheasant rump tied palmer style over dubbed portion of body.

Body: Rear two-thirds, flat silver tinsel and the front third, dubbed with #1 black African Angora goat.

Hackle: Guinea fowl barbs tied in at the throat.

Wing: Gray pheasant rump barbs tied short over the body.

Head: Black.

Silver Streak Spey

Hooks: AC80500BL or AC80501BL, sizes 2-8.

Thread: Black.

Ribbing: Oval silver tinsel.

Body Hackle: Gray tied palmer style over the body.

Body: Flat silver tinsel.

Hackle: Dyed light blue guinea fowl barbs tied in at the throat.

Wings: Bronze mallard sections tied low over the body.

Head: Black.

This is a Joe Howell creation.

Skagit Spey, Black

Hooks: AC80500BL or AC80501BL, sizes 1-4.
Thread: Black.
Tip: Flat gold tinsel.
Butt: Divided in two parts with first flat gold tinsel then orange floss.
Trailer: Orange calf tail tied on top.
Ribbing: Oval silver tinsel over front portion of body.
Body Hackle: Black marabou tied palmer style over the front portion of body.
Body: Dubbed with #1 black African Angora goat.
Hackle: Guinea tied on as a collar and tied back and down.
Wings: Bronze mallard sections tied low over the body.
Cheeks: J.C. or substitute.
Head: Black.

Skagit Spey, Orange

Hooks: AC80500BL or AC80501BL, sizes 1-4.
Thread: Black.
Tip: Flat gold tinsel.
Butt: Divided in two parts with first flat gold tinsel then orange floss.
Trailer: Orange calf tail tied on top.
Ribbing: Oval gold tinsel over front portion of body.
Body Hackle: Orange marabou tied palmer style over the front portion of the body.
Body: Dubbed with #53 fluorescent fire orange Bunnytron.
Hackle: Red marabou tied on as a collar with one full turn and tied back. A small bunch of barred teal barbs is tied in at the throat.
Wings: Bronze mallard sections tied low over the body.
Cheeks: J.C. or substitute.
Head: Black.

Skagit Spey, White

Hooks: AC80500BL or AC80501BL, sizes 1-4.
Thread: Black.
Tip: Flat gold tinsel.
Butt: Red floss.
Trailer: White calf tail tied on top.

Ribbing: Oval gold tinsel over front portion of body.
Body Hackle: Gray marabou tied palmer style over the front portion of the body.
Body: Sparsely dubbed with #13 gray Bunnytron over an underbody of flat gold tinsel.
Hackle: Barred mallard tied on as a collar and tied back and down.
Wings: Bronze mallard sections tied low over the body.
Cheeks: J.C. or substitute.
Head: Black.

Skagit Spey, Yellow

Hooks: AC80500BL or AC80501BL, sizes 1-4.
Thread: Black.
Tip: Flat gold tinsel.
Butt: Fluorescent fire orange floss.
Trailer: White calf tail tied on top.
Body Hackle: White marabou tied palmer style over the front portion of the body.
Body: Dubbed with #51 fluorescent yellow African Angora goat.
Hackle: Yellow marabou tied on as a collar with one full turn and tied back. Barred mallard and magenta hackle barbs are then tied in at the throat.
Wings: Bronze mallard sections tied low over the body.
Cheeks: J.C. or substitute.
Head: Black.

The Skagit Spey series was originated by John Farrar.

Skunk, Green Butt Spey

Hooks: AC80500BL or AC80501BL, sizes 1-6.
Thread: Black.
Tip: Flat silver tinsel. Now this may get complicated. After wrapping the tip, do not cut it off. Wrap down over the tip three quarters of the way with fluorescent green floss, wrapping your uncut end of tinsel with you. After returning your floss to the beginning and tying it off, wrap the free end of the tinsel over the floss creating three turns of ribbing. See, that was easy.
Tail: Scarlet red hackle barbs.
Ribbing: Oval silver tinsel.

Body Hackle: Black tied palmer style over the dubbing.
Body: Dubbed with #1 black African Angora goat.
Wing: White bucktail tied sparse over the body.
Hackle: Guinea fowl tied on as a collar and tied back.
Head: Black.

Steve Gobin of Marysville, Washington, certainly kissed the toad and turned it into a beautiful princess when he created this variation. Steve's skills will long be remembered in fly tying history.

Plate 13 — Skykomish Purple

Hooks: AC80500BL or AC80501BL, sizes 1-6.
Thread: Claret.
Ribbing: Oval gold tinsel.
Body Hackle: Purple tied palmer style over the dubbed portion of the body.
Body: Rear half, purple floss and the front half, dubbed with #30 purple Bunny-Blend.
Hackle: Dyed purple guinea fowl tied on as a collar and tied back.
Wings: Two natural red tips from a golden pheasant body feather tied flat over the body.
Head: Claret.

Originated by Michael Malloy of Everett, Washington.

Sol Duc

Hooks: AC80500BL or AC80501BL, sizes 1-6.
Thread: Black.
Tip: Flat silver tinsel.
Tail: Golden pheasant crest.
Ribbing: Flat silver tinsel.
Body Hackle: Yellow tied palmer style from the center of the body forward.
Body: Rear half, fluorescent orange floss and the front half, dubbed with #52 fluorescent orange African Angora goat.
Hackle: Barred teal tied on as a collar with one full turn and tied back.
Wings: Four fluorescent fire orange hackle tips tied over the body.
Topping: Golden pheasant crest.

Head: Black.

Sol Duc Dark

Hooks: AC80500BL or AC80501BL, sizes 1-6.
Thread: Black.
Tip: Oval silver tinsel.
Tail: Natural red golden pheasant body feather barbs.
Ribbing: Flat silver tinsel overwapped with a narrower oval silver tinsel.
Body Hackle: Yellow tied palmer style from the center of the body forward.
Body: Rear half, fluorescent orange floss and the front half, dubbed with #53 fire orange African Angora goat.
Hackle: Barred teal tied on as a collar with one full turn and tied back.
Wings: Four natural red golden pheasant body feathers tied over the body.
Head: Black.

Sol Duc Spey

Hooks: AC80500BL or AC80501BL, sizes 1-6.
Thread: Fluorescent red.
Ribbing: Flat silver tinsel.
Body Hackle: Salmon yellow tied palmer style over the dubbed portion of the body.
Body: Rear half, fluorescent orange floss and the front half, dubbed with #52 fluorescent orange African Angora goat.
Hackle: Dyed black pheasant rump tied on as a collar and tied back and down. Hackle should be equal in length to the palmered hackle.
Wings: Four fluorescent fire orange hackle tips tied over the body.
Head: Fluorescent red.

The three preceding patterns are creations of Syd Glasso. Also see his other Heron patterns in this chapter.

Spawning Purple Spey

Hooks: AC80500BL or AC80501BL, sizes 1-6.
Thread: Claret.
Tip: Flat silver tinsel.
Body: Fluorescent red floss tied over an underbody of flat silver tinsel.
Trailers: Five individual bunches of purple marabou barbs tied in at equal intervals,

starting from the center of the body to just behind the head.

Hackle: Purple tied on as a collar and tied back. This hackle should be tied long and extend back to the point of the hook.

Front Hackle: Barred teal wrapped on as a collar and tied back. Hackle length should equal the first.

Wings: Narrow sections of mottled brown turkey tied low over the body.

Cheeks: J.C. or substitute.

Head: Claret.

This pattern was developed in 1986 by John Shewey of Bend, Oregon. Looks both different and promising. As you can see this fly is a Spey in name only.

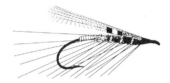

Spey Day

Hooks: AC80500BL or AC80501BL, sizes 1-6.

Thread: Black.

Tip: Oval gold tinsel.

Ribbing: Oval gold tinsel.

Body Hackle: Dark gray tied palmer style over the body. Wrap each turn of hackle alongside the ribbing.

Body: Dubbed in three equal parts starting at the rear with #9 orange, center with #53 fire orange, and at the front with #4 red Bunny-Blend.

Wing: Salmon yellow bucktail tied low over the body.

Cheeks: Black and white barred lemon woodduck sections.

Head: Black.

This pattern was originated by Scott Byner for summer-run fish in Alaska. After looking at it for a little while I am sure you will agree that it has potential elsewhere also.

Plate 13 — Spawning Silver

Hooks: AC80500BL or AC80501BL, sizes 1-6.

Thread: Black.

Tip: Flat silver tinsel.

Tail: Natural yellow golden pheasant plumage barbs.

Body Hackle: Gray tied palmer style over the body.

Body: Silver diamond braid.

Wings: White skunk tail tied over the body.

Topping: CH30 silver Crystal Hair.

Head: Black.

Spawning Spey

Hooks: AC80500BL or AC80501BL, sizes 1-6.

Thread: Black.

Tip: Flat silver tinsel.

Ribbing: Oval silver tinsel.

Body Hackle: Fluorescent fire orange tied palmer style from the second turn of ribbing.

Body: Rear third, fluorescent orange floss and then fluorescent red floss divided equally and the front two-thirds, dubbed with #52 fluorescent orange African Angora goat.

Hackle: Dyed purple barred teal tied on as a collar with one full turn and tied back.

Wings: Four purple hackle tips tied low and on edge over the body.

Topping: Two dyed purple golden pheasant crests.

Cheeks: J.C. or substitute.

Head: Black.

Created by Dave McNeese.

Plate 13 — Special Delivery

Hooks: AC80500BL or AC80501BL, sizes 4-8.

Thread: Black.

Tip: Flat gold tinsel.

Ribbing: Flat gold tinsel over front half of body.

Body Hackle: Black tied palmer style over the body.

Body: Rear half, fluorescent green floss and the front half, peacock herl.

Hackle: Guinea fowl tied on as a collar and tied back.

Wing: Four black hackle tips tied over the body.
Head: Black.

Originated by Ronnie Wilson of Alhambra, California.

Spring Spey

Hooks: AC80500BL or AC80501BL, sizes 1-6.
Thread: Olive.
Tail: Golden pheasant crest.
Ribbing: Oval gold tinsel.
Body Hackle: Gray pheasant rump tied palmer style over the body.
Body: Dubbed with #57 fluorescent chartreuse African Angora goat.
Hackle: Dyed fluorescent green barred mallard tied on as a collar and tied back and down.
Wings: Bronze mallard sections tied low over the body.
Head: Olive.

Originated by Randy Stetzer of Portland, Oregon.

Stratman Fancy

Hooks: AC80500BL or AC80501BL, sizes 1-6.
Thread: Black.
Tip: Flat silver tinsel.
Tail: Dyed purple golden pheasant tippet barbs.
Ribbing: Oval silver tinsel.
Body Hackle: Dyed fluorescent fire orange barred teal tied palmer style starting from the center of the body.
Body: Wrap a thin layer of purple floss over an underbody of flat silver Mylar tinsel. After ribbing is completed apply a coat of FLI-BOND cement to achieve a translucent effect.
Hackle: Dyed purple barred teal barbs tied in at the throat.
Wing: Four or five strands each of CH05 orange and CH19 purple Crystal Hair with an overwing of purple calf tail.
Head: Black.

A Dave McNeese pattern named in honor of his friend Roger Stratman.

Streak, Gold

Hooks: AC80500BL or AC80501BL, sizes 1-6.
Thread: Black.
Tip: Flat gold tinsel.
Ribbing: Oval gold tinsel.
Body Hackle: Dyed gray tied palmer style over the body.
Body: Rear half, orange floss and the front half, dubbed with #52 fluorescent orange Bunnytron.
Hackle: Dyed orange guinea fowl tied on as a collar and tied back.
Wings: Bronze mallard sections tied low over the body.
Head: Black.

Streak, Silver

Hooks: AC80500BL or AC80501BL, sizes 1-6.
Thread: Black.
Tip: Flat silver tinsel.
Ribbing: Oval gold tinsel.
Body Hackle: Dyed gray tied palmer style over the body.
Body: Flat silver tinsel.
Hackle: Dyed blue guinea fowl tied on as a collar and tied back.
Wings: Bronze mallard sections tied low over the body.
Head: Black.

Both the Gold and Silver Streak patterns are creations of Joe Howell.

Summer Spey

Hooks: AC80500BL or AC80501BL, sizes 1-6.
Thread: Black.
Tip: Oval gold tinsel.
Ribbing: Flat silver tinsel overwrapped with a narrower oval gold tinsel.
Body Hackle: Dyed gray tied palmer style over the body.
Body: Dubbed with #32 claret African Angora goat.
Hackle: Dyed claret guinea fowl tied on as a collar and tied back and down.
Wings: Bronze mallard sections tied low over the body.
Head: Black.

The Summer Spey was originated by John Hazel.

Sunday Spey
Hooks: AC80500BL or AC80501BL, sizes 4-8.
Thread: Black.
Tip: Oval silver tinsel.
Tail: Golden pheasant tippet barbs.
Ribbing: Oval silver tinsel.
Body Hackle: Brown tied palmer style over the body.
Body: Rear half, fluorescent yellow floss and the front half, dubbed with #21 golden olive African Angora goat.
Hackle: Peacock sword feather barbs tied in at the throat.
Wing: Mottled brown turkey quill sections tied low over the body.
Head: Black.

Plate 13 ## Super Spey
Hooks: AC80500BL or AC80501BL, sizes 4-8.
Thread: Black.
Tip: Flat silver tinsel.
Ribbing: Flat silver tinsel.
Body Hackle: Gray tied palmer style over the body.
Body: Hot pink floss.
Hackle: Dyed black pheasant rump tied on as a collar and tied back.
Wing: Dyed black squirrel tail tied low over the body.
Head: Black.

Originated by Danna Lamb.
Surestrike Coachman Spey
Hooks: AC80500BL or AC80501BL, sizes 1-8.
Thread: Black.
Tip: Oval gold tinsel.
Ribbing: Oval gold tinsel.
Body Hackle: Brown tied palmer style over the body.
Body: Peacock herl.

Trailers: Single strand of red floss tied in at the center of the body and extending along each side.
Hackle: Dyed dark brown pheasant rump tied on as a collar with one full turn and tied back.
Wing: Dyed dark brown bucktail tied low over the body.
Head: Black.

Years ago I started playing with an idea I got while in southern Oregon. The pattern I started from was one used in the lakes in that area. Later I started tying it in larger sizes for steelhead and today it has evolved into what you see here. This is an especially good pattern for all seasons.

Sweeter Orange
Hooks: AC80500BL or AC80501BL, sizes 4-8.
Thread: Red.
Tip: Oval silver tinsel.
Ribbing: Oval silver tinsel.
Body Hackle: Orange tied palmer style from the second rib.
Body: Fine fluorescent fire orange chenille.
Hackle: Dyed orange guinea fowl tied on as a collar and tied back.
Wing: Natural brown bucktail tied low over the body.
Head: Red.

Terry's Tiger
Hooks: AC80500BL or AC80501BL, sizes 1-6.
Thread: Black.
Tip: Oval gold tinsel.
Ribbing: Oval gold tinsel. Ribbing is applied to the rear half of the body only.
Body Hackle: Dyed black pheasant rump tied palmer style over the chenille.
First Wing: Sparse strands of CH07 fire orange Crystal Hair tied in at the center of the body and extending to the end of the hook.
Body: Rear half, burnt orange floss and the front half, fine black chenille.
Second Wing: Dyed orange gray squirrel tail tied low over the body.

Hackle: Dyed black pheasant rump tied on as a collar and tied back.
Head: Black.

This is a winter pattern that I have been developing since 1986. These colors work extremely well for me and others who have used them.

Tri•Colour

Hooks: AC80500BL or AC80501BL, sizes 2-6.
Thread: Black.
Tip: Oval silver tinsel.
Tail: Natural red golden pheasant breast barbs.
Ribbing: Flat silver tinsel overwrapped with a narrower oval silver tinsel.
Body Hackle: Gray tied palmer style over the front two-thirds of the body.
Body: Rear third, dubbed with #6 yellow African Angora goat, center third, dubbed with #34 silver doctor blue African Angora goat and the front third, dubbed with #4 red African Angora goat.
Wings: Natural brown bucktail tied sparse and low over the body.

This is a variation of an old Scottish pattern from the Dee. It probably was one of the more colorful ones of its time.

Trinity Beauty Spey

Hooks: AC80500BL or AC80501BL, sizes 1-6.
Thread: Black.
Body: Rear half, silver diamond braid and the front half, dubbed with #30 purple Bunnytron. The diamond braid should be extended down to also form a tip.
Body Hackle: Black tied palmer style over the front half of the body.
Wing: Gray squirrel tied sparse over the body.
Head: Black.

This Spey pattern was created and used in northern California by Bryant Cummings in 1981. Since then he has moved to New York where he reports it has done well for Atlantic salmon these past three years. We know it is still doing well here.

Trinity Prancer

Hooks: AC80500BL or AC80501BL, sizes 4-8.
Thread: Black.
Tip: Flat silver tinsel.
Ribbing: Flat silver tinsel
Body Hackle: Gray tied palmer style over the body.
Body: Rear half, yellow floss and the front half, light green floss.
Hackle: Barred mallard tied on as a collar and tied back.
Wing: Dark brown mottled turkey tail feather sections tied low over the body.
Head: Black.

Originated in 1963 by Herman Hellekson.

Plate 13 Trinity Teal

Hooks: AC80500BL or AC80501BL, sizes 4-8.
Thread: Black.
Tail: Barred teal barbs tied short.
Ribbing: Oval silver tinsel.
Body Hackle: Black tied palmer style over the body.
Body: Silver gray floss.
Hackle: Natural red golden pheasant plumage tied on as a collar and tied back.
Wing: Barred teal sections tied low over the body and extending to end of tail.
Head: Black.

Trinity Teal, Orange

Hooks: AC80500BL or AC80501BL, sizes 4-8.
Thread: Black.
Tail: Dyed orange barred teal barbs tied short.
Ribbing: Oval gold tinsel.
Body Hackle: Dyed black pheasant rump tied palmer style over the body from the second rib.
Body: Orange floss.
Hackle: Natural red golden pheasant plumage tied on as a collar and tied back.
Wing: Dyed orange barred teal sections tied low over the body and extending to end of tail.

Head: Black.

The two preceding patterns were originated by Bill Lane.

Turkey Jackson

Hooks: AC80500BL or AC80501BL, sizes 2-8.
Thread: Black.
Tip: Flat silver tinsel.
Ribbing: Flat silver tinsel.
Body Hackle: Black tied palmer style over the body.
Body: Dubbed with #1 black African Angora goat.
Hackle: Guinea fowl tied on as a collar and tied back.
Wing: Natural brown bucktail tied low and sparse over the body.
Head: Black.

This is a variation of a classic Atlantic salmon fly pattern.

Turkey Tracker

Hooks: AC80500BL or AC80501BL, sizes 1-8.
Thread: Black.
Ribbing: Embossed gold tinsel.
Body: Dubbed with #1 black Bunny-Blend.
Body Hackle: Brown marabou tied palmer over front third of body.
Wings: Dyed green highlander hackle tips tied low over the body.
Hackle: Purple hen hackle and barred teal tied on, with one full turn each, as a collar and tied back.
Head: Black.

Another of the Mike Kinney patterns. See Boulder Creek.

Winter Spey

Hooks: AC80500BL or AC80501BL, sizes 1-6.
Thread: Black.
Tip: Oval silver tinsel.
Body: Dubbed with #35 kingfisher blue African Angora goat.
Body Hackle: Kingfisher blue tied palmer style over the body.
Hackle: Gray pheasant rump tied on as a collar and tied back and down, followed by long kingfisher blue hackle barbs tied in at the throat.

Wings: Bronze mallard sections tied low over the body.
Head: Black.

The Winter Spey was originated by John Hazel.

Wintergreen Spey

Hooks: AC80500BL or AC80501BL, sizes 1-6.
Thread: Light olive.
Tip: Oval silver tinsel.
Tail: Dyed orange golden pheasant crest.
Ribbing: Oval silver tinsel tied over front body.
Body Hackle: Dyed yellow pheasant rump tied palmer style over the front half of the body.
Body: Rear half, flat silver tinsel and front half, dubbed with a 50/50 blend of #18 light olive and #6 yellow Bunny-Blend.
Hackle: Sparse dyed insect green pheasant rump tied on as a collar and tied back and down.
Wings: Narrow sections of dyed insect green turkey quill tied low over the body.
Cheeks: J.C. or substitute tied parallel to the body.
Head: Light olive.

This design is by Greg Scot Hunt of Redmond, Washington. I find that most often I have to bleach the hackle for this fly and then dye it the desired color.

Plate 13 Wanda

Hooks: AC80500BL or AC80501BL, sizes 4-8.
Thread: Black.
Tip: Oval silver tinsel.
Tail: Golden pheasant crest tied short.
Ribbing: Oval silver tinsel.
Body Hackle: Orange tied over front half of body.
Body: Rear half, flat silver tinsel and the front half, red floss.
Hackle: Dyed orange barred mallard flank tied on as a collar and tied back.
Wing: White skunk tail tied over the body.
Head: Black.

This pattern was named after one of my daughters. She illustrated this book.

Plate 13 ## Yarrow's Purple

Hooks: AC80500BL or AC80501BL, sizes 2-8.
Thread: Black.
Tip: Oval silver tinsel.
Ribbing: Oval silver tinsel.
Butt: Dubbed with #4 red lambs wool.
Body Hackle: Purple tied palmer style over the body.
Body: Dubbed with #30 purple African Angora goat.
Hackle: Dyed purple barred mallard tied on as a collar and tied back.
Wing: Gray squirrel tail tied over the body.
Head: Black.

Created by Stan Hellekson in 1990 for winter fishing in the Rogue River and named after Jim Yarrow.

Yuletide

Hooks: AC80500BL or AC80501BL, sizes 1-6.
Thread: Fluorescent orange.
Tip: Flat gold tinsel.
Ribbing: Oval gold tinsel. Entire body is ribbed, including butt.
Butt: Dubbed with #54 fluorescent hot pink Bunny-Blend. This section should be rather wide and consist of twenty percent of the body.
Body Hackle: Fluorescent hot pink tied palmer style over the body, including the butt.
Body: Dubbed with #15 insect green Bunny-Blend.
Hackle: Barred teal tied on as a collar and tied back.
Wings: Narrow sections of dyed insect green turkey quill tied low over the body.
Head: Fluorescent orange.

Created in 1984 by Michael Malloy of Everett, Washington.

Chapter 23

Pacific Salmon Flies

Having fished for salmon on both coasts I find they offer sheer sport on a fly rod regardless of where they are caught. Even the smaller cherry salmon of northern Japan are a formidable fish. Unfortunately our confused society has permitted the Atlantic salmon to steal much of the limelight and has it perceived as "the game fish of the century" and all others as food fish. How misinformed some of us are. Coupled with this, the steelhead steals even more than its share of glory. I will be the first to admit that there may be a very thin line when one speaks of fly fishing for Pacific salmon and steelheading, the two terms are synonymous with some folks.

Thinking of Pacific salmon as a food fish is greatly oversimplified for such a complex issue when they have proven themselves to be such a marvelous game fish. It is not about eating or not eating, we would all eat them if we were hungry enough. It is a question of respecting them for what they truly are. They are so removed from our environment that they are a mystery to us. They go mostly unseen in their watery world and even when we do see them, our view is often clouded by the quality of the water and the glare on the surface. We embrace an instinctive need that pulls us closer to their domain. It is through our fishing that we make contact with these mysterious creatures of the deep. The tying of flies to deceive, then partially entering their alien world when our trickery succeeds. For a moment we find ourselves gracefully dancing to and fro, a dance that is often intertwined between water and air, and again, a dive to the very depths of a clouded haven. After the fight is over, we are able to hold perfection in our hands, not too long lest we waste the life of a "gallant warrior."

Our Pacific salmon are found from Tomales Bay in California to the Bering Sea in Alaska. We try for them in the saltwater, tidal estuaries and in freshwater. The Chinook, silver, chum, pink and sockeye are the five species of salmon available to the angler. From this group of five we have selectively chosen the Chinook and silver as the top-of-the-line game fish.

The Chinook salmon, also known as the spring, king, or tyee, depending on where you are fishing, is the largest. At times they will grab at your fly without ceremony. At other times they lash at it first with their broad tail in a natural crippling maneuver—thinking it is a true baitfish. Normally, you will feel a faint tap on your line before they turn and finally seize your fly. Then they are off to parts unknown. This powerful run can take out a hundred yards or more of your line and backing. I learned long ago not to attempt to turn one of these monsters in his first run—they can be tackle busters. They seldom jump clear of the water when hooked and when fighting, they depend on sheer speed and strength in their bid for freedom.

The silver salmon, or coho, is much smaller but a much more active and volatile fighter. In fighting form and habits, the silver shares many characteristics of its cousin, the Atlantic salmon. They are a leaper, and probably as proficient a leaper as any. The first prick of your fly will make them jump—a clean jump, with head high in the sky. They can run as far as a hundred yards, hurdling periodically up and out of the water as much as a dozen times. Their jumps are the cleanest of all Pacific salmons, and for their size, the highest and longest. They can produce some great top-water action on a fly rod that often compares to a steelhead of comparable size.

My first real adventures with Pacific salmon in salt all started in the early 1950s. Puget Sound was the place and spotting birds and schools of herring and candlefish was the game. A keen eyed good-natured old man at the helm of the boat we were on for the day made the spot and positioned us accordingly. He told us, "Where there's herring or candlefish there's fish feeding on them." He went on to tell us, "The silvers drive them up to the surface as they try to escape the feeding frenzy." What he said made sense, but I got to thinking, "There is one hell of a lot more baitfish out there than salmon." At least this was true from my perspective as I witnessed a horrendous amount of boiling. Between the fish and the birds present that day, I gave wonder as to how my fly could ever find a place amongst the chaos.

In about an hour I had a fish on and my worries over the turmoil in the deep subsided. I had been using a Les Davis North Star pattern that was tied on a wire shank not unlike the Waddington. It was a seven pound silver and I was told that I was just lucky because my fly wasn't moving fast enough to entice a fish. I was further instructed we needed to be trolling.

For many fly rodders who have spent a good number of years pursuing fish in freshwater, it is hard for them to understand that Pacific salmon are also available in saltwater. For the most part many of the salmon taken in freshwater are fish which have been sighted first and then cast to. To most, the thought of casting a fly into a large expansion of water such as an estuary or the ocean itself is a blind affair. To me this is true salmon fishing and it certainly does not always have to be a sightless act.

With experience you are sure to develop a natural instinct for this type of fly fishing. It is much like other types of fly fishing, it is just the process of getting your fly to a hungry fish and in doing so correctly the fish will surely eat it.

I have always been able to regard my fishing for Pacific salmon as an off season or spontaneous affair when fishing here in northern California or southern Oregon. It is a time of year where one can retreat to the coast and escape the late summer heat. It is probably the only time of year that I welcome the early morning fog banks. Everyone finds themselves trouted out and it is usually too early for most of the steelhead.

This is the time of year when fish can be found in holding patterns and congregated at the mouths of the rivers. Nature has yet to trigger their final spawning run and they await the first rains of fall. This is a period when your fly offerings can be a mixed bag of natural and attractor patterns. Some estuaries will be teaming with natural food and I have found that salmon will take both types of patterns. They have essentially stopped eating, however, they will instinctively strike out at a baitfish pattern. I find this is also a good time to use small flies, even down to size eight or ten. A subtle fly, i.e., the Spade, Skunk or Black Boss will often as not do the trick. I find it confusing and intriguing at how indecisive these fish can be.

After the salmon enter the rivers one has to think of different tactics. They dominate the deeper pools so your flies need to be dressed sparse and fast sinking lines come into play. You may even find that steelhead have accompanied the run and are holding in the shallower tail water of the pool. This is when I start thinking of two species of fish and become a borderline salmon-steelheader, employing catch-as-catch-can methods. Once they enter the rivers they can also be successfully taken more easily on attractor type patterns. This is believed to be more of a territorial matter rather than a desire to eat. Here again, we find ourselves in the same old quandary—why do they strike?

Once this type of fishing gets into your blood there are always those unexplored waters further north. There has always been an unsatisfied desire to simply remain in Bella Coola or Ketchikan when I have been lucky enough to wonder there. Finding myself on an estuary, with the shoreline shrouded in green conifers, is not unlike many of the freshwater lakes that I have been on. Then when one passes the age of fifty there is that foreboding thought, "Will I ever be able to fish all such waters enough?"

In my mind, once these fish have reached the upper stretches of freshwater and have been there for a period—they are home free. They are spent or soon to be spent fish and should not be victimized for neither food nor sport. What I am speaking of here is that once a fish has changed into its spawning colors it deserves sanctuary. The state fish people in most areas do set aside some stretches of our streams as spawning grounds, but is this really enough?

Abe Snake has explained to some of the more novice fishermen the fact that spawning salmon go through a chemical change when they enter freshwater. Many of his patrons are malleable enough to associate the word "chemical" with something "toxic" and he just leaves it there not realizing what he has suggested, leaving yet another noble group with an unwarranted cause to deliberate.

There are those fishermen who will disagree with me about good protected spawning grounds, but they will also be holding a spinning rod in their hand or at least have obvious calluses from the extensive use of one. Hooking into and trying to fight, snagging the general practice, one of these fish is tantamount to sending an old man or woman to war. Their fight is power from the current of the water and their sheer size. At this point to try and justify them as a needed food fish is no more than admitting to eating carrion (road kill).

Trying to lay this book out into draft form became a tormenting affair. As aggravating as it was, I found courage enough to absorb my nice little chapter on Alaskan patterns elsewhere. When one sets out trying to define certain patterns as belonging to one type of fly fishing trouble follows fast. It is ingenuous for us to advocate that fish have any set rules with respect to the flies they like to eat. What it all boils down to is that there are no specific patterns for Alaska as such. If it works in the lower forty-eight, it will most likely work up there. That statement is sure to raise some concerns so I need to go further and try to clarify my point. There are patterns used in Alaska, and only in Alaska, that are only marginal down here. Most anglers who fish Alaska devote more attention to egg patterns, flesh flies, Woolly Buggers, wet flies and streamers of one kind or another.

Basically, that is part of how this chapter was born. That coupled with my strong desire to give our visiting Pacific quarry the ranking that they well deserve. The patterns used for Pacific salmon have little or no resemblance to those used for Atlantic salmon. The fact that salmon fly patterns were being developed for Atlantic salmon so many years in advance of those for Pacific salmon has little to do with this. One would think that the "monkey see monkey do" approach would have been applied. That was not a practical proposition in the beginning. Because of the scarcity of proper materials for the old world flies and earlier needs for subsistence this course of thinking had to be abandoned. Patterns that simulated baitfish or shrimp proved to be more provident for Pacific salmon. This feature is not evidenced in most Atlantic salmon fly patterns. I should mention however that with the eventful introduction in 1953 of the General Practitioner, a shrimp-like fly, both salmon and steelhead flies everywhere benefited—especially from the derivative offspring that it generated.

Pacific salmon flies are a breed of their own, and they are really in their infancy as far as established fly patterns are concerned. You could count on your ten fingers the total patterns that have gained any real undying acclaim. Nevertheless, with the abundance of food sources we have to emulate we are certain to be eventually discarding the chaff as new patterns continue to be developed.

I have not attempted to give you a zoological breakdown of these food forms, there are others who are much better qualified in that field. I have concentrated heavily on the baitfish and attractor patterns, knowing from my limited knowledge that these are among some of our most productive fly designs. Within the submarine kelp forest sanctuaries you will find populations of sardines, smelt, herring, sand lance and anchovies. Should you explore some of the other species on your own, you will be amazed at how simple a fly can be, yet still produce a deceptive form of another food source.

Tandem Style. The main advantage of this style is that it addresses most of the problems encountered with short strikes caused by the longer wings used on most streamer and streamer-like patterns. This method involves attaching a second hook behind the primary hook. This is most often done using heavy monofilament, however, I have seen others go to the extreme and use steel leader material. The method I have seen used most prevalently is securing a loop of leader to the fly body as it is being tied. Another that Ted Bentz showed me in Tacoma years ago is tying the loop in behind the eye of the primary hook using a knot to secure it much like the nail knot. This method leaves you with a bulky head which many are not in favor of. Both methods leave you with a loop of leader extending to the rear to attach your second hook.

I have heard a number of discussions that deal with whether the bend of the second hook should be up or down when attached to the rear of the primary fly. Personally, I prefer that the bend be up. This allows the wing to act as a weed guard of sorts and helps keep vegetation from collecting on your fly. Should the second hook be equal to or larger than the first, then naturally your fly may swim upside down. For that reason you should try to keep the second hook smaller in size than the first.

Tube Style. This style has some advantages that deserve our attention. This style of fly was created in Scotland around 1945 by Mrs. Winnie Morawski and was introduced into this country in the 1950s. Because the original flies that were tied on the tubes only suggested Atlantic salmon flies with treble hooks attached to them, they were not looked upon too favorably. With laws on the East Coast disallowing the use of trebles a "contrary" stigma was attached.

On the West Coast the tube style was received much differently. All at once a new method was there for Pacific salmon fly tiers to improvise on and get those longer, flashier bodies desired on the baitfish imitations they were trying to create. By using a simple piece of monofilament strung through the tube a fly was created that better preserved the fly. When a fish took the fly it was in essence pushed up the monofilament leader and out of harms way. Well, that works most of the time—not always.

The tube material used for this style is usually plastic or metal tubing. The British, in their meticulous manner, rate the metal tubes as weighted and plastic as unweighted. Tubes of all sorts are available in Europe so you can sense the competition generated to offer a better and more fishable tube. Here in North America we have the option of going to our local arts and crafts store and picking up our needs. The tube in your ball point pen is a desirable size, but there are no hard and fast rules regarding diameter or length used for your flies. This is dictated more on the basis of the size fly you want to tie.

Metal tubing is available in aluminum, copper and even stainless steel. Metal tubing has to be cut and finished just right or the ends will scuff your monofilament leader. My experiences with metal tubing have not been real outstanding. Even with a sophisticated tube cutting tool I manage to leave a burr on the ends. It is very time consuming trying to remove the unwanted rough burrs, so I opt for plastic. Any rough spots can easily be worked off with fine sand paper. By heating and softening the ends with a disposable lighter or other like heat source and then pressing it against a flat surface you are able to create an enlarged collar. This will assist in keeping your materials from slipping off. There are many obvious ways to build in any additional weight that might be desired.

It is relatively easy to figure out a method for holding your tube while the fly is being tied. I have been told that the English have even developed a commercial tool for this purpose. It took me about two minutes in my little workshop to find a nail of suitable diameter to fit snugly into the tubing I was using. I cut it off on both ends and flattened one end so it would clamp up in the jaws of my vise. That has worked for me for a long time and I know should I ever get larger tubing that does fit loosely I can always use a piece of masking tape to beef it up.

Shank Style 1.   *Shank Style 2.*

Waddington Shank Style. There are a number of styles which wear the "Waddington" name. Basically, it is a shank with an eye at each end, one for your leader and the other for attaching a hook of your desired style and size. Some European angling-writers have gotten a lot of mileage out of this style. Using a treble hook of course, they will emphasize the similarity it has to the tail of a fish; relate unending tales about tails and how much better a fly swims, etc., etc. I have to discount their theories and opt for this shank style, without trebles, for different reasons.

They can be used much like a tube style fly. These shanks are made in a wide range of sizes. The original selection I obtained from Gary Bell in England had eight different sizes included. Depending on the design of the shank and body thickness of the fly body, I often find it necessary to bend the eyes down even more to give the leader more clearance. They are used in this fashion when the fly design does not have obstructing materials tied in at the throat.

You may also see the term "articulated hook" being used. This is basically a ring eyed hook attached to one of these shanks. Tie a fly on the shank and consequently you have an "articulated fly," not a "Waddington."

Wing Harness. We all probably feel just this side of foolish when we have been playing a fly out behind the boat for some time and discover we have the wing of the fly entangled in the bend of the hook. This is not uncommon with salmon flies designed with longer wings. To help prevent this, tie in a loop of stiff monofilament when you tie your flies. The loop should be just stiff enough to support your wing, yet not be so stiff that it will knock the fly from the fish's mouth on a strike.

Eyes. There has been considerable discourse concerning eyes on flies ever since Jim Pray placed them on his first Optics. Some have claimed that fish avoid flies when they see their eyes, going on to speculate that our game fish prefer to attack baitfish only when they cannot see their eyes—inferring they prefer to back side them. This is really lowering your intellectual level to "thinking like a fish." The baitfish that I attempt to imitate all have eyes, they have evolved that way and there is nothing I can do about this natural feature. Should my fly be attacked while swimming away from a game fish, so much the better. If the theorists believe that these predators have such a high level of intelligence that they take advantage of such situations, so much the better. If I believe that eyes on flies cause me to feel that I am presenting the most natural imitation that I can possibly tie, so much the better. While the armchair gurus are wearing holes in their seats, I am going fishing with the best eyed flies I have available. Experience has told me in the past that such inattention to detail is a reckless and unnecessary approach.

Hooks. There are no definitive answers when it comes to suggesting specific hooks for these flies. The hook manufacturers have yet to make a hook that will satisfy the most of us, consequently those of us who tie these flies have had to lower our expectations. For the most part, I believe tiers would be very happy to see a 3X or 4X long shank stainless steel hook in a full range of sizes. At present I favor Mustad's 34039SS and 34044SS.

As you were reviewing Chapter 20 I am sure you were questioning the (s) coding of some patterns. This was my way of trying to tell you, "Hey, this pattern is also effective for Pacific salmon and is usually tied in larger sizes than those recommended for steelhead." Many of the patterns listed in this chapter are also effective for the Great Lakes region as well. Some of the patterns in this chapter have also been used successfully for many, many species off Baja and in other waters.

Plate 14   Ackerlund Humpy Fly

Thread: White.
Body: Wrapped with fine silver Mylar piping.
Wing: White bucktail with an overwing of fluorescent hot pink bucktail. Wing should be twice the length of the body.
Eyes: Silver bead chain.

Originated by Bill Ackerlund for summer pink salmon. When tied with a chartreuse overwing it is considered an effective fly for silvers.

Aid's Marabou Spiders

See Chapter 20.

Alaskan Polar Shrimp

Thread: Fluorescent fire orange.
Tail: Fluorescent fire orange hackle barbs.
Ribbing: Flat gold tinsel.
Body: Fluorescent fire orange chenille.
Hackle: Fluorescent fire orange marabou tied on as a collar and tied back.
Topping: Pearl Flashabou.
Head: Fluorescent fire orange.

Originated by George Cook.

Al's Salmon Streamer

Thread: White.
Body: Wrapped with fine silver Mylar piping.
Wing: Orange bucktail tied over the body with overwings of yellow bucktail, follow by orange bucktail. Badger hackles are tied in at each side of the wing.
Cheeks: Rounded pieces of sheet Mylar.
Head: Pearlescent blue.

Created by Alvin Trotter of McKinleyville, California. This pattern is usually tied tandem style.

Alaskan Candlefish

Thread: White.
Body: Flat silver tinsel.
Wing: White bucktail tied over the body with overwings of olive bucktail mixed with CH15 olive Crystal Hair with light blue bucktail tied on top.
Topping: Mixed CH08 pink and CH19 purple Crystal Hair.
Head: Pearlescent blue.
Eyes: White with red centers.

Plate 15   Alevin

Thread: White.
Tail: Frayed out end of body material.
Body: Pearl Mylar piping slipped over an underbody of white floss or yarn.
Throat (Egg Sac): Fat tuft of fluorescent fire orange marabou clipped at the end Glo Bug style.
Eyes: Silver bead chain.

Plate 15   Alevin, Brent's

Thread: Black.
Tail: Frayed out end of body material.
Body: Silver Mylar piping slipped over an underbody of white floss or yarn.
Throat (Egg Sac): Fat tuft of fluorescent orange Glo Bug yarn.
Wing: Sparse gray bucktail tied over the body.
Head: Black.
Eyes: Yellow with black centers.

Many of the salmon and steelhead waters on the West Coast and in the Great Lakes area will have an abundant number of these little guys as they go through their hatching process. This catches them still carrying their egg sac.

The egg sac is possibly the most important feature of this design and it is tied in a wide range of colors.

Plate 14   Anchovy

Thread: Black.
Body: Flat silver tinsel.
Wing: White bucktail tied over the body with an overwing of black bucktail and several strands of CH01 pearl Crystal Hair tied in at each side.
Topping: Peacock herl.

Head: Black.
Eyes: Tiny red dots.

Created by Jim Green for fishing off the coast of California.

Plate 15   Anchovy Streamer

Thread: White.
Wing: White bucktail tied over the body with overwings of CH30 silver Crystal Hair, green bucktail and blue bucktail tied on top.
Topping: Peacock herl.
Head: Green with a white throat.
Eyes: Yellow with black centers.

Wing should be tied equal to three times the length of the hook. This pattern was originated by Dennis Lee of Eureka, California.

Barbied Shrimp

See Chapter 17.

B.B.L.

Thread: White.
Body: Silver diamond braid.
Wing: Red bucktail tied over the body with an overwing of purple bucktail. Wing should reach just past end of hook.
Hackle: Teal blue tied in at the throat and extending the length of wing.
Topping: CH19 purple Crystal Hair.
Head: Pearlescent white.

A coho fly named for Bristol Bay Lodge.

Black Jack

Thread: Black.
Body: Black diamond braid wrapped over a tapered underbody of black floss or yarn.
Hackle: Black marabou tied on as a collar and tied back.
Head: Black.
Eyes: Tiny yellow dots.

Plate 14   Black Amos

Thread: Orange.
Tail: Black bucktail tied one and one half the length of the body.
Body: CC01 black Crystal Chenille.
Wing: Sparse strands of CH02 black Crystal Hair tied over the body and extending to the end of the tail.
Topping: Strands of peacock herl.

Hackle: Black tied on as a collar and tied back.
Head: Orange.

Originated by Irwin Thompson of Sebastopol, California.

Black ○ Blue Marabou

Thread: White.
Tail: Black marabou tied one and one half the length of the body.
Body: Rear three quarters, silver diamond braid and the front quarter dubbed with #35 kingfisher blue African Angora goat.
Hackle: Black tied on as a collar and tied back.
Head: Pearlescent blue.

Originated by Bob Guard of Eugene, Oregon.

Black Marabou Dancer

Thread: Red.
Tag: Red egg yarn.
Ribbing: Embossed silver tinsel.
Body: Black chenille.
Hackle: Red egg yarn tied in at the throat.
Wing: Black marabou tied over the body.
Head: Red.

Blonde Bucktails

See Chapter 18.

Blue Moon

Thread: Black.
Wing: Black marabou tied over the body with an overwing of CH01 pearl Crystal Hair and blue Flashabou.
Hackle: Dyed kingfisher blue schlappen tied on as a collar and tied back. The feather has the bottom fluff left on and is tied in by the butt.
Head: Black.

Originated by George Cook.

Plate 14 Blue Smolt

Thread: Black.
Butt: Red thread which secures body at rear.
Tail: Frayed end of body material.
Body: Silver Mylar piping slipped over and underbody of white floss or yarn.
Throat: Red hackle barbs.

Wing: White bucktail tied over the body with overwings of blue bucktail and a narrow barred teal flank feather tied flat on top.
Head: Black.
Eyes: Tiny orange dots.

Plate 15 Bodega Bay, Blue

Thread: White.
Body: CC01 pearl Crystal Chenille.
Wing: White bucktail tied long over the body with an overwing of blue bucktail.
Topping: CH13 blue Crystal Hair.
Head: Pearlescent blue.
Eyes: Small orange dots.

Plate 14 Bodega Bay, Green

Thread: White.
Body: CC01 pearl Crystal Chenille.
Wing: White bucktail tied long over the body with an overwing of chartreuse bucktail.
Topping: CH11 green Crystal Hair.
Head: Pearlescent green.
Eyes: Small orange dots.

Bodega Bay, Pearl

Thread: White.
Body: CC01 pearl Crystal Chenille.
Wing: CH10 light blue Crystal Hair tied long over the body with an overwing of white bucktail. Crystal Hair portion of wing should be about a dozen strands.
Topping: CH01 pearl Crystal Hair.
Head: White.
Eyes: Small black dots.

Wings for the Bodega Bay patterns should be twice the length of the hook.

Bodega Shrimp

See Chapter 17.

Bright Roe

Thread: Orange.
Ribbing: Silver diamond braid.
Body: Fluorescent fire orange chenille. Make fat.
Wing: Fluorescent fire orange egg yarn tied over the body with an overwing of CH07 fire orange Crystal Hair.
Head: Orange.

Bristol Bay Matuka

Thread: Fluorescent orange.
Body: Gold diamond braid over a tapered underbody of golden yellow floss.
Ribbing: Dyed gold monofilament.
Wing: Pair of fluorescent orange hackles inside of a pair of fluorescent red hackles tied Matuka style.
Cheeks: Fluorescent fire orange marabou tied in at each side.
Head: Fluorescent orange.

Created by Don Hathaway. This pattern, although originated for Alaska, has proven productive as far down the coast as northern California.

Plate 14 ## Cameron Baitfish

Thread: White.
Tail: White bucktail with red bucktail and the blue bucktail tied on top. Tail should be tied long as if you were creating a wing.
Body: Silver Mylar piping slipped over an underbody of either white yarn or floss.
Head/Butt: Pearlescent blue.

This pattern was originated by Chuck Cameron of Seaview, Washington. This fly actually represents a series of patterns tied in this design. The tail is tied in long, much like a wing, and full. Two of the other patterns consist of blue and white and green and white. Some tiers add a sparse wing to these flies of CH01 pearl Crystal Hair and claim that it is more successful.

Candlefish

Thread: White.
Body: Silver diamond braid.

Wing: White bucktail tied over the body with an overwing of green bucktail. CH23 chartreuse Crystal Hair is tied in at each side extending the length of the wing.
Topping: CH11 green Crystal Hair.
Head: Pearlescent green.
Eyes: Small red dots.

Plate 15 ## Candlefish Fly

Thread: White.
Body: Wrapped with fine silver Mylar piping.
Wing: White bucktail tied over the body with overwings of CH11 green Crystal Hair and blue bucktail on top.
Head: Pearlescent blue.
Eyes: Tiny red dots.

Plate 15 ## Candlefish, Lambuth

Thread: White.
Body: Flat silver tinsel.
Wing: Mixed light blue and light olive green bucktail tied long over the body with overwings of a small bunch of red bucktail and mixed gray and blue bucktail tied on top.
Head: Pearlescent blue.
Eyes: Tiny red dots.

This is a variation of the original pattern that was created by Letcher Lambuth in 1936. Other than my adding eyes and coloring the head, this is a reasonable recreation of what Roy Patrick gave me in the early 1960s. Lambuth's original pattern called for polar bear hair, however, even in the 1960s this was hard to come by. You will see many variations as many tiers get lazy and do not mix the hair colors properly. Also see Lambuth Candlefish.

Candy Cane

Thread: Fluorescent red.
Wings: Fluorescent red marabou mixed with CH30 silver and CH21 claret Crystal Hair. A second wing is then tied in duplicating the first.
Hackle: Fluorescent red hen hackle tied on as a collar and tied back.
Head: Fluorescent red.

George Cook developed this and other patterns in 1983 while working in

Alaska. This pattern is one in a series. The Crystal Hair helps keep the marabou from matting down when wet. Also, George's method of spacing the wings along the shank of the hook is helpful. The first wing is tied one-third back on the hook shank. The second wing of a shorted length is tied in front of the first and covers the head of the first. The third wing (on patterns calling for it) is tied long in front and covers over the first two. That is the general theory, but all are not tied in the same manner. Refer to each pattern for specific dressings. George calls some, if not all of these, the "Alaskabou series."

Chief Fat Dog

Thread: White.
Body: Silver diamond braid.
Wing: CH30 silver Crystal Hair tied over the body with an overwing of purple bucktail. Wing should extend to end of hook.
Throat: Fluorescent fire orange bucktail tied the length of the wing.
Head: Pearlescent blue.

This pattern was originated for freshwater coho and is thought to have come from Bristol Bay Lodge.

Christmas Tree

Thread: White.
Tail/Body: Green Flashabou pulled over body and ribbed with clear mono. Leave strands extending to the rear for tail.
Hackle: Green Flashabou tied on as a collar with silver Flashabou tied over.
Head: Pearlescent green.

Originated by Jonathan Olch.

Clouser Deep Minnow, Blue

Thread: White.
Bottom Wing: White bucktail.
Wing: Blue bucktail with a sparse underwing of CH01 pearl Crystal Hair.
Lead Eyes: Green with black centers.

Clouser Deep Minnow, Coho

Thread: White.
Bottom Wing: White bucktail.
Wing: Blue, green and yellow bucktail mixed with a sparse underwing of CH03 red Crystal Hair.
Lead Eyes: Green with black centers.

Clouser Deep Minnow, Green

Thread: White.
Bottom Wing: White bucktail.
Wing: Green bucktail with a sparse underwing of CH01 pearl Crystal Hair.
Lead Eyes: Green with black centers.

These are variations of the original Clouser Deep Minnows. See Chapter 18.

Coho

Thread: White.
Body: Silver diamond braid.
Wing: White bucktail tied over the body with overwings of CH01 pearl Crystal Hair and olive and gray mixed bucktail.
Throat: White bucktail and CH01 pearl Crystal Hair mixed.
Head: Pearlescent green.
Eyes: Tiny red dots.

Coho, Blue

Thread: White.
Body: Silver diamond braid.
Wing: White bucktail tied over the body with overwings of CH01 pearl Crystal Hair and blue bucktail on top.
Topping: CH14 dark blue Crystal Hair.
Throat: White bucktail and CH01 pearl Crystal Hair mixed.
Head: Pearlescent blue.
Eyes: Tiny red dots.

Coho, Russian River

Thread: Red.
Body: Silver diamond braid.
Hackle: White bucktail tied in at the throat and extending well past the hook.
Wing: Red bucktail tied over the body and extending to the end of white bucktail.
Head: Red.
Eyes: Tiny black dots.

Plate 14 — Copper Cousin

Thread: Black.
Body: Oval copper tinsel.
Wing: CH32 copper Crystal Hair tied over the body with an overwing of natural brown bucktail.
Throat: White bucktail tied in at the throat and extending to end of wing.
Head: Black.
Eyes: Tiny orange dots.

Originated in 1986 by Earl Hickman of Vallejo, California.

Crystal Candlefish

Thread: White.
Body: Silver diamond braid.
Wing: Mixed CH12 light blue and CH15 olive Crystal Hair tied long over the body with overwings of a small bunch of red bucktail and mixed gray and blue bucktail tied on top.
Head: Pearlescent blue.
Eyes: Yellow dots.

Plate 15 — Crystal Euphausid

Thread: White.
Tail: CH01 pearl Crystal Hair.
Body: Pearlescent Mylar tubing slipped over the body.
Hackle: CH01 pearl Crystal Hair tied in at the throat.
Head: White.

I generally tie this pattern in sizes 8-10.

Denali

Thread: Black.
Tail: Scarlet red hackle barbs.
Body: Copper wire.
Hackle: Yellow tied on as a collar and tied back and down.
Wing: Light blue bucktail tied over the body with overwings of orange and then light blue bucktail.
Head: Black.

Originated by Tom Elliott.

Dieker's Tandem Bucktail

Thread: White.
Wing: Strands of CH30 silver Crystal Hair with an overwing of blue bucktail.

Throat: White bucktail tied in at the throat and extending the length of the wing.
Head: Pearlescent white.
Eyes: Tiny red dots.

Originated by Mike Dieker of Pacific City, Oregon. Wing should extend past tandem hook.

Discovery Optic No. 1

Thread: White.
Ribbing: Oval silver tinsel.
Body: Flat silver tinsel.
Wing: White bucktail tied over the body with an overwing of light blue bucktail mixed with CH23 chartreuse Crystal Hair.
Head: Pearlescent white.
Eyes: Black with yellow centers.

Discovery Optic No. 2

Thread: White.
Ribbing: Oval silver tinsel.
Body: Flat silver tinsel.
Wing: White bucktail tied over the body with an overwing of orange bucktail mixed with CH04 yellow Crystal Hair.
Head: Pearlescent white.
Eyes: Black with yellow centers.

Discovery Optic No. 3

Thread: White.
Ribbing: Oval gold tinsel.
Body: Flat gold tinsel.
Wing: Yellow bucktail tied over the body with an overwing of red bucktail mixed with CH03 red Crystal Hair.
Head: Pearlescent white.
Eyes: Black with yellow centers.

Originated by A. J. McClane for fishing the Campbell River area of British Columbia. Original patterns called for a crimped nylon wing material but I have substituted Crystal Hair.

Dungeness Silver

Thread: Yellow.
Ribbing: Flat silver tinsel.
Body: Rear half, fluorescent orange yarn and the front half, fluorescent yellow yarn.
Wing: Fluorescent orange marabou tied over the body with an overwing of yellow marabou.
Head: Yellow.

The Dungeness Silver was originated by James Garrett, Sequim, Washington.

Egg Sac

Thread: Black.
Tail: Dyed black squirrel tail.
Body: Thinly tapered black floss.
Shoulder: Fluorescent red chenille.
Hackle: Black tied on as a collar and tied back.
Head: Black.

Originated by Bill Schaadt.

Fatal Attraction

Thread: White.
Tail: Silver Flashabou.
Body: Wrapped with pearl Mylar piping.
Hackle: White tied on as a collar and tied back and down.
Wing: White bucktail tied over the body with overwings of blue bucktail and CH01 pearl Crystal Hair. Keep all portions of wing sparse.
Eyes: Silver bead chain.

Originated by Dan Blanton.

Plate 15   Fire Cracker

Thread: White.
Tail/Body/Hackle: Silver Mylar piping slipped over the hook forming the body. Piping is frayed out and tied down at the rear to form tail and again at the front where it is tied down to form a hackle at the throat.
Wing: White bucktail tied over the body with an overwing of red bucktail.
Head: White.
Eyes: Tiny red dots.

Originated by Jonathan Olch.

Flash Fly

Thread: Red.
Body: Silver diamond braid.
Wing: Purple bucktail tied long over the body with an overwing of silver Flashabou.
Hackle: Scarlet red hackle tied on as a collar and tied back.
Head: Red.

Flashy Lady

Thread: White.
Wing: Pearl Flashabou and bucktail tied bullethead style.

Eyes: Black dots.

The Flashy Lady is basically tied in the bullethead streamer style. Pearl Flashabou is tied in first, followed by bucktail. Bucktail colors range from pink and purple to varying shades of blue and green. Crystal Hair and other like materials are also used in place of the Flashabou. See Thunder Creek, Chapter 18.

Ferguson's Green ○ Silver

Thread: Fluorescent green.
Tail: Clear (white) Miclon.
Body: Oval silver tinsel.
Shoulder: Fluorescent green chenille.
Wing: Clear (white) Miclon tied over the body with an overwing of CH30 silver Crystal Hair.
Head: Fluorescent green.

This is a variation of an original pattern that was created by Bruce Ferguson.

Ferguson's Marabou

Thread: White.
Tail: CH30 silver Crystal Hair.
Body: Silver diamond braid.
Wing: White marabou tied over the body with an overwing of CH30 silver Crystal Hair.
Topping: Strands of peacock herl.
Head: Pearlescent white.
Eyes: Tiny red dots.

Another variation of an original pattern created by Bruce Ferguson.

Plate 14   Frisco Streamer

Thread: White.
Body: Wrapped with fine silver Mylar piping.
Wing: White bucktail tied over the body with overwings of blue bucktail and then green bucktail on top.
Hackle: White bucktail tied in at the throat and extending back the length of the wing.

Cheeks: Red tags of yarn.
Head: Pearlescent blue.
Eyes: White with black pupils.

I have used this particular pattern from northern California to British Columbia since the 1950s. This is one of my favorites for silvers. I was given my first sample by a charter boat operator in Seattle.

Froggy's Herring

Thread: White.
Body: Silver diamond braid.
Wing: White bucktail tied long over the body with an overwing of mixed pearl and bronze Flashabou.
Topping: Strand of peacock herl.
Head: White.
Eyes: Black dots.

Originated by Steve Probasco of Raymond, Washington. This fly is usually tied tandem style.

Plate 14   Giloth Salmon Streamer

Thread: White.
Body: Silver Mylar piping slipped over an underbody of tapered white floss or yarn. Tie off at rear with red thread.
Wing: White bucktail tied over the body with an overwing of green bucktail.
Topping: CH13 blue Crystal Hair.
Head: White.
Eyes: Red with black centers.

Originated by Kirk Giloth of Lynnwood, Washington.

Ginger Jake

Thread: Orange.
Tail: Frayed out ends of body material.
Body: Silver Mylar piping slipped over an underbody of white floss or yarn.
Wing: White bucktail tied over the body with an overwing of orange bucktail.
Topping: Strands of CH07 fire orange Crystal Hair.
Head: Orange.

Green ◦ Black Marabou

Thread: Fluorescent green.
Tail: Green marabou tied long.
Body: Fluorescent green lace over an underbody of flat silver tinsel.
Shoulder: Black chenille.
Hackle: Fluorescent green tied on as a collar and tied back.
Head: Fluorescent green.

Originated by Bob Guard of Eugene, Oregon.

Greenhead

Thread: Fluorescent green.
Tip: Fluorescent green floss.
Tail: Dyed black squirrel tail.
Ribbing: Oval gold tinsel.
Body: Fluorescent fire orange floss.
Hackle: Fire orange tied on as a collar and tied back.
Eyes: Gold bead chain.
Head: Fluorescent green chenille wrapped through the eyes.

Originated by Red Collingsworth.

Green Weanie

Thread: Fluorescent green.
Tail: Black calf tail.
Body: Silver diamond braid.
Shoulder: Fluorescent chartreuse chenille.
Hackle: Fluorescent chartreuse tied on as a collar and tied back.
Eyes: Silver bead chain.

Herring Fly, Bales

Thread: Red.
Body: Red lace over an underbody of flat silver Mylar tinsel.
Wing: White bucktail tied over the body with an overwing of blue bucktail mixed with CH13 blue Crystal Hair.
Topping: Strands of peacock herl.
Head: Red.

Originated by Marc Bales.

Herring Fly, Hick's

Thread: White.
Body: Three layers of Mylar piping tied in at the front and pulled to the rear and tied together.
Wing: Several strands of peacock herl.

Throat: White bucktail tied in at the throat and extending to end of wing.
Head: Red.
Eyes: White with black centers.

Originated by Larry Hicks. This fly is normally tied tandem style, however, it is a good candidate for tube style also.

Herring Fly, Johnson's
Thread: White.
Tail: Frayed end of body material.
Body: Silver Mylar piping slipped over a well tapered (fat) underbody of white floss or yarn.
Wing: White bucktail tied over the body with an overwing of yellowish-olive bucktail. Pearl Flashabou strands are tied in at each side.
Hackle: Orange hackle barbs tied in at the throat.
Head: Pearlescent green.

Originated by Les Johnson.

Herring Fly, Lambuth's
Thread: White.
Body: Flat silver tinsel.
Wing: White and light green bucktail tied over the body with overwings of gray bucktail and bright green bucktail on top.
Topping: Strands of CH15 olive Crystal Hair.
Head: Pearlescent green.

Originated Letcher Lambuth of Seattle, Washington, in 1936. This is a variation, his fly called for polar bear hair.

Humboldt Bay Anchovy
Thread: Black.
Extended Body: Silver Mylar piping.
Tail: Gray squirrel tail mounted in end of piping.
Wing: White bucktail tied over the body with overwings of green bucktail and blue bucktail on top.
Topping: CH14 dark blue Crystal Hair.
Head: Pearlescent blue.
Eyes: Yellow with black centers.

Originated by Frank Woolner.

Humboldt Bay Salmon Fly
Thread: White.
Tail: White bucktail with green bucktail tied on top.
Body: Silver diamond braid.
Wing: White bucktail tied over the body with an overwing of yellow bucktail with green bucktail on top.
Cheeks: Wide strips of silver Mylar tied in at the sides and extending half the length of the wing.
Head: Pearlescent green.
Eyes: Tiny red dots.

Originated by Mike Foster of Miranda, California.

Humboldt Bay Streamer, Blue
Thread: White.
Body: Pearl Crystal Chenille.
Throat: White bucktail tied in at the throat and extending past hook bend.
Wing: White bucktail tied over the body with and overwing of CH13 blue Crystal Hair.
Cheeks: Red tags of yarn tied in at each side.
Head: Pearlescent blue.
Eyes: Yellow with black centers.

Humboldt Bay Streamer, Olive
Thread: White.
Body: Pearl Crystal Chenille.
Throat: White bucktail tied in at the throat and extending past hook bend.
Wing: White bucktail tied over the body with an overwing of CH15 olive Crystal Hair.
Cheeks: Red tags of yarn tied in at each side.
Head: Pearlescent green.
Eyes: Yellow with black centers.

Humpy Fly, Female
Thread: White.
Tail: Red hackle barbs.
Body: Flat silver tinsel.
Hackle: White tied on as a collar and tied back and down.
Wing: White marabou tied over the body.
Topping: Strands of peacock herl.
Head: White.
Eyes: Tiny black dots.

Humpy Fly, Male

Thread: White.
Tail: Red hackle barbs.
Body: Flat silver tinsel.
Hackle: Black tied on as a collar and tied back and down.
Wing: Black marabou tied over the body.
Topping: Strands of peacock herl.
Head: Red.
Eyes: Tiny yellow dots.

Originated in British Columbia by Bill Nelson.

Hurn's Candlefish

Thread: White.
Tail: Clear (white) Miclon.
Body: Oval silver tinsel.
Wing: Red bucktail tied over the body with a overwing of white bucktail and green bucktail tied on top.
Topping: Peacock herl.
Head: Pearlescent green.

Originated by David Hurn of Victoria, British Columbia.

Johnson's Beach Fly

Thread: Fluorescent orange.
Tip: Flat gold tinsel.
Ribbing: Flat gold tinsel.
Body: Fluorescent orange yarn.
Hackle: Badger hen hackle tied on as a collar (two turns) and tied back.
Wing: White calf tail with an overwing of clear (white) Miclon.

Originated by Les Johnson.

July Fly

Thread: White.
Wing: White bucktail tied over the hook shank with an overwing of green bucktail. Tie in strands of CH03 red Crystal Hair along each side.
Topping: Strands of peacock herl with CH30 silver Crystal Hair tied along each side.
Head: Pearlescent green.
Eyes: Black with yellow centers.

Originated by Bill Nelson.

Plate 15 King's Explorer, Black

Thread: Black.
Tail: Dyed black squirrel tail tied one and one half the length of the body.
Shellback: Black chenille.
Body: Silver diamond braid over a well tapered underbody of white floss or yarn.
Hackle: Black tied on as a collar and tied back.
Eyes: Silver bead chain.

Plate 15 King's Explorer, Red

Thread: Red.
Tail: Dyed black squirrel tail tied one and one half the length of the body.
Shellback: Red chenille.
Body: Silver diamond braid over a well tapered underbody of white floss or yarn.
Hackle: Red tied on as a collar and tied back.
Eyes: Silver bead chain.

The two preceding patterns were originated by Grant King of Santa Rosa, California.

Lambuth Candlefish

Thread: Black.
Body: Flat silver tinsel.
Wing: Light green and light blue bucktail tied over the body with an overwing of CH03 red Crystal Hair, followed with a mixed wing of blue bucktail and strands of CH11 green Crystal Hair.
Head: Black.
Eyes: Tiny red dots.

Also see Candlefish, Lambuth. This is just one more of many variations that are used for Pacific salmon. I have found that the combination given here is favored by many.

Lefty's Deceiver, Blue

Thread: White.
Wings: Six matched white saddles with a dyed blue grizzly saddle tied in at each side.
Collar: White bucktail tied in and extending well past hook bend.
Throat: CH03 red Crystal Hair tied in at the throat and extending to point of hook.
Topping: Strands of CH13 blue Crystal Hair with peacock herl tied on top.
Head: Pearlescent blue.

Plate 15 **Lefty's Deceiver, Green**

Thread: White.
Wings: Six matched white saddles with a dyed green grizzly saddle tied in at each side.
Collar: White bucktail tied in and extending well past hook bend.
Throat: CH03 red Crystal Hair tied in at the throat and extending to point of hook.
Topping: Strands of CH11 green Crystal Hair with peacock herl tied on top.
Head: Pearlescent green.

Lefty's Deceiver, Olive

Thread: White.
Wings: Six matched white saddles with a dyed olive grizzly saddle tied in at each side.
Collar: White bucktail tied in and extending well past hook bend.
Throat: CH03 red Crystal Hair tied in at the throat and extending to point of hook.
Topping: Strands of CH15 olive Crystal Hair with peacock herl tied on top.
Head: Pearlescent green.

Lefty's Deceiver, White

Thread: Red.
Wings: Six matched white saddles with a grizzly saddle tied in at each side.
Collar: White bucktail tied in and extending well past hook bend.
Throat: CH03 red Crystal Hair tied in at the throat and extending to point of hook.
Topping: Strands of CH03 red Crystal Hair with peacock herl tied on top.
Head: Red.

There are any number of fly patterns that bear the name "Lefty." These are the flies that I have found to be the most popular.

Little Herring

Thread: Black.
Body: Silver diamond braid.
Wing: Green bucktail tied over the body with overwings of sparse white and light blue bucktail. Grizzly saddle hackle is tied in a each side.
Topping: Strands of peacock herl.
Head: Black.
Eyes: White with black centers.

Originated by Kirk Giloth of Lynnwood, Washington. This is one of the patterns that I have learned to rely on more than most. It is one that I can recommend without reservation and I have used it from King Salmon, Alaska to California.

Midnight

Thread: Black.
Tail: Black bucktail.
Ribbing: Oval silver tinsel.
Body: Flat silver tinsel.
Wing: White bucktail tied over the body with an overwing of black bucktail.
Head: Black.
Eyes: White with black centers.

North Star

Thread: White.
Wing: Clear (white) Miclon tied over the shank with an overwing of green bucktail and sparse red bucktail tied in at each side.
Head: Pearlescent green.

As previously mentioned in the opening, this pattern was originally tied on a separate shank not unlike the Waddington. It is now often tied on a standard long shank hook.

Parr

Thread: White.
Body: Silver diamond braid.
Wing: Clear (white) Miclon tied over the body with an overwing of CH26 gray Crystal Hair.
Head: Pearlescent blue.
Eyes: Tiny black dots.

Payoff

Thread: Fluorescent fire orange.
Wing: Purple marabou with an overwing of a few strands of CH03 red and CH19 purple Crystal Hair.
Hackle: Dyed kingfisher blue schlappen tied on as a collar and tied back. The feather has the bottom fluff left on and is tied in by the butt.
Head: Fluorescent fire orange.

Originated by George Cook.

Pink Passion

Thread: Red.
Body: Rear two-thirds, pearl diamond braid and the front third, fluorescent red chenille.
Hackle: CH01 pearl Crystal Hair tied on as a collar with fluorescent hot pint tied on as a collar in front and tied back.
Head: Red.

Originated by Ken Fujii.

Pixie's Revenge

Thread: Claret.
First Wing: White marabou mixed with gold Flashabou and CH06 orange Crystal Hair. This wing should be tied in at the center of the hook.
Second Wing: Orange marabou mixed with gold Flashabou and CH06 orange Crystal Hair.
Third Wing: Duplicate the second wing.
Hackle: Magenta hen hackle tied on as a collar and tied back.
Head: Claret.

Originated by George Cook.

Plate 14 Point Arena Streamer

Thread: Black.
Tail: CH01 pearl Crystal hair.
Body: CC01 pearl Crystal Chenille.
Throat: White bucktail tied in at the throat and extending past hook bend.
Wing: Gray squirrel tail tied over the body.
Head: Black.
Eyes: White with tiny red dots.

Popsicle

Thread: Fluorescent red.
First Wing: Fluorescent orange marabou topped with CH19 purple and CH24 gold

mixed Crystal Hair. This wing should be tied in at the center of the hook shank.
Second Wing: Fluorescent red marabou.
Hackle: Purple marabou tied on as a collar and tied back.
Head: Fluorescent red.

Originated by George Cook.

Purple Bad Habit

See Chapter 20.

Rock Herring

Tail: White bucktail.
Body: Silver diamond braid.
Wing: White bucktail tied over the body with an overwing of magenta bucktail with chartreuse bucktail tied on top.
Head: Pearlescent green.
Eyes: Yellow with red centers.

Originated by Larry Green.

Salmon Creek Special

Thread: Fluorescent red.
Tail: Dyed black squirrel tail.
Ribbing: Flat silver tinsel.
Body: Fluorescent fire orange floss.
Wing: Fluorescent orange egg yarn tied over the body.
Topping: CH01 pearl Crystal Hair.
Hackle: Yellow tied on as a collar and tied back.
Head: Fluorescent red.

Originated by Irwin Thompson.

Salmon Fly

Thread: White.
Tail: White bucktail tied equal to one and one half the body length.
Body: Silver embossed tinsel.
Hackle: Scarlet red tied on as a collar and tied back.
Eyes: Silver bead chain.

Salmon Killer

Thread: White.
Tail: Purple bucktail with blue bucktail tied on top.
Body: Oval silver tinsel.
Hackle: Blue tied on as a collar and tied back.
Wing: Purple bucktail tied over the body with an overwing of black bucktail.
Head: Gold.

Eyes: White with red centers and tiny black dots.

The Salmon Killer was originated by Irwin Thompson of Sebastapol, California.

[Plate 14] Sand Lance
Thread: Black.
Body: Oval gold tinsel.
Wing: White bucktail tied over the body with overwings of CH03 red Crystal Hair with black bucktail tied on top.
Head: Black.
Eyes: Tiny red dots.

Sandstrom Baitfish
Thread: White.
Body: Silver diamond braid.
Wing: White bucktail tied over the body with an overwing of CH23 chartreuse Crystal Hair.
Head: Pearlescent green with a red band at wing base.

Originated by Gary Sandstrom of Tacoma, Washington.

Shimmering Blue
Thread: White.
Body: CC01 pearl Crystal Chenille.
Wing: White bucktail tied long over the body with an overwing of blue bucktail.
Head: Pearlescent blue.
Eyes: Tiny red dots.

Shimmering Green
Thread: White.
Body: CC01 pearl Crystal Chenille.
Wing: White bucktail tied long over the body with an overwing of olive bucktail.
Head: Pearlescent green.
Eyes: Tiny red dots.

Showgirl
Thread: Fluorescent red.
Wing: Fluorescent red marabou tied full and allowed to drape around the shank of the hook.
Topping: About two dozen strands of CH19 purple Crystal Hair.
Hackle: Purple tied on as a collar and tied back. This should be long, soft hackle which extends back over the wing at least half way.

Head: Fluorescent red.

Too simple you say, and I agree. But why make it difficult? This fly was designed by George Cook for Alaska and that explains the simplicity of it.

It doesn't take a New York chorus line dancer to fool fish in Alaska.

[Plate 14] Silver Minnow
Thread: White.
Body: Silver diamond braid.
Hackle: Scarlet red tied on as a collar and tied back.
Wing: White bucktail tied over the body with an overwing of peacock herl strands.
Eyes: Brass bead chain painted red with black centers.

This is a variation of an old Don Harger pattern.

[Plate 15] Silversides
Thread: Red.
Body: Pearlescent Mylar piping slipped over an underbody of white yarn or floss.
Tail: Frayed end of piping about 1/2" long.
Wing: White bucktail tied over the body with an overwing of blue bucktail with strands of silver Mylar tied in at each side. CH30 silver Crystal Hair may be substituted.
Head: Red.
Eyes: Yellow with black centers.

Originated by Bill Gallasch.

[Plate 14] Situk Special
Thread: Fluorescent pink.
Throat: Fluorescent pink FisHair tied in at the throat and extending past hook bend.
Wing: Blue Flashabou tied over the body with an overwing of silver Flashabou. Both wings should be twice the length of the hook shank.
Head: Fluorescent pink chenille wrapped through eyes.
Eyes: Brass dumb bells or bead chain.

Originated by Scott Byrne of Sacramento, California.

Skeena Nymph
See Chapter 20.

Stroud's Humdinger

Thread: White.
Body: Fluorescent green chenille.
Throat: Sparse white bucktail tied in at the throat and extending to end of wing.
Wing: White bucktail tied over the body and extending to end of tandem hook. Strands of CH30 silver Crystal Hair are tied in at each side.
Head: Pearlescent blue.
Eyes: Tiny red dots.

Originated by Carl Stroud. This fly is tied tandem style.

Tequila Sunrise

Thread: Fluorescent red.
First Wing: Pink marabou tied in one-third down the shank of the hook. Over this and to the sides is tied strands of CH06 orange Crystal Hair.
Second Wing: Fluorescent orange marabou tied in at the normal position on the shank. Over this and to the sides is tied strands of CH06 orange Crystal Hair.
Hackle: Large fluorescent red hen hackle tied on as a collar and tied back.
Head: Fluorescent red.

Another one of George Cook's large "marabou puffs." All of his patterns are intended for Alaskan conditions, however, when tied in the smaller sizes they have been equally productive elsewhere.

 Tillamook Bay Shiner, Blue
Thread: White.
Body: Pearlescent diamond braid wrapped over an underbody of white floss or yarn.
Wing: White bucktail tied over the body with an overwing of blue bucktail. CH13 blue Crystal Hair is tied in at each side.
Head: Pearlescent blue.
Eyes: White with red centers.

Tillamook Bay Shiner, Green

Thread: White.
Body: Pearlescent diamond braid wrapped over an underbody of white floss or yarn.
Wing: White bucktail tied over the body with an overwing of green bucktail. CH11 green Crystal Hair is tied in at each side.
Head: Pearlescent green.
Eyes: White with red centers.

Tillamook Bay Shiner, Pink

Thread: White.
Body: Pearlescent diamond braid wrapped over an underbody of white floss or yarn.
Wing: White bucktail tied over the body with an overwing of hot pink bucktail. CH08 pink Crystal Hair is tied in at each side.
Head: Pearlescent blue.
Eyes: White with red centers.

Plate 15 ## Tillamook Bay Shiner, Red

Thread: White.
Body: Pearlescent diamond braid wrapped over an underbody of white floss or yarn.
Wing: White bucktail tied over the body with an overwing of red bucktail. CH03 red Crystal Hair is tied in at each side.
Head: Pearlescent blue.
Eyes: White with red centers.

The Tillamook series was originated in 1971 by Martin Riley of Lincoln City, Oregon.

Volcano

Thread: Fluorescent fire orange.
Wing: Orange marabou with an overwing of CH03 red and CH31 gold Crystal Hair.
Hackle: Dyed red schlappen tied on as a collar and tied back. The feather has the bottom fluff left on and is tied in by the butt.
Head: Fluorescent fire orange.

Originated by George Cook.

Walker Shrimp, Black

Thread: Black.
Tip: Oval silver tinsel.
Tail: Black bucktail tied equal to one and half the length of the body.
Body: Black yarn.
Center Hackle: Black hen hackle tied on as a collar and tied back.

Hackle: Black hen hackle tied on as a collar and tied back.
Head: Black.
Eyes: Tiny red dots.

Walker Shrimp, Brown
Thread: Yellow.
Tip: Oval gold tinsel.
Tail: Natural brown bucktail tied equal to one and half the length of the body.
Body: Orange yarn.
Center Hackle: Yellow hen hackle tied on as a collar and tied back.
Hackle: Brown hen hackle tied on as a collar and tied back.
Head: Yellow.
Eyes: Tiny black dots.

Walker Shrimp, Gray
Thread: Black.
Tip: Oval silver tinsel.
Tail: Gray bucktail tied equal to one and half the length of the body.
Body: Gray yarn.
Center Hackle: Grizzly hen hackle tied on as a collar and tied back.
Hackle: Grizzly hen hackle tied on as a collar and tied back.
Head: Black.
Eyes: Tiny yellow dots.

Walker Shrimp, Olive
Thread: Olive.
Tip: Oval gold tinsel.
Tail: Olive bucktail tied equal to one and half the length of the body.
Body: Olive yarn.
Center Hackle: Olive hen hackle tied on as a collar and tied back.
Hackle: Brown hen hackle tied on as a collar and tied back.
Head: Olive.
Eyes: Tiny red dots.

Walker Shrimp, Orange
Thread: Fluorescent orange.
Tip: Oval silver tinsel.
Tail: Orange bucktail tied equal to one and half the length of the body.
Body: Fluorescent orange yarn.
Center Hackle: White hen hackle tied on as a collar and tied back.
Hackle: Fire orange tied on as a collar and tied back.
Head: Fluorescent orange.
Eyes: Tiny black dots.

The center hackle is tied in at the center of the body and should be under sized. This legendary series of shrimp patterns has been used along the northern coast of California for more than 50 years. No one has ever been able to come up with a plausible argument behind the name "Walker." It could have come from the name of a landing, creek or even a mine. Let us assume that there was a fly fisherman in the past with this name who had a hand in popularizing these flies. Much like with Woolly Worms, the variations are rather extensive.

Zonker, Black
Thread: Black.
Tail: Frayed end of Mylar piping from body.
Body: Pearl Mylar piping slipped over an underbody of white floss or yarn.
Wing: Dyed black rabbit fur strip tied Matuka style.
Hackle: Grizzly tied on as a collar and tied back.
Head: Black.

Zonker, Blue
Thread: White.
Tail: Frayed end of Mylar piping from body.
Body: Pearl Mylar piping slipped over an underbody of white floss or yarn.
Wing: Dyed blue rabbit fur strip tied Matuka style.
Hackle: Dyed blue grizzly tied on as a collar and tied back.
Head: Pearlescent blue.

Zonker, Cutthroat

Thread: Olive.
Butt: Red thread which secures body at rear.
Tail: Frayed end of Mylar piping from body.
Body: Pearl Mylar piping slipped over an underbody of white floss or yarn.
Wing: Dyed olive rabbit fur strip tied Matuka style.
Hackle: Scarlet red hackle tied on as a collar and tied back and down.
Head: Olive.

Zonker, Green

Thread: White.
Tail: Frayed end of Mylar piping from body.
Body: Pearl Mylar piping slipped over an underbody of white floss or yarn.
Wing: Dyed green rabbit fur strip tied Matuka style.
Hackle: Dyed green grizzly tied on as a collar and tied back.
Head: Pearlescent green.
See Chapter 18.

Chapter 24

Salmon and Steelhead Dry Flies

Should you review what we are doing in North America with respect to dry flies for salmon and steelhead, you will discover there is but very little difference between the two methods and the patterns used on both coasts. What I am speaking of here is the use of larger more massive creations and not the sometimes-used trout patterns. The only real differences may be a matter of dialogue. There are certainly recognizable local exceptions of course. The patterns offered here are some of those that are used for both Atlantic and Pacific salmon and steelhead wherever they might be found.

To my knowledge there is not, nor has there ever been, any real interest in Europe in the dry fly approach being used for salmon. I am sure that a few may have experimented, but it has never gained any notable degree of popularity. What we are doing today is more of our own shaping and many say that it is still in its rudimentary stages.

Years ago I found myself floating large caddisfly patterns below Martin's Ferry Bridge on the Klamath River and wondering if I was going to catch the dickens'. This certainly was not the conventional large wet fly approach that my elders had been preaching. My youthful innocence had taken command and common sense told me to work the hatch or at least the hatch that I was attempting to create. I had no explanation for why the fish, both salmon and steelhead, could be seen breaking water. In my mind, the rascals were hungry and if trout were suckers for a floating fly—why not?

No one had told me at the time that "those damn fish don't eat when they are spawning." Needless to say, I kept my mouth shut and in the evenings would play down any successful deceptions of the day. I was sure that I had put one over on the old man. Later back in Redding he pinned me down, wanting to know more about the fish I had been giving to the Indians. My token payment to them with an occasional fish in exchange for use of their dinghy for the day had left evidence of my youthful, then unorthodox, approach to fly fishing for steelhead and the occasional smaller salmon.

Although my father probably never approved of my methods, being a die hard wet fly man himself and always catching the most fish, we never spoke of it again. You have to remember that this particular generation measured a day on the river in pounds and not boyish entertainment often involving smaller fish. I believe that since that time the boy in many of us has refused to stand in the shadows of manhood and we have had some real exciting experiences with a dry. The take can often be most delicate, and it can also be a smashing blow, but in either case the explosion on the other end can be of hook straightening proportions.

While some approach the use of these larger flies as if they were visiting the local bass pond, using a seven weight or larger rod to throw the larger bugs, I also factor in a lighter rod into the challenge. If I can get away with a five weight it will be selected first, however, a six weight does become necessary when such flies are used in conjunction with the canyon winds. As nonsensical as it may sound, there always lurks in the back of my mind the possibility of giving a three weight a try—what a duel that would be.

The dry fly purists may find this particular form of fishing somewhat backwards or a reverse approach in the extreme. Where some can be found carrying an imitation for everything that flies over a trout stream, it is not an essential factor here. The fly patterns and methodology differs somewhat. One technique that we use is called a "damp" presentation. This is best described as fishing a dry fly "wet" or in the surface film. In other words, we allow our dry flies to get a little bit pregnant. I am sure that there are some that will identify this with wet fly fishing. I become amused, not displaying it of course, when I ask others to describe this form of fly fishing. They select their words oh so very carefully, yet the overwhelming pressures of exactness yields words that are vague and tinged with guilt. It is just as if you had asked about the cookie jar, received acknowledgment of its location, then a sheepish denial of entry.

As most of us know, most dry flies will eventually get waterlogged and have a tendency to sink into the surface film. This is what we are taking advantage of when we use these techniques. Forget the grease.

This may be one of those experiences that you have to encounter before it is fully understood. The damp method is one of my more favored fishing techniques. These partially drowned imitations may very well be imitating a natural in a more realistic manner than we are conscious of. I believe that our pattern of choice may not be of any real consequence when a fish elects to attack it on the swing. In those last seconds, while your fly is gaining momentum, very little opportunity is afforded the fish to make a close examination of your offering. After the take and the ensuing skirmish that follows, no man can eloquently describe the experience in words that are rational—you just have to live it.

Other approaches that are more commonly used do include grease. One involves casting across stream and allowing your fly to make a large arching wake over a large piece of water. Then we also tie some of our patterns so they will skate freely across the water. In both instances the fish are alerted to this disturbance and strike out of an instinctive food survival inclination or for territorial reasons. More presupposed reasoning on my part of course. Some say they strike because they are just naturally curious.

The distinction between the conventional dry fly approach as opposed to that used here is minimal. They both require the same amount of skill and the goals are equal. Some years ago I was amazed to learn from the Cortland sales representative, Joe Patterson, that his sales for bass poppers in Alaska exceeded that of California. Does this send a message or what?

I am not trying to suggest that we abandon the use of conventional trout flies when appropriate and that this is a new and more effective approach. Each piece of water is different, with one possibly dictating a size four Irresistible and another a size eighteen Blue-Winged Olive. An upstream cast, allowing our fly to pass by an awaiting fish is still probably one of the most practiced methods.

The hooks that I have suggested here are only that—suggestions. I find that there is a wide range of opinions on the proper hook to use for a particular pattern. Some will tell you that the use of any salmon fly style hook is unwarranted sugar coating and should be ignored. I have noted some very extensive use of conventional dry fly hooks in the larger sizes and it is not uncommon to see some patterns, especially the Bombers, tied on 3X and 4X long shank streamer hooks.

From the patterns offered here some skate beautifully across the top of the water while others create a seductive disturbance. You will also find many here, and in Chapter 20, that just beg to be fished "damp."

Air B.C.

Hooks: TMC7989, DAI2131 or DAI2421, sizes 4-8.
Thread: Orange.
Side Wings: Orange deer hair tied spent.
Tail: White calf tail.
Body: Orange deer hair spun on and clipped to a cigar shape.
Wing: Clump of white calf tail tied over the eye of the hook.

Originated by Bill McMillan in 1981.

Autumn Liner

Hooks: TMC7989, DAI2131 or DAI2421, sizes 4-8.
Thread: Tan.
Tip: Oval silver tinsel.
Tail: Light elk hair.
Ribbing: Oval silver tinsel.

Body: Dubbed with a 50/50 blend of #23 gold and #26 dark brown African Angora goat.
Hackle: Brown Hungarian partridge barbs tied in at the throat.
Wings: Narrow dark brown mottled turkey tail feather sections tied over the body with overwings of dark elk hair and light elk hair on top.
Head: Trimmed butt ends from hair wing extending over the eye of the hook. They should be fanned out and have cement applied to retain shape.

Originated by Jim Birrell of Seattle, Washington.

Plate 16 Beetle Bug Coachman

Hooks: TMC7989, DAI2131 or DAI2421, sizes 6-10.
Thread: Black.
Wings: White calf tail tied upright and divided.

Tail: Natural brown bucktail.
Body: Red floss.
Hackle: Dark brown tied on as a collar.

Originated in 1920 by John Dose. For those of you interested in the history of fly patterns it should be noted that this Wulff-like pattern was being tied a decade before any of today's Wulff patterns. It was possibly one of the first dry fly patterns used for steelhead. It is also tied with yellow or orange bodies. We should possibly be calling all such designs "Dose" rather than "Wulff." How does "Royal Dose" sound? See Gray Wulff further on.

Bi-Visibles

Bi-Visibles tied in larger sizes and heavily dressed will often bring good results when skated. See Chapter 7.

 ### Black Bee

Hooks: TMC7989, DAI2131 or DAI2421, sizes 6-8.
Thread: Black.
Wings: Dyed black squirrel tail tied upright and divided. Wings should slant forward over the eye of the hook.
Tail: Dyed black squirrel tail.
Body: Divided into three equal parts. Dubbed with #26 dark brown and a center joint of #6 yellow lambs wool.
Hackle: Black tied on as a collar.

This is a variation of Roderick Haig-Brown's Steelhead Bee.

 ### Bomber

Hooks: TMC5263 or DAI1720, sizes 4-8.
Thread: Black.
Wing: Clump of coastal blacktail deer hair tied over the eye of the hook.
Tail: Coastal blacktail deer hair.
Body Hackle: Brown tied palmer style over the body.
Body: Natural deer hair spun and clipped to a cigar shape.

This pattern is the one that I have always regards as the original of an endless series of Bombers. They are tied in several different color combinations. Elmer Smith of Prince William, N.B., Canada, is credited with tying the first of these flies. The patterns offered here are some of the more popular ones.

From the Bombers another simpler fly emerged, they are called Buck Bugs. They are tied the same except they have no forward protruding wing. Others have had the tail omitted and replaced with a butt.

Bomber, Black

Hooks: TMC5263 or DAI1720, sizes 2-8.
Thread: Black.
Wing: Clump of white calf tail tied over the eye of the hook.
Tail: White calf tail.
Body Hackle: Grizzly tied palmer style over the body.
Body: Black deer hair spun and clipped to a cigar shape.

Bomber, Orange

Hooks: TMC5263 or DAI1720, sizes 2-8.
Thread: Black.
Wing: Clump of white calf tail tied over the eye of the hook.
Tail: White calf tail.
Body Hackle: Brown tied palmer style over the body.
Body: Orange deer hair spun and clipped to a cigar shape.

Bomber, Purple

Hooks: TMC5263 or DAI1720, sizes 4-8.
Thread: Black.
Tail: Light purple elk hair.
Wing: Clump of light purple elk hair tied over the eye of the hook.
Body: Purple deer hair spun on and clipped to a fat cigar shape.

Originated by Bob Clay. There are several variations of this pattern. Another has black hackle tied palmer style over the deer hair body.

Bomber, Rusty
Hooks: TMC5263 or DAI1720, sizes 4-8.
Thread: Black.
Wing: Clump of fox squirrel tied over the eye of the hook.
Tail: Fox squirrel tail.
Body Hackle: Brown tied palmer style over the body.
Body: Rusty orange deer hair spun and clipped to a cigar shape.

Boxcar
Hooks: TMC7989, DAI2131 or DAI2421, sizes 4-8.
Thread: Black.
Tip: Flat silver tinsel.
Tail: Scarlet red hackle barbs.
Body: Peacock herl. Reverse wrap with fine gold wire.
Wing: White calf tail tied over the body.
Hackle: Brown tied on as a collar.

Originated by Wes Drain of Seattle, Washington.

Bulkley Mouse

Tied the same as the Disco Mouse except natural moose hair is used. It is not uncommon to discover many mouse imitations created for British Columbia's Bulkley River.

Caddis Flash
Hooks: TMC7989, DAI2131 or DAI2421, sizes 4-8.
Thread: Black.
Tail: CH06 orange Crystal Hair.
Body: CC07 fire orange Crystal Chenille.
Hackle: CH06 orange Crystal Hair tied in at the throat.
Wing: Dark brown deer hair. Hair is spun on allowing a small portion to go down over the hackle.
Head: Trimmed butt ends of wing.

Originated by John Shewey.

Chauncey
See Chapter 7.

Cigar Butt
Hooks: TMC5212 or DAI1280, sizes 6-8.
Thread: Black.
Tail: White calf tail.
Wing: Clump of white calf tail extending over the eye of the hook.
Body: Natural deer hair spun on and clipped to a cigar shape.

Originated by Keith Stonebreaker of Lewiston, Idaho. This pattern is also tied with a dark moose hair beard added.

Coal Car Dump
Hooks: TMC7989, DAI2131 or DAI2421, sizes 4-8.
Thread: Claret.
Wings: Dark moose body hair tied upright and divided. Wings should slant forward.
Tail: Dark moose body hair.
Tip: Flat gold tinsel.
Body: Rear 25%, orange floss, second 25% red floss, and the front half, dubbed with #1 black African Angora goat.
Hackle: CH21 claret Crystal Hair tied in at the throat with black hen hackle tied on as a collar.

Originated by John Shewey in 1986.

Colonel Monel
Hooks: TMC7989, DAI2131 or DAI2421, sizes 6-10.
Thread: Black.
Tail: Dark elk hair.
Ribbing: Red floss.
Body: Peacock herl.
Body Hackle: Grizzly tied palmer style over the body.
Hackle: Grizzly tied on as a collar.

Evening Coachman
See Chapter 20.

Disco Mouse
Hooks: TMC7989, DAI2131 or DAI2421, sizes 4-8.
Thread: Black.
Ribbing: Heavy black thread.

Tail/Body: Black deer hair laid parallel and wrapped with ribbing. Tips of body hair are left for tail.

Wings: Black deer hair tied over the body with a sparse underwing of CH01 pearl Crystal Hair.

Head: Trimmed butt ends of wing extending over eye of hook.

There are a number of mouse patterns.

Dr. Park

Hooks: TMC7989 or DAI2421, sizes 6-10.
Thread: Black.
Wings: White calf tail tied upright and divided.
Tail: White calf tail.
Body Hackle: Badger tied palmer style over the body. Keep tightly wrapped.
Hackle: Badger tied on as a collar.

Fluttering Termite

Hooks: TMC7989, DAI2131 or DAI2421, sizes 4-8.
Thread: Black.
Wings: Dark moose body hair tied upright and divided. Wings should slant forward.
Tail: Fox squirrel tail.
Ribbing: Well undersized blue dun hackle. Reverse wrap with fine gold wire.
Body: Orange yarn twisted with #10 orange stone African Angora goat.
Hackle: Dark blue dun tied on as a heavy collar.

Originated by Randy Stetzer of Portland, Oregon.

Plate 16   ## Grease Liner
Hooks: TMC7989, DAI2131 or DAI2421, sizes 4-8.
Thread: Brown.
Tail: Coastal blacktail deer hair.
Body: Dubbed with #24 brown African Angora goat.
Hackle: Long, soft grizzly hen hackle barbs tied in at the throat.
Wing: Coastal blacktail deer hair tied over the body.
Head: Trimmed butt ends of wing.

This pattern was designed by Harry Lemire of Black Diamond, Washington.

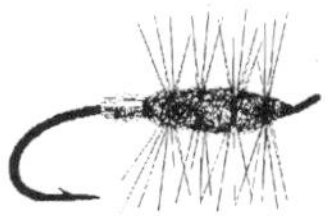

Plate 16   ## Green Machine
Hooks: TMC7989, DAI2131 or DAI2421, sizes 4-8.
Thread: Brown.
Butt: Fluorescent green yarn.
Body: Green deer hair spun on and clipped to a tapered shape.
Body Hackle: Brown tied palmer style over the body.

Humpy, S.H. Orange

Hooks: TMC7989, DAI2131 or DAI2421, sizes 4-10.
Thread: Orange.
Wings: Deer hair tied upright and divided.
Tail: Dark moose body hair.
Shellback: Deer hair.
Body: Orange floss.
Hackle: Brown tied on as a heavy collar.

See Chapter 7 for other Humpy patterns.

Irresistible

See Chapter 7.

Irresistible, Black Lemire's

Hooks: TMC7989, DAI2131 or DAI2421, sizes 4-8.
Thread: Black.
Wings: Dark moose body hair tied upright and divided.
Tail: Dark moose hair.
Body: Dyed black deer hair spun on and clipped to shape.
Hackle: Black tied on as a collar and clipped off on the bottom.

Originated by Harry Lemire.

Plate 16   ## MacIntosh
Hooks: TMC7989 or DAI2421, sizes 4-10.
Thread: Black.
Wing: Fox squirrel tail tied in at the center of the body.
Hackle: Brown tied on as a heavy collar.

This pattern was originated by Dan MacIntosh of Sherbrooke, N.S., Canada.

MacIntosh, Badger

Hooks: TMC7989 or DAI2421, sizes 4-10.
Thread: Black.
Wing: Gray squirrel tail tied in at the center of the body.
Hackle: Badger tied on as a heavy collar.

MacIntosh, Steelhead

Hooks: TMC7989 or DAI2421, sizes 4-10.
Thread: Black.
Tail: Dyed black squirrel tail.
Body Hackle: Black tied palmer style over the body. Hackle should be wrapped close.
Hackle: Dyed orange grizzly tied on heavy as a collar.

Originated by John Hazel.

Plate 16   Moose Turd

Hooks: TMC7989, DAI2131 or DAI2421, sizes 4-8.
Thread: Black.
Tail: White calf tail.
Wing: Clump of white calf tail tied over the eye of the hook.
Body: Black deer hair spun on and clipped to a cigar shape.

Originated by Bill McMillan in 1975.

Plate 16   Muddler, After Dinner Mint

Hooks: TMC7989, DAI2131 or DAI2421, sizes 4-8.
Thread: Black.
Tail: Scarlet red hackle barbs.
Body: Green diamond braid.
Wing: Dyed green gray squirrel tail with a small bunch of CH11 green Crystal Hair tied in on top. Mottled brown turkey quill sections are then tied over the body.
Head: Deer hair spun on and clipped into a sculpin shape.

This is a creation of Mark Noble of Vancouver, Washington. This fly is also tied in an orange version. See color plate.

October Caddis

Hooks: TMC7989, DAI2131 or DAI2421, sizes 4-8.
Thread: Black.
Wings: Fox squirrel tail tied upright and divided. Wings should slant forward.
Tail: Golden pheasant crest.
Body: Dubbed with #9 orange African Angora goat.
Hackle: Dark brown tied on sparse as a collar.

Originated by Bill Bakke.

Rat-Faced McDougall

See Chapter 7.

Soldier Palmer

Hooks: TMC7989 or DAI2421, sizes 6-10.
Thread: Black.
Tail: Scarlet red hackle barbs.
Ribbing: Flat gold tinsel.
Body: Red floss.
Body Hackle: Ginger tied palmer style over the body.
Hackle: Ginger tied on as a collar.

Plate 16   Speed Skater, Black

Hooks: TMC5212 or DAI1280, sizes 6-8.
Thread: Black.
Tail: Dark moose body hair.
Body: Dyed black deer hair spun on and clipped to a taper.
Hackle: Black tied on as a heavy collar.

Plate 16   Speed Skater, Gray

Hooks: TMC5212 or DAI1280, sizes 6-8.
Thread: Black.
Tail: Dark moose body hair.
Body: Natural deer hair spun on and clipped to a taper.
Hackle: Grizzly tied on as a heavy collar.

Plate 16   Speed Skater, Orange

Hooks: TMC5212 or DAI1280, sizes 6-8.
Thread: Black.
Tail: Dark moose body hair.
Body: Dyed orange deer hair spun on and clipped to a taper.
Hackle: Brown tied on as a heavy collar.

The Speed Skaters were originated in 1975 by Martin Maghnant of Napa, California.

Steelhead Bee

Hooks: TMC7989, DAI2131 or DAI2421, sizes 6-12.
Thread: Black.
Wings: Fox squirrel tail tied upright and divided. Wings should slant forward over the eye of the hook.
Tail: Fox squirrel tail.
Body: Divided into three equal parts. Dubbed with #26 dark brown and a center joint of #6 yellow lambs wool.
Hackle: Brown tied on as a collar.

Originated in the 1950s by Roderick Haig-Brown.

Steelhead Skater I

Hooks: TMC7989, DAI2131 or DAI2421, sizes 4-8.
Thread: Yellow.
Wings: Light elk hair tied upright and divided.
Tail: Light elk hair.
Body Hackle: Dyed yellow grizzly tied palmer style over the body.
Body: Dubbed with #6 yellow African Angora goat.
Hackle: Dyed yellow grizzly tied on as a collar.

Steelhead Skater II

Hooks: TMC7989, DAI2131 or DAI2421, sizes 4-8.
Thread: Brown.
Wings: Dark elk hair tied upright and divided.
Tail: Dark elk hair.
Body Hackle: Dyed brown grizzly tied palmer style over the body.
Body: Dubbed with #24 brown African Angora goat.
Hackle: Dyed brown grizzly tied on as a collar.

Thompson River Rat

Hooks: TMC7989, DAI2131 or DAI2421, sizes 4-6.
Thread: Black.
Tail: Chartreuse bucktail tied long.
Body: Natural deer hair spun on and clipped to a cigar shape.
Body Hackle: Sparse grizzly tied palmer style over the body.

Wings: Chartreuse bucktail tied along each side of the body and extending past the hook.

Originated by Ehor Boyanowski of Vancouver, British Columbia.

Plate 16 Waller Walker

Hooks: TMC7989, DAI2131 or DAI2421, sizes 4-8.
Thread: Black.
Wings: White calf tail tied upright and divided. Wings should slant forward.
Tail: Dark moose body hair.
Body: Alternating bands of colored deer hair which have been spun on and clipped to a cigar shape.
Hackle: Dark moose body hair tied in at the throat and extending past the hook bend.

Originated by Lani Waller of Novato, California. I have seen this fly tied with any number of body color combinations. I favor black and brown combinations, closely followed by black and white. Some tie it with deer, elk or moose hair wings. For visibility purposes I stick with white calf tail.

Stan Hellekson with summer-run steelhead.

Plate 16 Whiskey and Soda

Hooks: TMC7989, DAI2131 or DAI2421, sizes 6-10.
Thread: Black.
Tail: Two grizzly hackle tips.
Body Hackle: Grizzly tied very close over a thread underbody.

Wulff, Gray

Hooks: TMC7989, DAI2131 or DAI2421, sizes 4-10.
Thread: Black.
Wings: Deer hair tied upright and divided.
Tail: Natural brown bucktail.
Body: Dubbed with muskrat fur.
Hackle: Blue dun tied on as a collar.

Originated by Atlantic salmon guide Clarence Cains of Corner Brook, Newfoundland. Did that get your attention? I knew if I dug deep enough I would be able to reconstruct this bit of history that has been strongly rumored yet gone on for so many years uncorrected. They say if you tell a little boy that he is bad often enough and long enough he will be bad. This is what has happened to this pattern with respect to the "originator." The manifestation of this myth, after being repeated so many times, has caused many to believe Lee Wulff originated this fly.

Arguments based on interpretations, semantics and a host of other foundations became involved here. I have discussed this subject with Harry Darbee, Walt Dette, Andy Puyans and others through the years. Naturally one has to discount egos and other personal prejudices. I put this on the back burner and was content to let a sleeping dog lie as many others have done. When I started getting similar feedback on the Gray Wulff from the Canadians while researching Atlantic salmon flies I concluded it was time, I was compelled to kick the dog.

What supportable history tells us is Clarence Cains originated the fly and Lee Wulff took it and gave it the name, "Grey Wulff." See Lee Wulff's letter on page 160, Volume I, the spelling in that letter from Wulff with one "f" on the name has been rationalized as an error on the part of the typesetter at the time. There is no question that Wulff is not referring to an Atlantic salmon wet fly pattern.

As with the Royal Wulff whose origins were questioned earlier, we do have to credit Lee Wulff, Dan Bailey and others for popularizing this pattern. We cannot discount the power of mail-order catalogs either, and how they have written much of the history of fly fishing and the fly patterns associated with it.

Plate 16   Wulff, October

Hooks: TMC7989, DAI2131 or DAI2421, sizes 4-8.
Thread: Black.
Wings: Orange calf tail tied upright and divided.
Tail: Dyed black squirrel tail.
Body: Dubbed with a 50/50 blend of #6 yellow and #9 orange African Angora goat.
Hackle: Black tied on as a collar.

Originated by John Hazel. Also see other Wulff patterns in Chapter 7.

Yellow Ant

Hooks: TMC7989, DAI2131 or DAI2421, sizes 8-10.
Thread: Brown.
Tail: Coastal blacktail deer hair.
Body: Fluorescent yellow yarn.
Wings: Brown hackle tips tied delta style.
Hackle: Brown tied on as a collar.

Glossary of Terms

Adams. Fly pattern; also a term often used to describe a mixed grizzly and brown hackle as found on the Adams and other patterns.

Adult. The mature stage in the life cycle of the insects we try to simulate.

Aft. At, toward, or near the rear of the fly.

Amherst Pheasant Crest. Metallic red, stiff feathers from the top of the head of an Amherst pheasant. Used similarly to golden pheasant.

Amherst Pheasant Tippet. The neck hackle which is white with a black tip and a continuous bar across the feather. Used similar to golden pheasant.

Artificial. A type of fly created to imitate living creatures, i.e., insects or baitfish.

Attractor. Any fly pattern not designed to simulate an insect or baitfish, relying solely on form, brightness or flash to attract fish.

Barb. On a hook, the backward-projecting sliced point meant to prevent easy extraction. On a feather, the row of projecting fibers along the stem, or barbs.

Bead Chain. A metal flexible cord of small connecting beads; cut in pairs and tied to the head of the fly for eyes and added weight.

Beard. Small bunch of hackle barbs, hair or other like material tied below the hook and extending back from the head of the fly.

Bend. On the hook, the curved rear portion of the hook connecting to the barb and point.

Bobbin. Fly tying tool used to control thread supply.

Bodkin. Fly tying tool used to apply cement, cleaning the eye of the hook of excess cement, picking out dubbed bodies for buggy appearance, picking out unintentionally-wrapped down hackles, and other purposes expected of a third hand. Also referred to as a dubbing needle.

Body. The main portion of the fly constructed around or on the shank of the hook between the tail and the head.

Breast. Referring to birds, front of the body below the neck. Feathers from this general area are used as a material.

Bucktail. Of the deer family, used as a material for wings, tails and other purposes.

Butt. Material wrapped at the rear of the body of a fly.

Calf Tail. The tail from a young cow or bull. The hair is used in fly tying primarily for winging material. Sometimes referred to as either kip or impala. Both are a misnomer as calf tail hair is used as a substitute for these materials which have not been available in this country for fly tying for over 50 years.

Center Joint. That portion of the fly body just in front of the butt located in the center of the body.

Chenille. A soft fuzzy cord made of synthetic material used for body material on flies.

Clipped Hair. Refers to any natural or synthetic hair which is clipped, or shaped, by trimming. Used when constructing bodies and heads on flies.

Collar. Hackle wrapped completely around the shank portion of the hook in a specific spot.

Complete Metamorphosis. The life cycle of an insect which includes: egg, larva, pupa and adult.

Deer Hair. Hair from the body of a deer and the most used of all hairs in fly tying.

Divided Wings. Any two or more wings that are tied apart from each other.

Downwing. Wing or wings tied over or parallel to the body.

Dressing. Of fly tying, the act of constructing a fly; also the materials used except the hook.

Dry Fly. See *Chapter 7, Dry Flies*.

Dry Hackle. Hackle best suited for tying dry flies.

Dub. Is to transfer materials to a hook and making them secure with tying thread.

Dubbing. Natural or synthetic fur used for constructing bodies on flies; also the act of applying these materials. Other materials like marabou can also be used in this manner.

Dubbing Needle. See bodkin.

Dubbing Wax. A specially formulated tacky wax used to better induce dubbing material to adhere to the thread.

Dun. The first adult stage of a mayfly; also color, see *Chapter 2.*

Egg Sac. The butt portion of a fly body tied to simulate the female egg sack of an adult insect. "Sac" being the English spelling in old fly tying books from England which has carried on to our crafty art.

Emerger. An aquatic insect swimming or crawling to the surface of the water with the mission of hatching into an adult. With mayflies, from nymph to emerger to dun.

Eye. A portion of a feather such as a center dot; as painted or attached to the head of a fly; portion of the hook which attaches to the tippet.

Feather. One of the horny, elongated structures which form the body covering of birds and provide the flight surface for the wings. It consists of a central shaft composed of a hollow part near the body called the quill and a distal solid part, the rachis, along each side of which is a series of processes, the barbs. The barbs are provided with a fringe of smaller processes, the barbules, which in turn are equipped with barbicels, or hooklets, the whole composing the vane of the feather.

Figure Eight. A criss-cross wrapping technique used to secure and/or separate materials.

Floss. A fly body material made from rayon, nylon and silk into untwisted strands of many colors to include fluorescent.

Golden Pheasant Crest. Metallic gold, stiff feathers from the top of the head of the golden pheasant. Used primarily in fly tying for topping and tails on Atlantic salmon, steelhead, streamer and other wet fly patterns.

Golden Pheasant Tippet. The neck hackle which is golden orange in color with a black tip and black continuous bar across the feather. Used as a fly tying material in a number of applications, primarily tailing material.

Guard Hair. This is the hair that stands up above the underfur on fur bearing mammals as a guard. It is that glossy part that you see.

Hair Evener. A tool used to align the tip of hair prior to tying. Sometimes referred to as stacker, shaker or tamper, all being a misnomers as they neither stack, shake or tamp, if used correctly.

Half Hitch. A knot used to secure thread. This knot is used primarily when a bobbin is not used and of little consequence to those who use a bobbin.

Half Hitch Tool. A tool used to complete a half hitch. See *half hitch.*

Jamb Knot. A tying technique used to bind the thread to the shank of the hook when starting a fly. This same knot is used in wrapping the thread on the guides of your fly rod.

Marabou. Very soft, downy under feathers or the downy portion found at the base of feathers such as neck and saddle hackle. The English first started using the beautiful marabou stork and later had to give it up because of its scarcity. Today the feathers from white commercial turkeys are used and are consider to be of better quality than the stork. The supply is unlimited.

Mylar Tinsel. A thin flat metallic material used in the same manner as metal tinsels. A good material where lighter tinsel is desirable and it is virtually tarnish proof.

Mylar Piping. The same material as above except it has been machine woven into a tube with a cotton core. Available in three sizes and assorted colors. Sometimes available in very large sizes, however, they are always in very short supply and are expensive. Sometimes called tubing but the correct textile trade name is piping.

Palmer. A hackling technique used to wrap hackle spirally over the body of a fly. We have to assume that *"Palmer"* is the name of the person who first used this technique.

Parachute Style. Any fly which has the hackle wound on in a horizontal plane above or below the hook shank.

Ribbing. An open spiral of material over a portion of the fly, using tinsel, thread, hackle, or any other material that produces a segmented effect on the finished fly.

Thorax Style. A typical thorax style finds the wings mounted slightly further back, almost centered, on the hook shank that is usually found on conventional dry flies. Hackle collar is wrapped in a criss-cross fashion, often through the wings. The hackle barbs on the bottom are clipped off, allowing your fly to rest more naturally on the water. The position of the hackle and contact the thorax of the fly makes with the water gives it the name, *"Thorax Style."* I strongly suggest you visit Chapter 10 and apply this style of tying to many of the mayfly patterns offered. Not recommended for rough water.

Waterwalker Style. This technique consists of wrapping individual hackles on a pair of upright and divided wings not unlike the parachute style. The wings, preferably hair type, are mounted about one-third of the way back on the hook shank and should be tied perfectly upright and not slanted either forward or backwards, or you will have pigeon-toed flies. The angle between the wings should be approximately seventy degrees rather than the customary forty to fifty degrees. Hackles selected should be matching, having barbs of equal length to give your fly proper balance on the water.

The Waterwalker style gives flies the ability to stand naturally on the water, not lay on it, and places the imitation in a more natural field of vision. This style is best suited for flies tied in sizes 14 or larger. When I first introduced this style in 1975 I was overcome with enthusiastic discovery and did not check my information as carefully as I should have. Since that time I have been corrected a number of times and now have come to believe that this style of tying originated in France and was introduced into this country in the 1950s. I stand corrected. The French conceived this idea from the parachute style which was originated in Scotland in the 1920s.

When I reintroduced this style it did not become popular because proper hackle was not as readily available as it is today. Now, after twenty years, I am finally seeing new interest in this design. I could write a book on the fruition of the Waterwalker—it is complicated.

Wool. This is a term often used extensively in fly tying books. I believe this term originated with British fly patterns where Berlin wool (sheep's wool) was used extensively. Berlin wool was a yarn favored by the British. During the 1940s and 1950s wool yarn was readily available to the fly tiers in this country. Today we continue to see patterns which specify just *"wool."* One company calls their fly tying yarn *"nylon wool."* You will be safe using synthetic yarn on those patterns specifying wool. Now all I have to do is figure out what is really meant by *"pig's wool."*

Today, with the introduction of lamb's wool as a dubbing material, the term wool takes on a whole new meaning and means literally what it is. It is unprocessed fly tying material awaiting the skillful hands of the fly-artist.

Index